# Business Studies for AS

## Second Edition

Ian Marcousé

Andrew Gillespie    Barry Martin

Malcolm Surridge    Nancy Wall

Marie Brewer    Andrew Hammond

Ian Swift    Nigel Watson

Edited by

Ian Marcousé

## Hodder & Stoughton

A MEMBER OF THE HODDER HEADLINE GROUP

This Second Edition is dedicated to the
memory of Tim Gregson-Williams. He
will be sorely missed.

*Business Studies for AS Teacher's Book, Second Edition*
(ISBN: 0340-81113-7, publishing September 2003)
provides comprehensive and detailed answers to all the
questions and exercises in *Business Studies for AS,
Second Edition*.

Also available are *Business Studies, Second Edition*
(ISBN: 0340-81110-2) and *Business Studies Teacher's
Book, Second Edition* (ISBN: 0–340-81111-0, publishing
September 2003).

Orders: please contact Bookpoint Ltd, 130 Milton Park, Abingdon,
Oxon OX14 4SB. Telephone: (44) 01235 827720, Fax: (44) 01235
400454. Lines are open from 9.00 – 6.00, Monday to Saturday, with a 24
hour message answering service. You can also order through our
website: www.hodderheadline.co.uk

British Library Cataloguing in Publication Data
A catalogue record for this title is available from The British Library

ISBN 0 340 81112 9

First published 2001
Second edition published 2003
Impression number   10 9 8 7 6 5 4 3 2
Year                         2007 2006 2005 2004 2003

Copyright © 1999, 2003 Ian Marcousé, Andrew Gillespie, Barry Martin,
Malcolm Surridge, Nancy Wall, Marie Brewer, Andrew Hammond,
Ian Swift, Nigel Watson (© 1999 Clive Ruscoe)

Cover illustration from Jon H. Hamilton
Typeset by GreenGate Publishing Services, Tonbridge, Kent
Printed in Spain for Hodder & Stoughton Educational, a division of
Hodder Headline, 338 Euston Road, London NW1 3BH

# CONTENTS

iii

## OPERATIONS MANAGEMENT

## EXTERNAL INFLUENCES ON BUSINESS

## OBJECTIVES AND STRATEGY

## BUSINESS SKILLS AND EXAM TECHNIQUES

## INDEX

# INTRODUCTION

## What is Business Studies about?

Broadly, Business Studies is about management and enterprise. It looks at how businesses are created, develop, grow, survive crises and perhaps eventually decline. It focuses on the people whose skills affect this process. And uses theory to analyse the causes and effects of different management approaches. Typical issues of interest within the subject include:

- How did Manchester United come to dominate football in the 1990s?
- Just how massive is the money-making potential of the Internet?
- Why did Marks & Spencer hit trading difficulties in 1999/2000?
- Are brands such as L'Oreal really 'worth it'?

To tackle questions such as these, the starting point is to understand fully the basics of business. These include finance and accounting. What exactly does something cost to make or to distribute? What profit or loss is made at the end of the day? Accountants help provide data that can be used to make decisions on whether to invest in a new factory or whether to hire more staff. Once the financial facts are known, firms can consider how to maximise their marketing potential. This will involve analysing the needs and wants of customers, and the strengths and weaknesses of competitors and distributors.

As shown by the huge success of the Dyson Cleaner, marketing a product becomes easy if it is designed with a distinct product and visual advantage. So product innovation and design are important, as are the key operational requirements of supplying high quality products to the right place at the right time. This area – known as operations management – also draws upon perhaps the most important aspect of Business Studies – the management of people. The AS course looks at the psychological theory of how best to motivate people, and looks critically at the leadership styles adopted by many managers.

The internal functions of a business, then, are finance, marketing, operations and people. Management provides the cement that holds these four functions together (or fails to). From outside the business, however, comes a series of events and circumstances that can provide huge opportunities or serious threats to business success. An economic recession would cause a sharp fall in demand for luxury goods, while a sharp fall in the value of the pound would boost the demand for British exports. External influences such as these can push managers to make hasty or rash decisions. To prevent this, it is crucial for the business to have clear aims and objectives. In other words to be clear about what it is attempting to achieve. Figure 1 shows two possible objectives for an organisation: to grow by 25% within two years or to boost profit to £1 million in three years.

Figure 1

All these aspects of business are covered within AS Business Studies.

## What is AS level?

AS level is a new academic standard, introduced by the government in September 2000. In the government's own words, it is 'the level to be expected of a student half way through a two-year A level course'. In practice AS level is more than half way between GCSE and A level, because students need to take a step up from GCSE when starting AS level. In other words AS is not as hard as A level, but it is still quite tough. It requires many different academic skills, plus a great deal of subject knowledge. *Business Studies for AS* should help you greatly in acquiring both the knowledge and the skills.

AS Business Studies contains subject matter from each of the six main areas covered by the A level: Marketing, Finance, People, Operations, External Influences and Objectives and Strategy. Much of the hardest (especially numerical) material is left to the A level. Therefore the AS level is not too packed with things to learn. This leaves time and space for studying the material in relation to current media stories about business triumphs and crises.

AS Business Studies is examined in three main ways:

- short questions testing your factual knowledge, especially of definitions of business terms
- data response questions in which you are given stimulus material such as a newspaper article or a company's sales figures, and then asked a series of questions based on the data
- a case study, in which you are given the life story of a business – often one facing problems or a major decision. You are then given a series of questions that test your ability to analyse the business situation, then make judgements on what the business should do, or should have done. In some cases the basic story is provided in advance, so that it can be discussed in class; in others the exam is 'unseen', in other words you see the story for the first time when starting the exam.

*Business Studies for AS* provides a huge range of these three types of exam.

## What skills are needed for AS success?

AS is a stepping stone towards a full A level. Therefore the skills match those of A level. AS is made slightly easier, though, by demanding less evidence of the most difficult skills.

Business Studies exams focus upon four academic skills:

- **Knowledge and Understanding:** do you know the facts? Do you know the language of business? Do you understand what it means and can you explain it? Examiners regard this as the foundation skill: vital, but not that difficult to acquire.
- **Application:** can you apply your knowledge in practice? You may be able to define and explain

market research, but can you outline how research could benefit Virgin Atlantic, L'Oreal or a small business start-up?

- **Analysis:** can you look into cause and effect in depth, using the theory of the subject? This skill is largely related to the ability to construct a detailed argument, often by asking the question: Why? Why did the firm hit a crisis? Why is an understanding of psychology crucial to good people management?
- **Evaluation:** can you show good judgement within your arguments and in your conclusions? Such judgements can show through in the balance you bring to your arguments and in your understanding of the importance of one issue compared with another: what was the most important factor that caused the firm's collapse or triumph? Were there any key underlying reasons: great management? Or did luck (good or bad) play a part?

Examiners consider these four skills to be progressively more difficult, therefore the skill of evaluation is tested more thoroughly at A level than at AS. Broadly, the different exam boards test the four skills as shown in the table below.

Classroom teaching is a good way of providing knowledge and understanding; classroom exercises usually promote application and some analysis. For strong development of analysis, plus the skill of evaluation, the most important triggers are:

- classroom debate, especially if you are pushed to explain the reasons behind your own views
- reading newspapers, to give you a broader and deeper understanding of the real business world; good papers for AS level include the *Mail on Sunday* and the *Sunday Express*
- watching business TV, and being alert to business stories on main TV news programmes. The BBC has a long tradition of producing excellent business TV, notably series such as *Back to the Floor*, *Trouble at the Top* and *The Money Programme*. All give a wonderful insight into real business problems
- reading the whole of this book! (Sorry, but it is *all* relevant!) Nearer the exams, a second read through the 'Issues For Analysis' and the 'Evaluation' sections would be very helpful. These are towards the end of every unit, and summarise the key issues in a thought-provoking way.

| | AS LEVEL | A2 (2ND YEAR A LEVEL) | A LEVEL TOTAL |
|---|---|---|---|
| Knowledge and Understanding | **30%** | 20% | 25% |
| Application | **30%** | 20% | 25% |
| Analysis | **20%** | 30% | 25% |
| Evaluation | **20%** | 30% | 25% |
| Total | **100%** | 100% | 100% |

# Conclusion

AS Business Studies combines academic study with awareness and understanding of the real business world. This is its challenge, and it is this that makes it interesting. The exam also tests a combination of abilities and skills. Numerical questions are important, though written answers account for far more marks. The key skill for exam success is to be able to develop convincing written arguments based upon theory and the business context of the question. Then to weigh up those arguments, prioritising them and drawing judgemental conclusions.

# HOW TO USE THIS BOOK

This book is written for students of AS level Business Studies. It is also suited to the Advanced Certificate of Vocational Education and a wide range of professional courses. The 61 units of the book are organised into several main sections:

| | |
|---|---|
| Units 1–11 | Marketing |
| Units 12–21 | Finance |
| Units 22–31 | People in Organisations |
| Units 32–40 | Operations Management |
| Units 41–50 | External Influences on Business |
| Units 51–57 | Objectives and Strategy |
| Units 58–61 | Business Skills and Exam Techniques |

Within the first six sections of the book, the opening unit is introductory and the final unit is integrative. Within the latter units are a series of questions designed to help readers prepare for an examination.

Each unit is self contained. Therefore it is not necessary to read the units in the sequence in which they appear. Nevertheless references are made to other units, so that the reader can see where to find related topics.

The units have a common style. They start by defining key terms, move on to explain the key issues within the topic, then identify 'Issues for Analysis' and conclude with 'An evaluation'. Within the text are a number of 'In Business' up-to-date mini case studies, each selected to show how the textbook theory applies in the real world. At the end of each unit is a 'Workbook' section with revision questions and exercises. The book also has an exceptionally detailed index, to enable readers to quickly find what they need.

*Business Studies for AS* is written by a team of experienced teachers and examiners in the subject. It is up-to-date and full of real case material. Even so, the students who will get the most out of the book are those who are regularly reading extra business stories in newspapers or magazines. Business television programmes are also very useful. In every case, the chances of exam success are maximised by thinking, while watching or reading, about the textbook concepts implied by the material. A television programme on Japan might refer to the huge size of the market; the student should then think: 'economies and diseconomies of scale' or 'market segmentation'. Practising business concepts in this way is a valuable aid to memory and understanding.

## Note to students

What is a textbook for? It provides a useful reference book, of course, for when you need to know more about a topic to answer a case study question. It also provides a huge number of questions and exercises to enable you to test yourself in preparation for a test or exam. This book attempts to provide something more, however. It is written to be read. The text is intended to be a lively, relatively easy read. It contains plenty of real business examples and is always focused upon a key area of Business Studies. The book can be used, therefore, as a prime source of the wider reading that is at the heart of every student success.

Other valuable reading matter includes:

*The Complete A–Z Handbook of Business Studies 4th Edition* – Lines, Marcousé and Martin, Hodder & Stoughton

*Business Review* – a quarterly business magazine published by Philip Allan, Market Place, Deddington, OX15 0SE

Sunday newspapers such as the *Sunday Times*, *The Observer* and *The Mail on Sunday*.

If you decide to follow through to a full A Level course, the companion volume to this AS text is *Business Studies 2nd Edition* by Marcousé, Gillespie, Martin, Surridge and Wall, published by Hodder and Stoughton.

## Note to teachers

This book sets out to help develop a student's skills from GCSE standard up to AS level. No textbook can 'produce' A grades, but this one does aspire to help achieve high grades by combining an accessible style of writing with more demanding sections outlining the 'Issues for Analysis' and 'An evaluation'. The 'Workbook' sections also move up the skill levels from knowledge through application and analysis to demanding, evaluative questions.

*Business Studies for AS* is packed with questions. They broadly fall into three categories:

### 1. REVISION QUESTIONS

These are designed to be answered after reading a unit. They represent a moderately challenging way of getting students to reflect on the key terms and themes within the text. It is envisaged that this will be an effective way to introduce a topic (releasing teaching time for activities rather than chalk and talk). It will also, *in extremis*, be a way to achieve reasonable coverage of syllabus areas if timetable pressures mean that not everything can be taught.

## 2. DATA RESPONSE QUESTIONS

All the new specifications use data response as a form of assessment at AS level. It is worth bearing in mind that examiners make a great effort to write questions that require good use of the business context provided by the data. Candidates habitually prove weak at this. They regard repetition of a company name as contextualisation, rather than thinking through the service/manufacturing, large/small business featured in the article provided. The data response questions in this book attempt to replicate the exam-setting process, as shown by the marking schemes in the *Teacher's Book*.

The authors believe that there is no better data response question than one based on today's newspaper. Nevertheless these exercises will provide a useful fallback position for when current news is not as helpful as it might be.

## 3. CASE STUDIES

*Business Studies for AS* contains more than 50 new case studies. Most are tailored specifically to the syllabus material within a unit. For example, the Market Research unit contains a study on research at Braebourne Water. The focused nature of the cases should make them much easier to use than the broader, integrated cases supplied in case study books or photocopiable packs. Only the cases in the integrated units at the end of each section of the book have clear synoptic elements.

The *Business Studies for AS Teacher's Book* is also available (ISBN: 0–340–81113–7). It provides answers and mark schemes to the Workbook questions and also a reading list for every unit in the book. It is an invaluable resource.

## Progression to A level

If your students are continuing to A level, bear in mind that A2 exams are based upon the whole two-year course, not just the second year's work. Therefore it is vital to have complete coverage of the specification for revision purposes. This can be achieved by having an AS plus an A2 book, or by a complete A level text. What will not work is to give first-year students an AS text, then collect them in for the following cohort of first-year students.

For students carrying on from this AS book, the natural follow-up is *Business Studies 2nd Ed.* by Marcousé *et al*, published by Hodder & Stoughton. It includes the AS material from this volume (reassuring for revision purposes) plus full coverage of A2 subject content and exam-style exercises.

# Acknowledgements

Many people have contributed hugely to this book. Other than the authors, few put in as much work as the person responsible for the cover design: Pauline Stacey. This remarkable A level student put in hundreds of hours perfecting the design of the cover, the back cover and the spine. Professional designers then took over, but Pauline's energy and creativity was an example to anyone who doubts Herzberg's theory of motivation.

Other students have been helpful at various stages with the text itself. Taking pride of place are Vivien Wilson and Richard Thorburn. Intelligent and constructive criticism was also received from Chris Thompson, Melanie Coutinho, Hoshil Popat and Daniel Martyn. My thanks to them and my current students at Lambeth College.

The idea for the book emerged from many lunchtime sessions at the Hodder and Stoughton canteen between the late Tim Gregson-Williams and Ian Marcousé. Both knew there was a need for a new, more appropriate textbook for modern Business Studies courses. Finding the time was the hardest bit! After that problem was overcome, Ian designed the chapter structure and key features and put the writing team together. At GreenGate Publishing, David Mackin and Katie Chester performed miracles.

From the point of view of the authors, every family member has been inconvenienced and therefore deserves our gratitude and apologies. Probably Ian's family and dog suffered most, so a particular apology to Maureen, Claire, Jonny and Jumble.

It is also important to acknowledge that books such as this can only be written because of the wonderful resources of libraries such as the City Business Library, the Birkbeck Library and Senate House Library. The Financial Times Annual Reports service also deserves a special mention. The Internet is a wonder, but serious research cannot yet ignore the quality of the resources available on paper.

*Ian Marcousé*

The authors and publisher would like to thank the following for permission to reproduce copyright text material:

The Associated Examining Board for granting permission to reproduce Paper 3 (A/BUS/3), Summer 1998 on page 363. Also, for permission to reproduce brief extracts from the following mark schemes plus additional AEB material as detailed in text: Mark Scheme, Paper 3, Summer 1998 (A/BUS/3) and Mark Scheme, Paper 7, Summer 1998 (0650N).

Any answers or hints on answers are the sole responsibility of the author and have not been provided or approved by the AEB.

AQA pages 370, 374; The Benchmarking Exchange, page 232; *British Airways Reports and Accounts, 1997–1998*, page 174; Butterworth Heinemann Publishers, a division of Reed Educational & Professional Publishing Ltd., page 170; Capstone Publishing (extracts from *The Ultimate Book of Business Quotations*, Stuart Crainer, 1997), pages 2, 59, 149, 158, 165, 227, 239; *Caterer and Hotelkeeper*, page 337; Coca-Cola, page 171; Consumers' Association, *The Which? Hotel Guide 2002*, page 281; *The Engineer*, page 247; *Growing Business*, page 116; *Financial Times*, pages 16, 40, 158, 161, 166, 181, 209, 275, 299, 300, 314, 349; Frederick Herzberg, page 144; HarperCollins, pages 154–155; Institute of Business Ethics website, page 305; KPMG Consulting, page 250; Macmillan Publishers Ltd. (extract from *Mastering Accounting*, 1983), page 193; National Institute of Economic and Social Research, pages 281, 288, 319; Office for National Statistics, pages 263, 270, 272, 273, 276, 285, 286; © 1996 by James Womack and Daniel Jones, Pocket Books, a division of Simon & Schuster, page 227; *The Scotsman*, page 248; Texas Instruments website, pages 303, 304; *The Economist*, pages 278, 318; The European Commission, pages 278, 282; *The Grocer*, pages 15, 62–63, 134, 334; *The Independent*, page 275; *The Sunday Times*, pages 17, 289; *The Times*, pages 43 (© Times Newspapers Limited, 2002), 48 (© Times Newspapers Limited, 1998), 113 (© Times Newspapers Limited, 1998), 63 (© Times Newspapers Limited, 1998), 70 (© Times Newspapers Limited, 1998), 115, (© Times Newspapers Limited, 2002); The World Bank, page 261; West Yorkshire Trading Standards Service, page 296.

The authors and publisher would also like to thank the following for permission to reproduce copyright illustrative material:
© Amet Jean Pierre/Corbis Sygma, page 69; Associated Press, page 305; © W. Cody/Corbis, page 267; © Darama/Corbis, page 160; © Dave G Houser/Corbis, page 64; Corbis-Bettman, pages 37, 142; Dell Computer Corporation, page 61; Format Partners, page 285; © Gillette, page 238; © The Image Bank/Getty Images, page 264; © Zen Icknow/Corbis, page 262; © Bob Krist/Corbis, page 126; Life File, page 64; Microsoft Corporation, page 330 (Corbis/Wolfgang Kaehler); © Bruce Peebles/Corbis, page 213; Richmond Foods, page 137, 214; Sign UK/Faversham House Group Ltd, page 18; © Greg Smith/Corbis Saba, page 341; www.wembleystadium.com, page 212; © Ian Walton/Getty Images, page 59.

Every effort has been made to trace copyright holders but this has not been possible in all cases; any omissions brought to our attention will be corrected in future printings.

# MARKETING – INTRODUCTION AND OVERVIEW

## DEFINITION

Marketing is the process of learning about your customers and competitors, so that you can provide the right products at the right price in the right place, promoted in the right way to achieve your business objectives.

## 1.1 Where do you start?

The starting point is to gather accurate market knowledge. A successful business needs to understand its customers' needs, wants, habits and attitudes. For a small firm, this may be easy. The baker who bakes bread and cakes by night and serves customers by day will learn exactly how crusty and how airy the bread should be, how jammy the doughnuts and so on. Larger firms cannot reproduce this closeness between the decision makers and the customers. They require other approaches.

For the large firm, market knowledge consists of five main elements:

- knowing the size of the market (the value of purchases made by all the customers)
- knowing the competitors' market shares, their brand images and their strengths and weaknesses
- understanding your existing customers' habits, likes, dislikes and their image of your product compared with rivals; how loyal are they?
- understanding the image and attitudes buyers of rival products have towards yours; why are they not buying yours?
- knowing the key distribution methods and outlets.

Gaining this knowledge requires time, money and expertise. A great deal can be found through secondary and primary research (see Unit 4). Facts and figures can be gathered easily, though perhaps expensively. Much harder is to gain a full understanding of the psychology of the consumer. For example, when smokers of Benson & Hedges King Size are asked why they buy that brand, they usually suggest product quality and/or taste. In other words, they give an answer that sounds sensible. Yet in blind product tests (a taste test with the brand name removed), Benson & Hedges smokers cannot tell their brand from any other. Therefore the sensible answer is not the real one. Psychology-based research such as a group discussion is needed to reveal that image based reasons are the key in this case.

### Business in THE MIGHTY RED

Red Bull is a marketing phenomenon. Launched in 1995 to a baffled audience, its slogan 'Red Bull gives you wings' meant nothing until clubbers discovered its huge jolt of caffeine. Achieving shop distribution was difficult at first, despite providing retailers with far higher profit margins than on other drinks. Word of mouth and TV advertising helped push sales to £90 million by 2000. Then the Austrian owners found a way to boost sales further, by getting motorway service stations to sell it as a stimulant to help keep drivers from getting drowsy. Sales in 2001 ballooned to £150 million in Britain alone – a sales figure higher than the worldwide revenues generated by Manchester United plc. The Mighty Reds beaten by Mighty Red Bull.

Having acquired strong market knowledge, firms use it to analyse the marketplace. The main method is segmentation analysis. This means identifying the key characteristics within the market. This can reveal important sub-sectors within the market, such as super-premium lagers (extra strong lagers such as Carlsberg Special Brew). If sales within this sector are growing faster than the beer market as a whole, breweries will analyse the different needs of consumers within the sub-groups. This may lead to a new product aimed at a particular type of customer within the sector.

## 1.2 How do you decide what to do?

The key to all decision making is clear objectives. In other words, you must know exactly what you are trying to achieve. This sounds obvious, but the business reality is harder. A firm with a 17% market share wants to grow. It is tempted to set a target of 25% share within four years. Yet is it realistic? If it proves impossible to achieve, the consequences may be serious. After all, a **marketing** objective of growth may trigger increases in production capacity. In other words, extra machinery may be bought or even a new factory opened to cope with the expected increases in demand and therefore output. If the extra demand never comes, the firm will be left with expensive, under-used equipment.

Objectives must be set with sufficient optimism to make the targets challenging – but should never become unrealistic.

With objectives clarified, the next step is to identify the right strategy. Firms usually identify two or three alternative approaches. Then use market research to help make a choice. For example, sales growth may come from a new product launch, or a revamp of an existing product. Research will help forecast the effect on sales of each option. Unit 2 shows in more detail how firms make marketing decisions.

| MARKETING OBJECTIVES | POSSIBLE MARKETING STRATEGIES |
|---|---|
| Increase market share from 17% to 25% within 3 years | Reposition our Brand XYZ in the mass-market sector by cutting its price; launch new upmarket, high-price brands in each of the next 3 years |
| Within 2 years, to increase to 30% the proportion of our sales coming from new products | Increase the new product development budget by 50% and the market research budget by 30% |
| Reduce the proportion of over-60s among our market from 40% to 25% over the next 2 years | Relaunch our product with livelier, younger packaging and advertising; use direct mail to offer free samples to those who have just qualified to vote |

## 1.3 Are there any keys to marketing success?

Many markets change continually, as consumer tastes change, the ferocity of competition changes, or as a result of changing technology. Yet there are some marketing principles which always prove valuable.

### JUMP BEFORE YOU'RE PUSHED

Apple was the first provider of user-friendly personal computers. It enjoyed a cult status and huge brand loyalty, even in the face of fierce competition from the suppliers of IBM-compatible PCs. Even as Windows

### EXPERTS SAY:

'*Marketing is not a function, it is the whole business seen from the customer's point of view.*'
Peter Drucker, the ultimate management guru

'*Marketing is too important to be left to the marketing department.*'
David Packard, computer company founder

'*Marketing strategy is a series of integrated actions leading to a sustainable competitive advantage.*'
John Sculley, Pepsi chief

'*Every company should work hard to obsolete its own product line … before its competitors do.*'
Philip Kotler, marketing expert

'*The railroads collapsed because they thought they were in the railroad business, when really they were in the transportation business … they were product oriented instead of customer oriented.*'
Theodore Levitt, Harvard Business School marketing guru

'*While great devices are invented in the laboratory, great products are invented in the marketing department.*'
William Davidor, author

Source: The *Ultimate Book of Business Quotations*, Stuart Crainer, Capstone Publishing, 1997

software made PCs increasingly easy to use, Apple continued to assume its products were the best. Accordingly, it priced them high; typically they cost 25% more than PCs. Only when sales slid dramatically in 1996/97 did the company start to rethink. But too late. It only acted when pushed.

Contrast Apple's approach with that of Philip Morris, producer of the world's biggest selling brand – Marlboro cigarettes. Philip Morris boldly jumped to destroy the threat to its brand posed by price-cutting, discount brands – even at the short-term cost of a profit reduction of over $1 billion.

The lesson taught by these examples is that successful marketing is about anticipating change, not just reacting to it. Firms should not wait until established brands are slipping before devising a strategy for giving them a new lease of life.

### EXPLOIT YOUR ASSETS

Anyone can analyse a market to obtain market knowledge (given sufficient time and money). Therefore any firm can find out what customers want – and supply it. This means competition is fierce, so profit is hard to come by. For example, if a producer of fridges spotted an opportunity for red, instead of white, doors – a few months' of sales advantage would soon disappear when rivals copied the idea.

The answer is asset-led marketing. This means making decisions based not only on consumer needs, but also on the business's strengths. BMW researchers might find that its customers want a smaller, less powerful BMW for their 17–20-year-old sons and daughters. This opportunity may exist, but the firm may decide that a smaller, low cost BMW would make little or no use of the company's strengths. In this case it would have no advantages over Ford or Renault, and BMW would not want to compete.

Companies analyse the market, then see which opportunities allow them to draw on their strengths. A good example was when Mars investigated the ice-cream market in 1989. The company identified an opportunity for an adult-oriented, high quality, premium priced choc ice. The long-established Mars bar enabled a move into the ice-cream market from a position of strength (see Figure 1.1).

Some firms hold onto neither a market oriented nor an asset-led approach. They are still rooted in product orientation. This means that business decisions are

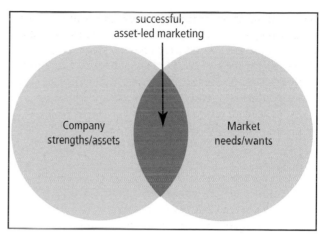

Figure 1.1

based upon the convenience and attitudes of the production staff, rather than the customer. This approach may work in certain situations. Where market change is constant, however, the firm will soon get left behind.

Of the three possibilities (product oriented, market oriented and asset-led), companies following the latter course are the most likely to succeed in the long term.

### KEEP AWARE OF CONSUMER PSYCHOLOGY

When sales are falling, firms often respond by cutting prices. This was Sainsbury's reaction to Tesco's achievement of market leadership in the mid-1990s. It is the reaction seen in every high street to a bad period of trading. The result is likely to be a sales increase. If prices are cut sufficiently, sales may leap ahead. Yet what is the point of a sales increase, unless profit is boosted too? As its chief executive explained in 1997, Sainsbury's '… panicked. Instead of reinforcing its leadership credentials – quality and choice – it competed on price … which led to lower profit margins.'

The problem with cutting prices is the effect on consumer image. A strong brand with a prestigious image may become an 'also-ran' if promoted regularly at hefty discounts. And once lost, a good image is hard to regain.

Consumer psychology is also affected by other messages, such as promotional offers. '25% extra FREE!' is attractive to everyone, but when offered too often, may devalue the key to long-term success – the strength of the brand name.

### BOB, BARNEY AND THOMAS

In 2002, HIT Entertainment made profits of nearly £25 million on sales of just over £100 million. Yet just a few years before it was losing money heavily. Why the turnround? At the heart of it was one man, *Bob the Builder*. HIT is the animation company behind *Bob the Builder* and *Barney the Dinosaur*. In 2001 Bob became a global phenomenon, propelling HIT to become the fourth largest children's video distributor in the massive American market. In 2002 Bob and Barney were joined by another star, as HIT bought the company with the rights to *Thomas the Tank Engine* for £130 million. HIT believes it now has the marketing strength to boost distribution and therefore sales of its products worldwide. If so, its brand new programme *Rubbadubbers* should clean up.

Characteristics of three types of firm

| MARKET ORIENTED | ASSET-LED MARKETERS | PRODUCT ORIENTED |
| --- | --- | --- |
| Monitors and responds to changing fashions | Monitors changing tastes; responds to long-term opportunities | Assumes changing fashions will return to square one – to the company's benefit |
| Wide range of product lines, pack sizes, colours and styles ('The customer's always right') | A few main product lines; wide range of options, but only supplies to order | One or two product lines with few options ('Trust us, we know best') |
| Promotional activity based upon special offers, competitions and eye-catching display | Promotional activity based on long-term, image-building advertising | Little promotional spending; focus on providing information through brochures |

Certain companies have achieved long-term, world-wide marketing success, for instance Levi's, Coca-Cola and McDonald's. All followed the same strategy: consistent, heavy spending on advertising campaigns to develop a strong consumer image of the brand. Unit 7 shows in more detail how a marketing strategy can be developed.

## BRANDS

Few assets are more important in modern marketing than strong brand names. Research among shoppers at Dixons showed these to be the top fashion brands.

**Top Ten Fashion Brands**

| | |
|---|---|
| 1 Calvin Klein | 6 Jasper Conran |
| 2 Gucci | 7 Nokia |
| 3 DKNY | 8 Tommy Hilfiger |
| 4 Sony | 9 Nike |
| 5 French Connection | 10 Burberry |

Source: 1,000 customers at Dixons Stores

## 1.4 Integrated marketing

Whenever a marketing decision is to be made, three questions must be asked:

- can we afford it?
- can we produce it?
- what knock-on effects may it have?

### CAN WE AFFORD IT?

Large firms have huge marketing budgets. Unilever, for example, spends over £3,000 million (yes, £3 billion) every year on advertising and promotions worldwide. A typical national TV advertising campaign costs in excess of £1 million. So firms have to work out the cost of achieving the marketing objectives they set themselves, and then make sure they can afford that level of expenditure. Often the strategy marketing managers want to adopt costs more than their budget allows. In which case they might – on occasion – request a budget increase. More often, though, they will trim their plans back to stay within their resources. Trimming back may leave them in too weak a position to compete effectively. If Coca-Cola is spending £8 million on TV, Pepsi may be wasting its money spending £3 million on the same medium.

### CAN WE PRODUCE IT?

Every marketing decision affects the operations of the business. A major advertising campaign may boost short-term demand by 40%. Have the extra units been produced in advance and stockpiled or is the factory prepared to increase production as soon as the extra demand arrives? Even major companies such as Nestlé

have been caught out by a level of demand they could not meet, causing empty shelves, dissatisfied customers and furious shopkeepers.

Long before a marketing strategy is put into action, therefore, it must be discussed with operations management – those responsible for meeting customer demand.

### WHAT ARE THE KNOCK-ON EFFECTS?

Large companies are complex organisations. Decisions made in one department or one country may have knock-on effects elsewhere. The decision by Carlsberg-Tetley in 1996 to market an alcoholic soft drink called 'Thickhead' brought a storm of complaint. It was said to taste of sherbet lemons, and therefore be particularly appealing to young children. Carlsberg-Tetley, like every large company, has many important dealings with government. Attracting howls of consumer and pressure group protest might make future dealings difficult or might start a consumer boycott. The company withdrew the brand.

ISSUES FOR **analysis**

When analysing why a firm pursues a particular marketing approach, or what strategy it might pursue in the future, it is useful to consider the following points:

- Successful marketing must be tailored to the market needs, wants and conditions; therefore no single approach will succeed in all markets at all times.
- Large, established firms have huge advantages over small, new firms; the latter can overcome these, though, if they listen to their customers and respond quickly, flexibly and innovatively to changing tastes.
- Large firms want to make decisions on the basis of quantified, 'scientific' evidence; the most brilliant marketing moves, however, are those requiring judgement or hunch (brilliant leaps into the unknown include Sony's development of PlayStation and Nokia's move from making car tyres to mobile phones!).
- Marketing strategies must change over time, as brands develop from their launch (birth) stage through growth towards maturity (see Unit 5).
- Long-term success comes from knowing your strengths and being consistent about exploiting and publicising them; the most important strength in marketing is a strong brand name.

## 1.5 Marketing
### an evaluation

Marketing lies at the heart of every successful business. Even firms with no marketing department have to be focused upon their customers if they are to succeed. It would be wrong to see marketing as purely passive, though. Marketing managers know they must respond to consumer tastes, but take exceptional delight in persuading people to buy what they do not need, or even want. Sunday colour supplements are full of advertisements for absurdly overpriced 'collectors' items' – and have been for 20 years. *Someone* must be buying! In a wealthy country such as Britain, the ethics of this matter little. Far more controversial is the success of firms such as Nestlé and Coca-Cola in persuading people in developing countries to spend scarce income on highly priced Western products. The power of advertising to persuade can give rise to fierce criticism of the role of marketing.

For most consumers, the great benefit of marketing is its effectiveness at finding out what they want – and then providing it. The huge choice of products in the modern supermarket is a tribute to the success of modern marketing.

**marketing** – the all-embracing function that links the company with customer tastes to get the right product to the right place at the right time. Marketing decisions are made through the marketing model, based on the findings of market research, and carried out through the marketing mix.

**product awareness** the proportion of all those within a target market who are aware of a particular brand/product. Brand leaders such as Coca-Cola may have almost 100% awareness, whereas only 60% of soft drink buyers are aware of 7-Up.

## Exercises

### A. REVISION QUESTIONS
*(40 marks; 80 minutes)*

Read the unit, then answer:

1 Explain the need for 'accurate market knowledge'. *(4)*
2 Distinguish between primary and secondary research. *(4)*
3 How might segmentation analysis help:
   a Tesco Stores decide on their future marketing strategy *(4)*
   b Heinz decide on the marketing of their salad cream. *(4)*
4 Suggest a suitable strategy to meet the following marketing objectives:
   a building up sales of Werther's Original through non-traditional outlets such as cinemas *(4)*
   b shifting the image of Marks and Spencer to make it younger and trendier. *(4)*
5 Identify two strengths and two weaknesses of product orientation. *(4)*
6 What is meant by the term 'consumer psychology'? *(3)*
7 Identify three problems that might arise from a failure to integrate marketing decisions into decisions made elsewhere in a business. *(3)*
8 What would you judge to be the most useful piece of marketing advice given in this unit? Explain and justify your answer. *(6)*

### B. REVISION EXERCISES

**B1 Case Study**
After a fruitless job hunt, Juan Olaria returned to college to start up a driving school business on-site.

He rented a small office opposite the student social area and set up a computer system for monitoring bookings and cash flow. Obtaining the cars was no problem, as his parents ran a second-hand car business. The arrangement was that Juan rented the cars for £30 per day, as and when he needed them.

Before opening, Juan had to decide on his marketing strategy. His primary target market was college students and his service would be based on second-hand cars. It was not hard to decide, therefore, that his prices should be relatively low. But how low? And did he need to promote his business, or could he rely solely on word of mouth?

Telephoning round the driving schools listed in *Yellow Pages* revealed prices of between £14 and £18 per hour. Some offered starter packages at £50 for five lessons, but there was little other evidence of promotional pricing. There were no driving advertisements in the local newspaper, so it seemed that directories such as *Yellow Pages* were the only form of advertising used by competitors.

Juan considered relying solely on word of mouth, but eventually decided to advertise on local radio. £300 bought him five spots but, more importantly, made it easier to write a more exciting press release for the local newspaper and radio journalists. The story of the student's bold move into business featured strongly over the following weeks. It achieved exactly what Juan had hoped for – several enquiries from students at other schools and colleges in the district. Juan's business was motoring.

## Questions                    (40 marks; 50 minutes)

1 Outline Juan's marketing objectives and strategy. (8)

2 How well suited was his strategy to his objectives?
(6)

3 **a** Explain the meaning of 'market segmentation'. (3)

3 **b** How effectively did Juan apply this approach? (6)

4 Why might driving schools use only directories
rather than other forms of media advertising?    (7)

5 To build his business in the medium term, Juan may
need to attract a wider market than just students.
What problems may he face if he attempts to
broaden his customer-base in this way?      (10)

## B2  Case Study

### Pizza the Action

In January 1998, David Di Mello left his job as marketing manager of Pizza Foods to start up his own pizza
business. He had noticed the shift in consumer demand
away from cheap frozen pizza slices and own-label pizzas. He believed the time was ripe for American-style
super-premium pizzas. Made with fresh dough which
rises in the oven, smells superb and tastes special.
Selling at a 20% price premium, these had already
swept through the American retail market.

   David's target was partly the major retail brands
such as McCain's and Goodfellas, and partly the buoyant take-away and delivery markets. His first year sales
target was to take 1% of the £400 million take-away
market and 2% of the main-meal pizza market.

   David had already signed an exclusive UK distribution
deal with a major American supplier of Mama Frescha
pizzas. To achieve effective sales and distribution, he
made an arrangement with Nestlé. The marketing he
would handle himself.

   He decided his target market was 25–30-year-olds
without kids. His budget allowed for £100,000 to be
spent on advertising in the first year, but how should it
be spent? On image-building colour magazine advertising or on door-to-door leaflets and special offers?
Now was the time to decide.

The UK pizza market: actual and forecast sales

|  | 1996 | 1999 (est) |
|---|---|---|
| Retail – main-meal pizzas | £177m | £210m |
| Retail – other | £73m | £70m |
| Restaurant | £540m | £590m |
| Take-away | £310m | £400m |
| Other | £88m | £100m |
| Total | £1,188m | £1,370m |

## Questions                    (20 marks; 25 minutes)

1 What value of sales does David expect for the first
year of his business?                           (3)

2 From the figures in the table, does David seem to
have targeted the right segments of the market? (3)

3 The three main producers in the retail sector of the
pizza market have a market share of over 40%
between them. What problems might that pose for
David's business?                              (5)

4 David's objective is to set up a business which will
be successful for at least 10 years. In the light of
this, consider which of the two promotional options
he should choose.                              (9)

# MARKETING OBJECTIVES AND DECISION MAKING

## DEFINITION

Marketing objectives are the marketing targets that must be achieved for the company to achieve its overall goals. Examples include 'Boosting sales from 600,000 to 1 million in two years' or 'Repositioning our product to make it appeal more to the under-25s'.

The link between marketing objectives and decision making is that decisions have to be based upon a clear sense of direction. That direction is provided by clear objectives.

## 2.1 How are marketing objectives set?

### AT A VERY SENIOR LEVEL IN THE COMPANY

In most firms, marketing is central to board-level strategic decisions. Not marketing in the sense of price cuts and promotions, but marketing in the sense of analysing growth trends and the competitive struggle within the firm's existing markets. And decisions about which markets the firm wishes to develop in future. For example, in early 1997, the business giant Unilever (Walls, Persil, Birds Eye, CK One and much else) set its sights on obtaining one-third of its world-wide sales from Asian markets by the year 2001. This goal was based upon observation of the rapid growth rates in economies such as Singapore, Taiwan and China.

Setting a company objective of growth in Asia enabled the directors to decide the marketing objectives. So, did this goal of one-third of sales coming from the Far East mean the *marketing* objectives were exactly the same? Not quite, because there were other options. Unilever had the financial strength to buy Asian businesses and therefore 'buy' sales. It may not have been necessary to increase sales in Asia on existing product lines. In fact they chose a combination of buying local firms and boosting the marketing on existing brands. The target was met by 2002.

### ROOTED IN THE COMPANY'S VISION OF ITS FUTURE (ITS MISSION)

A **vision** is a company's projection of what it wants to achieve in the future. It should be ambitious, relevant, easy to communicate and capable of motivating staff. Or even inspiring them. Bill Gates' 1980s vision for Microsoft was 'A computer on every desk and in every home'. Today, that seems uninspiring, even obvious. In the 1980s it seemed extraordinary.

A firm's marketing objectives need to reflect the firm's long-term aims/mission. The American car company Chrysler's mission statement says 'Our purpose is to produce cars and trucks that people will want to buy, will enjoy driving, and will want to buy again'. This sets the background for marketing objectives that focus on developing new, probably niche market, exciting rather than ordinary cars.

In his book *Even More Offensive Marketing*, Hugh Davidson suggests there are six requirements for a successful company vision. See the table on the following page.

### BY STRIKING A BALANCE BETWEEN WHAT IS ACHIEVABLE AND WHAT IS CHALLENGING

Objectives work best when they are clear, achievable, challenging and – above all else – when staff believe in them. To fit all these criteria, the firm must root the objectives in market realities.

In 1999 the Chairman of Iceland frozen food stores set a new objective. He wanted to reposition the stores to appeal to wealthier, middle class customers. All Iceland foods would be organic and GM-free. There would be no more Buy One Get One Free offers. By early 2000 the plan had flopped and the Chairman resigned. The company had attempted an objective that was out of line with marketplace reality. It was too ambitious.

Marketing objectives should not be set until the decision makers have a clear view of current customer behaviour and attitudes. This will probably require a lot of market research into customer usage and attitudes to the different products they buy and don't buy.

| REQUIREMENT | COMMENT |
|---|---|
| 1 Provides future direction | As shown in the above examples of Microsoft and Chrysler |
| 2 Expresses a consumer benefit | e.g. Prêt à Manger: 'Our mission is to sell handmade extremely fresh food …' |
| 3 Realistic | Realistic? Conservative Party 1997: 'Our mission is to create the greatest volunteer party in the Western democratic world.' Within five years party membership and morale collapsed. |
| 4 Motivating | The Body Shop: 'Tirelessly work to narrow the gap between principle and practice, whilst making fun, passion and care part of our daily lives.' |
| 5 Fully communicated | Easy to achieve if it's as simple as Kwik Fit's 'To get customers back on the road speedily, achieving 100% customer delight.' |
| 6 Consistently followed in practice | A company might claim to be at the leading edge of technology; it will lose all credibility if it reacts to the next recession by cutting spending on research and development |

Another key aspect is the marketing budget. How much can the business afford to spend on marketing? There is no point in setting a bold objective unless the resources are available to enable it to be met.

Once the marketplace and financial factors have been considered, objectives can be decided which stretch people, but do not make them snap. Cadbury's has had a 30% share of the UK chocolate market for decades. Setting a target of 35% for two years' time would be implausible. After all, will Mars or Nestlé just sit and watch? A wise marketing director might accept the challenge of 32% in two years' time – but would warn everyone that it might be very difficult to achieve this. (Note: each 1% of the chocolate market represents over £20 million of sales, so these matters are not trivial.)

## 2.2 Types of marketing objective

There are four main types of marketing objective:

- increasing product differentiation
- growth
- continuity
- innovation.

## ZARA

One day in 1998 saw an unusual event. The deputy editor of Vogue queued outside a new shop in London's Regent Street, waiting for it to open for the first time. Furthermore, this was a shop famed in Europe for its low prices, not for its designer labels. It was Zara, a retailer that never advertises and is run by a man who never gives interviews. He is also one of the richest men in Europe, with a £6,000 million fortune.

Amancio Ortega set up in business in 1963, with 5,000 pesetas (about £18). In 1975 he opened his first Zara store in Spain. Ortega built the business around the insight that modern women want fashionable, good quality clothes – and that being fashionable requires a production system that quickly translates catwalk fashions into new clothes on the shop rails. When a new look hits the fashion pages or the front pages of newspapers, Zara's versions are usually in its shops within two weeks.

Zara's progress throughout Spain, then continental Europe, then Britain, has been as rapid as that of Gap and H&M. Yet Zara is the most profitable by far. Its October 2002 opening of its largest store ever, in Oxford Street, London, saw a scrum of shoppers. For Zara, word of mouth has been enough to build a retail empire.

*Business IN*

## INCREASING PRODUCT DIFFERENTIATION

Product differentiation is the extent to which consumers see your product as different from the rest. It is the key to ensuring that customers buy you because they want you – not because you're the cheapest. It is a major influence on the value added and therefore profit margins achieved by the product.

To increase product differentiation requires a fully integrated marketing programme. Objectives must be set which separate your product from its rivals. These include:

- distinctive design and display
- unusual distribution channels – avoiding supermarkets, perhaps
- advertising based on image building, not sales boosting, e.g. television and cinema advertising rather than blockbuster sales promotions or competitions
- an integrated marketing programme focused solely upon the relevant age group or type of person.

## GROWTH

Some firms see growth as their main purpose and their main security blanket. They may reason that once they are Number 1, no-one else will be able to catch them. So they set sales or market share targets which encourage staff to push hard for greater success.

This is understandable but may prove self-defeating. A school or college pushing hard for rapid growth in student numbers would risk damaging its reputation. Class sizes would rise, hastily recruited new staff may be ineffective, middle management would be overstretched and quality standards would be at risk.

Just these things – and worse – happened during the 1980s and 1990s boom in private pensions. Giant companies such as Prudential were later condemned for mis-selling, as sales staff persuaded millions of people to abandon good, safe pension schemes. The sales staff were earning huge commissions on every sale, and the private pension companies were delighted by the sales growth. But in 1997 the new Labour government started naming and shaming the companies responsible for persuading people to buy an inferior pension. Years of building up the good name of a brand such as Prudential was being threatened. And the companies were forced to spend billions of pounds compensating those who had been sold an inappropriate pension.

Of course, the pursuit of growth does not have to lead to disaster. The rapid growth of Prêt à Manger in recent years was in response to buoyant consumer demand. If Prêt had not rushed to satisfy this demand for high quality sandwiches, other companies would have done so. Therefore the company's objective of rapid growth was very sensible. Too slow would have become too late.

## CONTINUITY FOR THE LONG TERM

The companies which own major brands such as Levi's, Bacardi or Cadbury's know that true success comes from taking a very long-term view. Unilever even tells its brand managers that their key role is to hand over a stronger brand to their successor. In other words they must think ahead 10 years or so.

Doubtless Bacardi could boost sales and profits this year by running price promotions with the major supermarkets and off-licences. Or next year by launching Bacardi iced lollies or bubble gum. But where would the brand's reputation be in a few years' time? Would it still be a classy drink to ask for at a bar?

Large firms think a great deal about their corporate image and the image of the brands they produce. They may try to stretch their brands a little, to attract new customers. Yet Cadbury's must always mean chocolate, not just snack products. Levi's must always mean jeans, not just clothes. Only in this way can the brands continue to add value in the long term.

## INNOVATION

In certain, major sectors of the economy, a key to long-term competitive success is innovation. In other words bringing new product or service ideas to the marketplace. There are two main categories of business where innovation is likely to be crucial: fashion-related and technology-related, as shown in the following table.

### — JD WETHERSPOON

JD Wetherspoon's growth has been astonishingly rapid within the mature, saturated pub market. From sales of less than £5 million in 1990, turnover rose to £89 million by 1997. To push sales and profits further, managing director John Hutson set the objective of boosting food sales in order to boost revenue per customer. The strategy was to hire food guru Egon Ronay to recommend how to improve food quality and consistency. He brought in new menus and a new staff training programme. The pay-off came quickly, with a sharp increase in food sales. By early 1998 food sales accounted for over 20% of sales, compared with 16% before the new strategy. This element in the company's growth plan helped drive sales forward to £484 million in 2001. With 522 outlets, JD Wetherspoon is now Britain's biggest pub chain.

| Business Category | Business Sector |
|---|---|
| Fashion-related | • The music business<br>• Clothing and footwear<br>• Entertainment, e.g. eating out |
| Technology-related | • Consumer electronics and IT<br>• Cars and aircraft<br>• Medicines and cosmetics |

| Timescale | Target (% of sales from products launched in past 5 years) | Strategy for Meeting Target |
|---|---|---|
| First year | 32 | One national new product launch plus another in test market |
| Second year | 35 | One national new product launch and two others in test market |
| Third year | 40 | Two national new product launches |

There are two key elements to innovation: get it right and get in first. Which is the more important? This is not possible to answer, as past cases have given contradictory results. The originator of the filled ice-cream cone was Lyons Maid (now Nestlé) with a product called King Cone. Walls came into the market second with Cornetto. In this case, getting it right proved more important than getting in first. In many other cases, though, the firm in first proved dominant for ever. The Boeing 747; the Sony Walkman; even the humble Findus Crispy Pancake (with its 80% market share); all have built long-term success on the back of getting in first.

## 2.3 Turning objectives into targets

The purpose of objectives is to set out exactly what the business wants to achieve. To ensure success, it is helpful to set more limited targets – staging posts en route to the destination. For example, a firm pursuing the objective of innovation may want at least 40% of sales to come from products launched within the past five years. If, at present, only 30% of sales come from this source, a jump to 40% will not be easy. The following targets may help, especially if – as in the table below – they are linked with the strategy for achieving them. Targets such as these:

- ensure that all the marketing staff know what to aim for
- provide a sound basis for cooperation with other departments (such as R&D and operations management)
- provide an early warning of when the strategy is failing to meet the objectives – should it be re-thought? Or backed with more resources?
- help psychologically; just as an end-of-year exam can concentrate the mind of a student, so a target can motivate managers to give of their best.

These benefits hinge on a key issue: have the targets been communicated effectively to the staff? This is an obvious point, but vital nonetheless. If the entire marketing department is based in one large office, it would be astonishing if anyone was unaware of new objectives. But what if it is a retail business and there are 400 branches around the country? Then a head office initiative can fall down at the local level, when a local manager thinks he or she knows best. Expertly considered **marketing targets** may fail unless they are communicated effectively to all the relevant staff.

## 2.4 Marketing objectives and the small firm

Do small firms set aside time to consider, set and write down objectives and targets? Very, very rarely. If you interviewed a dozen small-business proprietors, you might find none who found the time, and several who would regard such time as wasted.

There are two issues here:

1  In a very small firm, with all business decisions taken by the proprietor, the marketing objectives may be clear in the mind of the boss, even though they are not written down. That may work satisfactorily. When the firm gets 15 or more staff, it may have to change.
2  The bosses of small firms often find themselves swamped by day-to-day detail. Customers expect to speak to them personally, staff check every decision and may wait around for their next 'orders'. Only if they learn to delegate will they find the time to think carefully about future objectives and strategy.

There are some bright, young entrepreneurs, however, who apply a more thoughtful approach. Julian Richer identified a gap in the hi-fi market for high quality equipment sold by music enthusiasts at discount prices. This was intended to appeal to younger, more street-wise buyers. The target image was 'fun'. In the summer, customers receive free iced lollies; at Christmas, mince pies. The public face of Richer Sounds was that 'We have a laugh. We don't take ourselves seriously, but we do take our customers seriously'. Behind the scenes, though, careful target setting for stores and sales staff helped Richer Sounds achieve a *Guinness Book of Records* entry for the highest sales per square foot of any store in the UK.

## 2.5 Constraints on meeting marketing objectives

However well conceived, objectives do not lead automatically to success. Various factors may occur which restrict the chances of the objectives succeeding. These are known as **constraints**. They may occur within the firm (internal constraints) or may be outside its control (external constraints).

### INTERNAL CONSTRAINTS

1  Financial constraints affect virtually every aspect of every organisation. Even Manchester United has a budget for players, which the manager must keep within. A marketing objective might be set which is unrealistic, given the firm's limited resources. That is an error of judgement. Or the firm may have the finance in place at the start, but setbacks to the firm may cause budget cuts which make the objectives impossible to reach.
2  Personnel constraints may be important. The objective of diversifying may be appealing, but the firm may lack expertise in the new market. A recruitment campaign may fail to find the right person at a salary the business can afford. This may result in the project being delayed, scrapped or – worst of all – carried on by second rate staff.
3  Market standing. The marketing objectives may be constrained most severely by the firm's own market

position. The big growth sector in food retailing has been in chilled, prepared meals. So why no activity from the food giant Heinz? The answer lies in its success at establishing itself as *the* producer of canned soup and bottled salad cream and ketchup. The Heinz market image (its key marketing asset) is so narrowly focused that customer attitudes constrain it from competing effectively in chilled foods.

## EXTERNAL CONSTRAINTS

1 Competition is usually the main constraint outside the firm's control. It is the factor which prevents *The Sun* from charging 50p a copy. It is also the factor which makes it so hard to plan ahead in business. You may set the objective of gaining an extra 1% market share only to be hit by a price war launched by a rival.

2 Consumer taste is also important. If fashion moves against you, there may be little or nothing you can do to stop it. A logical approach is to anticipate the problem by never seeking fashionability. Reebok made the mistake of following Nike down the road of ever-more-trendy trainers. But being permanently trendy required huge promotional spending. Reebok's loss of market share forced it to pull back from the young end of the US trainer market.

3 The economy can also cause huge problems when setting medium-to-long-term objectives. This year's economic boom becomes next year's recession. Sales targets have to be discarded and a move upmarket comes to seem very foolish.

## 2.6 Marketing decision making – the marketing model

Successful marketing is not just about thinking. It is about decisions and action. Marketing decisions are particularly hard to make, because there are so many uncertainties. The following procedure, shown in Figure 2.1, is one of the most effective ways of ensuring the decision is well thought through.

Figure 2.1

The intention is to ensure that the strategy decided upon is the most effective at achieving the marketing objectives. In this process, market research is likely to be very important. It is crucial for finding out the

background data and again for testing the hypotheses. Test marketing may also be used. This is a way of checking whether the market research results are accurate, before finally committing the firm to an expensive national marketing campaign.

The **marketing model** is the way to decide how to turn a marketing objective into a strategy.

Marketing objectives are the basis for all marketing strategy. Therefore they will be central to almost every substantial exam question on marketing. For example, pricing decisions will depend upon the objectives. A firm pursuing growth might price a new product relatively cheaply, to ensure high market penetration and to discourage competition. Objectives will also affect the advertising approach: aimed at encouraging loyalty from existing users, or developing a new image/customer base.

To understand objectives fully, it is vital to be able to distinguish them from strategy. It is also important to remember that the setting of objectives cannot be done in isolation. The managers have to bear in mind the market situation, findings from market research and the financial resources and personnel the firm has available. Levi's objective of diversification foundered when it launched a range of two- and three-piece suits. On paper the objective may have looked fine; but in practice it became a classic marketing failure.

## 2.7 Marketing objectives
### an evaluation

What career are you aiming for? If you have a definite answer to that question, you probably have a clear idea how to achieve it. You are also likely to be very well motivated towards the qualifications you need. Most A level students have little idea of what they want to do. In other words they have no objectives. As a result, they have no plan and may struggle to find the motivation to succeed.

Marketing objectives are just as important. They allow a clear strategy to be devised, a plan to be set and give the motivation to succeed. Therefore they are the most important element of marketing.

**KEY terms**

**constraints** – factors which limit a firm's ability to achieve its objectives.

**marketing model** – a procedure for making marketing decisions in a scientific manner.

**marketing targets** – specific, measurable goals to be achieved within a relatively limited timescale.

**vision** – conceiving where the business wants to be in the future; the term implies something ambitious.

**2.8 Workbook**

## Exercises

### A. REVISION QUESTIONS
*(45 marks; 70 minutes)*

Read the unit, then answer:

1 Explain why it is important for a business to have clear marketing objectives. *(3)*
2 What do businesses mean by the term 'vision'? *(3)*
3 Why is it important that marketing objectives should be rooted in thorough market research? *(4)*
4 **a** State the four main types of marketing objective. *(4)*
   **b** Decide which one is most likely to be important for:
   **i** Coca-Cola
   **ii** Yorkie Bars
   **iii** Dyson Appliances *(3)*
5 Why might a firm seek to increase the product differentiation of one of its brands? *(3)*
6 What problems might a firm face if it focuses solely upon short-term objectives? *(5)*
7 Is it essential that marketing objectives should be written down in detail? Explain your answer. *(4)*
8 Explain the meaning of the terms:
   **a** internal constraints *(3)*
   **b** external constraints *(3)*
9 Outline two external constraints that might affect car sales over the coming months. *(4)*
10 Identify and explain two problems a firm might face if it makes marketing decisions without using a decision making framework such as the marketing model. *(6)*

### B. REVISION EXERCISES

#### B1 Data Response

#### Bzheanz Mzheanz Heinz

In Spring 1997 Heinz made its first move into the Russian food market. Although the economy was growing at that time, average wage levels were still very low – typically under £25 per week. Yet Heinz chose to price its baked beans at around 50p per can – the equivalent of charging £5 in Britain.

Heinz had set its sights on the long-term objective of building a prestigious brand name. When the famous beans first came to Britain in 1901 they were sold by Fortnum and Mason for £1.50 per can. Now Heinz was aiming to pull off the same trick again – nearly 100 years later.

Its target sales figure for year 1 was 12 million cans in Russia. This compares with 450 million cans in the UK each year. If the company's strategy is successful, Heinz beans may become the fashionable food to serve at Moscow dinner parties. Even before the move by Heinz, its products were available on the black market. It gained the status accorded to other Western products such as Coca-Cola and Levi's.

The company hoped that Russia would become one of the top five bean-eating countries in the world. This was before the August 1998 meltdown of the Russian economy that cut living standards sharply. Will Beanz still Mean Roubles? That remainz to be seen.

**Questions** *(30 marks; 40 minutes)*
1 Identify the company's marketing objective for its beans in Russia. *(3)*
2 State the target Heinz set as the test of whether its objective was met. *(3)*
3 **a** Explain the strategy Heinz chose to meet its objectives. *(4)*
   **b** Suggest and explain an alternative strategy it might have adopted. *(6)*
4 **a** Outline the external constraints faced by Heinz. *(5)*
   **b** Discuss how a business might react to changed external constraints, if it was determined to achieve its marketing objectives. *(9)*

#### B2 Case Study

Hoshil and Sunil's business started in rather dubious circumstances. While students they built up their capital by trading in 'second-hand' mobile phones. Their great friend Jayesh came up with the bright idea. They would open a night club aimed at young Asians. It would have two dance floors, one for Indian music and one for Western pop music. One of the bars would be alcohol-free, have pool tables and music soft enough to chat. It would be a night club, but with some of the benefits of a pub. The vision was clear: to provide a thriving social facility for young Asian men and women.

The investment outlay would be £150,000. Hoshil and Sunil put in £25,000 each and were fortunate that Hoshil's wealthy brother Satyam was able to put in the other £100,000. They would soon be ready to start.

Sunil and Jayesh planned their marketing strategy. The objective was clear: to maximise takings from day 1. They needed to pay back their borrowings as soon as possible. After carrying out market research at their local community centre, the boys decided to focus on better-off 16–24-year-olds. Prices would be kept relatively high, as there was no competition in the area. The location would be in the centre of Croydon, as the new Tramlink service would bring people by public transport from a long way away.

Despite the agreement to focus on the better off, when there was only a week until the opening night, Sunil panicked. Would there be enough people to create a good atmosphere? He printed 2,000 leaflets saying 'Half Price Drinks For All The First Week!' and distributed them through the local newsagents. The opening night went very well and on the following

Saturday it was impossible to move. By the second week, though, the numbers were dropping away. When research was carried out it showed that customers thought the drinks were expensive.

It took about six months to establish a really strong reputation as a top club. Large profits were being made and Hoshil's skills as a host were becoming well known. The national paper The Daily Jang ran a whole feature on him. He was very happy, while Sunil and Satyam were enjoying the large dividends on their investments. Jayesh congratulated them on their achievements, but was focused on his own, new computer business. It was bound to be a success.

**Questions** *(50 marks; 60 minutes)*
1 Outline the business importance of the following terms:
   a marketing strategy (5)
   b market research (5)
2 How important to the success of the club were the clear vision and objectives? Explain your answer. (10)
3 Discuss which of the four types of marketing objective were involved in this business success. (8)
4 How serious a risk did Sunil take by carrying out a marketing campaign that was at odds with the overall strategy? (10)
5 What do you consider to be the most important aspects of marketing for a small business? (12)

# ANALYSING THE MARKET

## DEFINITION

A market is a place where buyers and sellers meet. This may be in the street, a giant shopping centre or on the trading floor of a stock exchange. In marketing, though, there is a slightly different meaning for the phrase 'the market'. When businesses refer to the market for their products, they mean the customers. How many there are, whether the number is rising or falling, what their purchasing habits are and much else. Successful marketing relies on a complete understanding of the market.

## 3.1 What market are we in?

This sounds a daft question, but the marketing guru Theodore Levitt considers it vital. Is Liverpool FC in the football business, the sports business or the leisure business? Tottenham Hotspur nearly went into liquidation in the 1980s because of an unsuccessful diversification towards leisure clothing. Today Chelsea has its own hotel and restaurant complex. Barcelona FC runs an ice hockey team and a basketball side.

When looking at the size and growth of a market, it is essential to be clear on the market under consideration. As the above example shows, it can be difficult to decide on where the market's boundaries are. Even when that is settled, the market can probably be broken down into many sub-sectors. The car market, for example, can be broken down into luxury, executive, large family, small and sports vehicles. The issue of market segmentation is dealt with in more detail in Unit 6.

## 3.2 Market size and trends

Market size is the measurement of all the sales by all the companies within a marketplace. It can be measured in two ways: by volume and by value. Volume measures the quantity of goods purchased, perhaps in tonnes, in packs or in units. Market size by value is the amount spent by customers on the volume sold. So the difference between volume and value is the price paid per unit.

Take, for example, these figures for the UK yogurt market:

| | |
|---|---|
| *2001 market by value* | *£710 million* |
| *2001 market by volume* | *2,730 million servings* |
| *Average price per serving* | *26.0 pence (£710m/2,730m)* |

Source: Key Note Market Report 2002

Market size matters because it is the basis for calculating market share, i.e. the proportion of the total market held by one company or brand. This, in turn, is essential for evaluating the success or failure of a firm's marketing activities. Market size is also the reference point for calculating trends. Is the market size growing or declining? A growth market is far more likely to provide the opportunities for new products to be launched or new distribution initiatives to be successful.

In business, the most worrying markets are where volume is rising but value is falling. This means the average price paid is falling quite rapidly. Computer manufacturers have grown used to this situation. For most firms, though, it is very hard to cope with the combination of extra output/costs with lower value/revenue.

The table at the top of the next page gives an example of some different market sizes (by value), together with their most recent sales trends. The huge differences in market size give a good indication of the sales potential for a new company or a new product. The massive size of the soft drinks market means that the annual increase of 4.9% represents £117 million of extra sales. Plenty of room for new brands of the size of Lilt or Lucozade, which have sales of £20–30 million per annum.

Individual firms can do little to influence the overall growth of a market. Many factors are involved, mostly stemming from broader economic and social changes. The main factors affecting market growth are:

- economic growth, in other words the growth of real incomes throughout the economy; luxury markets will grow rapidly when people feel better off
- social changes, for example the move away from family meals at home has led to above average growth rates for markets such as fast-food, confectionery and prepared sandwiches
- changes in fashion, most obviously in the market for trainers; when fashion was an important influence, young people bought new trainers more often

| MARKET | 2001 UK MARKET SIZE | TREND (CHANGE SINCE 2000) | |
|---|---|---|---|
| Soft drinks | £2,481,544,000 | +4.9% | +£117 million |
| Bagged crisps & snacks | £1,836,016,000 | +2.1% | +£38 million |
| Hot drinks (tea, coffee, chocolate) | £1,049,619,000 | −4.0% | −£44 million |
| Soup | £373,328,000 | +2.5% | +£9 million |
| Ice-cream | £769,569,000 | +3.0% | +£23 million |

Source: *The Grocer*, 17/12/01 (quoting data from IRI InfoScan)

(increasing market size by volume) and were prepared to pay higher prices (increasing market value)

- the ability of the suppliers to identify and meet consumer requirements; the cinema market seemed in terminal decline until multi-screen, modern cinemas revitalised the market.

## 3.3 Market share

Market share is the proportion of the total market held by one company or product. It can be measured by volume, but is more often looked at by value. Among major companies in mature markets such as soft drinks or confectionery, market share is usually the focus of a great deal of attention. Famously, Coca-Cola's biggest marketing mistake was in response to a decline in its US market share from just 22.5% to 21.8% during the 1980s. Deciding that the taste of the product was less popular than Pepsi's, Coca-Cola changed its product formula and relaunched as New Improved Coca-Cola. The American population, brought up on *the original* Coke rejected the new product, forcing the company to reintroduce the old formula. The embarrassment was huge, as Pepsi gloated publicly about the better taste of Pepsi. All because of a slip of 0.7% in market share.

Market share is taken by most firms as the key test of their marketing strategy. Total sales are affected by factors such as economic growth, but market share only measures a firm's ability to win or lose against its competitors. As shown in the table below, rising market share can also lead to the producer's ideal of market leadership or market dominance. Kit-Kat has

market leadership among confectionery brands. Walkers has market dominance among crisps and snacks. Nestlé's position with Nescafé is stronger still, as the 'nearest competitor' is Nescafé Gold Blend.

There are many advantages to a business in having the top-selling brand (the **brand leader**). Obviously, sales are higher than anyone else's, but also:

- The brand leader will get the highest distribution level, often without needing to make much effort to achieve it. Even a tiny corner shop will stock Heinz. Success breeds success.
- Brand leaders will be able to offer lower discount terms to retailers than the Number 2 or Number 3 brands in a market. This means higher revenues and profit margins per unit sold. For example Nescafé may offer only an 8% margin to the retailer, whereas Maxwell House may need to offer 14%.
- The strength of a brand leading name such as Walls Magnum makes it much easier to obtain distribution and consumer trial for new products based on that brand name.

### FIGHTING FOR MARKET SHARE

Large firms operating in consumer markets focus a great deal on market share. Usually, every brand is looked after by a brand manager. He or she will have agreed targets for market share that must be met or beaten by the year-end.

At the start of the year, the brand manager will divide up his or her budget between above-the-line activity (media advertising), below-the-line promotions and market research. He or she will probably be

| LEADING BRAND IN ITS MARKET | SALES OF LEADING BRAND | MARKET SIZE (BY VALUE) | MARKET SHARE | SHARE OF NEAREST COMPETITOR |
|---|---|---|---|---|
| Walkers crisps | £488 million | £1,836 million | 26.6% | 7.4% |
| Nescafé | £153 million | £435 million* | 35.2% | 15.2% |
| Kit-Kat | £179 million | £2,553 million | 7.0% | 4.9% |
| Heinz soup | £133 million | £373 million | 35.7% | 11.4% |
| Wall's Magnum | £72 million | £770 million | 9.4% | 5.4% |

Source: *The Grocer*, 17/12/01 (quoting from IRI Infoscan)                     *Market for instant coffee

trying to strike a balance between this year's market share targets and the needs of future years. Media advertising boosts short-term sales but also strengthens brand awareness and image for years to come. Below-the-line activity merely strengthens short-term demand. A balanced approach might consist of two bursts of TV advertising during the year supported by trade promotions (to boost distribution), consumer price promotions, a consumer competition and an on-pack special offer. During the year, the market research budget will be used to check that the TV commercials achieve their objectives and to monitor customer attitudes to the brand (and its competitors).

If the marketing plan proves unsuccessful, with market share sliding by the mid-year, a rethink may be needed. The Autumn advertising budget may be cut back to provide more money for a big consumer promotion. Or on-pack special offer pricing may be needed to boost sales and market share. The risk with these actions is that rival firms may feel forced to respond, causing a flurry of promotional activity which cancels itself out.

## — TRAINER WARS

In 1987, Reebok was the dominant supplier of sports footwear to America. It had a 30% share – far in excess of the Number 2, Nike. Then, as the market size exploded in the early 1990s, Reebok found it increasingly difficult to compete. Nike kept hitting home with the smarter moves. With Michael Jordan and Tiger Woods, it was Nike who tied up the biggest star names. And Nike who proved one step ahead in new product development. By 1996 Nike was spending almost $1,000 million a year on marketing. Reebok could afford $400 million, but this was insufficient to prevent a slide in market share. By 2001, Reebok's market share fell to under 15% of the US market. By now Nike was the clear brand leader.

In early 1998 Reebok announced a change in strategy. No longer would it attempt to compete in the fashion-oriented youth market dominated by Nike marketing. Reebok would aim more at the adult market, accepting that lower market share would not matter as long as costs fell sharply enough.

Reebok was raising the white flag in the trainer wars. In Europe, it would be Adidas that would keep Nike on its toes, as shown in the Nike and Adidas TV advertising battle during the 2002 World Cup.

Source: Adapted from *The Financial Times*

## 3.4 Consumer usage and attitudes

Market analysis is rooted in a deep understanding of customers. Why do they buy Walkers crisps, not Golden Wonder? And who are the key decision makers? Purchasers (perhaps parents buying a multipack in Tesco) or the users (perhaps young teenage children slumped in front of the television)? Is the brand decision a result of child **pester-power**, or parental belief in the product's superiority? Knowledge of such subtleties is essential. Only then can the firm know whether to focus marketing effort on the parent or the child.

To acquire the necessary knowledge about usage and attitudes, firms adopt several approaches. The starting point is usually qualitative research such as group discussions. Run by psychologists, these informal discussions help pinpoint consumers' underlying motives and behaviour. For example, it is important to learn whether Kit-Kat buyers enjoy nibbling the chocolate before eating the wafer biscuit. In other words, to discover whether playing with confectionery is an important part of the enjoyment. This type of information can influence future product development.

The huge multinational Unilever has appointed a head of knowledge management and development (David Smith), to ensure that insights such as this can be spread around the business. As he says, 'The company's collective knowledge is potentially a great competitive advantage'. By encouraging improved communication and networking, Unilever believes it is benefiting from:

- improved decision making
- fewer mistakes
- reduced duplication
- converting new knowledge more quickly into added value to the business.

Among the other ways to gather information on customer usage and attitudes are quantitative research and obtaining feedback from staff who deal directly with customers. An example of the latter would be bank staff whose task is to sell services such as insurance. Customer doubts about a brochure or a product feature, if fed back to head office, might lead to important improvements.

Quantitative research is a common way to monitor customer usage and attitudes. Many firms conduct surveys every month, to track any changes over time in brand awareness or image. This procedure may reveal that a TV commercial has had an unintended side-effect in making the brand image rather too upmarket. Or that customers within a market are becoming more concerned about whether packaging can be recycled.

Business
IN

## 3.5 Consumer profiles

Marketing decisions are very hard to make without a clear picture of your customers. Who are they? Young? Outgoing? Affluent? Or not. From product and packaging design, through pricing, promotion and distribution – all these aspects of marketing hinge on knowing your **target market**.

A consumer profile is a statistical breakdown of the people who buy a particular product or brand, e.g. what percentage of consumers are women aged 16–25? The main categories analysed within a consumer profile are the customers' age, gender, social class, income level and region. Main uses of profile information are:

- for setting quotas for research surveys
- for segmenting a market
- for deciding in which media to advertise (*Vogue* or the *Sun*?).

A large consumer goods firm will make sure to obtain a profile of consumers throughout the market as well as for its own brand(s). This may be very revealing. It may show that the age profile of its own customers is becoming older than for the market as a whole. This may force a complete rethink of the marketing strategy. The company may have been trying to give the brand a classier image, but end up attracting older customers.

## 3.6 Market mapping

Having analysed consumer attitudes and consumer profiles, it is possible to create a market map. This is done by selecting the key variables that differentiate the brands within a market. Then plotting the position of each one. Usually this is done on a two-dimensional diagram as below. Here, the image of shoe shops has been plotted against the key criteria of price (premium–budget) and purpose (aspirational–commodity). For example, Bally shoes are expensive and are bought to impress others. Church's are expensive but bought because their buyers believe they are a top quality product.

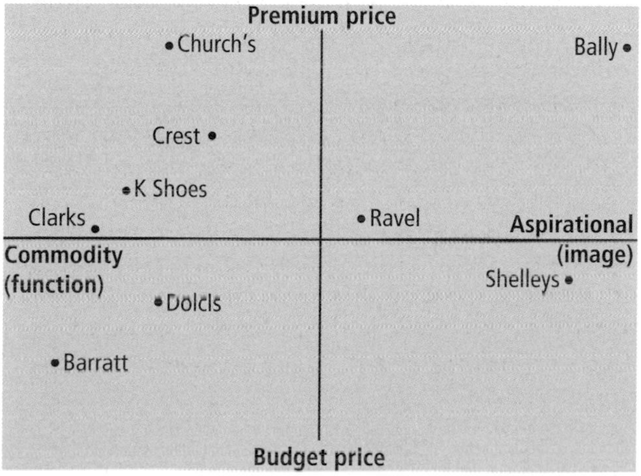


Source: author's estimates

**Figure 3.1**

Market mapping enables a firm to identify any gaps or niches in the market that are unfilled. It also helps monitor existing brands. Is the firm's image becoming too young and trendy? If so, booming sales in the short term might be followed by longer term disappointment. By monitoring the position of their brands on the market map, firms can see more easily when a repositioning exercise is required. This may involve a relaunch with a slightly different product, a new pack design and a new advertising campaign.

**IN Business**

### THE TOAST OF LONDON

Founded in 1945, Dualit built up a reputation for its toasters and kettles. Fierce competition from multinational electrical goods firms in the 1960s and 1970s forced it out of the consumer market. Instead of giving up, the company redesigned its products to aim for the catering trade. Dualit stainless steel, extra-durable toasters became the norm in cafes and hotel kitchens. Dualit's founder has explained that: 'I spotted a gap in the market and started to cater for the smaller demand in what was a niche area'. Remarkably, the elegant and robust design of the Dualit toaster made it fashionable in the 1990s. Despite costing more than £100, the Dualit made a comeback in a small segment of the consumer market. The company now employs 75 skilled workers in South London and makes more than £1.5 million profit on £10 million of sales.

Source: Adapted from *The Sunday Times*

## 3.7 Industrial versus consumer markets

Analysing **industrial markets** requires a slightly different approach. When selling to other firms, image is less of an issue. Traditionally, all that mattered was the right product at the right price at the right time. Today this will not always do. Firms are looking for more from their suppliers. They want complete solutions to problems or requirements. This may require the design of a brand new, tailor-made product. Or organising a series of suppliers to work together to supply a complete unit of production. For instance, a car manufacturer might want matching car seats, carpets and interior trim to be delivered to the right part of a production line at precise times.

To find out exactly what is needed, direct contact with potential and existing customers is essential. Fortunately it is also possible, as industrial markets are unlikely to have more than a hundred or so customers. Each may have slightly different requirements, so flexibility will be a key requirement. Visits to **trade exhibitions** should generate some contacts. Sales representatives should then follow these up by visiting the customer to discuss requirements.

Market analysis is therefore largely based on information gained from individual customers, rather than from general sources such as secondary research. The industrial supplier that waits for the phone to ring is likely to lose out in the short term. It will also fail to gather the market knowledge needed to keep improving the products in line with changing customer demand.

Trade exhibitions are important for generating contacts and raising a company's profile (© SignUK/Faversham House Group Ltd)

ISSUES FOR **analysis**

Among the main issues raised by this unit are:

- The importance to a firm of constantly measuring and rethinking its position in the market. This is why expenditure on market research needs to be regular; not just related to the latest new project.
- Given the importance of market knowledge, how can new firms break into a market? The answer is: with difficulty. Mars did remarkably well to break into the ice-cream market in 1990. But it has probably not yet made a profit on ice-cream in the UK market.
- If all companies follow similar techniques for market analysis, why don't they all come up with the same answers? Fortunately, there remains huge scope for initiative and intuition. Two different managers reading the same market research report may come up with quite different conclusions. The launch of the low cost airline easyJet in 1996 was one man's vision, Stelios Haja-Iaannou. At the time, British Airways predicted that easyJet would flop.

## 3.8 Market analysis
### an evaluation

Market analysis is at the heart of successful marketing. All the great marketing decisions are rooted in a deep understanding of what customers really want. From the marketing of The Spice Girls through to the 2001 launch of Sony PlayStation 2. These successes were rooted in an understanding of the consumer. The clever market stall trader acquires this understanding through daily contact with customers. Large companies need the help of market research to provide a comparable feel. Techniques such as market mapping then help clarify the picture.

Successful marketing strategies rely upon the firm's ability to target the real requirements of the customers. How it goes about this task (through the marketing mix) is a less important consideration.

**KEY terms**

**brand leader** – the brand with the highest market share. In fragmented markets such as chocolate, the brand leader may have no more than Kit-Kat's 7.0%.

**industrial markets** – those where products are sold only to other companies, e.g. heavy lorries.

**pester-power** – the ability of children to pester their parents into buying the products they want.

**product positioning** – deciding on the image and target market you want for your own product or brand.

**target market** – the type of customer your product or service is aimed at. For example the target market for Cherry Coke is 10–16-year-olds from both sexes.

**trade exhibitions** – annual events where suppliers display their products and services to the buyers who come to see what is new or improved.

# Exercises

## A. REVISION QUESTIONS
*(35 marks; 70 minutes)*

Read the unit, then answer:

1 What market would you consider each of the following businesses to be in?
   a  Müller Fruit Corner
   b  Rolls Royce Motors
   c  Virgin Trains                                                    *(3)*
2 What is the difference between market size by volume and market size by value?                                   *(3)*
3 In 1998, sales of Pringles rose 39% to achieve sales of £121 million. What share did this give it of the market for bagged crisps and snacks (see page 15)?         *(2)*
4 Identify three factors outside the control of a business that can influence its rate of growth.                  *(3)*

5 Why does the text suggest that whereas Kit-Kat has market leadership, Walker's has market *dominance*?  *(3)*
6 Why is it important to find out the way consumers use the products they buy?                               *(3)*
7 Identify four benefits a business may gain from effective knowledge management.                            *(4)*
8 a  Explain the meaning of the term 'consumer profile'.  *(3)*

   b  Why might the manager in charge of Sunny Delight find it useful to know the brand's consumer profile?  *(4)*

9 Read the In Business on the Dualit toaster. Briefly explain how the company benefited from analysing its market.                                               *(4)*
10 Explain how an industrial market differs from a consumer market.                                         *(3)*

### All outlets (grocery and impulse)

| | | | 52 w/e 02 Nov '97 Value Sales (£) | 52 w/e 01 Nov '98 Value Sales (£) | % chg |
|---|---|---|---|---|---|
| 1 | (1) | Nestlé Kit-Kat | 162,459k | 163,151k | 0.4 |
| 2 | (2) | Mars bar | 128,376k | 132,343k | 3.1 |
| 3 | (3) | Cadbury's Dairy Milk | 99,131k | 96,584k | −2.6 |
| 4 | (6) | Mars Maltesers | 81,242k | 89,382k | 10.0 |
| 5 | (5) | Mars Twix | 86,714k | 88,268k | 1.8 |
| 6 | (4) | Cadbury's Roses | 88,843k | 86,244k | −2.9 |
| 7 | (7) | Mars Snickers | 75,216k | 75,074k | −0.2 |
| 8 | (8) | Nestlé Quality Street | 65,511k | 68,415k | 4.4 |
| 9 | (9) | Mars Galaxy | 62,242k | 59,075k | −5.1 |
| 10 | (10) | Nestlé Aero | 58,471k | 58,995k | 0.9 |
| 11 | (11) | Cadbury's Milk Tray | 43,922k | 45,379k | 3.3 |
| 12 | (13) | Cadbury's Fruit & Nut | 43,507k | 43,726k | 0.5 |
| 13 | (15) | Nestlé Polo | 42,329k | 42,630k | 0.7 |
| 14 | (−) | Mars Celebrations | 12,830k | 42,478k | 231.1 |
| 15 | (14) | Mars Bounty | 42,475k | 41,800k | −1.6 |
| 16 | (16) | Cadbury's Crunchie | 40,401k | 37,299k | −7.7 |
| 17 | (19) | Cadbury's Whole Nut | 37,075k | 37,118k | 0.1 |
| 18 | (−) | Cadbury's Creme Egg | 32,590k | 36,863k | 13.1 |
| 19 | (18) | Nestlé Smarties | 38,594k | 36,467k | −5.5 |
| 20 | (17) | Cadbury's Time Out | 39,078k | 35,918k | −8.1 |
| **Total market value** | | | **3,189,707k** | **3,354,418k** | **5.2** |

### Sugar confectionery

| | | 52 w/e 02 Nov '97 Value Sales (£) | 52 w/e 01 Nov '98 Value Sales (£) | % chg |
|---|---|---|---|---|
| 1 | Nestlé Polo | 42,329k | 42,630k | 0.7 |
| 2 | Mars Opal Fruits | 29,804k | 35,475k | 19.0 |
| 3 | Trebor Softmints | 35,971k | 34,381k | −4.4 |
| 4 | Trebor Extra Strong Mint | 33,487k | 32,702k | −2.3 |
| 5 | Nestlé Rowntree Fruit Pastilles | 34,181k | 32,460k | −5.0 |

Source: IRI InfoScan

## B. REVISION EXERCISES

### B1 Data Response

Look at the table of data on the previous page.

**Questions** *(25 marks; 25 minutes)*

1 Explain the meaning of the term 'market value'. *(2)*

2 The outstanding new confectionery product success in 1998 was the launch of Mars Celebrations. It was designed to compete with Cadbury's Roses and Nestlé Quality Street. What reasons might explain why these products suffered little from this new competitor? *(5)*

3 Nestlé Smarties had a poor sales year. Outline two factors that might explain this. *(4)*

4 A new product success in 1998 was the launch of the Polo Supermint. Nestlé launched it at the younger end of the market than the traditional Polo buyer. What benefits might this have for Nestlé? *(5)*

5 Only two of the brands in the confectionery Top 20 have been launched in the past 10 years. Most are more than 50 years old. Consider why brand loyalties may be so stable in markets such as confectionery. *(9)*

### B2 Case Study

Graham Smith winked at Raya Farmer as the first guest signed in. She smiled cheesily. It had taken 10 months and £340,000 to get the Lakeside Coaching Inn open. Graham had found it hard to cope at times, but Raya's cool head helped to see it through. Now, with the lounge bar taking good business and the restaurant fully booked for tonight – opening night – the booking of a hotel room rounded off a very good start.

The idea had come about in a strategy meeting at Swallow Hotels, where Graham and Raya both used to work. Graham was operations manager and Raya the marketing manager. Raya had just completed a £50,000 market research programme to produce a market mapping exercise which no-one seemed interested in. Graham, though, had a quiet word with Raya afterwards. He said: 'Don't you think there's a market for a chain of reasonably priced hotels with character? At the moment you wouldn't know if you're in Torquay or Tokyo. They're identically dull.' She nodded keenly, making it clear that she had hoped the meeting would come to exactly that conclusion. Instead, over the following weeks, Graham and Raya talked it through together.

Having looked at market trends, Raya was convinced an opportunity existed. Graham had always yearned to be his own boss, so this seemed like the time to start.

Both he and Raya could find £40,000 of share capital. After discussions with NatWest Bank, the pair were offered a loan of £200,000, secured against hotel premises. Helped by £60,000 put into the business by Raya's uncle, they set out to buy their first outlet. It would be the first of perhaps a hundred 'traditional inns' they intended to link within their chain. Raya believed that would be enough to achieve a 4% share of the billion pound market for business travel.

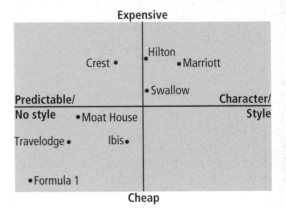

Market mapping – hotel chains in the UK

The intention was to guarantee certain service standards, such as all rooms have a bathroom, a TV and a telephone. Apart from that, though, the more original the inn the better. For example, one might be an old pub serving a wide range of real ales. Another might specialise in good local food. The travellers would be able to choose the one to suit their needs and tastes.

From the start the idea showed promise. The key, though, would be forming a national chain. While Graham looked after the business, Raya went to visit other pubs and inns to try to persuade their owners to join a marketing syndicate. Raya would organise the links with companies and business travel agents to ensure a regular stream of customers. Three months of hard, expensive travelling led finally to a breakthrough when a group of eight hotels in Somerset and Devon agreed to join. After that it became much easier to sell the concept and within six months she had signed up 100 traditional inns nationally.

### Press release – launch of Britain's newest hotel chain

**The Traditional Inns Group**

Business travellers are tired of dull hotels with formula food. Finance directors despair of the excessive prices charged by expense account hotels. The Traditional Inns Group will change all that. We are a national chain of a hundred hotels with character, warm hospitality, great beer and great food. Near Bath we have a seventeenth century coaching inn. Just outside Newcastle is a nineteenth century converted water mill. The Traditional Inns Group guarantees the service consistency business travellers demand, but in truly original settings. For further details phone …

At last there was a really strong story to send out as a press release to the travel trade magazines and in a direct mailing to businesses throughout Britain. The Traditional Inns Group had arrived. Marks & Spencer agreed to put the chain on its list of approved hotel groups for business travelling. The future seemed assured.

**Questions** *(40 marks; 70 minutes)*

1 Why was it important that Raya:
   a had conducted a £50,000 market research programme (5)
   b had a clear market share target? (5)
2 Consider why Swallow Hotels may have been uninterested in Raya's market mapping exercise. (10)
3 In the long term, the success of the Traditional Inns Group will depend upon satisfied customers, repeat purchase and good word of mouth. How might Graham and Raya set about achieving this? (10)
4 Discuss the importance of market mapping in the process of analysing a market. (10)

# MARKET RESEARCH

**DEFINITION**

Market research gathers information about consumers, competitors and distributors within a firm's target market. It is a way of identifying consumers' buying habits and attitudes to current and future products. Market research data can be numerical (such as what proportion of 16–24-year-olds buy *The Sun* every day?) or psychological (why do they buy *The Sun*?).

## 4.1 Researching into a new market

Where do you start? What do you need to know first? And how do you find it out?

The starting point is to discover the marketing fundamentals: market size, market potential and market shares.

Market size means the value of the sales made annually by all the firms within a market. For example, in 2001 the UK yoghurt market was worth £710 million. Market potential can be measured by the annual rate of growth. In the case of yoghurt, this has been at a rate of 6% per year, by value. This implies that, by the year 2005, the potential market size will be nearly £900 million.

When looking at a completely new market, these statistics will not be available. So research may be needed into other indicators. For example, the producer of an innovative new fishing rod would find out the number of people who go fishing regularly.

Market shares are also of crucial importance when investigating a market, as they indicate the relative strength of the firms within the market. In 2001, 28% of the yoghurt market was held by Müller, making it the leading brand by far. A benefit it received for its strong market share was a distribution level of almost 100% – nearly every grocery store stocked Müller. If one firm dominates, it may be very difficult to break the market.

So how can firms find out this type of information? The starting point is secondary research: unearthing data which already exists.

## 4.2 Secondary research

**Trade press:** All the above data about the yoghurt market came from an article in *The Grocer* magazine. Every major market is served by one or more magazines written for people who work within that trade. A subscription to *Caterer and Hotelkeeper* or to *The Grocer* soon provides a wealth of statistical and other information. The name and contact details of relevant magazines can be found in BRAD (British Rate And Data) – available at many public libraries.

**Trade associations:** These associations represent the interests of member companies within a market. For example, the Society of Motor Manufacturers and Traders collects production and sales statistics for the UK car market. It also speaks on behalf of the whole industry, perhaps when the Government is considering car tax increases. Trade associations represent a huge potential source of useful information on market size and trends. Most public libraries have their details listed in a directory called *Trade Associations and Professional Bodies of the United Kingdom* (published by Gale Research, 13th ed, 1997).

**Market intelligence reports:** These include data on market size by volume and value, market shares, sales trends, sales forecasts, market segmentation, details of advertising spending and distribution channels. They are hugely useful, but also hugely expensive. Fortunately, larger – business oriented – libraries often hold the reports produced by the big three: Keynotes, Mintel and Retail Business (EIU).

Other important sources of secondary data include:

- Government publications produced by the Office of National Statistics, such as the *Annual Abstract of Statistics*, *Social Trends* and *Economic Trends*. These provide data on population trends and forecasts (e.g. for a cosmetics producer to find how many 16–20-year-old women there will be in the year 2008); and on the amount consumers spend on different categories of product.
- Newspaper articles and special reports; for example, the *Financial Times* produces an eight-page report on information technology every three months. It gives the latest trends and ideas.

Once a firm has the necessary data on the market as a whole, a strategy can be developed for penetrating it. For example, if secondary data revealed that the average age of Bacardi drinkers was rising year on year, a rival company might decide an opportunity exists for a new white rum.

Having obtained background data, further research is likely to be tailored specifically to the company's needs, such as carrying out a survey among 18–25-year-old drinkers of spirits. This type of first-hand research gathers primary data.

| SECONDARY RESEARCH | | PRIMARY RESEARCH |
|---|---|---|
| Pros | • often obtained without cost<br>• good overview of a market<br>• usually based on actual sales figures, or research on large samples | • can aim questions directly at your research objectives<br>• latest information from the marketplace<br>• can assess the psychology of the customer |
| Cons | • data may not be updated regularly<br>• not tailored to your own needs<br>• expensive, but reports on many different marketplaces | • expensive, £5,000+ per survey<br>• risk of questionnaire and interviewer bias<br>• research findings may only be usable if comparable backdata exists |

## 4.3 Primary research

The process of gathering information directly from people within your target market is known as primary (or field) research. When carried out by market research companies it is expensive, but there is much that firms can do for themselves.

For a company that is up and running, a regular survey of customer satisfaction is an important way of measuring the quality of customer service. When investigating a new market, there are various measures that can be taken by a small firm with a limited budget:

- Retailer research – the people closest to a market are those who serve customers directly – the retailers. They are likely to know the up-and-coming brands, the degree of brand loyalty, the importance of price and packaging – all crucial information.
- Observation – when starting up a service business in which location is an all-important factor, it is invaluable to measure the rate of pedestrian (and possibly traffic) flow past your potential site compared with that of rivals. A sweet shop or a dry-cleaners near a busy bus stop may generate twice the sales of a rival 50 metres down the road.
- In-depth interviews – even if only with a few consumers, these can lead to ideas that would not otherwise have emerged, such as the importance of

a psychological price barrier ('Oh, I'd never pay over a tenner for a book.').

For a large company, primary research will be used extensively in new product development. For example, if a company were considering the possibility of launching Orange Chocolate Buttons, the development stages – plus research – would probably be those shown in the table below.

## 4.4 Qualitative research

Qualitative research is in depth research into the motivations behind the attitudes and buying habits of consumers. It does not produce statistics such as '52% of chocolate buyers like orange chocolate'; instead it gives clues as to why they like it (is it really because it's orange, or because it's different/a change?). Qualitative research is usually conducted by psychologists, who learn to interpret the way people say things as well as what they say.

Qualitative research takes two main forms:

**1 Group discussions:** Also known as focus groups, these are free-ranging discussions led by psychologists among groups of 6–8 consumers. The group leader will have a list of topics that need discussion, but will be free to follow up any point made by a group member. Among the advantages of group discussions are:

| DEVELOPMENT STAGE | | PRIMARY RESEARCH | |
|---|---|---|---|
| 1 | The product idea (probably one of several) | 1 | Group discussions among regular chocolate buyers – some young, some old |
| 2 | Product test (testing different recipes – different sweetness, orangeyness, etc.) | 2 | A taste test on 200+ chocolate buyers (on street corners, or in a hall) |
| 3 | Brand name research (testing several different names and perhaps logos) | 3 | Quantitative research using a questionnaire on a sample of 200+ |
| 4 | Packaging research | 4 | As 3. |
| 5 | Advertising research | 5 | Group discussions run by psychologists to discover which advertisement has the strongest effect on product image and recall |
| 6 | Total proposition test: testing the level of purchase interest, to help make sales forecasts | 6 | Quantitative research using a questionnaire and product samples on at least 200+ consumers |

- may reveal a problem or opportunity the company had not anticipated
- reveals consumer psychology, such as the importance of image and peer pressure
- a good way of shortlisting options from a number of possibilities; for example whittling six different pack designs down to two, which will then be researched quantitatively (see section 4.5).

## Business
### IN

## RESEARCHING HÄAGEN DAZS

Group discussions were used prior to the UK launch of Häagen Dazs. Groups of men and women were each given a half-litre tub of Häagen Dazs and asked questions about when, how and with whom they would like to eat it. Respondents spoke about sharing a spoon with their partner, feeding each other and 'mellowing out' in front of a video. This led to a breakthrough in food advertising: Häagen Dazs was advertised as a sensual pleasure to be shared. Its huge success when launched has become recognised as a success for qualitative research.

**2 In-depth interviews:** Informal, in-depth interviews between a psychologist and a consumer. They have the same function as group discussions, but avoid the risk that the group opinion will be swayed by one influential person.

*Typical research questions to be answered by:*

| *Qualitative research* | *Quantitative research* |
|---|---|
| • *Why do people really buy Levi's?* | • *Which pack design do you prefer?* |
| • *Who in the household really decides which brand of shampoo is bought?* | • *Have you heard of any of the following brands? (Ariel, Daz, Persil, etc.)* |
| • *What mood makes you feel like buying Haagen Dazs ice-cream?* | • *How likely are you to buy this product regularly?* |
| • *When you buy your children Frosties, how do you feel?* | • *How many newspapers have you bought in the past seven days?* |

## 4.5 Quantitative research

Quantitative research asks pre-set questions on a large enough sample of people to provide statistically valid data. Questionnaires can answer factual questions

such as 'How many 16–20-year-olds have heard of Chanel No 5?' There are three key aspects to quantitative research:

- sampling, i.e. ensuring that the research results are typical of the whole population, though only a sample of the population has been interviewed
- writing a questionnaire that is unbiased and meets the research objectives
- assessing the validity of the results.

### SAMPLING

The two main concerns in sampling are how to choose the right people for interview (sampling method) and deciding how large a number to interview (sample size). There are four main sampling methods:

**Random sample:** Selecting respondents to ensure that everyone in the population has an equal chance of being interviewed. This sounds easy, but is not. If an interviewer goes to a street corner one morning and asks passers-by for an interview, the resulting sample will be biased towards those who are not in work, who do not own a car and have time on their hands (the busy ones will refuse to be interviewed). As a result the sample will not be representative. So achieving a truly random sample requires careful thought.

Research companies use the following method:

- pick names at random from the electoral register, e.g. every 50th name
- send an interviewer to the address given in the register
- if the person is out, visit up to twice more before giving up (this is to maximise the chances of catching those who lead busy social lives and are therefore rarely at home).

This method is effective, but slow and expensive.

**Quota sample:** Selecting interviewees in proportion to the consumer profile within your target market, for example:

| ADULT CHOCOLATE BUYERS | | RESPONDENT QUOTA (SAMPLE: 200) |
|---|---|---|
| Men | 40% | 80 |
| Women | 60% | 120 |
| 16–24 | 38% | 76 |
| 25–34 | 21% | 42 |
| 35–44 | 16% | 32 |
| 45+ | 25% | 50 |

This method allows interviewers to head for busy street corners, interviewing whoever comes along. As long as they end up achieving the correct quota, they can interview when and where they want to. As this is a relatively cheap and effective way of sampling, it is the one used most commonly by market research companies.

**Stratified sample:** Only interviewing those with a key characteristic required for the sample. For example, the producers of Oil of Olay might decide to interview only women aged 30–45, the potential buyers of the future. Within this stratum/section of the population, individuals could be found at random (hence stratified random sample) or by setting quotas based on factors such as social class and region.

**Cluster sample:** Sampling only within a specified area/areas. For example, in selected university towns (perhaps for bank accounts) or in seaside resorts (for swimwear). This is not a common form of sampling, though valuable for student projects.

## SAMPLE SIZE

Having decided which sampling method should be used, the next consideration is how many interviews should be conducted? 10? 100? 1,000? The most high-profile surveys conducted in Britain are the opinion polls – asking people how they will vote in a general election. These quota samples of between 1,000 and 1,500 respondents are considered large enough to reflect the opinions of the electorate of 44 million. How is this possible?

Of course, if you only interviewed 10 people, the chances are slim that the views of this sample will match those of the whole population. Of these 10, seven may say they would definitely buy Chocolate Orange Buttons. If you asked another 10, however, only three may say the same. A sample of 10 is so small that chance variations make the results meaningless. In other words, a researcher can have no statistical confidence in the findings from a sample of 10.

A sample of 100 is far more meaningful. It is not enough to feel confident about marginal decisions (e.g. 53% like the red pack design, 47% like the blue one), but is quite enough if the result is clear cut (e.g. 65% like the name 'Spark'; 35% prefer 'Valencia'). Many major product launches have proceeded following research on as low a sample as 100.

With a sample of 1,000 a high level of confidence is possible. Even small differences would be statistically significant with such a large sample. A further benefit of large sample sizes is that they allow sub-groups to be analysed. For example, research into the sales prospects for a new product shows that 59% say they will definitely buy. But who exactly are the keen ones? Breaking the results down by age group may show that 71% of 16–20-year-old men will buy, but only 32% of 45–60-year-olds. In which case the advertising can be directed at the younger group. If the sample size is 100, each sub-group may contain fewer than 10 people, giving the findings no validity. A sample size of 1,000 provides large enough sub-groups to allow valid conclusions.

So why doesn't everyone use samples of 1,000? The answer is money. Hiring a market research agency to undertake a survey of 100 people would cost approximately £5,000. A sample of 1,000 people would cost three times that amount – good value if you can afford it, but not everyone can. As shown in the earlier example of launching Orange Chocolate Buttons, a company might require six surveys before launching a new product. So the spending on research alone might reach £90,000, if samples of 1,000 were used.

## QUALITATIVE UNDERSTANDING OF STATISTICAL SIGNIFICANCE

Market researchers know that no result from a sample can be relied upon 100%. You can only be 100% sure of the population's opinion if you ask all of them – but that would be impractical. Researchers have come to accept that 95% reliability is good enough, in other words they are willing to accept a finding that should be right 19 times out of 20 (95%). This is known as a 95% confidence level.

For example, a researcher may present the following findings to a client:

| | **PREFER** | | **PREFER** |
|---|---|---|---|
| Advertisement A | 48% | Brand name X | 31% |
| Advertisement B | 52% | Brand name Y | 32% |
| | | Brand name Z | 37% |

The researcher might say that, given the large sample size used for the advertising research, one can have 95% confidence in the preference for B, i.e. the result is statistically reliable. The apparent preference for brand name Z may not be reliable, however, if the sample size were relatively small. Therefore the researcher would recommend that the client should regard names X, Y and Z as liked equally. So the client should choose between them on other criteria, such as image.

## WRITING A QUESTIONNAIRE

Quantitative research is expensive and its results may influence major decisions such as whether to launch a new product. So a mistake in writing the questionnaire may prove very costly. For instance, the wording may influence respondents to sound more positive about a new product than they really feel. What are the key features of a good questionnaire?

- Clearly defined research objectives. What exactly do you need to find out?
- Ensure that questions do not point towards a particular answer.
- Ensure that the meaning of each question is clear, perhaps by testing (piloting) questions before putting them into fieldwork.

- Use mainly closed questions, i.e. ones with a limited number of pre-set answers that the respondent must tick; only in this way can you ensure quantifiable results.
- It is useful, though, to include a few open questions, to allow respondents to write a sentence or two, providing more depth of understanding.
- Ensure that the questionnaire finishes by asking full demographic and usership details, i.e. respondents' sex, age, occupation (and therefore social class) and buying habits. This allows more detailed analysis of sub-groups within the sample.

Having written a questionnaire in draft form, research companies trial it by getting experienced interviewers to try it out. Experienced researchers know that questionnaires are unlikely to be right first time. A question that seems clear to the writer may be interpreted in different ways by different people.

## 4.6 Other important considerations in primary research

**Response rate:** If a company sends out 2,000 questionnaires and only 200 people send back a response, the question must be asked: are those who respond typical of those who do not respond? Or is there a bias built into the findings as a consequence of the low response rate?

**Face-to-face versus self-completion:** In the past, most surveys were conducted by interviewers who asked the questions face-to-face. This had drawbacks such as cost and the risk of bias (a bubbly young interviewer may generate more positive responses). Clear benefits, however, included a high response rate and the assurance that the interviewer could help to explain an unclear question. Today, self-completion questionnaires are increasingly common.

## 4.7 Market research in the twenty-first century

Market research is increasingly influenced by technology. Instead of standing on windy street corners, interviewers are more likely to be sitting in a telephone booth in an office. There they can interview people over the phone, keying their answers directly into a computer. This provides results at the touch of a button at the end of a day's work. It is a cheaper and much quicker way to conduct quantitative research. Already most opinion polls are carried out this way.

An even stronger trend is towards database-driven research. Instead of finding the right people by trial and error, client firms supply research companies with database information on current or ex-customers.

Retailers such as Tesco and Sainsbury have millions of customer names on their databases, all grouped into categories such as regular/irregular shoppers, petrol buyers, disposable nappy buyers and so on. If Tesco wants to survey customer satisfaction with their baby products section, it knows exactly who should be contacted.

Manufacturers have learned from this and are rapidly developing the same database information. One of the major cigarette companies has developed a database of millions of its customers by logging every entry for a promotion or special offer. The same company has used this information to plot, by postcode, brand buying habits throughout the country. So instead of running poster advertising campaigns nationally, different brands are advertised on posters in different parts of the country.

The future of market research is clearly bound up in computers, the Internet, TV observation cameras and – quite soon – interactive cable TV. The basics will remain crucial, however: the avoidance of bias in the wording of questions, large enough sample sizes to provide valid data and intelligent analysis of the research findings.

ISSUES FOR **analysis**

When developing an argument in answer to a case study or essay question, market research offers the following main lines of analysis:

- The key role of market research in market orientation, i.e. basing decisions upon the consumer, rather than the producer's needs or opinions.
- The need for a questioning approach to data. When presented with a research finding one needs to know: Was the sample size large enough? Who paid for the research? Business people learn to ask questions about every 'fact' shown by research.
- The importance of market knowledge: large, established firms have a huge advantage over newer, smaller firms because of their knowledge of consumer attitudes and behaviour, built up from years of market research surveys.

## 4.8 Market research
### an evaluation

In large firms, it is rare for any significant marketing decision to be made without market research. Even an apparently minor change to a pack design will only be carried out after testing in research. Is this overkill? Surely marketing executives are employed to make judgements, not merely do what surveys tell them?

The first issue here is the strong desire to make business decisions as scientifically as possible. This dates back to the work of FW Taylor and is kept alive today through the concept of the marketing model (see Unit 2.6). Quantitative research, especially, fits in with the desire to act on science not hunch. Yet this can be criticised, such as by John Scully, former head of Apple Computers, who once said: 'No great marketing decision has ever been made on the basis of quantitative data.' He was pointing out that true innovations such as the Sony Walkman and great advertisements such as Levi's 'launderette' commercial were the product of creativity and hunch, not science.

The second issue concerns the management culture. In some firms, mistakes lead to inquests, blame and even dismissal. This makes managers keen to find a let-out. When the new product flops, the manager can point an accusing finger at the positive research results: 'It wasn't my fault. We need a new research agency.' In other firms, mistakes are seen as an inevitable part of learning. For every Sinclair C5 (unresearched flop) there may be a Sony Walkman (unresearched moneyspinner). In firms with a positive, risk-taking approach to business, qualitative insights are likely to be preferred to quantitative data.

## Exercises

### A. REVISION QUESTIONS
*(30 marks; 60 minutes)*

Read the unit, then answer:

1 State three ways in which a cosmetics firm could use market research. *(3)*
2 Outline three reasons why market research information may prove inaccurate. *(6)*
3 Distinguish between primary and secondary research. *(3)*
4 What advantages are there in using secondary research rather than primary? *(3)*
5 Which is the most commonly used sampling method? Why may it be the most commonly used? *(4)*
6 State three key factors to take into account when writing a questionnaire. *(3)*
7 Outline the pros and cons of using a large sample size. *(4)*
8 Why may street interviewing become less common in the future? *(4)*

### B. REVISION EXERCISES

#### B1 Market Research Assignment
Hampton is a medium-sized producer of health foods. Its new company strategy is to break into the £400 million market for breakfast cereals. It has thought up three new product ideas that it wishes to test in research before further development takes place. They are:

- Cracker: an extra-crunchy mix of oats and almonds
- Fizzz: crunchy oats which fizz in milk
- St James: a luxury mix of oats, cashews and pecan nuts

The research objectives are to identify the most popular of the three, in terms of product trial and regular usage; to identify price expectations for each; to find what people like and dislike about each idea and each brand name; and to be able to analyse the findings in relation to consumers' demographic profile and current usage patterns.

**Questions** *(30 marks; 35 minutes)*
1 Write a questionnaire based upon the above details, bearing in mind the advice given in section 4.5. *(12)*
2 Explain which sampling method you would use and why. *(6)*
3 Interview 6–8 people using your questionnaire, then write a 200 word commentary on its strengths and weaknesses. *(12)*

#### B2 Case Study
Braebourne Ltd supplies water coolers and mineral water to business customers. Started by a 22-year-old fresh from university in 1990, by 1997 its turnover was over £3 million and profit in excess of £400,000. The business has thrived from the 35% annual growth of the market as a whole, and from its excellent customer service. Braebourne only takes on customers who are within an hour's drive of one of their depots. Also, the delivery drivers are hired and trained for their customer-friendly approach.

When the business was small, the managing director had regular contact with all the customers and could therefore monitor customer satisfaction. Now he relies on regular surveys of customer opinion. Last month, 350 of Braebourne's 7,000 customers replied to the questionnaire. Here is an extract from the findings:

| WATER: | Awful | Poor | Fair | Good | V. Good | Excellent |
|---|---|---|---|---|---|---|
| Please rate the following: | | | | | | |
| taste: | 0% | 0% | 3% | 8% | 32% | 57% |
| clarity: | 0% | 1% | 6% | 9% | 41% | 43% |
| presentation of bottles: | 0% | 3% | 7% | 9% | 62% | 19% |

**4.9 Workbook**

| DELIVERY: | Awful | Poor | Fair | Good | V. Good | Excellent |
|---|---|---|---|---|---|---|
| Please rate your driver on the following: | | | | | | |
| courtesy: | 0% | 3% | 11% | 24% | 33% | 29% |
| helpfulness: | 1% | 3% | 15% | 28% | 34% | 19% |
| timekeeping: | 3% | 2% | 9% | 21% | 27% | 38% |

**Questions** *(15 marks; 30 minutes)*

1 How may the long term prospects of Braebourne be helped by effective use of market research? *(4)*
2 For what reasons may the reliability of this survey be called into question? *(4)*
3 What conclusions might the company draw from the above results? *(7)*

UNIT 4 | MARKET RESEARCH

# PRODUCT LIFE CYCLE AND PORTFOLIO ANALYSIS

## DEFINITION
The product life cycle shows the sales of a product over time.

## 5.1 What is the product life cycle?

The product life cycle shows the sales of a product over time. When a new product is first launched sales will usually be slow. If the product succeeds sales will then grow, until at some point they begin to stabilise. This might be because competitors have introduced similar products or because the market has now become saturated. Once most households have bought a dishwasher, for example, sales are likely to be relatively slow. This is because new purchases will mainly involve people who are updating their machine rather than new buyers. At some point sales are actually likely to decline. Perhaps because new technology means the product has become outdated. Or because competitors have launched a more successful model. The five key stages of a product's life cycle are known as: introduction, growth, maturity and decline and can be illustrated on a product life cycle diagram.

The typical stages in a product's life are shown in Figure 5.1 below.

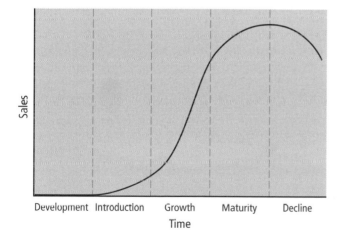

Sales / Time axis labels: Development, Introduction, Growth, Maturity, Decline

**Figure 5.1** Product life cycle

### MARKETING

| STAGE OF PRODUCT LIFE CYCLE | EXAMPLE OF A TYPE OF PRODUCT | EXAMPLE OF A PARTICULAR BRAND OF PRODUCT |
| --- | --- | --- |
| Introduction | Digital TV; 3G mobile phones; self cleaning glass | Wrigley's Extra Thin Ice (dissolving gum); Nestlé's Café Hazelnut, Café Caramel and Café Vanilla (speciality coffees); vanilla Coca-Cola; Nokia 6650 |
| Growth | Broadband internet access; digital cameras; MP3; organic chocolate; premium ice cream; laptops; coloured contact lenses; electric cars; supermini cars; videoconferencing; white chocolate cosmetic surgery | Harry Potter books; Sony PlayStation 2; Lego Mindstorm; Friends Reunited; BMW Mini |
| Maturity and saturation | washing machines; sliced white bread; tea; toothbrushes; brown chocolate | Coca-Cola; Cadbury's Dairy Milk; Typhoo; Tetley; Monopoly |
| Decline | Board games; 35mm cameras; high fat foods; artifical sweeteners; cigarettes | National Lottery (Lotto); Pokémon; Furby; Microsoft 2000; ONDigital (now shut down!) |

### ▬ NEW PRODUCTS: NOKIA

Few companies in business history have ridden a product life cycle as brilliantly (and profit ably) as Nokia did with 2G (2nd Generation) mobile phones between 1997 and 2002. So Nokia was desperately keen to be first to the market with Europe's first 3G handset. It managed this in 2002 with the 6650 model. It has a large colour screen and dual mode, meaning it can switch between the old 2G and the new 3G networks. It also has an in-built camera: users can take photos with their phones and send these to their friends. This is called photo messaging.

Despite the attractions of the 6650, sales were not expected to be particularly high in the short term. The company estimated it would have to wait until 2004 before 3G phones accounted for over 10% of its total sales. Partly this was due to technical problems; for example 3G requires large amounts of power which reduce the phone's battery life. Another issue was the price: in 2002 Nokia's 3G phone was priced at 800 euros (£480).

In 2002, 2G mobile phones were in their maturity phase, with sales flagging slightly. The birth of 3G was coming just in time for Nokia.

## 5.2 | What use is the product life cycle?

The concept of a product life cycle is useful because it highlights the need for a firm to alter its marketing policies at different stages of a product's life. In the growth phase the firm may be trying to increase its access to distribution channels. In the maturity phase it might develop new varieties of the product to maintain sales. In the decline phase it may have to reduce price to try to regain market share.

The product life cycle helps managers plan their marketing strategies. However, managers should realise that the duration of the life cycle will vary from one product to another. If, for example, the product is a fad (such as Pokémon) the overall life of the product will be quite short. Other products have very long life cycles. The first manufactured cigarettes went on sale in Britain in 1873. By chance, sales hit their peak (120,000 million!) exactly 100 years later. Since 1973 sales have gently declined.

It is also important to distinguish between the life cycle of a product category and the life cycle of a particular brand. Sales of wine are growing, but a brand that was once the biggest seller (Hirondelle) has virtually disappeared as wine buyers have become more sophisticated. Similarly, chocolate is a mature market but particular brands are at different stages in their life cycles: Mars bars are in maturity while Dream bars are in their growth stage.

Managers must also be aware that the pattern of sales from growth to maturity to decline is not inevitable. If they make the right decisions they can often keep sales growing. Just because sales begin to fall they must not assume that the product is entering a decline phase. It may well be a temporary or seasonal drop in sales. If managers believe their product is declining they may reduce their marketing efforts when in fact sales were about to increase! The life cycle model therefore needs to be treated with caution. It is a useful to tool to examine what has happened to sales and consider what might happen in the future. But managers must relate it to their own experiences, their own markets and any other information they have about future sales.

Features and implications of the different stages of the life cycle

| | INTRODUCTION | GROWTH | MATURITY | DECLINE |
|---|---|---|---|---|
| Sales | Low | Growing rapidly | At their highest | Falling |
| Costs per unit | High; no economies of scale | Falling; economies of scale | Low | Low |
| Competitors | Few | Growing | High | Falling |
| Product | One basic model | Product modifications and improvements | Diversify; new models | Remove weaker items |
| Promotion | Build awareness; high levels of promotion | Aim to generate interest; target new market segments | Stress differences with competitors | Lower budgets to keep costs down |
| Distribution | Limited | Growing number of outlets | High level of distribution | Reduce unprofitable channels |
| Price | May be skimming or penetration strategy | May keep penetrating the market or push prices up | May use competitive pricing | May increase prices, exploiting the loyalty of regular customers |

## 5.3 Cash flow and the product life cycle

In the development phase before a product is launched, cash flow will be negative. The firm will be spending money on research and development, market research and production planning, but no revenue is yet being generated. It may also decide to test market the product, which again costs money.

Once the product is on sale cash should begin to come in. However at this stage sales are likely to be low and the firm will still be heavily promoting the product to generate awareness. Overall cash flow is likely to continue to be negative. In many cases the cash flow will not become a positive figure until the growth stage of the life cycle. By then sales will be increasing and promotional costs can be spread over more units. This reduces costs per unit, making them

easier to cover. Cash flow should then continue to improve until the decline stage when the volume of sales and the amount of cash coming in begins to fall.

The changes in cash flow are related to the capacity utilisation of the firm. A large factory producing small quantities will be a drain on cash flow and profitability. In the early stages of a product's life the capacity utilisation is likely to be quite low. Therefore the cost per unit will be high. The combination of a high unit cost and low sales leads to negative cashflow. As sales grow, capacity utilisation increases and unit costs start to fall.

It is important, therefore, for firms to manage their cash flow effectively during the life cycle. Although a product may prove successful in the long term it may also cause the firm severe liquidity problems in the short term unless its finances are properly managed.

## 5.4 Extension strategies

The aim of an **extension strategy** is to prevent a decline in the product's sales. There are various means by which this can be achieved:

- By changing elements of the **marketing mix**; for example, new promotional techniques such as special offers can be used.
- By targeting a new segment of the market; when sales of Johnson and Johnson's baby products started to fall the company repositioned the product and aimed it at adults.
- By developing new uses for the product; the basic technology in hot-air paint strippers, for example, is no different from that of a hairdryer.

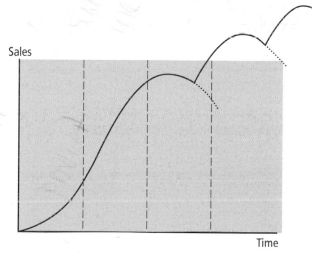

**Figure 5.3** The effect of extension strategies

The continued success of products such as Coca-Cola and Kellogg's cornflakes is not just due to luck. It is due to sophisticated marketing techniques which have managed to maintain their sales over many years despite fierce competition. The Kellogg's logo is regularly updated, new pack sizes are often introduced and various competitions and offers are used on a regular

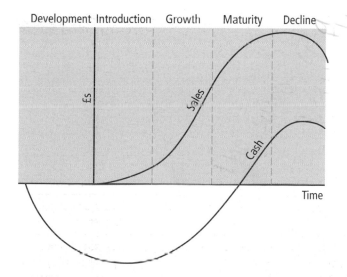

**Figure 5.2** Product life cycle and cash flow

basis to keep sales high. The company has also tried to increase the number of students and adults eating its products. It has run advertising campaigns to encourage people to eat the product throughout the day as well as in the morning.

## 5.5 Is a decline in sales inevitable?

In the standard product life cycle model it seems as if decline is inevitable. This may be true in some situations. For example, developments in technology may make some products obsolete. On the other hand the decline in sales may be the result of poor marketing. Effective extension strategies may ensure that a product's sales are maintained. The long-term success of products and services such as Monopoly and Kit-Kat shows that sales can be maintained over a very long period of time. Creative marketing can avoid the decline phase for a substantial period of time – but only if the product is good enough to keep buyers coming back for more. In 2002 Yorkie chocolate bars were relaunched with a tongue-in-cheek 'For Men Only' advertising campaign. Sales, which had been slipping for years, rose 27% and held their higher sales level into 2003.

One of the reasons for sales decline may be that some managers assume the product will fail at some point and so do not make enough effort to save it. This is known as 'determinism': managers think sales will decline and so sales do fall because of inadequate marketing support. Instead of adapting their **marketing strategy** to find new ways of selling the product they let it decline because they assume it cannot be saved.

It is important to remember that a life cycle graph only shows what has happened. It is not a prediction of the future. Top marketing managers try to influence the future, not just let it happen.

## 5.6 The product portfolio

Product **portfolio analysis** examines the existing position of a firm's products. This allows the firm to consider its existing position and plan what to do next. There are several different methods of portfolio analysis. One of the best known was developed by a firm of management consultants called the Boston Consulting Group and is known as the Boston Matrix.

The Boston Matrix shows the market share of each of the firm's products and the rate of growth of the markets in which they operate. By highlighting the position of each product in terms of market share and market growth the firm can analyse its existing situation and decide what to do next.

In Figure 5.4, product A has a high market share of a low growth market. The size of the circle depends on the turnover of the product. This type of product is known as a **cash cow**. An example of a cash cow might be Heinz baked beans. The overall market for baked

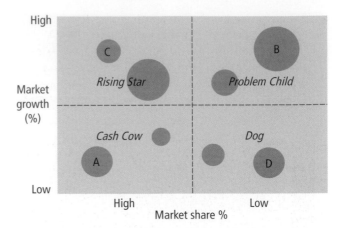

**Figure 5.4** Product portfolio: the Boston Matrix

beans is mature and therefore slow growing. Within this market the Heinz brand has a market share of about 50%. This type of product generates high profits and cash for the company because sales are relatively high whilst the promotional cost per unit is quite low. Consumers are already aware of the brand, which reduces some of the need for promotion. High and stable sales keep the cost per unit relatively low. Heinz can therefore 'milk' cash from baked beans to invest in newer products such as Heinz organic ketchup.

Product B, by comparison, is in a high growth market but has a low market share. This type of product is known as a **problem child**. It may well provide high profits in the future; the market itself is attractive because it is growing fast and the product could provide high returns if it manages to gain a greater market share. These products usually need a relatively high level of investment to keep them going. They may need relaunches to help find a profitable position in the market. Heinz organic baby food is in this position. Heinz hopes to persuade mothers to buy pre-prepared baby food rather than make their own but may not succeed.

A third type of product is known as a **star** or 'rising star'. These products (like C) have a high market share and are selling in a fast growing market. These products are obviously attractive – they are doing well in a successful market. However, they may well need protecting from competitors' products. Once again the profits of the cash cows can be used to keep the sales growing. Heinz organic soups are in this category. They are very successful with fast growing sales but still need heavy promotion to ensure their success.

The fourth category of products are known as **dogs**. These products (like D) have a low share of a low growth market. They hold little appeal for a firm unless they can be revived.

The purpose of portfolio analysis is to examine the existing position of the firm's products. Once this has been done the managers can plan what to do next. Typically this will involve four strategies:

- building – this involves investment in promotion and distribution to boost sales; this is often used with question marks

- holding – this involves marketing spending to maintain sales; this is used with star products
- milking – this means taking whatever profits you can without much more new investment; this is often used with cash cow products
- divesting – this involves selling off the product and is common with 'dogs'.

When analysing the importance of the product life cycle and portfolio model it might be useful to consider:

- product life cycle and portfolio analysis are used to examine the existing position of a firm's product or products in the market and plan what to do next
- the models do not in themselves tell the firm what to do; managers must interpret their findings and decide on the most effective course of action
- managers must avoid letting these models become self fulfilling e.g. deciding the product is in decline and so letting its sales fall
- product life cycles are generally becoming shorter due to the rapid developments in technology and the increasing levels of competition in most markets
- as well as the life cycle for a particular product we can also consider the life cycle of a category of products; for example, we might examine the life of Flora margarine and the life cycle for the whole margarine market.

## THE SWATCH PORTFOLIO

The Swatch Group Ltd in Biel (Switzerland) is the largest manufacturer and distributor of watches in the world. It has a 25% share of the world market and produces over 114 million watches a year. It has 160 production centres situated mainly in Switzerland, but also in France, Germany, Italy, USA, Virgin Islands, Thailand, Malaysia and China. It produces over 18 brand names offering watches in all price and market categories:

- Breguet, Léon Hatot, Omega, Longines and Rado in the luxury, prestige and the top range segment, where watches can be priced at £200 to £10,000+
- Tissot, Calvin Klein, Certina, Mido, Hamilton and Pierre Balmain in the middle segment, at prices between £50 and £200
- Swatch and Flik Flak in the basic segment of £10–£50.

**Business IN**

### 5.7 Product life cycle
#### an evaluation

Product life cycle and portfolio analysis are important in assessing the firm's current position within the market. This is known as a marketing audit. It is an essential step in the planning process. However, simply gathering data does not in itself guarantee success. A manager has to interpret the information effectively and then make the right decision.

Of the two approaches, product portfolio analysis is the more widely used. It helps a manager look critically at the firm's product range. Then decisions can be made on how the firm's marketing budget should be divided up. By contrast, product life cycle is found more often in textbooks than in the boardroom. It is a way of analysing what *has happened* to a product or brand. History can be useful or interesting, but it does not necessarily help you anticipate the future.

Think of all the fashions which died out, but then made a comeback. Then you realise anything is possible! There are no fixed rules in marketing. A product can start to grow and then sales suddenly fall. Alternatively sales may grow and grow for many years. A marketing manager needs to be flexible and use past data in connection with forecasts and even intuition.

The various strategies which are chosen will depend on the firm's portfolio of products. If most of the firm's products are cash cows, for example, it needs to be developing new products for future growth. If, however, the majority are problem children then it is in quite a high risk situation. It needs to try to ensure some products do become stars. If it has too many dogs then it needs to be investing in product development or acquiring new brands.

Both the product life cycle and product portfolio analysis are tools to help firms with their marketing planning. By analysing their existing situation they can identify what needs to be done to fulfil their objectives. However, like all planning tools, simply being able to examine the present position does not in itself guarantee success. Firms still have to be able to select the right strategy and implement it successfully.

**portfolio analysis** – an analysis of the market position of the firm's existing products; it is used as part of the marketing planning process.

**cash cow** – a product with a high share of a low growth market.

**dogs** – products which have a low share of a low growth market.

**star** – a product which has a high share of a fast growing market.

**problem child** – a product with a small share of a fast growing market.

**marketing mix** – the combination of variables through which the firm carries out its marketing strategy; for example, the product, the price, the place and the promotional mix.

**marketing strategy** – the way in which a firm aims to fulfil its objective, for example a firm may pursue a niche market or mass market strategy.

**extension strategy** – a strategy to prevent sales from declining.

# Exercises

## A. REVISION QUESTIONS

*(35 marks; 60 minutes)*

Read the unit, then answer:

1 Identify the different stages of the product life cycle. Give an example of one product or service you consider to be at each stage of the life cycle. *(4)*
2 Explain what is meant by 'extension strategies'. *(4)*
3 Outline the likely relationship between cash flow and the different stages of the life cycle. *(4)*
4 How is it possible for products such as Barbie to apparently defy the decline phase of the product cycle? *(6)*
5 What is meant by 'product portfolio analysis'? *(3)*
6 Distinguish between a cash cow and a star product in the Boston Matrix. *(4)*
7 Explain the likely relationship between capacity utilisation and the different stages of the life cycle. *(4)*
8 Firms should never take decline (or growth) for granted. Therefore they should never take success (or failure) for granted. Explain why this advice is important if firms are to make the best use of product life cycle theory. *(6)*

## B. REVISION EXERCISES

### B1 Data Response
**Golden Wonder**

Golden Wonder crisps was founded more than 50 years ago and grew to become the market leader. However, by the time Clive Sharpe led a management buyout from Dalgety in 1995 its sales were going backwards even though the market was still growing. Three years later, after a thorough shake up of the company, sales were back on the upward path. 'It's a great brand with a great reputation and we want to exploit it and take it into new territories', says Mr Sharpe.

Golden Wonder is best known for its crisps which are competing in a tough and mature market. Its main competitor is Pepsico, which has half the UK market with Walkers. Mr Sharpe claims Golden Wonder crisps beat Walkers 2:1 in blind tastings. But the group has a market share of just 19% including own-label brands for supermarkets – which Walkers does not make. Golden Wonder also makes branded snacks in which its best-known product is Wotsits. Pepsico has about a third of the snacks market, also under the Walkers brand. United Biscuits has a similar share with KP. This developing sector is where Golden Wonder is seeking most of its growth.

**Questions** *(30 marks; 35 minutes)*
1 What is meant by 'market share' ? *(3)*
2 How can the company exploit the Golden Wonder brand name to keep its sales up? *(6)*
3 If Golden Wonder beats Walkers in taste tests, as Mr Sharpe claims, analyse the possible reasons why Walkers has a bigger market share. *(9)*
4 The market size for bagged crisps and snacks in 1998 was £1,702 million. If Golden Wonder achieved its claimed market share, what level of sales revenue would that represent? *(4)*
5 In 1995 the sales of Golden Wonder were falling; afterwards they increased. Discuss whether this means the product life cycle model is wrong. *(8)*

## B2 Data Response
### Persil Tablets

In 1998 Lever Brothers launched Persil Tablets – a new way to do your washing. All you have to do is put two tablets in the bag, put them in your wash and turn the machine on. The launch was Lever's latest attempt to get ahead of Procter and Gamble's Ariel in the washing powder wars that have been going on for many years. Four years earlier the launch of Persil Power with a patented 'accelerator' ingredient turned into a disaster when it was discovered that it weakened fabrics and left the colours faded. Procter and Gamble delighted in showing clothes ruined by Persil Power and the product was quickly withdrawn.

After the Persil Power fiasco consumers are rather distrustful of innovative products in this market and so Lever played down the 'newness' of the tablets. Instead it stressed that the tablets reduce wastage because most people put too much powder or liquid into their wash. Less wastage means less sales as the product does not have to be bought as often. Lever, however, believes the fact people change their clothes more often means the market has underlying growth. Over time the tablets are expected to take 20% of the billion pound washing powder market. As Persil tablets were being launched, Procter and Gamble were busy test marketing their own Ariel Discs in Grimsby.

### Questions                          (30 marks; 35 minutes)

1  Distinguish between market share and market growth. (3)
2  Outline the factors that might determine the success of Persil Tablets in the market. (6)
3  Examine how the promotion of Persil Tablets might vary at different stages in its life cycle. (6)
4  Consider whether new product development is essential for success in the washing powder market. (6)
5  In the early 1980s the brand-leading detergent was Daz. By 1998 it was still fourth in the £750 million market for detergents, but with sales declining at a rate of 8% per year.
  a  Where would this place Daz on the Boston Matrix? (3)
  b  Given this placing, what factors should its owners, Procter and Gamble, take into account for the future marketing of Daz? (6)

## B3 Case Study

Freedom Publishing produces a range of magazines aimed at different segments of the market. For example it produces:

* *Shout it Out*, aimed at young men between the ages of 15 and 20
* *Cool It*, for 20 to 24-year-olds into the latest fashions, clubs, music
* *Active Living*, aimed at 30 to 35-year-olds interested in outdoor activities
* *Out and About*, aimed at pensioners who want to travel, go to exhibitions and have weekend breaks.

Another of its publications is *Girl Power*. This is aimed at teenage girls and focuses on fashion tips, the latest music, new bands, etc. The magazine was a best-seller for many years and became the cash cow of the company. It was one of the very first magazines it produced and helped finance the start-up of many others. However in recent months sales have been disappointing and some of the senior managers think it has had its day. The marketing manager of *Girl Power*, Sindy Beal, is considering what to do next. For example, should she get rid of it? Or try and boost sales?

| Year | Girl Power Sales (000s) |
| --- | --- |
| Four years ago | 190 |
| Three years ago | 240 |
| Two years ago | 260 |
| Last year | 265 |
| This year to date | 262 |

### Questions                          (30 marks; 40 minutes)

1  Draw a diagram of the product life cycle and highlight at which stage you think is *Girl Power*. State and justify your choice. (10)
2  What factors could influence what Sindy does next? (10)
3  If Sindy does decide to try and revive sales of *Girl Power*, suggest and explain an extension strategy she could try to adopt. (10)

# NICHE VERSUS MASS MARKETING

## DEFINITION

Mass marketing means devising products with mass appeal and promoting them to all types of customer. Niche marketing is tailoring a product to a particular type of customer. This limits the sales potential but makes the product more attractive to those in the target group.

## 6.1 Mass marketing

Mass marketing is the attempt to create products or services that have universal appeal. Rather than targeting a specific type of customer, mass marketing aims the product at the whole market. The intention is that everyone should be a consumer of the product. Coca-Cola is a good example of a firm that uses mass marketing techniques. The company aims its product at young and old alike. Its goal has always been to be the market leader, and it still is today. The ultimate goal of mass marketing is to achieve market domination. The ultimate prize of mass marketing is the creation of generic brands. These are brands that are so closely associated with the product that customers treat the brand name as if it were a product category. Examples include Hoover (vacuum cleaner) and Bacardi (white rum).

### THE ORIGINS OF MASS MARKETING

Mass marketing started alongside mass production at the turn of the twentieth century. The architect was Henry Ford and the product was the Model T. Before the Model T, cars were too expensive to be owned by more than a handful of rich Americans. Ford decided that he wanted to see every American family owning a

Push assembly line, 1913: dropping the Ford engine into the Model T chassis (© Corbis-Bettman)

Ford car. To do this profitably Ford had to revolutionise the way that cars were produced. By producing a standardised product from standardised parts Ford was able to reduce his costs. Ford did not even offer a choice of colour. Ford famously joked that you could have a Model T in 'any colour, so long as it's black'.

As costs fell Ford cut his prices. This brought the car within the budget of more American families. So demand grew further. Ford cut his prices continuously between 1909 and 1916. As a consequence sales rose by an astonishing 4,594% during the same period.

By the early 1920s Ford's mass marketing and mass production strategies had given the company over 50% of the US car market. Ford managed to create a virtuous reinforcing circle (see Figure 6.1). If mass marketing is carried out successfully it can be highly profitable. Even today many firms still set out

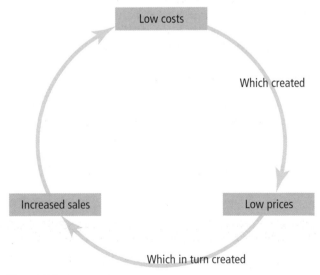

Figure 6.1

to be high volume, low margin operators and achieve handsome profits. However, it is important to note that mass marketing does not have to go hand in hand with low prices. For example, Calvin Klein, producer of CK One, took the decision to target its latest fragrance at the mass market. First, by taking the unusual step of aiming its latest fragrance at both men and women the target market was doubled at a stroke. The decision to attract the mass market was also evident in terms of distribution policy. Calvin Klein decided to sell the fragrance through record shops as well as the more traditional distribution outlets of boutiques and department stores. By doing this Calvin Klein increased the chance of trial purchase from those who might not have considered buying fragrances before. The company's mass marketing strategy was vindicated by phenomenal sales and profitability. A highly effective advertising campaign featuring the supermodel Kate Moss provided the necessary **product differentiation** to sell high sales volumes without the need to cut prices.

## PAN-EUROPEAN AND GLOBAL MARKETING

Many firms have looked to exploit the fact that the world is shrinking. Modern communications and travel have created a situation where consumers of all nationalities are developing common habits and wants. Brands such as Levi's, Sony, McDonald's and Coca-Cola are available everywhere. The result is a global mass market for standardised consumer products. The **global marketing** approach involves selling the same product with the same marketing strategy the world over. McDonald's aims to create the same brand identity for its products the world over. Individual elements of the marketing mix may be adjusted slightly to suit local conditions but the general thrust of the marketing strategy does not vary from region to region. For example, the price of a Big Mac in Budapest is considerably lower than in London, but this is just a reflection of the differences in living standards between the two cities rather than anything more significant. Global marketing is therefore just an example of mass marketing but on a larger scale than even Henry Ford could have imagined.

## THE BENEFITS OF GLOBAL MARKETING

- A global approach to marketing will increase the potential size of the target market. If the marketing strategy proves to be successful the rewards are massive in terms of sales volumes and profits. Western businesses such as Volkswagen and Tesco

have targeted the undeveloped markets of Eastern Europe for this very reason.
- In markets where product differentiation is low, survival against international competitors may require cost-reducing economies of scale. Most domestic markets are not large enough to create the output level required to generate these vital economies of scale. Global competition has also created severe pricing pressures. One way of coping with these pressures is to market your products on the largest possible stage, spreading costs and creating revenues across the globe. So therefore firms need to export. Firms selling a mass market product need to think globally just to survive.
- Standardising a marketing strategy can help to cut costs. First, a global strategy can be implemented more rapidly. Second, by selling the same product in the same manner everywhere, advertising and packaging costs need not be duplicated. Recently Mars the confectionery manufacturer renamed their famous Opal Fruit brand 'Starburst' for this very reason. The cost savings created by this type of strategy can be translated into lower worldwide prices giving the firm yet another source of competitive advantage.
- Due to rapidly advancing technology, product life cycles in many markets are getting shorter. If firms are not to be left behind they must attempt to develop more new products. However, new products are still very expensive to develop. Today, new products must repay their development costs more quickly if the firm is to make a profit on its new product launches. The extra sales generated by a global marketing strategy are important in terms of shortening the payback times on new products.

## 6.2 Niche marketing

### INTRODUCTION

A market niche is a small segment of a larger market. Niche marketing is the process by which firms attempt to, first, find and then exploit new or under-served market sectors. It involves aiming at a relatively small target market with a specialised product designed to

The potential problems of going global

| DIFFICULTY | KEY QUESTION | EXAMPLE |
| --- | --- | --- |
| Cultural problems | Does the product fit the lifestyle and values of every nationality? | McDonald's struggled at first in France, as the French took meals too seriously for fast-food |
| Brand names | Does the name translate effectively? | Vauxhall were forced to change their Nova brand name in Spain. 'No va' in Spanish means 'no go'. Not a helpful brand name for a new car! |
| Consumer preference for local producers | Is the brand seen as 'foreign', or is it given the image of a local product? | Ford is widely seen as British, even though it is an American firm which imports many of its cars into Britain |

meet the specific needs of that niche. A simple example is the holiday firm Saga, which aims only at the over-50s.

Firms adopting a niche market strategy must make their profits from a relatively small sales volume. This presents a problem as overheads cannot be spread over a high output level. So fixed costs per unit are high. Firms using niche marketing need high prices to compensate. Therefore the product must be highly differentiated and highly valued by the niche it is aimed at.

## NICHE MARKETING IN THE MOTOR INDUSTRY

There are many reasons why firms in the motor industry have chosen to adopt niche marketing strategies.

- Niche markets can act as safe havens for small firms. In the mass market the small firm will always struggle against the economies of scale of larger firms. To survive, small firms often operate in niches that are too small for large firms to be interested. A small car manufacturer using this strategy is Morgan Cars. This England-based company makes hand-built sports cars aimed firmly at the nostalgic enthusiast. Morgan's sales of 500 cars per year give it a market share of below 0.05%. This niche is profitable for Morgan, but companies like Ford feel they can use their resources more effectively elsewhere. This is particularly true when the larger firms are making good profits in their mass markets. Why develop a new product for a tiny niche market when one aimed at the mass market will have far more sales potential?
- Large firms may switch to a niche marketing approach when a market has stopped growing. In a mature market the only way to gain further sales is to take market share from competitors. One way of

achieving this is by using niche marketing tactics. Ten years ago Ford would have rejected the idea of developing a car aimed at a niche capable of sales of only 5,000 units per year. However this is exactly what Ford is doing today. It has a separate new product development division (called the Special Vehicle Team). It specialises in niche market vehicles with projected sales of less than 5,000 cars per year. By producing cars that tap into unmet needs, Ford has a better chance of tempting customers from their rivals. Niche products are being used by Ford in order to break existing brand loyalties.
- Niche marketing can also be used to help improve the sales of mass market products sold by the same manufacturer. Jaguar launched the high performance XJ220 partly to provide additional glamour to the family brand name. Niche market products can be highly profitable in their own right. However their effect on overall company profits can be even more substantial. The XJ220 created a 'halo effect' that added value and sales volume to the more established Jaguar models.

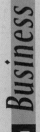

## HOT STUFF IN A NICHE MARKET

In 1985, Andrew Palmer spotted a gap in the food market. Heinz dominated soup sales, but the market was slowly declining. He decided to market a range of fresh, chilled 'home-made' soups which would be expensive but with a distinctly better taste than from cans or packets. Prices would be three times those of canned soup, but the quality of the soups would add the value required to justify the price. Palmer found the necessary capital and the 'New Covent Garden Soup Company' was born.

It started in London, but spread nationwide by 1990. Quickly, Marks & Spencer and Sainsbury's copied the style of packaging and product, but the company kept introducing new flavours and survived the competition. In the year to June 1997, sales of £16 million yielded operating profits of over £2.4 million. Then a medium-sized food group called S Daniels offered £22 million to buy the business. Andrew Palmer became a millionaire.

## HOW DO FIRMS GO ABOUT IDENTIFYING NEW MARKET NICHES?

The approach used to identify niche markets varies from company to company. However there are some general lessons to be learned.

## NICHE RADIO

In August 2002 the BBC launched a new niche market digital radio station called 1Xtra. According to Wilber Wilberforce, the station's programme editor 1Xtra is aimed at urban 16 to 25 year olds who enjoy a combination of hip-hop, raga, drum 'n' bass and UK garage that is collectively known as 'Black Music'. Unfortunately for the BBC, research conducted just prior to the station's launch revealed that ownership of digital radios is very low amongst urban 16 to 25 year olds. Consequently, despite the undoubted popularity of 'Black Music', 1Xtra is likely to remain a tiny niche market radio station until cheap digital radios become available.

**If possible be close to your own market:** Small firms may have an advantage over larger firms in terms of identifying market niches. This is because smaller firms are said to be closer to their consumers. But what exactly does this mean?

- Many ideas for niche market products come from direct customer feedback at the point of sale. 'Off the cuff' comments on likes and dislikes about the present product range can provide valuable insights and ideas for new niche products. In small firms the manager is more likely to pick up these ideas. They are in more regular contact with customers and their front-line staff. A customer complaint or request may spark an idea for a totally new product or service.
- Small specialist firms are often run by enthusiasts. Indeed, the idea to set the business up in the first place may have come from the experiences of the owner as a consumer. An example of this was James Dyson who decided to design a bagless vacuum cleaner that would not suffer from suction problems.

## AIMING HIGH

The world market for wristwatches is exceptionally fragmented. Most people choose their watch largely on the basis of design and price. Brand names count for little in the mass market. An exception is Swatch – the Swiss brand which has sold over 250 million watches since its 1983 launch.

At the top end of the market, most of the prestige brands such as Cartier sell in very small volume. Only Rolex combines high price with relatively high volume (rumoured, says the Financial Times, to be 700,000 units per year). Citizen of Japan has tried to break away from general competition by designing watches to meet specific market niches. This allows it to charge £100+ instead of its more usual £50. An example is the Altichron. This watch gives a climber the height above sea level as he or she ascends a mountain. A useless feature for most people, but real added value to a climber. And a nice way for a Japanese firm to break into the Swiss home market.

IN **Business**

**Utilise modern secondary market research information:** Both manufacturers and retailers have always been keen to swop sales figures in order to gain valuable **market intelligence** information. The fact that many shoppers use retail loyalty cards has added even more value to this data. Databases can now be merged and cross-referenced so that retailers and manufacturers know not only what has been sold but also the identity of the buyer. Knowing the identity of a potential buyer is vital for targeting promotion. If a firm knows the names and addresses of potential consumers they can be contacted via direct mail. Advances in technology now make it possible to target with a precision that was once inconceivable. Precision reduces direct mail costs substantially because it reduces wastage. It avoids the huge expense of a mass medium such as television advertising. Secondary market research information held on complex databases can also be used to conduct market mapping exercises. This process is described in detail in Unit 3.

ISSUES FOR **analysis**

- It is useful to analyse niche marketing in relation to price elasticity. Niche market products are invariably designed to meet the needs of customers looking for something different. This means that buyers of niche market goods are likely to be less price sensitive than consumers of mass market brands. This is especially true for the first brand to open up a niche market. Consumers may regard the originator of the market segment as 'the real thing'. An example would be Haagen Dazs in the super-premium ice-cream sector. On average, niche products are less price elastic than mass market products. Therefore higher prices can be charged.
- Fundamentally there are two approaches to making profit. The first is to be a high volume, low margin operator. The second is to charge higher prices and be a low volume, high margin operator. This is the route taken by those who adopt niche marketing tactics.
- In developed economies there is a trend away from mass to niche marketing. It will be difficult for large firms to be profitable in niche markets unless they can find a way to produce efficiently in small batches. Niche marketing implies a move away from mass production.

## 6.3 Niche versus mass marketing
### an evaluation

Which is better? Mass or niche marketing? The answer is that it depends. In the bulk ice-cream market, large packs of vanilla ice-cream have become so cheap that little profit can be made. Better by far, then, to be in a separate niche, whether regional (Mackie's Scottish ice-cream) or upmarket such as Rocombe Farm or Häagen Dazs. The latter can charge 10 times as much per litre as the mass market own-label bulk packs.

Yet, if one looks at the marketing of films or books, would a firm rather be selling a critic's favourite or a blockbuster smash hit? The latter, of course. Film-makers such as Steven Spielberg have shown not only mastery over the technical side of film production and direction but also a sure marketing touch. They can tell whether a story will appeal to a mass audience. Conventional businesses such as Heinz, Kellogg's and even Chanel show that mass marketing does not have to mean devaluing a brand name.

**global marketing** – marketing throughout the world as if it is one market, for instance using the same brand name and brand advertising.

**market intelligence** – useful information about consumers, distributors or competitors.

**pan-European marketing** – marketing throughout Europe as if it is a single market, i.e. same brand name and advertising.

**price elasticity** – the responsiveness of demand to a change in price.

**product differentiation** – the extent to which consumers perceive your brand as being different from others.

# Exercises

## A. REVISION QUESTIONS
*(30 marks; 60 minutes)*

Read the unit, then answer:

1 Identify three advantages of niche marketing over mass marketing. *(3)*
2 Give three reasons why a large firm may wish to enter a niche market. *(3)*
3 Why do small firms frequently appear better at spotting and then reacting to new niche market opportunities? *(4)*
4 Give two reasons why average prices in niche markets tend to be higher than those charged in most mass markets. *(2)*
5 Many firms have developed global marketing strategies during the 1990s. Outline three of the motivations for such a move. *(6)*
6 Outline two factors a firm should consider before embarking on a global marketing strategy. *(4)*
7 State three reasons why information technology has made niche marketing a more viable option for large firms. *(3)*
8 Explain why it is important for a large firm to be flexible if it is to operate successfully in niche markets. *(5)*

## B. REVISION EXERCISES

### B1 Data Response

**The New Beetle**

> Volkswagen is drawing up contingency plans to build its new Beetle model in Europe as a result of soaring demand for the Mexican-built car in North America and a global queue of more than 2,000 would-be buyers.
>
> A decision on whether to proceed, and at which of the group's plants that should be, will be made by May, Ferdinand Piech, chairman, told the Financial Times at the European launch of the car. VW will start selling the new VW in Europe on November 27 at prices starting from DM34,950 (£12,650).

> The original Beetle, launched in 1945, has sold more than 21 million units and is still produced at Puebla in Mexico, mainly for developing world markets. Although production of the new Beetle is still climbing from the start-up phase, more than 40,000 have been delivered to North American buyers. A decision was taken several months ago to lift capacity at Puebla from 121,500 to 162,000 a year.
>
> With VW's executives in the US indicating that North American markets alone could absorb most of the Mexican output, only around 80,000 new Beetles will be allocated for sale in Europe next year, 45,000 of them for Germany.
>
> The UK market will not receive right-hand drive versions of the new Beetle until the end of 1999, although VW will offer 1,000 left-hand drives in the Spring to customers who have already ordered.
>
> **Source:** Adapted from *The Financial Times*, 9/11/98

**Questions** *(25 marks; 30 minutes)*

1 Explain the meaning of the terms:
   a contingency plan *(2)*
   b capacity. *(2)*
2 Volkswagen planned the Beetle as a niche market product aimed at trendy young drivers. It was to sell at a price premium over cars such as the Golf (approx £10,000) and the Seat (approx £9,000).
   a Given that approach, how might Volkswagen promote the Beetle when it is launched in Britain in late 1999? *(6)*
   b How might the company's marketing strategy change if the Beetle's sales success persuades Volkswagen to mass market the product in Britain? *(8)*
3 Discuss the business consequences of a continued failure by Volkswagen to produce enough cars to meet the demand for this new Beetle. *(7)*

## B2 Case Study

### A Niche Interest in Computers

The IT revolution has created opportunities for both large and small firms. When Mike Penfield and Dianne Tomkinson met during their last year at university they discussed the idea of setting up their own business together. They felt that many large studios had overlooked a potentially profitable niche within the design market. Mike and Dianne shared a background in design and IT. Their idea was to offer affordable access to high quality computer facilities, backed up by advice and help. They planned to cater for the needs of small firms who wanted to hire the technology required to produce their own distinctive posters and brochures rather than having to buy it or sub-contract the work out. In other words they planned to benefit from being small.

The couple provided most of the necessary start-up capital to set up Desire Design Ltd. With the aid of a bank loan the business opened its first outlet in Croydon in 1998 with seven Apple Macs, two printers and a scanner being available for hire. Fortunately for the couple, the business proved to be a roaring success. The concept of hiring proved popular for two reasons. First, entrepreneurs appreciated the cost savings that came from doing design work in house rather than having to pay expensive design studio fees. Second, hiring was also a more viable option than outright purchase for the majority of small firms as clients only paid for what they used.

Dianne was keen to pursue growth. So a decision was made to reinvest most of the firm's profits in new equipment. Today, Desire has more than 50 fully equipped workstations to hire out and the couple are looking to diversify. One of their current ideas is to offer a budget website design service targeted specifically at small firms.

### Questions                    (30 marks; 60 minutes)

1 Describe the niche Mike and Dianne identified.    (4)
2 Explain why the profit margins in niche markets are frequently higher than in the mass market.    (5)
3 Outline three key criteria for successful operation in a niche market.    (6)
4 Consider the problems Desire may run in to as a result of Dianne's policy of growth.    (7)
5 Discuss whether a small operator such as Desire Design can only survive by competing in niche markets.    (8)

## B3 Case Study

### The Niche Marketing of BMW's New Mini

In the summer of 2001 BMW launched the new Mini. The new car was designed so that it resembled the original Mini, the best selling car that was a design icon of the 1960s and 70s. However, the new model was bigger, safer and more luxurious than its predecessor. These improvements were intended to create a car that was right up to date but without losing the character, fun and excitement of the original Mini.

The new Mini was a strategically important new product for BMW. The aim being that this new car would enable BMW to capitalise on the growing small car segment of the car market. By diversifying in this way the company would no longer be so dependent upon sales of its luxury cars for the bulk of its profits.

The car was aimed at creating a new market niche by appealing to twenty and thirty-somethings with high disposable incomes who want a funky, more stylish alternative to mass-market small cars. According to BMW promotional material the new Mini was 'for individuals who were not interested in following the crowd'.

BMW's marketing department used persuasive advertising to promote the brand. The 'Mini Adventures' TV advertising campaign was based around a series of humorous story lines featuring good looking young people having fun and adventure in their new Mini. In addition to the above-the-line activity, BMW used a variety of innovative below-the-line tactics. For example, part of Gatwick South's departure lounge was transformed into a shrine devoted to the new Mini. Passengers waiting for their flights were given access to a colourful and stylish Mini lounge area equipped with terminals offering free Internet access to www.mini.co.uk. Tactics like this helped to create exactly the sort of trendy image that BMW wanted for the brand.

The new Mini had a very successful first year in terms of sales: 30,000 cars were sold in the UK alone and in America the car was so popular that waiting lists developed. To address the supply and demand mismatch, BMW plan to increase the annual production of the new Mini by 15 to 20% in order to cope with demand levels that have clearly caught the company by surprise.

### Questions                    (30 marks; 35 minutes)

1 Explain how BMW might have gone about identifying whether a niche market opportunity existed for the new Mini.    (6)
2 How can large firms like BMW benefit from selling niche market products like the new Mini?    (8)
3 The new Mini was priced at £11,000 in the UK when it was launched in 2001. Discuss whether BMW should consider increasing the price of the car in the future.    (10)
4 To be successful, niche market products must be differentiated. Explain how BMW went about creating the product differentiation needed to ensure the new Mini's success.    (6)

# MARKETING STRATEGY

DEFINITION

Marketing strategy is a carefully evaluated plan for future marketing activity that balances company objectives, available resources and market opportunities.

## 7.1 What is strategy?

Strategy is the plan of the medium- to long-term actions required to achieve the company goals or targets. Marketing strategy is the marketing contribution. The term strategy implies that the plan has been carefully thought out. Successful marketing requires careful planning. This requires an understanding of the nature, possibilities and potential of the business and the environment in which it is operating. Marketing strategy is finding a fit between the company objectives, customer requirements and the activities of competitors.

### WHY HAVE STRATEGY?

The aim of this planning is to shape the company's activities and products to generate the best returns for the business. It ensures that marketing activity makes the best possible contribution to the success of the business. Marketing strategy is about *adding value*. It takes advantage of any unique selling points. It helps the business to identify the right mix of design, function, image or service.

### STRATEGY IS ABOUT THE FUTURE

The term 'strategy' implies looking to the future. It is important not to look at what is working well now but at what future prospects are. The Ford Motor Company recognised that rising petrol prices meant large cars were likely to go out of fashion. It started to invest in the production of small cars. If it had continued to invest in the most profitable part of the business it would have continued to expand production of large cars.

### STRATEGY MUST BE ACHIEVABLE

Strategy is concerned with what is possible not just desirable. It must take into account market potential and company resources. The company needs to recognise its own limitations and potential. It also needs to consider economic and social circumstances. Many UK firms held back from developing new export markets when the pound was strong between 1997 and 2002. In America, the popularity of products such as Bacardi Breezer and Smirnoff Ice is leading to calls for advertising bans, as they are said to encourage underage drinking.

### STRATEGY IS COMPANY SPECIFIC

Each company will have a different marketing strategy. This will reflect its individual circumstances. Different companies within the same industry may be pursuing different goals. They will develop different strategies. Within the same industry, one company may be aiming to increase market share whilst another looks for cost reductions in order to compete on price. The tyre industry is a good example of this. The market leaders were faced with increasing price competition from developing countries. They had to develop new marketing strategies. Their responses differed. Goodyear reduced costs. Michelin put its effort into innovation and widened its product range. Pirelli decided to concentrate on the market for luxury and speed.

> *Marketing strategy is the marketing plan of action which:*
>
> - *contributes to the achievement of company objectives*
> - *finds the best fit between company objectives, available resources and market possibilities*
> - *looks to the future*
> - *is carefully thought out*
> - *is realistic*

## 7.2 Strategy versus tactics

Strategy is not the same as tactics. Strategy is an overall plan for the medium to long term. Tactics are individual responses to opportunities or threats. They tend to be short term. The marketing strategy may be to increase sales by developing a new market segment. One of the tactics used may be to undercut a competitor on price in a price sensitive segment of the market.

| Defining strategy: | |
|---|---|
| Business review | • Where are we now? |
| Objectives | • Where do we want to be? |
| Strategy | • How shall we get there? |
| Plans | • Ways and means of carrying out strategy |

## 7.3 Developing a marketing strategy

The strategic planning process is at the heart of marketing. It involves laying down clear plans for marketing activities. If the strategy is to work it requires an excellent knowledge of the business, its markets and its customers.

To develop a marketing strategy it is necessary to:

1 define overall company objectives
2 analyse the existing business
3 understand the market
4 analyse available resources.

Company objectives identify priorities for the organisation. They take account of the external climate and the state of the business. Marketing strategy should contribute to the achievement of these objectives. The marketing element will not be independent. To be effective it needs to work with the other business functions. Doubling market share may require an increase in production. This involves operations, finance and personnel.

If the strategy is to work there must be a clear understanding of the existing business and the market in which it is operating. The two are interlinked. Sales may be increasing. This may be due to better products. It could be poor performance by a competitor. The analysis will include the whole business but concentrate on marketing. There are several tools that can be used. These include:

**1 Statistical analysis:** A good starting point is to look at past performance. Figures need to be gathered for sales, market share and contribution, ideally broken down by product. The trends can be analysed. This analysis should help to explain the patterns. This will be useful for estimating future sales.

**2 Market research:** The statistical analysis should be supported by market research. An understanding of customer buying behaviour will help explain sales patterns. It will indicate future buying patterns. Market research will also provide information about the state of the total market and the behaviour of competitors.

**3 SWOT analysis:** This is a tool used to audit the internal and external business environments. SWOT stands for Strengths, Weaknesses, Opportunities and Threats.

### Business IN

## TOO MANY SEATS?

2002 was a record year for cinemas. Audience figures reached 174 million matching the previous record set in 1971. This success, partly due to the release of successful films such as *The Lord of the Rings* and *Star Wars Episode 2*, masks an underlying problem in the industry.

After years of audience decline customers started returning during the early 1990s. This led to an expectation of even further growth, leading to huge investment into new multiplex complexes. The result is that in spite of record attendance, most big cities such as Manchester and Birmingham have too many cinema screens. In 2000 the number of screens rose by 200 or 6% while seat sales only grew by 2.8%. This growth is expected to slow and analysts are suggesting that there will be some consolidation in the market. There have already been signs of this. In 2001 ABC cinemas bought the Odeon chain resulting in the closure of 36 cinemas. In spite of these closures the feeling of industry experts is that 'it is a question of being selective about locations and getting the right size of cinema'. Cinema owners are also looking at new developments such as the screening of live events, e.g. music and sport.

Source: *The Times*, 24/8/02

### Internal review

The internal audit looks at what the business is doing well (strengths) and what it could do better (weaknesses).The emphasis is on marketing but other aspects are important. A company with inefficient production processes will have high costs. It will find it difficult to compete on price. Each business will have its own problems and areas of excellence. Key areas include:

- Company reputation – what is the reputation of the business? Marks and Spencer has a reputation for quality. Microsoft has a reputation for innovation. But Skoda? Or Iceland? What reputations have they?
- Market representation – is the business strong or weak in any particular market or market segment?
- Brands – does the company have any strong brands?
- New products – does the business have any new products ready for the market?
- Distribution – are the products widely available in the market?

### External review

The external review looks at the business environment.

The opportunities and threats audit will look at issues such as:

- **State of the economy** – is the economy growing or in recession? Are any sectors of the economy performing differently? A period of recession may be a threat to a company supplying luxury goods but an opportunity for a manufacturer supplying own label goods to supermarkets.
- **Market** – are there any gaps in the market? Are new markets available? What are competitors doing? An aggressive marketing campaign by a competitor will be a threat. The failure of a competitor will be an opportunity.
- **Technology** – how may technological change affect the business? Are products keeping pace with change? Is technology opening up new markets? Video conferencing is an opportunity for telecommunications firms. It could be seen as a threat to the business travel industry.
- **Demography** – how will changes in population structure affect the market and the business? The growth in the number of old people has provided opportunities for businesses providing goods and services required by the elderly. The falling number of young people coming into the job market may be a threat to industries that rely on young people for their workforce.

### ANALYSIS OF AVAILABLE RESOURCES

The marketing strategy cannot be finalised without considering available resources. The strategy must be realistic and achievable. Company resources will include products, finance and human resources. A strategy to expand into overseas markets will fail unless the company can commit the resources needed to penetrate that market. When certain skills are not available it may be possible to purchase them from external specialists. The growth of advertising agencies is a reflection of this.

## 7.4 Marketing strategy – the final piece of the jigsaw

Finding the best marketing strategy is like finding the last piece of the jigsaw. All of the other pieces are now in place. The company objectives, available resources and an understanding of the business and the environment in which it is operating. The final piece to deliver business success is the strategy. The strategy should flow naturally from the situation that the company is in and the prospects for the future. It should take advantage of the company strengths and the available market opportunities. It cannot try to do

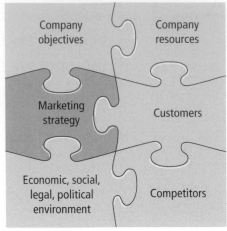

**Figure 7.1**

everything but should pick out priorities according to the circumstances. A good strategy will link together analysis of customer preferences to the company's strengths. This is known as *asset-led marketing*.

---

*Marketing strategy should:*

- *be part of the overall business strategy*
- *add value*
- *be asset led – use the company's strengths*
- *take advantage of market opportunities*
- *address the company's weaknesses*
- *be prepared to react to any threats*

---

## 7.5 Types of strategy

There are many possible strategies for any one business. The strategy may be specific to a particular product. It may focus on the whole product range, or be focused on new products or new markets. At any one time the business could be pursuing several different strategies. A business may have one strategy for one product and another for a different product.

Among the main marketing strategies are the following:

**Market penetration:** This is about increasing market share. It is the most common and safest strategy. It concentrates on existing markets and products. The business should have good knowledge of these. The strategy will involve finding ways of increasing sales. This may be by:

- Finding new customers – perhaps by widening the product's appeal to attract additional buyers.

- Taking customers from competitors – this may be achieved by aggressive pricing or by offering additional incentives to the customer.
- Persuading existing customers to increase usage – many food companies give recipes with their products to suggest additional ways of using the product. Shampoo manufacturers introduced a frequent wash shampoo to boost product usage.

**Market development:** This is about finding new markets for existing products. It is a more risky strategy as it involves dealing with new customers and markets. It may be done by:

- **Repositioning** the product – this will target a different market segment. This could be by broadening the product's appeal to a new customer base. Rover's traditional market for Land Rovers was farming and military use. It has now repositioned the product to appeal to town dwellers.
- **Moving into new markets** – many British retailers have opened up outlets abroad. Some, such as Tesco and Laura Ashley, have opened up their own outlets. Others have entered into joint ventures or have taken over a similar operation in another country.

### REPOSITIONING HOVIS

By 2001, the Hovis brand name was becoming tired. It was still much-loved and trusted, yet market research showed it to be seen as old fashioned. Unsurprisingly, sales were slipping. The brand owner, British Bakeries, called in a specialist packaging design company to re-position the brand. Out went the traditional wheat sheaves and 'warm', brown colours. In came a dramatic new look, with bright packaging covered in pictures of baked beans, cucumber, and other foods that people eat with bread. It gave the brand a much younger feel, and beat rival brands hands-down for visual display and appeal in-store. Since then, Hovis brown and white bread have become the brand leaders for the first time in the company's 115 year history, boosting sales by a value of 31% since the relaunch.

**Product development:** Most companies continually develop their products. In some industries, such as electronics or pharmaceuticals, innovation is essential. In highly competitive markets companies use product development to differentiate their product from the competitor's product. Strategies may include:

- Changing an existing product – this may be to keep the products attractive. Washing powders and

shampoos are good examples of this. The manufacturers are continually repackaging or offering some 'essential' new ingredient.
- Developing new products – Mars ice-cream bar is a classic example of a new and successful product development.

## 7.6 Marketing strategy in different markets

### INDUSTRIAL VERSUS CONSUMER MARKETS

Although exams tend to focus on consumer products and services, there are sometimes questions on firms which sell to industrial and business customers. Examples include firms producing heavy lorries, metal components or services such as security or cleaning. There are some differences between consumer and industrial marketing. Often because the number of potential buyers may be far fewer. A supplier of metal components may have only 12 potential customers in the country.

Developing strategies will, however, be a very similar process. It will still need an excellent understanding of the product and the market. To a great extent the differences will depend on how competitive the market is. In some industrial markets there may be only one customer or one product. This will clearly result in different strategies. It may require working directly with the buyer to develop the product. Where customers are limited the industrial business may have no alternative but to look to overseas markets if it wishes to expand. If the market for its products is stagnant or saturated the business may need to develop new products.

For many industrial products there will be little difference to the consumer market. There will still be a need for **competitive differentiation** and correct positioning of the product.

## 7.7 Marketing strategy – a risky business?

Making changes in any business carries a certain amount of risk. Careful evaluation of the business and market situation will reduce the risk involved. Some strategies are more risky than others. The closer the business stays to its existing market and products the lower the risk. As it moves away from these known areas so the risk increases. Ansoff shows this in his matrix (see Figure 7.2).

As Ansoff's matrix shows, the least risky strategy is market penetration. Both the market and products are known to the business. With both product development and market development the risk is increased as the business moves into new areas. **Diversification** is the most risky strategy. Here both products and the market are new to the business.

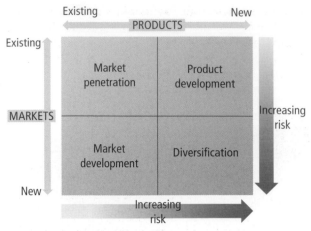

**Figure 7.2** Ansoff's matrix

## 7.8 Marketing strategy – a continual process

Once the strategy has been developed it needs to be constantly reviewed. An idea that looks good on paper will not necessarily work in action. There may need to be some testing of strategies, especially if they are risky. Market research and monitoring are necessary to ensure that the actions are producing the desired results. Evaluation of results will feed back into the system and in turn contribute to the development of revised objectives and strategies. This ongoing cycle is known as the **strategic cycle**.

**Figure 7.3** The strategic cycle

### STRATEGY NEEDS TO BE RESPONSIVE

A company's marketing strategy does not exist in a vacuum. It may provoke responses from competitors. Market opportunities will be changing constantly. If the company is to be successful it needs to be responsive and to adjust the strategy to cope with any changes in the environment or within the company. For example, the giant Heinz company found that its

approach to global marketing was ineffective – it shifted strategy to become more local. Only in Britain were baked beans an important seller, so the baked bean pizza was developed for the UK alone. In Korea, people love to pour ketchup on pizza, so a deal with Pizza Hut put a Heinz bottle on every table.

### BRITISH AIRWAYS THREATS AND STRATEGIES

British Airways has had more than its fair share of threats. During the 1990s, airline deregulation in Europe led to a growth in cut-price airlines. The huge success of these cheap, no-frills operations led British Airways to set up its own cut-price operation called 'Go'. Go was successful and BA sold it in 2001 to a management buyout team for £110 million saying that it was impractical for one company to run two businesses. (It was resold to easyJet for £400 million in 2002).

It wasn't long before BA was faced with a more substantial threat to its existence. The terrorist attacks in September 2001 had a devastating impact on the airline industry. BA was reported to be losing £2 million a day and many analysts feared that the airline would go bankrupt. Then, in 2003, BA was hit again by the war in Iraq plus the SARS virus in the Far East. However, although bruised, it has survived. The key to survival has been to cut costs and for the first time in its history to offer low priced, short-haul fares that compete with prices offered by the low cost airlines.

The low cost airlines still remain a threat; the scale of which can be seen in the number of orders for new planes. At the same time as British Airways has 20 planes mothballed in the Mojave Desert, Ryanair and easyJet have both placed orders for new aircraft. Analysts expect the discounters' share of the market to rise to 12–15% by 2010. If it is to survive, British Airways will need an imaginative and successful marketing strategy.

**IN Business**

### ISSUES FOR analysis

Issues that may need to be considered in response to case study or essay questions are:

● The relative importance of strategic market planning in different types of businesses. Can small firms possibly devote the time, thought and resources to strategy that would be spent by firms such as Heinz?

● The extent to which it is possible to develop clear strategies in a constantly changing marketplace.

- The influence of individuals may be important. The degree of risk in a firm's strategy may depend partly on the personality of the key decision maker. An entrepreneurial marketing director may achieve breakthroughs (or disasters) which a more cautious person would avoid.
- How do businesses find a balance between what is desirable and what is achievable? In some firms, the balance is determined at the top (by directors who may not understand fully the market conditions). Others adopt a more participative style, in which directors consult junior executives to get a clear idea of what can be achieved.

## 7.9 Marketing strategy
### an evaluation

It would be nice to think that businesses carefully evaluate the marketing environment and then devise a strategy that fits in with overall company objectives. In reality the strategy may be imposed by management, shareholders or even circumstances. In some instances

the only business objective may be survival. Strategy may then be reduced to crisis management. The other reality is that the business environment is not always clear and logical so it may be very difficult to generate realistic and effective strategies.

**KEY terms**

**competitive differentiation** – making your product or buying experience different from that of your competitors.

**demography** – the study of populations.

**diversification** – when a company expands its activities outside its normal range. This may be done to reduce risk or to expand possible markets.

**repositioning** – changing the product or its promotion to appeal to a different market segment.

**7.10 Workbook**

## Exercises

### A. REVISION QUESTIONS
*(30 marks; 70 minutes)*

Read the unit, then answer:

1 What is marketing strategy? *(3)*
2 What is the difference between marketing strategy and marketing tactics? *(3)*
3 What is a unique selling point? Give two examples. *(4)*
4 What is meant by product differentiation? *(3)*
5 What are the four steps in developing a marketing strategy? *(4)*
6 What is a SWOT analysis? *(3)*
7 Why is it important for a firm to examine its internal resources before deciding on a strategy? *(3)*
8 What is meant by 'market penetration'? *(3)*
9 What is the difference between market development and product development? *(4)*

### B. REVISION EXERCISES

#### B1 Activities
This can be a group or individual exercise.
Select a current advertisement from the TV or from a magazine or newspaper.

#### Questions
1 Analyse the advertisement in detail. You will want to look at issues such as:
  a What is the advertisement about? A product, a service, an improvement to an existing product, a special offer?
  b What is the message in the advertisement? Identify the key features such as price, quality, comparisons with rivals, etc.
  c Who is it aimed at? What is the target group or groups?
  d Is it a new or existing product?
  e Does the product have any rivals? If so, is the company trying to differentiate its product? How?
2 Research the market for this product. You might attempt to do this via the Internet, or visit a good business library. (A full list of available resources and libraries is given in the *A–Z Coursework Handbook* 3rd edition, Marcouse I, Hodder and Stoughton, 2003.) Visit the appropriate retail outlet and carry out a comparison of the shelf space, prices and display strengths of this product in relation to its competitors.
3 Decide what you believe the marketing strategy is for this company or product. Try to determine how this advertisement will fit into an overall marketing strategy.
4 Prepare your conclusions and analysis as a marketing presentation.

## B2 Data Response

### Shoppers Are Going Upmarket

According to research done by the British Retail Consortium shoppers are switching away from discount products to more upmarket goods. This trend towards quality rather than quantity is most evident in the electrical goods sector with shoppers opting for more expensive household gadgets. Of the 1,000 adults surveyed, 71% of those who said they were spending more on electrical goods said the extra had gone on better quality goods.

The food sector has also seen a change from traditional foods to exotic foreign and health foods. About half of those who said they were spending more on food said they were buying more upmarket products.

Source: *The Times*, 21/8/98

**Questions** *(30 marks; 35 minutes)*

1 What is meant by discount goods? *(3)*
2 a What do customers seem to want from electrical goods? *(3)*
   b How might an electrical goods retailer react to these findings? *(6)*
3 What changes might a food manufacturer make to its marketing strategy, as a result of the information in the article? *(8)*
4 As a food manufacturer, what other information would you like to have before deciding on a new marketing strategy? Explain your answer. *(10)*

# ELASTICITY OF DEMAND

## DEFINITION

Elasticity measures how the demand for a product changes in response to a change in a variable such as price or income.

## 8.1 Introduction

The demand for goods and services is determined by a wide variety of factors. The demand for a new Rover 200 car, for example, will be influenced by its price, the price of similar small cars, the amount spent on advertising, seasonality and many other factors. Elasticity measures the degree to which one of these variables affects demand.

Each variable that affects demand has its own relevant elasticity. A price rise is almost certain to cut demand and an increase in advertising spending is likely to increase it. So the price and advertising elasticities of demand can be calculated. The elasticities most commonly used in business are price and income.

## 8.2 Price elasticity of demand

In the short term, the most important factor affecting demand is price. If Coca-Cola raised the price of Coke, sales would almost certainly fall. Some consumers would switch to a cheaper brand. Others would purchase Coke less frequently. If a 10% price increase caused demand to fall by only 1%, Coca-Cola could benefit hugely by increasing the price.

So the crucial question is *how much* will demand fall when the price increases? This question can be answered by calculating the price elasticity of demand for Coca-Cola. Price elasticity is not about whether demand changes when price changes, it is about the *degree* of change. Consequently, price elasticity is a unit of measurement rather than being a thing in itself. A price cut will not cause price elasticity to fall. Instead the price elasticity figure explains the effect the price cut is likely to have on demand. Will demand rise by 1%, 5% or 25% following the price cut? The answer can only be known by referring to the product's price elasticity of demand. Price elasticity measures the *responsiveness* of demand to a change in price.

Some products are far more price sensitive than others. Following a 5% increase in price the demand for some products may fall greatly, say by more than 20%. The demand for another type of product may fall by less than 1%.

Price elasticity can be calculated by using the following formula:

$$\text{price elasticity} = \frac{\%\text{ change in quantity demanded}}{\%\text{ change in price}}$$

Price elasticity measures the percentage effect on demand of each 1% change in price. So if a 10% increase in price led demand to fall by 20%, the price elasticity would be 2. Strictly speaking, price elasticities are always negative, because price up pushes demand down, and price down pushes demand up. For example:

$$\frac{-20\%}{+10\%} = -2$$

The figure of −2 indicates that for every 1% change in price, demand is likely to change by 2%. All price elasticities are negative. This is because there is a negative **correlation** between price and quantity demanded. In the short term, a price cut will always boost sales and a price rise will always cut sales. The only exception to this is when a price rise on a luxury good helps to boost its long-term status to a potential buyer.

## 8.3 Using price elasticity information

Price elasticity of demand information can be used for two purposes:

### 1 SALES FORECASTING

A firm considering a price rise will want to know the effect the price change is likely to have on demand. Producing a sales forecast will make accurate production, personnel and purchasing decisions possible. For example, when News International cut the cover price of *The Sun* by 25% from 25p to 20p, sales rose 16% to more than 4 million copies per day. The price elasticity of *The Sun* proved to be:

$$\frac{+16\%}{-20\%} = -0.8$$

This information could be used by News International to predict the likely impact of future price changes. A price cut of 10% could lead to a rise in circulation of 8% ($-10\% \times -0.8 = +8\%$). This is valuable information to know. Before implementing the price cut the company would check the current production capacity. It would be foolish to cut price only to find that the new higher demand level cannot be met.

## 2 PRICING STRATEGY

There are many external factors beyond a firm's control that determine a product's demand and therefore profitability. For example, a soft drinks manufacturer can do nothing about a wet summer that hammers sales and profits. However, the price the firm decides to charge *is* within its control. And it can be a crucial factor in determining demand and profitability. Price elasticity information can be used in conjunction with internal cost data to forecast the implications of a price change on profit.

**Example:**
A second-hand car dealer currently sells 60 cars each year. On average each car costs him £2,000 to buy. Annual overheads are £18,000. Currently he charges his customers £2,500 per car. This means the business makes a profit of:

$$\text{total revenue} = £2,500 \times 60 = £150,000$$
$$\text{total cost} = £18,000 + (2,000 \times 60)$$
$$= £138,000$$
$$\text{total profit} = £150,000 - £138,000$$
$$= £12,000$$

From past experience the salesman believes the price elasticity of his cars is approximately 0.75. The dealer is thinking about increasing his prices to £3,000 per car. An increase of 20%. Using the price elasticity information, a quick calculation would reveal the impact on profit:

$$\text{percentage change in demand} = +20\% \times -0.75$$
$$= -15\%$$

A 15% fall in demand on the existing sales volume of 60 cars per year will produce a fall in demand of 9 cars per year:

$$\frac{60}{100} \times 15 = 9 \text{ cars per year}$$

So demand will fall to 51 cars per year after the price increase. On the basis of these figures the new annual profit would be:

$$\text{total revenue} = \text{new price} \times \text{new sales volume}$$
$$= £3,000 \times 51 \text{ cars}$$
$$= £153,000$$
$$\text{total cost} = £18,000 + (51 \times £2,000)$$
$$= £120,000$$
$$\text{new profit} = £33,000$$

So following the 20% increase in price, profits should increase by:

$$\frac{£33,000 - £12,000}{£12,000} \times 100 = 175\%$$

Obviously in this case the car dealer should change his pricing strategy. However, this is all based on two assumptions:

1 that the price elasticity of the cars actually proves to be −0.75
2 other factors that could also affect demand remain unchanged following the price increase.

## 8.4 Classifying price elasticity

### PRICE ELASTIC PRODUCTS

A **price elastic** product has a price elasticity of above one. This means that the percentage change in demand is greater than the percentage change in price that created it. For example, if a firm increased prices by 5% and as a result demand fell by 15%, price elasticity would be:

$$\frac{-15\%}{+5\%} \times 100 = -3$$

The figure indicates that for every 1% change in price there will be a 3% change in demand. The higher the price elasticity figure the more price elastic the product is. Cutting price on a price elastic product will boost total revenue. This is because the extra revenue gained from the increased sales volume more than offsets the revenue lost from the price cut. On the other

### INELASTIC NEWSPAPERS?

In September 2002 *The Daily Telegraph* raised its cover price from 50p to 55p. In the same month the price of a copy of *The Sunday Times* went up by 20p. These price increases were in sharp contrast to the price-cutting strategies used by the broadsheet dailies during the 1990s. Ivan Fallon, the Chief Executive of the *Independent*, claimed that his newspaper lost £1 billion in the previous decade as a result of price cuts. This change in pricing strategy reflects the fact that newspaper owners now believe that their broadsheets are price inelastic rather than price elastic. The strong brand loyalties that exist within the market mean that price increases, rather than price decreases, are the route to higher revenues and profits. This point was backed up by the fact that following the *Telegraph*'s decision to increase price by 10%, circulation fell by only 1.77%.

*IN Business*

hand, a price increase on a price elastic product will lead to a fall in total revenue.

Although a price cut on a price elastic product will increase revenue, it might not boost profits. Total revenue will increase. However, a price cut that increases sales volume will also increase costs as more of the product now has to be produced. To predict the impact on profits one must also have access to cost information. It is also important to note that price cutting can damage brand image. First, customers often associate high prices with high quality. Second, a price cutting decision is usually difficult to reverse due to consumer resistance to price increases. Finally, the actions of the competition must also be taken into account. If your price cut prompts a price war, the much needed gains in sales volume might not arise.

PRICE INELASTIC PRODUCTS

## PRICE INELASTIC PRODUCTS

**Price inelastic** products have price elasticities below one. This means the percentage change in demand is less than the percentage change in price. In other words, price changes have hardly any effect on demand. Perhaps because consumers feel they *must* have the product or brand in question. The stunning dress, the trendiest designer label, or – less interestingly – gas for central heating. Customers feel they must have it, either because it really is a necessity, or because it is fashionable. Firms with price inelastic products will be tempted to push the prices up. A price increase will boost revenue because the price rise creates a relatively small fall in sales volume. This means the majority of customers will continue to purchase the brand but at a higher, revenue-boosting price.

## 8.5 Strategies to reduce price elasticity

All businesses prefer to sell price inelastic products. Charging more for a price inelastic product guarantees an increase in short-term profit. Cutting price on a price elastic product, however, increases total revenue in the very short term but may hit profit. A sharp rise in sales will probably be at the expense of competitors. They will have little choice but to respond. A price war may result.

It is important to realise the price elasticity of a brand is not set in stone. Price elasticity is not an external constraint. Firms use a variety of strategies to try to reduce the price elasticity of their products. The most important influence on a brand's price elasticity is substitutability. If consumers have other brands available that they think deliver the same benefits, price elasticity will be high. So to make a brand price inelastic the firm has to find ways of reducing the number of substitutes available (or acceptable). How can this be done?

## INCREASING PRODUCT DIFFERENTIATION

Product differentiation is the degree to which consumers perceive that a product is different (and preferably better) than its rivals. Some products are truly different, such as a Jaguar car. Others are differentiated mainly by image, such as Coca-Cola. The purchasers of highly differentiated products like Coke often remain brand loyal despite price rises.

## HORIZONTAL INTEGRATION

This occurs when two firms in the same industry and at the same stage of production decide to merge or when one decides to take the other over. In 2003 low-cost airline Ryanair bought the rival Buzz. Horizontal integration decreases rivalry and consumer choice. Many analysts predicted that this decrease in competition would lead to an increase in air fares.

## PRICE FIXING

Some markets are less competitive than they first appear. This is because firms in the same industry decide to form a **cartel**. Instead of competing against each other, the cartel members behave as if they were one large monopolist. Consumers might have a theoretical choice of who to purchase from. But the suppliers may have agreed to charge very similar prices. By reducing genuine choice and competition, cartels can successfully reduce price elasticity.

## 8.6 Techniques used to estimate price elasticity of demand

There are two main techniques that can be used to estimate a brand's price elasticity of demand.

| Year | Price Change (%) | Demand Change (%) | Estimated Price Elasticity of Demand |
|---|---|---|---|
| 1999 | +2 | −2.4 | $\dfrac{-2.4\%}{+2\%} = -1.2$ |
| 2001 | +2.5 | −2.9 | $\dfrac{-2.9\%}{+2.5\%} = -1.16$ |
| 2002 | −4 | +5 | $\dfrac{+5\%}{-4\%} = -1.25$ |

## PAST SALES FIGURES

A simple way to estimate price elasticity is to consider what happened to sales the last time the firm changed its prices.

### Example:

A firm manufacturing washing machines has changed the price of its leading model three times in recent years. Sales responded in the manner shown in the table at the foot of page 51.

By taking the average value of the price elasticities over the period, the firm could get an idea of the overall price elasticity for the product. In this case it would be:

$$\frac{-2 + -1.16 + -1.25}{3} = -1.20$$

The danger of this approach is that it ignores the other factors affecting demand besides price. For example, when the firm cut its prices in 2002 demand increased. The critical question, though, is whether the price cut created *all* 5% of the demand increase that followed. Were other factors at work? Maybe some of the increase in demand would have happened anyway even if prices had not been cut? Some of the increase in demand may have been created by competitors cutting back on advertising support or by cuts in UK interest rates.

### PRIMARY QUANTITATIVE MARKET RESEARCH

Before launching a new product firms use representative matched samples. Each sample of potential consumers is then asked how much they would be prepared to purchase at a given price level. The price levels quoted will vary between samples. By identifying the differences in the quantities the samples intend to purchase, the price elasticity can be estimated.

## 8.7 Income elasticity of demand

**Income elasticity** of demand measures the responsiveness of demand to a change in the overall spending power of consumers. This is measured by comparing income increases with inflation. If incomes rise 6% while inflation is 4%, spending power has risen 2%. This measurement of spending power is known as *real income*. A 2% rise in real incomes might lead consumers to spend 10% more on eating out. If so, eating out would be considered a highly income elastic activity.

Income elasticity is calculated as follows:

$$\text{income elasticity} = \frac{\text{\% change in quantity demanded}}{\text{\% change in real income}}$$

Economic growth tends to fluctuate due to the effects of the trade cycle. Economic booms are followed by downturns which can become recessions. Income levels follow this pattern, with profound effects on the demand for most goods and services. These effects can vary greatly from product to product. During booms, when incomes grow rapidly, the demand for some types of good will increase greatly, whilst the demand for other types of good may actually fall.

## 8.8 Classifying income elasticity

Products and services can be grouped into three categories of income elasticity. Unlike price elasticity, income elasticity figures are not always negative.

### NORMAL GOODS

As real incomes increase the demand for normal goods will also increase. This means that a normal good will have a positive income elasticity that is below one. A typical example of a normal good is petrol. As real incomes increase, many people may feel that they can now afford more weekend trips out in the car. So following a 2% increase in real income the demand for petrol might rise by 0.5%. On the basis of these figures the income elasticity of petrol would appear to be:

$$\frac{+0.5\%}{+2\%} = +0.25$$

This figure of +0.25 indicates that a 1% increase in real income will create an increase in demand of 0.25%. So when real incomes rise the demand for normal goods will also rise, but at a slower rate.

### LUXURY GOODS

Luxury goods also have a positive income elasticity. However, unlike a normal good the income elasticity

### Business IN

**SALES OF LUXURIES RECOVER IN SOUTH KOREA.**

The economy of South Korea was hit badly by the Asian crisis of 1997, which led to a high unemployment rate and falling consumer income levels throughout the country. Since the beginning of 2000 the economy of South Korea has recovered. In 2001 real incomes increased by 3.3% and were forecast to increase by as much as 5.8% in 2002.

This recovery had a profound effect upon the sales of premium branded goods in South Korea. For example sales of imported Gucci clothes increased by over 44% during 2001. According to the company, sales rose because the disposable incomes of South Korea's middle class population increased. It appears from this information that the income elasticity of Gucci clothes may be as high as +13 (44% ÷ 3.3%).

figure will be above one. The demand for luxury goods will grow at a faster rate than the increase in real income that created the change in demand. This responsiveness will also apply in reverse. During recessions, when real incomes fall, the demand for luxury goods will fall sharply. By a far bigger percentage than the initial fall in real income. As a result the demand for luxury goods tends to be more volatile than that of normal goods during a typical trade cycle.

## INFERIOR GOODS

Inferior goods have a negative income elasticity. So people buy less of these products or services when they are better off. And more of them when they hit hard times. They are cheap substitutes for products they prefer to buy when they can afford to. Such as 'no frills' baked beans.

For example, If real incomes grew by 2% the demand for a budget own-label tin of baked beans might actually drop by 10%. In this case the own label would have an income elasticity of:

$$\frac{+10\%}{+2\%} = -5$$

ISSUES FOR **analysis**

In examinations, elasticity of demand is a key discriminator between good and weak candidates. Really weak candidates never bring the concept into their answers at all. Better candidates apply it, but imprecisely. Top grade students see where it is relevant and show a clear understanding of the concept and its implications. Here are some of the ways elasticity can be used for business analysis:

- When answering a question about pricing, elasticity is a vital factor. Even if a firm faces severe cost increases, a price rise will be very risky if its products have a high price elasticity. Pricing decisions must always start with careful consideration of price elasticity.
- People naturally assume that marketing (especially advertising) is always about trying to increase sales. In fact, most firms are far more interested in their image. A glance at any commercial break will confirm this. Companies focus upon their image because that is the way to differentiate themselves from others. That, in turn, is the way to reduce price elasticity and therefore give the company stronger control over its pricing.
- Good students rarely refer to 'elasticity'. They refer to price elasticity or income elasticity. This is because it is quite wrong to assume that products have the same level of price and income elasticities. A luxury car such as a Rolls Royce has a very low price elasticity, but its income elasticity is very high. In the 1991 recession, Rolls Royce sales fell by more than 30% when real incomes fell by less than 3%!

- When considering any question about business strategy, income elasticity is an important issue. A firm selling luxury products may be very vulnerable to recessions, as the income elasticity of its products is likely to be high. Therefore it should ensure that its financial position (its balance sheet) is always strong – because recessions are not easy to predict. The business could also consider diversifying.

## 8.9 Elasticity of demand
### an evaluation

For examiners, elasticity is a convenient concept. It is hard to understand, but very easy to write exam questions on! But how useful is it in the real world? Would the average marketing director know the price elasticities of his or her products?

In many cases the answer is no. Examiners and textbooks exaggerate the precision that is possible with such a concept. The fact that the income elasticity of Rolls Royce cars appeared to be around +10 in 1991 does not mean it is always that high. Price elasticities change over time as competition changes and consumer tastes change. Income elasticities may vary as products come to seem more or less of a necessity.

Even though elasticities can vary over time, certain features tend to remain constant. Strong brands such as Levi's and Coca-Cola have relatively low price elasticity. This gives them the power over market pricing that ensures strong profitability year after year. For less established firms, these brands are the role model. Everyone wants to be the Coca-Cola of their own market or market niche.

**KEY terms**

**cartel** – an agreement by producers to limit supply to keep prices high.

**correlation** – the relationship between one variable and another.

**income elasticity** – the effect on demand of changes in consumer spending power.

**price elastic** – a product which is highly price sensitive, so price elasticity is above 1.

**price inelastic** – a product which is not very price sensitive, so price elasticty is below 1.

# Exercises

## A. REVISION QUESTIONS
*(40 marks; 80 minutes)*

Read the unit, then answer:

1  a  If a product's sales have fallen by 21% since a price rise from £2 to £2.07, what is its price elasticity? *(4)*
   b  Is the product price elastic or price inelastic? *(1)*

2  State two methods Nestlé might take to reduce the price elasticity of KitKat chocolate bars. *(2)*

3  A firm selling 20,000 units at £8 is considering a 4% price increase. It believes its price elasticity is −0.5.
   a  What will be the effect upon revenue? *(4)*
   b  Give two reasons why the revenue may prove to be different from the firm's expectations. *(2)*

4  Explain three ways a firm could make use of information about the price elasticity of its brands. *(6)*

5  Identify three external factors that could increase the price elasticity of a brand of chocolate. *(3)*

6  A firm has a sales target of 60,000 units per month. Current sales are 50,000 per month at a price of £1.50. If its products have a price elasticity of −2, what price should the firm charge to meet the target sales volume? *(4)*

7  Why is price elasticity always negative? *(2)*

8  Why may the manager of a product with a price elasticity of −2 be reluctant to cut the price? *(3)*

9  When the recession hit, a 3% fall in consumers' real incomes caused sales of a firm's product to rise from 40,000 to 44,800.
   a  Calculate the product's income elasticity. *(4)*
   b  Suggest the type of product it is. *(1)*

10  Suggest two brands that:
   a  have low price elasticity but high income elasticity *(2)*
   b  have low income elasticity but high price elasticity. *(2)*

## B. REVISION EXERCISES

**B1  Data Response**  *(20 marks; 30 minutes.)*
A firm selling Manchester United pillowcases for £10 currently generates an annual turnover of £500,000. Variable costs average at £4 per unit and total annual fixed costs are £100,000. The marketing director is considering a price increase of 10%. Given that the price elasticity of the product is believed to be −0.4, calculate:
1  the old and the new sales volume *(3)*
2  the new revenue *(3)*
3  the expected change in profit following the price increase *(6)*

4  if the firm started producing mass-market white pillowcases, would their price elasticity be higher or lower than the Manchester United ones? Why is that? *(8)*

**B2 Case Study**
A firm producing ice-cream has recently cut the price of two of its leading brands by 10%. One of its brands, Spice Spangle, is a budget mass-market product which is targeted at children. Finesse is sold in a totally different market segment. Its premium price creates far higher margins from a relatively low sales volume. The table below shows the impact the price cuts have had on the two brands.

**Questions**  *(40 marks; 70 minutes)*
1  Complete the gaps in the table. *(8)*
2  From the data above, calculate the price elasticity of the two brands. *(6)*
3  Discuss the wisdom of the two respective price cuts. *(10)*
4  What additional sales would be needed on the Finesse brand to pay for the 10% price cut? *(6)*
5  Should pricing decisions always be based upon the impact they have on short-term profits? *(10)*

| | Spice Spangle Pre-price cut | Post-price cut | Finesse Pre-price cut | Post-price cut |
|---|---|---|---|---|
| Sales volume (000) units | 5,000 | 7,000 | 1,000 | 1,050 |
| Sales value (£000) | 2,000 | 2,520 | 1,500 | 1,418 |
| Variable cost of goods sold (£000) | 1,000 | 1,200 | 750 | 788 |
| Gross profit (£000) | 1,000 | | 750 | |
| Advertising, administration and distribution expenses (£000) | 600 | 750 | | 90 |
| Net profit | 400 | 570 | 650 | 540 |

## C. ESSAY QUESTIONS

1 'Reducing price elasticity should be the number one goal of any firm's marketing strategy.' Discuss the validity of this statement.

2 As marketing director of a successful company, explain how you would go about reducing the price elasticity of one of your leading confectionery brands. What external and internal constraints are you likely to encounter along the way?

3 Outline and evaluate the factors that might affect the price elasticity of demand for a fitness centre. Why might managers wish to change the price elasticity of the centre?

# MARKETING MIX

## 9.1 How is it used?

Marketing managers look at each of the ingredients in the mix. They decide what marketing actions need to be taken under each of the headings. If marketing activity is to be effective each ingredient needs to be considered. It will be constrained by the budget available for marketing activity. For each market situation there will be an optimum combination of the ingredients. This will give a balance between cost and effectiveness. The ingredients need to work with each other. A good product poorly priced may fail. If the product is not available following an advertising campaign the expenditure is wasted.

A successful *mix* will produce customer satisfaction. It will achieve the marketing objectives.

## 9.2 For each market situation there will be a different mix

The mix will ensure that the marketing effort is correctly targeted. There are different markets. Industrial markets are different from consumer markets.

### INDUSTRIAL MARKETS

In industrial markets, one business is supplying another. The products will be:

- materials and parts, including raw materials, part-finished goods, component parts, supplies such as packaging, office supplies
- capital goods, including machinery, vehicles, buildings, office equipment
- services such as banking, insurance, distribution.

Businesses purchase these products in order to produce their own products for the market. They will have concerns about cost, reliability, quality and availability. In industrial markets the product may have exact specifications agreed with the customer. There will be less scope for modifying the product.

### CONSUMER MARKETS

The consumer market supplies the final consumer (the 'end-user'). It is a much larger and more complex market. In order to understand this market businesses look at:

**Buying habits:** Most purchases fall into two categories:

- Convenience goods – these are bought frequently. They include most non-durable goods. They are consumed when used. They can be:
  - regular purchases
  - impulse purchases
  - emergency purchases.
- Shopping goods – the customer will take longer to choose. They include durable goods such as cars and household goods. They are used over and over again.

**The type of consumer:** Customers can be categorised in several ways. Such as by:

- Spending power – customer expectations and buying patterns vary with spending ability. Lower income households will look for less expensive hotels with family sized rooms. Higher income families will look for more exclusive locations and better facilities.
- Age – there are some products such as toys or sheltered housing that are age specific. Businesses sometimes modify the product to make it appeal to other groups. Johnson and Johnson repositioned its baby products. It changed its promotion to encourage women to buy.
- Gender – many products are gender specific. If the product is sold as 'unisex' there will be a larger market. Calvin Klein sells perfumes for men and women. The marketing however suggests some of them can be used by males or females. Some products can be modified slightly and marketed to appeal to a different gender group. Cosmetics companies have developed cosmetics for men. These are similar products to those sold to women. The packaging and market support have been changed to appeal to men.

### WITHIN EACH MARKET THERE MAY BE MANY DIFFERENT SEGMENTS

The differences in customers and buying habits result in many 'markets within markets'. These are known as market segments. Each segment will require its own marketing mix. The fashion industry is an example. At one end, cheap, cheerful with mass availability is the key. At the other end exclusivity and quality workmanship are important.

## 9.3 The ingredients are not equally important

In most cases the product is the vital ingredient. No amount of marketing effort will make a poor product succeed. However a good product without good support may also fail. The balance will vary. In a price-sensitive market, pricing will be important. This is seen in the petrol market. If one company reduces its price the others follow rapidly. In industrial markets reliability and quality may be the overriding considerations.

## 9.4 Product

A product is something that is offered to the market. Businesses need to understand what the product is and what it means to the consumer.

A product can be:

- a good such as a washing machine or shampoo
- a service such as accountancy or hairdressing
- a place such as a tourist destination
- a person such as a football player or pop star.

Understanding the type of product is important. Businesses will need a different marketing strategy to sell a chocolate bar than a washing machine. For the chocolate bar the location and the wrapping may be important features. For the washing machine, design and performance are more likely to be significant to the customer.

### WHAT THE PRODUCT MEANS TO THE CUSTOMER

Products are not just physical things. They *do* something for the customer. Mobile phones are not just communication devices. They are also fashion accessories. Look at Nokia's range of interchangeable mobile phone covers.

Products provide both *tangible* and *intangible* benefits. Tangible benefits are those that can be measured. Cars have different performance levels. A Ford Focus will not give the same speed performance as a Porsche 911. Intangible benefits cannot be measured. They include things such as pleasure, satisfaction or peace of mind. Häagen-Dazs ice-cream advertising does not emphasise the nutritional value of the ice-cream. It concentrates on building an image for the brand. Building society advertisements emphasise security (an intangible benefit) above convenience (a tangible benefit).

### BRAND VALUES

On 2 October 2002 EMI proudly announced 'the biggest record deal in British history'. Robbie Williams had agreed to record his next six albums with EMI in return for a payment of between £50 and £80 million. The media loved the deal and so did the stock market. The name Robbie Williams was enough to push up the share price of EMI. Few noticed, though, the announcement just two days later that Guy Chambers would no longer be writing songs with or for Williams. Chambers' songs such as 'Millennium' and 'Rock DJ' were a vital part of Williams' success. EMI said 'there are plenty of good songwriters who Robbie could work with', but it raised the question of whether Robbie Williams – the brand name – is more important than the Robbie Williams music.

### MAKING THE PRODUCT FIT THE MARKET

Good marketing means developing products that 'fit' the market. They need to be designed correctly and then developed to keep pace with market changes. Businesses use market and product research to tailor products to customer requirements. *Market research* is essential. It will help to understand the customer and the product. It will tell the business:

- who the customer is
- how the customer makes their purchasing decisions
- what the customer wants from the product
- if there are gaps in the market
- what rival products are in the market
- what competitors are doing.

*Product research* concentrates on the product in order to:

- produce new products
- modify existing products.

### THE ROLE OF NEW PRODUCTS

New products are important to businesses. They give competitive advantage. They bring new customers. New products may come from product research. They may have been developed to fill a gap in the market. When a new product is developed it should take account of market and customer requirements. Test marketing is useful. The product may be launched in a small area to test customer reactions. Modifications can then be made before the final launch.

### MANAGING EXISTING PRODUCTS

Once a product is in the market the business needs to monitor customer and competitor reaction regularly.

It is essential that the product is developed as necessary. This will maintain the life of the product. It will ensure that it does not get overtaken by rival products. Car manufacturers introduce new models on a regular basis. They also modify their existing models continually. These modifications keep the product 'fresh' in the eyes of the customer.

In a highly competitive market it is essential to make the product stand out from its rivals. In order to attract customer attention businesses try to differentiate their product from other products. Some are easier to differentiate than others. The secret is to find the modification that will have the most customer appeal. Understanding what customers want helps to ensure that the modifications are effective. When video recorders were first introduced manufacturers kept adding more complex features. This differentiated their products in a highly competitive situation. Some manufacturers realised that customers wanted a machine that was easy to use. This has now become a standard product feature.

Modifications can be made to:

- the design, such as shape or colour
- the performance, such as adding extra features or making the product easier to use
- service levels, such as improving after-sales care or the guarantee period.

Businesses may also modify existing products to make them attractive to a different market segment. This may be just repackaging. Products sold to overseas markets will often require repackaging. In other cases the product may be altered. Heinz introduced a range of tinned products with lower sugar content to appeal to the health conscious customer. These are sold alongside its normal products.

## 9.5  Price

(Pricing is dealt with more fully in Unit 10.)

Price plays a critical part in marketing activity. Incorrect pricing policy could:

- Lose customers – if the price is not 'right' customers will buy rival products. Consumers have a fair idea of what is the correct price for a product.
- Lose revenue – obviously lost customers mean lost revenue. Revenue can also be lost if the price is too low. There needs to be a balance between sales and revenue. An understanding of **price elasticity of demand** will help businesses to make correct pricing decisions.

Pricing involves a balance between being competitive and being profitable.

### PRICING STRATEGIES

Pricing strategies will depend on the product and the market. There are different strategies for new and existing products.

Strategies for new products include:

- Skimming – setting a high price when the product is introduced. This maximises initial returns.
- Penetration – setting a low price to guarantee entry into the market.

For existing products there are other strategies:

- Price leader – the business will set the market price.
- Price taker – the business will match the market price.
- Predator – the business will undercut the market price.

Once the strategy has been determined there are many different pricing *tactics* that can be used. These include:

- Loss leaders – prices are set deliberately low, possibly below cost. This encourages buyers, who then purchase related products. This in turn generates profits. Supermarkets often offer some products at below cost in order to attract customers into the store. These customers will hopefully then fill their baskets with these and other goods. Similarly, car manufacturers make most of their profits on parts sales rather than the initial sale of the car.

## BATTLE OF THE CONSOLES

In August 2002 Sony and Microsoft announced price cuts on their games consoles, as part of the war for dominance of this £20 billion world market. The two companies, together with Nintendo, vie with each other to produce ever more sophisticated machines. The current winner is the Sony PlayStation 2, which has sold more than 33 million machines since its launch in March 2000. This is eight times more than its rivals the Microsoft Xbox and Nintendo's GameCube.

Once the battle of technology has been fought, the companies keep the product alive by cutting prices and the battle moves to level 2. Microsoft had to reduce the price of its Xbox very soon after its launch because Sony reduced its price. In this latest move Sony is in a strong position. It has already covered its development costs and can afford to reduce prices to maintain its domination. Microsoft clearly feels that it cannot allow Sony any more competitive advantage at this stage in the product life cycle of Xbox and so is matching the price reduction.

The battle looks likely to continue well into the future. Sony is expected to have its new generation game machine on the market by 2005 and the press has reported that Microsoft is looking to launch Xbox2 in 2004.

Business IN

- Psychological pricing – prices are set just below psychological price barriers such as £10. A price of £9.99 seems lower than £10.00.
- Special-offer pricing – this includes offers such as 'three for the price of two'.

## 9.6 Promotion

This is about communication. It is about telling potential consumers about a product. The aim is to persuade customers to buy the product. The extent to which this ingredient is important will depend on:

- The competitiveness of the market – where no alternatives are available the consumer will have less choice. There will be less need to persuade the customer to buy.
- Availability – if the product is in short supply there will be little need to promote it. In Russia, toilet paper is scarce. Russian customers are less concerned about the thickness, softness or number of sheets in the roll than people in the West, where several products are competing for customer approval in crowded markets.
- How easily the product can be differentiated in the market – if the differences are obvious to the customer there may be less need for promotion.
- The stage of the product life cycle – a new product will usually need promotional support. Promotion will tell customers that the product is available. It will persuade them to try the new product. If the product has been altered, promotion will tell customers of the changes.

Promotion should be:

- informative
- persuasive
- reassuring.

There are many forms of promotion. It is not just advertising!
Promotion includes:

- Advertising – this includes direct advertising such as through the TV, radio and newspapers. It also includes indirect advertising such as product placement.

> '*I know half the money I spend on advertising is wasted, but I can never find out which half.*'
>
> Lord Leverhume, *British industrialist*

Source: *The Ultimate Book of Business Quotations*, Stuart Crainer, Capstone Publishing, 1997

- Direct selling – customers are approached directly. This may be by direct contact. Telesales is a growing business.
- Direct marketing – this will include mailshots, perhaps supported by sales catalogues.

The London Marathon: sponsorship as a promotional and PR exercise (© Ian Walton/Getty Images)

- Point-of-sale – promotional material is often used where the product is being sold. It may include displays, free samples or special offers.
- Incentives – these include loyalty cards, bonus points and sometimes price incentives.
- Public relations – this is not direct marketing but involves ensuring that the company or product name is known and is well thought of by customers. This will include activities such as sponsorship of sport or arts.

Promotion is often talked about as being above- or below-the-line. Above-the-line is direct advertising through consumer media such as press, TV, cinema and radio. All other forms of promotion are considered below-the-line activity. This would include direct selling and promotional activities such as incentives. Businesses will not just use one method of promotion. They will have a mixture of activities. This is known as the promotional mix. The mix will need to be balanced to be as effective as possible. The mix of promotional activities will depend on:

- the size of the market
- the type of product
- the cost.

Promotion needs to be effective. Being effective means getting a balance between coverage and cost. TV advertising is expensive but has huge coverage. There is no point in advertising table tennis equipment on TV at peak viewing times. It is more effective to use a specialist magazine for table tennis players. If players belong to clubs they could also be targeted by direct mail.

## 9.7 Place

This is about availability. It includes the physical place, availability and timing.
The key questions facing firms are:

- What are the best outlets for reaching potential customers?
- How can I convince those outlets to stock my products?

- What is the most effective way to get my products to those outlets?

Compare, for a moment, McVitie's Jaffa Cakes and Burton's Jammie Dodgers. Both are well-known biscuit brands, but the former is distributed in 90% of retail outlets whereas the latter is in only 64%. Clearly this restricts sales of Jammie Dodgers, because few customers would make a special journey to find them. Both companies have a similar view of the right outlets for their products (supermarkets, corner shops, garages, canteens and cafés). So why may Burton's be losing out to McVitie's in this particular race? Possible reasons include:

- Jaffa Cakes have higher consumer demand, therefore retail outlets are more willing to stock the product
- Jammie Dodgers may have more direct competitors; high product differentiation may make Jaffa Cakes more of a 'must stock' line
- If Jaffa Cakes have more advertising support, retailers know customers will ask for the product by name while the advertising campaign is running
- McVitie's have a much larger market share, therefore the company is in a stronger position to cross-sell (i.e. persuade a shopkeeper to buy a range of McVitie brands).

In this case, both firms were clear about the target outlets for their product. This is not always the case – there may be important decisions to be made. If you are launching the world's first robotic lawnmower, would you want it in every garden centre, DIY outlet, department store and Argos catalogue? That would depend on

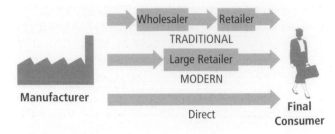

**Figure 9.1** Channels of distribution

your overall strategy. Perhaps you feel that, while the only supplier, you should price high to enjoy high profit margins to recoup your investment (skimming the market). In which case you should perhaps only distribute through department stores. Later, you could bring the price down and strike a deal with B&Q. Persuading retailers to stock your product is never easy. For the retailer, the key issues are opportunity cost and risk. As shelf space is limited, stocking your chocolate bar probably means scrapping another. Which one? What revenue will be lost? Will one or two customers be upset? ('What! No Coffee Walnut Whips any more!') These factors represent the opportunity cost of stocking your product. The other consideration is risk. A brand new chocolate bar endorsed by a supermodel may be a slimmer's delight, but high initial sales may then flop, leaving the shopkeeper with boxes of slow-moving stock.

The remaining issue to consider is the distribution channel. In other words, how the product passes from producer to the consumer. Sold directly, as with pick-your-own strawberries? Or via a wholesaler, then a retailer, as with newspapers bought from your local shop? There are three main channels of distribution:

1 Traditional – in the days before hypermarkets and superstores, shops bought their stock from wholesalers, who in turn bought from producers. The profit mark-up applied by the 'middle man' added to the final retail price, but wholesalers had many other advantages. They 'broke bulk', meaning that they might buy a container load of Andrex, but be happy to sell in boxes of 48 packs to shopkeepers. This ensured that small shops did not need to hold high stock levels.
2 Modern – Sainsbury's, B&Q and WH Smith do not buy from a wholesaler. They buy direct from producers and then organise their own distribution to their outlets. Their huge selling power gives them huge buying power. Therefore they are able to negotiate the highest discounts from the producers.
3 Direct – years ago, door-to-door selling was an important distribution method. Today this has given way to many other approaches. Retailers of home computers in Britain and America are being hit hard by fierce competition from direct sales companies such as Dell. By cutting out the wholesaler and the retailer, Dell is able to offer low prices for up-to-date machines. Already very successful at

## THE DISTRIBUTION OF CK ONE

The hugely successful launch of the fragrance CK One had many unusual features. In an era of niche marketing, Unilever targeted a multi-racial, multi-ethnic, ageless, genderless audience. Yet it applied this apparently mass market approach through completely unorthodox distribution channels. A fragrance on sale in a record shop? Or in a night club? Why not? In this way CK One acquired an image of being young and different – yet it sold to both sexes and many age groups. And having established a general brand name in the fragrance market, young consumers who like experimenting can choose from a range of CK products.

Source: Adapted from *Unilever Magazine*, no. 106

Dell Computers advertised on the Internet (© Dell Computer Corporation)

attracting customers through its media advertising, Dell now gets three quarters of its orders via the Internet. This low-cost form of promotion gives Dell a major competitive edge. Dixons and Computer World have huge overheads to pay; Dell has very few.

## 9.8 Where does the marketing mix fit into marketing planning?

The marketing mix should follow on from the marketing strategy. Managers need an excellent understanding of the market if they are to *mix* the ingredients effectively.

- Statistical analysis should highlight trends. Investigation will reveal the reasons for them.
- Market research should provide:
  - an understanding of the product's place in the market, the market segments and target customers
    customers' views on the product
  - reasons for the success or failure of the product
  - an understanding of competitive activity.
- **SWOT analysis** will identify internal strengths and weaknesses. It will highlight external opportunities and threats.
- The marketing strategy should follow from this analysis. The marketing mix will put the strategy into practice (see the table at the bottom of the page).

### EVALUATING THE MARKETING PLAN

The marketing mix can also be used to evaluate the marketing plan. Marketing activities can be reviewed

using the marketing mix to ensure that the marketing objectives will be achieved (see Figure 9.2).

**Figure 9.2** Where do the four Ps fit into marketing planning?

ISSUES FOR **analysis**

When answering questions on the marketing mix consideration should be given to the following:

- How well the mix is matched to the strategy; only if every aspect of the mix is coordinated and focused will it be effective. The giant Unilever (Wall's) flopped with its UK launch of Ranieri luxury Italian ice-cream because the product was distributed through mass market outlets such as Tesco before it had built its prestige through smaller, more exclusive outlets.
- The relative importance of the ingredients in the marketing mix. Although the product is likely to be the most important element of the mix, every case is different. Taste tests show Coca-Cola to be no better than Pepsi. Yet Coke outsells its rival by up to 20 times – in nearly every country in the world.
- How each of the mix ingredients can be used to achieve effective marketing. The mix elements must be tailored to each case. One product may require (and afford) national television advertising. In another case, small-scale local advertising might be supported by below-the-line activity to increase distribution. There is never a single answer to a question about the marketing mix. The best approach depends on the product, its competitive situation, the objectives and the marketing budget.

| MARKET ANALYSIS | STRATEGIC RESPONSE THROUGH MARKETING MIX |
|---|---|
| • Statistical analysis shows sales are falling; research identifies the cause as competitors' pricing | • Redesign products to have lower costs, then reposition at a lower price level |
| • The SWOT analysis identifies an advanced product feature as the reason current buyers are purchasing our product | • Focus heavily upon this in advertising and at the point of sale |
| • Criticism is made of the lack of availability of our product | • Switch resources from advertising to improving incentives to retailers to stock our product |

The concept of marketing mix has remained unchanged since it was first introduced in the 1950s. It has proved to be a useful marketing tool. It still serves the useful purpose of focusing marketing activity. However many believe that there are strong arguments for adding a fifth ingredient – people. Many also feel that it should not be presented as a list of equally important parts but that the mix should be seen with the product at the core, supported by the other ingredients.

With the growing importance of customer service and of good sales staff, it is legitimate to extend the marketing mix to include people. Businesses can support and differentiate their product by the people they employ. Any business based on day-to-day contact with customers cannot ignore the importance of its employees. Retail outlets rely on their salesforce to enhance the shopping experience. A customer who feels the salesperson is rude or lacks knowledge will go elsewhere.

Asda supermarkets use one of the staff as a greeter. They stand at the entrance of the store to 'greet' customers. The type of people employed and their attitude can be used to support corporate identity. Disney employees have to be smart, without facial hair, and be 'upbeat'. The leading accountancy firms insist that their employees dress smartly. Well-trained salespeople ensure that the customer has a satisfactory buying experience. A customer buying a computer wants reassurance that the salesperson knows about the product. This gives them confidence to buy.

Although the four Ps are presented as a list there is no doubt that in almost every case the product is the most important ingredient. A successful marketing mix should be matched to the marketing strategy. And that strategy is rooted in how well the product is matched to the segment of the market being targeted.

In the future, it is likely that the marketing mix will be product plus marketing support. Marketing support will be a mix of price, promotion, place and people.

### KEY terms

**marketing planning** – producing a schedule of marketing activities based upon decisions about the marketing mix. This will show the when, what and how much of a product's advertising, promotions and distribution drives over the coming year.

**price elasticity of demand** – a measure of how sensitive demand is to changes in price.

**SWOT analysis** – analysing the Strengths, Weaknesses, Opportunities and Threats facing a business or a product.

# Exercises

## A. REVISION QUESTIONS
*(30 marks; 60 minutes)*

Read the unit, then answer:

1 What are the four ingredients of the marketing mix? *(4)*
2 What is the difference between industrial and consumer markets? *(2)*
3 What is the difference between shopping and convenience goods? *(2)*
4 List three ways in which businesses categorise customers. *(3)*
5 What is meant by a market segment? *(3)*
6 List three ways, with examples, of how a business can differentiate the product. *(3)*
7 Why are new products important to a business? *(4)*
8 List three different ways of promoting the product. *(3)*
9 What is meant by the promotional mix? *(3)*
10 What are the three main channels of distribution? *(3)*

## B. REVISION EXERCISES

### B1 Data Response

### Milk Tray Revamped as Competition Intensifies

Cadbury spent 18 months planning a relaunch of Milk Tray – its boxed chocolate brand. This was the first major change to the product in over four years. The chocolates are now presented in a box with a patented curve to one side and updated graphics. The same design is also used for another brand, Darkness, that was launched in 1996. The new packaging is said to provide 'a more sophisticated and desirable gift for the modern consumer' and is expected to add 10% growth to sales.

The marketing director, Alan Palmer, said that the activity was to fight off increasing competition from other sectors. 'Milk Tray is mostly bought as a gift. In recent years chocolate has been losing out to other gifts such as wine and flowers. The brand must be seen to be as relevant and contemporary as those products.'

The market for boxed chocolate assortments grew by 8% in value in 1996. 3% was due to volume growth and the remainder was a result of higher raw material costs. This is in spite of heavy competition from 'twist wraps' such as Roses and Quality Street. Alan Palmer feels that the traditional presentation of the twist wraps may be their downfall. He believes consumers want a fresh approach.

The price of the newly packaged chocolates was about 5% higher than previously. The range was also widened to include larger sized boxes and special limited editions at Christmas time. The relaunch was supported by a £3 million campaign. This promotional spending was almost double the amount spent in the previous year.

Source: *The Grocer*, 26/4/97

Milk Tray – rebranding to compete against the competition

## Questions
(25 marks, 30 minutes)

1 Why did Cadbury feel it was necessary to relaunch Milk Tray? (4)
2 Explain, using a numerical example, the statement 'The market for boxed chocolate assortments grew by 8% in value in 1996. 3% was due to volume growth and the remainder was a result of higher raw material costs.' (5)
3 Why might the firm have decided to relaunch the product rather than launch a new product? (5)
4 Why has the advertising budget been doubled? (2)
5 Evaluate the actions taken by Cadbury using the marketing mix as a guide. (9)

## B2 Data Response

### Cellnet

BT's Cellnet mobile phone network has over 3 million subscribers. Early in 1998 it launched its largest advertising campaign since it was formed in 1985. Cellnet has been troubled by a high level of lapsed customers. This 'churn', as it is known in the industry, runs at about 20–30% a year for the whole market. Cellnet's loss of customers has been at the higher end of the range. The marketing team estimates that the campaign will pay for itself easily in the first year if the new initiative brings this disconnection rate down to nearer the 20% level.

The £20 million advertising and direct mail campaign was planned to draw attention to a range of new initiatives. These include:

- a discount programme similar to BT's 'Friends and Family'
- ending minimum contract periods
- compensating customers if they sign up to an inappropriate plan
- a new scheme called 'First for Firms' which gives discounted call rates to businesses when calling 10 selected numbers
- additional discounts for business customers choosing longer term contracts
- tariff cuts
- introduction of a new pre-pay package.

The managing director explained that the new 'First' programmes had been developed in the USA so that rivals would not get to hear about the scheme before it was launched. He said that the aim of the scheme was to end confusion in the market.

Cellnet hopes that the new initiatives backed by the promotional spending will reduce the loss of customers to rivals and increase their subscriber base.

Source: Adapted from *The Times*, 28/5/98

## Questions
(25 marks; 30 minutes)

1 What might be the reasons for the high level of 'churn' in the mobile phone market? (4)
2 Why did Cellnet develop the 'First' programme in the USA? (2)
3 Use the marketing mix to review Cellnet's campaign. (8)
4 State and explain Cellnet's marketing objective. (4)
5 How important do you think the £20 million advertising campaign will be to the success of the whole campaign? (7)

# PRICING

## 10.1 How important is price?

Price is important. It is one of the main links between the customer (demand) and the producer (supply). It is the focus of marketing activity to add value to the product. And is fundamental to a firm's revenues and gross profit margins.

As part of the marketing mix it plays a strong role in marketing the product. It is fundamental to most consumer buying decisions. The importance of price to the customer will depend on several factors:

- customer sensitivity to price
- the level of competitive activity
- the availability of the product.

### CUSTOMER SENSITIVITY TO PRICE

Consumers have an idea of the correct price for a product (see Figure 10.1). They balance price with other considerations. These include:

- The features of the product such as its design and performance – customers will pay more for a car with a larger engine or better comfort.
- The quality of the product – products seen as having higher quality can carry a price premium. This may be real or perceived quality.
- How much they want it – all purchases are personal. Customers will pay more for goods they need or want.
- Their income – customers buy products within their income range. Consumers with more dispos-

able income are less concerned about price. Uncertainty about future income will have the same effect as lower income. In a recession even those who are working will be more sensitive to price. They are aware of the possibility of losing their income.

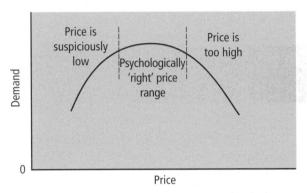

**Figure 10.1** The 'right' price

Pound Stop Ltd: an example of low pricing (© Life File/Emma Lee)

Chanel: an example of the high quality designer market
(© Corbis/Dave G Houser)

## THE LEVEL OF COMPETITIVE ACTIVITY

In a competitive market price is important. Customers have more choice in a competitive market. Price is one element in that choice. Businesses may use price to differentiate their product. They may also use price as part of their promotional activity. For some products such as **branded goods** the price is kept higher to reinforce the brand's value. In a **monopoly** the business is able to charge higher prices.

## THE AVAILABILITY OF THE PRODUCT

If the product is readily available consumers are more price conscious. They know they can go elsewhere and find the same product – perhaps cheaper. Scarcity removes some of the barriers to price. This can be seen in the art world where huge prices are paid for paintings. Shortage of the product forces the price up.

## 10.2 Price determines business revenue

Pricing is important to the business. Unlike the other ingredients in the marketing mix it generates revenue. Sales revenue is arrived at using a simple formula:

sales revenue = price per unit × number sold

Getting the price right is therefore vital. Price is important in persuading customers to buy. Price determines demand. If the price is not right the business could:

- Lose customers – lost customers mean lost revenue. Demand is directly related to price (see Unit 8). If the price is too high, sales and therefore revenue will be lost. If goods remain unsold costs of production will not be recovered.
- Lose revenue – revenue can also be lost if the price is too low. The business will not be maximising its revenue. There needs to be a balance between sales and revenue. If lower prices mean higher sales the business may be able to take advantage of **economies of scale**. This will generate additional profit. Understanding the relationship between demand and price is fundamental.

Pricing involves a balance between being competitive and being profitable.

## 10.3 How do businesses decide what price to charge?

At certain times during a product's life cycle pricing is especially important. Incorrect pricing when the product is launched could cause the product to fail. At other stages in the product's life pricing may be used to regenerate interest. It may also be used to avoid the product being overtaken by rivals.

### Business in
## ― THE RISK OF UNDERPRICING

Chris and Becky Barnard risked everything on opening a restaurant in the country. Their sales projections convinced their bank to provide a £40,000 overdraft (on top of a £110,000 mortgage on the property). They decided on the upmarket name Avins Bridge Restaurant and set their price at £17 a head for a three-course meal. The restaurant opened in August.

Although evening trade proved reasonable, lunchtimes were dead. By February the situation was very worrying. With an average of just 16 meals a day (perhaps one table of four at lunch and three in the evening) the business was operating well below break-even. Drastic action was needed. A failed special offer of a free dessert proved that their relatively elderly, affluent customers were not price sensitive. So the Barnards decided to push prices up – and to cut costs by running the restaurant without any outside staff.

Although things are still a struggle, the higher prices are helping to keep the restaurant going while the Barnards wait for word-of-mouth to bring in new customers.

There are two basic pricing decisions:

- pricing a new product
- managing prices throughout the product life.

Both decisions require a good understanding of the market – consumers and competitors.

Businesses need to know what competitors are charging and how customers feel about price. For price changes they need to know how their customers and competitors will react. They need to understand how other market factors, such as changes to the economy, affect purchasing.

There are several ways that businesses obtain market information:

- market research can provide consumer reactions to possible price changes
- competitive research tells the company about other products and prices
- analysis of sales patterns shows how the market reacts to price and economic changes
- sales staff can report on customer reactions to prices.

Pricing decisions also require an understanding of costs. These costs must include purchasing, manufacturing, distribution, administration and marketing.

Cost information should be available from the company's management accounting systems.

The lowest price a firm can consider charging is set by costs. Except as a temporary promotional tactic (a loss leader), businesses must charge more for the product than the variable cost. This ensures that every product sold contributes towards the fixed costs of the business.

The market determines the highest price that can be charged. The price that is charged will need to take account of the company objectives. The right price will be the one that achieves the objectives.

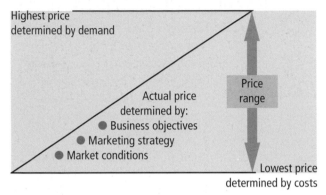

**Figure 10.2** Determining the price

When making changes to product prices the business needs to understand the relationship between price changes and demand. Demand for some products is more sensitive to price changes than others. Price elasticity of demand measures how sensitive demand is to price changes (see Unit 8). If demand for a product is sensitive to price changes an increase in price could cut total revenue.

## 10.4 Pricing methods

There are several different pricing methods.

### COST-PLUS

This is the most commonly used method. The average cost is calculated. This is total cost divided by the number of units. Total cost will include both fixed and variable costs. A mark-up is then added to give the selling price. The level of mark-up should take into account market circumstances. Businesses often set target mark-ups. These may need to be reduced if the price is too high for the market. They can also be increased if there is an opportunity to raise prices.

**Example:**
A business is manufacturing educational CDs. The overheads or fixed costs are £40,000. The variable costs for each CD amount to £5. The business is producing 20,000 units.

The total costs will be:

£40,000 + (20,000 × £5) = £140,000.

The average cost for each CD will be:

$$\frac{£140,000}{20,000} = £7$$

This is the minimum price that could be charged if the company is to break even.
In this case the company adds a 200% mark-up.
The selling price will be £7 + (7 × 200%) = £21.

The mark-up that is used varies from product to product. Grocers add an average of about 25%. Clothes shops look for a 100% mark-up. For cosmetics the mark-up can be as high as 2000%!

This method ensures that some profit is made. It is sometimes known as *absorption pricing*. This is because all costs are accounted for in the price.

### CONTRIBUTION PRICING

The price is calculated using variable costs plus a contribution. It is also known as *marginal pricing*.

**Example:**
In the example above the variable costs are £5. The minimum price has to be above £5.

Any price over £5 will make a contribution to overheads. When sufficient units have been sold to pay for the overheads any further sales will contribute to profit.

If the business charges £6 for the product the contribution will be £1.

The fixed costs are £40,000. The first 40,000 units will pay for fixed costs. Any sales above this will provide profit.

If the price were £10 the contribution would be £5. The first 8,000 units would contribute to fixed costs.

Profit is only ensured if there are sufficient sales to cover fixed costs. The level of mark-up over variable costs needs to take market conditions into account. This method is often used for special order pricing. If the business already has sufficient sales to cover fixed costs, special orders can be sold at a lower price. Care needs to be taken that the lower price does not harm the existing market. (Covered in detail on page 98.)

### COMPETITIVE

This method sets the price in relation to competitors' prices. This approach is used on products which have little or no market power. In other words they lack the reputation or brand loyalty to allow them to set their own price.

There are two main types of competitive pricing:

- Pricing at the prevailing market price – for example, if every local petrol station is charging 79.9p per litre of petrol, you have little alternative but to adopt that price. If you price higher your sales volume will be very low. If you price lower, you may start a price war.

- Pricing at a discount to the market leader. How do Lee or Wrangler price their jeans? How do Crosse and Blackwell or Sainsbury's price their salad cream? All price at a discount to the market leader. If Levi's price 501s at £49.99, Wrangler will price their equivalent at £39.99.

## PRICE DISCRIMINATION

All markets can be broken down into different segments. In some cases, these segments can be identified and separated from the mass market. Then it may be possible to use price discrimination to charge different prices to different people for the same product.

Rail travel is a good example. Business travellers have little choice but to travel in peak times. Prices are therefore kept high. At other times of the day the train operators want to attract customers. They therefore offer cheaper prices for off-peak travel. This approach will only be successful if the segments can be clearly defined and are separate. If customers from one segment can buy from a cheaper segment, they will surely do so. That is why price discrimination is only effective with services which must be used by an individual. Goods such as Mars bars are inappropriate. If you charge more for Mars bars in London than in Middlesborough, a trader will buy up the northern supplies and sell them down south.

## 10.5 Flexibility is the best method

Although it helps to explain each method separately, many businesses use a combination of methods. They may start with cost-plus. In the long term revenue must be greater than costs. However there are risks in using this rigidly, ignoring competition. Businesses need to be flexible when setting prices. The core of the business may be based on cost-plus pricing but there may be opportunities to make additional profit using other methods. One-off deals may be made at lower than normal prices. These sales generate additional

### ── FULHAM FAN FLOP

When Fulham Football Club won promotion to the Premier League in 2001, season ticket prices were held constant at an average of £260. This was to help ensure that the ground was full. Then for the 2002/2003 season, season ticket prices rocketed to £480 – an increase of 85%! The consequence was that instead of selling 13,000 season tickets in 2001/02, the club sold only 10,000 tickets. This boosted ticket revenue from 13,000 × £260 (£3.38 million) to 10,000 × £480 (£4.8 million), but at the cost of falling sales of complimentary products such as programmes, football shirts and other merchandise.

profit, providing the core business covers fixed costs. Businesses also need to have the flexibility to deal with changes in market circumstances. Pricing should also ensure that there is sufficient margin to enable the company to cope with unexpected events. Sudden cost increases or competitive pressure could tip the balance between profit and loss.

## 10.6 Pricing strategies

Pricing strategies will depend on the product and the market. Different strategies will be needed for new and existing products.

### STRATEGIES FOR NEW PRODUCTS

There are two main pricing strategies: skimming and penetration.

Skimming is used when the product is innovative. As the product is new there will be no competition. The

Advantages and disadvantages of different pricing methods

| METHOD | ADVANTAGES | DISADVANTAGES |
|---|---|---|
| Cost-plus | • Ensures all costs are covered<br>• Effective way to set own price for products with market power | • Only works if all output is sold<br>• Inflexible; may miss opportunities to price higher |
| Contribution | • Ensures variable costs are covered<br>• Flexible; especially useful with special-order pricing | • Must be careful to ensure fixed costs are covered<br>• Flexibility may upset regular customers |
| Competitive | • Sensitive to the market<br>• Little alternative for unbranded products | • May not cover costs<br>• Undesirable to be at the mercy of competitors |
| Discrimination | • Good way to maximise revenue and profit<br>• A way of rationing a scarce resource such as peak-time rail tickets | • Difficulties with customer leakage<br>• Those paying full price may resent being discriminated against, and look for a different supplier |

price can therefore be set at a high level. Customers interested in the new product will pay this high price. The business can recoup some of the development costs. It will also be able to gauge market reaction. If sales become stagnant the price can be lowered to attract customers who were unwilling to pay the initial price. The price can also be lowered if competitors enter the market.

Penetration pricing is used when launching a product into a market where there are similar products. The price is set lower to gain market share. Once the product is established the price can be increased. Hopefully, high levels of initial sales will recover development costs.

### STRATEGIES FOR EXISTING PRODUCTS

For existing products there are several pricing strategies. These are:

- Price leader – the price is set above the market level. This is possible when the company has strong brands or there is little effective competition.
- Price taker – the price is set at the market level. This happens in highly competitive markets. Businesses want to avoid a price war that will reduce profits.
- Predatory (or destroyer) pricing – this involves undercutting the market price with the specific intention of driving weaker producers out of the market. It is an aggressive strategy aimed at taking market share. Short-term profit is sacrificed to strengthen the firm's long-term position. Stronger firms set prices at a level that the other company cannot match without getting into financial difficulties. They use their financial security to underwrite the price reduction. It is also used to prevent new entrants gaining market share. In the 1990s British Airways was accused by Richard Branson of adopting this approach to hurt Virgin Atlantic.

The choice of pricing strategy will depend on the competitive environment. The grid in Figure 10.3 shows how the choice of pricing strategy will vary according to the level of competition.

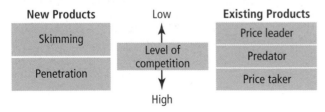

| New Products | Low | Existing Products |
|---|---|---|
| Skimming | ↑ | Price leader |
| | Level of competition | Predator |
| Penetration | ↓ | Price taker |
| | High | |

**Figure 10.3** Pricing strategy and level of competition

### 10.7 Pricing tactics

Once the strategy has been determined there are many different pricing tactics that can be used. They can be part of normal pricing or used as promotional tactics.

They include:

- Loss leaders – prices are set deliberately low. This may be below costs. The idea is to encourage customers to buy other products or **complementary goods** that generate profit. Supermarkets commonly use this tactic. Baked beans have been sold as low as 5p per can to attract custom. Children's sticker albums may be offered very cheaply – but the packs of stickers to go inside are often expensive.
- Psychological pricing – prices are set at a level that seems lower to the customer. A price of £19.99 seems more than 1p less than £20.
- Special-offer pricing – buy one get one free. Or offers made for a period of time or to clear stocks.
- Discounting – discounts are offered in a variety of ways. They may be for:
  - early payment
  - quantity purchased
  - seasonal offers
  - trade business.

### PRICING MAKES HITS

Record companies use a range of marketing tactics to turn a newly released single into a hit. The company wants to sell albums as they are very profitable. Hits increase the popularity of the artist. The record companies lose money on singles but they are a way of marketing albums. The record companies use pricing to get singles to the Number 1 spot. They offer special deals to the retailers. For example one company gives its dealers a free single for every one they buy. This enables the dealers to offer huge discounts to the customer and still make good profits. One problem is that cheap singles now threaten to undermine the album market. If singles with 4 tracks are sold for £1.99 why should customers pay £12.99 for an album with 12 tracks?

IN **Business**

### ISSUES FOR analysis

When answering a question on pricing it is important to understand:

- The relationship between price and demand.
- The role of pricing as one part of an overall marketing strategy.
- The influence of price upon profitability. Many products have profit margins of only 20%. Therefore a 10% price cut will halve profit per unit. It would take a huge increase in demand to compensate.

- The factors influencing pricing such as cost, customer psychology and competitors.
- The role of pricing in achieving company objectives.
- How to choose the most appropriate pricing policies and tactics for different market situations.

Economists think of price as a neutral factor within a marketplace. Its impact upon demand can be measured, predicted and captured in the concept of price elasticity. Many businesses would disagree – especially those selling consumer goods and services. The reason is that consumer psychology can be heavily influenced by price. A '3p off' flash makes people reach for the Mars bars. But if they are half price people wonder whether they are old stock or have suffered in the sun. They are *too* cheap.

When deciding on the price of a brand new product, marketing managers have many options. Pricing high might generate too few sales to keep retailers happy to stock the product. Yet pricing too low carries even more dangers. Large companies know there are no safe livings to be made selling cheap jeans, cheap cosmetics or perfumes.

If there is a key to successful pricing, it is to keep it in line with the overall marketing strategy. When Häagen-Dazs launched in the UK at prices more than double those of its competitors, many predicted failure. In fact the pricing was in line with the image of adult, luxury indulgence and Häagen-Dazs soon outsold all other premium ice-creams. The worst pricing approach would be to develop an attractively packaged, well made product and then sell it at a discount to the leading brands. In research people would welcome it, but deep down they would not trust the product quality. Because psychology is so important to successful pricing, many firms use qualitative research rather than quantitative – to obtain the necessary psychological insights.

Häagen-Dazs – priced to match the luxury image
(© Amet Jean Pierre/Corbis Sygma)

**KEY terms**

**branded goods** – goods with a brand name or identity. This may be a business name such as Mars or a product name such as Ariel.

**complementary goods** – products bought in conjunction with each other, such as bacon and eggs or Gillette shavers and Gillette razors.

**economies of scale** – reductions in unit costs made possible by increased scale of production.

**monopoly** – a market dominated by one supplier.

| BUSINESS OBJECTIVE | PRICING STRATEGY | EXPLANATION |
|---|---|---|
| Profit maximisation | Price discrimination | Maximising takings from every segment of the market |
| Long-term profit growth | Penetration pricing | Building market share to strengthen long-term profit potential |
| Diversification | Cost-plus | Imposing quite a high mark-up to generate the profits to finance diversification |
| Survival | Contribution | When a recession or a price war threatens survival, pricing may have to be below average costs (variable plus fixed) for a while |

# Exercises

## A. REVISION QUESTIONS

*(25 marks; 50 minutes)*

Read the unit, then answer:

1 How can price be used to differentiate a product? *(3)*
2 How does the availability of the product affect pricing? *(3)*
3 Why might businesses lose revenue if the price is not set correctly? *(4)*
4 List two problems caused by setting the price too low. *(2)*
5 What determines the highest price and lowest price that can be charged for a product? *(4)*
6 What is meant by cost-plus pricing? *(3)*
7 What is a discount? *(2)*
8 What is meant by a 'complementary product'? Give two examples. *(4)*

## B. REVISION EXERCISES

### B1 Data Response – Filling the Train

British Airways has been hit by the introduction of Eurostar. BA estimate that it has lost 61% of its Paris market and 52% of the Brussels traffic. In spite of this apparent success, Eurostar lost £180 million in 1997 and is not expected to make a profit until at least 2001. The major problem is that the trains are running half empty. The average load on the Paris run is 50% and only 35% on the trips to Brussels. Only Friday night and Sunday night trains are full. After the initial impact on the airlines the situation now seems to have stabilised and the airlines are again seeing growth in their market.

Analysts feel that the only way forward for Eurostar is to attract more customers, and that will probably involve reducing prices. This is a problem for Eurostar whose main marketing thrust has been to attract business customers. It has recently introduced Premium First. This service offers improved service and increased flexibility. Customers can, for example, switch to a different train or even to a British Midlands flight if necessary. The fare for this service of £399 is below the £422 that BA charges for its fully flexible return air ticket to Paris. The normal first class fare compares well with the cost of air travel. £319 compared to an average price of £358 for the airlines operating on the London to Paris route.

This new pricing structure has increased Eurostar's profit per passenger from 40% last year to 55% this year.

### Questions
*(30 marks; 35 minutes)*

1 On the Premium First ticket, what is the average profit per passenger? *(3)*
2 How can Eurostar make a profit of 55% per passenger but make an overall loss of £180 million? *(5)*
3 Why do analysts say that Eurostar needs to increase passenger numbers? *(6)*
4 How might Eurostar set about attracting more passengers? *(6)*
5 Discuss the possible consequences of Eurostar deciding to reduce its prices in order to attract more customers onto the trains. *(10)*

### B2 Data Response

#### Supermarket Price Wars

1999 is expected to see strong competition between supermarkets. During 1998 the supermarkets were subjected to strong criticism in the press when a survey showed that food prices in the UK were generally higher than in other parts of Europe and the USA. The supermarket chains reacted by saying the comparisons were unfair. Nevertheless it is expected that future marketing will concentrate on price. Any price war will be damaging. It is likely that the two largest supermarket chains, Sainsbury and Tesco, will begin the price cutting. Sainsbury has already started its preparation by cutting out £100 million in costs by reorganising regional management.

If a full-blown price war begins there are likely to be casualties. Asda's unique selling point of low prices will be hard to sustain. Safeway is considered vulnerable and unlikely to cope with a prolonged reduction in prices. Another casualty could be the discounters such as Aldi and Netto. Their margins are already low and it is difficult to see what they could do to re-establish the pricing gap. They may be forced to change tactics. Kwik Save and Somerfield have moved upmarket following their recent merger. They have increased prices and are offering a better quality range of products together with improved service.

Source: Adapted from *The Times*, 7/12/98

**Questions** *(30 marks; 35 minutes)*

1 How will the cost cutting undertaken by Sainsbury help if there is a price war? *(5)*

2 Why might Safeway be unable to sustain a long period of price cutting? *(5)*

3 What is meant by Asda's 'unique selling point' and why might this be lost? *(6)*

4 What do the actions of Somerfield and Kwik Save following their merger tell you about the role of price in marketing? *(6)*

5 The American retail giant Walmart is considering entering the British grocery market with a strategy of penetration pricing. What does this mean and what are the implications of this for the other grocery chains? *(8)*

# INTEGRATED MARKETING

## 11.1 Marketing – an overview

### INTRODUCTION

Which is more important to a firm – revenue or costs? You might say that they are equally important. Or you might say that a firm must have revenue – therefore revenue is the key. Yet students revise costs (finance and accounting) far more thoroughly than revenue (marketing). This is partly because they feel weaker at finance and wish to improve; also, they underestimate the analytic demands (and importance) of marketing.

Firms can have many different objectives, but profit making is clearly a vital aspect of business activity. The most important formula in this subject is the one for profit.

**profit = total revenue – total costs**

or, to use the expanded form:

**profit = (price × quantity) –
([variable cost × quantity] + fixed costs)**

Marketing decisions have a direct influence upon:

- the price and quantity of goods sold
- the variable cost per unit (as bulk-buying discounts are affected by sales volume)
- fixed costs, as they include marketing expenditures such as advertising and promotions.

In other words, marketing influences every aspect of the profit formula.

### WHAT IS MARKETING?

- Is it about responding to consumers or persuading them?
- Is it about creating competition or attempting to avoid it?
- Is it ethical or unethical?

Every textbook has its own definition. A definition such as 'to fulfil consumer needs, profitably' suggests that marketing is about identifying and meeting needs, and is therefore serving the consumer's best interests. Is this true? Always? Do consumers need Snickers chocolate or Apple Hooch?

Marketing today is seen as the all-embracing function that acts as the focal point of business activity. Top business consultant Richard Schonberger describes the best modern firms as those that 'build a chain of customers'. In other words marketing forms the link between the firm and its customers. It therefore determines the type and quantity of goods to be designed and produced.

### 'A' GRADE MARKETING

Marketing consists of a series of concepts and themes (such as the marketing mix). All good students know these; better ones can group them together and relate them to one another. They can be grouped as follows:

- An understanding of markets – the price mechanism, price elasticity, market segmentation, and competitive tactics.
- An understanding of consumer behaviour – psychological factors in product pricing and image, brand loyalty, consumer resistance.
- Product portfolio analysis – product life cycle, Boston Matrix.
- Marketing decision making – the marketing model, market and sales research and analysis, the need to anticipate, not just reflect, consumer taste.
- Marketing strategy – both in theory and in practice through the marketing mix/four Ps.

'A' grade marketing requires a grasp of big underlying issues such as those that follow. These are areas of discussion for conclusions to answers or case studies. They represent ways of evaluating the wider significance of concepts such as the product life cycle.

### ISSUE 1    Is marketing an art or a science?

Is marketing about judgement and creativity, or scientific decision making? If it is a science, the numerate information provided by market research would lead to a 100% success rate with new products. The reality, of course, is different. Kellogg's researched Pop Tarts heavily – and spent millions advertising a flop – while Bailey's Irish Cream became a worldwide best-seller even though research said women would not buy a whisky-based liqueur.

Marketing relies upon anticipating consumer behaviour. Research can help enormously, but the final decision on strategy is a judgement. Therefore individual flair and luck play an important part.

## ISSUE 2  Does marketing respond to needs or create wants?

It is easy to see the importance of marketing to the firm. But what are its effects upon the consumer/general public? Is it just a way of encouraging people to want things they do not need?

Health issues are important in this debate. McDonald's may make your day, but is it what your stomach needs? And is it right that children should pester their parents for Potato Waffles, when potatoes are cheaper and more nutritious? You must form some views on these questions. You may feel that the marketeers' pursuit of new products, flavours, trends and glitz makes life fun. Or you may feel that marketing can manipulate people, and that its most persuasive arm (TV advertising) needs to be controlled. The Government's recent decision to ban cigarette advertising implies that they favour control.

## ISSUE 3  Has market orientation gone too far in Britain?

The trend towards a market-led approach was good for companies which produced the same products in the same way, year after year. Market orientation brought in new ideas and more attractive product design.

However, it also encouraged Ford to focus too much on the styling and imagery of their cars while BMW and Honda concentrated upon their production quality and reliability. Money that had once been spent on research and development was now spent on market research. The number of engineering graduates declined as the numbers on marketing and accounting courses ballooned. Manufacturing industry depends upon high quality engineers and a skilled workforce. Marketing is not enough.

# Marketing

## A.  SHORT-ANSWER QUESTIONS

1  Why is a reduction in price unlikely to benefit a firm whose products are price inelastic? (2)
2  Distinguish between primary and secondary research. (2)
3  Why might a firm's long-term pricing policy differ from its short-term one? (3)
4  Explain the term 'product differentiation'. (2)
5  Give two reasons why a firm may sell, for a limited period of time, part of its product range for a loss. (2)
6  List three factors a firm should consider when determining the price of a new product. (3)
7  Give two ways in which decisions made within the marketing department might affect activities in the personnel department. (2)
8  Distinguish between marketing objectives and marketing strategy. (3)
9  Identify three factors that are likely to influence the choice of distribution channel for a product. (3)
10  Give two examples of ethical dilemmas a marketing manager might face. (2)
11  Distinguish between product orientation and market orientation. (3)
12  A business decides to reduce the price elasticity of its product from £3.00 to £2.75. As a result, sales rise from 2,500 to 3,000 units. Calculate the price elasticity of demand for its product. (3)
13  Explain what is meant by 'negative income elasticity'. (2)

14  State two business objectives, other than profit maximisation, that will influence a firm's marketing strategies. (2)
15  The price of a good is 100p of which 40p is the contribution. If the price is cut by 30%, how much extra must be sold to maintain the same total contribution? (3)
16  Only one in five new product launches are successful. Why? Give three reasons. (3)
17  State three ways of segmenting a market. (3)
18  What is a marketing budget? (2)
19  Suggest three possible extension strategies for a brand of bottled lager for which sales have levelled out. (3)
20  State two strategies a firm might adopt to defend itself if a price war broke out. (2)

## B.  DATA RESPONSE

A manufacturer of footballs has sales of 100,000 units a month and fixed costs of £240,000 a month. Raw materials are £3.00 per unit and the pricing method is a 100% mark-up on variable costs. When it last increased its prices, price elasticity proved to be about 0.6. Now it is thinking of a further 10% price rise.

a  Calculate the effect on profit of this 10% rise. State your assumptions.
b  What factors may have caused the price elasticity to have changed since the time it was measured at 0.6?

## C. CASE STUDY

You are the brand manager of Cardew's Dairy Milk chocolate. Your share of the milk chocolate sector is high, but slipping slightly. The sector itself is only just hanging on to sales in the face of strong growth in bagged chocolates such as Maltesers. Your boss, the marketing director, has set you the objective of boosting sales of Cardew's Dairy Milk by 5% per year for each of the next two years. She wants you to send her a report detailing:

**a** two alternative marketing strategies you are considering, as ways to achieve the objective

**b** the market research programme you recommend, giving a full explanation of your reasoning

**c** the pricing methods you have considered, and which one you recommend

**d** your analysis of the potential threat to the brand, if the sales slide cannot be reversed.

Write a 750-word report to the marketing director covering these issues.

## D. ROLE PLAYS AND SIMULATIONS

### Should Schweppes launch this new product?

As joint marketing directors:

**1** Decide what you recommend and why.

**2** Prepare an OHP presentation to explain your views.

### Appendix A – Briefing document

> Sparkler is a brand new, sparkling, exotic fruit drink. It is aimed at the mass market, and will sell at the same price as Coca-Cola (35p). Schweppes has developed the product, registered the trademark and is about to hold a meeting to decide whether or not to launch it.

### Appendix B – Market research findings

Regular drinkers of:

| | Pepsi | Coke | Sparkling orange | Other fruit flavours | TOTAL |
|---|---|---|---|---|---|
| Sample size | 80 | 340 | 170 | 50 | 640 |
| Will definitely try | 24% | 21% | 32% | 39% | 26% |
| Will probably try | 36% | 37% | 39% | 38% | 37.5% |
| **Following product trial:** | | | | | |
| Will definitely buy regularly | 21% | 17% | 35% | 47% | 27% |
| Will probably buy regularly | 37% | 31% | 32% | 36% | 32% |

Source: Adapted from Gallup Poll Research Company

## Appendix C – Cost data

| | Production of cans per week | | |
|---|---|---|---|
| | Up to 99,000 | 100,000–499,000 | 500,000+ |
| Sparkler production cost per can | 3.3p | 3.0p | 2.8p |
| Sparkler delivery cost per can | 2.7p | 2.0p | 1.2p |

**Weekly fixed costs:**

| | |
|---|---|
| Salaries and administration | £20,000 |
| Marketing costs | £40,000 |
| Other expenses | £10,000 |

## Appendix D – Market size and share data

| | Market size | Coca-Cola | Pepsi | Orange | Other fruit |
|---|---|---|---|---|---|
| 3 years ago | £2.5 bn | 23.4% | 8.9% | 7.4% | 4.6% |
| 2 years ago | £2.7 bn | 23.9% | 8.7% | 7.7% | 4.9% |
| Last year | £3.1 bn | 24.1% | 8.6% | 7.9% | 5.3% |

## Appendix E – Sales information

| Forecast sales volume | If research is positive | If research is negative |
|---|---|---|
| Year 1 | 400,000 pw | 200,000 pw |
| Year 2 | 600,000 pw | 300,000 pw |
| Year 3 | 700,000 pw | 280,000 pw |
| Year 4 | 750,000 pw | 200,000 pw |

## E. INTEGRATED CASE STUDY

### Lastminute.com

The start of the millennium year proved to be a period when extraordinary fortunes were made extraordinarily quickly. It took Bill Gates eight years at Microsoft before he became a millionaire. In January to March 2000 it seemed a daily event that a loss-making internet start-up would float on the stock market, making the owners hugely rich. The most high-profile of all of these was Lastminute.com.

Lastminute.com was founded in 1998 by two young entrepreneurs who spotted the potential for an on-line travel agent targeted at people with busy lifestyles (like themselves). Brent Hoberman and Martha Lane Fox were in their twenties, came from wealthy backgrounds and worked in management consultancy. In March 1998 they wrote a business plan that persuaded a venture capital company to invest £600,000. This funded the work required to get the site up and running in October 1998. With a good eye for publicity, they pushed their business to become Britain's second best-known website (after Amazon). Nevertheless, in the six months to 31 December 1999 sales turnover of £1.24 million was swamped by high operating expenses, leading to a pre-tax loss of over £17 million. In normal circumstances, there would have been no possibility of raising money from the stock market.

Towards the end of 1999, however, a wave of internet millionaires created in California led UK investors to become increasingly keen (desperate, even) to get on the dot.com bandwagon. By February 2000 rumours of Lastminute.com's flotation were accompanied by an amazing number of press photographs and stories about the photogenic Martha. The *Observer* newspaper playfully began an unofficial count of media mentions of Martha, which peaked at 435 in the third week of March.

During this period, the company was also running a substantial above-the-line advertising campaign. Bus-sides, poster hoardings and the national press shouted the slogan *Do Something Lastminute.com* alongside visuals of airplanes, hotels or famous restaurants. Between January and June 2000 the company spent an astonishing £13 million on media advertising (far more than its annual turnover). This raised the question: if the internet is such a successful channel for distribution and advertising, why the need for so much old-fashioned promotion?

On 1 March 2000, merchant bankers Morgan Stanley announced that Lastminute.com would be floated at between 190 and 230p per share, valuing the business at £300–350 million. Thirty three million shares would be sold, equivalent to 22% of the enlarged share capital. A week later, massive demand for the shares encouraged the merchant bank to increase the launch price by 67% to 380p. This placed a value of £570 million on a firm with a turnover of little more than £1 million and massive operating losses. It was an extraordinary gamble on the growth potential of the internet and the capabilities of two young managers. It was the equivalent of meeting someone with £1,000 and saying 'Here's £570,000, take it and please invest it wisely for me.'

On 14 March, the first day of trading, the shares went to a 28% price premium, making Brent and Martha's shares worth £150 million. Soon afterwards, however, disenchantment set in. Within a fortnight the share price sagged to 280p. City analysts queued up to gloat. 'Overpriced, oversold and over-optimistic,' said one. Another said, 'If Lastminute was run by a 51-year-old man with a toupee it wouldn't have been valued at £570 million'. A few weeks later the collapse of Boo.com led to further dips in the market price of internet shares. On 22 May Lastminute.com shares dropped to 122p, valuing the company at little more than the £131 million of cash it had raised from its stock market flotation.

Despite the dismal performance of the shares, the huge publicity gained in the first half of the year boosted the number of subscribers. At the end of December 1999 there were 572,000 registered users (though only 29,000 people had been converted into buyers). By the end of March this total had risen to 1.4 million, and with a slightly better than 5% conversion rate. Nevertheless, an analyst calculated that the company would need '30 million subscribers and a conversion rate of around 20%' by 2010 to create the cash flow necessary to justify the £570 million launch price.

To Brent Hoberman, such ambitious targets are not impossible to achieve. Unusually for a UK internet business, Lastminute.com is a true original. It is not just a copy of an American site. So it has the opportunity to become a worldwide brand. Brent explains that keeping ahead of the competition is '... all to do with pace, innovation and creativity ... scale is also important. We're building what I'd like to think of as a global *Lastminute* marketplace. Maintaining our lead calls for keeping our brand position, watching funding, recruiting the best people and nurturing the best relationships.'

Despite the embarrassment of the company's share price slide, the crucial thing for the long-term funding of the business was to raise over £100 million in March 2000. To grow rapidly, a stock market flotation is a marvellous option. It can bring in substantial capital resources without having to sacrifice day-to-day control of the business. In a case such as Lastminute.com, where only 22% of the shares were sold, control is unaffected. From an investor's point of view, however, cases such as this point to the classic Latin phrase *caveat emptor*, 'let the buyer beware'. By November 2000 Lastminute's shares were 75p, a massive fall from the 380p paid by investors at the time of the float. The company, of course, was unaffected by this, as it had the cash safely in the bank.

Is the internet *the* future, or only a part of the future? How important, strategically, is first-mover advantage? And how much value can be created by hype? These three important business issues were raised by the flotation of Lastminute.com. It is hoped that Brent Hoberman, Martha Lane Fox and nearly 200,000 small shareholders will be able to look back with amusement at a tricky start to a very successful business.

## Questions                                    *(80 marks; 90 minutes)*

1 Consider why Lastminute.com may have thought it valuable to spend £13 million on above-the-line media advertising during Jan–June 2000. *(14)*

2 **a** Explain the meaning of the term 'venture capital'. *(3)*
  **b** Evaluate the main questions the venture capital company is likely to have asked Brent and Martha before putting £600,000 at risk. *(12)*

3 Identify and explain what you believe to have been Brent Hoberman's marketing aims, objectives and strategy. Did he also use marketing tactically? If so, how and why? *(15)*

4 **a** Other than flotation, what alternative sources of finance might have been available to Lastminute.com during the first half of 2000? Which one of these do you think would have been the most promising? *(12)*
  **b** Analyse the advantages and disadvantages of a stock market flotation for Lastminute.com, in comparison with the best alternative method of capital raising. *(12)*

5 Why is cash flow such a problem for small business start-ups such as Lastminute.com? To what extent could the problem be eliminated if a firm used strict budgeting procedures? *(12)*

# INTRODUCTION TO FINANCE AND ACCOUNTS

## DEFINITION

Accounting can be defined as the collection, recording, compiling and forecasting of financial information. Accounting is split into two distinct areas – financial accounting and management accounting.

Financial accounting describes the process of gathering and publishing information of financial record. All limited companies must publish a set of accounts for each financial year. These accounts are available for public inspection at Companies' House.

Management accounting is the term used to describe accounting statements produced and used for management purposes. The main uses of management accounts are planning, decision making, review and control.

## 12.1 Why do businesses need accounts?

Kelly Thomson left college determined to set up her own business. Her brother, James, an engineer, had designed a revolutionary new lawnmower. At the flick of a switch, it could dig out weeds whilst cutting grass. Between them they had £5,000 saved. That was enough to cover the cost of building a working prototype. By September the prototype was ready, so Kelly and James arranged an appointment with their bank manager. Kelly had calculated that they would need £15,000 to rent a small workshop and hire another person to help manufacture the mower. The bank manager insisted on seeing a business plan before lending them the money.

Two weeks later, they returned with a business plan including a projected profit and loss account, balance sheet and cash flow forecast. Having seen these, the bank manager granted the £15,000 loan. Production began immediately and by the start of November they were ready to sell their unique new product.

The problem they now faced was that no-one wanted to buy a lawnmower in November. They continued producing 50 mowers a week in anticipation of a demand surge in the spring. Just after Christmas a supplier demanded payment for the debt they had built up with him. Sadly, the £15,000 was gone and the trickle of revenue was just enough to cover the interest on the loan. When the bank manager refused to grant them an overdraft, they were forced to close down the business, having sold fewer than 100 lawnmowers. James managed to sell the patent for the mower to a large garden tools manufacturer for £15,000, just

enough to repay the loan. However, £5,000 of savings was lost as a result of poor financial planning. A proper approach to accounting could have saved their business.

Kelly's tale illustrates the importance of careful financial planning. Without a clear idea of when, and how much, cash is going to enter or leave a business, failure is likely. In order to run any business it is vital to make sure the firm has enough cash to pay its bills and buy-in stock. Without stock firms have nothing to sell. Unpaid bills may mean no electricity or telephone.

Management accounting ensures that firms keep a careful check on their cash flows. Careful monitoring means firms are able to plan ahead, perhaps arranging an overdraft or discussing a delay in payments to their suppliers.

In addition to keeping a check on a firm's day-to-day finance – its **working capital** – managers can use accounting to:

- identify the costs involved in making a product – this can be the first step in deciding the selling price
- work out how many products they need to sell to make a profit
- measure how well their staff have performed
- keep tight control over the way in which the firm's money is spent.

Along with these uses of management accounting, the role of financial accounting is also important. Kelly's story shows how hard it can be to raise finance. This is true for existing as well as new firms.

Barclays Bank lends over £1 billion a year to small businesses. Any existing business looking for a loan from Barclays will need to submit previous years' profit and loss accounts and balance sheets.

Graham Howie, an experienced business banker at Barclays, says: 'I would not lend to an existing business which is unable to supply copies of previous years' audited accounts.'

Financial accounts have one key advantage over management accounts for external users. Published accounts have to be audited by an independent accountant. This means they are checked to see that they show a true and fair view of the company's financial position. In addition, management accounts are rarely seen by any external users, so it is clear that financial accounts play a key role in business.

| MANAGEMENT ACCOUNTING | FINANCIAL ACCOUNTING |
|---|---|
| Focuses on the present and the future | Reports what happened in the past |
| Is for internal users | Is for external users |
| Needs to be easy to use, relevant and up to date | Needs to be reliable, accurate and consistent |
| Is ruled by managers' requirements | Is ruled by accounting conventions and legal requirements |
| Covers departments and divisions | Covers the whole firm |

## 12.2 Major accounting documents

The following units explain in detail all the main accounting documents. To provide an overview, here is a brief explanation of each.

### FINANCIAL ACCOUNTING

**Balance sheet:** This is a snapshot of a firm's assets, liabilities and sources of capital at any moment in time. It helps answer questions such as:

- What is the business worth?
- Can it afford to expand?
- Is it a safe investment?

**Profit and loss account:** This shows the level of profit made in the most recent trading period (usually the financial year). Profit is calculated by subtracting costs and expenses from revenue. This helps answer questions such as:

- Is the firm trading successfully?
- Are the senior managers proving effective?
- Is it likely to be a profitable investment?

**Cash flow statement:** This is required in the published financial accounts of public limited companies only. It shows where cash has come from and where cash has been used over the course of the past year. It answers these questions:

- How easily was the firm able to find the cash to finance its recent activities?
- Was the finance generated from within the business, or was outside finance needed?

### LOSING ON AND OFF THE PITCH

Leeds United announced an annual loss of £34 million for the 2001–2002 season. No business can continue operating in the long term without doing something to address such losses. Along with the announcement of these figures, Chairman Peter Ridsdale made it clear that the club would be seeking to reduce its running costs and provide one-off revenues by selling more of its star players. August of 2002 saw Leeds sell Rio Ferdinand to Manchester United and Robbie Keane to Tottenham Hotspur in deals which generated a combined figure of £37 million – too late to offset the 2001–2002 loss but helping the club in its next financial year.

In addition to cutting costs by shedding the substantial salaries commanded by these 2 stars, Leeds also planned to trim the squad by 6 players, in order to reduce the wage bill by at least £1 million per year. The long term future of the club, as with many other football clubs, is dependent upon being able to halt their losses and cover their costs.

Later in 2002, Ridsdale was dismissed.

### MANAGEMENT ACCOUNTING

**Cash flow forecasts:** These estimate what the firm's bank account will look like in each month of the coming year. If a serious overdraft is predicted, it can be discussed with bankers to ensure that the deficit is financed.

**Budgets:** These are financial plans which can be set for costs and/or revenues. They are a way of coordinating, motivating and controlling the key activities of the business over the coming year.

**Contribution statements:** These set out the contribution to overheads made by each division or department of a firm. This helps in making decisions about allocating resources between the different parts of the business, e.g. providing more capital to finance expansion of the most profitable product area.

**Investment appraisal:** These calculations help decide whether a prospective investment project is financially attractive. Investment decisions from buying new machinery to building a new factory are made using the techniques of investment appraisal.

**Break-even charts:** These indicate revenues and costs and therefore profit at all possible levels of output. They enable the break-even point, where neither a profit nor a loss is made, to be identified. They can be useful in decision making on issues such as pricing, cost cutting or expansion.

Figure 12.1 shows the main strands of both financial and management accounting.

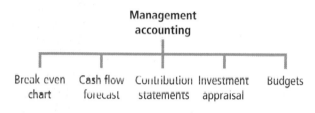

**Figure 12.1** Financial and management accounting

## 12.3 Users of published accounts

There are three main groups of users of published accounts. Each may be looking for different information, but all hope to find it in the same set of documents: largely the profit and loss account and the balance sheet.

- Internal management – uses published information largely as a matter of record. Possibly as public recognition for its own achievements. The actual contents (such as the profit made and any successes at cutting stock or debt levels) would have been known internally for some months before the figures are published.
- Other internal users – perhaps employees or trade unions who can check a firm's published accounts if threatened with redundancy or when putting in a pay claim. Only the most open, self-confident managements share current management accounting data with staff. So most have to wait until the published figures to be sure of the firm's financial performance.
- External users – also have access to the published accounts of limited companies. Groups such as suppliers, customers, banks or potential investors can use the accounts to gain an overall picture of the firm's efficiency and stability.

Figure 12.2 shows the categories of users.

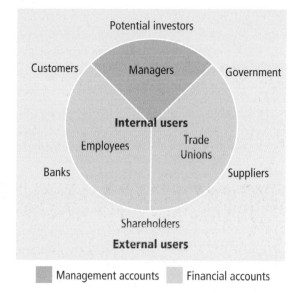

**Figure 12.2** Users of accounts

**IN Business**

### ENRON – AN ACCOUNTING FIASCO

The years 2001 and 2002 saw a number of huge accounting scandals. The collapse of Enron, the American energy provider, sent shock waves throughout the world's financial markets and raised a number of questions about the accounting and financial reporting practices of the firm. The fundamental cause of the problem was that Enron had been 'hiding' its debts in the accounts of other companies – companies that had been set up by Enron but whose accounts were kept separate. Sooner or later these debts had to come out and, as they did, the whole firm came tumbling down.

Job losses ran into the thousands, not just Enron employees but employees at Enron's suppliers whose debts were never met by the American giant. A further consequence was that shareholders in Enron, many of whom were staff who had invested their life savings in the company they believed in, lost everything. The case of Enron led to much examination of accounting regulations, both in the US and the UK and pressure to ensure that such a scandal could not be allowed to occur again. This will require a tightening of the rules and regulations covering how firms compile and present their accounts.

**Short-term (under 1 year):**

| | |
|---|---|
| ● Bank overdraft | *Allowing the firm's bank account to go into the red up to an agreed limit. Flexible and easy to arrange but interest charges are high.* |
| ● Trade credit | *Suppliers agree to accept cash payment at a given date in the future. Failure to pay on time can present problems on future orders.* |
| ● Debt factoring | *A firm selling on credit 'sells' its debt to a factor. The factor is responsible for collecting the debt. The firm receives 80% of the debt in cash from the factor immediately and the balance, minus the factor's fee, when the debt is collected.* |

**Medium-term (2–4 years):**

| | |
|---|---|
| ● Bank term loan | *Banks lend sums of capital, often at a fixed rate of interest, to be repaid over a fixed period. Makes financial planning easy but interest rates can be high, particularly for small firms.* |
| ● Leasing | *Firms sign a contract to pay a rental fee to the owner of an asset in return for the use of that asset over a period of 2–4 years (usually). Expensive, but avoids large cash outflows when buying new assets.* |

**Long-term (5+ years):**

| | |
|---|---|
| ● Owners' savings | *Most small businesses are set up with the owners' savings. They are 'interest free' but will be lost if the business fails. Banks will not provide a loan or overdraft unless the owners are sharing the financial risk.* |
| ● Sale of shares | *Private and public limited companies can sell shares in the ownership of the company. In return, shareholders gain a say in how the firm is run and are entitled to a share of profits.* |
| ● Reinvested profits | *Profits are the most important source of long-term finance. This form of finance is good because there are no interest payments to be made.* |
| ● Venture capital loans | *These specialist providers of risk capital can provide large sums. The finance is usually partly loan capital and partly share capital.* |
| ● Government loans | *Although much paperwork is involved and only some firms are eligible, national government and the EU do offer grants and loans for firms. Less than 3% of business finance stems from this source.* |
| ● Debenture loans | *Long-term loans repayable on a certain date are called debenture loans. These are secured on specific assets and carry fixed interest payments.* |

## 12.4 Raising finance

The story at the beginning of this unit illustrated another key issue in accounting – how to raise finance. The finance may be used for a variety of purposes. A firm may seek long-term finance for building a factory or buying out another business. Short-term finance may be used to buy extra stock or get through periods where cash flow is poor due to seasonal factors. The above table shows the sources of finance available to firms.

## 12.5 Accounting in the twenty-first century

Computers have taken much of the number crunching out of accounting. A vast array of specialist accounting software packages exist, simplifying the process of accounting for managers of small and large businesses alike. Furthermore, sophisticated information recording systems, such as EDI (**electronic data interchange**) enable firms to compile statements of costs and revenues, daily, just hours after the day's trading is over.

This process is becoming even cheaper and easier through the use of **intranets**. These advances mean that management accounting has become more complex, yet more useful. The forecasts involved in producing sales or cost budgets gain in accuracy as the quality of past information improves. The time has already arrived when most large firms have completely computerised accounting systems. The first decade of the twenty-first century is likely to see most small businesses follow suit. The good news is that as IT advances, accounting packages become easier to use for those with little accounting experience. However, the theory behind accounting is unlikely to change significantly for a long time to come. IT can make accounting easier, but it is still vital to understand what accounts actually show.

A further development in recent years, which is set to continue, is the growing use of social **auditing**. Pioneered in the UK by firms such as The Body Shop, a social audit attempts to include non financial factors in a firm's accounts. Conventional accounts judge a firm's performance purely on measures such as profit and revenues. Social accounting includes measures such as pollution emissions and labour turnover to try to show a fuller picture of a firm's performance. Recently, major multinationals such as Shell and BP have begun to publish social audits. The accounting profession is working on a set of common social accounting standards. Nevertheless, the practice is unlikely to become widespread until a change in the law forces firms to include social measures in their annual published accounts.

ISSUES FOR **analysis**

Key issues for analysis include:

- The difference between cash and profit can lead to excellent analytical comment. Firms which sell on credit record a profit on items for which no cash has yet been received. The importance of cash was made clear earlier in this unit. Without cash, bills go unpaid and stocks are not bought. So it is possible for profitable firms to run out of cash and go out of business. In examinations, many students treat cash flow and profit as if they are the same thing. Distinguishing clearly between the two is a helpful starting point for strong analysis of a financial issue.
- Also important is to have a broad range of accounting information. With more information, a clearer picture can be built up. Several years' of figures are needed to identify trends in revenues, costs or profits. If similar information about competitors is also available, the accounts you are analysing can really be put into context.
- A third key form of analysis is to place any accounting question firmly in the context of the business. Is it small or large? Is it largely dependent on just one product or customer? Is its marketplace fast-moving, with short product life cycles and fierce competition? Are the managers experienced, prudent and looking towards the long-term future?

## 12.6 Finance and accounts
### an evaluation

Reliability is a key issue when looking at any accounts. Management accounts, such as cash flow forecasts and investment appraisals, are predictions. In other words, they are not statements of fact but educated guesses. This means that they should be used only as a guideline. Questions need to be asked, such as who drew up

*'The accounts are a snapshot of the business at a moment in time. Take a picture the following day and the scene may look very different. As with many of us, companies try to look their best when they are photographed and sometimes dress for the occasion'.*

MA Pitcher (quoted in Pocket Accounting, C Nobes, Penguin Books, 1995)

the accounts? Do they have an interest in making the accounts point in a particular direction? Budgets are also open to a certain degree of bias based upon personal interest. Financial accounts are supposed to present a true and fair view of a firm's financial position. They are checked by an independent auditor. However, creative accounting techniques exist which can be used, legally, to muddy the waters.

A second key point to remember is how accounts fit into the big picture of Business Studies. Feel the weight of this book. There are several units dedicated to accounting, but a great number of units cover other areas of business activity. Accounts are good at dealing with financial, quantitative information. They are, however, notoriously poor at dealing with qualitative issues. How should you value the experience of managers in a firm's accounts? How much is a brand name like Guinness worth? The growing awareness of qualitative issues in accounting has led to the growth in the use of social audits, but accounts are limited in terms of what they can say.

Look at the accounts, but don't forget the people behind them.

**KEY terms**

**auditing** – an independent check on the methods and procedures used to draw up a company's accounts.

**Companies' House** – where the Registrar of Companies holds the records for all the limited liability companies in the country. These include the latest financial statement.

**electronic data interchange** – computers linked by a permanently open telephone line which enables them to swop data. This system, for example, enables Dixon's to know the sales total from all their stores within minutes of closing time on a Saturday.

**intranets** – an internal, closed version of the Internet. Companies can set up their own intranet which can only be accessed by company staff. This enables quick, cheap electronic communication of data such as sales figures.

**working capital** – the finance available for the day-to-day running of the business.

# Exercises

## A. REVISION QUESTIONS

*30 marks; 60 minutes*

Read the unit, then answer:

1 Give two examples of situations in which firms would use:
   **a** short-term
   **b** medium-term
   **c** long-term
   sources of finance (6)
2 Explain what is meant by 'working capital'. (3)
3 Give three functions of management accounting. (3)
4 State how each of the following groups might use a firm's accounts:
   **a** trade unions
   **b** shareholders
   **c** suppliers
   **d** potential investors
   **e** rival companies. (5)
5 Briefly explain the purpose of auditing accounts. (3)
6 What are the main problems involved in preparing a social audit? (3)
7 State three benefits that the use of information technology has brought to accounting. (3)
8 Explain one advantage and one disadvantage to a firm of having large sums of cash for a long period of time. (4)

## B. REVISION EXERCISES

### B1 Data Response

Khilna and Co manufacture women's fashionwear in a large factory in South London. It employs 1,000 local semi-skilled staff in a run-down area in the borough of Lambeth. The managing director has expressed her desire to retire soon and has been experiencing growing problems in her dealings with union representatives at the factory. Before passing the leadership of the firm on to her successor, Khilna plans to borrow £4 million to invest in new machinery, costing a total of £6 million – to be paid over three years.

This investment is possible given the current favourable trading conditions. These have led to record profits over the past three years – profits which, rumour has it, have made the firm an attractive takeover target for various larger clothing firms.

**Questions** *(25 marks; 30 minutes)*
1 State four groups or individuals who may be interested in seeing the financial accounts of Khilna and Co. (4)
2 For the four users identified in your answer to question 1, explain why each one would be interested in seeing the accounts. (12)
3 Why might those considering a takeover bid be interested in seeing the management accounts as well? (9)

### B2 Case Study

Barakat Ltd needs to borrow £10,000 to finance the purchase of a new machine. The managers hope that the machine will make enough money to pay for itself after 12 months. If there are problems, however, it could take as long as 18 months.
The finance director is considering two options:

- Arrange an overdraft facility with the bank for £10,000. In return, the bank will charge interest at 15% per annum on the overdraft. This is charged at 1.25% per month on the sum outstanding at the start of the month.
- Arranging a loan with the bank for the £10,000. The money will be paid back in 18 equal instalments of £587 over a year and a half.

**Questions** *(25 marks; 30 minutes)*
1 How much interest will the firm pay in total if the loan option is taken? (2)
2 In the end, the firm decided to use the overdraft. The new machine boosted profits by £1,000 per month. The firm used these extra profits to pay off the overdraft, so the amount owed gradually fell.
   **a** How long did the machine take to pay for itself? (2)
   **b** Complete the following table, indicating the amount of interest paid on the overdraft: (10)

| Month | Overdraft Outstanding at End of Month | Interest Paid on Overdraft this Month |
|-------|------|------|
| Jan | £9,000 | £125 |
| Feb | £8,000 | |
| Mar | | |
| Apr | | |
| May | | |
| Jun | | |
| Jul | | |
| Aug | | |
| Sep | | |
| Oct | | |

3 How much did the firm pay in interest, in total? (2)
4 Was it better to use the overdraft or the loan? (2)
5 If the machine had not operated as effectively as hoped, and it had taken 18 months to pay back the £10,000 cost – which option would have been the more attractive? (7)

# REVENUE, COSTS AND PROFIT

**DEFINITION**

Revenue is the value of total sales made by a business within a period, usually one year. Costs are the expenses incurred by a firm in producing and selling its products. These include expenditure upon wages and raw materials.

There are a number of types of profit but, in broad terms, profit can be defined as the difference which arises when a firm's sales revenue exceeds its total costs.

## 13.1 Business revenues

The revenue or income received by a firm as a result of trading activities is a critical factor in its success. When commencing trading or introducing a new product, businesses may expect relatively low revenues for several reasons:

- their product is not well known
- they are unlikely to be able to produce large quantities of output
- it is difficult to charge a high price for a product which is not established in the market.

At the start of each year, most firms plan the management of their finances. The starting point is an assessment of the income or revenue they are likely to receive during the coming financial year. Businesses calculate their revenue through use of the following formula:

sales revenue =
volume of goods sold × average selling price

You can see that there are two key elements which comprise sales revenue: the quantity of goods that are sold and the prices at which they are sold. A firm seeking to increase its revenue can plan to sell more or aim to sell at a higher price. Similarly, firms often maintain high prices, even though this policy may reduce sales. Such companies, often selling fashion and high technology products, believe that this approach results in higher revenue and profits.

To sustain a high revenue from relatively few sales a company has to be confident that consumers will be willing to pay a high price for their product. And that direct competition will not appear – at least in the short term. This is a strategy employed by major pharmaceutical companies. They spend huge amounts on researching and developing new products and then protect them with patents. This then allows them to earn high profits by accepting relatively low sales but at high prices. A high price/low output strategy offers

the additional benefit of keeping down the cost of producing the goods.

**Business IN**

### BRITISH AIRWAYS EXPECTS REVENUES TO FALL WHILE PROFITS RISE

British Airways has announced that it expects its revenues to fall during the 2002–2003 financial period. The company said that revenue had fallen by 10% during the last quarter of the previous year and it could not forecast when it would rise again. British Airways has suffered declining demand for its flights due to increasing competition from low cost airlines such as Ryanair and easyJet. A further factor depressing sales has been the gloom in the international travel market following terrorist attacks, the Iraq war and the SARS virus. British Airways has, however, managed to maintain its profitability as a consequence of a tough cost cutting programme.

The alternative way of boosting revenue is to charge a low price in an attempt to sell as many products as possible. In some markets this may lead to high revenues and profits. Firms following this approach are likely to be operating in markets where the goods are fairly similar and consumers do not exhibit strong preferences for any brand. This is true of the overseas holiday market where competition is fierce and businesses seek to maximise their sales and revenue.

Businesses adopt a **revenue oriented** approach for different reasons. If the company has few costs which vary with the level of its output, then it will seek to maximise revenue. Because its costs are not sensitive to the level of its sales, then maximising sales will result in maximum profits. This is the position for companies operating the Government's rail franchises. A full train has few extra costs than a half empty one, so the franchise holders seek high revenues.

---

### The new venture

*Paul Merrills has achieved his lifetime ambition of opening a restaurant specialising in French cuisine in south London. Paul is a highly regarded and experienced restaurateur and wants to create a unique atmosphere in his new venture. How would you advise him to maximise his revenue in these circumstances? What factors influenced your advice?*

---

You will have realised from the analysis so far that price, cost and volume are all important elements of a firm's planning and success. Each of these factors affect each other and all of them together determine the profitability of a business.

If a business cannot control its costs then it will be unable to sell its products at a low price. In turn, this will mean a low sales volume. This will mean that overhead costs such as the rent of a factory will be spread over a low output, causing further pressure on costs of production.

It is to the costs of production that we now turn our attention.

## 13.2 The costs of production

There are many definitions of the term 'costs'. Economists often assess the cost of something in terms of the foregone alternative, the **opportunity cost**. For example, the cost of new computer-aided design technology may be the retraining programme which had to be postponed as a result of the decision to purchase the CAD equipment. An accountant is more likely to consider the **accounting costs**. He or she would talk in terms of the value of the resources involved. Thus the cost of the new CAD equipment might be £50,000. Throughout this unit we will be referring to accounting costs.

Costs are a critical element of the information necessary to manage a business successfully. Managers need to be aware of the costs of all aspects of their business for a number of reasons:

- They need to know the cost of production to assess whether it is profitable to supply the market at the current price.
- They need to know actual costs to allow comparisons with their forecasted (or budgeted) costs of production. This will allow them to make judgements concerning the cost efficiency of various parts of their enterprise.
- They also need to know if they have sufficient finance to afford the expected costs.

## 13.3 Fixed and variable costs

This is an important classification of the costs encountered by businesses. This classification has a number of uses. For example, it is the basis of calculating break-even, which is covered in a later unit.

### FIXED COSTS

Fixed costs are any costs which do not vary directly with the level of output. These costs are linked to time rather than to the level of business activity. Fixed costs exist even if a business is not producing any goods or services. An example of a fixed cost is rent, which can be calculated monthly or annually. It will not vary, whether the office or factory is used intensively to produce goods or services or is hardly utilised at all.

If a manufacturer can double output and still use the same factory (but more intensively) the amount of rent will not alter – thus it is a fixed cost. In the same way, a factory's rent will be unchanged during the period when the factory is closed for the annual summer holiday. As these costs stay high even when business is slack, it is important for firms to use their facilities (especially their premises) intensively. This is true because the firm's fixed costs do not alter as facilities are used more intensively, yet it is likely that revenue will as it sells its increased output of goods or services.

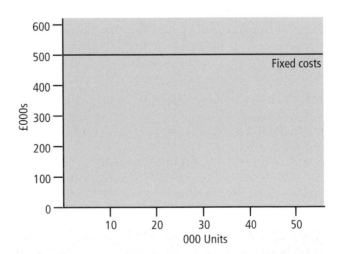

**Figure 13.1** Fixed costs of £500,000

In Figure 13.1, you can see that the firm faces fixed costs of £500,000 irrespective of the level of output. Contrast two levels of annual output. How much would the fixed cost of production be for each unit if production were (a) 10,000 units a year and (b) 50,000 units a year? What might be the implications of this distinction for the managers of the firm?

Other examples of fixed costs include the uniform business rate, management salaries, interest charges and depreciation.

In the long term, fixed costs can alter. The manufacturer referred to earlier may decide to increase output significantly. This may entail the renting of additional factory space and the negotiation of loans for additional capital equipment. Thus rent will rise, as may interest payments. We can see that in the long term fixed costs may alter, but that in the short term they are – as their name suggests – fixed!

## VARIABLE COSTS

Variable costs are those costs that vary directly with the level of output. They represent payments made for the use of inputs such as labour, fuel and raw materials. If our manufacturer doubled output then these costs would rise significantly. There would be extra costs for the additional raw materials and fuel which would be required. Also more labour would most probably be required, incurring extra costs in the form of wages.

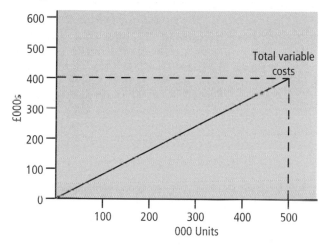

**Figure 13.2** Variable costs of 80p per unit

The graph in Figure 13.2 shows a firm with variable costs of 80p per unit. This means variable costs rise steadily with, and proportionately to, the level of output. Thus a 10% rise in output will increase variable costs by the same percentage.

## SEMI-VARIABLE COSTS

The classification of costs into fixed and variable is simple and very convenient. In businesses, however, not all costs can be classified so simply. Take the case of a delivery vehicle operated by a local bakery. Many of the operating costs of this vehicle are fixed. These include the costs of insurance and the road fund licence. However, if demand rises sharply, transport costs will rise as the business increases its deliveries. More fuel will be needed, servicing will be required more regularly as its mileage increases and wear and tear will be greater. In these circumstances we should say that this vehicle's cost is semi-variable, i.e. part fixed and part variable.

## 13.4 Total costs

When added together, fixed and variable costs (plus any semi-variable costs) give the total costs for a business. This is, of course, a very important element in the calculation of the profits earned by a business.

The relationship between fixed, variable and total costs is straightforward to calculate but has important implications for a business. If a business has relatively high fixed costs as a proportion of total costs, then it is likely to seek to maximise its sales to ensure that the fixed costs are spread across as many units of output as possible. In this way the impact of high fixed costs is lessened. Similarly, if variable costs rise less than proportionately with output, due to, say, the benefits of bulk-buying raw materials and fuel, then a business will seek to produce the highest level of output possible.

The table below shows the costs incurred by the The Norfolk Brewery Ltd in producing a single brand of beer – Yarmouth Ale. Can you explain why the average cost of producing a gallon of Yarmouth Ale alters according to the level of output? What is the significance of this for the management team of the Norfolk Brewery?

| LEVEL OF OUTPUT (GALLONS) | FIXED COSTS (£000) | VARIABLE COSTS (£000) | TOTAL COSTS (£000) | COST PER GALLON (£) |
|---|---|---|---|---|
| 5,000 | 100,000 | 10,000 | 110,000 | 22.0 |
| 10,000 | 100,000 | 20,000 | 120,000 | 12.0 |
| 15,000 | 100,000 | 30,000 | 130,000 | 8.7 |
| 20,000 | 100,000 | 40,000 | 140,000 | 7.0 |
| 25,000 | 100,000 | 50,000 | 150,000 | 6.0 |
| 30,000 | 100,000 | 60,000 | 160,000 | 5.3 |
| 35,000 | 100,000 | 70,000 | 170,000 | 4.9 |
| 40,000 | 100,000 | 80,000 | 180,000 | 4.5 |

## 13.5 Direct and indirect costs of production

Direct costs are those which can be directly attributed to the production of a particular product or service and allocated to a particular cost centre. Raw materials and piece-rate wages are examples of direct costs.

Indirect costs are the opposite of direct costs. They are those costs which cannot be directly attributed to a particular production line or cost centre. These costs can sometimes be difficult to control and managers have to be aware of this and not allow indirect costs to become disproportionately high. Examples of indirect costs include depreciation, management, administration, marketing and some expenses such as rent, business rates and telephone charges.

Thus, fixed costs are normally the same as indirect costs but variable costs can be direct or indirect.

Another term for indirect costs is 'overheads'. Overheads are costs that are not generated directly by the production process. The term can be used interchangeably with indirect costs. Overheads are not always fixed costs, though they are usually.

Examples of fixed overheads include administrative costs, lighting and heating, whilst the commission payments to a salesforce or the postage costs incurred by a mail order company are examples of variable overheads.

| DESCRIPTION | TYPE | £000 |
| --- | --- | --- |
| Gross profit: the revenue earned by a firm less the cost of achieving the sales. These costs are essentially direct costs such as wages and raw materials | Sales revenue<br>– Cost of sales<br>= Gross profit | 760<br>510<br>250 |
| Operating profit: this is the firm's gross profit minus the overheads associated with production, for example rent and rates | – Overheads<br>= Operating profit | 75<br>175 |
| Pre-tax profits: the business's operating profit plus one-off items such as the costs of staff restructuring, including redundancy payments | + One-off items<br>= Pre-tax profits | (25)<br>150 |
| Profit after tax: not surprisingly this is simply pre-tax profits less tax which is levied on company profits (called corporation tax) | – Tax<br>= Profit after tax | 40<br>110 |

## 13.6 Profits

Having considered revenues and costs, it is now appropriate to focus upon a prime motive for business activity – profit. Profit is a *comparison* of revenues and costs. This comparison determines whether or not an enterprise makes any profit. As we saw at the beginning of this unit the key formula is:

profit = total revenue – total costs

### THE TYPES OF PROFIT

Although profit is always revenue – costs, there are different types of cost which can be allowed for. This leads to different types of profit. These are set out in the table below.

Perhaps the most important of these various types of profit is profit after tax, since this is the profit which the business can decide how to allocate. The most important uses to which this profit can be put are:

- payments to shareholders in the form of dividends
- reinvestment into the business to purchase capital items such as property and machinery.

### BIRDS EYE WALL'S CUT COSTS

Birds Eye Wall's has announced that it plans to cut 320 jobs from its factory in Gloucester during 2003. The job losses will be part of a 'restructuring programme' aimed at lowering the company's costs. The changes (part of a plan to cut costs by up to £12 million a year) involve making fewer ice cream products and moving from a 7-day to a 5-day working week. The changes are expected to reduce significantly the company's variable costs in the long-term, though there are likely to be additional costs in the short-term.

About 770 people are currently employed at the firm's ice cream manufacturing business at Gloucester. In line with its commitments to trade unions, Birds Eye Wall's vowed there would be no compulsory redundancies before September 2003, except by agreement.

Birds Eye Wall's Chairman, Mr James Hill, said that any employees made redundant would receive a generous settlement package, well in excess of the legal minimum.

## THE IMPORTANCE OF PROFIT

Undeniably, profits are important to the majority of businesses. Profits are usually assessed in relation to some yardstick, for example the capital invested or sales revenue. They are important for the following reasons:

- they provide a measure of the success of a business
- they provide funds for investment in further fixed assets
- they act as a magnet to attract further funds from shareholders enticed by the possibility of high returns on their investment
- profit is the source of more than 60% of all the finance used to help companies grow; without profit, firms would stand still.

## MIXED MESSAGES ON PROFITS FROM THE HIGH STREET

High street fashion clothing retailer Next has announced a substantial rise in its profits for the six months to July 2002. The company reported a 24% rise in profits to £93 million; during the same period sales revenue rose by 26%. The company enjoyed rising sales in its catalogue business as well.

However, over the same six months the John Lewis Partnership saw its profits fall from £44 million to £34 million. John Lewis runs 26 department stores as well as the Waitrose food shops. Despite a 5% growth in sales the group's profits fell because of increased costs.

The group's store refurbishment scheme pushed up costs and made a severe dent in the level of profits.

A profitable, thriving business community will attract other, new businesses who seek to benefit from the commercial vitality of the region. The new businesses may in turn create more prosperity. A virtuous, upward spiral of prosperity can result.

## 13.7 Profit quality and the utilisation of profit

### PROFIT QUALITY

Profit quality refers to the likelihood of a source of profit continuing into the future. If a profit has arisen as a result of a one-off source (such as selling assets for more than their expected value), its quality is said to be low since it is unlikely to continue. A good example is profits from foreign exchange transactions. One year, a firm might make 20% of all its profit from this source. The following year it is just as likely to make losses from the exact same source.

High quality profit is trading profit which can be expected to be sustained into future years. Clearly, high quality profit is more attractive to managers and particularly to potential investors who may be seeking high returns into the future.

### PROFIT UTILISATION

The profits generated by a business can be put to two broad uses:

- paid to shareholders in the form of dividends
- retained within the company for future (or immediate) investment.

Profit paid to shareholders in the form of dividends is termed 'distributed profit'. It is important that a company pays shareholders a sufficient dividend in order to be able to attract share capital into the company. Many shareholders are interested in short-term returns and not the long-term benefits which they may derive from the company reinvesting profits.

Companies retain profits they do not pay to shareholders (undistributed profits) in their reserves. These reserves may be used in a number of ways. They could be used to finance new business activities such as the building of a new factory or a major programme of research and development. Alternatively, they may be held as a precaution against less profitable years. In these circumstances the reserves may be utilised to pay shareholders dividends.

ISSUES FOR **analysis**

When analysing costs, revenues and profit, there are some key issues to consider:

- Is the information based upon the firm's actual experience, or is it being estimated as part of a business plan? Many new businesses underestimate operating costs and are all too optimistic about potential revenues. No answer can impress unless it shows a clear grasp of whether the figures are actual or forecast.
- A key element with respect to the revenues earned by a business is the relationship between the price charged and the volume of sales achieved. This relates to many marketing issues, but it is worth noting that choosing a price is an exercise requiring considerable judgement. Simply raising price will not necessarily provide more revenue for a firm. This statement is true because as a firm raises its price it can reasonably expect to lose some sales as customers switch to cheaper brands. Factors influencing consumers' decisions will include the quality of the products in question and the availability of competitors' products.
- Calculations of revenues or profits are always based upon a series of assumptions, such as ignoring the possible effect of bulk buying on variable costs per unit. These assumptions should always be stated as part of a good exam answer.

## B. REVISION EXERCISES

### B1 Data Response
*(30 marks; 35 minutes)*

The Highland Manufacturing Company (HMC) Ltd is concerned at its low profitability. This is not only a disappointment to shareholders, but it is also threatening the firm's ability to fund the expenditure it needs on new technology. Chief Executive Mr B Martin wants to close the Torrans product line and concentrate on producing just Sporrans and Warrens. Yet he realises that if he stops producing Torrans, the other two products will have to pay for £20,000 of extra fixed overheads. In other words the company's £60,000 of fixed overheads will not go away. He is usually very decisive, but this time he is uncertain.

### Questions
*(30 marks; 35 minutes)*

1  **a** Explain what is meant by 'direct costs'. *(3)*
   **b** Give two possible examples of 'other direct costs'. *(2)*
2  **a** From the table of figures, calculate the total contribution and the profit generated by each of the three products. *(6)*
   **b** Use this data and the text to discuss whether to stop the Torrans production line. *(10)*
3  Apart from discontinuing Torrans, outline *three* other ways in which HMC Ltd could boost the total contribution from its products. *(9)*

|  | Sporrans | Torrans | Warrens | Total |
|---|---|---|---|---|
| Revenue | £45,000 | £80,000 | £120,000 | £245,000 |
| Materials | £15,000 | £40,000 | £40,000 | £95,000 |
| Other direct costs | £10,000 | £25,000 | £45,000 | £80,000 |
| Fixed overheads | £10,000 | £20,000 | £30,000 | £60,000 |

### B2 Case Study

The Bakery de Bologna had been a fixture in Cardiff for more than 30 years. Two years ago, Zino Mancini handed the bakery over to his daughter Serena and her husband. Serena worked tirelessly to build the business up, but there seemed a relentless customer trend towards one-stop shopping at the huge Tesco, Sainsbury and Asda stores nearby. Her introduction of innovations such as freshly baked pizzas helped to build up her lunchtime trade, but the steady decline in bread sales continued. She tried cutting the price of bread by 20% on Monday to Wednesday, but despite a 25% rise in sales, she noticed that profits seemed worse than ever.

Serena decided to set out exactly what she knew about the costs of baking each product, to compare them with the prices she charged. This is set out on the following page.

The picture confirmed Serena's impression that the business was making enough for them to live on, but nothing like enough to build the capital to finance expansion. And if bread sales kept sliding, the profitability of the business would fall away dramatically.

Then came a phone call. A hugely successful South Wales restaurant chain needed a new supplier of bread rolls. Their previous supplier's quality had slipped and they had been sacked. The sales volumes would be huge. 400 rolls per restaurant per day, times 5 outlets times 6 days would mean 12,000 rolls per week! The contract price would be 6p per roll, delivered to each restaurant.

Serena's first thought was that it was hopeless. With a total contribution of only £120 per week, the delivery overhead costs would make the contract a loss maker. Serena's husband was not so sure, though. He phoned the supplier of the flour they used for rolls to see whether a bulk discount could be offered if they pushed their order up by 1,200%! Unsurprisingly, the supplier offered a much cheaper price. Prompted by this, Serena phoned her bakery equipment suppliers and found out about a super-fast machine for mixing and shaping bread rolls. This automation would enable her to cut the direct labour cost per roll. After much pressing of calculator keys, both were convinced they could cut the direct cost per roll to 3p and hold the addition to overheads to £160 per week.

The following morning Serena drove to the restaurant's head office with a basket full of freshly baked rolls. She handed them over confidently and was given an appointment straightaway. Thirty minutes and two cappucinos later, Serena headed home with a signed contract in her hand.

| | Bread | Rolls | Filled Rolls | Speciality Bread | Pizzas | Cakes | Total |
|---|---|---|---|---|---|---|---|
| Price | 90p | 20p | £1.00 | £1.25 | £3.50 | 80p | |
| Direct costs | 40p | 5p | £0.30p | £0.50p | £1.10 | 30p | |
| Contribution p.u. | 50p | 15p | 70p | 75p | £2.40 | 50p | |
| Sales per week | 800 | 1000 | 500 | 400 | 250 | 400 | |
| Total contribution | £400 | £150 | £350 | £300 | £600 | £200 | £2,000 |
| Weekly overheads | | | | | | | £1,600 |
| Weekly profit | | | | | | | £400 |

**Questions** *(50 marks; 70 minutes)*

1 Outline three other pieces of information it would be useful to have to assess the bakery's financial position. *(6)*

2 a Calculate the price elasticity of the Bakery de Bologna's bread. *(5)*

 b Calculate the effect of the price cut on the profitability of the bread, as measured by its total contribution. *(6)*

 c Explain why the price cut might still have been worthwhile for the business as a whole. *(6)*

3 Calculate the effect on the bakery's overall weekly profits of accepting the restaurant's order. *(6)*

4 a Taking into account the information in the text and the data table, consider two other strategies Serena might adopt in future, to build up the profitability of her business. *(12)*

 b Then decide and explain which one of the two you would recommend and why. *(9)*

# CASH FLOW MANAGEMENT

## 16.1 Importance of cash flow management

Managing cash flow is one of the most important aspects of financial management. Without adequate availability of cash from day to day, even the most successful company could fail. As bills become due it is essential that there are sufficient funds to pay them. If a company delays paying its suppliers they may be reluctant to deliver further supplies. Workers will be very unlikely to tolerate not being paid. If bills remain unpaid then the **creditors** of the business may take the company to court. This could result in the company being made insolvent. A sole trader could be made bankrupt.

Cash flow problems are the most common reason for business failure. This is particularly true for new businesses. It is estimated that 70% of businesses that collapse in their first year fail because of cash flow problems.

Cash flow is not the same as profit. Profit is the difference between revenue and costs. It is available:

- to the owners as the return on their investment, or
- can be retained in the business for development of the business.

Cash flow is the movement of money through the business. It is possible for a company to be cash rich but unprofitable. A company may also be profitable but unable to pay its suppliers (creditors). Figure 16.1 shows how a small firm might suffer cash flow difficulties when receiving a large order. It will eventually make £10,000 profit on the order, but in the short term goes £40,000 into the red.

In the short term, cash flow plays a vital role. Businesses can survive without making profit for some time. For long-term survival and – especially – growth, profit is essential.

### MANAGING CASH FLOW

To manage cash flow, businesses need to continually review their current and future cash position. They can review their future position by forecasting future cash flows. This will enable them to:

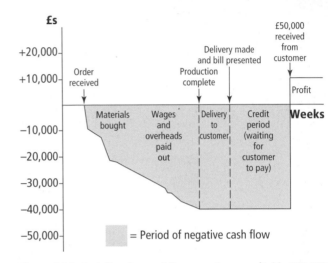

**Figure 16.1** Cash flow for small firm accepting a profitable £50,000 order

- anticipate the timing and amounts of any cash shortages
- arrange financial cover for any anticipated shortages of cash
- review the timings and amounts of receipts and payments.

They can review their current cash flow position by:

- comparing the actual situation with the forecast
- analysing when their **debtors** are due to pay
- taking any necessary measures to correct cash shortfalls.

## 16.2 Cash flow forecasts

A cash flow forecast sets out the anticipated cash inflows and cash outflows over the coming months. Each column shows money coming into and out of the business in that month. The forecast then shows the effect of each month's cash flows upon the firm's cash balance/total. It is like a mini bank statement. One essential rule when constructing a cash flow forecast is that money is shown when it is received or paid. The cash flow forecast will show if there is sufficient cash available each month. A negative cash flow in any time period will indicate that the company has insufficient funds. If the firm has an overdraft facility, this may be sufficient to cope with the period of negative cash flow. If not, preventative action must be taken quickly.

Banks always request a cash flow forecast when considering an application for a loan from a new or an existing business. They do this in order to ensure that the business:

- has enough cash to enable it to survive
- is able to pay the interest on the loan
- will be able to repay the loan
- is aware of the need for cash flow management.

### SOLVING CASH FLOW PROBLEMS

If the cash flow forecast predicts a cash shortage the business can take actions to avoid the problem. It can do this in several ways:

**1 Speeding up cash inflows:** This can be done by:

- Negotiating shorter credit for customers – the average producer in the UK has to wait 75 days to be paid. If customers agree to pay for the goods earlier, cash is received earlier. In a very competitive market the length of credit may be a competitive issue. Large companies often insist on longer credit. Some companies offer discounts to encourage early payment of bills.
- Credit management – businesses can improve cash flow by ensuring that payment is received on time.

This is likely to involve writing reminder letters and making phone calls to persuade customers to pay promptly.

- Factoring – it may be possible to factor the debt. By factoring the company is able to receive 80% of the amount due within 24 hours of an invoice being presented. The factor then collects the money from the customer when the credit period is over. And pays the seller the remaining 20% less the factoring fees. These depend on the length of time before the payment is due, the credit rating of the creditor and current rates of interest. The fees are usually no more than 5% of the total value of the sale.

**2 Delaying cash outflows:** This can be done by:

- Negotiating longer credit for supplies – this postpones cash outflows, which can help the firm get through a difficult period. The length of credit will often depend on the stability of the company. New companies often have difficulty in negotiating credit.
- Leasing rather than buying equipment – expenditure on fixed assets is a substantial drain on cash, especially for new businesses. By leasing rather than buying, the cash can remain in the business.
- Renting rather than buying buildings – this also allows capital to remain in the business.

**3 Cutting or delaying expenditure:** Ways of decreasing expenditure include:

- decreasing levels of stock
- cutting costs
- postponing expenditure, e.g. on new company cars.

**4 Finding additional funding to cover cash shortages:** This can be done by:

- Using an overdraft – an overdraft is arranged with a bank. It allows the business to overdraw up to an agreed limit negotiated in advance. Overdrafts usually incur high rates of interest. As much as 6% over **base rate**. As Figure 16.2 shows, however, an overdraft ensures the firm only borrows money on the days it really needs it. It is a very flexible form of borrowing. This makes it suitable for small or short-term shortages of cash. Although it should only be used to fund short-term problems, a recent study of firms in Bristol found that 70% of small firms had a permanent overdraft. A risky aspect of an overdraft is that the bank can withdraw the facility at any time and demand instant repayment. So, when a firm needs it most, such as in a recession, it may find the bank has withdrawn it.

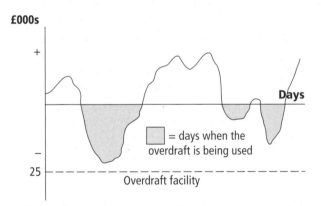

**Figure 16.2** Daily cash balances for a firm with a £25,000 overdraft

- Taking out a short-term loan – this incurs a lower rate of interest than an overdraft. Although less flexible than an overdraft, short-term loans offer more security and are cheaper.

- Taking out a long-term loan – this is more appropriate when the financial need is for a longer term, for example a three-year loan to help fund a new computer network.
- Sale and leaseback of assets – if a business has fixed assets it may be possible to negotiate a sale and leaseback arrangement. This will release capital and give an immediate inflow of cash. The equipment will be paid for through a leasing arrangement. This will be a regular and ongoing cost that must be budgeted for.

Whatever measure is chosen it needs to be effective in the short term. The action chosen will depend on the firm's circumstances at the time.

## 16.3 How reliable are cash flow forecasts?

Although they are useful, cash flow forecasts are only as good as the estimates they are based on. Businesses need to be aware that the figures are estimates and to build in some safety margins.

Companies should ask themselves what would happen if:

- sales were lower
- the customer did not pay up on time
- prices of materials were higher than expected.

Using spreadsheets enables companies to look at some of these possibilities. With the use of spreadsheets it is possible to adjust both the timings and amounts. This enables a business to evaluate the most likely and the worst case situations.

As well as being useful for ensuring successful start-ups, cash flow forecasts can also be used to provide an ongoing check on future cash flow. They can also be used to evaluate the effect of accepting a special order.

**Example:**

Treasured Memories produces commemorative pottery. It has been approached by a London store to supply a limited edition of 1,000 plates for a royal wedding. The plates will sell to the store for £35 each. The cost of materials is £9 per plate and labour costs

Cash flow forecast for Treasured Memories

| | SEPT. | OCT. | NOV. | DEC. | JAN. | FEB. | MARCH |
|---|---|---|---|---|---|---|---|
| Cash in | | | | | | | £35,000 |
| Cash out | | | | | | | |
|   Wages | £2,000 | £2,000 | £2,000 | £2,000 | | | |
|   Materials | | £2,250 | £2,250 | £2,250 | £2,250 | | |
|   Other costs | £750 | £750 | £750 | £750 | | | |
| Total outflow | £2,750 | £5,000 | £5,000 | £5,000 | £2,250 | | |
| Opening balance | 0 | (£2,750) | (£7,750) | (£12,750) | (£17,750) | (£20,000) | (£20,000) |
| Closing balance | (£2,750) | (£7,750) | (£12,750) | (£17,750) | (£20,000) | (£20,000) | £15,000 |

are £8 each. Additional costs will be £3 per plate. The store wants to have the plates available for sale from next January. The store will pay for the goods next March. The plates will take four months to produce so production needs to start this September. Production will be spread evenly over four months. Suppliers will give one month's credit for the materials. The order seems too good to refuse but the finance manager is worried. He has produced the cash flow forecast shown at the bottom of page 104.

The cash flow forecast shows that although the order is profitable it could cause serious cash flow problems. If the company is to accept the order, the bank manager needs to be asked to provide an overdraft facility of at least £20,000. It also needs to include any interest costs in the decision making.

**Overtrading** is when firms try to expand without having sufficient financial backing. Many firms try to finance growth by using working capital. This is a risky strategy that may result in cash flow problems. In some cases it is possible to expand the business using cash available topped up with overdrafts, but this could put the business at risk. Any delay in payment or unexpected problem may result in severe cash flow problems. It is generally considered better for firms to finance growth by using long term capital such as retained profit or business loans.

ISSUES FOR **analysis**

When answering a question on cash flow management, it is important to understand that the figures are only the starting point for analysis and decision making. Consideration needs to be given to:

● The validity of the figures – who constructed the forecast? Is he or she unbiased? Reliable?
● What the figures show.
● The possible solutions to any problems.
● The advantages and disadvantages of the possible solutions.
● The need to take full account of the circumstances of the business. If sales are to a foreign country such as Russia, payment may not be certain and even if it arrives, changes in currency values may make cash inflows worth fewer pounds than forecast.
● The differences between cash flow and profitability.

## 16.4 Cash flow management
### an evaluation

There is no doubt that cash flow management is a vital ingredient in the success of any small business. For a new business, cash flow forecasting helps to answer key questions. Is the venture viable? How

much capital is needed? Which are the most dangerous months? For an existing business the cash flow forecast identifies the amount and timing of any cash flow problems in the future. It is also useful for evaluating new orders or ventures.

Nevertheless, completing a cash flow forecast does not ensure survival. Consideration needs to be given to its usefulness and limitations. It must be remembered that cash flow forecasts are based on estimates. These estimates are not just amounts but also timings. The firm must be aware that actual figures can differ wildly from estimates – especially for a new, inexperienced firm. When preparing cash flow forecasts managers need to ask themselves 'what if?'. A huge mistake is to only look at one central forecast. Far better to look at best case and worst case scenarios. Spreadsheets allow for easy manipulation of data. It is easy to see the impact of single and multiple changes to the forecast figures. This should help to reduce the risks. It does not guarantee results. Continual awareness of the economic and market climate is just as important as number crunching.

**bankruptcy** – applies to individuals. If a sole trader or partnership is unable to pay its bills the creditors can take the debtor to court and have the individual declared bankrupt.

**base rate** – the interest rate set by the Bank of England which high street banks use to set their savings and loan interest rates.

**credit control** – the management of debtors. It includes vetting potential customers for creditworthiness, following up on late payment and pursuing bad debts.

**creditors** – individuals or other businesses that are owed money by the business.

**debtors** – individuals or companies who owe money to the business.

**insolvency** – applies to companies. When unpaid creditors take a debtor to court the company is declared insolvent. It may be closed down, which is known as liquidation. It could be put into receivership.

# Exercises

## A. REVISION QUESTIONS
*(35 marks; 70 minutes)*

Read the unit, then answer:

1  What is meant by 'cash flow'? (4)
2  Why is it important to manage cash flow? (5)
3  What is a cash flow forecast? (3)
4  What benefit might a firm get from reviewing its current cash position? (4)
5  Explain two limitations of cash flow forecasts. (4)
6  Give two reasons why a bank manager might want to see a cash flow forecast before giving a loan to a new business. (2)
7  Identify three ways a business might benefit from factoring its debts. (3)
8  How might a firm benefit from delaying its cash outflows? (3)
9  What problems might a firm face if its cash flow forecast proved unreliable? (3)
10  How might a firm benefit from constructing its cash flow forecasts on a computer spreadsheet? (4)

## B REVISION EXERCISES

### B1 Data Response

#### Kerri's soft drinks
Kerri has been helping a friend to refill drinks machines. She now has the opportunity to take on the franchise as the friend is going to college. The franchise is fairly simple. She must purchase a minimum quantity of juice each month. The minimum is £150. This has to be paid immediately, as the supplier does not allow any credit. With this amount of stock her friend has been making sales of £450 per month. This, however, is not received until two months later.

Other expenses include van rental of £100 per month and other costs which total £100 each month.
Kerri has £50 cash in the bank. Her father has offered her a loan of £400.

**Questions** *(30 marks; 35 minutes)*
1  Assuming that Kerri starts the business in January, construct a cash flow forecast for the first six months. (10)
2  Comment on the cash flow. (5)
3  Suggest and discuss possible solutions to any problems you can see. (9)
4  Do you think she should take on the franchise? (6)

### B2 Data Response

#### Merlin Construction
Merlin Construction has planning permission to convert an old office block into four flats. The directors managed to borrow £130,000 from the bank in January. They used £100,000 to buy the building that month. The work will start in January and take nine months to complete. The plan is to build and sell the two upstairs flats in June and then complete the ground floor flats. These will be sold in September. The flats should sell for £60,000 each. Materials are estimated to cost about £10,000 a month with one month's credit. Wages and salaries will be £4,000 a month. Interest charges will be £1,000 a month. Other expenses will be £1,000 a month.

**Questions** *(30 marks; 35 minutes)*
1  Construct a cash flow forecast for the business for January to September. (10)
2  What does this cash flow forecast show? (4)
3  Suggest and discuss three possible courses of action. (12)
4  Outline two ways in which the cash flow forecast might be unreliable. (4)

## B3 Data Response

### Statutory Interest for Late Payments

The Labour government has announced that it is planning to help small businesses by introducing legislation to control late payment by debtors. Large companies are accused of delaying payment of bills. This puts pressure on the cash flow of small firms. One idea that has been suggested is to make compulsory interest payments due on overdue debts.

Industry views are divided. While many think that this will be helpful to small firms there is concern about how it would be enforced and the size of company that would be affected. Others are worried that as small firms tend to be net debtors they could face interest charges if they are late with payments. Another problem is that if the bill only covered small firms this would put them at a disadvantage compared to larger firms when negotiating sales.

**Questions** *(30 marks; 35 minutes)*

1 Explain how late payment affects businesses. *(6)*
2 Why is the government trying to help small businesses? *(6)*
3 Why is it necessary to introduce legislation to encourage businesses to pay their bills promptly? *(4)*
4 What is meant by the suggestion that small firms tend to be 'net debtors'? *(4)*
5 Do you agree that small firms would be at a competitive disadvantage if the bill were introduced? Explain your answer. *(10)*

# CONTROL OF WORKING CAPITAL

## 17.1 What is working capital?

All businesses need money. It is required by the business to buy machinery and equipment. This expenditure on **fixed assets** is known as *capital expenditure*. The business also needs money to buy materials or stock and to pay wages and the day-to-day bills such as electricity and telephone bills. This money is known as *working capital*.

Managing working capital is about ensuring that cash available is sufficient to meet the cash requirements at any one time. This is also known as having enough *liquidity*. If the bills cannot be paid on time there are serious consequences. In the worst situation the business may fail. Insufficient working capital is the commonest cause of business failure. Managing working capital is therefore a vital business activity.

## 17.2 The liquidity cycle

Managing working capital is a continuous process. When a business starts up it takes time to generate income. Money to pay for stock and the running costs will need to be found from the initial capital invested in the business. As the business cycle gets going, income from customers will be available to pay for expenditure. The firm needs to ensure that there is always sufficient cash to meet daily requirements. If the business is expanding or takes on a special order, extra care needs to be taken. Sufficient funds are needed to pay for the additional expenditure until the revenue arrives. This continuous process is known as the liquidity cycle. This is shown in Figure 17.1, which also shows why working capital is sometimes referred to as circulating capital.

As can be seen from Figure 17.1, managing working capital is about two things:

- ensuring the business has enough finance to meet its needs
- keeping cash moving rapidly through the cycle, so there is enough to meet future orders.

Each business will have its own distinct cycle.

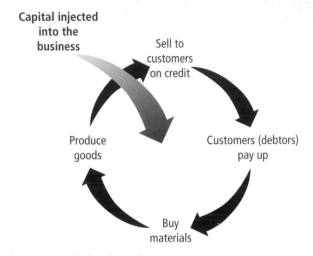

**Figure 17.1** The liquidity cycle

Businesses will also be subject to unexpected events and need to be able to cope with these. Therefore it is helpful to have a generous overdraft limit, which can be drawn upon when needed.

## 17.3 Problems caused by insufficient working capital

- With suppliers – a firm with too little working capital will struggle to pay its bills on time. It has no spare cash. It may resort to delaying payments. It may need to borrow more money. Delaying payment means that suppliers are not paid on time. They may reduce the **credit period** or refuse credit for a future order.
- With banks – if the business is resorting to borrowing it will have the additional cost of interest charges. If the bank is concerned about the liquidity situation it may impose higher charges. The business will find it more difficult to get loans. Any lender will want to be assured that the company is managing its working capital.
- Opportunities may be missed – the business may not be able to buy supplies in bulk. This removes the advantage of lower bulk-buying prices. Even more importantly it may have to refuse a large

order because it cannot finance the extra working capital requirement.

In the longer term, shortage of cash means that no funds are available for development. The business will not be able to grow. In extreme cases creditors may ask for the business to be declared insolvent. A sole trader or partnership will be declared bankrupt. Most creditors will only take this action if they feel that there is little hope of being paid. They will look at the future prospects and past performance of the business.

## 17.4 How much working capital do businesses need?

The working capital requirement varies from business to business. It depends on:

- The length of the business process. There are huge variations in the length of the liquidity cycle for different businesses. A fruit stall market trader buys supplies for cash from a wholesaler in the morning and sells everything (for cash) by late afternoon. The cycle takes less than a day. By contrast, a small construction firm building four houses may take a year between starting the project and having cash paid by a new homeowner.

  The length of the business cycle is a combination of:

  - The length of the production process. This depends on the product. A service industry such as a restaurant has a very short production time. To construct a road bridge takes a little longer. The time taken to get the product to the market. Overseas markets have a longer distribution process. Seasonal products may be manufactured but not delivered for many months.

- The credit given to purchasers. This depends on market conditions. As a general rule business customers expect longer credit than private customers. A retail business receives payments sooner than a manufacturer or wholesaler. The relationship between firms also affects the credit period. A large, important customer may demand longer credit. A sole supplier can insist on early payment.

- The credit given for purchases of materials or stock. Most businesses obtain credit for their purchases. The length of time allowed before payment depends on:

  - how established the firm is (an established firm can negotiate longer credit than a new firm)
  - its credit record (a firm with a good record of paying can negotiate longer credit)
  - its credit worthiness (a firm that appears solvent can obtain longer credit than a firm that is struggling)
  - market conditions (the credit period varies from industry to industry; credit is often used as part of the sales package)

  - the size of the order (larger orders may get longer credit)
  - regular orders (regular customers expect longer credit than occasional customers).

The business needs to take into account both the timing and the amounts involved when working out its working capital requirements. It also needs to include an allowance for uncertainty. An extra 10% on top of the expected cash requirement would usually be sufficient. For a new small firm such as a new restaurant, though, a bigger safety net can be wise. It can take months for word to spread sufficiently to push the business above its break-even point.

## 17.5 Can a business have too much working capital?

In America and Britain it is thought important that a business should not have too much working capital. The term 'too much' implies that the capital would be wasted. In some ways this is true. There is no point in having too much capital tied up in stock or giving too much credit to customers. There is a problem, though, in defining what 'too much' actually means.

Japanese and German firms have always tended to adopt a very cautious approach to their finances. In the early 1990s many were criticised by English analysts. They questioned why firms such as Honda and Sony had billions of dollars of cash lying idle on their **balance sheets**. Why so much working capital? Fortunately for companies in both countries, their caution helped them enormously when severe recessions hit them (especially Japan) in the mid-1990s.

It should always be remembered that whereas you can have too much stock or too many debtors, you can never have too much cash!

## 17.6 How can a business manage its working capital?

Maintaining good liquidity in a business is about managing the elements of the liquidity cycle. There are several ways that the business can minimise its working capital needs. These are centered on:

- Controlling cash.
- Obtaining maximum possible credit for purchases – delaying payment of bills will allow time for receipt of income from customers.
- Getting goods to the market in shortest possible time – the sooner goods reach the customer the sooner payment is received. Production and distribution should be as efficient as possible.
- Collecting payments efficiently – the business should aim to collect payment as soon as possible.

It can do this by increasing the proportion of cash customers.

i If cash payment is not possible because of market conditions the firm should give the shortest possible credit period. Early payment should be encouraged by offering incentives such as discounts for early payment.

ii If credit is granted the business should control its debtors – confusingly this is known as credit control. Credit control involves:
 – ensuring the debtor is creditworthy before granting credit (by getting a bank reference)
 – constantly reviewing the credit position of existing customers
 – following up on non-payment.

• Minimising spending on fixed assets – this keeps cash in the business. The business must balance its need for cash and its need for fixed assets. A compromise is to lease rather than buy equipment. This increases expenses but conserves capital.

• Controlling costs – this can be done by keeping administrative and production costs to a minimum. Efficient production reduces costs. Savings may be possible by upgrading machinery to replace labour. This has an impact on short-term capital availability but reduces the working capital requirements over the longer term.

• Stock management (see Unit 39) – stocks, whether raw material or finished goods, tie up money. If the business minimises its stock levels, working capital requirements will be lower. Stock management includes:
 – ensuring an efficient production process, minimising work in progress
 – ensuring goods are delivered promptly, minimising stocks of finished goods
 – minimising stock losses, for example by efficient stock rotation.

Longer term improvements can stem from a move to just-in-time production (see Unit 35). This should reduce stocks of raw materials, work in progress and finished goods. The firm must balance the cost of stockholding with incentives to buy in bulk. Together with JIT purchasing, this helps to minimise stock losses from obsolescence. Good warehousing and security reduces other losses.

## 17.7 Causes of liquidity problems

Many liquidity problems are a result of the firm not setting aside sufficient money for working capital. This results in a hand-to-mouth existence. If short-term funds are used for purchasing fixed assets this could cause working capital problems. There will be constant pressure to find the money to repay the borrowing.

Good management of liquidity and an awareness of external events will be all that is necessary for most businesses to avoid liquidity problems. However, there is always a need to be prudent. Businesses can experience

### DELL ON LINE

Dell Computer Corporation is the world's no. 1 personal computer manufacturer with an estimated 14% of the global market. It has an enviable record of success. One factor in this success is the careful management of stock. Computers are made to the customer specification. At the assembly plant they do not keep stocks of finished machines, only component parts. After an order is received the computer is constructed. It is then shipped to a distribution centre. Here it meets up with its various peripherals. These items such as monitors and keyboards are not held in stock but are delivered to the distribution centres directly from the suppliers.

Minimising its investment in working capital in this way has helped Dell to finance and maintain its incredible growth. It has also helped the company to avoid the problems of holding stocks of computers when a change in technology makes yesterday's models obsolete and slashes their value.

unexpected problems. A firm may feel confident in its liquidity position until a major customer goes into liquidation. Suddenly the debtors payment expected next week becomes a bad debt. Often when one firm goes under, others are dragged down with it.

Internal causes of liquidity problems can include:

• Production problems – interruptions to production delay the product reaching the market. Prolonged delays such as strikes are a major problem.
• Marketing problems – if demand for a product is slow, sales staff may offer longer credit terms to try to shift unsold stocks.
• Management problems – poor stock or production management can result in additional costs.

External causes of liquidity problems include:

• Changes to the economic climate – this may include inflation, recession or changes to taxation.
• Lower demand – this may be caused by recession, changes in fashion or seasonal factors.
• Unexpected non-payment by customers – this may be a payment delay or may become a bad debt if the customer goes out of business.

## 17.8 Dealing with liquidity problems

Any business may be faced from time to time with a liquidity emergency. In this situation there are several measures that can be taken. The following table shows the measures, the result of them and possible pitfalls.

Dealing with working capital shortages

| MEASURE | RESULT | DRAWBACKS |
|---|---|---|
| Discounting prices | • Increases sales<br>• Reduces stock<br>• Generates cash | • May undermine pricing structure<br>• May leave low stocks for future activity |
| Reduce purchases | • Cuts down expenditure | • May leave business without means to continue |
| Negotiate more credit | • Allows time to pay | • May tarnish credit reputation |
| Delay payment of bills | • Retains cash | • Will tarnish credit reputation |
| Credit control – chase debtors | • Gets payments in and sooner | • May upset customers |
| Negotiate additional finance | • Provides cash | • Interest payments add to expenditure<br>• Has to be repaid |
| Factor debts | • Generates cash<br>• A proportion of the income is guaranteed | • Reduces income from sales<br>• Costs can be high |
| Selling assets | • Releases cash | • Assets are no longer available |
| Sale and leaseback | • Releases cash<br>• Asset is still available for use | • Increases costs – lease has to be paid<br>• Company no longer owns asset |

## 17.9 Working capital in the balance sheet

One of the ways a firm can monitor its working capital is by use of its **balance sheet**. On the balance sheet working capital is **current assets** minus current liabilities. It is also known as *net current assets*.

> *current assets*
> =
> *stock (raw materials, part-produced goods and finished goods)*
> +
> *debtors (money owed to the business)*
> +
> *cash (cash held in the business or in bank accounts)*

> *current liabilities*
> =
> *creditors*
> *(money owed by the business for goods or services)*
> +
> *short-term loans/overdrafts*
> *(to be repaid within one year)*

### Example:
P Perfect Ltd manufactures scientific instruments. The assets section of its balance sheet for last year showed:

| | | |
|---|---|---|
| Fixed assets | | £750,000 |
| Stock | £95,000 | |
| Debtors | £65,000 | |
| Cash | £10,000 | |
| Current assets | | £170,000 |
| Creditors | £80,000 | |
| Overdraft | £20,000 | |
| Current liabilities | | £100,000 |
| Working capital | | £70,000 |
| Assets employed | | £820,000 |

This shows the business has £70,000 of working capital. In other words, of the £820,000 invested in the business, £750,000 is tied up in fixed assets. Only £70,000 is available for the day-to-day running of the firm. Despite having only £70,000 available, the firm has managed to obtain £170,000 of current assets. This is because it has obtained £100,000 of short-term finance from credit given by suppliers (creditors) and a bank overdraft.

If a rush order required the purchase of £100,000 more stock, where could the money come from? P Perfect has only £10,000 of cash. Perhaps the creditors or the overdraft levels could be increased? If not, the firm would need to increase its working capital.

### WAYS OF INCREASING WORKING CAPITAL

- sell some fixed assets for cash, i.e. switch resources from fixed capital to working capital
- raise a long-term loan to increase the assets employed, but leave the extra cash in current assets
- raise more share capital – this will also increase assets employed and current assets
- over the coming months, ensure that trading profits are retained in the business to build up the cash total.

## 17.10 How useful is the balance sheet?

Basing working capital management on balance sheet ratios has its limitations. The balance sheet gives only a snapshot view. It does not give any indication of timing. Perhaps the money owed has to be paid tomorrow, but the debtor payments are not due for three months. If working capital is to be well managed it needs to be considered continually. What bills are due next week? What cash is available and how much do we expect to receive?

The balance sheet is also historic. It is a record of what has happened in the past. Good management of working capital is about looking at the future. It has been known for firms to boost their working capital position just before the balance sheet is prepared. This window dressing will make the liquidity situation seem better.

A more useful tool for managing working capital is the cash flow forecast. It gives the business an indication of the expected flow of cash in and out of the business. It will highlight any danger times when there appears to be a cash shortfall (see Unit 16).

ISSUES FOR **analysis**

To analyse working capital management in a business case study or data response question it is important to remember:

- For small firms especially, the liquidity cycle is the equivalent of blood circulating round the body. If the cash dries up, the firm dies.
- The problems caused by too little or too much working capital.
- How businesses can cope with poor working capital situations and the pitfalls of any actions.
- Business requirements for working capital will depend on the nature of the business. It is also necessary to understand that managing working capital is not just about cash management. It goes far deeper and involves most aspects of the business. As in most Business Studies situations, care should be taken to relate the answer to the circumstances of the particular business.

It would be nice if there were a perfect, 'right' level of working capital. But there is not. Sainsbury's has operated very successfully for decades with a hugely negative working capital. This is because it sells its stock quickly, yet gets a long credit period from suppliers. So the creditors' item (a liability) is huge, but stocks (an asset) are low. As it is a cash-rich business, it is always confident that enough cash will come through today's tills to pay yesterday's bills. So the tell-tale sign about working capital is not whether it is high or low, positive or negative. The key issues are: can the firm fund the short-term actions it would like to take, and is the working capital position improving or worsening?

## 17.11 Control of working capital
### an evaluation

Managing working capital is very important for every business. As in many other areas of business it is about getting the balance right. Too much liquidity is wasteful – too little can be disastrous. Businesses need to consider working capital requirements right from the outset. Most new businesses underestimate their working capital needs. Typically, firms only allow £20 of working capital for every £100 of fixed capital (assets). Accountants usually advise a £50:£50 ratio.

Managing working capital is not just about managing cash flow. The timing and amounts of cash flow are important, but working capital management goes beyond that. It is about managing the whole business. In this respect it is an integrated activity. It involves each aspect of the company. Efficient production keeps costs to a minimum and turns raw inputs into finished goods in the shortest possible time. Effective management of stock can have considerable impact on working capital requirements. Effective marketing ensures that the goods are sold and that demand is correctly estimated. This avoids wasted production. Cash then flows in from sales. Efficient distribution gets the goods to the customer quickly. The accounting department can help to control costs. Effective credit control improves cash flow. Each of these can reduce the need for cash and/or ensure that sufficient cash is available for the business to meet its objectives.

**KEY terms**

**bad debts** – payments that are long overdue and cannot be expected to be received.

**balance sheet** – a statement of the assets and liabilities of the business at a point in time (usually the end of the financial year). It shows where the money is in the business and where it came from.

**bankruptcy** – applies to individuals. If a sole trader or partnership is unable to pay its bills the creditors can take the debtor to court and have the individual declared bankrupt.

**credit period** – the length of time allowed for payment.

**current assets** – cash or assets that can be turned into cash. This includes stock and money owed to the company.

**factoring** – obtaining part-payment of the amount owed from a factoring company. The factoring company will then collect the debt and pass over the balance of the payment.

**fixed assets** – items that are used over and over again by the business. They include buildings, equipment and vehicles.

**insolvency** – applies to companies. When unpaid creditors take a debtor to court the company may be declared insolvent.

# Exercises

## A. REVISION QUESTIONS

*(40 marks; 70 minutes)*

Read the unit, then answer:

1 What is working capital? (3)
2 What is capital expenditure? (3)
3 What does it mean when it is said that a firm has enough liquidity? (3)
4 What is working capital used for? Give two examples. (5)
5 What problems might arise if a firm is operating with very low working capital? (4)
6 Why might a business be unable to get a loan or overdraft if it has working capital difficulties? (4)
7 Explain two factors that influence the amount of working capital required by a firm. (4)
8 Outline three ways in which a business can improve its working capital situation. (6)
9 How does better stock management help a firm to control its working capital requirements? (5)
10 List three ways in which stock levels can be reduced. (3)

## B. REVISION EXERCISES

### B1 Data Response

#### Small Businesses Hit by Economic Downturn

It is normally expected that small businesses are the hardest hit by any economic downturn. However, Barclays Bank has reported that the number of small firms closing down in the third quarter of 1998 was less than the previous quarter despite the slow-down in economic growth. There was, in fact, a net gain in the number of businesses. The number of new business start-ups was 118,000 in the period from July to September whilst the number of closures was 110,000. Barclays' conclusion was that the economic downturn was having more impact on larger businesses and that smaller businesses might not feel the impact until the following year.

A different survey by a firm specialising in factoring showed a slightly different picture. Its research indicated that the hardest hit firms were those with turnover above £50 million or below £2.5 million. They highlighted several problems faced by businesses:

- In order to combat fierce competition, firms were having to discount prices. This caused a reduction in profitability.

- Firms have reduced their stock levels, including raw materials, work in progress and finished goods.
- There was a high level of cancelled orders.
- Payments were being received on average 23 days after their due date. This situation was unchanged from the previous year except in the clothing industry where payments had slipped a further 10 days.
- Exporters were having a difficult time. They were hard hit by the strong pound and were experiencing the longest payment delays since the last recession.

Source: Adapted from *The Times*, 10/11/98

**Questions** *(30 marks; 35 minutes)*

1 Explain the meaning of the term 'factoring'. (3)
2 Barclays feels that small firms would be hit by the economic downturn in the following year (1999). What changes might firms need to make to their working capital management to prepare for a period of falling demand? (6)
3 How do increased payment delays affect a firm's working capital? (8)
4 On average, customers pay their bills 23 days late. In fact, some will pay early, others on time and some very late indeed. How might factoring be of use to a firm in this situation of uncertainty? (5)
5 What are the advantages and disadvantages of firms reducing stocks in times of economic downturn? (8)

### B2 Case Study

#### Hatta Lighting

Hatta Lighting plc makes component parts for the car industry. It started out making bulbs but now also supply a range of electrical and electronic components. The company started as a family-run business but expansion has meant that five years ago it became a public limited company. During the last two years its performance has been mediocre and dividends paid to shareholders have been falling. The share price has also fallen. One of the largest shareholders has decided that change was necessary and has managed to exert enough pressure to replace the established chairman. The new chairman has a strong financial background but has been involved in the retailing industry for many years. He has asked the management team to produce some information. The team has come up with the following:

| | Last year | This year | Industry average |
|---|---|---|---|
| Stock turnover materials | 44 days | 48 days | 40 days |
| Stock of finished goods | £780,000 | £910,000 | £700,000 |
| Average days before payment | 38 | 54 | 42 |
| Working capital at year end | £560,000 | £380,000 | Not available |

After examining these figures the new chairman is very concerned about the liquidity situation of the company. Several large debts totalling £500,000 are due to be paid shortly. The firm does not have sufficient cash available to pay these. He sees this as being the most urgent issue facing the company and he has arranged an urgent meeting of all the managers. He has asked each of the three department heads (marketing, finance and production) to come up with ideas to solve the problem.

**Questions** *(45 marks; 60 minutes)*

1 What might be the reasons for the increase in the stock of finished goods and materials? *(6)*
2 Consider what suggestions the production director might make? Explain your reasoning. *(10)*
3 The finance director sees slow payment as his major problem. Examine the ways in which the firm might tackle this problem. *(10)*
4 Outline the contribution the marketing department might make to help improve the liquidity situation. *(9)*
5 Apart from tackling the issue of slow payment, consider what other short-term measures the firm might take to overcome the immediate liquidity crisis. *(10)*

# SOURCES OF FINANCE

DEFINITION
All businesses need money invested in them. Sources of finance are the origins of that money. They are where the money in the business comes from.

## 18.1 The need for finance

Whether a business is starting out or developing, it needs money. Businesses starting up need money to invest in fixed assets such as buildings and equipment. This is known as *capital expenditure*. They also need money to purchase materials or to buy in finished goods. The money used to purchase stock and to pay the bills is known as **working capital**. Both the working capital and money for capital expenditure has to be found before the business starts to generate any income.

Once the business is established the income from customers should provide sufficient working capital plus some profit. This profit can be returned to the investors in the business or it could be reinvested in the business. If the business wants to expand it will probably need to find additional finance. Sometimes businesses have problems. They may have a cash problem caused by changes in market conditions. They will need to find additional funding to enable them to continue.

## 18.2 Sources of finance

The type and amount of finance that is available will depend on several factors. These are:

- **The type of business** – a sole trader will be limited to the capital the owner can put into the business plus any money he or she is able to borrow. A partnership will have the resources of all the partners. A limited company will be able to raise share capital. In order to become a plc it will need to be of a certain size and have a track record of success. This will make borrowing easier.
- **The stage of development of the business** – a new business will find it much harder to raise finance than an established firm. As the business develops it is easier to persuade outsiders to invest in the business. It is also easier to obtain loans as the firm has assets to offer as security.
- **How successful the firm is** – a track record of success will encourage both lenders and investors. Lenders will have more confidence that their loan will be returned. Investors will be keen to invest so they can share in the rising profits.

- **The state of the economy** – when the economy is booming business confidence will be high. It will be easy to raise finance both from borrowing and from investors. In a recession the opposite will be true. It will also be more difficult for businesses to find investors when interest rates are high. They will invest their money in more secure accounts such as building societies. Higher interest rates will also put up the cost of borrowing. This will make it more expensive for the business to borrow.

Finance for business comes from two main sources:

1 inside the business – known as internal finance
2 outside the business – known as external finance.

### INTERNAL FINANCE

### Retained profit

Once the business starts to generate sales it will hopefully make some profit. This provides a return on the investment in the business. However it is also a source of finance. Research shows that over 60% of business investment comes from reinvested, retained profit.

### Squeezed out of working capital

By cutting stocks, chasing up debtors or delaying payments to creditors, cash can be generated from a firm's working capital. This is an internal source of finance. However, when cash is taken from working capital for a purpose such as buying fixed assets, the liquidity position worsens.

### Sale of assets

An established business has assets. These can be sold to raise cash. The business loses the asset but has the use of the cash. It makes good business sense for businesses to dispose of redundant assets. They can finance development without extra borrowing. If the asset is needed, it may be possible to sell it, but imme-

*Reuters, the media company, is looking at releasing £100 million of capital from the sale and leaseback of its London offices. It has appointed NM Rothschild to investigate the options available. Rothschild recently advised the BBC on a £1 billion deal which allowed the broadcaster to raise funds to develop the White City studios at no cost to the licence fee payer.*

(The Times, 16 August 2002)

diately lease it back. In this way the business has use of the money and the asset. This is known as sale and leaseback. Recently Marks & Spencer, Safeway and the BBC have used their property to release cash in this way.

## EXTERNAL FINANCING

Few firms are able to operate without some external finance, i.e. finance from outside their own resources.

## External finance for day-to-day working capital:

### Trade credit

This is the simplest form of external financing. The business obtains goods or services from another business. It does not pay for these immediately. The average credit period is two months.

### Bank overdrafts

This is the commonest form of borrowing for businesses. It is an effective short-term source of finance. The bank allows the firm to overdraw up to an agreed level. This has the advantages of:

- flexibility
- the firm only needs to borrow what it needs.

It is, however, an expensive way of borrowing, and can be withdrawn instantly by the lender.

### Factoring

A factoring company might provide a firm with 80% of its invoiced sales within 24 hours. It then provides the other 20% (minus a fee) after collecting the debt from the firm's customer. This is a common way to finance small, rapidly growing firms with high profit margins.

## External finance for growth and expansion:

### Leasing

This is a common way to finance the acquisition of new fixed assets. Instead of buying a new fleet of company cars for cash, for example, they are leased. A contract is signed committing the firm to pay a monthly sum for the next three years. The cars never become the firm's property. The business has use of the asset without the capital expenditure.

### Loan capital, such as a bank loan

Banks offer a range of loans. They may be medium term or long term with variable or fixed interest rates. Banks will only lend if they are confident the loan will be repaid. They will insist on a well thought out business plan. They are also likely to ask for collateral, i.e. some form of security. For a sole trader this is a personal asset such as a house, which can be sold to repay the debt if the business fails. For other businesses the assets of the business may suffice. The bank may call in the loan if it fears that the business is in trouble.

If the business is unable to get a loan because it is unable to provide security it may be able to take

## — CARDPOINT TAKES AIM

Cardpoint was formed in 2001 when two companies Cash Card and Direct Cash merged. The company supplies cash machines to various retailers such as corner shops, hospitals and petrol stations. The founder and chief executive Mark Mills came up with the idea when he was on holiday in the US. He was impressed with the idea of putting cash machines in convenient places. This, he felt, would benefit both the customer and the owner of the location. He set up the company in 1999 and has seen turnover grow to £250,000 each month. In order to fund the next stage of its expansion the company floated on the Stock Exchange AIM (Alternative Investment Market) in June 2002. In spite of the general downturn in the stock market the sale was oversubscribed, easily raising the £2.5 million that the company was looking for.

Source: *Growing Business* July/August 2002

advantage of the Department of Trade and Industry (DTI) guaranteed loan scheme. Loans from £5,000 to £250,000 are available for periods of between two and ten years. The DTI will guarantee 70% of the loan (85% if the business has been trading for more than two years). The borrower negotiates the terms of the loan with the lender. They pay a premium to the DTI of 1.5% of the outstanding balance. This facility has several exclusions. It is, for example, only available to businesses with an annual turnover below £1.5 million (£3 million for a manufacturer) or 200 employees.

### Debentures or corporate bonds

These are loans to the business by individuals or financial organisations. They are for a specified length of time, typically 25 years, and secured against a specific asset (usually property) and carry a fixed rate of interest. They are the business equivalent of a mortgage.

### Owners equity (also known as share capital)

This is the money put into the business by the owner or owners. For new businesses this is the most likely source of finance. Many businesses are started with individual savings. This money has the advantage that it has no interest charges. The money is also at risk. If the business fails the money is likely to be lost.

### Venture capital

This is a way of getting outside investment for businesses that are unable to raise finance through the stock markets. Venture capitalists invest in smaller,

Business
IN

riskier companies. They may make a loan or become part-owners. It is a much riskier form of investment.

### Grants

There are many different grants available to businesses. These are sponsored by the Government, the EU and other agencies such as The Prince's Trust. Growth Resourcing Associates offer an Internet advisory service for obtaining grants. They estimate that there are over 1,000 different grants available. Research shows, however, that fewer than 3% of all new firms are financed by grants.

## 18.3 Finance should be adequate and appropriate

Having adequate funding means ensuring the business has sufficient access to finance to meet its capital and working capital requirements. When a business starts up it needs sufficient funds to enable it to survive until it starts to generate enough income. Expansion also requires the purchase of additional equipment and additional working capital needs.

Appropriate financing means matching the type of finance to its use. A distinction is made in company financing between short- and long-term finance (see Figure 18.1). Short term finance is usually considered to be for less than one year. Medium-term is one to five years. Long-term finance is longer than five years. Short-term finance should not be used to finance long-term projects. Using short term finance such as overdrafts puts continual pressure on the company's working capital.

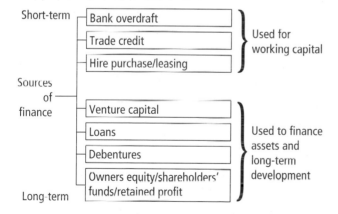

**Figure 18.1** Short- and long term sources of finance

It is appropriate to use an overdraft to cope with irregularities in working capital. If the overdraft becomes permanent then it is effectively funding the provision of assets. A machine should not be purchased with the aid of a short-term loan. The machine will generate income over its lifetime, and this should provide sufficient return to repay the loan and any interest payments plus some contribution to its replacement.

When a business expands without a solid financial foundation it is known as **overtrading**.

## 18.4 Financing growth

Growth is often seen as a natural development for a business, but it can be risky. If it is not managed well it can destroy a successful business. There are a number of reasons why growth should take place:

- a business may need to expand to take advantage of economies of scale, to keep pace with competitors or to supply a market where demand is not satisfied
- a larger business will find it easier to ride out fluctuations in economic activity, to cope with setbacks, to compete and to raise finance
- a business with a mixture of activities will have a spread of risk
- a business may be below break-even level.

Whatever the motive for growth it requires financial back-up. Ideally the growth should generate additional profit. But before profit comes the cash investment in the assets and personnel needed to succeed.

### GROWTH REQUIRES ADEQUATE FINANCING

Cash flow planning is just as important when a business is looking for growth as at any other stage of its life. Not only is capital required for the purchase of new assets but the firm must ensure that there is adequate working capital. This is required to fund the additional raw materials, labour costs and general overheads until the increased business activity generates sufficient income. A promising long-term growth opportunity could, if the funding is inadequate, cause the business to fail in the short term. Such failures are usually due to overtrading.

Overtrading means growing faster than can be sustained by a firm's capital base. A small firm may have been producing goods for years when, suddenly, there is a surge in demand. This happened to Doc Martens shoes in the 1980s and again in the 1990s. It happened to the toy importer Kids' Biz in the yo-yo boom of 1998–1999. Step by step, overtrading happens as follows:

1 a demand upsurge hits a firm with small stocks and a small production capacity
2 it uses its overdraft to fund the extra sales and soon reaches 100% capacity
3 as sales shoot ahead, today's costs are rising rapidly, but cash inflows from customers lag behind
4 excess demand means capacity must be increased, causing a huge cash requirement
5 and so on.

### MAKING GROWTH WORK

Although growth can significantly improve a company's fortunes, growth for growth's sake is not desirable. Many companies that expanded in the past are now

## FINANCING GROWTH

How do rapidly growing small firms finance their growth? By venture capital? By loans? To find an answer to this question, Hamish Stevenson from Templeton College, Oxford, looked at 100 of the fastest growing firms of the 1990s. One of these is R Frazier, a firm which recycles computers. Its sales grew from £294,000 to £7,400,000 in just three years. An increase of more than 2,400%! In common with the majority of the firms, R Frazier's early growth was self-funded, in other words from reinvested profits, overdrafts and trade credit. 'These are the real entrepreneurs,' says Stevenson. 'They grab money where they can. It is fly-by-the-seat-of-their-pants finance.' The 54 firms which used this method were doing so 'through default not by design', according to the research.

Twenty-one of the firms were helped by equity finance; 15 from venture capital houses and 6 from business angels. Just 10 used long-term bank debt.

Having survived, even thrived, through these hectic early years, as many as 40 of the firms are looking at, or in the process of, floating their firms on the London Stock Market. This would secure the finance for the next stage of growth.

looking to return to their '**core business**' activity. Many successful companies have collapsed in the process of expansion.

For most businesses, growth can have significant advantages. It is essential that the financial aspects be managed carefully. Any new venture carries an element of risk. So, too, does rapid growth in existing markets. The firm needs to evaluate this to minimise the impact of the risk.

Ideally, businesses should look to grow steadily. Each step should be established with secure funding. This careful approach will minimise risk. It spreads the need for funding and makes finance easier to obtain.

Any business that is keen to grow needs to recognise that it is not always beneficial. It needs to:

- estimate the timing and value of additional sales
- estimate timing and amounts of all additional costs
- do a cash flow forecast to ensure that it has the necessary working capital
- perform an investment appraisal to ensure that the return from the project is acceptable.

If it still feels that the development is worthwhile then it needs to ensure that:

- the amount of any funding covers both capital and working capital needs
- that the funding is available for long enough to enable it to repay the loan from profits generated by the expansion.

It also needs to ensure that it has looked at other aspects of the business such as marketing, distribution and staffing.

ISSUES FOR **analysis**

When analysing or suggesting appropriate sources of finance, the key issues are:

- Whether the business itself is risky or stable. If risky (such as a low cost airline), the form of financing should be as safe as possible. The collapse of the world's first major, low cost airline (Laker Airways) was due to high capital gearing for a business caught in a price war.
- Whether the founding family of the business is determined to hold onto power. If so, it will be very reluctant to sell more than 49% of the shares. This may force it to finance growth by borrowings rather than safer share capital. Rupert Murdoch's media empire grew in this way, and was fortunate to survive the early 1990s' recession.
- For what reason is the business seeking finance? The key here is to ensure that the finance is adequate and appropriate. The type of finance should be matched to the capital need. For example, long-term asset purchases might be financed by a long-term bank loan.

## 18.5 Sources of finance
### an evaluation

Finding finance may involve balancing conflicting interests. Internal sources of finance may be too limited to provide opportunities for business development. If retained profit is used, shareholders wanting a return on their investment may not be satisfied.

Obtaining external financing increases the money that is available. However, it has its downsides. Borrowing increases risk. Raising extra share capital dilutes the control held by existing shareholders.

The cost of finance will also reduce the company's net profit and, in the case of limited companies, reduce dividends paid to shareholders. If the growth is successful this may prove nothing worse than a short-term problem. The problem comes if costly growth leads to costly failure. This happened to Carlton and Granada TV when they flopped with ITV Digital in 2002.

Having adequate and appropriate finance at each stage in the firm's development will ensure it stays healthy. Decisions about where to obtain the finance will be a matter of balancing the business objectives, the reasons for the funding and the need for a safety cushion, in case of crisis.

**core business** – the basic business activity. The core business is the major activity of the business.

**overtrading** – when a firm expands without obtaining appropriate funding.

**private limited company** – a business with limited liability whose shares are not available to the public

**public limited company (plc)** – a company with limited liability and shares which are available to the public. Its shares can be quoted on the Stock Exchange.

**Stock Exchange** – a market for stocks and shares. It supervises the issuing of shares by companies. It is also a second-hand market for stocks and shares.

**working capital** – the money needed to finance the day-to-day running of the business. It allows stock to be bought and wages and bills to be paid.

## Exercises

### A. REVISION QUESTIONS

*(25 marks; 50 minutes)*

Read the unit, then answer:

1 What is meant by 'capital expenditure'? (2)
2 What is the importance to firms of working capital? (3)
3 What is meant by 'retained profit'? (2)
4 Outline two ways in which businesses can raise money from internal sources. (4)
5 Explain the term 'factoring'. (3)
6 Outline two sources of finance that can be used for long-term business development. (4)
7 Why might a new business find it difficult to get external funding for its development? (3)
8 What are the advantages and disadvantages of raising capital by selling shares? (4)

### B. REVISION EXERCISES

**B1 Activity**

**EBS: A Business for Our Times**

> Executive Business Services is a modern day business success story. It was started by Val Hood in 1990. She had been made redundant from her job when she was two months pregnant. She did not qualify for redundancy payments. Working from a bedroom at home using a PC and a printer she built up a client base by offering to take on their excess typing work. Her main selling point was that she would do the work within 24 hours. Inevitably this meant working very long days. Although at times she had too much work she could not afford to pay staff.

> This changed in 1995 when she tendered for work from an insurance company that wanted to close down its typing pool. Winning the contract allowed her to expand. She took on three more staff, all mothers who worked from home. In 1998 the business made a profit of £50,000. It now operates from offices in South London, employs 26 home-based workers and has a client list of 60 firms.

> Mrs Hood believes that this type of work will grow in the future. As businesses seek to reduce costs they will increasingly outsource routine work such as typing. This is now made easier with the use of computer-based technology. As the business has grown, she has ensured that both the equipment and the skills have developed. The firm uses e-mail and has software that is compatible with that used by the clients. In addition to typing, the firm will take shorthand, translate and transcribe. It collects and delivers work but also has work dictated over the telephone.

> Mrs Hood's next venture is to launch a recruitment agency providing security-cleared temps to those firms who do not wish to have work leaving the office.

> (**Source:** Adapted from *The Times*, 15/12/98)

This business is typical of the way in which many businesses start and grow. At each stage in the development of the business it will have needed money to finance the development.

**Questions** *(30 marks; 35 minutes)*
1 Identify the stages in the development of the business. *(4)*
2 For each stage in the development identify the financial needs. *(4)*
3 Investigate possible sources of funding for each stage. *(8)*
4 Consider the pros and cons of these sources. *(8)*
5 Finally identify and justify the best way of financing the latest expansion plans. *(6)*

### B2  Data Response

#### Mayday Printers

Mayday Printers specialises in last minute printing for firms. Its major selling point is that it will turn a job around within 24 hours providing the artwork is ready. Mayday is able to charge a premium for this service and is seldom short of work. The firm does, however, need to be extremely flexible. This means having a flexible work force and very reliable machines. It has had to turn away several large jobs lately because of a lack of machinery and now the managers are considering buying an additional large printer. Although they know that this will not be used at full capacity they are worried that turning away business will damage their reputation and lead to a loss of business in future. The company is in good financial health with a strong cash flow, though the cash position can be strained sometimes when there is a rush of work. To complete an order Mayday might have to pay bonus wages to staff, often before payment is received.

The finance director has come up with two proposals that he will present to the next Board meeting. The first is to buy a new printer and to fund the purchase with a bank loan. The printer will cost £100,000 so he suggests taking out a loan for that amount. The loan will be at bank rate plus 8% and will be for 10 years. The bank rate is currently 4%.

The alternative proposal is to rent this new machine. He has found a company who will do this. The cost of the rental including a maintenance contract would be £1,500 per month. The marketing department expects to pick up at least 5 additional contracts during the first year. These should generate at least £20,000 of revenue, but just as importantly will protect the company's reputation and existing business.

**Questions** *(20 marks; 30 minutes)*
Prepare a report for the Board outlining the advantages and disadvantages of each proposal. End your report with a clear recommendation.

# BUDGETING

DEFINITION
A budget is a target for costs or revenue that a firm or department must aim to reach over a given period of time.

## 19.1 Introduction

Budgeting is the process of setting targets covering all aspects of costs and revenues. Budgeting is a method for turning a firm's strategy into reality. A budgeting system should allocate and monitor costs and revenues. Most firms use a system of budgetary control as a means of supervision.

The process starts with an assessment of likely sales revenues for the coming year. Then a cost ceiling is set that allows for an acceptable level of profit. This budget for the whole company's costs is then broken down by division, department or by cost centre. The budget may then be broken down further so that each manager has a budget and therefore some spending power.

## 19.2 What is budgeting for?

- To ensure that no department or individual spends more than the company expects, thereby preventing unpleasant surprises.
- To provide a yardstick against which a manager's success or failure can be measured (and rewarded). For example, a store manager may have to meet a sales budget of £450,000 at a maximum operating cost of £320,000. As long as the budget holder believes this target is possible, the attempt to achieve it will be motivating. The company can then provide bonuses for achieving or beating the profit target.
- To enable spending power to be **delegated** to local managers who are in a better position to know how best to use the firm's money. This should improve and speed up the decision making process – and help motivate the local budget holders. The management expert Peter Drucker refers to 'management by self-control'. He regards this as the ideal approach. Managers should have clear targets, clear budgets and the power to decide how to achieve them. Then they will try everything they can to succeed.

## 19.3 Setting budgets

Setting budgets is not an easy job. How do you decide exactly what level of sales are likely next year? Furthermore, how can you plan for costs if the cost of your raw materials tends to fluctuate? Most firms treat last year's budget figures as the main determinant of this year's budget. Minor adjustments will be made for inflation and other foreseeable changes. It is very unlikely that budgets will fall if this method is being used. The great advantage of this method is that very little time needs to be spent on the budget setting task.

An alternative approach is **zero budgeting**. This approach sets each department's budget at zero and demands that budget holders, in setting their budget, justify every pound they ask for. This helps to avoid the common phenomenon of budgets creeping upwards each year. The advantages and disadvantages of this method are set out below.

### Advantages of zero budgeting:

- Helps to identify those departments that no longer need as large a budget. This can release funds for growth areas elsewhere within the organisation.
- Can work effectively as a way of cutting the entire cost base of the organisation. This may be necessary in times of recession.

### Disadvantages of zero budgeting:

- In order to justify every pound of every budget, a great amount of management time is spent on the budget setting process. This time could be used, perhaps more effectively, elsewhere.
- Fails to overcome the age-old problem that some managers are more devious than others in trying to justify a larger budget than is really needed.

The best criteria for setting budgets are:

- To be clear about the firm's objectives and the strategy for achieving them. Departments with a key role to play in achieving objectives might expect an increase in the year's budget. Departments where no extra activity is required can expect their budget to be frozen, or perhaps cut back a little to release funds.
- To involve as many people as possible in the process. People will be more committed to reaching the targets if they have had a say in how the budget was set.
- To make the process as transparent as possible, so that everyone knows how decisions are reached. In a school or college, for example, an allowance of £20 per student per subject is far clearer than encouraging every department head to go and haggle with the Principal.

## 19.4 Advantages and disadvantages of budgeting

### ADVANTAGES

Budgets are a way to control and monitor costs. Senior managers will approve each department's budget and can then allow the budget holders to run their departments day by day. Only departments which are over budget need attract the regular attention of senior management.

A company-wide system of departmental budgets can be drawn together to give an overall picture for the firm. This is a vital tool in coordinating a firm's diverse activities. This is easy to achieve on modern computer networks or intranets. Every departmental budget spreadsheet can be linked with the company's master budget. The chief executive can therefore find out at the touch of a button what's going well or badly, and who is responsible.

Budgets are often said to have a motivational effect on staff. Budget holders who have the authority to decide how the budget is spent will feel valued and trusted. Meanwhile, the budget can be used as a target for departments, whether they are attempting to exceed budgeted sales or keep costs under the budgeted figure. Success gives a sense of achievement to those who have met their targets.

### DISADVANTAGES

Budgeting is not an exact tool because it is based on assumptions and predictions which are subject to error. If a budget is set incorrectly, it can be very demoralising for a manager who is attempting to achieve the impossible.

Clever (or powerful) managers may be able to convince their bosses to provide a higher budget than is really necessary. The incentive is clear; if you are given plenty of spending power it becomes easier to do well at your job. For example, a brand manager with a large advertising budget should be in a strong position to achieve the sales target. Unfortunately, managers with influence in the boardroom may achieve generous budgets at the cost of insufficient budgets for products or departments with higher growth prospects.

Managers may take short-term decisions that help meet current budgets at the cost of damaging future customer goodwill. For example, costs could be trimmed back to meet the budget by using materials of a slightly lower quality. This kind of short-termism may be particularly likely if managers are offered large bonuses for meeting or beating their budgets.

## 19.5 Other types of budgeting

### FLEXIBLE BUDGETING

Flexible budgeting adjusts the budgeted figures in line with the actual sales volume achieved. This ensures that variances show changes in costs rather than a mixture of costs and sales volumes. In the example below, how can a manager identify the cause of the cost overrun?

|  | Budget | Actual | Variance |
|---|---|---|---|
| Factory cost | £120,000 | £132,000 | £12,000 Adverse |

Costs are £12,000 higher than forecast, but that would be understandable if demand were up 10%. But if demand was as expected, the extra £12,000 costs must be due to paying more for the materials or for labour. Flexible budgets get round this problem. They automatically adjust all variable items to allow for changes in sales volume. For example, if this company had enjoyed a 10% rise in sales in the month, the flexed budget would adjust the budgeted figure by +10% and show:

|  | Budget | Actual | Variance |
|---|---|---|---|
| Factory cost | £132,000 | £132,000 | £0 |

## 19.6 Budgetary variances

Variance is the amount by which the actual result differs from the budgeted figure. It is usually measured each month, by comparing the actual outcome with the budgeted one. It is important to note that variances are referred to as adverse or favourable – not positive and negative. A **favourable variance** is one which leads to higher than expected profit (revenue up or costs down). An **adverse variance** is one which reduces profit, such as costs being higher than the budgeted level.

The following table shows when variances are adverse or favourable:

| VARIABLE | BUDGET | ACTUAL | VARIANCE |
|---|---|---|---|
| Sales of X | 150 | 160 | 10 Favourable |
| Sales of Y | 150 | 145 | 5 Adverse |
| Material costs | 100 | 90 | 10 Favourable |
| Labour costs | 100 | 105 | 5 Adverse |

The value of regular variance statements is that they provide an early warning. If a product's sales are slipping below budget, managers can respond by increasing marketing support, or by cutting back on production plans. In an ideal world, slippage could be noted in March, a new strategy put into place by May and a recovery in sales achieved by September. Clearly, no firm wishes to wait until the end of-year profit and loss account to find out that things went badly. An early warning can lead to an early solution.

## MANAGEMENT BY EXCEPTION

In a large company, with many separate cost centres, senior managers will have hundreds of budget statements to review each month. In order to avoid information overload, most budgeting systems work on the basis of management by exception. Senior managers will only concern themselves with departmental budgets which show large variances (probably adverse). In large companies management authority is usually delegated down through the organisation. Senior managers only get involved with problem areas or areas of great success.

ISSUES FOR **analysis**

- Variances are the key to analysing budgets. Once a variance between budgeted and actual figures has been identified, the analysis can begin. The important step is to ask why that variance occurred. Does the person responsible know the reason? Is it a one-off, or does this same person offer a different excuse each month for poor performance?
- Variance analysis is a means of identifying symptoms. It is down to the user of the variance figures to make a diagnosis as to the exact nature of any problem, and then to suggest the most appropriate cure.
- Although budgets and variances sound very focused upon numbers, they are rooted in everyday actions by people. Sales budgets will only be achieved if the salesforce is enthusiastic and well managed. Production costs will only be kept down if wastage is low and commitment is high. When analysing budgetary problems, therefore, managers soon find themselves looking at the quality of management in departments such as marketing and production.

## 19.7 Budgeting
### an evaluation

Budgets are a management tool. The way in which they are used can tell you a lot about a firm's **culture**. Firms with a strict autocratic culture will tend to use a tightly controlled budgetary system. Managers will have budgets imposed upon them and variances will be watched closely by supervisors. Organisations with a more open culture will use budgeting as an aid to discussion and empowerment.

Whatever the culture, if a manager is to be held accountable for meeting a budget, he or she must be given influence over setting it and control over reaching it.

Although budgets are set for future time periods, analysis of actual against budgeted performance can only take place after the event. This is true of all financial monitoring and this leads to doubts as to its effectiveness as a planning tool. Other measures may be far more reliable in predicting future performance – market research indicating growing levels of customer complaints may well be more useful in predicting future performance.

From an even broader perspective, it could be argued that budgets and other financial measures are unhelpful in some circumstances. Perhaps firms should look at their objectives before deciding on the most useful measure of performance. Financial measures are fine for firms attempting to maximise their profits, but sales figures will be more relevant for firms pursuing an objective of growth, whilst customer complaint levels will be particularly relevant to firms aiming for excellence in their levels of service.

**KEY terms**

**adverse variance** – when the variance between actual and budgeted figures results in lower profit.

**culture** – the attitudes and approaches that typify the way staff carry out their tasks.

**delegate** – pass authority down the hierarchy.

**favourable variance** – when the variance between actual and budgeted figures results in higher profits.

**variance analysis** – studies variances between actual and budgeted figures, looking for causes of those variances with a view to suggesting solutions.

**zero budgeting** – a system of setting budgets to zero every year and expecting budget holders to justify every pound of their budget.

**19.8 Workbook**

**UNIT 19 | BUDGETING**

# Exercises

## A. REVISION QUESTIONS
*(30 marks; 60 minutes)*

Read the unit, then answer:

1 Explain the meaning of the term 'budgeting'. *(2)*
2 List three advantages that a budgeting system brings to a company. *(3)*
3 Why is it valuable to have a yardstick against which performance can be measured? *(3)*
4 Explain what Peter Drucker means by calling budgeting 'management by self-control'. *(4)*
5 What are the disadvantages of a zero-based budgeting system? *(3)*
6 How might a firm respond to an increasingly adverse variance in labour costs? *(4)*
7 Explain what is meant by a 'favourable cost variance'. *(2)*
8 Why is management by exception a useful time-saving measure for management? *(3)*
9 Briefly explain how most companies actually set next year's budgets. *(3)*
10 Why should budget holders have a say in the setting of their budgets? *(3)*

## B. REVISION EXERCISES

### B1 Data Analysis

|  | January | | | February | | |
|---|---|---|---|---|---|---|
|  | B | A | V | B | A | V |
| Sales revenue | 140* | 150 | 10 | 180 | 175 | ? |
| Materials | 70 | 80 | (10) | 90 | 95 | ? |
| Other direct costs | 30 | 35 | (5) | 40 | 40 | 0 |
| Overheads | 20 | 20 | 0 | 25 | 22 | ? |
| Profit | 20 | 15 | (5) | ? | 18 | ? |

*All figures in £000s

**Questions** *(20 marks; 20 minutes)*
1 What are the five missing numbers from the variance analysis above? *(10)*
2 Outline one financial strength and two weaknesses in this data, from the company's viewpoint. *(6)*
3 How might a manager set about improving the accuracy of a sales budget? *(4)*

### B2 Data Response
Budget Data for Clinton and Collins Ltd. (£000s)

**Questions** *(25 marks; 30 minutes)*
1 Use the data to explain why February's profits were worse than expected. *(5)*
2 Why might Clinton and Collins Ltd have chosen to set monthly budgets? *(5)*
3 Explain how the firm might have set these budgets. *(6)*
4 The directors of Clinton and Collins Ltd knew that the recession was causing problems for the firm but were unsure as to whether things were improving or worsening. To what extent does the data suggest an improvement? *(9)*

### B3 Case Study
Foxbury Ltd is a manufacturer of bicycle parts, set up by three old friends in Oxfordshire:

- Russ Day is trained as an accountant and therefore fills the role of finance director
- Nigel Pearce is marketing director
- Nick Johns handles production and fulfils the role of managing director.

When they set up the business, two years ago, Russ convinced the others of the need for a budgetary system. They were won over by his arguments and a system was established whereby the three directors were given control of a budget – one for marketing, one for production and one for finance and administration. Russ monitored performance closely and was disappointed to see Nigel's marketing department overspending its budget. By the end of the first year's trading, Russ complained several times to Nigel that he was spending too much, but Nigel insisted that the frequent trips he made to Holland and Hong Kong were vital to building up a good relationship with customers. Before the start of the next financial year, the three directors met to try to agree next year's budget. Nigel insisted that the previous year's budget had been set too low. Russ again suggested that Nigel had failed to control his expenditure effectively.

Nick intervened, suggesting that as sales were buoyant, they could afford to increase all three budgets by

|  | January | | February | | March | | April | |
|---|---|---|---|---|---|---|---|---|
|  | B | A | B | A | B | A | B | A |
| Sales revenue | 160 | 144 | 180 | 156 | 208 | 168 | 240 | 188 |
| Materials | 40 | 38 | 48 | 44 | 52 | 48 | 58 | 54 |
| Other direct costs | 52 | 48 | 60 | 54 | 66 | 62 | 72 | 68 |
| Overheads | 76 | 76 | 76 | 78 | 76 | 80 | 76 | 80 |
| Profit | (8) | (18) | (4) | (20) | 14 | (22) | 34 | (14) |

the 20% that Nigel wanted. Nick felt that this was appropriate since labour and material costs had both increased substantially since last year. Russ was also happy with the suggestion, because although he didn't need any extra money this year, he would be happy to drive a larger company car and spend a little more on decorating his office. The directors agreed and the budget was set. At the end of that year, profits fell by 75% despite a healthy increase in sales.

**Questions** *(25 marks; 50 minutes)*

1 Explain the arguments Russ might have used to convince his colleagues of the need for a budgeting system. (6)
2 What problems does the case study indicate may arise from such a system? (5)
3 How might Foxbury Ltd's management seek to overcome these problems? (8)
4 Explain why profits fell so dramatically despite an increase in sales. (6)

# COST AND PROFIT CENTRES

## DEFINITION

A cost centre is a section, product or department of a business that can be held accountable for some of the costs of the business.

A profit centre is a part of the business for which a separate profit and loss account can be drawn up.

## 20.1 The purpose of cost centres and profit centres

**Cost centres**, like **profit centres**, are sections of a business than can be seen as being distinct from other operations of the firm. In a school, each subject department can be seen as a cost centre. The Business Studies department has its own salary, stationery and textbook costs. By dividing a large organisation into cost centres, it is possible to hold individual managers to account for the costs incurred in their departments.

The total costs of the business can be divided up among each of these cost centres. Similarly, part of the firm's revenues can be seen to be due to the operations of each profit centre. Cost centres can be the basis for deciding the price to charge for a product. Or even which products to continue producing, and which to kill off. The idea of using separate centres, instead of just looking at the firm as a whole, has several purposes:

- Accounting – management accounting depends on the availability of accurate information to be able to monitor the activities in all the areas of a business. By using cost centres for separate products or areas, individual performances can be more easily

The Max Factor cosmetics counter at the Daimaru department store in Kyoto (© Bob Krist/Corbis)

analysed. This allows firms to take corrective action wherever necessary.
- Organisational – the use of cost centres allows managers to see which areas of the business are working well, and which are underperforming. This helps senior managers make the right decisions to improve the overall running of the firm.
- Motivational – theorists argue that giving middle managers control over a distinct area of the firm's operations motivates them more strongly to fulfil their responsibility. They will be spurred on to make their area the most profitable in the business.

| ADVANTAGES OF COST AND PROFIT CENTRES | PROBLEMS OF COST AND PROFIT CENTRES |
|---|---|
| • Some control of operations is delegated to the local level, which can be motivating | • Parts of the firm can put themselves before the business as a whole |
| • The successes and failures of individual departments can be identified clearly | • The reason for good or bad performances may be external to the cost centre, and not under its control |
| • Problems can be traced more easily | • Not all costs and revenues can be associated directly with a particular part of the firm |
| • Decision making is aided, for example on setting prices | • They can create extra pressure on more junior managers |

Note that cost centres and profit centres are largely the same thing. The only difference is that cost centres only incur costs. Profit centres also generate revenues, therefore their profit can be calculated. For instance the Heinz market research department generates no sales and is therefore a cost centre. The soups division generates costs and revenues and can therefore be a profit centre.

## 20.2 Establishing cost and profit centres

The way in which a business divides itself up into cost centres will vary according to the circumstances of the firm. Some of the more common bases for cost centres are:

- A product – where a firm has several products that can be easily differentiated from each other, then the different products can each form a cost centre.
- A group of machines – a particular work area for which the inputs and outputs can be observed.
- A department – an area of activity within the business that performs a specific function.
- A location – if the firm is geographically spread, each separate location can be used as a cost centre.
- A person – some individuals may have responsibility for a specific area of operation and spending, and could be accountable themselves for the costs involved.

If a firm wishes to use cost centres, it will choose a basis that is appropriate for its own situation. A firm with several factories spread around the country may use location as the basis for its cost centres. One which produces a range of different products may be more interested in how each of its products are doing. So it will use the products as individual cost centres.

The aim of using cost centres is to provide managers with information to monitor the performance of the individual parts of the company. The choice of cost centre must be appropriate to the situation of the firm.

## 20.3 Types of cost

For the purpose of allocating costs to the various cost centres of the business, it is necessary to know which costs are direct, and which are indirect.

> *Direct costs are those costs which are linked completely to a specific product or area of operation.*

For example, a car manufacturer will have clear direct costs when it buys components from an outside firm, such as headlights or tyres. These costs can be attributed directly to the specific make and model of car being produced. This will provide managers with a

precise breakdown of the money spent on this product.

Alongside the direct costs of producing a car, the firm will also have costs that are not linked directly to the production of a particular item. These costs are often referred to as overheads. They cover a range of the firm's activities. For example, building a new factory that will produce a range of different models will be a cost the firm must pay, even though the money paid is not associated clearly with any one model.

> *Indirect costs are costs that are general to some or all areas of the business.*

Note that the distinction is not always a clear one – costs such as wages, depreciation and so on can be either direct or indirect, depending on individual circumstances.

> *Some common direct costs:*
> - *Wages of factory labour*
> - *Materials*
> - *Components*
> - *Depreciation of specialised machinery*
> - *Marketing specific to one product/cost centre*
>
> *Some common indirect costs:*
> - *Supervisors'/managers' wages/salaries*
> - *Running service departments such as personnel*
> - *Heating and lighting*
> - *Depreciation of general machinery*
> - *Administration costs*
> - *General marketing*
> - *Running expenses, such as telephone bills, rent*

## 20.4 Profit centres and financial rewards

Having divided up a large business into individual profit centres, it seems a logical step to offer bonuses related to the profits achieved. Each profit centre manager might be offered a bonus worth 5% of the annual profit achieved. Or every employee might be given an annual bonus based upon a proportion of the division's profit.

This method has advantages, because it provides incentives within teams small enough for each individual to feel that her/his own efforts matter. If you are one among 5,000 staff, you know that however hard you work, your own effort cannot have any significant effect on overall profit and therefore bonus levels; whereas if you are in a team of 18 people, individual effort and the team spirit will count for a great deal.

Problems arise, however, because business rarely runs smoothly. As an example, take the company

Cadbury Schweppes. In a hot summer, sales of chocolate slump while soft drink sales boom. So the Cadbury's Dairy Milk profit centre – whose staff may have been working hard and effectively all year – can find its profit and bonuses slumping for a reason outside its control. Fat cheques picked up by Schweppes staff would not help the mood of their Cadbury colleagues.

Furthermore, what if a new product developed by the New Product Department (a cost centre) was passed on to Brand Management Team C (a profit centre) for the latter to launch? And what if it was a huge success? How would the new product engineers feel about seeing the Team C marketing executives in their new Mercedes sports cars?

The point being made is a simple but crucial one. All financial reward systems risk creating a sense of acute unfairness or injustice. When they work well they can be highly effective, but they must always be thought through with very great care.

Analysis shows depth of understanding through the process of breaking things down. 'Profit' can be analysed by breaking it down into revenue and costs. Similarly, cost and profit centres can be analysed by showing a clear recognition that cost centres have different characteristics from profit centres. They are not one and the same, despite their similarities.

Cost centres generate no revenue (directly). Therefore costs can only be controlled in relation to a target or budget. This usually means that firms do not set up financial incentives for those who work within cost centres. The manager may receive praise for keeping costs within budget, but little else. Profit centres, on the other hand, can become hothouses. Managers press staff hard to achieve, achieve, achieve – all for the sake of the bonuses (and the greater status) that come from success.

Generally, this does not matter. Visitors to TGI Fridays know that the staff will press them to spend heavily. Some will enjoy the experience, others may find it offputting. No harm done. More serious, though, is when people are pressed hard to buy a type of mortgage or pension that is profitable to the supplier, but poor value for the consumer's money. This could blight a family's finances or a person's retirement. Profit centres can be too 'successful' at incentivising staff. Cost centres would rarely, if ever, share that drawback.

## 20.5 Cost centres
### an evaluation

The use of cost centres and the various methods for allocating overheads needs to be used with care. It ought not to be taken in isolation from all the other aspects of the firm. Determining the full cost of a product is difficult. Therefore it is vital to allow for other factors such as the marketing, human and social implications of a decision.

It is perhaps better to think of the costing methods as ways of finding out which questions to ask, rather than actually providing answers. If one product has a large share of the physical area of the business, does it use this space effectively? Are the large numbers of workers in a cost centre efficient, or would the product, and the firm as a whole, benefit from some capital investment? Only when such matters are considered can valid judgements about products or other cost centres be made.

**KEY terms**

**cost centre** – a department or section of an organisation to which specific costs can be allocated.

**costing** – dividing up production and selling costs into direct and indirect components.

**direct costs** – costs that can be attributed directly to a cost centre.

**indirect costs** – overheads such as rent which cannot be attributed to a specific cost centre.

**profit centre** – a department which generates costs and revenues, allowing a profit and loss account to be drawn up.

# Exercises

## A. REVISION QUESTIONS

*(25 marks; 30 minutes)*

Read the Unit, then answer the following.

1 State two benefits of dividing an organisation into profit centres. *(2)*
2 What is the difference between a cost centre and a profit centre? *(2)*
3 Why may the use of cost and profit centres help staff motivation? *(2)*
4 Cost centres help identify the cost per unit of each product made by a firm. Outline two possible benefits to the firm of having this data. *(4)*
5 Section 20.2 suggests five ways in which a firm can split itself up into cost or profit centres. Which would you think is the most appropriate for:
   a WHSmith retail division
   b Cadbury's chocolate products
   c a large department store, such as Harrods?
   Briefly state your reasoning. *(6)*
6 Explain the difference between direct and indirect costs. *(2)*
7 Decide whether each of these costs are direct or indirect:
   a a corporate advertising campaign
   b the salaries of the personnel department
   c the ingredients to make a product
   d the interest charges on the firm's loans
   e the electricity used to make the product. *(5)*
8 Broadly, the concept of direct and indirect costs can be said to be similar to the division between fixed and variable costs. Which is the best match?
   a Direct costs are similar to _____ costs. *(1)*
   b Indirect costs are similar to _____ costs. *(1)*

## B. REVISION EXERCISE

### B1 Data Response

Charli Beale started up beauty.com with just £2,000 while studying for her A Levels. The website started by offering cosmetics imported from Paris and Milan, although six months ago Charli started offering an own label range called C.B. From the start she made C.B. a separate profit centre and appointed an enthusiastic young executive to manage the brand. His first target was to achieve a break-even level by month six, which he has just managed (see figures for the latest month in the following table).

| | Imported | C.B. | Total |
|---|---|---|---|
| Revenue | £47,000 | £25,000 | £72,000 |
| Materials | £11,500 | £5,500 | £17,000 |
| Direct labour | £18,500 | £10,500 | £29,000 |
| Other direct costs | £8,000 | £6,000 | £14,000 |
| Total direct costs | £38,000 | £22,000 | £60,000 |
| Fixed costs | £5,500 | £3,000 | £8,500 |
| Profit | £3,500 | £0 | £3,500 |

**Questions** *(30 marks; 35 minutes)*

1 Explain what is meant by the term profit centre. *(2)*
2 Outline two reasons why a small business start-up may benefit especially from the use of profit centres. *(6)*
3 Examine how the 'enthusiastic young executive' might use the profit centre figures for the C.B. range? *(6)*
4 Using profit centres has allowed Charli to delegate authority.
   a What does this mean? *(2)*
   b Outline two possible disadvantages to Charli of delegating authority to her profit centre managers. *(6)*
5 Discuss whether traditional methods, such as profit centres, are really needed in the modern world of 'dot.com' businesses. *(8)*

### B2 Case Study

Nigel and Roger began their business – Schools Alive Ltd. – in 1994. It specialised in organising and running travel for student groups to Eastern Europe. Roger was brilliant at the organisational detail, while Nigel was expert at researching new destinations. Back in 1994 they provided dedicated tours of Prague and Budapest, aiming at three student sectors: art, history and business studies.

The business grew steadily, but really took off in 1997 when the boys were joined by two new shareholder/directors, Andrew and Siobhan, who injected £100,000 of additional finance into the business. At that point, Roger decided the complexity of the accounting process was making it harder to measure and control costs. He was no longer sure exactly what the costs were of a six day coach trip to Prague compared with a five day tour by plane to Moscow. At the same time, the rapid growth in the business was making it harder to price trips consistently. The problems came to a head when teachers at schools from Bristol and Middlesborough met in Prague and found that one group was being charged £165 and the other £220 for the exact same programme. Quite simply, Andrew had not known what Nigel was agreeing to.

Accordingly, Roger devised a new budgeting system. All air tours would come within a profit centre and be controlled by Nigel. All overseas coach tours would be controlled by Siobhan within her own profit centre. All other business, including new ideas for student trips and conferences in Britain, would fall within a profit centre led by Andrew. Roger's role would be to run the general office and to support the others by helping with costing and administration.

**Schools Alive Ltd. Sales and profit 1994–2000 (£m)**

There were some hiccups with the new system, because it relied on a much more organised, efficient approach to paperwork and invoices (which Nigel hated). Nevertheless, as shown in the sales figures, it helped the business grow dramatically.

**Questions** *(60 marks; 70 minutes)*

1 The text states that it was hard to 'measure and control costs'. Outline the implications of this for a small firm such as Schools Alive Ltd. *(8)*

2 Explain two possible reasons why a system of profit centres helped Schools Alive Ltd. *(8)*

3 An alternative way of organising the centres would have been to divide the schools in the country by region, and give Nigel the South East, Andrew the Midlands and the South West and Siobhan the North and Scotland. Consider the strengths and weaknesses of this approach compared with the one chosen by Roger. *(12)*

4 a Estimate the % change in sales and in profit between 1998 and 2000. Show your workings for both of these calculations. *(8)*

   b The bar chart shows two ways in which growth can be measured: sales and profit. Which do you consider to be the better way of measuring growth? Explain your reasoning. *(12)*

5 The text suggests that the new system of profit centres 'helped the business grow dramatically'. Evaluate the other financial and marketing factors that would be needed to achieve this result. *(12)*

# INTEGRATED FINANCE

## 21.1 Finance – an overview

### INTRODUCTION

Finance is an area of the syllabus people love or hate. Many students worry about the maths and so tend to avoid finance when possible. The maths is not all that complicated and it is worth putting some effort into learning how to do the financial calculations. A correct finance calculation can get you full marks. This is much harder to obtain with a written answer.

The calculations in themselves are only a means to an end. Businesses do financial calculations to help them to manage the business. In both coursework and examinations you should treat the figures the same way. When answering questions on finance and, even when revising, ask yourself:

- What do they show?
- What do they not show?
- What other information would help to explain the situation?

It is always worth considering that the finance answer is only part of the information needed to make an assessment of the situation. Remember that in a business, finance does not stand alone. It is always connected with other aspects of the business such as marketing or production. Controlling costs is not just important for profit. It also contributes to the marketing effort by enabling competitive pricing. If the business is to keep ahead, sufficient funds need to be generated both through profit and external finance raising.

### WHY STUDY FINANCE?

Finance is about managing the business. It is about the management of money in the business. The management techniques perform several functions:

- Some tell managers how the business is performing. These include profit and loss accounts and balance sheets.
- Some help managers to make decisions. Investment appraisal, break-even, cost and contribution analyses are included here.

- Some help managers to control the business. These include cash flow, budgeting and cost accounting.
- Some, such as accounting ratios, help managers to compare their business with other businesses or to look at how business performance is changing.

Finance is pretty fundamental to the whole business. A successful company will have sufficient day-to-day funds and will be achieving its objectives.

### WHO IS CONCERNED ABOUT FINANCE?

Finance is very much an internal activity. Unlike marketing there is no direct interaction with the consumer. However, external groups are interested in and affected by the financial health of the business. All stakeholders have a vested interest.

- Workers rely on the viability of the business to ensure that their jobs continue and that their wages remain competitive.
- Customers will look to the business to provide good quality goods at reasonable prices. This means that the company must remain financially viable so that it can invest in R&D and new machinery.
- Controlling costs will enable the business to control prices. Continuing viability is also important to the customer who needs aftercare or continuity of supply.
- Investors will be looking for a return on their capital and will want to know that the business is being financially well managed.
- Prospective investors will be interested in the past performance of the business and its potential in the future.
- The Government will want the business to succeed both as a source of employment and as a tax payer.
- The local community will also benefit from a viable business in its midst.

So a well-managed business will have a wide impact. Finance as a tool for good management will play its part. Financial decisions will impact on other aspects of the business and therefore are indirectly a part of the relationship with the customers and other external groups.

Getting the sums right is obviously the first requirement for the 'A' grade finance answer. However, getting higher grades requires more than just being able to do the calculations. It also requires an understanding of what the figures mean. The first part of this understanding is knowing where the figures came from. This will help in two ways.

1  If the numbers you are given to make the calculation are not exactly the ones you are used to, you will be able to get back to the figures you need. For example, investment appraisal calculations are normally based on net cash flow figures. An understanding of how net cash flow is calculated will enable you to do the calculation if you are given cost and revenue figures.

2  If you understand where the figures came from you will be able to make some assessment of their validity. Are the basic figures actual or estimated? Knowing this will help you to comment sensibly on the results. A cash flow forecast will nearly always be based on estimated figures. However, the revenue figures may be contractually agreed with the customer and will therefore be much more reliable than best guesses.

Another important consideration is understanding what is included in the figures and what is not. The figures may not tell the whole story. An 'A' grade student will know that the figures may be only part of the picture and will look for other information. Two businesses may have identical sales this year but what about future prospects? One may be facing fierce competition from a new rival or experiencing a period of labour unrest. The other may have no threats and so faces a much more healthy outlook. So the 'A' grade student will put the figures into the wider perspective before commenting on the results. This is particularly important in case study and report papers and is necessary to demonstrate an understanding of the integrative nature of business.

## ISSUES IN FINANCE

There are several recurrent themes in finance. Being able to discuss these will often help to give a deeper, more evaluative, answer, to a finance question.

### ISSUE 1    The importance of profit

Profit is clearly important to a business. It is necessary for the business to continue and an essential requirement for growth. However, it does not have to be the overriding consideration and many businesses balance other objectives with the profit motive. Some small businesses may fulfil a personal need to survive financially with other personal needs such as enjoying work. Larger businesses may balance the profit made with the requirement to maintain good public relations.

Businesses may forego immediate profit in order to put in place strategies for growth or survival or increased profit in the future.

Profit also does not have to be continuous. Many new businesses take some time to become profitable. Many existing businesses may have periods when they make no profit and may even show losses. As long as liquidity is maintained the business will be able to survive making a loss at least in the short term.

### ISSUE 2    The ethics of profitability

Newspapers contain much discussion about the ethics of profitability. Businesses need profit, but how much and at what cost? What balance should be achieved between profit and issues such as the environment or exploitation of workers? Answering this question will require a balancing of the various interests involved. When answering a question involving ethics it is important to look at all sides of the issue and to avoid becoming emotionally involved with one point of view. This may be very difficult if you have strong beliefs about an issue such as animal welfare. By all means express your views but remember to balance them with the other side of the case. Animal welfare is important but what about the jobs of people in the industries? What about increased costs passed on to consumers who may not be able to afford to pay more? Should the views of one small group change things for everyone?

### ISSUE 3    The importance of liquidity

Understanding this issue requires an understanding of the difference between liquidity and profit. Liquidity is about having access to sufficient cash on a day-to-day basis to meet the business's commitments. Even if the cash is not available within the business, all is not lost if it is able to generate the required cash from external sources. Poor liquidity is not just a short-term problem. Unless the business is properly funded the problem will keep returning. It is essential that the business has sufficient working capital for its short- and long-term needs.

### ISSUE 4    Is financial management only for large businesses?

While larger companies have the resources to employ financial experts, good financial management is essential for all businesses. Many new businesses fail because of poor financial management. This is the commonest cause of early business failure. Smaller businesses may well need tighter financial management. They will not have the resources to buffer the business if mistakes are made. They are also less likely to have access to outside funding to bail them out in difficult times. Small firms may also have a smaller product range which means financial risks are more concentrated. However, as the business grows there will be a widening gap between ownership and control. Financial management systems will be necessary to keep control of this growing business. Financial analysis will enable the business to evaluate new developments and ensure that they contribute positively to the business.

## ISSUE 5 Financial information cannot be trusted

Many people suspect that the published accounts of large firms are manipulated. They show what the company wants the outside world to see. To some extent this is true. Firms can 'massage' the figures to a certain extent to make the liquidity or profitability look more or less favourable. They may wish to do this to even out profitability over several years to minimise the tax payable. They may wish to convince outsiders that the company is in a better position than it really is. However, the scope for this window dressing is limited. Businesses have to legally conform to certain financial reporting requirements. All limited company reports must be audited by an independent accountant. This generally ensures that the figures are accurate and a true representation of the company's position. However, there may be situations where the auditors are unaware of questionable business activities. As auditors are outside agencies they depend on the company giving them correct information. Their scope for investigation is limited. Although this was the defence given by Arthur Andersen when blamed for the collapse of Enron in 2001/2002, few were willing to accept it. These days, accounting statements must be right.

•••••••••••••••••••••••••••••••••••••••••••••••••••••

# Finance

## A. SHORT-ANSWER QUESTIONS

1 List three uses for company accounts. (3)
2 Why is profit important to a business? (2)
3 What is the difference between profit and cash flow? (2)
4 How can an understanding of contribution help a business? (2)
5 State two possible causes of a negative materials variance. (2)
6 List the two most likely sources of finance for a new business. (2)
7 List and discuss two ways a business could finance expansion. (6)
8 What does a cash flow forecast show? (2)
9 How can cash flow forecasts help a business? (4)
10 Identify and discuss two ways a firm can deal with a predicted future cash flow shortage. (6)
11 What does break-even analysis show? (2)
12 Distinguish between fixed and variable costs. (2)
13 How do you calculate unit contribution? (2)
14 What is the purpose of budgeting? (2)
15 What is a cost centre? (1)

## B. DATA RESPONSE QUESTIONS

UNIT 21 | INTEGRATED FINANCE

### B1 Massey Boots

Massey Boots produces boots for working men but have recently began selling their boots for general wear. It has been surprised by the interest shown by teenagers and young adults. At the moment it produces three types of boots, but increased demand has placed considerable strain on the production facilities. The production manager believes that if the company only produced two types of boot, the production facilities could be used more efficiently. Then some of the problems it is facing at the moment could be reduced. It has decided to cut the range to two models and needs to decide which models to continue producing. It is confident of selling all the boots it makes. The machinery and labourforce can be used to manufacture any of the boots without the need for additional expenditure. The maximum number of boots that can be produced is 300,000 pairs. The finance department has produced the following figures.

| Type of boot: | Toughman | Roughneck | Cruncher |
|---|---|---|---|
| Sales per year | 150,000 | 80,000 | 70,000 |
| Selling price | £45 | £40 | £60 |
| **Costs** | | | |
| Direct materials per boot | £12 | £8 | £18 |
| Direct labour per boot | £13 | £10 | £12 |
| Total fixed costs are £600,000. | | | |

**Questions**

**1** Calculate the unit and total contribution for each type of boot. *(6)*
**2** If the factory only made one type of boot calculate the break-even level of production for each of the three types. *(6)*
**3** Using the calculations comment on the production manager's suggestion. *(8)*

## C. CASE STUDY

### The Café at All Saints

The Café in the crypt at All Saints Church has had a very successful first year. The director of the vegetarian café is Bill Sewell. He has overseen the development of this new venture. The bulk of the £1.7 million investment came from English Heritage, the Heritage Lottery Fund and fund-raising initiatives at All Saints. Situated in the centre of the market town of Hereford, the Café is conveniently placed for shoppers and tourists. The only other vegetarian restaurant, The Pulse, closed in the spring. Bill Sewell doesn't think that All Saints caused The Pulse to close, but its closing has left the field clear. Sales for the first year are expected to be £240,000. This compares with Sewell's prediction of £100,000 and the bank's more cautious estimate of £70,000.

The pattern of trade varies considerably. August was busy, September very quiet and December staggeringly busy. The winter months were very quiet. But with visitors coming back to the town in spring and summer, the Café is now having problems fitting everybody in.

The average spend per head rarely goes above £2.50 so numbers are critical to the success of the business. Bill Sewell attributes the high demand to its position, the attractiveness of the interior and the food on offer. Customer surveys have revealed quite a few people coming to Hereford specifically because of the Café. The two main customer groups are elderly people and mothers with babies and small children. Bill Sewell hopes to attract professionals to the Café by targeting them with advertising in the coming year. He has decided not to operate a sandwich round to local offices as it is too time consuming and would strain the limited kitchen space and staff.

Although initially there was a cool response from local traders to the Café, most are now convinced it is an asset to the town. Many local growers want the Café to use their produce. Bill sees this as a good development and sees the possibility of Hereford developing as a centre for delicious food and, of course, the local product, cider.

As well as underestimating the sales Bill also underestimated the costs. They are about double his original estimate. Food costs are about 25% of turnover and staffing about 40%. Other costs are about £45,000. Some of these, such as laundry costs, relate to turnover. Others are fixed overheads, but still seem too high. Bill is hoping to reduce the labour figure to 35% of turnover and to reduce the other costs by 10%. The raw material costs are unlikely to change as Bill feels that it is important to maintain quality.

The staff at All Saints are optimistic for the future. They are trying different approaches to widen the customer base. One initiative has been special one-off evening meals. Bill believes these have been successful even though they have not been profitable. They have been useful as publicity and to test the market. Bill feels that the strategy for the second year should be to continue steadily with no radical moves.

**Source:** *The Grocer,* 11/6/98

**Questions** *(50 marks; 70 minutes)*
**1** In what way is this enterprise different from most businesses in terms of its funding? *(2)*
**2** How might a similar business raise finance? *(4)*
**3** Using the figures given, calculate the first year profit. *(4)*
**4** If turnover remains the same and Bill achieves his cost reductions, what is the estimated profit for the second year? *(2)*
**5** Both turnover and cost figures were underestimated. Why might this have happened? *(8)*
**6** How should the business forecast next year's figures? *(8)*
**7** In spite of its obvious success, the Café clearly faces some business challenges. Identify two of these and evaluate ways that the business might tackle them. *(12)*
**8** Bill has no specific plan for next year but plans to continue the same way as last year. Do you think this is a good idea? *(10)*

# PRODUCTIVITY AND PERFORMANCE

### DEFINITION

Productivity is a measure of efficiency; it measures the output of a firm in relation to its inputs.

## 22.1 Productivity – what is it?

The productivity of a firm is a measurement of its efficiency. It measures output in relation to inputs. A firm can increase its efficiency by producing more with the same inputs or producing the same amount with fewer inputs.

The most common measure is **labour productivity**. This measures the amount a worker produces over a given time. For example, an employee might make 10 pairs of jeans in an hour. Measuring productivity is relatively easy in manufacturing where the number of goods can be counted. In the service sector it is not always possible to measure anything tangible. Productivity in services can be measured in some cases (the number of customers served, number of patients seen, the sales per employee). But how can the productivity of a receptionist be measured?

When considering a firm's efficiency it is important to distinguish between productivity and total output. By hiring more employees the firm may increase the total output, but this does not necessarily mean that the output per employee has gone up. Similarly, it is possible to have less total output with higher productivity because of a fall in the number of workers. Imagine, for example, 20 employees producing 40 tables a week in a furniture company. Their productivity on average is 2 tables per week. If 5 employees make 15 tables the overall output has fallen, but the output *per worker* has risen. This situation of falling output but rising productivity happened in many manufacturing companies in the UK in the early 1990s. Faced with high interest rates, high exchange rates and a recession, many companies were forced to rationalise their organisations. This led to high levels of redundancies and extra work for those who still had a job. The result was that there were fewer people working but at the same time there was often higher output per person.

### PRODUCTIVITY

In 2002 for the sixth year in succession Nissan's Sunderland factory was acknowledged as the most productive in Europe. Its productivity level of 95 cars per worker per year was more than double the rates achieved by European rivals such as Rover, Volkswagen and Peugeot. However, even the Sunderland plant achieves only half the productivity of the world's best – operated by Mitsubishi Motors of Japan. Of the top 10 plants in the world, the first 9 are in Japan. The tenth is in South Korea. Each worker at Mitsubishi's best plant produces almost 180 cars per year. The most efficient plant in North America – Honda's Marysville factory in Ohio – is similarly behind its Asian rivals, producing 96 cars per employee.

What might explain the productivity differences? The age of the factories provides a part-explanation, with those at the top tending to be the newest plants. The type of car is also important. There is more work in producing a Jaguar than a Fiat. Researchers usually conclude, though, that the main explanation is the quality of management.

## 22.2 Why does productivity matter?

The output per employee is a very important measure of a firm's performance. It has a direct impact on the cost of producing a unit. If productivity increases, then, assuming wages are unchanged, the labour cost per unit will fall. Imagine that in one factory employees make 5 pairs of shoes a day but in another one they make 10 pairs a day. Assuming the wage rate is the same this means the labour cost of a pair of shoes

| | DAILY WAGE RATE | PRODUCTIVITY RATE (PER DAY) | WAGE COST (PER PAIR) |
|---|---|---|---|
| Factory 1 | £50 | 5 | £10 |
| Factory 2 | £50 | 10 | £5 |

will be halved in the second factory (see the table above). With lower labour costs this firm is likely to be in a better competitive position.

By increasing productivity a firm can improve its competitiveness. It can either sell its products at a lower price or keep the price as it was and enjoy a higher profit margin. This is why firms continually monitor their productivity relative to their competitors and, where possible, try to increase it. However, they need to make sure that quality does not suffer in the rush to produce more. It may be necessary to set both productivity and quality targets.

## 22.3 How to increase productivity

### INCREASE INVESTMENT IN MODERN EQUIPMENT

With more modern or more sophisticated machines and better production processes, output per worker should improve. Many modern factories have relatively few production workers. Mechanisation and automation are everywhere. However, firms face financial constraints and should be cautious about assuming that mechanisation guarantees higher profits. In the 1980s the American car giant General Motors invested billions of dollars in robotic production lines. Breakdowns meant they never proved as efficient as intended. More importantly, when customer buying habits switched to smaller cars, the machines proved much less flexible than humans. The investment proved unprofitable and by the early 1990s the company was close to financial failure.

It is also true to say that many people call for new technology when in fact more output can be squeezed out of the existing equipment. It may prove more efficient to run the machines for longer, spend more on careful maintenance to prevent breakdowns and discuss how to improve working practices. Firms can often achieve significant productivity gains without new equipment. This is the reason for the success of the **kaizen** approach taken in many firms. Important benefits can be achieved from what seem like relatively small changes to the way the firm operates rather than large-scale investment in technology.

### IMPROVE THE ABILITY LEVEL OF THOSE AT WORK

To increase productivity a firm may need to introduce more training for its employees. A skilled and well-trained workforce is likely to produce more and make fewer mistakes. Employees should be able to complete the task more quickly and not need as much supervision or advice. They should be able to solve their own work-related problems and may be in a better position to contribute ideas on how to increase productivity further.

However, firms are often reluctant to invest in training because employees may leave and work for another firm once they have gained more skills. Training also involves higher costs in the short run, which the business may not be able to afford, and the actual training period may cause disruptions to the normal flow of work. There is also a danger that the training will not provide sufficient gains to justify the initial investment. So any spending in this area needs to be properly costed and researched. Simply training people for the sake of it is obviously of limited value. However, in general, UK firms do not have a particularly good record in training. More investment here could probably have a significant effect on the UK's productivity levels.

It should also be remembered that elaborate training may not be necessary for a firm which recruits the right people. Great care must be taken in the selection process to find staff with the right skills and attitudes. A firm with a good reputation locally will find it much easier to pick the best people. This is why many firms take great care over their relations with the local community.

### IMPROVE EMPLOYEE MOTIVATION

Professor Herzberg once said that most people's idea of a fair day's work was less than half what they could give. If they wanted to. The key to success, he felt, was to create the circumstances in which people wanted to give all they could to the job. His suggestions on how to provide job enrichment are detailed in Unit 23.

There is no doubt that motivation matters. A motivated salesforce may achieve twice the sales level of an unmotivated one. A motivated computer technician may correct twice the computer faults of an unmotivated one. And, in both cases, overall business performance will be affected.

### THE ROLE OF MANAGEMENT

The management's style and ability can have a significant impact on motivation and on how effectively resources are used. Good managers can bring about substantial productivity gains through well-organised work, the effective management of people and the coordination of resources. Bad managers can lead to wastage, inefficiency and low productivity.

Perhaps the key management role is to identify increasing productivity as a permanent objective. For example, the Japanese bulldozer company Komatsu set a target of a 10% productivity increase every year, until the world-leading American producer Caterpillar had been overhauled. In many firms, productivity is not a direct target. The focus, day by day, is on production, not productivity. After all, it is production which ensures customer orders are fulfilled. An operations manager, faced with a 10% increase in orders, may simply ask the workforce to do overtime. The work gets done; the workforce is happy to earn extra money; and it's all rather easy to do. Harder by far to reorganise the workplace to make production more effective. Managers whose main focus is on the short term, therefore, think of production not productivity.

## 22.4 Problems increasing productivity

Firms often struggle to increase their productivity. In some cases this is because managers are failing to use their resources effectively. In other cases there are genuine obstacles. The firm's equipment and the quality of its workforce, for example, can limit the maximum output per worker. In the long run the firm can invest in training and more modern technology (assuming it has the necessary funds) but in the short run it may well be constrained.

Managers may also face resistance from the workers. This is because productivity gains may be at the expense of jobs. If new working practices enable employees to produce 10% more but the overall number of orders has not increased, the firm may have to make some employees redundant. By increasing productivity, therefore, the employees may in effect be working themselves out of a job. Consequently, when management talk of the need to increase productivity, employees are often quite suspicious. On the other hand, if productivity is not increased, the firm may struggle to compete and *everyone's* job may be under threat.

The need to be competitive seems to be increasingly clear to employees, possibly because of much greater international competition than in the past. As a result, negotiations between management and workers over productivity have tended to become more cooperative. Both sides now appear to appreciate the need to improve the firm's performance and to realise that this requires greater productivity. This may not lead to unemployment provided the firm can increase its overall number of orders – and to do this it must increase competitiveness! Greater productivity may, therefore, increase long-term job opportunities rather than destroy them. It is certainly true that a firm which fails to boost productivity as much as its rivals will find it harder to compete.

If greater productivity does lower the unit cost and lead to a higher profit margin, workers are naturally eager to share in these gains. This is why pay and productivity are often linked in pay negotiations. Employees may accept the need to boost productivity but in return negotiate a pay increase.

The end of a production line © Richmond Foods

When answering a case study or essay it might be useful to consider the following points:

- Productivity is an important determinant of a firm's international competitiveness because it can have a significant impact on unit costs.
- High productivity does not in itself guarantee that a firm is competitive – it also depends on other factors such as the cost of materials, product quality, product design, good marketing and external factors such as the exchange rate.
- The productivity within an industry will depend on a combination of factors such as training, capital equipment and production techniques. The productivity of UK firms is typically quite low compared with American, German or Japanese competitors.

The importance of productivity to a firm depends primarily on the level of value added involved. Top-price perfumes such as Chanel have huge profit margins. Production costs are a tiny proportion of the selling price. Therefore a 10% productivity increase might have only a marginal effect on profit and virtually none on the competitiveness of the brand. For mass market products in competitive markets, high productivity is likely to be essential for survival. A 5% cost advantage might make all the difference. Therefore, when judging an appropriate recommendation for solving a business problem, a judgement is required as to whether boosting productivity is a top priority for the business concerned.

## 22.5 Productivity and performance
### an evaluation

Greater labour productivity can lead to greater efficiency and higher profitability. This is because, other things being equal, it lowers the labour cost per unit. However, productivity is only one factor which contributes to a firm's success. A firm must also ensure it produces a good quality product, that it is marketed effectively and that costs are controlled. There is little point increasing productivity by 20% if at the same time you pay your staff 30% more. Similarly, there is no point producing more if there is no actual demand. Higher productivity, therefore, contributes to better performance but needs to be accompanied by effective decision making throughout the firm.

**KEY terms**

**capacity** – total output which could be produced with existing resources.

**capital intensive** – high level of capital equipment compared to labour.

**kaizen** – a Japanese term meaning 'continuous improvement'. Regular, small increases in productivity may achieve more (and be less disruptive) than major changes to working methods.

**labour intensive** – high level of labour input compared to the amount of capital equipment.

**labour productivity** – output per worker.

# Exercises

## A. REVISION QUESTIONS
*(40 marks; 70 minutes)*

Read the unit, then answer:

1 What is meant by the term 'productivity'? (3)
2 Why may it be hard to measure the productivity of staff who work in service industries? (4)
3 How does productivity relate to labour costs per unit? (4)
4 Explain how a firm might be able to increase its employees' productivity. (4)
5 How can increased investment in machinery help to boost productivity? (3)
6 Identify two factors which help and two factors which constrain your productivity as a student. (4)
7 Outline the likely effect of increased motivation on the productivity of a teacher. (5)
8 Calculate the change in productivity at BDQ Co since last year: (4)

|  | Output | Number of Staff |
| --- | --- | --- |
| Last year | 32,000 | 50 |
| This year | 30,000 | 40 |

9 Explain how motivation and productivity might be linked. (4)
10 Explain how productivity can be linked to unit labour costs. (5)

## B. REVISION EXERCISES

### B1 Data Response

**Productivity**

In 1997, Europe's most efficient car plant was the Nissan factory in Sunderland. Its productivity level of 98 cars per worker was three times higher than Rover's Longbridge plant. The implications of this difference are enormous. Assuming workers at both plants are paid £25,000 a year, the labour costs per car are as follows:

|  | Labour Cost per Worker | Cars per Worker* | Labour Cost per Car |
| --- | --- | --- | --- |
| Nissan, Sunderland | £25,000 | 98 | £255 |
| Rover, Longbridge | £25,000 | 33 | £758 |

*Source: Economist Intelligence Unit, 1998

Clearly, having labour costs which are treble the Nissan figures makes it much harder for Rover to compete effectively in the mass market.

Among the explanations offered for this big difference in productivity are:

● better design – Japanese cars are designed with fewer components than British ones

● more reliable plant – Nissan's Sunderland plant has an exceptionally low rate of stoppage, partly because it is quite new and partly because of careful maintenance

● excellent workforce management and motivation at Nissan.

**Questions** *(30 marks; 35 minutes)*
1 Explain how productivity affects labour costs per unit. (4)
2 Outline how each of the three 'explanations offered for this big difference' could affect productivity. (12)
3 Explain two other possible reasons why the Sunderland plant has higher productivity than Rover. (6)
4 Analyse the benefits Nissan can derive from being able to compete more effectively in the market than Rover. (8)

### B2 Case Study

**Going Potty**

Fabienne de Bruges was trying to explain the need to boost productivity to the employees at her ceramics factory, FB Ltd. Relations between Fabienne and her staff had not been good in recent years. The company was not doing well and she blamed the workers. 'On average you work 8 hours a day at £5 an hour and produce around 160 pots each. Meanwhile at Frandon I am told they produce 280 pots a day. Can't you see that this makes it cheaper for them and if things go on like this we'll be out of business? You need to work much harder to get our unit costs down! I know you are expecting to get a pay rise this year but I cannot afford it until you produce more; then we'll think about it.'

Jeff Battersby, the spokesperson for the employees, was clearly annoyed by Fabienne's tone. 'Firstly, Ms de Bruges, have you ever considered that if you paid us more we might produce more for you? I'm not surprised productivity is higher at Frandon – they get about £56 a day. There's no point demanding more work from us if you are not willing to pay for it – we're not slaves you know. If you paid us £7 an hour like Frandon I reckon we could increase productivity by 50%. However, that's not the only issue: they've got better equipment. It's not our fault if the kilns don't work half the time and take an age to heat up. Sort out the equipment and our pay and you'll soon see productivity improve. Why not *ask* us next time instead of jumping to conclusions?'

**Questions** *(60 marks; 75 minutes)*
1 a FB Ltd employs 50 pot makers whilst Frandon Ltd employs 30 people in production. Calculate the total output for each of the two companies. (4)
  b With reference to FB Ltd and Frandon Ltd, explain the difference between 'total output' and 'productivity'. (6)

**2 a** Calculate the average labour cost per pot at FB Ltd if employees are paid £5 an hour and their daily output is 160 pots each. *(4)*

**b** What is the wage cost per pot at Frandon? (Assume an 8-hour day.) *(3)*

**c** Analyse the short- and long-term benefits to Frandon of its lower labour costs per unit. *(12)*

**d** Jeff Battersby claims that if the employees at FB Ltd were paid £7 an hour their productivity would increase 50%. What would the unit wage cost be then? *(5)*

**3** Would you recommend Fabienne increases the pay of her employees to £7 an hour? Justify your answer. *(12)*

**4** Discuss the possible gains from involving employees in discussions about how to improve productivity. *(14)*

# MOTIVATION IN THEORY

## DEFINITION

One key theorist (Professor Herzberg) believes motivation occurs when people do something because they want to do it. Others think of motivation as the desire to achieve a result. The difference between these two definitions is important and should become clear during this unit.

## 23.1 Introduction

In February 1996 Fulham Football Club was placed 95th in the League, one place away from relegation to the Vauxhall Conference. When the club's centre forward was booked in a home game, the home fans shouted off, off, off! The club's manager was shuffled to one side and a new one appointed, Micky Adams.

One year later Fulham sat on top of the 3rd division and the centre forward was the fans' hero – one of the Football League's top goal scorers. What had happened?

The new manager had made a few free transfer signings, but the team was largely the same. Their pay had not risen, nor had a new bonus scheme been introduced. The key difference was in the players' motivation. They had found a new spirit, a new confidence, a new will to win. The transformation was purely psychological.

Later, Micky Adams did the same again at Brighton and at Leicester City. In football, so in business. Motivation matters. This is why it merits a unit to itself – and why many consider motivation theory to be the most important topic within Business Studies.

## 23.2 FW Taylor and scientific management

Although there were earlier pioneers, the starting point for the study of motivation is FW Taylor (1856–1917). As with most of the other influential writers on this subject, Taylor was American. His influence over the twentieth century world has been massive. Much business practice in America, Europe, Japan and the former Communist countries is still rooted in his writing and work.

A recent biography of Taylor is titled *The One Best Way*. This sums up neatly Taylor's approach to management. He saw it as management's task to decide exactly how every task should be completed. Then to devise the tools needed to enable the worker to achieve the task as efficiently as possible. This method is evident today in every McDonald's in the world. Fries are cooked at 175 degrees for exactly three minutes, then a buzzer tells employees to take them out and salt them. Throughout every McDonald's are a series of dedicated, purpose-built machines for producing milkshakes, toasting buns, squirting chocolate sauce and much else. Today, one hundred years after his most active period working in industry, FW Taylor would feel very much at home ordering a Big Mac.

So, what was Taylor's view of the underlying motivations of people at work? How did he make sure that the employees worked effectively at following 'the one best way' laid down by managers?

Taylor believed that people work for only one reason – money. He saw it as the task of the manager to devise a system which would maximise efficiency. This would generate the profit to enable the worker to be paid a higher wage. Taylor's view of human nature was that of 'economic man'. In other words people were motivated only by the economic motives of self-interest. Therefore a manager could best motivate a worker by offering an incentive (a 'carrot') or a threat (the 'stick'). One can view Taylor as a manipulator or even a bully. But he believed his methods were in the best interests of the employees themselves.

Taylor's influence stemmed less from his theories than his activities. He was a trained engineer who acted as a very early management consultant. His methods were as follows:

- Observe workers at work, recording and timing what they do, when they do it and how long they take over it (this became known as time and motion study).
- Identify the most efficient workers and see how they achieve greater efficiency.
- Break the task down into small component parts which can be done quickly and repeatedly.
- Devise equipment specifically to speed up tasks.
- Set out exactly how the work should be done in future; 'each employee', Taylor wrote, 'should receive every day clear-cut, definite instructions as to what

he is to do and how he is to do it, and these instructions should be exactly carried out, whether they are right or wrong.'

- Devise a pay scheme to reward those who complete or beat tough output targets, but penalises those who cannot or will not achieve the productivity Taylor believed was possible.

As an engineer, Taylor was interested in practical outcomes, not in psychology. There is no reason to suppose he thought greatly about the issue of motivation. The effect of his ideas was profound, though. Long before the publication of his 1911 book *The Principles of Scientific Management*, Taylor had spread widely his managerial practices of careful measurement, monitoring and – above all else – control. Before Taylor, skilled workers chose their own ways of working and had varied, demanding jobs. After Taylor, workers were far more likely to have limited, repetitive tasks; forced to work at the pace set by a manager or consultant engineer.

To maximise the efforts put in by workers, Taylor devised an incentive system known as differential **piece-rate**. This offered a meagre payment per unit produced. Beyond a threshold, though, the payment became generous. For example:

- 2p per unit for the first 500 per day
- 5p per unit all those above 500 per day.

The threshold was set at a level at which those producing 500 received barely a living wage. Those unable to keep up even that pace would have no alternative but to find another job. The incentive to achieve 700 or so

per day was massive. It would mean earning double the rate earned by those on 500 per day. Despite Taylor's enthusiasm for this approach, it was resented so bitterly by workers that it usually had to be abandoned soon after introduction. Piece-rate itself, of course, lives on today.

Among those influenced by Taylor was Henry Ford. His Model T was the world's first mass produced motor car. By 1911 the Ford factory in Detroit, USA was already applying Taylor's principles of high **division of labour**, purpose-built machinery and rigid management control. When Ford introduced the conveyor belt in 1913, he achieved the ultimate Taylorite idea – men's pace of work dictated by a mechanical conveyor belt, the speed of which was set by management.

Beyond America, Mussolini was an admirer of Ford. So was Stalin. Communist factories in Eastern Europe, Russia and China imitated Taylor's methods. In every case the result was a huge improvement in productivity for several years. Though it was also commonly the case that workers eventually rebelled against being treated like machines. **Trade union** membership thrived in factories run on Taylorite lines, as workers wanted to organise against the suffocating lives they were leading at work. Fortunately, in many Western countries further developments in motivation theory pointed to new, more people-friendly approaches.

## TAYLOR LIVES ON

*Business*

*IN*

In June 2002 Websense announced a boom in sales of their software for monitoring and blocking staff access to web sites. Apparently the software is bought by human resource managers to check up on staff. What do sales of 'web spies' say about modern business? Nearly 100 years ago the Ford Motor factories employed 'spotters' to monitor the number of breaks taken by each worker, and to check on workers' interest in, or membership of, trade unions. Ford had followed FW Taylor's insistence upon controlling every aspect of the workplace. If staff are so bored that surfing the web seems fun, perhaps human resource departments should consider enriching the job rather than putting tougher control systems in place.

### 23.3 Elton Mayo and the human relations approach

Elton Mayo (1880–1949) was a medical student who became an academic with a particular interest in people in organisations. An Australian, he moved to America

Early days of mass production at Ford: the assembly line
(© Corbis–Bettman/UPI)

in 1923. His methods were heavily influenced by FW Taylor. An early investigation of a spinning mill in Pennsylvania identified one department with labour turnover of 250% compared with 6% elsewhere in the factory. His Taylorite solution was to prescribe work breaks. These had the desired effect.

Mayo moved on to work at the Hawthorne plant of Western Electric Company in Chicago. His investigations there are known as the Hawthorne Experiments.

He was called in to Hawthorne to try to explain the findings of a previous test into the effects of lighting upon productivity levels. The lighting conditions for one work group had been varied while those for another had been held constant. The surprise was that whatever was done to the lighting, production rose in *both* groups. This proved that there was more to motivation and efficiency than purely economic motives.

Between 1927 and 1932 Mayo conducted a series of experiments at Hawthorne. The first is known as the Relay Assembly Test. Six volunteer female assembly staff were separated from their workmates. A series of experiments was carried out. The results were recorded and discussed with the women. Every 12 weeks a new working method was tried. The alternatives included:

- different bonus methods, such as individual versus group bonuses
- different rest periods
- different refreshments
- different work layout.

Before every change, the researchers discussed the new method fully with the operators. Almost without exception productivity increased with every change. At the end, the group returned to the original method (48-hour, 6-day week with no breaks) and output went up to the highest yet! Not only that, but the women claimed they felt less tired than they had at the start.

The experiments had started rather slowly, with some resistance from the operatives. Progress became much more marked when one member of the group retired. She was replaced by a younger woman who quickly became the unofficial leader of the group.

## MAYO'S CONCLUSIONS

- The women gained satisfaction from their freedom and control over their working environment.
- 'What actually happened was that six individuals became a team and the team gave itself wholeheartedly and spontaneously to cooperation in the experiment' (E. Mayo, 1949).
- Group norms (expectations of one another) are crucial and may be influenced more by informal than official group leaders.
- Communication between workers and managers and worker-to-worker influences morale and output.
- Workers are affected by the degree of interest shown in them by their managers; the influence of this upon motivation is known as 'the Hawthorne effect'.

The consequences of Mayo's work were enormous. He influenced many researchers and writers, effectively opening up the fields of industrial psychology and industrial sociology. Many academics followed Mayo's approach in what became known as the human relations school of management.

Businesses also responded to the implications of Mayo's work for company profitability and success. If teamwork, communications and managerial involvement were that important, firms reasoned that they needed an organisational structure to cope. In Taylor's era, the key person was the engineer. The winners from Mayo's work were personnel departments. They grew throughout America and Britain in the 1930s, 40s and 50s as companies tried to achieve the Hawthorne effect.

## 23.4 Maslow and the Hierarchy of Needs

Abraham Maslow (1908–1970) was an American psychologist whose great contribution to motivation theory was the 'Hierarchy of Needs'. Maslow believed everyone has the same needs – all of which can be organised as a hierarchy. At the base of the hierarchy are physical needs such as food, shelter and warmth.

| MASLOW'S LEVELS OF HUMAN NEED | BUSINESS IMPLICATIONS |
| --- | --- |
| - Physical needs, e.g. food, shelter and warmth | - Pay levels and working conditions |
| - Safety needs, e.g. security, a safe structured environment, stability, freedom from anxiety | - Job security, a clear job role/description, clear lines of accountability (only one boss) |
| - Social needs, e.g. belonging, friendship, contact | - Teamworking, communications, social facilities |
| - Esteem needs, e.g. strength, self-respect, confidence, status and recognition | - Status, recognition for achievement, power, trust |
| - Self-actualisation, e.g. self-fulfilment; 'to become everything that one is capable of becoming', wrote Maslow | - Scope to develop new skills and meet new challenges and to develop one's full potential |

**Figure 23.1** Maslow's Hierarchy of Needs

When unsatisfied, these are the individual's primary motivations. When employees earn enough to satisfy these needs, however, their motivating power withers away. Maslow said that 'It is quite true that humans live by bread alone – when there is no bread. But what happens to their desires when there is bread?' Instead of physical needs, people become motivated to achieve needs such as security and stability – which Maslow called the safety needs. In full, Maslow's hierarchy consisted of needs as shown by the diagram above.

Ever since Maslow first put his theory forward (in 1940) writers have argued about its implications. Among the key issues raised by Maslow are:

- Do all humans have the same set of needs? Or are there some people who need no more from a job than money?
- Do different people have different degrees of need, for example are some highly motivated by the need for power, while others are satisfied by social factors? If so, the successful manager would be one who can understand and attempt to meet the differing needs of his or her staff.
- Can anyone's needs ever be said to be fully satisfied? Perhaps the hierarchy diagram (see Figure 23.1) should have an open top to suggest that the human desire for achievement is limitless.

Maslow's work had a huge influence on the writers who followed him, especially McGregor and Herzberg. The Hierarchy of Needs is also used by academics in many subjects beyond Business, notably Psychology and Sociology.

## 23.5 Herzberg's two factor theory

The key test of a theory is its analytic usefulness. On this criterion, Herzberg's theory is the strongest by far.

The theory stems from research conducted in the 1950s into factors affecting workers' **job satisfaction** and dissatisfaction. It was carried out on 200 accountants and engineers in Pennsylvania, USA. Despite the

limited nature of this sample, Herzberg's conclusions remain influential to this day.

| *Key quotes from Professor Herzberg:* | |
|---|---|
| *On the two factor theory* | *'Motivators and hygiene factors are equally important, but for different reasons'* |
| *On movement* | *'If you do something because you want a house or a Jaguar, that's movement. It's not motivation'* |
| *The risks of giving bonuses* | *'A reward once given becomes a right'* |
| *The importance of training* | *'The more a person can do, the more you can motivate them'* |
| *The importance of always treating staff fairly* | *'A remembered pain can lead to revenge psychology … They'll get back at you some day when you need them'* |
| *On communication* | *'In industry, there's too much communication. And of course it's passive … But if people are doing idiot jobs they really don't give a damn'* |
| *On participation* | *'When participation is suggested in terms of control over overall goals, it is usually a sham'* |

Herzberg asked employees to describe recent events which had given rise to exceptionally good feelings about their jobs. Then probed for the reasons why. 'Five factors stand out as strong determiners of job satisfaction', Herzberg wrote in 1966, 'achievement, recognition for achievement, the work itself, responsi-

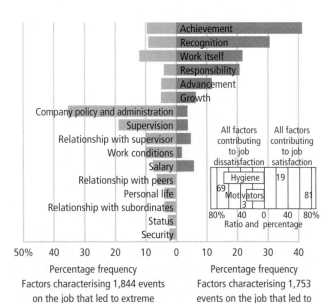

**Figure 23.2** Comparison of satisfiers and dissatisfiers

| Motivators (can create positive satisfaction) | Hygiene Factors (can create job dissatisfaction) |
| --- | --- |
| • Achievement | • Company policy and administration (the rules, paperwork and red tape) |
| • Recognition for achievement | • Supervision (especially being over-supervised) |
| • Meaningful, interesting work | • Pay |
| • Responsibility | • Interpersonal relations (with supervisor, peers, or even customers) |
| • Advancement (psychological, not just a promotion) | • Working conditions |

bility and advancement – the last three being of greater importance for a lasting change of attitudes.' He pointed out that each of these factors concerned the job itself, rather than issues such as pay or status. Herzberg called these five factors 'the motivators'. The researchers went on to ask about events giving rise to exceptionally bad feelings about their jobs. This revealed a separate set of five causes. Herzberg stated that 'the major dissatisfiers were company policy and administration, supervision, salary, interpersonal relations and working conditions.' He concluded that the common theme was factors which 'surround the job', rather than the job itself. The name he gave these dissatisfiers was '**hygiene factors**'. This was because fulfilling them would prevent dissatisfaction, rather than causing positive motivation. Careful hygiene prevents disease; care to fulfil hygiene factors prevents job dissatisfaction.

## THANK HEAVEN IT'S MONDAY!

Poor Jason Fitzgerald. Every Friday evening he has to drag himself away from work to get back to reality – a bit of cooking, seeing friends and so on. But on Monday morning he's up early to get back to his job as Communications and Development Executive on Sony PlayStation 2. He spends his days playing games, to make sure that he is in touch with any new trends or innovations. As video games take 2 years and £2–£3 million to develop, he organises consumer trials of games in development, to make sure that the moves are fun and challenging. At present his main focus is on multi-player games.

As Herzberg would say, he is motivated by the challenging, interesting work. He enjoys the teamworking and financial aspects of the job, but they are not the motivators. His motivations are intrinsic, in other words they come from his love of the job.

### SUMMARY

Motivators have the power to create positive job satisfaction, but little downward potential. Hygiene factors will cause job dissatisfaction unless they are provided for, but do not motivate. Importantly, Herzberg saw pay as a hygiene factor, not a motivator. So a feeling of being underpaid could lead to a grievance; but high pay would soon be taken for granted. This motivator/hygiene factor theory is known as the *two factor theory*.

### MOVEMENT AND MOTIVATION

Herzberg was keen to distinguish between movement and motivation. Movement occurs when somebody does something; motivation is when they *want* to do something. This distinction is essential to a full understanding of Herzberg's theory. He did not doubt that financial incentives could be used to boost productivity: 'If you bully or bribe people, they'll give you better than average performance.' His worries about bribes ('carrots') were that they would never stimulate people to give of their best; people would do just enough to achieve the bonus. Furthermore, bribing people to work harder at a task they find unsatisfying would build up resentments which might backfire on the employer.

Herzberg advised against payment methods such as piece-rate. They would achieve movement, but by reinforcing worker behaviour, making them inflexible and resistant to change. The salaried, motivated employee would work hard, care about quality and think about – even welcome – improved working methods.

### JOB ENRICHMENT

The reason why Herzberg's work has had such impact on businesses is because he not only analyses motivation, he also has a method for improving it. The method is job enrichment, which he defined as 'giving people the opportunity to use their ability'. He suggested that, for a job to be considered enriched, it would have to contain:

• A complete unit of work – not just a small repetitive fragment of a job, but a full challenging task;

Herzberg heaped scorn upon the 'idiot jobs' that resulted from Taylor's views on the merits of high division of labour.

- Direct feedback – wherever possible, a job should enable the worker to judge immediately the quality of what they have done; direct feedback gives the painter or the actor (or the teacher) the satisfaction of knowing exactly how well they have performed. Herzberg disliked systems which pass quality inspection off onto a supervisor: 'a man must always be held responsible for his own quality'. Worst of all, he felt, was annual appraisal – in which feedback is too long delayed.

- Direct communication – for people to feel committed, in control and to gain direct feedback, they should communicate directly – avoiding the delays of communicating via a supervisor or a 'contact person'. For a Business student, this leads to an important conclusion: that communications and motivation are interrelated.

### CONCLUSION

Herzberg's original research has been followed up in many different countries, including Japan, Africa and Russia. An article he wrote on the subject in the *Harvard Business Review* in 1968 (called 'Just One More Time, How Do You Motivate Employees') has sold more than one million reprinted copies. His main insight was to show that unless the job itself was interesting, there was no way to make working life satisfying. This led companies such as Volvo in Sweden and Toyota in Japan to rethink their factory layouts. Instead of individual workers doing simple repetitive tasks, the drive was to provide more complete units of work. Workers were grouped into teams, focusing on significant parts of the manufacturing process, such as

ISSUES FOR **analysis**

In an exam context, the starting point is usually to select the most appropriate theory to answer a question. If a case study context suggested poor relations between management and workforce, Elton Mayo's would be very suitable. If motivation was weak, Herzberg's theory provides a comprehensive analysis.

When applying a theory, the analysis is strengthened by using a questioning approach. Herzberg's theory is admirable, but it is not perfect. It provides insights, but not necessarily answers. And certainly not blueprints. A job enrichment programme might be highly effective in one situation, but a disappointment in another.

This leads on to another key factor. The success of any new policies will depend hugely on the history of trust – or the lack of it – in the workplace. Successful change in the factors involved in motivation may be very difficult and slow to achieve. There are no magic solutions.

Accordingly, when a firm faces a crisis, changes in factors relating to motivation will rarely provide an answer. A crisis must be solved in the short term, but human motivation requires long-term strategies.

assembling and fitting the gearbox. And then checking the quality of their work. Job enrichment indeed.

## 23.6 Motivation
### an evaluation

Most managers assume they understand human motivation. But they have never studied it. As a result they may underestimate the potential within their own staff. Or unthinkingly cause resentments that fester.

The process of managing people takes place in every part of every organisation. By contrast, few would need to know the financial concept of gearing in their working lives. So lack of knowledge of motivation theory is particularly unfortunate – and has exceptionally widespread effects. In some cases, ignorance leads managers to ignore motivation altogether. They tell themselves that control and organisation (i.e. paperwork!) are their only concerns. Other managers may see motivation as important, but fail to understand its subtleties.

For these reasons, there is a case for saying that the concepts within this unit are the most important in the whole subject.

### BIBLIOGRAPHY

E Mayo, *The Social Problems of Industrial Civilisation*, Routledge 1975 (1st edition 1949).
AH Maslow, *Motivation and Personality*, Harper Collins 1987 (1st edition 1954).
F Herzberg, *The Motivation To Work*, Wiley International 1959.

**KEY terms**

**division of labour** – subdivision of a task into a number of activities, enabling workers to specialise and therefore become very efficient at completing what may be a small, repetitive task.

**hygiene factors** – 'everything that surrounds what you do in the job' such as pay, working conditions and social status. All potential causes of dissatisfaction, according to Herzberg.

**job satisfaction** – the sense of well-being and achievement gained from doing a satisfying job.

**piece-rate** – the rate of payment for piecework.

**piecework** – work that is paid per 'piece' produced. Workers' pay is therefore directly related to the amount they produce.

**trade union** – an organisation that represents the interests of the workforce in a particular trade or profession.

# Exercises

## A. REVISION QUESTIONS
*(50 marks; 75 minutes)*

Read the unit, then answer:

1 Which features of the organisation of a McDonald's could be described as Taylorite? (3)
2 Explain the meaning of the term 'economic man'. (3)
3 What is meant by 'time and motion study'? How did Taylor make use of this method? (5)
4 Explain the difference between piece-rate and differential piece-rate. (3)
5 Identify three main consequences of Taylor's work. (3)
6 Give a brief outline of Mayo's research methods at the Hawthorne plant. (5)
7 How may 'group norms' affect productivity at a workplace? (3)
8 Explain the meaning of the term 'the Hawthorne effect'. (2)
9 Explain two effects upon firms of Mayo's work on human relations. (4)
10 Which two levels of Maslow's hierarchy could be called 'the lower order needs'? (2)
11 Describe in your own words why Maslow organised the needs into a hierarchy. (4)
12 State three business implications of Maslow's work on human needs. (3)
13 Herzberg believes pay does not motivate, but it is important. Why? (3)
14 How do motivators differ from hygiene factors? (3)
15 What is job enrichment? How is it achieved? (4)

## B. REVISION EXERCISES

### B1 Data Response
Study Figure 23.2. It shows the results of Herzberg's research into the factors which cause positive job satisfaction and those which cause job dissatisfaction. The length of the bars shows the percentage of responses. Their width indicates how likely the respondent was to say that the effect was long term.

**Questions** *(20 marks; 25 minutes)*
1 Which of the factors had the least effect on satisfaction or dissatisfaction? (1)
2 One of Herzberg's objectives was to question whether good human relations were as important in job satisfaction as claimed by Elton Mayo. Do you think he succeeded? (6)
3 Responsibility had the longest lasting effects on job satisfaction. Why may this be the case? (5)
4 Discuss which of the factors is the most important motivator. (8)

### B2 Case Study
Tania was delighted to get the bakery job and looked forward to her first shift. It would be tiring after a day at college, but £32 for 8 hours on a Friday would guarantee good Saturday nights in future.

On arrival, she was surprised to be put straight to work, with no more than a mumbled 'you'll be working packing machine B'. Fortunately she was able to watch the previous shiftworker before clocking-off time, and could get the hang of what was clearly a very simple task. As the 18.00 bell rang, the workers streamed out, but not many had yet turned up from Tania's shift. The conveyor belt started to roll again at 18.16.

As the evening wore on, machinery breakdowns provided the only, welcome relief from the tedium and discomfort of Tania's job. Each time a breakdown occurred, a ringing alarm bell was drowned out by a huge cheer from the staff. A few joyful moments followed, with dough fights breaking out. Tania started to feel quite old as she looked at some of her workmates.

At the 22.00 mealbreak, Tania was made to feel welcome. She enjoyed hearing the sharp, funny comments made about the shift managers. One was dubbed 'Noman' because he was fat, wore a white coat and never agreed to anything. Another was called 'Turkey' because he strutted around, but if anything went wrong, went into a flap. It was clear that both saw themselves as bosses. They were not there to help or to encourage, only to blame.

Was the bakery always like this, Tania wondered? Or was it simply that these two managers were poor?

**Questions** *(25 marks; 30 minutes)*
1 Analyse the working lives of the shiftworkers at the bakery, using Herzberg's two factor theory. (8)
2 If a managerial follower of Taylor's methods came into the factory, how might he or she try to improve the productivity level? (7)
3 Later on in this (true) story, Tania read in the local paper that the factory was closing. The reason given was 'lower labour productivity than at our other bakeries'. The newspaper grumbled about the poor attitudes of local workers. Consider the extent to which there is some justification in this view. (10)

# MOTIVATION IN PRACTICE

## DEFINITION

Assessing how firms try to motivate their staff and how successful these actions appear to be. In this context, companies take 'motivation' to mean enthusiastic pursuit of the objectives or tasks set out by the firm.

There are three main variables which influence the motivation of staff in practice:

- the company culture
- its approach to managing its people
- the financial reward systems.

All three will be analysed using the theories outlined in Unit 23.

## 24.1 Company culture

Company culture means the accepted set of attitudes, values and habits within an organisation – its ethos. Every business has its own culture, as does every college and every classroom. Within an hour of joining a new class, its culture becomes apparent. Is it purposeful? Cooperative? Open? Challenging? Self-disciplined? Or just disciplined? In most workplaces, the culture emerges quite quickly. In some retail businesses, young part-timers get their enjoyment from pranks and sarcasm; in others the satisfaction comes from doing the job well.

### HOW DOES CULTURE RELATE TO MOTIVATION?

Company culture can be positive or negative in many ways. Most affect motivation, either directly or indirectly. For example, the traditional police force culture was often sexist and racist. This may have boosted the team spirit of the white males involved. Yet their motivation may have been towards 'solving' crime in a manner determined by their prejudices rather than by police procedure. For instance, stopping and searching young blacks rather than solving burglaries.

The most obvious direct impact of culture upon motivation is through what Elton Mayo called **group norms** (see Unit 23). FW Taylor conceived the notion of 'a fair day's work for a fair day's pay', but Mayo was the theorist who analysed the social factors affecting what staff regard as fair. The work culture in one office may be so weak that idle chatting, social phone calls, tea breaks and computer game playing may halve the productivity compared with a similar office in another firm. Where the culture is strong, a slack period of the year is treated as the opportunity to

improve systems or to carry out research into new customer needs. Where the culture is weak, a slack period means still slacker behaviour. Mayo pointed out that the difference in attitude was often to do with the unofficial leader or leaders of the staff concerned. It is also to do with tradition and – of course – the company or departmental culture.

### HOW CAN A FIRM ACHIEVE THE CULTURE IT DESIRES?

If a new managing director wanted to shift a company's culture from being 'safety first, risk free, nine-to-five' to a more entrepreneurial, flexible one, where would he or she start? It should be accepted at the start that this will not be easy. A dull, safe company will have been recruiting dull, safe people for years. They will have become used to a culture in which failure means blame (even though, as fewer than one in four new products succeed in the marketplace, three failures in a row may not be unreasonable). They will probably be used to checking every decision with their boss; and spending much of their day looking forward to five o'clock.

Changing the culture will require four key factors:

1 clear communication to all staff about why and how change is to be achieved
2 a new organisational structure, with fewer layers of supervisory management and therefore more delegation of authority to more junior staff
3 identifying staff training needs and meeting them – both now and regularly in the future
4 a genuine change in attitude at the top, the effects of which will eventually spread throughout the business. Key indicators will be the types of managers who are promoted and demoted in the reorganisation and how the first major mistake is treated.

Source: *The Ultimate Book of Business Quotations*, Stuart Crainer, Capstone Publishing, 1997

## 24.2 Effective management of people

Good management can mean different things in different circumstances. Sometimes decisive leadership is called for. At other times careful planning and good organisation are the key factors. Effective management of people comes from a boss who has the experience, the foresight and the skills to ensure that staff feel confident and prove competent or better in their day-to-day tasks.

### JOB ENRICHMENT

Professor Herzberg defines job enrichment as 'giving people the opportunity to use their ability'. A full explanation of his theory is outlined in Unit 23.

How can job enrichment be put into practice? The key is to realise the enormity of the task. It is not cheap, quick or easy to enrich the job of the production line worker or the supermarket checkout operator. The first thought might be to provide more variety to the work. The supermarket worker might switch between the checkout, shelf stacking and working in the warehouse. Known as job rotation, this approach reduces repetition but still provides the employee with little challenge. Herzberg's definition of job enrichment implies giving people 'a range of responsibilities and activities'. Job rotation only provides a range of activities. To provide job enrichment, workers must have a complete unit of work (not a repetitive fragment), responsibility for quality and for self-checking and be given the opportunity to show their abilities.

Full job enrichment requires a radical approach. Take a conventional car assembly line, for example (see Figure 24.1). Workers each have a single task they carry out on their own. One fits the left-hand front door to a car shell which is slowly moving past on a conveyor belt – one car every 22 seconds. Another worker fits right-hand front doors and so on. Job enrichment can only be achieved by rethinking the production line completely.

**Figure 24.1** Traditional production line

Figure 24.2 shows how a car assembly line could be reorganised to provide more enriched jobs. Instead of working in isolation, people work in groups on a significant part of the assembly process. An empty car shell comes along the conveyor belt and arrives at the Interior Group Area. Six workers fit carpets, gloveboxes, the dashboard and much else. They check the quality of their own work, then put the vehicle, now looking significantly more like the finished product, back on the conveyor belt. Not only does the teamwork element help meet the social needs of the workforce, but there are also knock-on effects. The workers can be given a time slot to discuss their work and how to improve it. When new equipment is needed, they can be given a budget and told to meet potential suppliers. In other words, they can become managers of their own work area.

**Figure 24.2** Enriched groupworking line

Such a major step would be expensive. Rebuilding a production line might cost millions of pounds and be highly disruptive in the short term. There would also be the worry that teamworking might make the job more satisfying, yet still be less productive than the boring but practical system of high **division of labour**.

## JOB ENLARGEMENT

Job enlargement is a general term for anything that increases the scope of a job. There are three ways it comes about:

1  Job rotation – increasing a worker's activities by switching between tasks of a similar level of difficulty. This does not increase the challenge, but may reduce the boredom, of a job.
2  Job loading – increasing workload, often as a result of redundancies. It may mean having to do more of the same, but often entails one or two extra activities that have to be taken on.
3  Job enrichment – this enlargement of the scope of the job involves extra responsibilities and challenges as well as extra activities/workload.

Of these, only job enrichment is likely to provide long-term job satisfaction. Employers may like to use the term 'job enrichment', but often they are really carrying out job rotation or job loading.

## EMPOWERMENT

Empowerment is a modern term for delegation. There is only one difference between the two. The empowered worker not only has the authority to manage a task, but also some scope to decide what that task should be. An Ikea store manager has power delegated to him or her. But head office rules may be so rigid that the manager has little scope for individual judgement. An empowered store manager would be one who could choose a range of stock suited to local customers, or a staffing policy different from the national store policy.

Empowerment means having more power and control over your working life. Having the scope to make significant decisions about how to allocate your time and how to move forward. It is a practical application of the theories of Herzberg and McGregor. It may lead to greater risks being taken, but can also lead to opportunities being identified and exploited. Above all else, it should aid motivation.

One major worry about empowerment in recent years has come from the financial services industry. A trader called Nick Leeson carried out a series of reckless trades which lost hundreds of millions of pounds and brought about the collapse of Barings Bank. In the stock market shake-out of 2001/2002 a series of other speculative failures emerged. In most cases, a fundamental problem was that the company bosses did not understand fully the risks that were being taken. Empowerment is highly dangerous in a situation of ignorance.

## TEAMWORKING

Teamworking is the attempt to maximise staff satisfaction and involvement by organising employees into relatively small teams. These teams may be functional (the 'drive-thru crew' at a McDonald's) or geographic. The key features of such teams are that they should be:

- multi-skilled, so that everyone can do everyone else's job
- working together to meet shared objectives, such as to serve every customer within a minute or produce a gearbox with zero defects
- encouraged to think of the future as well as the present, in a spirit of kaizen (**continuous improvement**).

From a theoretical point of view, teamworking fits in well with Mayo's findings on the importance of group working and group norms. It can also be traced back to Maslow's emphasis on social needs. In practical terms, modern managers like teamworking because of the flexibility it implies. If worker A is absent, there are plenty of others used to dealing with the job. Therefore there is no disruption. Teamworking also gives scope for motivating influences such as job enrichment and quality circles.

## GENBA-SHUGI

Genba-shugi is a Japanese phrase meaning 'respectable shop floor'. It points out that, even though Japanese managers are very status-conscious, working on the shop floor is a dignified and necessary part of building a career. Toyota recruits graduates and puts them on the production line so that they learn exactly what it is like to make a car. For 2 or 3 years staff may be switched from department to department to gain a full understanding of the shop floor aspects of the whole business. The British approach of occasionally putting a boss 'Back to the Floor' for a week makes good television (it's a BBC series) but is no substitute for learning the hard way.

Above all else, genba-shugi means staff know that managers really understand their problems. A hotel manager who has spent three months in the kitchens knows the importance of air conditioning and top quality equipment. A Toyota boss who has spent a year on the production line knows the value of cell production and empowerment. For effective management of people, genba-shugi is a term worth remembering.

**Business IN**

Professor Charles Handy suggests in his book *Inside Organisations* (BBC Books, 1990) that 'a good team is a great place to be, exciting, stimulating, supportive, successful. A bad team is horrible, a sort of human prison'. It is true that the business will not benefit if the group norms within the team discourage effort. Nevertheless, teamworking has proved successful in many companies in recent years. Companies such as Rolls Royce, Treboi, Rover and Komatsu have reported large improvements in absenteeism and labour turnover, and significant shifts in workforce attitudes.

## 24.3 Financial reward systems

### PIECEWORK

Piecework means working in return for a payment per unit produced. The payment itself is known as piece-rate. Pieceworkers receive no basic or shift pay, so there is no sick pay, holiday pay or company pension.

Piecework is used extensively in small-scale manu-facturing, for example of jeans or jewellery. Its attraction for managers is that it makes supervision virtually unnecessary. All the manager need do is operate a quality control system which ensures the fin-ished product is worth paying for. Day by day, the workers can be relied upon to work fast enough to earn a living (or a good) wage.

Piecework has several disadvantages to firms, how-ever:

- Scrap levels may be high, if workers are focused entirely on speed of output.
- There is an incentive to provide acceptable quality, but not the best possible quality.
- Workers will work hardest when they want higher earnings (probably before Christmas and before their summer holiday). This may not coincide at all with seasonal patterns of customer demand.
- Worst of all is the problem of change. Herzberg pointed out that 'the worst way to people is piece-rate … it reinforces behaviour'. Focusing people on maximising their earnings by repeating a task makes them very reluctant to produce something different or in a different way (they worry that they will lose out financially).

### PERFORMANCE-RELATED PAY (PRP)

Performance-related pay is a financial reward to staff whose work is considered above average. It is used for employees whose work achievements cannot be assessed simply through numerical measures (such as units produced or sold). PRP awards are usually made after an appraisal process has evaluated the perfor-mance of staff during the year.

A 1991 survey found that 56% of private sector firms used PRP for clerical and managerial staff. Merit pay was the 'big idea' of the 1980s. The use of PRP has grown slightly since then (to 60%), but the method is increasingly being questioned. In 1996, for example, Scottish Amicable loosened its link between pay and performance.

On the face of it, PRP is a highly attractive system for encouraging staff to work towards the organisa-tion's objectives. The usual method is:

1. establish targets for each member of staff/manage-ment at an appraisal interview
2. at the end of the year, discuss the individual's achievements against those targets
3. those with outstanding achievements are given a Merit 1 pay rise or bonus worth perhaps 6% of salary; others receive between 0% and 6%.

Despite the enthusiasm they have shown for it, employers have rarely been able to provide evidence of the benefits of PRP. Indeed, the Institute of Personnel Management concluded in a report that:

> *'It was not unusual to find that organisations which had introduced merit pay some years ago were less certain now of its continued value … it was time to move on to something more closely reflecting team achievement and how the organisation as a whole was faring.'*

This pointed to a fundamental problem with PRP. Rewarding individuals does nothing to promote team-work. Furthermore, it might create unhealthy rivalry between managers – each going for the same Merit 1 spot.

Among other problems for PRP systems are:

- Whether the incentives are large enough to moti-vate – to keep costs down, firms usually allow no more than 2–3% of the wage bill for merit pay. The HSBC Bank system, for instance, provides between 0% and 6% as a performance-related reward.
- Perceived fairness/unfairness – staff often suspect that those awarded the maximum are being rewarded not for performance but out of favouritism. This may damage working relations and team spirit.
- Whether they have a sound basis in human psy-chology – without question, Professor Herzberg would be very critical of any attempt to influence work behaviour by financial incentives. A London School of Economics' study of Inland Revenue staff found that only 12% believed that PRP had raised motivation at work, while 76% said it had not. Herzberg would approve of the researchers' conclu-sion that 'the current system has not succeeded in motivating staff to any significant degree, and may well have done the reverse'.

As the last point illustrates, a key assumption behind PRP is that the chance to be paid a bit more than other employees will result in a change in individual behaviour, in increased motivation to work. A survey for the Government publication *Employment in*

*Business* IN

## PRP AND HSBC BANK

HSBC Bank uses a performance-related pay system for its 40,000 clerical staff. It is based on appraisal linked to customer service. It gives each employee one of the following ratings:

- unacceptable (U)
- improvement required (I)
- good (G)
- high achievement (H)
- outstanding (O).

Oustanding achievers receive an extra 6% per year on their salary whereas category I staff receive no performance bonus. Those in category U receive no pay increase at all, not even a rise to keep up with inflation.

HSBC's head of compensation, Pam Wood, believes the system 'focuses people's attention on performance on the job, rather than just turning up and being paid'. The bank's trade union takes a different view. It believes every employee has a right to an annual pay rise. It also suspects the proposals give an unhealthy amount of power to the managers of the clerical staff.

*Britain* found that 'pay incentives were thought important for hard work by less than one in five and for quality standards by less than one in ten'.

So why do firms continue to pursue PRP systems? There are three possible reasons:

- to make it easier for managers to manage/control their staff (using a carrot instead of a stick)
- an underlying Theory X view on the part of senior managers – a 1996 survey found that two-thirds of personnel managers saw monetary incentives as a good way to motivate employees
- to reduce the influence of collective bargaining and therefore trade unions.

## PROFIT SHARING

A different approach to financial incentives is to provide staff with a share of the firm's annual profit. This puts staff in the same position as shareholders as, in effect, they are paid an annual dividend. This offers clear psychological benefits:

- Staff can come to see profit positively – before they may have regarded it as an unfair way of diverting pay from their own pockets to those of shareholders.
- Herzberg and other theorists warn that financial incentives distort behaviour. For example, if you pay a striker £500 per goal, wave goodbye to passing in the penalty area. Profit sharing, however, is more of a financial reward than an incentive. It may encourage people to work harder or smarter, but should not stop them working as a team.
- If paid to staff in the form of free shares, the employees may develop a strong sense of identity with the company and its fortunes.

Profit sharing can represent a substantial bonus on top of regular earnings. For instance, the John Lewis Partnership pays an annual bonus which is usually worth over 20% of an employee's earnings. In 2002 the John Lewis Partnership shared nearly £250 million among its 37,500 employees! In other cases, such as Tesco, the profit share is well below 5%. At such a low level it is clearly more of a thank you than a serious incentive.

## SHARE OWNERSHIP

On the face of it, this is a far more radical approach to financial reward. It has the potential to achieve the business ideal: workers, managers, directors and shareholders thinking as one. Without question it has a pedigree. In his book *The Way Ahead*, Bill Gates suggests that employee share ownership has been fundamental to the success of Microsoft. The promise of a shareholding helps Microsoft attract the brightest graduates to work for it – and helps keep them focused on the company's success.

There are two main ways of providing employee share ownership:

1 Save as you earn – this is usually a five-year scheme in which staff save perhaps £50 per month. At the end of the five years they can convert their cash savings into shares at the price the shares were at the start of the five-year period. Often this will pro-

Pros and cons of profit sharing

| PROS | CONS |
|---|---|
| • Encourages staff to think about the whole business, not just their own job | • If the employee share is only a small proportion of annual profit, the payouts may be meaninglessly small |
| • Encourages thinking about cost saving as well as revenue raising | • Large payouts, though, may either hit shareholder dividends or reduce the investment capital for long-term expansion |
| • Focus on profit may make it easier for staff to accept changes in working practices, i.e. it may lessen resistance to change | • Because no single individual can have much impact on overall profits, there may be no incentive effect |

vide a substantial, immediate profit. Most employees hold onto the shares, hoping they will prove a sound long-term investment.

2 Share options – senior managers are often given the option to buy a substantial number of the company's shares at a discounted price at some agreed date in the future. For example, today's share price is 100p. A manager is given the option to buy 50,000 shares at 80p in 3 years' time. Three years later, a boom in share prices has taken the price to 280p. The manager buys the 50,000 shares at 80p and sells them for 280p. Profit: 50,000 × £2 = £100,000. Very nice for the manager, but very annoying for others in the department who may feel they work harder than their boss – and should also be allowed to enjoy this substantial perk. In 2002 the massive corporate collapses of Enron and Worldcom were blamed, in part, on the greed of senior executives with huge share options.

## FRINGE BENEFITS

These are forms of reward other than income. Some managers have generous expense accounts. Many have company cars. Usually all maintenance and running costs are paid by the company. In some cases, even petrol for private mileage can be charged to the employer. Other fringe benefits include:

- membership of clubs or leisure centres
- low interest rate loans or mortgages
- discounts on the company's products, such as the British Airways' perk of air fares at 90% off!

In all cases, fringe benefits are offered to encourage staff loyalty and to improve human relations.

ISSUES FOR analysis

The key ways to analyse motivation in practice are:

- To select and apply the relevant motivation theory to the method being considered. Often modern methods appear to be based upon an understanding of human psychology, but careful scrutiny reveals they are not. Good analysis of methods such as performance-related pay or job rotation would require a critical eye.
- To question the publicly stated motives of the organisation or manager concerned. Businesses can be very loose in their use of words such as 'motivation' or 'empowerment'. They can be euphemisms for tougher targets and greater pressure. If the recent history of a firm makes employees sceptical of the goodwill of managers, students should be equally questioning.
- As John Kotter has said, 'Motivating people over a short period is not very difficult.' The key test of a new approach to motivation is over a 2–5 year period, not the early months of a new initiative. So always consider the timescale.

There are many aspects of business studies which point solely towards money. How profitable is this price or that? What is the forecast net cash flow for April? And so on. In such circumstances it is understandable that human implications may be forgotten. A high price for an AIDS cure may be profitable, but life-threatening to those who cannot afford the medicine. April's positive cash flow might be achieved only by sacking temporary staff.

When covering motivation in practice, there is little excuse for ignoring the implications for people. Exaggerated commissions or performance-related pay can lead sales staff to oversell goods or services which may cause customers huge difficulties later on, such as cosmetic surgery or questionable investments. Also within the workplace, serious problems can arise. Bullying to 'motivate' staff into working harder, or creating a culture of overwork which leads to stress.

Fortunately there are many businesses in which the management of motivation is treated with respect. Companies which know that quick fixes are not the answer. Successful motivation in the long term is a result of careful job design, employee training and development, honesty and trust. It may be possible to supplement this with an attractive financial reward scheme. But money will never be a substitute for motivation.

**KEY terms**

**continuous improvement (kaizen)** – moving productivity and product quality forward in regular, small steps.

**division of labour** – subdividing a job into small, repetitive fragments of work.

**group norms** – the types of behaviour and attitude seen as normal within a group.

# Exercises

## A. REVISION QUESTIONS
*(40 marks; 70 minutes)*

Read the unit, then answer:

1 Explain the business meaning of the term 'culture'. *(3)*
2 Outline the culture in any company you have worked for. *(5)*
3 How should a manager deal with a mistake made by a junior employee? *(4)*
4 State three reasons why job enrichment should improve staff motivation. *(3)*
5 Distinguish between job rotation and job enrichment. *(4)*
6 How does 'empowerment' differ from 'delegation'? *(4)*
7 Identify three advantages to an employee of working in a team. *(3)*
8 State two advantages and two disadvantages of offering staff performance-related pay. *(4)*
9 What might be the implications of providing share options to senior managers but not to the workforce generally? *(5)*
10 What problems might result from a manager bullying staff to 'motivate' them? *(5)*

## B. REVISION EXERCISES

### B1 Data Response
In 1998, Britain's most successful car factory was Nissan UK's plant in Sunderland. Its productivity level of nearly 100 cars per worker per year was three times higher than rivals such as Rover. So, how was this achieved? Of course, there were many operational factors, such as high investment and effective lean production. Also important, though, has been the effective management and motivation of personnel.

From the time it opened in 1986, Nissan took care to establish a positive staff culture. Young, enthusiastic staff were recruited who had no preconceptions about making cars. Heavy emphasis was placed on training and continued education for staff. When production started, the views and suggestions of staff were welcomed. Each production department had a kaizen (continuous improvement) unit, manned by dedicated staff. Supervisors were empowered to interview, select and organise their staff. This encouraged a sense of responsibility and commitment. The result has been the acceptance by staff that Nissan's success is not only the company objective but also their own. 'Everybody takes a defect personally', says Craig Douglas, a supervisor in the plant's engine shop.

Mr Cushnaghan, the plant's deputy managing director, is clear that Nissan's success would have been much harder to achieve if trying to change practices in an older factory, because of 'cultural hangover'. 'That culture is an immense drag on a company's ability to make progress,' he says, 'Here, because we created the culture from day one, that drag doesn't exist. This place is full of change.'

### Questions *(30 marks; 35 minutes)*
1 Outline the workplace culture at Nissan, as suggested by the text. *(4)*
2 How well has the approach adopted by Nissan fitted Herzberg's model of job enrichment? *(6)*
3 Consider the advantages to a business of empowering supervisors to interview and select their staff rather than leaving this task to the personnel department. *(8)*
4 Nissan staff are well paid, but receive only a salary. There are no financial reward systems that encourage them to work harder. How, then, can they be the most productive workforce in the British car industry? *(6)*
5 Consider how managers might attempt to tackle a 'cultural hangover' from an earlier period. *(6)*

### B2 Data Response

#### Gambling on People

Procter and Gamble is the world's biggest advertiser and one of America's most respected companies. It is the company behind such brands as Fairy Liquid, Ariel, Crest, Max Factor, Head & Shoulders, Vidal Sasoon, Pringles, Sunny Delight and hundreds more. Behind its marketing success lies an exceptionally strong company culture and an advanced approach to the management of its people.

Procter and Gamble (P&G) was an early advocate of motivating staff by empowerment and job enrichment. Dave Swanson was the principal architect of the organisational design of the system. Swanson joined P&G in the early 1950s after studying at the Manchester Institute of Technology (MIT). While at MIT he had been inspired by the lectures of Professor Douglas McGregor. McGregor attacked the theory of command-and-control management, advocating empowerment. When Swanson had the opportunity to design a new detergent plant in Atlanta, Georgia, he enlisted McGregor's help.

Processes were put in place to make communications and control flow up, down and sideways in a very easy, uninhibited way. They emphasised knowledge of the business and learning new skills for all employees of the plant. The objective was to push the Augusta plant to be as unstructured as possible. 'We were trying to take away the rule book and substitute principle for mandate … We wanted people to reach for responsibility,' Swanson said. They did. Factory productivity went up 30% and the system was expanded to other P&G plants.

In his book *What America Does Right*, Robert Waterman describes P&G as a pioneer in pushing leadership, responsibility and decision making down to the plant floor.

Source: *P&G99*, Decker C, HarperCollins 1998

## Questions                               *(30 marks; 35 minutes)*

1 How might motivation be affected by 'taking away the rule book'? *(6)*

2 Explain the importance to staff motivation of freely flowing, accurate communication. *(6)*

3 Explain how the views of McGregor given in the text compare with his Theories X and Y. *(8)*

4 In this case, high motivation boosted productivity by 30%. Discuss whether increased motivation need always result in increased productivity. *(10)*

## B3  Activity

Write a questionnaire for self-completion by full-time employees. Your research objectives are to discover:

- whether there are any policies in place for encouraging workplace involvement/consultation
- whether job enrichment or job rotation measures exist (and what is their effect)
- how your respondents would describe the workplace culture
- whether there are any financial bonuses available, such as piece-rate or performance-related pay, and what is their effect on motivation
- how highly motivated the employees feel themselves to be
- how highly motivated they believe their colleagues to be.

This questionnaire should be conducted on at least 10 respondents. It is preferable for them to be face-to-face, but if that is not possible, self-completion is acceptable.

When the research is completed, analyse the results carefully and write a summary of them in report form.

# LEADERSHIP AND MANAGEMENT STYLES

DEFINITION
Management involves getting things done through other people. Leadership, at its best, means inspiring staff to achieve demanding goals. According to Peter Drucker, a manager does things right; a leader does the right thing.

## 25.1 Introduction

The way in which managers deal with their employees is known as their management style. For example, some managers are strict with workers. They always expect deadlines to be met and targets to be hit. Others are more relaxed and understanding. If there is a good reason why a particular task has not been completed by the deadline, they will be willing to accept this and give the employee more time. Although the way in which everyone manages will vary slightly from individual to individual, their styles can be categorised under three headings: **autocratic**, **democratic** and **paternalistic**.

Autocratic managers are authoritarian; they tell employees what to do and do not listen much to what workers themselves have to say. Autocratic managers know what they want doing and how they want it done. They tend to use one-way, top-down communication. They give orders to workers and do not want much feedback. Democratic managers, by comparison, like to involve their workers in decisions. They tend to listen to employees' ideas and ensure people contribute to the discussion. Communication by democratic managers tends to be two-way. Managers put forward an idea and employees give their opinion. A democratic manager would regularly delegate decision making power to junior staff.

The delegation of authority which is at the heart of democratic leadership can be approached in one of two main ways:

1 Management by objectives – the leader agrees clear goals with staff, provides the necessary resources, and allows day-to-day decisions to be made by the staff in question; this approach is advocated by Peter Drucker (see Unit 27) and by Douglas McGregor (see below) in his support for what he called the Theory Y approach to management.
2 Laissez-faire, meaning 'let it be' – this occurs when managers are so busy or so lazy that they do not take the time to ensure that junior staff know what to do or how to do it. Some people might respond very well to the freedom to decide on how to spend their working lives; others may become frustrated.

It is said that Bill Gates, in the early days of Microsoft, hired brilliant students and told them no more than to create brilliant software. Was this a laissez-faire style or management by objectives? Clearly the dividing line can be narrow.

A paternalistic manager thinks and acts like a father. He or she tries to do what is best for the staff/children. There may be consultation to find out the views of the employees, but decisions are made by the head of the 'family'. This type of manager believes employees need direction but think it is important that they are supported and cared for properly. Paternalistic managers are interested in the security

Assumptions and approaches of the three types of leader

| | DEMOCRATIC | PATERNALISTIC | AUTOCRATIC |
|---|---|---|---|
| Style derived from | Belief in Maslow's higher order needs or in Herzberg's motivators | Mayo's work on human relations and Maslow's lower and middle order needs | A Taylorite view of staff |
| Approach to staff | Delegation of authority | Consultation with staff | Orders must be obeyed |
| Approach to staff remuneration | Salary, perhaps plus employee shareholdings | Salary plus extensive fringe benefits | Payment by results, e.g. piece-rate |
| Approach to human resource management | Recruitment and training based on attitudes and teamwork | Emphasis on training and appraisal for personal development | Recruitment and training based on skills; appraisal linked to pay |

and social needs of the staff. They are interested in how workers feel and whether they are happy in their work. Nevertheless it is quite an autocratic approach.

## 25.2 McGregor's Theory X and Y

In the 1950s Douglas McGregor undertook a survey of managers in the USA and identified two styles of management, which he called Theory X and Theory Y. Theory X managers tend to distrust their subordinates; they believe employees do not really enjoy their work and that they need to be controlled. In McGregor's own words, many managers believe 'The average human being has an inherent dislike of work and will avoid it if he can.' Note that McGregor is not putting it forward as a theory about workers, but about managers. In other words, Theory X is about the view managers have of their workforce. Theory Y managers, by comparison, believe that employees do enjoy work and that they want to contribute ideas and effort . A Theory Y manager is, therefore, more likely to involve employees in decisions and give them greater responsibility. The managerial assumptions identified by McGregor as Theory Y included:

- 'Commitment to objectives is a function of the rewards associated with their achievement.'
- 'The average human being learns, under proper conditions, not only to accept but to seek responsibility.'
- 'The capacity to exercise a relatively high degree of imagination, ingenuity and creativity in the solution of organisational problems is widely, not narrowly, distributed in the population.'

**Source:** *The Human Side of Enterprise*, D McGregor, Penguin Books 1987 (first published 1960)

It is clear that Theory Y managers would be inclined to adopt a democratic leadership style. Their natural approach would be to delegate authority to meet specific objectives.

The Theory X approach is likely to be self-fulfilling. If you believe people are lazy, they will probably stop trying. Similarly if you believe workers dislike responsibility and fail to give them a chance to develop, they will probably stop showing interest in their work. They end up focusing purely on their wage packet because of the way you treat them.

In his book *The Human Side of Enterprise*, McGregor drew upon the work of Maslow and Herzberg. It need be no surprise that there are common features to the theories of these three writers. McGregor's unique contribution was to set issues of industrial psychology firmly in the context of the management of organisations. So whereas Herzberg's was a theory of motivation, McGregor's concerned styles of management (and thereby leadership).

So, which is the 'right' approach? Clearly a Theory Y manager would be more pleasant and probably

| Theory X managers believe: | Theory Y managers believe: |
|---|---|
| • *Employees dislike work and will avoid it if they can* | • *Putting some effort into work is as natural as play or rest; employees want to work* |
| • *Employees prefer to be directed, want to avoid responsibility and have little ambition* | • *Employees want responsibility provided there are appropriate rewards* |
| • *Employees need to be controlled and coerced* | • *Employees are generally quite creative* |

more interesting to work for. As outlined in the 'In Business' on Harold Geneen, however, a Theory X approach can work. It is especially likely to succeed in a business employing many part-time, perhaps student, workers, or in a situation where a business faces crisis.

### — HAROLD GENEEN

Harold Geneen, who died aged 87 in 1998, was the man who made ITT one of America's most powerful multinational corporations.

When Geneen became President of ITT in 1959, the company was a loose-knit empire with modest profits. By the time he left he had bought 350 companies in 80 countries and created America's 11th biggest firm with sales of $17 billion. Geneen introduced a system of incredibly strict accountability. His system involved monthly meetings at which executives had to explain their results and achievements to Geneen. The ordeal of being cross-questioned in these meetings made some managers physically ill. According to Geneen the skill of management lay in being able to 'smell' the truth. He liked complete control, relied only on 'unshakeable facts' to make logical decisions and insisted, 'I want no surprises'.

## 25.3 Team-based management

The role of managers is changing in many firms, which are now encouraging employees to work in teams. In this system managers are increasingly seen as a support to employees rather than as a supervisor. In the words of Tom Peters (see Unit 30), they are 'coaches and facilitators' not 'policemen'; they are there to help employees fulfil their potential. This approach relies on a high degree of trust between employees and managers and a common sense of purpose.

To gain this trust managers must show that they want employees to contribute and take greater responsibility for decision making. They must show they value the workers' input. In companies such as Rover and Unipart, for example, employees are encouraged to take control over their own work and develop ways of improving the process for themselves. In such organisations there is a conscious effort to remove the distinction between managers and workers (or 'them and us'). At Rover, for example, everyone is called an associate; at Unipart everyone is a 'team member'.

Although a simple change of name could in itself be a gimmick, it reflects a move away from the traditional company hierarchy. All Unipart employees are salaried (rather than being paid wages or piece-rate) and have the same terms and conditions as managers. Salaries differ according to different skills and responsibilities, but everyone is treated in the same way, i.e there is **single status**. In the past, people would eat in different canteens according to their rank within the organisation. They would have different car parking areas and would have different sickness benefits. In many companies such obvious distinctions no longer exist.

Strangely, though, this progressive move has coincided with a rapid increase in share options and other financial incentives for directors and senior managers. Huge payouts for those at the top of an organisation must undermine the desire to build team spirit.

## LEADER OF THE PACK

In December 2002 Judy Gibbons took her executive team at MSN, Microsoft's Internet business, to spend a week in the South African bush. It was the high point of a leadership programme developed by Judy from Jim Collins' book *Good To Great*. Collins believes great leadership is not based on personal charisma, but on a blend of personal humility and professional determination.

Judy's job as Head of the Europe, Middle East and Africa regions of MSN means leading a staff of 350 in 16 countries. Knowing that she cannot personally 'lead' all these people, her concern is to encourage best practice in her senior team.

The first two days were spent on a leadership course based in the South African bush. The most inspiring part was instruction on an African tribal custom called 'indaba'. When the tribal leaders meet with the chief on a specific concern, each person speaks, and this continues round with each person having an opportunity to speak in turn, again and again. Gradually people shift their position and a consensus emerges.

After this, several days in the Kruger National Park kept up the feeling of shared experiences and teamwork. Judy's approach shows that skilled leadership need not be based on power, or on 'establishing who's boss'. It can succeed through a combination of democratic and paternalistic styles.

Adapted from *The Financial Times*, 19/12/02

## 25.4 What is the best style of management?

Each style of management can work well in different situations. If there is a crisis, for example, people often look for a strong leader to tell them what to do. Imagine that sales have unexpectedly fallen by 50%, causing uncertainty, even panic, within the organisation. The management needs to take control quickly and put a plan into action. An autocratic style might work well at this moment. In a stable situation where employees are trained and able to do their work successfully a more democractic leadership style might be

'*When the effective leader is finished with his work, the people say it happened naturally.*'
Lao-Tzu (604–531BC), Chinese philosopher

'*The quality of a leader is reflected in the standards they set for themselves.*'
Ray Kroc (1902–1984), the man behind McDonald's

'*Leadership is practiced not so much in words as in attitude and in actions.*'
Harold Geneen (b. 1910) famous chief executive of the huge American corporation ITT

'*A leader shapes and shares a vision, which gives point to the work of others.*'
Charles Handy (b. 1932), management thinker

'*The leader's job is to help everyone see that the platform is burning, whether the flames are apparent or not.*'
Larry Bossidy (b. 1935), chief executive of Allied Signal Corporation

Source: *The Ultimate Book of Business Quotations*, Stuart Crainer, Capstone Publishing, 1998

more appropriate. It is often said that countries elect very different types of leaders when there is a threat of war or economic instability than when the country is doing well. Similarly, think about how people react when they are learning to drive. For the first few lessons they are uncertain what to do and are grateful to be told. Once they have passed their test and have driven for several years they will no doubt resent anyone telling them how to drive better!

The best style of management at any moment will depend on an enormous range of factors such as the personalities and abilities of the manager and the workers, and the nature of the task (see Figure 25.1). Imagine a confident manager who knows his or her job well but is faced with an unusually difficult problem. If the staff are well trained and capable, the manager would probably ask for ideas on what to do next. If, however, the manager was faced with a fairly routine problem he or she would probably just tell the employees what to do because there would be no need for discussion.

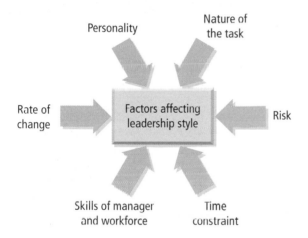

**Figure 25.1** Factors affecting leadership style

A manager's style should, therefore, change according to the particular situation and the people involved. It will also vary with the time and degree of risk involved. If a decision has to be made urgently and involves a high degree of risk, the manager is likely to be quite autocratic. If there is plenty of time to discuss matters and only a low chance of it going wrong the style may well be more democratic.

## 25.5 Does the style of management matter?

The way in which a manager deals with his or her colleagues can have a real impact on their motivation and how effectively they work. An experienced workforce which is used to being involved in decisions may resent a manager who always tries to tell them what to do. This might lead to a reduction in the quality of their work, a fall in productivity and an increase in

labour turnover. If, however, these employees were involved in decision making, the firm could gain from better ideas and a more highly motivated workforce. This does not mean that everyone wants to be involved or indeed that it is appropriate. Employees may lack the necessary training or experience. Therefore a democratic approach might simply mean taking longer for management to reach the decision it was going to make anyway.

## 25.6 What is the most common style of management?

The style of management which people adopt depends on many factors such as their personality, the particular circumstances at the time and the culture of the organisation. Although we have discussed three main styles the actual approach of most managers is usually a combination of all of them, depending on the task or the nature of the situation. If an order has to be completed by tomorrow and time is short, for example, most managers are likely to be autocratic to make sure it gets done. If, however, there is plenty of time available the manager may be more democratic. No-one is completely autocratic or completely democratic, it is simply a question of degree. However, some managers do tend to be more autocratic than others. This often depends on their own experiences (What was their boss like? What worked well when they were being trained?) and their personality (Do they like to be in control of everything? Are they willing to delegate? Do they value the opinions of others?).

In general the move has been towards a more democratic style of management in the UK in recent years. This is probably because employees expect more from work than they did in the past. They are better educated, have a higher basic standard of living and want more than just money in return for their efforts. Having satisfied their lower level needs they are now looking to satisfy their higher level needs. The growth of **democratic management** and greater participation has also increased with the move towards lean production and the emphasis on techniques such as total quality management. These methods of production require much more involvement by the employees than in the past. Employees are given control over their own quality, given the authority to make decisions over the scheduling of work and are expected to contribute ideas on how to improve the way they are working. This approach requires much more trust in employees than was common many years ago. It has to be matched with a more democratic leadership style.

Just one style of management
(© Darama/Corbis)

ISSUES FOR  analysis

Among the main lines of analysis are:

- Management style can have a significant impact on the way people work. By adopting the right approach employees are likely to be more motivated and show greater commitment. Therefore effective analysis of leadership should be rooted in the theories of writers such as Mayo and Herzberg.
- The 'correct' management style will depend on factors such as the task, the people involved and the amount of risk. There is no one style which is always appropriate. Therefore the context of the business case is always relevant.
- It may not be easy for managers to change their style. There may be situations in which managers should be more democratic; this does not necessarily mean they will be. Effective management training could be a useful way to persuade managers to be flexible.
- There is some debate about the extent to which you can train people to become effective managers or leaders. One extreme

view is that good managers and leaders are born that way – if this is true companies have to put their resources into finding the right sort of person. It is more likely that a good leader is a combination of training and personal characteristics.

## 25.7 Management styles
### an evaluation

All firms are seeking effective managers. Good managers make effective use of the firm's resources and motivate the staff. They provide vision and direction and are therefore a key element of business success. Look at any successful company and you will usually find a strong management team. The problem is knowing what it is that makes a good manager and what is the 'best' management style. Even if we thought we knew the best style, can we train anyone to adopt this approach or does it depend on their personality? There are, of course, no easy answers to these questions. The 'right' style of management will depend on the particular circumstances and the nature of the task and while it is possible to help someone develop a particular style it will also depend on the individual's personality. As employees have benefited from a higher standard of living in the UK and have higher expectations of work, managers have generally had to adopt a more democratic style to motivate people. However, there are plenty of autocratic managers who also succeed.

**KEY terms**

**autocratic management** – autocratic managers keep most of the authority to themselves; they do not delegate much or share information with employees. Autocratic or authoritarian managers tend to tell employees what to do.

**democratic management** – democratic managers take the views of their subordinates into account when making decisions.

**paternalistic management** – a paternalistic manager believes he or she knows what is best for the employees. Paternalistic managers tend to tell employees what to do but will often explain their decision. They are also concerned about the social needs of employees.

**single status** – occurs when all employees are given the same rights and conditions, e.g. the same rights to pension and sickness benefits.

**team-based management** – decisions are made by teams rather than workers being told what to do by a supervisor.

# Exercises

## A. REVISION QUESTIONS

*(30 marks; 60 minutes)*

Read the unit, then answer.

**1** Distinguish between autocratic and paternalistic management. *(4)*

**2** Identify two features of democratic management. *(2)*

**3** Identify one advantage and one disadvantage of an autocratic management approach. *(4)*

**4** Distinguish between McGregor's Theory X and Theory Y. *(4)*

**5** Why is it 'clear that Theory Y managers would be inclined to adopt a democratic leadership style'? *(4)*

**6** Why is trust so important for successful teamworking? *(4)*

**7** Why have many firms introduced teamworking in recent years? *(4)*

**8** Explain a circumstance in which an authoritarian approach to leadership may be desirable. *(4)*

## B. REVISION EXERCISES

### B1 Data Response

### Unipart

When John Neill shows you around Unipart's headquarters be prepared for some rather unusual features – the lecture theatre, the technical library, the in-house TV studio, the squash courts and fitness centre. Not forgetting the aromatherapy and reflexology suites and the shower rooms. The company was bought off Rover by a management buy-out group led by Neill (managing director) in 1987. It remains an unquoted company which means it does not have to focus simply on short-term shareholder value but can think and plan long term.

Neill is a champion of lean production techniques and his Japanese enthusiasm extends to employee relationships In the past he cannot recall any forced redundancies at Unipart. And when he hires consultants to help reorganise the firm, he guarantees employment of those whose jobs vanish. However, Neill is no soft touch for the workers. Back in the 1970s when labour relations in the UK car industry were poor he routinely fired workers for going on strike. In 1987, at the time of the buyout, he cut the workforce sharply to eliminate overstaffing. Finally, in 1992, he ended union recognition altogether.

In some respects Neill's approach is old-style paternalism. Hence his insistence on making shares available to workers. For those who hold shares over the long haul the gains are a reward for loyal service. 'I'm a very strong believer in the free enterprise system. The way we're trying to do it is the capitalist sytem on the moral ground. If a warehouseman can retire and buy a cottage or put his kids through higher education, that's what we're trying to do'.

Source: Adapted from *The Financial Times*, 6/2/98

**Questions** *(30 marks; 35 minutes)*

**1** Explain the meaning of the following terms:
  **a** union recognition *(3)*
  **b** old-style paternalism. *(3)*

**2** Outline the evidence that John Neill is a paternalistic manager. *(8)*

**3** Consider the possible effects of a switch by John Neill to a more democratic leadership style. *(10)*

**4** What do you think influences the way in which someone manages? *(6)*

### B2 Assignment

#### An Investigation into a Leader

**1** Arrange to interview an employee. Preferably this person should be a full-timer who has worked for at least a year. The employee could be a manager but should not be a director.

**2** Your objective is to gain a full understanding of the leadership style prevailing at the employee's workplace, and the style employed by the individual's own manager.

**3** Devise your own series of questions in advance, but make sure to include the following themes:
  **a** How open are communications within the business?
  **b** Are staff encouraged to apply a questioning or critical approach?
  **c** Are there any forums for discussion or debate on important policy issues affecting staff?
  **d** What does the organisational hierarchy look like? Where is your employee on that diagram? How powerful or powerless does he or she feel?
  **e** How exactly does the employee's boss treat him or her? Is there delegation? Consultation? How effective is communication between the two of them?

Write at least 600 words summarising your findings and drawing conclusions about how well the experience conforms to the leadership theory dealt with in this unit.

## B3 Case Study

'If you take your eyes off them for one minute they'll probably walk off with half the shop,' said Brian Brimpton to Frank Shore. Frank was a business colleague of Brian who found it difficult to hide his surprise that Brian was talking about his own workforce! 'I pay them well to make sure they get out of bed in the morning but I watch them all the time. I've had too much money taken out of the tills and stolen from the shops in the past to be able to relax for one minute,' continued Brian. 'I've got security cameras in all my shops and they're focused on the tills not the shoppers! I make them empty their pockets in the morning and put everything in their lockers so if I ever catch them with money on them I know they've stolen it. I do random checks every day and not surprisingly I'm catching more and more of them doing it.'

Frank pointed out that he did not have any of these policies but that theft in his stores was much lower than in Brian's. 'You're either lucky and have managed to find some honest employees or more likely you haven't discovered how much is being stolen yet!' said Brian. 'You know, Brian, I used to think like you,' continued Frank, 'but a few years ago I changed my approach. I started listening to my staff and found that much of what they said was valuable. I've now decided that you should always try to involve your employees more in making decisions. It's worked for me.' 'So far, may be,' said Brian, 'but just you wait and see. Trust me, Frank, I know. They always bite the hand that feeds them.'

**Questions** *(30 marks; 45 minutes)*

1 In what ways could Brian be described as a Theory X manager? *(4)*
2 Outline the problems that might result from a Theory X approach. *(6)*
3 Is Frank right when he says 'you should always try to involve your employees more in making decisions'? *(8)*
4 Consider whether Frank would be able to cure the security problems if he took over as manager at Brian's business. *(12)*

# ORGANISATIONAL STRUCTURE

## DEFINITION

Organisational structure is the formal and systematic way the management of a business is organised. When presented as a diagram, it shows the departmental functions and who is answerable to whom.

## 26.1 Introduction

Soon after the start of the industrial age, organisations became larger and more complex. Early management thinkers, such as FW Taylor and H Fayol, began to consider how best to design the structure of an organisation. Both these writers had production and engineering backgrounds. They saw the function of organisations as converting inputs, such as money, materials, machines and people, into output. Therefore designing an organisation was like designing a machine, the objective being to maximise efficiency. Their thinking was mechanistic; the principles of good management were like the principles of physics. Their approach was prescriptive. Early managers wanted to be told the best way to manage. And the organisational structure which would be the most effective.

## 26.2 The formal organisation: a hierarchy

The first significant attempt at organisational structure is the classical or formal hierarchy, as in Figure 26.1. Such a diagram looks familiar today and is very much part of the way we now think about organisations. It is probably the first way many people would think of describing the structure of the organisation in which they work. The diagram has many advantages. It gives a quick and simple way of gaining a mental map of an organisation. It is based on the main managerial functions and is controlled from the top layer of senior management. It suggests how all the parts and people fit together and defines each person's place and role.

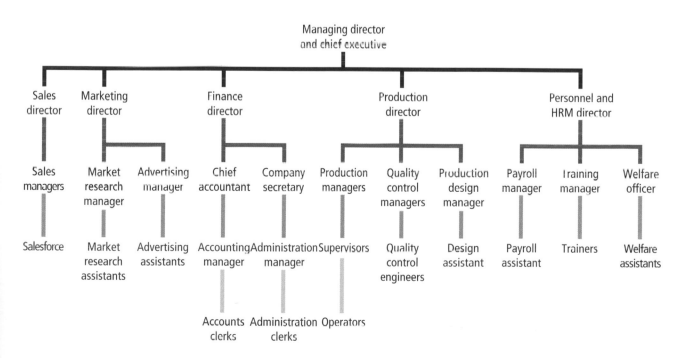

**Figure 26.1** Classical or formal hierarchy

## 26.3 Principles of management and organisational structure

Figure 26.1 also gives a good insight into many of the fundamental characteristics of the theory and principles of management and organisation structure. These are set out below.

### SOME PRINCIPLES AND CHARACTERISTICS OF MANAGEMENT AND ORGANISATIONAL STRUCTURE

**Managerial functions:** Management is an activity which can be divided neatly into functions: production, marketing, sales, accounting and finance, human resources and so on. The job of the managing director, and the other directors, sitting at the top of the 'pillars', is to ensure that all these functions are coordinated. So if each function, or department, plays its part properly, the whole organisation will succeed.

**Chain of command:** In a hierarchy, the vertical chain of command can be seen. The salesforce reports to the sales manager and the directors report to the managing director. Information is communicated up the hierarchy through the layers and orders are communicated down.

**Authority:** Authority flows from position in the hierarchy and is a source of power. The production manager has formal authority over the supervisors, who have authority over the operators below them.

**Accountability and responsibility:** A hierarchy and defined lines of authority lead to clear accountability and responsibility. A subordinate is accountable to a manager who must be responsible for him or her. Whereas authority can be delegated to a junior manager, responsibility rests at the top.

The clearer and more tightly defined the organisation chart and the organisation's rules and procedures, the more likely are accountability and responsibility to rest with named individuals. This can be positive as personal accountability can lead to high motivation. However, in an atmosphere of mistrust or in difficult times, such accountability can be a threat and reduce morale.

**Span of control:** The number of subordinates reporting to a manager. Fayol thought the span should never exceed five. A narrow span of control means tight supervision, less discretion and therefore less chance of mistakes. This may be suitable where tasks are straightforward, relatively unchanging and easily checked and measured. For instance, production of components to given tolerances, or the checking of standardised application forms and paperwork. A narrow span may mean more levels in the hierarchy or ranks, and therefore greater promotion prospects. A wide span of control reduces supervision and leads to greater **delegation** and job enrichment.

**Levels of hierarchy:** The number of layers in a hierarchy will reflect the number of supervisory and managerial levels, ranks or grades. The more there are and the taller the organisation structure, the greater the opportunities for miscommunication, or distorted or deliberately filtered communication. Also the more remote the top and bottom of the hierarchy are from each other.

**De-layering:** The removal of one or more layers from a hierarchy as organisations attempt to become leaner and fitter. This can assist communication, cut out bureaucracy and overhead costs, and motivate staff by increasing individual authority and responsibility. However, it can widen the span of control, reducing supervision and lead to overwork and perhaps stress. De-layering is sometimes a convenient term for redundancies.

**Centralisation:** Centralisation means that only the top levels of the hierarchy have the authority to take decisions. In an organisation which is spread geographically, for example, it implies that all key decisions will be taken at head office. This can ensure tight financial control since targets will be set for the whole organisation from the centre. It can lead to coherent strategies in marketing and production and sharing of resources. Also it can simplify and speed up decision making. However, centralisation reduces the opportunities for input from the lower levels of the hierarchy or the more distant parts of the organisation. This can lead to poor communication and demotivation.

**Decentralisation:** This implies widespread **delegation** and the passing of power down to lower levels in the hierarchy for decision making. This can motivate and empower junior managers and supervisors and can lead to greater innovation and enthusiasm. It also reduces the need for tight control and communication. However, it can lead to loss of control by senior managers and head office. It can also lead to lack of direction or less consistency (which may damage the corporate identity).

**Bureaucracy:** A bureaucracy is where the work of the organisation closely follows rules and procedures. Precedent is important in making decisions. Anything unusual will be referred up the hierarchy. Job descriptions will be tightly and narrowly defined. Individuals will have little discretion. Work will probably be broken into small tasks which are measured and checked. Paperwork and forms will be common. Overt respect for authority will be high. The strongest source of power will be position power in the hierarchy. Conformists are likely to be successful, ensuring a stable corporate culture.

## 26.4 Organisational behaviour

Do people in organisations actually behave as the formal hierarchy suggests?

In reality, businesses, or the people in them, do not always behave in the way the organisation chart would suggest. Communication may not always be upwards but sideways; employees in different functions find it better to talk direct rather than 'through the proper channels', i.e. via their boss.

The objectives of staff in different parts of a business may not always match the corporate objectives because of personal interests or rivalries:

- sales staff may believe they do all the hard work while marketing executives merely dream up fanciful campaigns
- production managers may pursue product quality for its own sake rather than that required by the customers
- accountants will see budgets as an objective which others see as constraints
- position power, for example that held by the chief executive's personal assistant, may be used to filter communication. Informal groups may influence individual behaviour away from formal objectives.

Organisational success relies upon bringing staff together in a shared vision of what needs to be done and everyone's role in achieving it. Diagrams of organisation hierarchies may give little clue about the reality of who is contributing most to business success.

---

'*Hierarchies just get in the way of business, cutting off managers from their customers, insulating them from the market and creating slow bureaucracies.*'
Percy Barnevik, former chief of the industrial giant ABB
(Asea Brown Boveri)

'*In a hierarchy, every employee tends to rise to his own level of incompetence.*'
Lawrence Peter, creator of The Peter Principle

'*There has to be some degree of hierarchy, because decisions actually have to be taken.*'
George Bull, chief executive

'*Middle managers, as we have known them, are cooked geese.*'
Tom Peters, management guru

'*If you look at General Motors today versus yesterday, they've slimmed a little bit. They had 29 layers. Which means that nobody could really be considered for a top management job before the age 211.*'
Peter Drucker, management guru

Source: *The Ultimate Book of Business Quotations*, Stuart Crainer, Capstone Publishing, 1997

---

## 26.5 Factors influencing optimal organisational structure

Modern management thinking has moved away from the view that there is one organisational structure which will suit all organisations at all times. What is the best structure for one organisation will depend on many factors. Organisations have vastly different environments in which they operate. Some are reasonably stable while others are constantly changing.

Organisations also differ greatly in size and in objectives. As Charles Handy explained in *Understanding Organizations*, within all large organisations, a culture develops which greatly influences the type of structure which is appropriate. This culture can be thought of as an organisational ideology, a set of norms or a way of life, which is pervasive. The culture of a sixth form college is very different from that of an army officer training school. Similarly, working in the research department of a giant pharmaceutical company is likely to be very different from working as a foreign exchange dealer in a city bank. Indeed, within large organisations, there will be different cultures – the bank's foreign exchange dealing room will work quite differently from the mortgage lending department where a financial adviser patiently explains complex matters to a first-time house buyer.

Some organisations have a culture which is very formal, where there is a strict dress code, where punctuality is all-important or staying late is normal. In some organisations everything operates through committees; rules and procedures are very important. In other, more informal, organisations, individuals rather than committees make decisions. Initiative rather than conformity or obedience is usual. People are judged on results rather than adherence to precedent or established practice. All organisations have signs of power – do people seek expense accounts, a large office, a bigger company car, or share options? Answers to these types of question tell much of the culture of an organisation.

## 26.6 Organisational structures for different organisational cultures

Following Handy, we can identify four different sets of circumstances or 'cultures', as set out in the table at the top of the next page. Each requires a different organisational structure.

### THE FORMAL HIERARCHY

When is this the best structure? The formal hierarchy (see Figure 26.1) is best suited to the role culture. In this culture the role, or job description, is often more

| CULTURE | STRUCTURE |
|---------|-----------|
| Role culture | Formal hierarchy |
| Task culture | Matrix |
| Power culture | Web |
| Person culture | Cluster |

important than the individual who fills it. Performance over and above the job description is not required. Tasks are clearly defined, as are accountability and responsibility. There is a clear chain of command. Position power is the major source of power in this culture.

Other features of the role culture are:

- Individual departments or functions can be very strong and self-contained, guarding their own power.
- Roles will be precisely defined using clear job descriptions and definitions of authority.

## Business IN

### IKEA

Ikea's huge success in Europe comes from a high degree of central control. Maintenance, internationally, of consistency of the Ikea brand name and image is all-important. This often causes tension between the satellite stores in the UK and head office in Sweden. Local stores want to follow local market trends but this conflicts with the central objective of a consistent brand image everywhere. A good example is store design and product development, which are both run from Sweden. This policy of tight central control has worked so far and no doubt has enabled growth. The policy may well be severely tested if there is a major change in the business environment, such as new competition or a widespread recession.

Source: Adapted from *The Financial Times*

- There are set ways of communicating, such as standard memos with defined circulation lists and 'usual channels', e.g. subordinate to superior and no-one else. There may also be accepted ways of addressing others, such as calling the boss 'Mr' or 'Mrs' instead of using Christian names.
- Decision making will be based largely on precedent.
- There are likely to be many layers of hierarchy in a bureaucratic structure in which there is a narrow span of control.

Managerial functions will need to be strongly coordinated at the top by senior management. Then, if the departments do their job, as laid down by the rules and procedures, the results should be as planned.

### THE TASK CULTURE: MATRIX STRUCTURE

The task culture is job or project oriented. Its accompanying structure can be best seen as a matrix. So the matrix organisation, as shown in Figure 26.2, is a common structure for organisations with a task culture.

This attempts to avoid the major disadvantage of the formal hierarchy in which only senior levels of management communicate and work together. In a matrix the functional departments still exist. But people from those departments have the flexibility to work on projects with or for other departments. The development of a new product would require product research and design, consumer and market research, as well as production and management accounting. So a researcher whose **line manager** is the head of research may spend half their time working on a project run by the head of new products. Those who favour formal hierarchies would worry about an employee having two bosses. Japanese firms such as Toyota have proved, however, that working together on projects saves time and therefore allows new products to be brought to the market more quickly.

Matrix management is likely to work best in a business with a relatively wide span of control and relatively few layers of management hierarchy. The structure aims to bring people and resources together and let them get on with particular tasks. Individual capability rather than age or formal status determines people's standing in the task culture. Rules, procedure

| | Finance department | Marketing department | Research and development department | Production department |
|---|---|---|---|---|
| | Finance specialist | Marketing specialist | Research and development specialists | Production specialist |
| Project manager A | | | | |
| Project manager B | | | | |
| Project manager C | | | | |
| Project manager D | | | | |

**Figure 26.2** Matrix or net structure

and precedent are less important. Authority flows more from competence on the task rather than place in the hierarchy.

### Advantages:

- Task culture is appropriate where flexibility, creativity and teamwork are important qualities. This would be where the market is volatile or product life cycles are short. Being job or project oriented, the task culture is based on the expertise of a well-trained professional staff and its strength lies in its adaptability.
- Different teams across the functions can be combined as appropriate to meet the needs of different projects. This adds interest and variety to working life and can therefore act as a motivator.

### Disadvantages:

- Much of the power and influence in a matrix system lies at quite low levels in the management hierarchy. This gives rise to power groups at lower levels with specialised knowledge and expertise. Senior managers no longer know everything.
- Control may be difficult in the task culture. Dilution of power and control are the price paid by senior managers for fast response and more teamwork.

### POWER CULTURE AND THE ENTREPRENEURIAL OR WEB STRUCTURE

A power culture or web is often found in small businesses or entrepreneurial organisations and in some property and trading and finance companies. A power culture is usually dominated by a strong central figure, typically the founder or chairman. Its structure is best pictured as a web (see Figure 26.3). Alan Sugar's company Amstrad was run in this way. Sugar's speed of decision making was the key to success in the early

**Figure 26.3** Power culture and the web

stages of the markets for personal computers and satellite dishes.

This culture depends on a central power source radiating power and influence. It may also depend on a few key individuals trusted by the leader. Few decisions are taken collectively or in a committee. This organisation works on precedent, and on anticipating the wishes and decisions of the central power sources. As the views of middle managers carry little or no weight, few of them will be employed. Therefore there are likely to be few layers of hierarchy and a relatively wide span of control. Usually this kind of structure encourages delegation or **empowerment**. Here, though, the control exerted by the leader means that decision making power remains firmly at the top.

### THE PERSON CULTURE

The fourth culture is an unusual one. It will not be found pervading many organisations. Its structure is as minimal as possible; a cluster is the best word for it – or perhaps a galaxy of individual stars (see Figure 26.4).

The person culture may be seen where any kind of formal structure seems largely absent. The organisation exists simply to assist as administrative back-up for 'star-performer' individuals. Handy gives barristers' chambers, architects' practices, and some management consultancy firms as examples. Possibly one might include hospitals and universities where cutting-edge research is undertaken, or the creative departments of advertising agencies.

**Advantages:** The person culture thrives where rules, procedures and precedent are virtually non-existent as new ground is being broken all the time. Creativity is the watchword. The cluster will be successful where

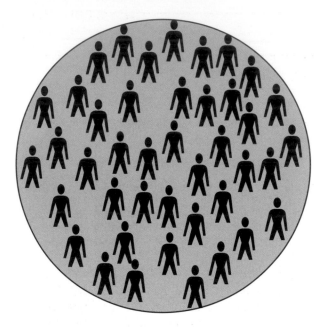

**Figure 26.4** The person culture and the cluster

work is often very specialised, with each case unique. And where quick reactions to ever-changing and new events are needed, together with rapid risk taking and decision making.

**Disadvantages:** Specialised departments of large organisations which operate as unstructured person cultures can become divorced from the main business and become self-running. It may be difficult to set targets or keep them in line with organisational objectives. The department's spending may be difficult to control and its end results may not be apparent. This culture is not often found in manufacturing companies, or large-scale organisations generally.

---

ISSUES FOR **analysis**

Work experience, part-time work or project coursework provide good opportunities to examine the structure of an organisation. This applies whether commercial or non-profit making, for example a school or college. The formal structure is often recorded and published in a chart. It will be revealing to analyse the chart to see if the organisation really does work along the lines set out in the chart. How do the people at the top attempt to set objectives and keep the organisation on course? What controls are in place? Is the organisation hierarchical, with rules and procedures, or does it just seem to happen?

All organisations have a culture. A useful exercise would be to classify it and to analyse whether it matches the structure which has been chosen.

Finally, in your organisation or organisations under review, are there powerful groups or individuals not appearing in the formal structure. One good question is this: if you want something done, who do you go to?

---

The choice of the appropriate organisational structure will depend on many factors, especially culture, but also history and ownership, size of organisation, technology, goals and objectives, the business environment and the people.

Structure can be extremely important and must be chosen very carefully. In situations which are subject to rapid change, the rigid procedures of a formal hierarchy may well frustrate competent people who will want to see proper change and development. Too many levels of management may also demotivate good ambitious young managers who feel that red tape and 'dead wood' are blocking their way. However, a person culture with the free-wheeling deregulated structure of the cluster organisation would hardly suit the armed forces with their responsibility for highly powerful and potentially dangerous equipment and armaments. Nor would air passengers feel secure if air traffic controllers and airline pilots did not follow the rules and procedures of a relatively formal organisation.

Handy should have the last word. Perhaps, as he suggests, large firms should contain the various cultures within themselves. So a formal structure and hierarchy could deal with routine and mundane procedures such as processing orders or paying invoices. These make up the majority of any organisation's activity. However, some parts of the organisation, such as the policy or strategic planning section, product design or research and development, or creative marketing, should be organised as a matrix or even cluster. So the best organisation will have different structures to meet its ongoing needs.

---

**KEY terms**

**delegation** – passing power and authority down the hierarchy. It involves giving junior managers greater trust and authority, and requires the superior to release control.

**empowerment** – a more advanced form of delegation whereby subordinates have more wide-ranging control over their work.

**line manager** – a manager with specified authority for meeting key operational objectives. Subordinates will be specifically accountable to him or her.

**staff manager** – manager that does not have line responsibility, but is likely to perform research, advisory or problem-solving functions, such as work study or consultancy services, for line managers.

# Exercises

## A. REVISION QUESTIONS

*(30 marks; 70 minutes)*

Read the unit, then answer:

1 Give three ways in which an organisation chart might be useful. *(3)*
2 Identify two observers outside an organisation who might want to see its organisation chart. Suggest reasons why they might want to see it. *(5)*
3 Distinguish between accountability and responsibility. *(4)*
4 Is there an ideal span of control? Explain your answer. *(5)*
5 Explain in your own words the term 'bureaucracy'. *(3)*
6 What is organisational culture? Is an organisation's culture really 'the way things are done round here' by the most powerful group? *(6)*
7 What organisational structure is most suited for an organisation in a stable environment? *(2)*
8 What organisational structure is most suited for an organisation facing a rapidly changing or unpredictable environment? *(2)*

## B. REVISION EXERCISES

### B1 Data Response

Deeton & Co has three directors answerable to the chief executive.

- One director is in charge of two accountants.
- The second has five managers answerable to her, each of whom has four subordinates.
- The third has four managers, each with two subordinates.
- One of the managers is answerable to both the second and third directors.

**Questions** *(15 marks; 20 minutes)*
1 Draw the organisational hierarchy. *(5)*
2 What is the second director's span of control? *(1)*
3 Explain any weaknesses you can identify in this hierarchy. *(9)*

### B2 Activity

Consider an organisation you know well. This could be your school or college. Draw an organisation chart to describe in the form a classical hierarchy.

Explain to the rest of your group how realistic a description this chart is of the organisation.

You may find it useful to consider:

- How stable is its environment?
- Have there been new targets, constraints, competition?
- How much internal change has there been in the last two years?
- Has there been a change of leadership?
- How do you get things done in the organisation?
- Is there a powerful informal group?
- Is there a group with power based on knowledge, experience or expertise?
- Is tradition important – 'we've always done it this way'?
- Is promotion usually internal or external or a mix?
- How does communication take place?
- Is it effective?
- Do the departments or sections communicate much with each other?

### B3 Case Study

A light engineering business, making plastic components, employs you as a management consultant. Its organisation chart, drawn by the personnel officer, is shown below. The business has been in a stable environment for many years and sells most of its output to a major consumer goods manufacturer. Your friend has just started as a management accountant and tells you that profitability is falling and that administrative overheads seem to be rising as a percentage of sales revenue.

**Questions** *(30 marks; 45 minutes)*
Write a report on the suitability of the organisational structure. Your terms of reference are to include any recommendations for change.

Within your report, indicate what assumptions you make and any other information you would like. Ensure that your recommendations include suggested amendments to the organisation chart.

You should consider at least the following: the number of departments, clarity of lines of accountability and responsibility, suitability of lines of accountability and responsibility, span of control, fit between structure and actual and potential business environment. Bring in any other relevant points or arguments. *(25)*

Your report should have at least the following headings: 'To/from', 'Date', 'Subject', 'Terms of reference', Conclusions', Recommendations'. *(5)*

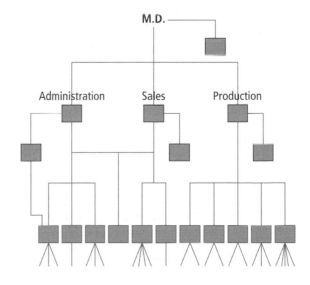

# MANAGEMENT BY OBJECTIVES (MBO)

**DEFINITION**

A system of mutually agreed targets between managers and employees which is intended to ensure that everyone is working towards the organisational goals.

## 27.1 What is management by objectives?

Every large organisation has problems coordinating the activities of all of its employees. Senior managers may have a clear idea of what they want to achieve. Others within the organisation may not be so sure. If you ask employees in most organisations what they think the overall **objective** of the business is, you are likely to get very different answers. Senior managers may have tried to explain the corporate objectives, but many staff will still be unclear. They may wonder what they are supposed to be doing or how their work helps the business fulfil its overall target. Even if people do understand their role there is a danger that they will be more interested in their own targets rather than those of the firm as a whole. By increasing the size of their own department, for example, individual managers may well gain more power, even if this is not necessarily in the interest of the business. Such problems often increase with the size of the firm. It becomes more difficult to keep in constant and personal contact with people and to check on what they are doing.

The originator of much modern thinking on management by objectives was Peter Drucker. In his 1973 book *Management: Tasks, Responsibilities and Practices* (© Butterworth Heineman Publishers) he wrote that:

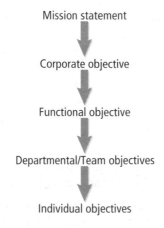

Mission statement

↓

Corporate objective

↓

Functional objective

↓

Departmental/Team objectives

↓

Individual objectives

**Figure 27.1** Management by objectives

'A manager, in the first place, sets objectives. He determines what the objectives should be. He determines what the goals in each area of the business should be. He decides what has to be done to reach these objectives. He makes the objectives effective by communicating them to the people whose performance is needed to attain them.'

Drucker went on to stress that managers must also establish yardsticks to enable staff to focus 'on the performance of the whole organisation and which, at the same time, focus on the work of the individual and help him to do it.' In other words, it is not enough to establish objectives. At the same time a system must be established to let people see for themselves how they are performing against the targets set. By delegating power in this way, bosses no longer need to check regularly on what each employee is doing.

## 27.2 From mission to MBO

The overall reason for the firm's existence is known as its corporate aim or mission. This is often written out in a **mission statement**. For example, the firm might set out to be 'the lowest cost producer in Europe', 'the world's favourite car hire firm' or simply 'to be the best in the industry'. The mission is usually a fairly general target. It sets out the overall purpose of the firm without much detail. Remember Star Trek's 'To boldly go where no man has been before'? This is a typical mission statement – it is meant to inspire and define the underlying purpose of the organisation.

Whilst a mission statement may be motivating, it lacks the specific information needed for planning. What does being the 'best in the industry' mean? The most profitable? The biggest? The fastest growing? To plan properly the firm needs to turn the mission into a corporate objective. This will specify exactly what the firm wants to measure, how much of an increase it wants and when it wants to achieve the target. For example, the firm might set out to 'increase profits by 20% over a five-year period'.

The firm then has to turn this overall objective into more detailed targets for individual departments and managers. To achieve the corporate objective all the different functional managers (such as marketing, finance, operations and human resources) must have their own targets. For example, the marketing objective might be to increase sales, whilst the operations department might try to reduce costs. These func-

Coca-Cola in China

tional objectives then lead to further targets within each business area. To increase sales, for example, the marketing managers might decide to increase the level of promotional activities; to reduce costs the operations manager might aim to reduce the number of reject products. Every time an objective is set, the next level of managers must decide how this is to be fulfilled. If everyone meets their targets successfully then the firm will achieve its overall objective. If the number of defects is reduced, for example, this will decrease costs which in turn will help the firm increase its profitability.

Once managers have agreed their objectives it is possible to develop appropriate strategies. The **strategy** is the plan which shows how to fulfil the objective. If, for example, the objective is to generate 25% of sales from new products, the strategy might be to invest more heavily in research and development.

## 27.3 How does MBO work?

The MBO system is based on mutually agreed objectives. A manager will discuss with subordinates what needs to be achieved in their particular section of the firm. Between them they will agree specific targets for each subordinate. For the MBO system to work effectively it is important that the objectives are agreed by the subordinates and not simply imposed on them. This is because a target means nothing unless the individual feels committed to achieving it. It is good practice, therefore, to allow staff to set objectives for themselves subject to the superior's approval. They are likely to be much more committed to them because they will feel that they 'own' these targets for themselves. The parent who sets a struggling A level student the objective of 2As and a B is unlikely to generate a positive response.

## 27.4 Advantages of MBO

- By adopting a system of management by objectives, each manager knows exactly what he or she has to do. Everyone has a clear set of targets which will help them decide on their own priorities and allocate their resources effectively. This is crucial. A busy executive starts every day with mail, e-mail, voicemail, faxes and scribbled notes left on the desk. Many get bogged down in responding to the requests and problems involved. The stars are the ones who prioritise effectively. They concentrate on the issues which matter most in achieving their – and the company's – objectives.

- The MBO system also acts as a motivator. Individuals are able to track their own performance and measure it against the agreed targets. Theorists such as Herzberg made clear their belief that responsibility is a vital motivator. Peter Drucker believed that the most effective way to give people a sense of responsibility for their working lives was to enable them to decide for themselves how to achieve their objectives.
- At the same time, the targets act as a control mechanism for the organisation. Everyone's performance can be judged against the targets. The potential impact of any variance from these can be identified or anticipated.
- The MBO system should also ensure that employees in every department are all working towards common goals. Without this their efforts may be well intentioned but actually conflict with each other. Attempts by marketing to promote an exclusive image might contradict the attempts of the production department to cut costs by using cheaper packaging. MBO allows delegation to be achieved in a coordinated way.

## 27.5 Problems of MBO

While the MBO system sounds appealing in theory, in practice it can become bureaucratic and time consuming. Managers and subordinates can spend hours in meetings trying to agree targets which may be unrealistic anyway. There is no point in setting Ryan Giggs the objective of a goal every two games. There are too many factors outside his control to enable him to believe in such a target. Setting targets does not guarantee that they are achieved. In some cases, companies introduce MBO but individual managers are unwilling to delegate fully to their subordinates. This results in frustration as the executive feels they will be held responsible for something they do not fully control.

Another problem is that the objectives can become out of date and inappropriate very quickly. This is especially true if the environment in which the firm operates is changing rapidly. With new competitors, new product offerings, new technology and new legislation the world in which a firm operates can be very dynamic. Targets may soon become irrelevant. Consequently some managers think it is more important to set out the general direction the firm wants to move in. Not try to be too specific about the exact

route. Tying managers down to specific objectives may mean they end up pursuing a target which is inappropriate in a changed environment. Much better, some say, to let managers react for themselves to the situation in which they operate.

### Business IN TOO MANY TARGETS

In 2002 the National Health Service (NHS) Confederation asked the Government to cut the number of targets it had been set and give managers and doctors the space to deliver its aims. In the same year it was revealed that parts of the NHS had been manipulating waiting lists in order to achieve targets and cut waiting times. The National Audit Office, a government watchdog, found 'pressure to reduce waiting lists has led a significant number of consultants to treat some patients before others with higher clinical priority'. Nine NHS trusts had 'inappropriately adjusted' their waiting lists – 3 of them for 3 years or more – affecting 6,000 patient records. The adjustments varied in seriousness from junior staff following 'established but incorrect' procedures to 'deliberate manipulation or mis-statement' of figures. While in some cases there was little or no impact on patient care, in other cases patients with a serious illness were forced to wait longer for treatment.

## 27.6 The features of a good objective

A good objective has five main features. It should be:

- Specific – this means it must be clear what the firm is trying to achieve. For example, managers may want to increase sales, increase profit or increase customer satisfaction.
- Measurable – this means that all objectives should include a quantifiable element. For example, the firm might aim to increase profit by 30%. This means that the managers can easily check whether the target has been achieved.
- Agreed – targets need to be agreed by the different people who are involved in the process. There is no point imposing a target on someone. For example, if you were simply told to work harder it is unlikely to have any effect unless you can see the point of it and have a chance to discuss how much additional work you can realistically do.

- Realistic – a target should always be achievable. If you set an objective which cannot be achieved people will not be motivated by it. It may even discourage them because they know the target can never be reached anyway. To work well employees must believe that their efforts can be successful.
- Time specific – all objectives should state quite clearly when they should be achieved. Managers need to know exactly how long they have so that they can plan accordingly.

Imagine you were set an objective of 'increasing sales'. This is a very poor objective. You do not know how long you have to do it or by how much you have to increase sales.

## UNILEVER: PATH TO GROWTH

In February 2000 Unilever announced a 5 year strategic plan called 'Path to Growth'. The plan focused on a series of initiatives concentrating on fewer stronger brands to accelerate growth. By 2004 the company is committed to delivering:

- Revenue growth of 5-6% per annum
- Operating profit margins of more than 16% (compared to 11% before the start of Path to Growth)
- Double digit growth of earnings per share

The company has set out to achieve these targets by focusing on its leading brands such as Lipton tea, Dove soap and Hellmann's mayonnaise, and supporting them with an increased marketing budget. At the same time it is selling off its under-performing businesses. For example it has already put up for sale brands such as Elizabeth Arden, Calvin Klein and Karl Lagerfeld, Nautica, Vera Wang, Valentino and Cerruti.

### ISSUES FOR analysis

- Management by objectives provides a valuable means of coordinating the firm's activities and improving decision making. It is therefore an invaluable way of combatting the diseconomies of scale which can harm the economic performance of large businesses.
- Management by objectives provides a system for managers to review their progress to date and consider how they can contribute to the overall success of the organisation. It can therefore be seen as fundamental to McGregor's ideas on Theory Y leadership, and as a way of implementing Herzberg's desire for job enrichment.
- To work effectively, the targets must be mutually agreed and used as part of a regular appraisal system.

- Management by objectives may restrict managers' efforts; they may focus on the particular targets and not use their initiative.
- Objectives may become out of date quite rapidly in a fast-changing environment. Therefore the business context is an important consideration. For instance, when tackling a business case study you would be most inclined to recommend the use of MBO for a large firm in a relatively stable market.

## 27.7 Management by objectives
### an evaluation

The aim of management by objectives is to coordinate the decisions of all the different parts of the firm. This is needed to bring about a consistent approach and ensure that a workforce of perhaps 50,000 people are all heading in the same direction. It can also form part of a regular appraisal system in which managers and workers meet to review performance and set new targets. However, in recent years MBO has been rejected in many organisations because it can act as a constraint on management thinking. Once certain targets have been set managers may only focus on these areas of their job and may neglect other business opportunities which present themselves. Given the increasing pace of change targets can quickly become out of date, which limits the value of the system.

An even more important issue is that MBO may cause problems to a business with a weak corporate culture. In the 1980s and 1990s, many large financial businesses such as Prudential found severe problems with sales staff. In the pursuit of their sales objectives, the staff had been mis-selling private pension plans to people who would have been better off staying in the state pension scheme. The employees' short-term pursuit of their objectives led the companies into years of bad publicity and very expensive refunds to customers. Management by objectives can give the green light to **short-termist** decision making unless a positive long-term vision is clearly in place.

### KEY terms

**mission statement** – a statement of the firm's overall reason for its existence.

**objective** – a quantifiable target which helps to coordinate activities.

**short-termist** – pursuing an objective without considering the longer term impact.

**strategy** – a plan which shows how to achieve an objective.

# Exercises

## A. REVISION QUESTIONS
*(30 marks; 50 minutes)*

Read the unit, then answer:
1 Explain what is meant by 'management by objectives'. *(3)*
2 Why is it 'not enough to establish objectives'? *(4)*
3 What are the possible advantages of using a management by objectives approach? *(4)*
4 What are the possible disadvantages of using a management by objectives approach? *(4)*
5 Outline three features of an effective objective. *(6)*
6 What is meant by the term 'delegation'. *(3)*
7 Why is delegation an important part of MBO? *(3)*
8 Distinguish between an objective and a mission. *(3)*

## B. REVISION EXERCISES
### B1 Data Response: British Airways

> Our aim is to provide … customers, whoever they are with the finest service to be found anywhere. We want to offer them the widest choice of fares, of routes and of times of their flights. And because air travel has now become a truly global industry we are determined to forge ever closer links with airlines of like mind throughout the world to deliver together the service our customers desire …
>
> We are a British airline, and proud of it. But that alone is not enough. We have global obligations – to our customers, to our staff in 85 countries, to our shareholders, and to the world itself.
>
> British Airways will fulfil its mission to be the undisputed leader in world travel. We cannot, however, achieve that alone. While boundaries exist on the ground we must join other airlines in other parts of the world in bringing the highest possible standards of safety, style, comfort and service to the people of every nation around the globe.
>
> Source: *British Airways Report and Accounts*, 1997–8

**Questions** *(30 marks; 35 minutes)*
1 British Airways' mission is 'to be the undisputed leader in world travel'. Why do some firms have mission statements? *(5)*
2 Distinguish between a firm's mission and its objectives. *(3)*
3 Examine two possible influences on a firm's objectives. *(6)*
4 A firm's strategy aims to fulfil its objectives. Outline British Airways' strategy. *(9)*
5 Could British Airways' commitment to its shareholders conflict with its commitment to its staff? Explain your answer. *(7)*

### B2 Case Study: George McGarry
George McGarry works as a sales representative for Magnox Computers, a local computer specialist which sells computer networks to companies in Oxford. George has been working there for nearly a year now and is very eager to succeed. Although he enjoys his work he finds that it is not always clear exactly what he should be doing. Obviously his job is to sell the computer systems, but which areas should he be concentrating on? Should he focus on selling more to his existing customers or finding new business? Should he try and sell one or two big orders or try and find more smaller contracts?

Although his boss seems very pleased with him, George is not entirely certain what he is doing! Take last week, for example. George did very few deals, but did manage to make a number of new contacts. His boss was delighted and said that this was good 'for long-term growth'. Only a few months ago, however, George had been criticised for spending too much time on the future and not enough on increasing his weekly sales total. To make matters worse, in his six monthly appraisal he had been given a 20% bonus but he had no idea how this had been calculated.

He had, of course, asked his boss what his targets should be at any given moment. 'It's not as simple as that, George. The messages come down to me from on high and I never know what they're going to be. One month we may want to push a particular product, next month we have hit our overall target and can concentrate on generating new business. Just carry on what you're doing; if there are any problems I'll let you know. There's really no point us sitting down and agreeing long-term targets because they'll only change week to week.'

**Questions** *(30 marks; 45 minutes)*
1 Analyse the possible gains from introducing management by objectives at Magnox Computers. *(10)*
2 What problems might occur if management by objectives were introduced at Magnox Computers? *(10)*
3 To what extent should firms concentrate on the future rather than the present? *(10)*

## C. ESSAY QUESTIONS

1 Bantron plc is a conglomerate which operates in several countries. Despite its rapid growth, Bantron's profitability has been falling. Consider the possible advantages of introducing management by objectives at this time.
2 'In a bureaucratic organisation, management by objectives becomes a checklist. Just another form to be filled in.' How might a business leader make sure that management by objectives becomes a way of driving the business forward?
3 Discuss whether management by objectives is a means of controlling or a means of empowering employees.
4 To what extent is it likely that employees will welcome or resist the introduction of management by objectives within a business?

# HUMAN RESOURCE MANAGEMENT

The purpose of human resource management (HRM) is to recruit, develop and utilise an organisation's personnel in the way which is most appropriate to the achievement of that firm's objectives.

## 28.1 Introduction

Research regularly shows that the most successful organisations are those that make the best use of their staff. So the management of human resources (staff) should be one of the highest-profile, highest status jobs in the business world. In reality this is not the case. Twenty years ago 'personnel managers' began a campaign to increase their influence within companies by emphasising that 'human resources' were at least as important as financial resources. Therefore 'human resource directors' were needed in the boardroom to help make and implement important strategic decisions.

This renaming of the personnel function has been implemented in many firms. It remains very questionable, though, as to whether it has any greater significance. Many UK firms remain dominated by accountants and – less often – marketing experts. Therefore the need to get the best out of staff is more a feature of foreign-owned firms, such as those from Japan, Germany and America.

In theory, HRM is about strategic decisions based upon the skills of the workforce. Day by day, however, it concerns recruitment, training, performance appraisal and the attempt to manage staff performance, plus occasional issues of redundancy, dismissal and industrial relations.

## 28.2 Recruitment and selection

The purpose of the recruitment and selection process is to acquire a suitable number of employees with appropriate skills, in order to meet the manpower requirements of the organisation. It is in the interests of the firm to achieve this goal at a minimum cost in terms of both time and resources.

There are three stages to this process:

1 determining the human resource requirements of the organisation
2 attracting suitable candidates for the vacancy
3 selecting the most appropriate candidate.

### 1 DETERMINING THE HUMAN RESOURCE REQUIREMENTS OF THE ORGANISATION

Recruitment and selection procedures need to fit in with the overall workforce plan. Workforce planning starts by auditing the current staff. How old are they (how many will be retiring over the next 18 months?)? What are their skills? And how many are prepared to take on new tasks or challenges? This information must be compared with an estimate of the future workforce needs, based on the firm's overall strategy for the next year or two. A sales push into Europe might require more French speakers; planned factory closures may require redundancies and redeployments. The workforce plan must then show how the business can push staff from where they are now, to where they need to be later on.

Efficient workforce planning requires managers to question the existing employment structure at every opportunity. This can occur when:

- an individual leaves the firm because of retirement or finding alternative employment
- an employee is promoted within the business, creating a vacancy
- an increase in workload occurs
- the development of a new product, or an emerging technology, which means that the organisation requires employees with additional skills.

Many businesses fill vacancies automatically with no analysis of alternative actions. However, it may be more effective to consider reorganisation of job responsibilities. Now that Jim has retired we can consider whether his job should be rather different today. A good human resource manager will look ahead to the future needs of a department before just advertising for a replacement. Should Jim's successor be able to speak French? Indeed, is a full-time employee needed? Should the business opt for increased flexibility by shifting to the use of part-time employees? Or contract Jim's tasks out to a specialist firm?

### 2 ATTRACTING SUITABLE CANDIDATES FOR A VACANCY

Once the firm's human resource provision has been considered and the need for a new recruit established,

## WORKFORCE PLANNING AT TESCO

Britain's largest private sector employer is Tesco, with more than 200,000 employees. In October 2002 it announced headline details of its workforce plan for the coming 6 months. It would be hiring 17,000 extra staff before Christmas, 5,000 of whom would be kept on permanently to work in 62 new stores. Tesco's retail director, David Potts, said this came on top of 9,000 jobs created to cope with busier trading conditions at existing stores.

it is necessary to find a method of attracting suitable candidates.

The first step in this process is to develop a *job description*. This will usually consist of:

- a job title
- a statement outlining how the job fits into the overall structure of the organisation
- details of the job's content, such as the tasks which must be performed and the responsibilities involved
- an indication of the working conditions the post holder can expect. This includes details of pay, hours of work and holiday entitlement.

Many firms will then choose to produce a *person specification*. This details the qualities of the ideal candidate, such as 'highly numerate'. This should help to identify the criteria to use to shortlist and then select the best candidates from those who apply.

At this point the business must decide if the post will be filled from within the company or from outside it. Internal recruitment ensures that the abilities of candidates will be known. In addition, other employees will be motivated by the evidence of promotion prospects within the firm. However, external recruitment will provide a wider pool of applicants from which to select. It can also introduce new thinking to the organisation.

The recruitment process can be expensive. It includes not only the cost of the advertising, but also the administration of, perhaps, hundreds of applications. Then there is the management time spent in the shortlisting and interviewing phases. The insurance giant Standard Life spends over £500,000 a year to recruit 50 management trainees. That is over £10,000 each!

The successful management of human resources demands that the effectiveness of recruitment advertising should be monitored. The most common method adopted is to calculate the cost of attracting each new employee. The appropriateness of recruits is also a concern. This can be judged by keeping a record of the proportion of candidates recruited by the firm who remain in employment six months later. Standard Life is rightly proud that 99% of the graduate trainees they employ are still with them two years later.

### 3 SELECTING THE RIGHT PERSON FOR THE JOB

The selection process involves assessing candidates against the criteria set out in the person specification. The most frequently employed selection process is to:

- shortlist a small number of applicants based on their application forms
- ask for a reference from their previous employers/teachers
- call for interview the individuals whose references are favourable.

The choice of who will be offered the job is made by the interview panel, based on which candidate they feel most closely matches the person specification for the post. Research suggests that the use of interviews is not a very reliable indicator of how well an individual will perform in a job. This is largely because interviewers are too easily swayed by appearance, personal charm and the interview technique of applicants. A number of other selection techniques have therefore been developed to complement, or replace, the use of this selection procedure.

The interview is a common form of selection

**Testing:** There are two types of test. *Aptitude tests* measure how good the applicant is at a particular skill, such as typing or arithmetic. *Psychometric tests* measure the personality, attitudes and character of an applicant. They give an indication of whether the applicant will be a team player or a loner, passive or assertive, questioning or accepting, and so on. The firm can make a selection judgement on the appropriate type of person from experience, and from the specific requirements of the job. This approach is particularly common in management and graduate recruitment.

Many doubts have been raised about the accuracy and validity of psychometric tests. Do they give an unfair advantage to certain people? Certainly the questions must be checked to remove social, sex or racial bias. There is also concern about whether firms are right to want all their managers to have similar characteristics. A wide range of personalities may lead to a more interesting, sparky atmosphere with livelier debates and better decisions.

**Assessment centres:** Assessment centres are a means of establishing the performance of job candidates in a range of circumstances. A group of similar applicants are invited to a centre, often for a number of days, for an in-depth assessment. They will be asked to perform tasks under scrutiny, such as role playing crisis situations. This is a good way to assess leadership qualities.

Research suggests this approach is the most effective selection technique for predicting successful job performance. Although the use of these centres is growing they are expensive and time consuming. Only large firms can afford to use this recruitment strategy and it is only appropriate for individuals who will potentially fill senior positions within a firm in the future.

Whichever selection procedure is adopted, a growing number of organisations are encouraging line managers to become involved in the recruitment decision. The role of the human resource department is increasingly one of providing support to functional departments rather than driving the recruitment process itself. Line managers are more aware of the key requirements of a post because they see it being carried out from day to day.

## 28.3 Training and development

Training is the process of instructing an individual about how to carry out tasks directly related to his or her current job.

Development involves helping an individual to realise his or her full potential. This concerns general growth, and is not related specifically to the employee's existing post.

An organisation which introduces a training and development programme does so in order to ensure the best possible return on its investment in people.

The four key objectives of training and development are:

1 To help a new employee reach the level of performance expected from an experienced worker. This initial preparation upon first taking up a post is known as 'induction' training. It often contains information dealing with the layout of the firm's operating facility, health and safety measures and security systems. An attempt may also be made to introduce the individual to key employees and give an impression of the culture of the organisation. The firm's induction training should aim to drive each employee along their own personal learning curve as quickly as possible (see Figure 28.1).

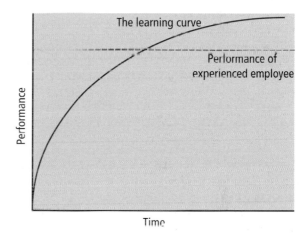

**Figure 28.1** Objective of induction training

2 To provide a wide pool of skills available to the organisation, both at present and in the future (see Figure 28.2).

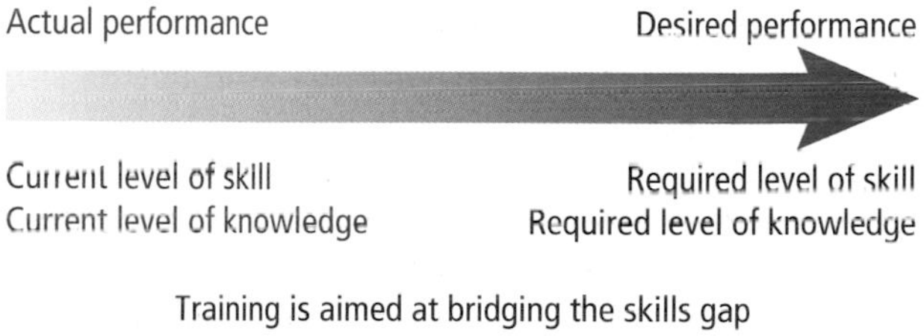

Actual performance → Desired performance

Current level of skill → Required level of skill
Current level of knowledge → Required level of knowledge

Training is aimed at bridging the skills gap

**Figure 28.2** The training gap

3 To develop a knowledgeable and committed workforce.
4 To deliver high quality products or services.

### TYPES OF TRAINING

**On-the-job training** involves instructing employees at their place of work on how a particular task should be carried out. This may be done by an experienced worker demonstrating the correct way of performing a task, or by a supervisor coaching an employee by talking them through the job stage by stage. Job rotation involves switching an employee around a range of tasks in order to develop their skills in more than one area.

**Off-the-job training** is any form of instruction which takes place away from the immediate workplace. The firm itself may organise an internal programme based within on-site facilities, or send employees to a local college or university for an external development scheme. This approach to training is more likely to include more general skills and knowledge useful at work, rather than job-specific content.

## THE COST OF NOT TRAINING

If an organisation chooses not to train its workforce it will be faced with additional recruitment costs. This is because when new skills are required existing employees will have to be made redundant and new people employed with the right skills or experience.

Untrained staff will not be as productive, or as well motivated, as those who are trained. They will be unable to deal with change because their skills are specific to the present situation. There may be more accidents in the workplace if the workforce is unskilled. In addition, employees are less likely to know, and work towards, achieving the organisation's aims and objectives.

## TRAINING IN PRACTICE

A wide range of research has indicated that organisations in the UK, both in the private and public sector, fail to invest appropriately in training and development. Many organisations view training only as a cost and therefore fail to consider the long-term benefits it can bring.

Rather than planning for the future by anticipating the firm's knowledge and skill requirements, many businesses only develop training programmes as an answer to existing problems. The Government has responded to the reactive nature of UK training by launching the Investors In People (IIP) campaign. This encourages firms to develop a more strategic view of training and development. An organisation can gain IIP accredited status if it analyses its training and development needs, plans and implements a programme in response, and evaluates the effectiveness of its provision.

## TRAINING AND MARKET FAILURE

Business people and economists like to emphasise the efficiency of 'the market'. This is the mechanism that ensures that consumer demand for eggs or Smarties is met by the right amount of supplies by the producers. In other words, 'the market' is the matching of supply and demand. Economists believe that the market

### INVESTORS IN PEOPLE

Ten years ago, business at the 62-bedroom Park Hotel in Liverpool was poor. Profit had fallen to £60,000 and the occupancy was only 30%. Ron Jones, general manager, decided that the fundamental problem was lack of repeat and recommended (word-of-mouth) business. The cause of this seemed to be the lukewarm efforts of staff.

He responded by bringing in an expert to retrain staff and build morale. And then went for the Investors In People (IIP) award. The first step was to devise a SWOT analysis in conjunction with staff. Then heads of department explained their objectives and the staff skills required to achieve it. Every member of staff had a personal development plan drawn up and was given the training they required.

By the time of receiving the IIP award, the hotel had already gained in many ways. Labour turnover fell to 5% (compared with 35% for the industry nationally). Occupancy rose to 72% and profit was in excess of £500,000 on turnover which had doubled to £1.4 million.

The hotel's general manager, June Matthews, is certain that Investors In People stimulated higher participation and more positive attitudes among staff: 'Without a shadow of doubt it was worth it.'

*Business IN*

works best when the government allows it to operate freely, without intervention.

The labour market is the supply and demand for labour. This is also allowed to operate quite freely. There are some laws to regulate the ability of employers to hire and fire or to discriminate against certain types of people. Broadly, though, the government allows firms a great deal of freedom.

The free market has served Britain very well in many ways. It can be at its weakest, however, when requiring firms to make long-term investments, such as in top quality staff training. The problem is that it may be cheaper for an individual firm to train no-one, merely hiring in new, experienced staff. In this way, the firm suffers none of the short-term costs and disruption involved in training staff who may leave once their training is complete. However, if several firms adopt this approach, companies offering good training will find that their young staff are 'poached' as soon as they become experienced. This becomes a major disincentive for firms in general to provide high quality training.

In a case such as this, the market can lead to inefficiency rather than efficiency. So it may be desirable for the government to intervene, perhaps by offering tax incentives for firms to train their own staff.

## 28.4 Appraisal of performance

Appraisal is a formal assessment of the performance of a member of staff. It involves establishing clear objectives for each employee and evaluating actual performance in the light of these goals. The most important element of an appraisal system is usually a one-to-one discussion between an individual and his or her manager. This can be held frequently, but is usually once a year. The discussion may consider specific performance measures such as individual output. Or involve a more general review of the contribution the employee makes to the smooth running of the business.

The main objectives of an appraisal system are:

- to improve the performance of the employee
- to provide feedback to the individual about his or her performance
- to recognise the future training needs of the individual
- to consider the development of the individual's career
- to identify employees in the organisation who have potential for advancement.

An appraisal system provides information which allows the business to plan and develop its human resource provision.

### APPRAISAL IN PRACTICE

Research suggests that approximately 80% of UK organisations have some form of appraisal system. The current trend is to extend schemes beyond managers and supervisors to clerical and shop-floor workers. This is being partly driven by the Investors In People initiative. This demands that all employees must be involved in, or have the option of joining, an appraisal system if it is to be recognised by the project.

Use of appraisal does not seem to be limited to large firms. Evidence suggests that the majority of firms employing less than 500 people have in place some form of appraisal system. There is some evidence, however, that linking appraisal with pay can cause disharmony in the workplace.

## 28.5 Reward systems

### FINANCIAL REWARD PROCESS

A reward system consists of financial rewards and employee benefits. Together these two elements make up an individual's total **remuneration**.

- Base pay – the level of wage or salary which represents the rate for the job. It will be based on internal comparisons which reflect the importance of the job within the organisation. Also external comparisons will reflect the market rate for the equivalent post in other firms.
- Additions to base pay – these are influenced by variables such as skill, performance and experience. For example, merit pay reflects an assessment of the individual's level of performance.
- Employee benefits – these include holiday entitlement, pension schemes, sick pay, insurance cover and company cars.

### NON-FINANCIAL REWARD PROCESS

Non-financial rewards are the benefits the employee receives in addition to total remuneration. These can include a feeling of achievement, recognition, personal influence and increased responsibility.

The key objectives of a reward system are:

- to ensure individuals with the appropriate levels of skill and motivation are available to the organisation when they are needed
- to communicate to employees what qualities and actions the organisation values
- to encourage and support planned changes within the firm
- to provide value for money.

In order to achieve these goals a reward system must be regarded by employees as 'internally fair' and 'externally competitive'.

### PAYMENT SYSTEMS IN PRACTICE

Research suggests that the reward systems employed by UK organisations in the 1970s and 1980s failed to recognise the role of pay as a strategic tool. Emphasis was placed on the need to attract and retain employees, rather than on any wider strategic implications. During the 1990s, performance-related pay became popular. This approach involves the payment of a bonus, or salary increase, which is awarded in line with an employee's achievements over a range of indicators. Today, more emphasis is placed on rewarding the individual's skills, knowledge and competence, while at the same time placing greater significance on non-financial rewards.

ISSUES FOR **analysis**

When analysing a firm's existing approach to managing human resources, or the strategy it might choose to adopt in the future, it is useful to consider the following points :

- Is the business planning ahead to identify its future workforce requirements, or is it responding to short-term events and allowing these to shape human resource policy?

- Is the organisation preparing job descriptions and person specifications in order to ensure the recruitment process selects individuals with the most appropriate skills for the vacant post?
- Have a range of selection techniques been employed by the firm, or is a single method being used? Is an effort made to match the process adopted to the requirements of the job?
- Does the organisation have an employee appraisal system in place? If it does, is the main objective of the process to develop individuals, or to link performance to reward?
- Has the organisation's reward system been designed in a way which motivates employees to help achieve the firm's aims and objectives?
- Does the reward system use non-financial rewards in addition to pay?

## 28.6 Human resource management
### an evaluation

Managing people effectively is the single most common factor that links successful organisations. Is that the same thing as effective human resource management? Some observers consider that once managers start to think of people as 'human resources', they are on a slippery slope towards hiring and firing staff as casually as they might buy or sell raw materials or shares. In many organisations the staff feel that 'H.R.' are 'them', not 'us'. This is because human resource managers may have been responsible for contracting work to outside suppliers, causing redundancies. Or they may have set up performance-related pay systems that force staff to do tasks they do not wish to do, or even disapprove of.

HRM can be used as a tool of a Theory X management, to impose a control system on an unwilling workforce. Or it can be a way to ensure that staff needs and talents become a fundamental part of decision-making in a Theory Y organisation. Clearly, when going for job interviews, the wise applicant judges a firm not by whether the interviewer is a HR manager, but whether the attitudes to staff seem open, positive and participative.

**KEY terms**

**off-the-job training** – any form of training not immediately linked to a specific task. It may take place within the firm, perhaps in conference facilities, or away from it, for example at a local technical college.

**on-the-job training** – the process of instructing employees at their place of work on how a particular job should be carried out. This usually involves watching an experienced operative carry out a task, or actually undertaking the activity and being guided as to appropriate technique.

**remuneration** – the whole package of rewards offered by an organisation to an employee. This will include additional benefits, such as a pension scheme, share options, company car and so on, as well as basic pay.

**selection methods** – the process by which organisations choose to differentiate between the applicants for a specific job in order to pick out the most appropriate candidate. The most commonly used technique is interview, but a range of different approaches (e.g. personality testing) are being used more frequently in order to complement traditional methods.

**workforce planning** – the process of anticipating in advance the human resource requirements of the organisation, both in terms of the number of individuals required, and the appropriate skill mix. Recruitment and training policies are devised with a long-term focus, in order to ensure the firm is able to operate without being limited by a shortage of appropriate labour.

# Exercises

## A. REVISION QUESTIONS

*(35 marks: 70 minutes)*

Read the unit, then answer:

1 Why is it important that an organisation challenges its existing employment structure each time an opportunity to do so emerges? *(4)*
2 Why do 'job descriptions' and 'person specifications' play an important part in the selection of appropriate personnel? *(4)*
3 What advantages does the process of internal recruitment offer to the business over the appointment of individuals from outside the organisation? *(4)*
4 Identify three benefits to a firm of using assessment centres in selecting key staff. *(3)*
5 What might be the costs of not training:
   a new supermarket checkout operators *(4)*
   b crowd stewards at Manchester United. *(4)*
6 How can a form of 'market failure' result when a firm is considering training its employees? *(4)*
7 What is the main purpose of 'induction' training? *(4)*
8 What benefits might a firm derive from achieving an Investors In People award? *(4)*

## B. REVISION EXERCISES

### B1 Data Response

### Recruited by Bill Gates

The richest man in the world, feted by presidents and prime ministers, Bill Gates sees no activity as more important than meeting superior candidates to convince them they should join Microsoft. He even targets the graduate trainees, inviting all 600 in groups to his $60 million home. Mingling with the young guests, he answers questions, gives advice and reinforces the excitement of a career with Microsoft.

Recruitment at Microsoft has two main strands. The first is picking the best of the year's 25,000 computer science graduates. Microsoft creates a shortlist of 8,000 CVs which are reviewed to identify the 2,600 targeted for campus interviews. 800 of these are invited to Microsoft's head office at Seattle.

Each candidate is then interviewed by between three and ten 'Microsoftees'. This lengthy and expensive process provides about 400 graduates each year who join Microsoft.

But this accounts for only 20% of Microsoft's annual recruitment. Most of the remaining 2,000 staff hired each year are the best and brightest people working elsewhere. To identify and track these potential assets, Microsoft maintains a full-time team of 200 recruiting experts. Their job is to head hunt the industry's most talented people and then build and maintain a relationship with them.

The pursuit is relentless, if subtle. Regular telephone calls at discreet intervals, invitations to informal dinners – anything to keep open the lines of communication with the potential candidate. Mike Murray, Microsoft's head of human resources, says 'One day he will be ticked off with his current organisation. That day, he'll call us.'

Mike Murray also makes sure to monitor the performance of the 200 recruiters. When it comes to human resources, Microsoft leaves nothing to chance.

Source: *The Financial Times*, 28/7/98

**Questions** *(30 marks; 35 minutes)*

1 Many firms state that 'Our most important asset is our people'. What evidence is there that Microsoft actually believes it? *(6)*
2 a Apart from interviewing the candidates for the management trainee posts, how else might Microsoft have selected the right person for the job? *(4)*
   b Which of these methods might have been most suitable for a large computer software company such as Microsoft? Explain your answer. *(8)*
3 Microsoft head hunts staff from other firms using a method known as 'poaching'.
   a What benefits might Microsoft derive from poaching staff from other firms? *(4)*
   b Why might poaching lead to a reduction in the level of training generally in an industry? *(4)*
4 Outline two ways in which Mike Murray might evaluate the performance of the 200 recruiters. *(4)*

## B2 Case Study

### Human Resource Development at Prest Ltd

In the early 1990s Prest Ltd, manufacturer of electronic components, closed three factories and concentrated its operations on a single site. At the same time it reorganised the remaining plant to cut costs and improve product quality. Before modernisation, 50% of the machinery being used at the site had been over 15 years old. This was replaced with the latest equipment. The new production line was designed to run continuously with operators being expected to take 'first level' decisions at the point of production to keep it functioning. As a result, tasks such as fault finding and machine maintenance became an important part of the job of each worker.

The modernisation of the plant signalled a shift to teamworking, in order to encourage employee flexibility. Multi-skilled operators were needed with a deeper understanding of the production system. The employees needed to know how the new machinery could best be used to ensure consistently high levels of production quality. These changes had clear implications for the human resource department at Prest. Recruitment would have to focus on a new type of employee, and existing employees would need to be retrained.

The human resource manager conducted a feasibility analysis in order to review the strengths and weaknesses of the company's existing workforce and its ability to handle the new situation. This concluded that both shop-floor supervision and the engineering section needed strengthening. In response, 15 new engineers were recruited and 5 staff redeployed to improve production supervision.

As an answer to the immediate need for greater skill levels, a comprehensive training programme in quality control was introduced for all staff. Machine operators were encouraged to mix with engineers during this exercise, helping to break down barriers between the two groups. For many individuals this was the first formal company training they had ever received. The development initiative was successful enough to stimulate requests for further learning opportunities. As a result, Prest created a link with a local technical college to provide more extensive instruction for those who wished to learn more about modern production techniques.

Although the benefits of the training were clear, three problems emerged which Prest had not anticipated. The greater knowledge of the operators made them anxious to put their acquired skills into practice. After nine months the new production line had only reached 80% efficiency. Senior managers believed employees were losing interest when machinery was functioning normally. In addition, some workers felt the extensive training they had received was not reflected in enough increased responsibility. Their expectations of a more interesting job had been raised, but the reality seemed little different than before. Finally, 12 newly trained staff left the company because they could now apply for more highly paid posts at other firms in the area.

Prest also considered the long-term human resource implications of the move to a more sophisticated form of production. The workforce knew little about new production technology, so the firm's training school ran a course on robotics. The decision was also taken to provide a sponsorship scheme to encourage new recruits to study on an engineering degree course at university. The firm wished to ensure it did not face a shortage of talent in the long term.

### Questions (40 marks; 60 minutes)

1 Analyse the significance for each of the four stages of the human resource cycle created by the introduction of new technology and different working practices at Prest Ltd. (10)
2 What human resource issues might emerge as a result of the feasibility study conducted at Prest Ltd? (8)
3 Evaluate the development programme introduced by Prest Ltd in the light of the problems identified by the feasibility study. (6)
4 Consider whether the difficulties experienced after staff training at Prest Ltd suggest that employees can receive too much training. (10)
5 Has the HR Department at Prest Ltd created a 'horizontal fit' between each of the four elements of the human resource cycle in the programme which has been introduced? (6)

# CHANGE MANAGEMENT

**DEFINITION**

The management of change is the process of planning, implementing, controlling and reviewing the movement of an organisation from its current state to a new position which is believed to be more desirable.

The most extreme change would involve abolishing the existing way of doing things and starting again. More often, adjustments are made to the present approach in order to fit a new position. For example, many companies did this in reorganising their management structure in response to recession in the early 1990s.

All change, from introducing a new piece of machinery to restructuring the organisation, has implications for employees. The management of people is the largest problem which faces those who are trying to move the business successfully to a new position.

## 29.1 Change

The rate of change in organisations has increased rapidly in the last 15 years. For example, the development of information technology is so great that for many employees their house will soon also be their place of work. The computer firm Digital already has in excess of 1,000 of its 4,000 workforce operating from home.

Today, change is a permanent characteristic of business activity. In some cases it can be anticipated and therefore planned for, in others it is unexpected. For example, a rapid growth in sales may demand extensive change. If it can be foreseen, this will allow the process of expansion to be managed more effectively. Even when a business cannot control the change, anticipating it will allow plans to be made. This is why Nike has always employed an army of young people it calls 'coolhunters'. Their job is to keep in touch with the opinions and attitudes of American youth, and then keep Nike up to date.

In contrast, some changes may be impossible to forecast. For example, the impact of the Foot and Mouth crisis on UK farmers. The effect will be heightened when the factors driving change fall beyond the control of the business, as was true in this case. Shifts in the external business environment are often the most difficult changes which face firms. New consumer tastes, the rise of competitors, reform of legislation, or economic fluctuations are examples of these movements. A firm's managers can try to influence these changes through actions such as advertising or pressure group activity, but their attempts may fail.

The arrow in Figure 29.1 illustrates the direction of growing uncertainty (low to high), and therefore risk, to the organisation associated with different types of change.

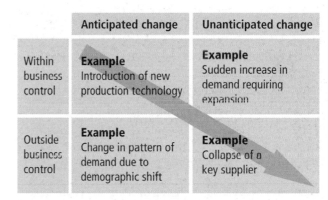

|  | Anticipated change | Unanticipated change |
|---|---|---|
| Within business control | **Example** Introduction of new production technology | **Example** Sudden increase in demand requiring expansion |
| Outside business control | **Example** Change in pattern of demand due to demographic shift | **Example** Collapse of a key supplier |

**Figure 29.1** Types of change

## 29.2 Managing a change programme

Figure 29.2 illustrates the four phases involved in managing change.

**PLANNING**

The first step when organising a change programme is the recognition that a new approach to a given prob-

**Figure 29.2** Managing change

lem is required. It is then necessary to find a solution which matches the policy to be adopted, to changed circumstances.

For example, consider an organisation which manufactures plastic moulded products, such as the cases for CDs and video games. The company has greater production costs than its immediate competitors and is experiencing difficulties with high absenteeism amongst its shop-floor employees.

The three key questions when planning change management are:

- **Where are we now?**
  e.g. high costs and high absenteeism
- **Where do we want to be?**
  e.g. reduced costs and lower absenteeism
- **How do we get there?**
  e.g. introduce teams producing in work 'cells'.

A change of this kind has many implications:

- jobs would have to be redesigned
- the shop-floor layout changed
- workers trained in new skills
- the recruitment policy adjusted to employ workers with greater potential for moving flexibly between tasks within the cell.

The process of implementing these changes will be made much easier if the people affected by them are involved in identifying the initial problem and evaluating the proposed solution.

### IMPLEMENTATION

People implement change, but they are also the most important barrier to its success. Resistance to change may occur in the process of putting the planned developments into action.

Individuals may resist the implementation of change:

- To preserve existing routine.
- To protect pay and employment – if payment is based on output produced, workers may find themselves earning less after the change. This is because it will take time to get used to the new way of doing things.
- To avoid threat to security and status – change can endanger a person's position of authority. As a result they may try to preserve their area of power and influence by resisting the development.
- To maintain group membership – workers may resist change because they are worried about what others may think if they do not. The 'norms', or accepted views, established by a group of employees who work together can be very strong. If some people see a change of production as threatening they may influence the attitudes of the other people around them.

**Overcoming resistance to change:** There are two key ways in which managers can help individuals overcome their natural resistance to change (see Figure 29.3).

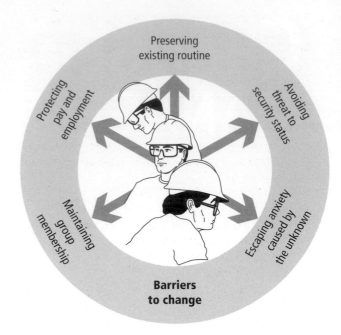

**Figure 29.3** Individuals resist the implementation of change

### TAXING TIMES AT THE INLAND REVENUE

The Inland Revenue is a government department which organises the collection of tax in the UK. When it introduced a reorganisation of its offices and functions, there seemed to be a positive impact on customer satisfaction.

However, the changes introduced made its employees very unhappy. Two successive surveys of staff attitudes showed widespread hostility on the part of employees to the developments introduced. MORI, the opinion polling company, commissioned by the Board of Inland Revenue, found that 56% of staff 'feel change is happening too rapidly' and only one member of staff in 50 agreed that change had been 'well managed'. A second survey of employee feeling was undertaken by the Industrial Society, again at the request of department officials. It reported 'there is a tremendous thirst for information from senior management ... this leads to a widespread belief that information is being deliberately withheld'.

One workforce representative described staff as experiencing a 'deep-seated crisis in morale', because they are 'starting to feel they are losing sight of their core activity'. He suggested that in the future large numbers of inspectors would leave the department, unable to cope with the change.

IN **Business**

1   Involve those affected by change at every stage of the decision making process. So they understand why a new approach is necessary. Acting in this way develops the commitment of individuals to a decision. If they are involved in the development of the idea from an early stage they have a personal stake in its success.

This approach is used extensively in Japanese companies and is known as 'ringi'. When a decision is to be made, a proposal passes between all the employees who will be affected by it. They are asked to comment on the idea or even suggest a different approach. Gradually agreement about the best way forward emerges and a final plan is developed. Of course, management by consensus is much less useful if rapid change is needed in response to a crisis.

2   Keep all those people affected by a change informed of what is happening at each stage of the process. Make sure everyone is aware of the options available. Many of the difficulties caused by a new situation are the result of a fear of the unknown. By informing those involved some of the uncertainty can be removed.

### CONTROL

When a change is introduced the process must be controlled. The final outcome of the programme should be the situation which was identified as 'where we want to be' at the end of the planning phase. Targets should be set for each step of the implementation phase in order that progress is focused and does not lose momentum.

It is important that each target is measurable. It must be possible to say with certainty that it has been achieved. An example of a suitable target is: 'By 31 December this year, 40% of the CD cases produced in this factory should be made by employees working in teams'. This is a measurable target, which can be communicated clearly, understood and therefore used for control purposes. If the outcome of each stage is clearly defined, action can be taken quickly if the process shows any sign of moving out of control.

### REVIEW

When the change programme has been implemented the new situation must be analysed. What should be the next phase of the organisation's development? For example, the CD case manufacturer must consider if the movement to cell production has reduced both costs and absenteeism. What new initiatives are required to improve further the competitive position of the company?

A process of constant review is essential because a business which stands still risks moving backwards in the marketplace. New technology, more sophisticated customer requirements and increasing competition may threaten established competitive advantage.

## — CHANGE FOR THE BETTER

**Business IN**

Catomance Technologies, a 60-year-old chemicals manufacturer, nearly hit the buffers in 1999 with a loss of £300,000 on its £4 million turnover. The staff level had halved to 72 employees yet the business still had 6 directors and 4 layers of management. After the managing director led a management buy out in May 2000, he set about a process of change. The hierarchy was flattened, first to 3 layers, then to 2. New people were brought in who were able to make changes without any 'emotional baggage' caused by long experience of the business and its staff. The sales force was given more authority, enabling the business to act more flexibly when facing competition from major European chemical manufacturers. The changes are working and the business is now profitable.

## 29.3  Change and the organisation

Businesses consist of individual people who relate to each other within a framework of established customs and practices. These may sometimes be written rules, but are often simply 'the accepted way of doing things'. These traditional approaches can also act as barriers to change, because the organisation shows collective resistance to new developments. This may result in a failure both to recognise the need for change and to implement it effectively (see Figure 29.4).

**Figure 29.4** Organisations resist the implementation of change

## OVERCOMING ORGANISATIONAL RESISTANCE TO CHANGE

In order to overcome resistance to change within an organisation it is necessary to develop a **change management programme** which creates an atmosphere of trust amongst employees. It would help managers to bear in mind Maslow's insights into human psychology. Resistance to change is inevitable if basic human needs are threatened such as security, social ties and personal esteem. It is therefore necessary for managers to consider the human implications of change. If these are understood, they can be planned for, and actions taken to make implementation of the programme as trouble free as possible.

Initially a business must identify the process which is to be altered by the change programme. This may be a particular operating activity, such as production of a given product. Or it may be an organisational issue, for example the way in which communication takes place within the firm.

The 'diamond change management' model shown in Figure 29.5 illustrates the four key elements which should be considered in order to develop an effective programme aimed at overcoming organisational resistance to change.

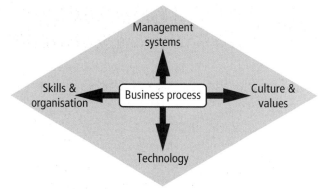

**Figure 29.5** The diamond change management model

**Management systems:** The objectives of any change introduced should be clearly defined and communicated to employees. The means of informing employees of the goals of a development should be considered carefully. If the purpose of innovation is not clear, individuals will attribute aims which may be false. Rumours about the impact of change will emerge and these will be hard to overcome at a later point once they have gained some acceptance. Planning is also necessary to decide on the extent to which the pay and reward system will be used. For example, staff who must acquire new skills may be encouraged to do so by a pay increase.

**Culture and values:** Leadership style will have a key impact on the success of a change programme. McGregor's Theory Y manager, who believes that individuals can be stimulated by their work and will be interested by new developments, will try to encourage employees to get involved in planning change and foster their commitment to its objectives. In contrast, the Theory X manager will consider what steps must be imposed upon employees to ensure the change is adopted with as little resistance as possible. This approach is more likely to use the reward system to facilitate innovation and may resort to coercion or threat. (For example, the possibility of redundancies if change is not accepted).

The organisation's culture will also have to be considered. There may be a long tradition of working in a particular way. It will be important to recognise this and make the need for change very clear.

**Technology:** The introduction of new technology will often accompany change and at times it will be its main purpose. A change management programme must investigate carefully the potential for introducing supporting information technology. Then ensure continuing research and development to keep one step ahead of the competition.

**Skills and organisation:** Significant human resource planning issues will often result from major change. The correct number of employees, with appropriate skills, must be in place to implement a change programme successfully. This has important implications for both recruitment and training within the business.

A wide-ranging programme of change may demand a major restructuring of the organisation. For example, the introduction of project teams taking members from different functional departments. In order for such an approach to prove effective employees must be provided with the support required to adjust to changing responsibilities and work practices.

## MANAGING THE EXISTING BUSINESS DURING CHANGE

When developing a change management programme it is vital to ensure that existing operations continue to function efficiently. In their enthusiasm to introduce new business processes managers may lose sight of the present position of the firm. Any single change may involve only 10% of the staff. Yet more than 50% of senior management time may be devoted to it. Managers may lose sight of the basics of business life such as customer service. This could be more costly than any resistance to change.

Figure 29.6 illustrates the way in which 'managing the existing business' must be combined with 'managing change' through the three key phases of a change management programme.

By showing a commitment to existing operations, any perceived threat to employee security will be reduced and the introduction of new ideas is therefore more likely to be accepted throughout the organisation.

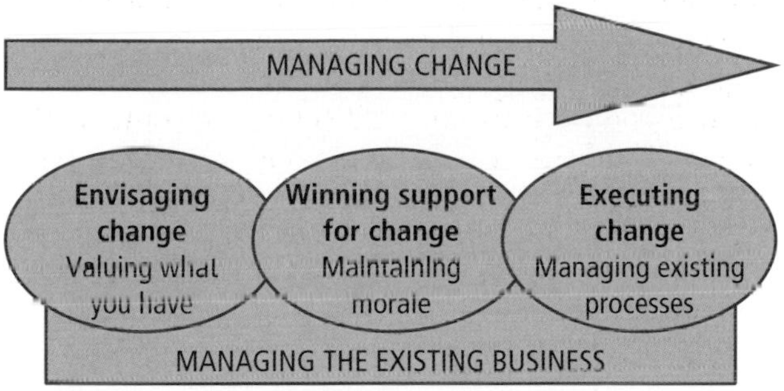

Source: Marcousé (November 1997)

**Figure 29.6** Managing the business during change

## MANAGING ORGANISATIONAL CHANGE AT HEWLETT PACKARD

Lew Platt is chief executive of Hewlett Packard, a major North American firm in the computer industry. Although the company is experiencing increasing profits and is in 'fundamentally good shape' he is always looking to guard against complacency.

Platt comments that 'People ask: "What do you think about when you're in the shower or shaving?" Well, I think about how easy it is to just keep doing what you are doing today for a little bit too long. General Motors, Sears, International Business Machines were the greatest companies in their industries, the best of the best in the world. These companies did not make gigantic mistakes. They were not led by stupid, inept people. The only real mistake they made was to keep doing whatever it was that had made them successful for a little too long.'

He believes that 'the real secret is to build an organisation that isn't afraid to make changes while it is still successful, before change becomes imperative for survival.' Platt adopts a leadership style which encourages his managers to be 'always looking over your shoulder at the competition, always thinking about the next move'. He believes that a policy which makes the company successful today, might work for a year, or at the most two, but beyond this to stick to it will 'kill' the company. His approach to management signals to employees that resistance to change and failure to constantly adapt to new market conditions is why large companies fall from their position of market dominance.

Business IN

When analysing a firm's approach to managing change it is useful to consider the following points:

- On implementation of a change programme what signs of individual resistance to change are evident?
- Has the organisation made sure that those directly affected by a change are involved in its planning?
- Have employees been kept informed about the change throughout its implementation and are they aware of all the options open to the organisation?
- Have targets been set to control the change? Are the outcomes measurable?
- Has the organisation reviewed the policy for change after implementation and moved forward to further development, i.e. is the change programme evolving?
- Has the change programme met with resistance from the organisation as a whole?
- Is there evidence that 'management systems', 'business culture and values', 'technology' and 'skills and organisation' have been considered in designing the change programme?
- Has sufficient attention been paid to managing the existing business during the change?

## 29.5 Change management
### an evaluation

All organisations must manage change. In order to do so successfully it is necessary to analyse the impact on people. Without employee support no innovation will succeed. The single most important issue is therefore the extent to which trust can be developed between a workforce and the organisation. This will demand a long-term approach, in which individuals are both consulted and kept informed about developments within the business. Resistance to change will emerge if the basic needs of security, social ties, and self-esteem are threatened.

A firm may choose to move towards a programme of gradual change, which Japanese managers call 'kaizen'. An approach of this kind involves every employee being willing to review their role in the business in order to suggest potential improvements to the processes they are directly involved with. Individuals must adjust to a series of continuous improvements, which means that the working environment is one of constant change. In contrast, some firms employ 'step' change. This means trying to establish periods of stability, interspersed by a small number of major innovations. The most appropriate method of change management will depend on the nature of the business environment the firm operates within.

To remain competitive over time any business must be prepared to change. The ability of employees to manage this process therefore holds the key to the future success (or failure) of all organisations.

**anticipated change** – when organisations can foresee future developments, either within or outside the business, they can plan their response in advance. This will reduce the risks associated with change and make it more likely that any resistance by individuals, or the organisation as a whole, can be overcome successfully.

**change management programme** – a series of steps designed to move the organisation forward to a new operating position. Four key phases are involved in developing an initiative of this type. These are planning, implementation, control and review.

**individual resistance to change** – pressure from individuals who attempt to oppose the implementation of new developments within the organisation, and maintain the existing situation.

**organisational resistance to change** – pressure from groups of people within the business, or even the whole work-force, which attempts to resist the implementation of new developments within the organisation, and maintain the existing situation.

**unanticipated change** – many future developments, particularly in the firm's external environment, cannot be foreseen. For example, changes in consumer tastes, interest rate movements or exchange rate fluctuations are all factors which it will be hard for the business to influence and which may not behave in the manner expected. Planning and implementing change in response to developments of this type will be more difficult and there is therefore a much greater risk of failure.

188

UNIT 29 I CHANGE MANAGEMENT

29.6 Workbook

# Exercises

## A. REVISION QUESTIONS
*(35 marks; 70 minutes)*

Read the unit, then answer:

1 Outline why unanticipated change causes organisations difficulty in planning. (4)
2 What are the three key questions managers should ask when planning change? (3)
3 a If a new Head decided that all staff and students should wear the same blue overalls as the school/college 'uniform', how do you think staff would react? (4)
  b How might the Head overcome any resistance to the change? (4)
4 Distinguish between a measurable target and one which would be ineffective in the process of monitoring change. (3)
5 a Suggest four ways in which organisations create barriers to introducing change. (4)
  b To what extent are these more difficult to overcome than those erected by individuals? (5)
6 Why is organisational culture an important factor in change management? (3)
7 Outline how the 'diamond change management' model might be used to design a change management programme. (5)

## B. REVISION EXERCISES

### B1 Case Study

**Major Changes**
Sarah bit her lip to stop herself. She wanted to reply to Nilesh but knew it wouldn't help. He had spent 40 minutes moaning about his colleagues and customers. She excused herself and left.

As she left her office that evening, Sarah thought back over her first fortnight at Cartright's. Being appointed chief executive at 34 was a huge thrill, but already it was wearing off. She had been warned that Cartright's was dull, bureaucratic and inward-looking, but the reality was still a shock. She had been round every department, talking one-to-one to over 100 staff. Most were cautious, bored and focused only on paper-work, not on creating something new or better. The temptation was to leave things be. After all, the busi-ness was highly profitable, thanks to a huge 10-year contract supplying the Saudi Arabian government. Why shake things up?

Sarah slept on it, and by the morning had decided. People like Nilesh would be scared of change, they would fight against it and therefore her, but they must be forced to accept it. In the long term, all would benefit. Their working lives would become more interesting and they would have a better chance of keeping their jobs when the Saudi Arabian contract ran out in four years' time.

Having convinced the chairman that her approach was right, she called a board meeting. She announced a new corporate objective: 'to develop new products and customers so that the Saudi Arabian contract provides only 50% of turnover within three years'. To achieve this, there would need to be a complete reorganisation of the board and senior management to reflect the reduced importance of those involved in the Saudi contract. Every manager in the business would have to reapply for his or her job, to prove their commitment to the new approach. Sarah's final presentation slide said 'The culture must change or the business will die'.

Many of the directors were furious at the implied criticism. And worried about their own future. Major Chris Thompson, the finance director, said: 'Cartright's has been successful for 40 years. It may need sharpening up; it doesn't need a revolution. Our staff will never be go-getters. This plan risks everything.'

By the end of the day, rumours had spread throughout the building. There were stories of mass redundancies and a widespread belief that Sarah would be bringing in her own management team. Sarah's response was to call together all 600 staff and tell them her concerns about the future and her plans for change.

Within a few weeks the plan was underway. The interview panel quizzed managers on their strengths and weaknesses, their ideas for the future and on the management style they would like to employ in the future. Only a quarter met the standards set by Sarah. These were given important positions and the other managers were given 12 months to try to change their approach.

The short-term impact of the upheaval was awful. Close contacts with the Saudi government encouraged a very hostile reaction from Cartright's biggest client. Staff sick leave rose dramatically and three long-standing clients were lost.

Ten months later, however, things looked rather better. Nilesh, of all people, had become a key figure. He developed a completely new product that would offer a high service level at a sharply lower cost than before. His team of six were buzzing with ideas. Another star was Vivien, who developed an internal Internet (an 'intranet') which provided all staff with full access to all the sales and production data for the business. This helped staff make better-informed decisions, and emphasised the change from the secretive approach of the old management team.

Twelve months from the start of the programme, half the directors and one-third of the old management team had left. But Cartright's was on course to meet its sales objective. There had been times when Sarah had suffered from terrible stress. Now she felt proud of her enthusiastic team – and very proud of herself.

## Questions     (60 marks; 80 minutes)

1 Explain the meaning of the terms:
  a bureaucratic
  b culture.     (6)
2 a How may organisations become as bureaucratic as Cartright's?     (7)
  b Analyse why Sarah was so concerned to change this culture of bureaucracy.     (10)
3 Consider how well the process of change at Cartright's fits the diamond change management model (Figure 29.5).     (15)
4 Discuss why many directors and staff at Cartright's resisted Sarah's plan for change.     (10)
5 Sarah made radical changes to Cartright's. Consider whether she would have been wiser to have made changes more gradually.     (12)

# PEOPLE AND ORGANISATIONS – MANAGEMENT GURUS

## 30.1 Modern management gurus

### IGOR ANSOFF

| | |
|---|---|
| *Born:* | 1918 |
| *Area of study:* | Objectives and strategy |
| *Key text:* | Corporate Strategy, *McGraw-Hill, 1965* |

**Major contribution to the study of business:**

Ansoff was the first writer to develop an understanding of the role of strategic planning in business. He argued that a firm is a 'resource converter'. Human, physical and financial resources are translated into products or services as efficiently as possible. In order to do this managers must develop a formal strategy which matches the strengths of the organisation to its competitive environment.

This decision making process takes place under conditions of 'partial ignorance' because the future of the firm and its environment cannot be anticipated completely. So shaping strategic policy is a high risk process which involves making unique, non-repetitive choices. As such it is quite different from other management decision making problems of an operational nature.

Ansoff's early work provides a series of checklists which managers can employ when developing a strategic position. However, critics suggested this approach is too rigid. It ignores the fact that many organisations develop a competitive advantage based on strategies which emerge over time, rather than being formally planned. Ansoff responded by emphasising the need for strategy to be adapted on a real-time (near immediate) basis to deal with changing competitive environments. This recognised the dynamic nature of strategic decision making. In business, today's correct decision can look foolish tomorrow.

Ansoff now accepts that formal strategic planning is a complex issue which cannot be dealt with by providing a series of rules for managers to follow. Nevertheless he still defends his original contribution to the subject, that formal strategic planning is vital for long-term business success.

### EDWARD DEMING

| | |
|---|---|
| *Born:* | 1900 |
| *Died:* | 1993 |
| *Area of study:* | Operations management |
| *Key text:* | Out of the Crisis, *Cambridge University Press,1986* |

**Major contribution to the study of business:**

Deming is regarded by many people as the originator of the idea of total quality management. He recognised that reducing variability in a process is the key to improving both quality and productivity. This can be achieved by the application of statistical process control, which involves using simple numerate analysis to ensure that a process is proceeding efficiently and at high quality standards. The approach can be applied not just in production, but to service and administrative activities as well.

The principles of Deming's ideas were summarised in his 14 points for management (see the table on the following page). Aimed at senior decision makers, they ranged widely over operations and people management.

He continually stressed the need for an organisation to be customer driven, claiming 'the customer is the most important part of the production line'.

These concepts were far more influential in postwar Japan than in his own country until the late 1970s. Deming visited the Far East on a lecture tour in 1950 and his ideas provided the basis for Japanese industrial success. He challenged the Western idea that quality adds to costs; that quality and productivity must be traded off against each other. When Japanese products such as cameras, cars and copiers began to penetrate North American markets in substantial quantities, Western managers realised the potential of his contribution to business thinking. Almost too late for some firms such as the giant General Motors, which almost went under in the 1980s as car buyers switched to Japanese and German cars. Since then quality has become one of the most significant issues facing modern organisations.

*Deming's 14 points for management:*

1 *Encourage continual improvement in the work-place.*

2 *Adopt Japanese management techniques where appropriate.*

3 *Stop making defects by ensuring products are made 'right first time' and therefore reduce the need for quality inspection.*

4 *Consider quality as well as price when deciding upon suppliers.*

5 *Do not see the goal of improvement as reaching a desirable finishing point, change should continue forever.*

6 *Use modern training techniques for all employees, including management.*

7 *The role of a leader is to enable others to do their job better.*

8 *Eliminate fear by keeping employees informed through a process of two-way communication.*

9 *Encourage line and staff employees to work together by breaking down barriers between the two.*

10 *Do not constantly warn the workforce about the need for increased effort, only demotivation results.*

11 *Do not use numerical performance targets, instead provide help and guidance.*

12 *Do not employ appraisal systems, or management by objectives; these reduce the pride of employees in their own work.*

13 *Encourage employees to improve themselves through a process of continuous education.*

14 *Show clear senior management support for the principles outlined above.*

internal workings of what was then the largest organisation in the world, General Motors. This experience set a pattern for his later writing which often draws on the case histories of large organisations such as General Electric and IBM.

The management of organisations by a hierarchy of objectives (MBO) is one of Drucker's most influential ideas. He suggests these targets should fall into five key groups dealing with market standing, innovative performance, productivity, liquidity and profitability. It is his view that large firms can only be managed effectively by setting clear goals for subordinates and then delegating tasks to them. With this approach in mind, Drucker was also one of the first writers to develop the principle of using a mission statement to inspire employees to take appropriate action.

Setting clear objectives is the first of five key roles which a manager must undertake identified by Drucker. The other four are to organise, motivate, measure performance and develop people. To motivate, he stressed the need to create 'responsible workers'. The aim of this approach is to help employees develop knowledge, because this represents the possibility for the organisation to improve productivity, quality and performance in parallel. In this sense Drucker's concept of the 'knowledge worker' can be seen as the forerunner of the 'learning organisation' principle which is popular in management theory today.

Drucker has also made contributions to the understanding of the key role which marketing plays in an organisation's success. For example, he identifies the purpose of business as 'the creation of customers and their subsequent satisfaction'. As a result he argues that concern and responsibility for marketing lies with all employees.

One theme connects the wide range of ideas which Peter Drucker has developed about business. It is that human resources must be used effectively to create and sustain a successful organisation. His influence on other writers and practising managers, over a 40 year period, has been wide ranging and significant.

## PETER DRUCKER

| | |
|---|---|
| *Born:* | *1909* |
| *Area of study:* | *Objectives and strategy/people* |
| *Key text:* | The Practice of Management, Heinemann, 1955 |

## CHARLES HANDY

| | |
|---|---|
| *Born:* | *1932* |
| *Area of study:* | *People* |
| *Key text:* | Understanding Organisations, *Penguin, 1976* |

### Major contribution to the study of business:

Peter Drucker was one of the first writers to give the study of business intellectual respectability. His work has been at the forefront of business thinking over many years. He has influenced developments in a wide range of subject areas. His early working life included a period in a merchant bank and employment as a journalist. Then he spent 18 months studying the

### Major contribution to the study of business:

Charles Handy is a leading authority on *organisation culture*. He has written extensively about the future of business and the nature of work. He has industrial experience as an executive at BP. More recently he has worked as an academic, a writer and a broadcaster.

In the late 1980s Handy suggested that organisations will increasingly contract out work and require employees to work flexibly. This proved an accurate forecast of exactly what happened in the 1990s in Britain and America. He described the 'shamrock' organisation of the future as consisting of three employee types:

- Core workers – these are likely to be qualified professionals, technicians or managers, providing the source of organisational knowledge which is key to the functioning of the business. These individuals will be expected to have a long-term commitment to the firm.
- Contract workers – these are contracted to the organisation to complete a specific task; they will not be employed on a long-term basis.
- Peripheral workers – a flexible labour force employed on a part-time or temporary basis in order to meet the organisation's short-term needs.

Handy suggested that this type of organisation will grow as firms seek ever greater flexibility to changes in demand or competition. If he is right, it will mean a steady reduction in the number of people with secure, full-time, salaried employment.

The four types of organisation culture defined by Handy have also had an important impact on academic thinking in this area of business theory. His view is that either 'power', 'role', 'task' or 'person' cultures can be identified in all firms. This approach is reflected in the work of other writers dealing with relationships between employees. (For a more detailed explanation of each type of culture, see Unit 26.)

Charles Handy is currently Britain's leading management guru. Recently he has turned his attention to the need for companies to adopt a 'broader social responsibility' with respect to its employees. To consider the impact of its actions, particularly in the case of the large number of redundancies associated with the trend for firms to downsize. Time will tell if his work in this area will show the foresight evident in his earlier writing.

## SIR JOHN HARVEY JONES

| | |
|---|---|
| *Born:* | *1924* |
| *Area of study:* | *People* |
| *Key text:* | Making it Happen, *Collins, 1984* |

### Major contribution to the study of business:

Sir John Harvey Jones is a practising manager, rather than an academic. He became chairman of the chemicals giant ICI in 1982, when the firm was suffering from the impact of a severe recession. He was chairman until 1987. During this time he was responsible for restructuring the company. He created three customer-based divisions rather than a much more complex, product oriented framework, which existed previously. The success of this strategy led to subsequent opportunities for him to outline his views on management, both as an author and TV presenter.

The ideas which Harvey Jones presents are often outspoken, but generate a good deal of interest among fellow managers. He suggests that 'management is an art', in which no one unique solution exists which can be applied to every company. The manager's role is to understand existing business theory and select those elements most appropriate to the organisation's specific position. The aim must be to encourage constant change, at the greatest pace which the firm, and the people within it, can deal with. In order to achieve this, the smallest possible number of levels of hierarchy should be adopted within the organisation structure. Each layer must be clearly seen to be adding value and doing only their own job, and not those of individuals at other levels. In this way, from top to bottom of the organisation, individuals will be stretched in their jobs, resulting in high motivation to achieve.

The advice which Sir John offers is that the 'aim of the business leader must be to be the best'. He argues this will take time because people will not change rapidly. Three to five years is needed for a manager to have a radical impact on an organisation. Despite this, his suggestions, both in books and the BBC TV series *Troubleshooter*, provided practising managers with a clear understanding of what it takes to achieve such an ambitious target.

## ROSABETH MOSS KANTER

| | |
|---|---|
| *Born:* | *1943* |
| *Area of study:* | *People* |
| *Key text:* | The Change Masters, *Allen and Unwin, 1984* |

### Major contribution to the study of business:

Kanter is a leading academic authority on the subject of managing change within organisations. She developed the idea that large organisations should have few layers of hierarchy, and contain 'new ventures' which operate as small companies in their own right. This makes the firm more flexible, allowing it to respond to change more quickly. Making success more likely in competitive global markets.

The managers of these organisations play the key role of team leaders. They must *empower* employees who represent a source of knowledge and value to the business. This process implies a degree of self-regulation; giving individuals the freedom to decide what to do and how to do it. In so doing people are motivated and become catalysts for change. Kanter identifies individuals she describes as 'change masters'. They have the ability to move beyond the organisation's established practices and drive the process of innovation. This does not necessarily involve just new products or services. It may equally concern the introduction of technology, or work practices, which are radically different to those being currently employed by the firm. These managers are capable of building teams of employees to put these visions in place and shape the organisation's future.

Kanter has promoted her vision of the role of manager in the twenty-first century, both as a former editor of the influential *Harvard Business Review* and as a Professor of Business Administration at Harvard University. Her ideas about the importance of empowering people have had an important impact on current business theory. Large companies are showing a great deal of interest in empowerment. Whether this really makes a difference in the workplace remains to be seen.

## HENRY MINTZBERG

| | |
|---|---|
| *Born:* | *1939* |
| *Area of study:* | *Objectives and strategy* |
| *Key text:* | *Mintzberg on Management, Macmillan, 1989* |

### Major contribution to the study of business:

Henry Mintzberg is a Canadian academic best known for his work dealing with the structure and culture of organisations, and the styles employed by their managers. He is an outspoken critic of the idea that the strategic direction of a business can be planned formally over a long period of time. It is his view that strategy 'emerges' as a pattern in management action over time. Not as a series of 'designed' steps. This belief led to a public disagreement between Mintzberg and Ansoff.

Mintzberg's early work involved the study of what managers actually do. He rejected the traditional view that their role consisted of defined tasks such as planning, organising, coordinating and controlling. He concluded that they spend very little time thinking ahead. Half the activities they were involved with each day were small tasks which required less than nine minutes of their time and dealt with existing problems. Thus managers in reality are 'fire-fighters', coping with short-term emergencies. He identified three types of managerial role on the basis of his observations, these were 'interpersonal' (e.g. acting as leader), 'informational' (e.g. acting as spokesman) and 'decisional' (e.g. deciding upon resource allocation). His writing places emphasis on the need for greater managerial training to deal with these different functions.

The most influential of Mintzberg's later work identifies five main business structures:

- **entrepreneurial** structure, in which the chief executive officer exercises a good deal of personal power
- **machine bureaucracy**, in which decision making is centralised and formal

- **divisionalised**, where semi-autonomous business units share a common administrative structure
- **professional bureaucracy**, which operates by relying on the skills and knowledge of highly trained employees
- **adhocracy**, involving flexible project teams working to develop innovative solutions to the problems facing the business.

Mintzberg continues to write extensively about the role of managers and the way in which they make decisions. His recent work has focused on the extent to which decision makers are able to identify small, but significant, changes in the organisation's environment and respond to the opportunities these present.

## TOM PETERS

| | |
|---|---|
| *Born:* | *1942* |
| *Area of study:* | *People* |
| *Key text:* | *In Search of Excellence, Harper and Row, 1982 (co-author: Robert Waterman)* |

### Major contribution to the study of business:

The work of Tom Peters is more likely to be found on the desk of a practising manager in the UK than that of any other business writer. His text *In Search of Excellence*, written with Bob Waterman, is the world's best-selling business book. Peters worked for the United States management consulting firm McKinsey, before leaving to become an author and leading speaker. He has become well known for his almost evangelical platform performances presented to groups of practising managers. Companies are prepared to pay large fees to hear his outspoken views of what brings business success.

*In Search of Excellence* identified 43 companies which had remained in the top half of their industry over a 20-year period. These 'excellent' organisations were then analysed in order to detect common features which generated success. Eight factors emerged:

- the use of small project teams
- elimination of bureaucracy
- the ability to listen to and learn from the customer
- support for individuals willing to innovate
- recognition of employees as the firm's core asset
- a clear outline of the organisation's mission
- tightly held common values but room for employees to act within them
- an ability to identify and concentrate on the core business.

The credibility of this work was dealt a heavy blow because within five years more than half of these companies had fallen from favour on Wall Street. Nevertheless, Peters' reputation was established by this book.

Tom Peters has produced a range of texts in the intervening period. These use case studies to illustrate his views on what represents good management practice. They are written in a way which communicates his evident enthusiasm for business subjects. The main theme of his later work is the need for rapid change in the new, increasingly competitive, business environment. He regards substantial reorganisation on a regular basis as the way in which customer loyalty can be 'captured' and maintained. He argues that organisation structures should be flat, with functional barriers broken down, and supervisors giving way to self-managed teams. This approach encourages task orientation, innovation and commitment, and focuses the minds of employees. The key to business success is to involve everyone within the firm in virtually everything. Peters believes there are no limits to the ability of individuals to contribute to business success.

Many of the ideas which Tom Peters presents are not original. But his ability to bring them to life for practising managers by using real examples, combined with his undoubted communication skills, mean he may be the most influential current management guru.

## MICHAEL PORTER

| | |
|---|---|
| **Born:** | 1947 |
| **Area of study:** | Objectives and strategy |
| **Key text:** | Competitive Advantage, Free Press, 1985 |

### Major contribution to the study of business:

The work of Michael Porter on competitive advantage, for businesses and even for countries, has had a great impact on managers and politicians over the last 10 years. He is currently the most influential business academic. His work emerged at a key point in the development of United States industry. The growing success of Japan in penetrating export markets created a desire for a new understanding of the nature of competition. Porter offered a series of business tools which managers could employ to analyse their own company and its competitive environment. Then devise a strategy for success.

Porter developed a model called 'the five forces' to analyse the competitive space within which a business operates. This technique offers a means by which managers can identify opportunities and threats, and therefore potential profitability, in their industry. Its five key elements are the extent of rivalry between existing competitors, the likelihood of new market entrants, the bargaining power of both suppliers and buyers, and finally the danger of substitute products emerging.

In order to understand the internal strengths of a business, Porter developed the concept of the 'value chain'. Each activity in a production and supply process is identified. This allows the identification of those actions which fail to add value for the organisation, leading to cost reductions when they are eliminated. Careful study by managers should help identify how specific activities can be performed better than by competitors, and as a result prove a source of advantage over them.

Porter suggests that the strengths of the business, represented by activities within the value chain, must be 'matched' to opportunities in the organisation's environment. Then a strategy can be built around cost leadership or product differentiation. These two generic strategies can be focused on a niche, or used for mass marketing purposes.

Porter's 'diamond' is a model seeking to explain 'the competitive advantage of nations' by applying the ideas found in his 'five forces' theory to countries rather than industries. A careful study of 10 national economies, including the UK, allowed him to build up an understanding of why some nations were able to grow and increase living standards, while others stagnated. The four key elements within this analysis are the structure, strategy and rivalry of firms in the nation's domestic economy, conditions of demand in the home market, availability and quality of factors of production and the interrelationships between supporting industries. One key factor in national success is the ability to build 'clusters' of related industries which serve each other.

Porter is currently Professor of General Management at Harvard Business School, but his work first gained national prominence as a result of his appointment to President Reagan's Commission of Industrial Competitiveness in the mid-1980s. He still works actively as a management consultant and continues to develop his extensive body of research work.

# INTEGRATED PEOPLE IN ORGANISATIONS

## 31.1 People – an overview

### INTRODUCTION

A common phrase uttered by managers in the modern business world is that 'people are our most valuable asset'. Twenty years or more ago, the opposite seemed to be true. Businesses appeared to run despite the best attempts of 'the workers' to take high wage increases in return for less and less work. The business world was characterised by an attitude of 'them and us'.

Since then, massive changes have taken place in a short period of time. They cover a wide range of topics connected to people in business organisations, such as:

- motivation
- communication
- labour relations
- job design
- workplace design.

People management is perhaps changing more rapidly than any other area of Business Studies. Old assumptions are quickly being overturned. Today's workers are developing different expectations in their working lives which need to be fulfilled if businesses are to operate effectively.

The implications of accepting the phrase 'people are our most valuable asset' as a basis for decisions are wide ranging. They can be costly to firms and threatening to managers and, perhaps, workers as well. The changing style of personnel management is one that goes to the very heart of any business and its corporate culture.

### HOW ARE PEOPLE MANAGED IN BUSINESS ORGANISATIONS?

People in business organisations can be treated by managers on a variety of levels.

- At its simplest, there is the mechanistic function involved in administrating the working lives of all the firm's employees, such as payroll, contracts and so on.
- On a second level, the personnel department can be involved in the preparation of the workforce for their jobs through induction, training and appraisal.
- On a higher level, the work of the personnel/HR department can be a key ingredient in the establishment of the culture of the whole organisation. Management styles, the organisation of the workplace and lines of communication can all fall within the range of work covered by this department.

Of course, the work of managing people must form a single part of the whole jigsaw that makes up the work of a business. Nevertheless, it can be argued that the way a business treats its workers sets the tone for all the activities in the business. Levels of service to customers, relations with suppliers, levels of worker efficiency and commitment can all be traced back to people management.

### 'A' GRADE PEOPLE IN ORGANISATIONS

The study of people in business organisations is made up of several distinct areas, each of which has its own body of theory and empirical evidence. Motivation, communication, employee relations and the internal organisation of the business are often treated as separate topics. Better students are able to go beyond these separate areas and develop arguments that follow key themes through each of the areas. A question on changing management styles may have implications for the motivation techniques used and therefore employee relations, which may in turn require different lines of communication, and so on. Adopting an approach such as this demonstrates overall understanding of the subject and a full grasp of its integrated nature.

A common distinction between 'A' grade writing and answers that attract lower grades lies in the approach undertaken to personnel issues. It is possible to argue for empowerment, job enrichment and so on because they seem to be the 'right' or 'nice' thing to do. Better answers will relate the relevant theory to more tangible benefits. The key effect of motivation, for example, will not be a happier workforce, but one that has a higher labour productivity as shown by concrete calculations.

'A' grade people in business organisations requires a grasp of big underlying issues such as those that follow.

These are areas of discussion for case study conclusions. They represent ways of evaluating the wider significance of the concepts covered in this area.

## ISSUE 1 Has the management of people improved in recent years?

Most research suggests that it has not. The pace of organisational change has been compounded by frequent changes to personnel practices. Human resource management (HRM) was supposed to give personnel issues a bigger strategic voice. In fact HRM has often been a banner under which labour flexibility has become associated with insecurity and uncertainty.

A key feature of modern firms is the huge gulf between personnel approaches. Some firms are far-sightedly developing staff through extensive training and interesting initiatives in consultation. Other firms are creating atmospheres of fear and mistrust. A recent survey of 1,300 managers was run jointly by UMIST and the Institute of Management. It showed the negative view of recent changes held by many managers – especially those working in the public sector (see the table below).

What has been the effect of organisational change?

| PERCENTAGE SAYING THAT: | ALL | PRIVATE SECTOR | PUBLIC SECTOR |
| --- | --- | --- | --- |
| Decision making is faster | 29% | 31% | 25% |
| Morale has decreased | 64% | 53% | 81% |
| Motivation has decreased | 49% | 39% | 65% |
| Sense of job security has decreased | 65% | 52% | 80% |

## ISSUE 2 Is Japanisation a passing fad?

The adoption of 'modern' personnel management techniques has followed a seemingly logical course. In the 1970s UK firms were losing out in competition with rivals from Japan. One reason identified for the better performance of Japanese firms was the production techniques used and the way in which workers formed an integral part of the production process. It seemed clear that kaizen groups, quality circles and the like were the way to compete in the international market.

How long will this trend be followed? For every firm that has successfully adopted these techniques there are examples of other firms that have tried and failed. Adding to the unease on these 'miracle' techniques is the growing economic crisis in Japan and its Far Eastern neighbours. Time will tell if the current push for these 'modern' management techniques will prove themselves as reliable tools, or if the management gurus will develop new ideas that will take centre stage in the future.

## ISSUE 3 Are people the main assets of a business?

A simple answer to this must be 'yes'. Without people there would be no business. However, people on their own could not produce efficient productive units making highly complex technological products, so capital machinery can be seen as being equally important. The argument can follow, then, that all aspects of business are equally important.

This line of reasoning, however, neglects the crucial fact of personnel management. The work of the personnel department sets the tone for the whole culture of the organisation. A happy, content and committed workforce will be more productive than one in which workers feel oppressed and under-valued. On the sporting field and in armed conflicts, victory has often gone to the side that was more committed and unified in its aims than the one with the better individuals or better equipment.

In a competitive environment staff motivation and effectiveness can make the crucial difference between success and failure.

# People in organisations

## A. SHORT-ANSWER QUESTIONS

**1** Give two reasons why a manager might delegate authority to a subordinate. *(2)*

**2** State two factors that might influence the effective span of control in a business organisation. *(2)*

**3** Give two benefits to an organisation from employing a 'flatter' organisation structure. *(2)*

**4** Give three examples of how a firm may set out to satisfy the lower level needs of its employees. *(3)*

**5** Distinguish between job enlargement and job enrichment. *(3)*

**6** Define the term 'decentralisation' as used in organisation theory. *(3)*

**7** Which motivation theorist highlighted each of the following:
  **a** the two-factor theory: motivators and hygiene factors
  **b** the Hawthorne effect
  **c** the hierarchy of needs *(3)*

**8** State three reasons in support of employee participation in the decision making of a business enterprise. *(3)*

**9** Explain two benefits a firm might derive from its employees participating in quality circles. *(4)*

**10** Give three symptoms of unsatisfactory recruitment procedures in a business enterprise. *(3)*

**11** What factors might be taken into account when preparing a wages budget? *(2)*

**12** Give four reasons why a firm might promote from within the existing workforce rather than appoint from outside. *(4)*

**13** Give four examples of monetary payments that may be received by a manual worker in addition to the basic wage. *(4)*

**14** List two reasons why a business enterprise might attach importance to a training programme for staff. *(2)*

## B CASE STUDY

### Modern Working Life

A recent study on the UK labour market, entitled 'Different Jobs, Different Lives', forecasts significant changes in the types of jobs available and the type of person needed to fill these posts. Traditional manufacturing jobs will shrink to 3 million by 2006. Growth will come from the 'creative professions' such as the music business, design or professional sport. It is thought that by 2001 there will be 4.5 million managers, 2.6 million professionals, such as doctors and lawyers, and another 1.9 million 'associate professionals', such as legal executives and computer programmers. These are the highest paid categories, with average earnings ranging up to £569 per week for a male manager. These occupations also demand the highest level of qualifications. Four-fifths of professionals and a third of managers and administrators have degrees.

At the other end of the scale, demand is expected to grow in some lower paid jobs as well. The report foresees 2.7 million people in occupations such as health care and catering. The number working in childcare is expected to rise significantly to half a million by 2006.

Such figures suggest that not only is working life changing, but also the structure of companies is changing too. For some time company chairpeople have said that 'people are the most important asset of a business' and that 'knowledge workers are the way forward'. Now organisational structures may be changing to match these trends.

Studies show that some firms are developing corporate structures based on people rather than physical assets. This involves the creation of a business without a recognisable centre. Instead, there is a network structure with a core in which the various elements are connected through internal and external alliances. Such an organisation has leaders throughout its operations who focus on themes such as people, values, strategy, customers and learning.

The function of the 'global core' as differentiated from the centre of an organisation is to create a sense of purpose, creating a context for growth. It sets the tone rather than dishing out orders, and aims to add value rather than overheads. The functions of the core are:

- identifying the organisation's strengths
- encouraging business units to build on those strengths
- providing strategic leadership
- minimising the cost of capital
- exercising control on behalf of the board and shareholders.

For this decentralised structure to work, a different kind of organisation must be developed. It must be flexible and capable of working effectively with the various units and outside organisations who are linked via strategic alliances.

Source: Adapted from *The Independent*, 16/4/98, *Independent on Sunday*, 12/4/98.

**Questions** *(35 marks; 60 minutes)*

**1** Define the following terms:
  **a** labour market *(3)*
  **b** corporate structure *(3)*
  **c** decentralised structure. *(3)*

**2** Explain the phrase 'people are the most important asset of the business'. *(6)*

**3 a** What are the implications for individual workers of the changes in corporate structure described here? *(10)*
  **b** How do these changes compare with Handy's theory of the shamrock organisation? *(10)*

## C. ROLE PLAYS AND SIMULATIONS

Should Sierra close a plant – if so, which?

### Appendix A – Briefing document

> Sierra Foods plc has made a name for itself supplying own-brand pizzas to national supermarket chains. They operate three plants, two in Lancashire, one of which acts as company headquarters, and a third in South Wales.
>
> Recently the company has come under increasing pressure, particularly from international competitors, who are regularly introducing innovative product ideas at prices below those Sierra wishes to charge.
>
> A proposal has been made to rationalise production on two of the existing sites, closing a third.

As Joint Personnel Directors:

1 Decide what you would recommend and why.
2 Prepare a presentation to explain your views.

### Appendix B – Operational data for the three plants (averages for the last four years)

|  | Leyland (HQ) | Wigan | Pontypool |
|---|---|---|---|
| Labour productivity | 22,500 | 23,000 | 18,913 |
| Capacity usage | 0.87 | 0.6 | 0.77 |
| Annual output | £45m | £18.4 | £28.37 |
| Waste levels | 2% | 2.3% | 3.1% |

### Appendix C – Market size and market share

|  | 3 years ago | 2 years ago | Last year | This year |
|---|---|---|---|---|
| Total market sales | £125m | £130m | £137m | £160m |
| Sierra total sales | 19% | 16% | 16% | 17% |

### Appendix D – Employee relations data (last four years)

|  | Leyland (HQ) | Wigan | Pontypool |
|---|---|---|---|
| Average working days lost due to industrial action | 0 | 0 | 5 |
| Absenteeism rate | 4% | 3% | 6% |
| Labour turnover | 14% | 17% | 28% |

### Appendix E – UK economic trends

|  | 3 years ago | 2 years ago | Last year | This year |
|---|---|---|---|---|
| GDP indexed (5 years ago = 100) | 104 | 105 | 109 | 116 |
| Unemployment | 2.9m | 2.7m | 2.4m | 2m |
| Inflation | 2.5% | 2.4% | 2.7% | 3.1% |

# ECONOMIES AND DISECONOMIES OF SCALE

## DEFINITION

Economies of scale are factors which cause average unit costs to fall as the scale of output increases. Diseconomies of scale are factors causing average costs to rise as the scale of output increases.

## 32.1 Two ways firms can grow

- Internal growth occurs when a firm expands its own sales and output. Firms growing in this manner must invest in new machinery and usually take on extra labour too. Firms that are successful in achieving internal growth have to be competitive. Companies like Sony have grown rapidly by taking market share from their less efficient competitors.
- External growth is created by takeover and merger activity. In early 2003 the low-cost airline Ryanair bought smaller rival Buzz. The intention was to cut costs by pooling overheads (such as booking systems). Also Ryanair gained market share by acquiring the many routes Buzz had established to France and Italy.

The trend towards increased industrial concentration has been largely due to external growth. There are many reasons why firms may wish to grow by takeover or merger. One of the most significant is that many managers believe growth will create cost savings for their firms. They anticipate benefiting from economies of scale. Unfortunately, this is not always true. Many mergers and takeovers actually reduce efficiency. Any economies of scale prove to be outweighed by diseconomies. Research has shown consistently that, on average, takeovers and mergers fail to improve efficiency.

## 32.2 Economies of scale

When a firm grows there are some things it can do more efficiently. The group term given to these factors is 'economies of scale'. When firms experience economies of scale their unit costs fall. For example, a pottery which could produce 100 vases at £5 each produces 1,000 vases at £4.50 per unit. The total cost rises (from £500 to £4,500) but the cost per unit falls. Assuming the firm sells the vases for £6 each, the profit margin rises from £1 per vase to £1.50.

Economies of scale are, in effect, the benefits of being big. Therefore, for small firms, they represent a threat. If a large-scale producer of televisions can sell them for £99 and still make a profit, there may be no chance for the small guy.

There are five main economies of scale. These are discussed below.

### BULK-BUYING ECONOMIES

As a firm grows larger it will have to order more raw materials and components. This is likely to mean an increase in the average order size the firm places with its suppliers. Large orders are more profitable to the supplier. Both the buyer and the potential suppliers are aware of this. Consequently, firms who can place large orders have significant market power. The larger the order the larger the opportunity cost of losing it. Therefore the supplier has a big incentive to offer a discount. Big multinational manufacturers like

### THE $3,000 MILLION DISCOUNT

How much would you be willing to pay for a brand new 150-seater Airbus 319? Film stars such as John Travolta strip out the seats and furnish the interior luxuriously. The list price for an Airbus 319 is $50 million. Yet in October 2002 easyJet struck a deal to buy 120 of these aircraft at a 50% discount. Aircraft priced at $6,000 million were bought for just $3,000 million. This bulk buying benefit helped to justify easyJet's boldness in taking over the rival discount airline 'Go'. Together, the purchasing power of easyJet plus Go made it far easier to pressure the European makers of Airbus, and thereby benefit from purchasing economies of scale.

Volkswagen have been relentless in demanding larger discounts from their component suppliers. This has helped Volkswagen reduce its variable costs per car.

## TECHNICAL ECONOMIES

When supplying a product or service there is usually more than one production method that could be used. As a firm grows it will usually have a greater desire and a greater ability to invest in new technology. Using more machinery and less labour will usually generate cost savings. Second, the new machinery may well be less wasteful. Reducing the quantity of raw materials being wasted will cut the firm's variable costs.

These cost savings may not be available to smaller firms. They may lack the financial resources required to purchase the machinery. Even if the firm did have the money it may still not invest. Technology only becomes viable to use if the firm has a long enough production run to spread out the fixed costs of the equipment. For example, a small company may wish to buy a new computer. As the firm is small it may end up using it for only two days a week. The total cost of the computer will be the same whether the firm uses it one day or five days per week. So the average cost of each job done will be high as the small firm is unable to make full use of its investment. **Capital investment** becomes more viable as a firm grows because capital costs per unit fall as usage rises.

## MANAGERIAL ECONOMIES

When firms grow there is greater potential for managers to specialise in particular tasks. For instance, large firms will probably have enough specialised personnel work to warrant employing a full-time personnel specialist. In many small firms the owner has to make numerous decisions, some of which he or she may have little knowledge of, for example accounting. This means the quality of decision making in large firms could be better than in small firms. If fewer mistakes are made, large firms should gain a cost advantage.

## FINANCIAL ECONOMIES

Many small firms find it difficult to obtain finance. Even if banks are willing to lend they will tend to charge very high rates of interest. This is because logic and experience shows that lending to small (especially new) firms is more risky. They are more likely to go into liquidation than large firms. There are two main reasons for this:

- Successful small firms grow into large firms. Consequently, large firms tend to have more established products and have experienced teams of managers.
- Small firms are often over-reliant on one product or one customer; larger firms' risks are more widely spread.

The result of all this is that large firms find it far easier to find potential lenders. Second, they also pay lower rates of interest.

## MARKETING ECONOMIES

Every aspect of marketing is expensive. Probably the most expensive, though, is the salesforce. These are the people who visit wholesale and retail outlets to try to persuade them to stock the firm's goods. To cover the country, nothing less than six sales staff would be realistic. Yet that would cost a firm around £200,000 per year. For a small firm with sales of under £1 million a year, this would be a crippling cost. Larger firms can spread the costs over multi-million sales, cutting the costs per unit.

### BUSINESS CONCENTRATION

In early 2003 a take-over battle began as each of the major supermarkets tried to buy Safeway.

But how important is scale? Does the biggest firm have such an advantage that others can never catch up? By no means. J&P Coats was once Britain's largest manufacturing company. Today it forms one small part of a medium-sized business. Looking at it the other way, today's monster companies include many that were small or did not even exist 30 years ago. These include Microsoft, Intel, Philip Morris (Marlboro) and Toyota.

It is not even true to say that large firms are taking a larger share of national output. The heyday of large firms was in the 1970s, as the table shows:

**Percentage share of manufacturing output by the largest 100 manufacturers**

|  | 1918 | 1970 | 1990 |
|---|---|---|---|
| US | 2% | 33% | 33% |
| Japan | 23% | 22% | 21% |
| Germany | 17% | 30% | 23% |
| UK | 17% | 40% | 36% |

Source: Adapted from City University Business School Working Paper

The point is, therefore, that despite the apparent benefits from economies of scale, very large firms have no guarantee of permanent success. They often became the biggest due to mergers or takeovers, and can shrink again when managerial problems become overwhelming.

Size matters, but size is no guarantee of success.

UNIT 32 I ECONOMIES AND DISECONOMIES OF SCALE

## 32.3 Other benefits of size

Apart from achieving cost-reducing economies of scale there are some other benefits attached to size.

### REDUCED RISK

If a firm grows by diversifying into new markets the firm will now be less dependent on one product. A recession might cause sales in one area of a business to fall. However, if the firm also manufactures products which sell strongly in recessions, the overall turnover of the organisation may change little. In recent years a high percentage of takeovers and mergers have involved firms operating in totally different industries. When Volvo bought out Procordia, a firm in the processed food business, Volvo was seeking a wider product base. This helps the company avoid the risk inherent in 'having all your eggs in one basket'.

### INCREASED CAPACITY UTILISATION

Some firms may wish to grow in order to increase their **capacity utilisation**. Capacity utilisation measures the firm's current output as a percentage of the maximum the firm can produce. Increasing capacity utilisation will spread the fixed costs over more units of output. This lowers the total cost per unit.

## 32.4 Diseconomies of scale

When firms grow, costs rise. But why should costs per unit rise? This is because growth can also create diseconomies of scale. Diseconomies of scale are factors that tend to push unit costs up. Large organisations face three main types of diseconomy of scale.

### POOR EMPLOYEE MOTIVATION

When firms grow, staff may have less personal contact with management. In large organisations there is often a sense of alienation. If staff believe that their efforts are going unnoticed a sense of despondency may spread. According to the motivation theorist Elton Mayo, employees enjoy working for managers who pay an interest in them as individuals. This is the so-called 'Hawthorne effect'. In large firms some managers may feel they do not have sufficient time for frequent informal chats with their staff. Professor Herzberg also believes that recognition for achievement is vital for employee motivation. If managers do not take this into account the likelihood is that staff motivation will fall. A falling level of work effort will increase the firm's costs. Poor motivation will make staff work less hard when they are actually at work. Absenteeism is also a consequence of poor motivation. This means that the firm may have to employ more staff to cover for the staff they expect to be absent on any given day. In both cases output per worker will fall. As a result, labour costs per unit will rise.

### POOR COMMUNICATION

Communication can be a significant problem when a firm grows. First, effective communication is dependent on high levels of motivation. Communication is only effective if the person being communicated with is willing to listen. If growth has left the workforce with a feeling of alienation, communication can deteriorate alongside productivity. A second reason for poor communication in large organisations is that the methods chosen to communicate may be less effective. As a firm grows it may become necessary to use written forms of communication more frequently. Unlike verbal communication, written communication is less personal and therefore less motivating. Written messages are easier to ignore and provide less feedback. Relying too much on written forms of communication could result in an increase in the number of expensive mistakes being made.

### POOR MANAGERIAL COORDINATION

In a small firm coordination is easy. The boss decides what the goals are, and who is doing what. As firms grow, it becomes harder for the person at the top to control and coordinate effectively. The leader who refuses to **delegate** 'drowns' under the weight of work. The leader who delegates finds (later) that manager A is heading in a slightly different direction from manager B. Regular meetings are arranged to try to keep everyone focused on the same goals through the same strategy. But not only are such meetings expensive, they are also rather ineffective. Coordination is effective and free in a small firm, expensive and hugely ineffective in large corporations.

## 32.5 Combining economies and diseconomies of scale

It is important to realise that growth normally creates both economies and diseconomies of scale. If growth creates more economies than diseconomies then unit costs will fall. On the other hand, if the growth creates more diseconomies, the opposite will happen (see Figure 47.1).

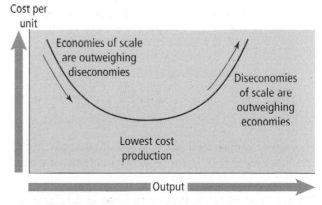

**Figure 47.1** Production costs and production scale

Normally, when a firm is small, initial bouts of growth will create more economies of scale than diseconomies. So growth pushes average costs down.

## WHAT CAN MANAGERS DO ABOUT DISECONOMIES OF SCALE?

Diseconomies of scale are to a certain extent inevitable. However, this does not mean that managers should just accept them. With careful planning, many diseconomies may be minimised or avoided completely. They key point is that diseconomies are more likely to arise either when growth is unplanned or when it is too rapid. When a firm embarks on a programme of growth it is vital that managers recognise the need to change and adapt.

| Diseconomies of Scale | Corrective Action Required |
|---|---|
| Poor motivation | • Delegate decision making power<br>• Job enrichment<br>• Split the business up by using the following:<br>– profit/cost centres<br>– cell production |
| Poor communication | • Improve employee motivation as above<br>• Send managers on attitudinal training courses<br>• Create new communication structures such as works councils |
| Poor coordination | • Decentralise<br>• Empowerment<br>• Wider spans of control |

**KEY terms**

**capacity** – the maximum output possible from a business over a specified period of time.

**capacity utilisation** – actual output as a proportion of maximum capacity.

**capital investment** – expenditure on fixed assets such as machinery.

**delegate** – hand power down the hierarchy to junior managers or workers.

**Theory X** – Douglas McGregor's category for managers who think of workers as lazy and money-focused.

Economies of scale is a concept used frequently by students in examinations. When using it to analyse a business situation, the following points should be considered:

• In most business circumstances, a rise in demand cuts average costs because of improved capacity utilisation. In other words, if a half-used factory gets a big order, unit costs fall because the fixed overheads are spread over more output. This is great, but should not be referred to as an economy of scale. It is simply an increase in capacity utilisation. The term 'economies of scale' refers to increases in the scale of operation, e.g. when a firm moves to new, bigger premises.

• The cost advantages from bulk buying can be considerable, but are often exaggerated. A medium sized builder can buy bricks at much the same cost per brick as a multinational construction company. It should also be remembered that materials and components form quite a low proportion of the total costs for many products. For cosmetics or pharmaceuticals, bought-in materials would usually cost less than one-tenth of the selling price of the product. So lively minds dreaming up new products will count for far more than minor savings from bulk buying.

• Traditionally, managers of growing or merging companies have tended to predict economies of scale with confidence, but to turn a blind eye to diseconomies. In the medium to long term, though, managerial problems of coping with huge organisations have tended to create more diseconomies than economies of scale.

## 32.6 Economies and diseconomies of scale
### an evaluation

Three important issues should be considered:

• If diseconomies are all people problems, why can't they be better managed?

Most diseconomies of scale are caused by an inability to manage people effectively. When firms grow managers must be willing to delegate power in an attempt to avoid the problems caused by alienation. Some types of manager might find it hard to accept the need for delegation. If the manager has strong status needs and has **Theory X** attitudes, he or she may find it difficult to cope.

Enriching jobs and running training courses are expensive in the short term. These costs are also easy to quantify financially. The benefits of job enrichment and training are more long term. Second, they are harder to quantify financially. This means that it can be quite hard for the managers of a company to push through the changes required to minimise the damage created by diseconomies of scale. Public limited companies may find this a particular problem. Their shares can be bought freely and sold on the stock market. This means that considerable pressure is put on the managers to achieve consistently good financial results. The penalty for investing too much in any one year could be a falling share price and an increased risk of takeover.

- Do economies of scale make it impossible for small firms to survive?

In highly competitive markets it is difficult for small firms to compete with large established businesses. Especially if they try to compete with them in the mass market. In this situation the small firm will lose out nine times out of ten. The small firm will not be able to achieve the same economies of scale. As a result, its prices will have to be higher to compensate for its higher costs.

To a degree this view is correct. However, the fact that the majority of firms within the economy have less than 200 employees proves that small firms do find ways of surviving, despite the existence of economies of scale.

- The importance of being unimportant.

Many small firms do not need economies of scale to survive. They rely upon the fact that they do not compete head on with their larger competitors. Small firms often produce a highly specialised product. These products are well differentiated. This means the small firm can charge higher prices. So even though they have higher costs their profit margins can be healthy. The larger firms in the industry are frequently not interested in launching their own specialist products. They believe there is more money to be made from the much larger mass market. By operating in these smaller so-called niche markets, many small firms not only survive but often prosper. By being small and by operating in tiny market segments they are not seen as a threat to the larger firms. As a consequence they are ignored because large firms see them as unimportant.

# Exercises

## A. REVISION QUESTIONS
*(35 marks; 70 minutes)*

Read the unit, then answer:

1 Identify three managerial motives for growth. (3)
2 Give three examples of managerial economies of scale. (3)
3 Explain why large companies are frequently able to command larger discounts from their suppliers than are smaller firms. (4)
4 Give three examples of managerial diseconomies of scale. (3)
5 Explain the likely consequences for a large firm of a failure to control and coordinate the business effectively. (4)

6 Many car manufacturers like Nissan are attempting to reduce the complexity of their designs by using fewer parts in different models. With reference to the concept of economies of scale, explain why this is happening. (4)
7 Give three reasons why employee morale can deteriorate as a consequence of growth? (3)
8 Give three examples of corrective measures that managers could decide to undertake in order to tackle these morale problems. (3)
9 Explain how economies of scale could give a firm a considerable marketing advantage. (4)
10 What is meant by 'the importance of being unimportant'? (4)

## B. REVISION EXERCISES

### B1 Data Response

Geoff Horsfield and his sister Alex are worried about whether they can compete effectively with their big local competitor, Bracewell plc. Alex believes that Bracewell's economies of scale mean that Horsfield Trading cannot compete head-on. Therefore she wants to switch the company's marketing approach away from the mass market towards smaller niches.

Geoff is not sure of this. He knows that Bracewell has a more up-to-date manufacturing technique, but has heard of inefficiencies in the warehousing and office staff. He doubts that Bracewell is as efficient as Alex supposes. Therefore he argues that Horsfield Trading can still compete in the mass market.

Fortunately the employment of an accountant from Bracewell plc has enabled direct comparisons to be made. These figures, shown below, should help Geoff and Alex decide on Horsfield's future strategy.

| | Horsfield Trading Ltd | Bracewell plc |
|---|---|---|
| Capital investment | £240,000 | £880,000 |
| Factory employees | 28 | 49 |
| Other employees | 7 | 21 |
| Guarantee claims per 100 sales | 1.2 | 2.1 |
| Output per employee (units per day) | 21 | 23 |

**Questions** *(30 marks; 35 minutes)*

1 Calculate the capital investment per employee at each company. What do the figures tell you? *(6)*
2 Outline the probable reasons for Alex's wish to aim at smaller market niches. *(5)*
3 a What explanations may there be for the differences between the guarantee claims of each business? *(8)*
  b What may be the short- and long-term effects of these differences? *(6)*
4 Outline any other evidence in the case of diseconomies of scale at Bracewell plc. *(5)*

### B2 Case Study: Expanding European Airways

European Airways is a successful cut-price airline offering scheduled services to the major cities of Europe. The company's director, Daniel Addana, had always been keen on planes and flying. He had inherited a chain of hotels based in mainland Europe, but sold it to raise enough money to purchase his first aircraft.

His business plan came as a result of his experiences as a customer. On his travels around Europe Dan felt aggrieved about the high prices he was often asked to pay for what were relatively short journeys. He then struck upon the idea of setting up his own airline that would be able to undercut the established competi-

tion. Initially Dan targeted the London to Amsterdam route. By offering low fares Addana filled nearly every seat, so despite his low prices he made handsome profits. The key to the company's success has been its ability to achieve a high seat occupancy rate. In the airline industry load factors are crucial. Aircraft are expensive to purchase, they are also costly to run. Therefore to be efficient, every single seat must be filled in order to dilute these costs so that profits can be made from prices that are competitive.

The company has subsequently expanded and now has 10 Airbus A300s in the fleet.

Dan Addana believes that the company's winning formula can also be applied to a new destination. The only choice Addana has to make is which type of aircraft the company will buy to service the route. The finance director advises buying an A340. The A340 is much larger than the A300 and can carry 400 passengers rather than 255. However it does burn 15% more fuel per kilometre than the A300. Despite this apparent superior efficiency, Addana has two doubts about buying the A340. The first is that the A340 will only deliver its technical economies of scale if load factors remain high. Second, if the airline buys a new type of aircraft, economies of scale might be lost in maintenance, spare parts and training.

**Questions** *(40 marks; 60 minutes)*

1 Using the above information, prove that economies of scale will be generated if the A340 is bought for the new route. *(6)*
2 Using examples from the case study, distinguish between gains in efficiency created through high capacity utilisation and efficiency gains created though economies of scale. *(12)*
3 Explain the logic behind Addana's second concern about buying the A340 over the A300. *(6)*
4 What actions could Airbus Industrie take in order to minimise the loss of maintenance, spare parts and training for customers like European Airlines? *(6)*
5 Identify and then evaluate the external threats that could affect the success of Addana's latest expansion plan. *(10)*

## C. ESSAY QUESTIONS

1 Small firms are often said to have better internal communications than larger organisations. Does this mean that growth will always create communication problems? If so what can be done about these difficulties?
2 MHK plc is a large manufacturer of semiconductors. Discuss the opportunities and problems it may face if it decides on a strategy of growth through centralising production.
3 Given the existence of economies of scale, how do small firms manage to survive?

## B3 Case Study:

### The Drugs Deal That Went Wrong

In 2000 Glaxo and SmithKline, two giants of the phar-maceutical industry merged. The goal was to create cost saving economies of scale that would hopefully boost profitability. City analysts claimed that the deal might create economies of scale worth as much as £1.8 billion. It was also hoped that the merger would create a dominant and innovative industry Goliath, that would be able to generate new products at a rate that the competition could not match.

Unfortunately, GlaxoSmithKline discovered that in business size matters but not in the way they had hoped. Bigger does not always equate to better because growth can create problems that, if not tack-led, will push costs up. Like many companies before them, GlaxoSmithKline forgot that growth creates both economies and diseconomies of scale.

By 2002 these diseconomies began to emerge. Poor profitability, the loss of patents on top selling products and the loss of key skilled personnel led to a halving of the share price. The rumour on the stock market was that the new company was struggling to adjust to its new scale of operation. Overheads soared following the merger. A good example was the new Head Office which was so big that it required a permanent team of window cleaners. There were many corporate luxuries for the staff at Head Office. In addition to cafés and shops, staff had the pleasure of a river that ran through the middle of the site.

The growth created by the merger also led to a change in organisational culture. Prior to the merger both companies were known for their innovative and entrepreneurial approach. This culture began to wane in the new organisation, as the company became pro-gressively more and more bureaucratic. For example, staff selection for crucial middle-management positions began to favour those with strong organisational skills over those possessing the qualities of vision and inspi-ration.

Growth also created co-ordination and control prob-lems for the London-based management. Their centralised business empire now consisted of 104 manufacturing sites in 40 countries and a further 24 research and development centres in seven countries. With an organisation this large, attempts to monitor the performance of every division proved unsuccessful. Under-performing overseas divisions were not spotted fast enough; so corrective action was sometimes taken too late to prevent losses.

### Questions                    (25 marks; 35 minutes)

1 Define what is meant by the term 'diseconomies of scale'. (2)

2 Outline the diseconomies of scale that came about as a result of the GlaxoSmithKline merger. (6)

3 Growth through merger and takeover has become an increasingly common business objective in the past 15 years. Apart from the desire to achieve economies of scale can you explain why this might be so? (7)

4 Most business theorists believe that diseconomies of scale are not inevitable. Discuss the actions GlaxoSmithKline should have taken in order to min-imise potential diseconomies of scale. (10)

# CAPACITY UTILISATION

**DEFINITION**

Capacity utilisation is the proportion of maximum possible output that is currently being used. A football stadium is at full capacity when all the seats are filled. A company producing 15,000 units a week when the factory is capable of 20,000 units has a capacity utilisation of 75%.

## 33.1 How is capacity utilisation measured?

Capacity utilisation is measured using the following formula:

$$\frac{\text{current output}}{\text{maximum possible output}} \times 100$$

What does capacity depend upon? The amount a firm can make is determined by the quantity of buildings, machinery and labour it has available. The level of output achieved when the firm is making full use of all the buildings, machinery and labour available is the maximum output. The firm is said to be working at full capacity, or 100% capacity utilisation.

For a service business the same logic applies. Though it is much harder to identify a precise figure. This is because it may take a different time to serve each customer. In a shop or a bank branch, demand may exceed capacity at certain times of the day. In which case queues will form. At other times the staff may have little to do. A service business wishing to keep cost competitive will measure demand at different times of the day and then schedule the staffing level to match the capacity utilisation.

Many of these service businesses are better able to cope with fluctuating demand by employing temporary or part-time staff. A glance at employment figures for the UK will show the growing importance of temporary and part-time jobs in the UK. These employees bring a far greater degree of flexibility to employers. Part-time hours can be increased or extra temporary staff can be employed to increase capacity easily. If demand falls, temporary staff can be laid off without redundancy payments or part-time staff can have their hours reduced, thus reducing capacity easily and cheaply. This flexibility is good for businesses, helping to reduce spare capacity. However the situation may not be as appealing for employees who have fewer rights than their full-time salaried predecessors.

## 33.2 Fixed costs and capacity

It is vital to understand clearly the relationship between fixed costs and capacity utilisation. Fixed costs are fixed in relation to output. This means that whether capacity utilisation is 50% or 100%, fixed costs will not change. The implication of this is clear. If a football club invests in a huge, expensive playing staff (whose salaries are a fixed cost) but matches are played to a half-empty stadium, the fixed costs will become a huge burden. This is because the very fact that fixed costs do not change *in total* as output changes means that they do change *per unit* of output/demand. A half-empty stadium means that the fixed costs per unit are double the level at maximum capacity. For example:

|  | FULL STADIUM 50,000 FANS | HALF EMPTY 25,000 FANS |
|---|---|---|
| Weekly salary bill (fixed costs) | £250,000 | £250,000 |
| Salary fixed cost per unit | £5 (£250,000/50,000) | £10 (£250,000/25,000) |

When the stadium capacity utilisation is at 50%, then, £10 of the ticket price is needed for the players' wages alone. The many other fixed and variable costs of running a football club would be on top of this, of course.

The reason why capacity utilisation is so important is that it has an inverse (opposite) effect upon fixed costs per unit. In other words, when utilisation is high, fixed costs are spread over many units. This cuts the cost per unit. Which enables the producer either to cut prices to boost demand further, or to enjoy large profit margins. If utilisation is low, fixed costs per unit become punishingly high. As Disneyland Paris found when it opened up in 1992 and demand proved lower than expected.

The ideal level of capacity utilisation, therefore, is at or near 100%. This spreads fixed costs as thinly as possible, boosting profit margins. There are two key concerns about operating at maximum capacity for long, however. These are:

- the risk that rising demand could be met only by competitors, as you are already producing flat out
- the risk that you will never have the time to service machinery, change/improve production methods or train/retrain staff; this may prove costly in the long term, and may increase the chances of production breakdowns in the short term.

The production ideal, therefore, is a capacity utilisation of around 90%.

### 33.3 How to get towards full capacity

If a firm's capacity utilisation is an unsatisfactory 45%, how could it be increased to a more acceptable level of around 90%? There are two possible approaches.

1 Increase demand (in this case, double it!). Demand for existing products could be boosted by extra promotional spending, price cutting or – more fundamentally – devising a new strategy to reposition the products into growth sectors. If supermarket own-label products are flourishing, perhaps offer to produce under the Tesco or Sainsbury's banner. If doubling of sales is needed, it is unlikely that existing products will provide the whole answer. The other approach is to launch new products. This could be highly effective, but implies long-term planning and investment.

2 Cut capacity. If your current factory and labour force is capable of producing 10,000 units a week, but there is only demand for 4,500, there will be a great temptation to cut capacity to 5,000. This might be done by cutting out the night shift, i.e. making those workers redundant. This would avoid the disruption and inflexibility caused by the alternative, which is to move to smaller premises. Moving will enable all fixed costs to be cut (rent, rates, salaries and so on), but may look silly if, six months later, demand has recovered to 6,000 units when your new factory capacity is only 5,000.

A key factor in deciding whether to cut capacity or boost demand is the underlying cause of the low utilisation. It may be the result of a known temporary demand shortfall, such as a seasonal low point in the toy business. Or it may be due to an economic recession which (on past experience) may hit demand for around 18–24 months. Either way, it might prove a mistake in the long run to cut capacity. Nevertheless, if a firm faces huge short-term losses from its excess fixed costs, it may have to forget the future and concentrate on short-term survival.

Figure 33.1 shows the proportion of UK business operating at full capacity over the five years from January 1993 to October 1998. The graph implies a strong correlation between the trade cycle and the number of firms with spare capacity. In times of recession, there are fewer firms operating at full capacity. As recovery begins more firms are able to get close to full capacity, until the economy enters a period of prosperity, when the majority of firms are operating at full capacity.

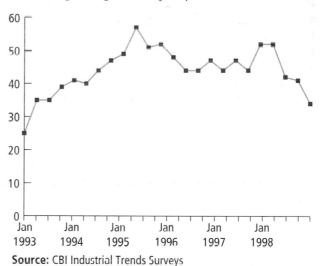

**Source:** CBI Industrial Trends Surveys

**Figure 33.1** % of UK firms operating at full capacity (Jan 93–Oct 98)

### 33.4 Why and how to change capacity

Firms may find themselves with **excess capacity** if demand for their products slows down. Unless the reduction in demand is just a short-term glitch, a firm will seek to find ways to reduce its maximum capacity. This process is commonly called **rationalising**. It means reorganising in order to boost efficiency (though cynics call 'rationalising' a polite way of saying redundancies).

Clearly, if capacity is dependent on the amount of buildings, machinery and labour available to a firm, a change in capacity must mean a change in one or more of these resources. In the case of buildings, the firm may decide to sell off a factory or part of a factory if it feels it will not need that space in the future. Or the firm may decide to lease out factory space to other companies, on a short-term basis. This will enable it to get the extra space back if demand improves.

Machinery can be sold off second-hand or for scrap. In both cases, though, it is likely that the firm will be unable to gain the true financial value of the machinery when it is sold. A more flexible solution is to rent machinery rather than buy it outright in the first place. This would enable the firm to return machinery in times when capacity needs to be reduced.

Redundancy is the obvious answer for a firm whose workforce is too large. It is important to remember that making staff redundant is an expensive business for firms. Wherever possible, firms may look to reassign their employees to other roles or, if money allows, send staff on training programmes while they are not needed for production. Many firms with excess labour will cut down the length of time worked by employees, perhaps by shortening shifts. In October 2002 Jaguar put their X-type car workers at Halewood on a 4 day week to cut production levels.

---

## *Business* IN

### ▬ RATIONALISING THE SKIES

A process of rationalisation is always likely to follow a sudden fall in demand within an industry. Just such a demand shock followed the 11 September 2001 attacks, in the airline industry. In a market which already had too many seats for the passengers it was attracting, an estimated 10% fall in worldwide demand in the year following the attacks was the cue for a round of rationalisation.

Older aircraft were retired in order to cut running costs, whilst many firms followed the lead of Virgin Atlantic and put craft into a kind of hibernation in massive airliner parks, mothballed until demand picks up. Some companies, such as Swissair and Belgium's Sabena, found themselves unable to shed capacity fast enough and went bankrupt. Meanwhile, in America, airlines sought help through government loans and subsidies as a way of covering their costs in the hope that demand would recover. This course of action was all that was left as attempts to cut costs were met by determined trade union opposition within the US.

Recovery had begun by late 2002 with European carriers such as Lufthansa, BA and SAS beginning to emerge from the setback. However, American companies remained in dire straits, expecting several bankruptcies along with further capacity cutting by individual firms.

Source: Adapted from the *Guardian*

---

## *Business* IN

### ▬ OVERCAPACITY IN CARS

Jaguar and Land Rover, both owned by Ford, announced a programme of redundancies on 19 September 2002. Both firms appeared to have excess production capacity at their plants within the UK. They are both seeking voluntary redundancies among production staff as a way of reducing their cost base – reducing their fixed costs. These announcements came despite news that sales of both brands of car were healthy and production levels were not expected to fall as a result of the redundancies. Trade union representatives were not surprised by the announcements, suggesting that more could be in the pipeline. Jaguar will also be introducing a 4-day week for production personnel at their Halewood plant – a further indication of overcapacity in the car market.

---

## 33.5 Advantages and disadvantages of full capacity

### ADVANTAGES

- If a firm is working at full capacity, its fixed costs per unit are at the lowest possible level. The firm is producing as many units as possible so fixed costs are spread as widely as they can be. The result is that the amount of fixed costs borne by each unit is at its lowest possible level.
- At full capacity, the firm is assumed to be using all its fixed assets as effectively as possible. Since fixed assets generate profit, profits should be high.
- A firm working at full capacity will be perceived as a successful firm. Full capacity utilisation implies that demand for the firm's products is healthy. This perception will have positive internal and external effects. Internally, workers will feel secure in their jobs and may well feel a certain pride in working for a successful organisation. Externally, customers and potential customers will feel that if the firm is working at full capacity, it must be manufacturing a good product.

## DISADVANTAGES

- Firms working at full capacity may need to turn away potential customers. Even if the firm does not turn customers away, the prospect of a long wait for the firm's products may well lead to customers going elsewhere.
- Workers who are working at full capacity will have little, if any, time to relax and will need to work as hard as possible at all times. This may make some workers feel overworked.
- Managers may be subject to high stress levels if the firm is operating at full capacity. With no time available to make up for mistakes, it is vital that production planning is accurate and effective.
- If a firm is working at full capacity, its machinery is assumed to be working all the time. This means that there is no **down time** available when routine maintenance can be carried out. Without regular maintenance, most machinery is more likely to break down, causing a complete halt.

It follows, therefore, that firms which are enjoying high capacity utilisation should consider investing to boost their total production capacity. From the viewpoint of the economy as a whole, there can be economic growth and long-term increases in prosperity only if firms increase their capacity.

ISSUES FOR **analysis**

When developing an argument in answer to a case study or essay question, the following lines of analysis should be considered:

- The importance of considering the time frame of the question. Is spare capacity caused by a short-term fall in demand or is there a longer term downward trend? Only if the demand decline is a long-term trend should capacity be cut. It must be remembered, though, that it is always hard to be sure of these things. In the 1980s and early 1990s, falling football crowds meant that when clubs such as Manchester United and Newcastle rebuilt their stadiums, they cut the crowd capacity. Looking back it is easy to say they were wrong. At the time they made what seemed the right decision. So consider the timescale, but be careful of sounding too definite about the 'right' solution.
- The link between capacity utilisation, fixed costs per unit and profitability. If dealing with a question about how to improve profitability, increasing capacity utilisation could well be a valid solution. If profits are poor, be sure to ask what capacity utilisation is at present.
- Modern production theory praises systems such as just-in-time, **flexible specialisation** and lean production. Successful management of all three of these approaches is likely to mean capacity utilisation that is well below 100%. This is because all three approaches require flexible responses to customer requirements/orders. In turn, this requires spare capacity. How can any firm afford to operate deliberately at a low level of average capacity utilisation? By keeping fixed costs down and by charging relatively high prices for the products.

## EXPANDING CAPACITY

In the mid-1990s, Electro Furnace Products (EFP) was enjoying buoyant demand for its output of insulating materials for the heating elements in electric kettles and washing machines. After careful forecasts of future demand, the company took a big risk by investing £4.2 million to quadruple production capacity. From 4,000 tonnes per year, capacity reached 18,000 tonnes. Fortunately the expected sales increases came about, allowing EFP to operate at 80% of capacity. Its bold decision allowed export sales to rise 170% within three years. No wonder the company received the Queen's Award For Export Achievement in 1998.
Source: *The Financial Times*

*In Business*

## 33.6 Capacity utilisation
### an evaluation

Most firms will aim to operate close to full capacity, but probably not at 100%. A small amount of spare capacity is accepted as necessary, bringing a certain degree of flexibility in case of need. In this way, sudden surges of demand can be coped with in the short run by increasing output, or down time can be used for maintenance. Spare capacity can be a good thing, particularly in small doses.

Firms operating close to full capacity are those who may be considering investing in new premises or machinery. This is often the scenario in which questions on investment appraisal are set. In addition to considering whether demand is stable in the long run, the firm must also consider the length of time between deciding to build extra capacity and when the extra capacity is available for use. Building new factories takes time as well as huge quantities of money. Can the firm afford to wait 18 months for its capacity to be expanded? Perhaps the firm would be better served subcontracting certain areas of its work to other companies, thus freeing capacity.

Capacity utilisation also raises the difficult issue of cutting capacity by **rationalisation** and, often, redundancy. This incorporates many issues of human resource management, motivation and social responsibilities. There are fewer more important tests of the skills and far-sightedness of senior managers.

When tackling case studies, it is important that you take a step back from any case study dealing with such a situation to consider the cause and the effect. Is **excess capacity** the problem or an indicator of another problem such as declining market share? By showing the broader picture in this way you can also show the skill of evaluation.

**KEY terms**

> **down time** – any period when machinery is not being used in production. It is used for carrying out maintenance, so some down time for all machinery is necessary. However, too much down time indicates a low level of capacity utilisation.
>
> **excess capacity** – when there is more capacity than justified by current demand, i.e. utilisation is low.
>
> **flexible specialisation** – a production system based upon batches of goods aimed at many market niches, instead of mass production/mass market.
>
> **rationalisation** – reorganising in order to increase efficiency. This often implies cutting capacity to increase the percentage utilisation.

**33.7 Workbook**

**210**

UNIT 33 | CAPACITY UTILISATION

# Exercises

## A. REVISION QUESTIONS

*(25 marks; 50 minutes)*

Read the unit, then answer:

**1** What is meant by the phrase '100% capacity utilisation'? *(3)*

**2** At what level of capacity utilisation will fixed costs per unit be lowest for any firm? Briefly explain your answer. *(4)*

**3** What formula is used to calculate the capacity utilisation of a firm? *(2)*

**4** How can a firm increase its capacity utilisation without increasing output? *(3)*

**5** If a firm is currently selling 11,000 units per month and this represents a capacity utilisation of 55%, what is its maximum capacity? *(4)*

**6** Use the following information to calculate profit per week at 50%, 75% and 100% capacity utilisation:

| | |
|---|---|
| Maximum capacity | 800 units per week |
| Variable cost per unit | £1,800 |
| Total fixed cost per week | £1.5 million |
| Selling price | £4,300 *(9)* |

## B. REVISION EXERCISES

### B1 Data Response

K Leonard and Co was founded 50 years ago. It has a successful history of manufacturing high quality bicycle chains which are supplied direct to retailers. In recent years, orders from retail customers have fallen, meaning that the firm is now only manufacturing and selling 12,000 chains per month.

The following cost information has been made available:

| | |
|---|---|
| Materials cost per unit: | 80p |
| Shop-floor worker's salary: | £10,000 p.a. |
| Salary paid to other staff: | £12,000 p.a. |
| Manager's salary: | £32,000 p.a. |
| Maximum capacity: | 20,000 units per month |
| General overheads: | £40,000 p.m. |
| Current selling price: | £5.80 |
| Number of managers currently employed: | 3 |
| Number of shop-floor staff currently employed: | 10 |
| Number of other staff currently employed: | 4 |

The finance manager has called the other two managers to a meeting to discuss the firm's future. She puts forward two alternative courses of action:

- Make four shop-floor and two other staff redundant, thus cutting the firm's fixed costs, and reducing maximum capacity to 12,000 units per month.
- Sign a contract to supply a large bicycle manufacturer with a fixed quantity of 8,000 chains per month at £5.80 each for the next four years. Breaking the contract will lead to heavy financial penalties.

**Questions** *(30 marks; 35 minutes)*

**1** What is the firm's current monthly profit? *(5)*

**2** Calculate the monthly profit which would result from each of the two options. *(10)*

**3** Explain the advantages and disadvantages of each option. *(10)*

**4** State which of the two options you would choose and list any other information you would need before making the final decision. *(5)*

## B2 Case Study

European car manufacturers still lag behind the US and Japan in the key matters of quality, productivity, profitability, matching production capacity to demand and producing cars with genuine worldwide appeal. However, most European motor bosses are united in their refusal to accept that sales are about to dive, or that they are doomed to be victims of overcapacity. A recent Economist Intelligence Unit (EIU) report suggested that Europe is carrying sufficient idle capacity to produce 3 million extra cars on top of the 13 million made in the previous year. Other estimates of overcapacity in Europe range from 1 million cars per year to 6 million. The EIU report recommends savage cost cutting based on factory closures and job losses.

Chrysler chairman, Bob Lutz, has been quoted as saying: 'You have to bite the bullet, the US car industry has been through a fundamental shake-up in recent years. It is hard but you have to shut down excess plants. Too many European factories have been built on the basis of production and jobs coming first, with the hope that you can find the customers for the cars later. But manufacturing must flow from demand.'

European car makers are operating in a flat market. They have struggled to break into other markets in the way their US and Japanese rivals have done. Some action is beginning to happen – Renault has just closed a factory in Belgium, amid political uproar over job losses. Renault's executive vice-president, Carlos Ghosen, told last week's *Financial Times* conference: 'It is true that there is overcapacity in Europe, but you have to know where your break-even point is. If it is near full capacity you are in trouble. But if you can make a profit, you can keep spare capacity for a rise in the market.'

Overall, most experts agree that manufacturers need to cut capacity in Europe, in addition to improving the way they match capacity to demand. Rover is currently suffering from chronic overcapacity for its larger cars but cannot meet demand for its MGF sports car.

**Source:** Adapted from an article by Joanna Walters published in *The Observer*, 14/9/97

### Questions                         *(40 marks; 60 minutes)*

1 Explain what is meant by the phrase 'estimates of overcapacity in Europe range from 1 million cars a year to 6 million'. *(4)*
2 Why might car manufacturers be reluctant to reduce capacity by closing factories? *(8)*
3 Explain why 'you are in trouble if your break-even point is near full capacity'. *(6)*
4 Discuss the problem faced by Rover, with excess large-car capacity yet not enough production of MGF sports cars. *(12)*
5 Assess the importance of the statement by Bob Lutz that 'manufacturing must flow from demand'. *(10)*

# TYPES OF PRODUCTION

**DEFINITION**

The type of production is the method by which goods and services are produced.

## 34.1 Introduction

Operations management is concerned with the transformation of inputs into outputs (see Figure 34.1). People, materials, machines, money and technology are all combined to produce goods and services. During this transformation process value is added to the materials. £10 worth of wood becomes a chair selling for £65. The aim of operations management is to ensure the efficiency of this process of adding value.

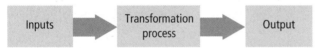

| Inputs | Transformation process | Output |

**Figure 34.1** Transformation of inputs into outputs

There are many different types of production: restaurants producing meals; construction workers building a house; a manufacturing company producing aluminium cans. All of these are involved in one form of transformation process or another. Although there are many production methods they tend to be classified as job, batch, flow or lean production. Lean production is dealt with in Unit 35.

## 34.2 Job production

**Job production** occurs when firms produce items which meet the specific requirements of each customer. Every time you order a meal in a good restaurant, for example, it will be made just as you want it. Similarly, a tailor-made suit is designed to fit one particular customer rather than being bought 'off the peg' in a retail outlet. Major constructions such as Wembley Stadium are also one-off items which are designed and produced to meet a specific order.

Job production is very flexible in that each product is made to order. At the same time, it is often an expensive production process. Instead of setting up machines and letting them run for hours on end, producing hundreds or thousands of items, a firm involved in job production is producing a new item or offering a new service each time. Imagine you are a solicitor, for example. Each client's situation will be unique and you

## THERE'S ONLY ONE WEMBLEY

After almost 7 years of political and financial problems it was finally announced in July 2002 that work was about to begin on the new Wembley stadium. The old stadium would be knocked down and a new one built with a capacity of 90,000. This would take about 3 years and is a good example of one-off job production.

The estimated costs associated with Wembley have spiralled from £185 million to more than £750 milion since it was first proposed, making it the most expensive stadium project in history, and putting it on a par with the ill-fated Millennium Dome. The last match was played at the old stadium in October 2000.

The costs include:

- £120 million of lottery money which was largely used to buy the site of the current derelict stadium.
- Construction costs of around £452 million, including £80 million to demolish the old stadium.
- £80 million for design, legal and financing fees.
- Developing the infrastructure and transport links around the new stadium.

The new Wembley stadium ©www.wembleystadium.com

will offer specific advice to that person. This provides a highly personalised service but is very labour intensive.

In manufacturing, job production requires highly skilled staff and a wide range of equipment because the firm must be able to adapt to different requests. Typically, the firm will have a series of machines which are grouped according to their function. By changing the route of any item from one type of machine to another, a unique product can be produced each time. Alternatively a skilled worker may carry out the job without any purpose-built tools. A potter, for example, can produce a specially shaped vase using only his or her hands and a potter's wheel.

The management of job production tends to be quite complex because each order is unique. Therefore the organisation of orders can become difficult to coordinate. However the level of motivation is usually quite high. This is because each job is different – providing employees with variety in their work. Employees also have a very direct input into the production process. They can see the result of their efforts because there is a usually a clear start and finish to a job. Today a worker starts to build a garden wall; by Friday the task is complete and the customer (and worker) satisfied.

## 34.3 Batch production

**Batch production**, by comparison, produces a group of items at one time. Each group undergoes one stage of the process before being moved on to the next stage. For example, when baking bread a batch of loaves will be prepared, then cooked and finally wrapped and dispatched. Similarly, a fish and chip shop is based around a batch process. A batch of chips or fish is prepared and then cooked ready for customers. When this is

Batch production © Bruce Peebles/Corbis

gone another batch is prepared. Alternatively imagine that you are running a printing company. You will set up the printing presses to print the pages of one particular book. These will be printed then glued together then moved on to be bound, trimmed and despatched. New printing plates will be placed on the presses and a new book produced in the same way.

The advantage of batch production is that more items are produced at any one time than in the job system. This allows the firm to spread its overheads and so reduce the unit costs. However, it is obviously less flexible than job production. Once a batch is in production it cannot easily be changed to produce something else. Switching from one to another takes time and involves a loss of output.

### McJIT

In the late 1990s, McDonald's introduced a new 'made for you' system bringing just-in-time production techniques to the service industry. The system (which costs $25,000 to install) speeds up the time taken for a customer to receive his or her order. This helps McDonald's respond to the success of competitors, such as Burger King, which have stressed in their promotion that their customers can choose exactly what they want and how they want it cooked. In the past, McDonald's franchises cooked their food in batches ready for the busy periods. This meant that some of it sat around before being eaten and so lost some of its flavour. The 'made for you' system includes new technology and a re-engineering of the old process. It includes equipment which toasts buns in 10 seconds and ovens which keep burgers fresh for up to 20 minutes. Everything is designed to increase the speed of service and cut the maximum customer waiting time to 90 seconds.

Batch production can also lead to high stock levels as items wait to move on to the next stage of the process. This takes up space, involves an opportunity cost and creates the possibility of items deteriorating or being damaged.

## 34.4 Flow production

The third type of production is '**flow**' or 'mass' production. With this system an item moves from one stage of the process straight on to the next stage. Oil refining or bottling plants are both examples of a flow process. In a bottling plant, for example, the bottles move

Flow production © Richmond Foods

continuously from the cleansing operation to the actual bottling, to capping, labelling and despatch. The flow from one stage to the next is achieved either by conveyor belts or – in the case of liquids – by pipeline.

Flow production is highly capital intensive. It involves a high level of investment in modern machinery and computer-controlled equipment. The process produces a standardised product in high volumes, such as the Mars factory in Slough which produces three million Mars bars per day. The advantage of this type of process is that the high initial costs can be spread over thousands or millions of units. This generates technical and purchasing **economies of scale**. But to be profitable it relies on high and stable demand. Perfect for producing long-term big sellers such as Kit-Kat, Heinz baked beans or cars such as the Renault Megane.

A custom-built flow production line is difficult and expensive to alter. The system is efficient but inflexible. The firm must therefore be certain that the market will remain large enough to be profitable. The management of people on a flow process can also cause difficulties. Work is often repetitive and relatively unskilled. Staff have little direct input into the way the product is made. The process is also vulnerable to stoppages. Any problem at any stage will hold up the entire production process. Yet the machines need to be running to enable the firm to recoup the high level of initial investment.

## 34.5 Job, batch and flow

The different types of production can be analysed in terms of a product–process matrix (see Figure 34.2). If, for example, the product is a unique one-off item, then the most suitable production process is job production. If the product needs to be standardised and

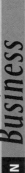

### MASS PRODUCING CHOC ICES

The production process starts by mixing a huge vat of vanilla ice-cream mixture. This is semi-frozen and then squeezed out of a rectangular pipe facing downwards towards a conveyor belt. A mechanical arm slices through the ice-cream mixture, so that slices drop onto the conveyor belt – three semi-frozen, white ice-cream bars per second. The conveyor then enters a refrigerated chamber where the ice-cream circulates slowly until, 15 minutes later, it is frozen rock hard. The conveyor emerges and deposits the bars onto another conveyor which takes each bar through two sheets of warm, liquid chocolate. The chocolate sticks instantly to the frozen bar, which then goes through a little chocolate bath to coat the underside.

After a brief spell in another refrigerated chamber, the conveyor takes the bars to an automated wrapping machine. Three wrapped choc ices per second are packed into cardboard outer boxes and put into cold store awaiting the refrigerated delivery vans. The whole process has taken no more than 45 minutes. No-one has touched the ice-cream. Only six operators are needed to produce more than 10,000 choc ices per hour.

*Business* IN

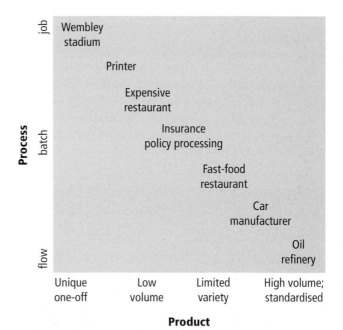

**Figure 34.2** Product–process matrix

| | JOB | BATCH | FLOW |
|---|---|---|---|
| Quantity of products: | One-off item | Group of products produced together | Large quantities |
| Variety of products: | Very flexible | Can vary from batch to batch | Not flexible |

produced in large volumes, then the most appropriate production process would be flow production.

## 34.6 Technology

Developments in technology such as computer-aided design, computer-aided manufacture and the use of robots have allowed firms to design, develop and produce products more rapidly. They have also allowed companies to build greater variety into their production process. Car companies, for example, can now build several models of car based on the same basic features. Similarly, many personal stereos have few differences between them; by changing only certain features a firm is able to produce a wide range of 'different' models. These are mass produced products which look tailored to the needs of individuals.

### — MASS CUSTOMISATION

When Henry Ford launched the Model T Ford over 90 years ago customers were delighted with the low price made possible by mass production. The only problem was the lack of choice ('any colour as long as it's black'). As time has gone on customers have come to expect more and more variety, and producers in all sectors need to be as responsive as possible to customer needs. At the same time they must try to keep production as simple as possible to benefit from economies of scale.

The solution is 'mass customisation' whereby firms offer customers the ability to choose from a number of standardised parts. By combining these parts in different ways customers feel they are getting a tailor-made product, but the actual production process does not become too complex. Cars, washing machines, fridges and computers are all being produced in this way. One of the leaders in mass customisation is Dell Computers. Dell customers specify what features they want on their PC and pay upfront by credit card. The machine is then assembled and dispatched, usually arriving within 3 days. Dell PCs can be put together in about 4 minutes flat, with a further 90 minutes needed to load up the software. Most of the customisation comes from the software that is chosen. This formula has allowed Dell to grow by 20% a year in recent years, even as the PC industry as a whole has been growing by less than 10%.

When analysing the type of production process a firm should adopt, it is useful to consider the following points:

- The most appropriate type of production will depend on the nature of the market. If the firm wants to produce large volumes of standardised products it will move towards a flow process. If it wants unique tailor-made products it will need to adopt a job process.
- Many firms would like the cost advantages of low volumes combined with the ability to produce different products for different markets. Technology is giving firms more flexibility so they can produce various models from the same basic design and production process.
- Only large firms can afford the high capital outlay to set up automated or robot-operated production lines. But small firms are the only ones with the flexibility to design and produce the exact specifications wanted by the one-off customer.

## 34.7 Types of production
### an evaluation

The differences between job, batch and flow production are becoming blurred. Companies such as Dell Computers, for example, can build the product you want in a few hours. Although a production line approach is used, it now has the flexibility to assemble slightly different versions of the same basic computer. In the past, job (and, to a lesser extent, batch) production has been the mainstay of the small firm. So, is the flexibility of modern robotic technology a threat to the future of the small firm? In some cases, yes. Though there will always be a need for the small-scale, highly skilled business which can produce the uniquely designed, tailor-made wedding dress, or Elton John's next swimming pool.

Crucially, flow production means mass production which means mass marketing. This will always struggle to add as much value as specialised, tailor-made, craft skills. Niche marketing implies batch production rather than flow. And the smallest niche of all is one-off production to meet one-off demand. Argos will always sell more rings than a specialist jewellers. But not everyone wants to buy the ring that everyone else buys.

In a recent staff newsletter Schmid explained the situation to her staff in the following way:

'Competing in today's global marketplace requires us to keep moving forward as quickly and efficiently as possible. We must cut our costs if we are to survive. The easiest way to do this would be to make cutbacks. We do not propose to do this. Instead, we intend to reduce our costs by eliminating wastage. In particular we want to target 'track time'. This is the total time for a unit to go from raw materials to finished product. By finding ways of reducing track time we will be able to squeeze out more finished product from the same overheads, therefore our unit costs will fall.'

'At present the track time for our basic 385 model is 31 minutes 22 seconds. It breaks down as follows:

Time to load and unload sub-assemblies: 12 mins 25 secs
Time to clamp and unclamp parts: 2 mins 10 secs
Ram cutting: 12 mins 35 secs
Ram return time: 4 mins 12 secs.

Our objective is to reduce the track time of the 385 model by at least 20% within the next 12 months. We intend to implement the following strategy in order to achieve this objective:

- Cell production – at present we spend too much time on handling components. We already have the right equipment; the problem is that it's in the wrong location.
- Preventative maintenance and in-process inspection – at present we waste too much time fixing machinery that has gone wrong. We want this issue to be given Number One priority in future. We shall look for answers from the weekly quality circle discussion groups.
- Identifying new suppliers who will be more reliable.

These ideas will be discussed in next week's works council meeting before any final decisions are made.'

**Questions** *(50 marks; 60 minutes)*

1 Explain why Huttledorf Engineering is attempting to reduce its 'track time'. *(6)*
2 How will a move towards cell production help the firm in terms of achieving its goal of a 20% time reduction? *(10)*
3 Consider how the staff at Huttledorf Engineering might benefit from Schmid's proposals. *(10)*
4 Many British firms prefer to employ temporary or part-time workers to 'do a job', rather than get involved in consultation exercises such as works councils or quality circles. Why may this be? *(12)*
5 In the context of this case study discuss whether all firms have to constantly adapt and change in order to survive. *(12)*

## C. ESSAY QUESTIONS

1 Discuss the difficulties and dilemmas faced by managers who are considering a switch to lean methods of production.
2 In some companies, lean production is viewed as just being another in a long line of management fads. In others it is embraced with enthusiasm by the staff. Why may this be so?
3 Why do some firms seem far better than others in terms of their ability to successfully implement lean production techniques?
4 Discuss the benefits, and the possible disadvantages, of lean production methods being utilised by an aircraft manufacturer. How might the balance between the benefits and the possible disadvantages change in the long term?

# KAIZEN (CONTINUOUS IMPROVEMENT)

## DEFINITION

Kaizen is a Japanese term meaning continuous improvement. Staff at firms such as Toyota generate thousands of new ideas each year – each aimed at improving productivity or quality. Over time, these small steps forward add up to significant improvements in competitiveness.

## 36.1 Introduction

> 'If a man has not been seen for three days his friends should take a good look at him to see what changes have befallen him.'

This ancient Japanese saying seems to sum up **kaizen** quite nicely. Continuous improvement or 'kaizen' is a philosophy of ongoing improvement based around small changes involving everyone – managers and workers alike.

There are two key elements to kaizen:

- Most kaizen improvements are based around people and their ideas rather than investment in new technology.
- Each change on its own may be of little importance. However, if hundreds of small changes are made, the cumulative effects can be substantial.

An example of a kaizen improvement comes from Barclaycard. In processing billions of pounds of credit card transactions per year, a major problem is fraud. An employee suggested a way of analysing bogus calls to the company's authorisation department. This has saved Barclaycard over £100,000 a year. The precise method is secret, but it works by blocking the credit card numbers of callers trying to buy goods fraudulently. It can also trace the callers, resulting in the arrest of the fraudsters involved.

In the 1990s, continuous improvement became one of the main operations management strategies in Britain. A 1997 study by *IRS Employment Trends* found that 70% of private sector service businesses and 62% of manufacturers claimed to use kaizen. Nine-tenths of these firms had introduced this approach since 1990.

## 36.2 The components of the kaizen philosophy

Describing kaizen as just 'continuous improvement' is simplistic. To work effectively kaizen requires a commitment from management to establish a special, positive culture within their organisation. This culture must be communicated and accepted by all those working at the company. It must permeate the whole organisation. What are the characteristics of this culture or philosophy?

### ONE EMPLOYEE, TWO JOBS

According to the Kaizen Institute the goal of any kaizen programme should be to convince all employees that they have two jobs to do – doing the job and then looking for ways of improving it. The kaizen culture is based on the belief that the production line worker is the real expert. The worker on the assembly line does the job day in day out. This means knowing more about the causes of problems and their solutions than the highly qualified engineer who sits in an office. The kaizen philosophy recognises the fact that any company's greatest resource is its staff. Good ideas can be shared. Arthur Anderson, for example, uses a computer network to spread information around its staff about best practices. Staff are encouraged to post any good ideas that they might have onto the network.

### TEAMWORKING

To operate kaizen successfully employees cannot be allowed to work as isolated individuals. Teamworking is vital to the process of continuous improvement. These teams are composed of employees who work on the same section of the production line as a self-contained unit. Each team is often referred to as a 'cell'. The members of a cell are responsible for the quality of the work in their section. Over time the cell becomes expert about the processes within its section of the production line. Kaizen attempts to tap into this knowledge by organising each cell into a quality circle. The members of each cell meet regularly to discuss problems cropping up within their section. The circle then puts forward solutions and recommendations for the management to consider.

---

## TESCO – EVERY LITTLE HELPS

How would you react if Lidl or Aldi announced the intention of becoming Britain's number one, high quality grocery chain? The better you know the stores, the more you would laugh at the thought. Yet that was largely the position of Tesco when it decided to move upmarket in the early 1980s. It had been famous for being a cheap, low cost, low quality alternative to Sainsbury's.

Over the following two decades it had a mountain to climb, yet stumbled upon the slogan 'Every Little Helps'. This not only became the clever advertising line when introducing initiatives such as Clubcard and 'Only One In the Q' (or we'll open another aisle). It also became vital behind the scenes, as staff started to realise that small steps forward were appreciated by management.

By the mid 1990s Tesco was bigger, better and more profitable than Sainsbury's. It was Britain's number one by miles. It even had the confidence to show little concern when the world's biggest company (Wal-Mart) bought Asda, to bring itself in competition with Tesco. A kaizen approach to management looked even cleverer in 2003, when Morrison's bid for Safeway put further pressure on Britain's number two – Sainsbury's.

*Business* IN

---

### EMPOWERMENT

Empowerment is essential to any kaizen programme. Empowerment involves giving employees the right to make decisions that affect the quality of their working lives. Empowerment enables good shop-floor ideas to be implemented quickly.

Once the necessary kaizen apparatus is in place good ideas and the resulting improvements should keep coming. The number of suggestions made each month should improve over time once employees see the effects of their own solutions. At LucasVarity (motor components) there are over 125 different kaizen groups in their UK-based cable division. Over 2,000 kaizen suggestions are implemented each month and the rate of suggestions is still rising.

However, if quality circles and teamworking are to be truly effective employees must be given real decision making power. If good ideas are constantly being ignored by management they will eventually dry up as the employees become disillusioned with the whole process.

---

## USING TEAMWORKING TO CREATE KAIZEN CUSTOMER SERVICE BENEFITS

Julian Richer is a strong believer in the merits of teamworking and kaizen. Richer is the owner of a highly innovative and successful hi-fi retailing chain called Richer Sounds. Apart from offering excellent value for money Richer has utilised the creative ideas of his staff to create customer service with a difference. For the benefit of every Richer Sounds customer each outlet is equipped with its own free coffee and mint dispensing machine. Each shop has its own mirror which says 'You are looking at the most important person in this shop' and a bell that customers can ring if they feel that they have received excellent service. Many of these innovations have come from Richer's own style of quality circle. Once a month staff at each outlet are encouraged to talk to each other about new ideas. To lubricate this process Mr Richer gives each of his staff £5. This is because at Richer Sounds they hold their kaizen discussions at the pub!

*Business* IN

---

### PERFORMANCE TARGETS

Setting performance targets and then monitoring achievement is also a key component of kaizen. A very simple device that supports this process is the 'level-up' chart. OKI, a Japanese-owned manufacturer of computer printers, uses daily performance targets as an integral part of its kaizen programme. At OKI each production cell is given daily quality targets. They are based on maximum defect rates. These targets are then displayed publicly on a large chart inside the factory. The chart is updated regularly to show each cell's performance in relation to its target. This is sometimes called the level-up chart.

Target setting and monitoring creates three benefits:

- If quality problems do occur it should be easier to trace the fault so that causes can be identified. Those involved at that particular stage of production can then put forward solutions to be discussed.
- Targets can be used to judge whether a kaizen change has been successful.
- Setting and then monitoring quantitative targets can enable benchmarking surveys to take place. (See Unit 37.)

## Words of wisdom – kaizen

> 'Continuous improvement is better than delayed perfection.'
>
> Mark Twain, famous American writer

> 'If there's a way to do it better ... find it.'
>
> Thomas Edison, inventor

> 'If you're not making progress all the time, you're slipping backwards.'
>
> Sir John Harvey Jones, former chief of ICI

> 'I believe that there is hardly a single operation in the making of our car that is the same as when we made our first car of the present model. That is why we make them so cheaply.'
>
> Henry Ford, legendary car maker

> 'Our company has, indeed, stumbled onto some of its new products. But never forget that you can only stumble if you're moving.'
>
> Richard Carlton, former chief at American giant 3M

> 'Be not afraid of going slowly; be only afraid of standing still.'
>
> Chinese proverb

Source: *The Ultimate Book of Business Quotations*, Stuart Crainer, Capstone Publishing, 1997

---

### Business IN — REPEAT KAIZENS

An American engineering firm called FNGP experimented with a three-day Kaizen workshop in 1992. Factory workers were encouraged to suggest ways of improving productivity and product quality. The results were so impressive they held five more Kaizen events over the following three years. The results are shown in the table below.

Note that accident levels fell 92% over this period and the capital expenditure required to make the improvements amounted to less than $1,000.

Source: Adapted from *Lean Thinking* by J Womack and D Jones (1997). Reprinted with the permission of Pocket Books, a Division of Simon & Schuster

---

## 36.3 Potential problems of implementing a successful kaizen programme

### CULTURE

In order for kaizen to really work, employees must be proud to contribute their ideas to the company. Japanese companies do not offer financial rewards in return for suggestions. Their attitude is that employees are told that kaizen is part of the company policy when they are recruited. For them employee commitment to kaizen is gained via genuine staff motivation rather than by financial bonuses. Creating the right organisational culture is therefore vital for success. Resistance can come from two quarters:

- Management resistance – managers with autocratic tendencies may be unwilling to pass decision making power down the hierarchy. Empowerment, de-layering, quality circles and other tools to promote industrial democracy can be seen as a threat to their own status and power.
- Employee resistance – a history of poor industrial relations and a climate of mistrust can create resistance to change among the staff. Employees may not view the delegation of power as a chance to do a more interesting job. Instead, the 'new empowerment programme' may be seen by the workforce as just the latest in a long line of cynical attempts to get more out of the staff for less. The result? Reluctant cooperation at best, but little in terms of real motivation.

### TRAINING COSTS

Mistakes made by managers in the past can have severe long-term effects. Changing an organisation's culture is difficult as it involves changing attitudes. The training required to change attitudes tends to be expensive. It can also take a very long time to change attitudes. Consequently, the costs are likely to be great.

### JUSTIFYING THE COST OF KAIZEN

The training cost and the opportunity cost of lost output is easy to quantify. It may be harder to identify and prove the financial benefits of a kaizen programme. Managers can quite easily produce financial

Results of FNGP kaizen experiment

| | FEB 92 | APR 92 | MAY 92 | NOV 92 | JAN 93 | JAN 94 | AUG 95 |
|---|---|---|---|---|---|---|---|
| Number of staff | 21 | 18 | 15 | 12 | 6 | 3 | 3 |
| Units per worker | 55 | 86 | 112 | 140 | 225 | 450 | 600 |
| Total output | 1,155 | 1,548 | 1,680 | 1,680 | 1,350 | 1,350 | 1,800 |
| Space utilised (sq ft) | 2,300 | 2,000 | 1,850 | 1,662 | 1,360 | 1,200 | 1,200 |

estimates of the benefits of capital investment. It is much harder to assess programmes designed to develop the stock of human capital within the company. Consequently, in firms dominated by the accountant it can be very difficult to win budgets for kaizen programmes.

## 36.4 Business process re-engineering: an alternative approach to kaizen improvement

**Business process re-engineering** (or BPR for short) was a fashionable 1990s' buzzword for something that is as old as the hills. Michael Hammer, author of *Re-engineering The Organisation* calls the approach 'rethinking and redesigning business processes to bring about sharp increases in performance'. According to the re-engineering approach, managers should not attempt to just tinker with existing systems in order to make marginal improvements. Instead, managers should seek genuine breakthroughs, usually through heavy programmes of capital expenditure. These breakthroughs are achieved by scrapping existing systems rather than modifying them. Many BPR programmes can thus be seen as revolutionary, whereas kaizen is evolutionary.

Managers (or management consultants) engaged in BPR programmes are encouraged to rethink everything. For those who believe in BPR, this system has a major advantage over kaizen. Their argument is that starting with a clean slate ensures managers will not be held back by tradition. According to BPR everything should be questioned. This is the way to make major breakthroughs.

This approach is very attractive to company bosses, especially new ones. They can sweep old traditions away and establish an entirely new approach. Fashioned in the image of the leader. Graham Souness did exactly this when he took over as manager of Liverpool Football Club. A number of superb players were sold off; new ones came, and the playing tactics changed dramatically. If it had worked he would have been the hero. It would have been the Souness team, not the Liverpool team. The re-engineering failed, however.

Figure 36.1 shows the effect kaizen has on productivity compared with BPR. Large-scale reorganisations take time to implement, especially if they are based on new machinery and plant. Consequently the firm using BPR may be constantly behind its kaizen competitors and never able to catch up, never mind overtake. The crucial point is that kaizen is all about continuous change. The problem faced by the BPR firm is that by the time the new plant and process are operational the plant may be already out of date. The cause being the changes made by the kaizen competitor in the interim period.

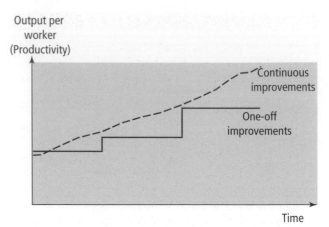

**Figure 36.1**

## 36.5 The limitations of kaizen

### DIMINISHING RETURNS

Some managers argue that the improvements created through a kaizen programme will invariably fall as time goes on. The logic is that the organisation will seek ways of solving the most important problems first. So by implication the problems that remain will become progressively less important. If this is the case it might prove to be difficult to maintain staff enthusiasm. However, supporters of kaizen would reject this criticism on the grounds that there is no such thing as a perfect system. According to them, even the best system is capable of being improved. Cadbury Schweppes' chief executive John Sunderland was asked which management theory was the most overrated. He replied 'If it ain't broke don't fix it. Everything can be improved.' This is a perfect statement in favour of kaizen.

### RADICAL SOLUTIONS

Sometimes radical solutions implemented quickly are necessary in order to tackle radical problems. Kaizen may not be appropriate in all situations. The solution might have to be more dramatic than yet another change to an old system. It may be time to throw out all of the old and replace it with something totally new. This is usually the case in industries facing radical changes brought on by a rapid surge in technology.

A perfect example is the Dutch electronics manufacturer Phillips. During the 1980s the company's product range aged. By the end of the decade the firm was in a real crisis. Both market share and profitability had sunk. Something radical needed to be done and quickly. The senior management at Phillips devised a company-wide BPR project which they called the Centurian programme. The objective of the programme was to re-engineer Phillips' new product development processes. The goal being to reduce design lead time so that Phillips' new products got onto the market first – before the competition. Without this rapid and fundamental rethink of the design process Phillips may not have been able to survive.

- Kaizen improvements to a product are more likely to be effective in the earlier stages of a product's life cycle. If the kaizen programme is started too late it may only slow down the rate of decline rather than reverse it.
- If BPR is to be effective, the restructuring process will need to be ongoing. If the firm pauses too long between each reorganisation, the programme will just be an exercise in catching up. This is why firms that have adopted the kaizen philosophy are often the leaders. Lagging behind the competition can be very expensive, as Sainsbury's discovered in 1999–2001.
- In the short run, the cash flow impacts of BPR can be severe. This is because of the reliance upon technology as the method for seeking major improvement. Struggling firms should therefore be aware of the dangers of BPR. The heavy programmes of capital expenditure required will create immediate outflows of cash. If the radical changes fail to work, the consequences may prove severe.

In the circumstances it is not surprising that those who are afraid of anything too radical choose kaizen over BPR. Kaizen is less threatening. This is because each improvement is relatively small in relation to a massive one-off BPR reorganisation. The attraction of kaizen may be that managers can pretend their firm is 'committed to excellence', yet use kaizen as an excuse to reject any idea that is too radical and which may rock the boat. In summary, when those with bureaucratic tendencies embrace kaizen the result can be very little in terms of meaningful change.

Are kaizen and BPR mutually exclusive? It is possible to use both approaches. Even in Japan kaizen is not used exclusively. The Japanese even have their own word for BPR. They call it 'kaikaku' which roughly translated means 'a radical redesign'. In practice, many Japanese firms use kaikaku as a source of a major breakthrough when one is required. They then follow this up with a kaizen programme in order to perfect and then adapt this new system to suit new conditions as they emerge.

## 36.6 Kaizen
### an evaluation

Does the kaizen approach encourage bureaucracy? In the global market of the 21st century, managers have come to realise that an ability to adapt and change is vital if the firm is to survive. However, many managers and many businesses have great problems with change management. The main issue is that many individuals are frightened of the uncertainty that usually goes hand in hand with change. Some managers seek security, stability and predictability in their own working lives. So which method of change management should managers like this use, kaizen or BPR?

**KEY terms**

**business culture** – the attitudes prevailing within a business.

**business process re-engineering (BPR)** – redesigning key aspects of a business from scratch, often at the cost of job losses.

**kaizen** – continuous improvement.

**suggestion scheme** – a formal method of obtaining written employee suggestions about improvements in the workplace.

# Exercises

## A. REVISION QUESTIONS
*(35 marks; 70 minutes)*

Read the unit, then answer:

1 Give three reasons why kaizen improvements can prove to be cheaper than improvements gained via business process re-engineering. *(3)*
2 State three limitations of the kaizen philosophy. *(3)*
3 Explain why a re-engineering programme can lead to a deterioration in employee morale within the organisation being re-engineered. *(3)*
4 Why might some managers find it harder to implement kaizen than others? *(4)*
5 Give three reasons why it is vital to involve both management and shop-floor staff in any programme of continuous improvement. *(3)*
6 To be truly effective why must kaizen programmes be ongoing? *(3)*
7 Why is it important to set and monitor performance targets when attempting to operate kaizen? *(4)*
8 Explain how kaizen can help to create a better motivated workforce. *(4)*
9 Why might some managers believe that kaizen brings diminishing returns over time? *(4)*
10 Read the In Business headed 'Kaizen Stock Control'. What benefits may Acuson have gained from the improvements to the accuracy of its stock records? *(4)*

## B. REVISION EXERCISES

### B1 Data Response

**Hail The Star**

Julian Hails was once a star player in lower league football teams such as Southend. He believed in teamwork, in training and in continuous improvement. He joined Star Electronics as a sales manager, but became managing director after just three years – promoted over the head of the chairman's son, Richard Star. His enthusiasm was infectious, and his kaizen programme soon bore fruit. This was fortunate because a slump in Star's sector of the electronics market caused a decline in market size.

At the latest board meeting, Julian presented figures recording the impact of the company's kaizen programme. Young Richard Star took the opportunity to snipe at Julian's achievements, saying: 'So after this programme of continuous upheaval, I see our total costs per unit are higher than they were two years ago.'

|  | Two Years Ago | Last Year | This Year |
|---|---|---|---|
| Rejects per unit of output | 7.8 | 6.8 | 6.2 |
| Assembly time (minutes) | 46 | 43 | 39 |
| Stock value per unit of output | £145 | £128 | £111 |
| Direct costs per unit | £42.50 | £39 | £36.50 |
| Overhead costs per unit | £64 | £67 | £72 |

**Questions** *(30 marks; 35 minutes)*

1 Explain the links between 'teamwork' and 'continuous improvement'. *(4)*
2 Analyse the data provided above to evaluate the key successes of Julian's policies. *(12)*
3 Explain what Richard Star meant by his use of the term 'continuous upheaval'? *(6)*
4 What further information is needed to assess the validity of Richard Star's claim? *(8)*

### B2 Case Study

**Continuous Improvement at Dray Technologies**

When Neryn Gaul took over an electrical cable business in 1992 he diagnosed that it was failing fast. 'On my first day here I was shocked by the poor working conditions the staff were expected to put up with. The walls were burnt black and the floor was so dirty your shoes stuck to it.' The previous manager, Mr Smith, had also left a management regime that was highly autocratic. Employees were not trusted or given any decision making power. The management accounts figures also made depressing reading. During Gaul's first month in charge, market share fell for the sixth consecutive month. Urgent action had to be taken to improve the situation.

Gaul's first step was to interview every member of staff to collect ideas and opinions on the causes of the firm's problems and what could be done about them. Gaul started by talking to the production manager, Mr Giles. Giles argued that the cause of the drop in sales was an inability to compete with cut-price competition from the Far East. In order to compete, Dray must find a way of cutting its unit labour costs. Giles' preferred method was to scrap the existing plant and purchase the latest computer-aided manufacturing equipment. 'By investing in this new equipment we will be able to lay off 50 staff and still manage to produce the same volume as we do today. This modernisation programme is essential. We can't pay the same wage rates as our competitors in the East. The only solution is to invest in the new technology that will allow us to improve our productivity by reducing the head count at the factory.' Gaul listened with interest to Giles' argument. However he did feel that this radical modernisation programme was highly risky. Dray's capital gearing was already 65% and due to the company's private limited status the only realistic way of raising the necessary finance would be more loan capital.

Gaul then began to interview the staff and a different picture emerged. The climate of fear created by Mr Smith had stifled innovation and change at Dray. Staff devoted all their energies into self defence and job preservation. No-one was keen to come up with new ideas on how to adapt existing systems to improve productivity because of concerns about the job losses that might follow. Consequently the result was stagnation. Now Gaul felt he had found the true cause of the firm's problems. Gaul decided to reject Giles' advice. Rather than relying on a massive one-off burst of capital expenditure Gaul decided to build the company's future around its staff instead. The next step would be far harder. How was he to set about changing the organisation's culture so that employee ideas would flow?

### Questions                          (50 marks; 70 minutes)

1 What were the probable reasons for the loss of market share suffered at Dray Technologies prior to Mr Gaul's takeover?                                      (8)

2 Using the arguments put forward by Mr Giles, explain how investment in new technology can enable firms to compete against firms operating from low-wage economies?                         (8)

3 Identify and assess the drawbacks of Mr Giles' proposals.                                          (10)

4 How could a firm in the same position as Dray Technologies set about changing its organisational structure in order to encourage greater employee participation?                                      (9)

5 Using the text as a starting point, evaluate the merits of continuous improvement over business process re-engineering.                                 (15)

## C. ESSAY QUESTIONS

1 Two years ago the management team at Lynx Engineering commissioned a benchmarking survey to assess its relative position within the marketplace. To their horror the managers discovered that they were lagging behind their competition in terms of both cost and product quality. In an attempt to rectify the situation a massive £2 million re-engineering programme was announced. Two years later things have still not improved. Assess what could have gone wrong. What should the company do next?

2 How might a firm set about improving its efficiency? What factors are likely to affect the success of any strategy designed to achieve this goal?

3 'It has been proven time and time again that in order to survive firms must be willing to initiate change successfully within their own organisations. Firms that are afraid of change will fail because those that are more adventurous will always leave them behind.' To what extent do you agree or disagree with this statement?

# BENCHMARKING

DEFINITION

Benchmarking is a management tool which helps companies improve their performance. It involves comparing aspects of business performance with those of other companies. The purpose is to identify the best achievements, for instance in terms of delivery reliability. The business will then change some or all of its practices in order to try to match the best company.

## 37.1 How did it develop?

Benchmarking arose from a recognition that profitability and growth come from improving performance. This is not just year on year improvement. It needs to be improvement compared with the best performers. Benchmarking developed during the 1980s when businesses in Europe and the USA faced strong competition from Japanese companies. They were losing their home markets to imported products. To survive they had to compete. This meant discovering why they were losing business. Two major issues were identified:

1  The Japanese companies produced better quality products. Customers received a more reliable product and a higher standard of service.
2  Japanese companies were more efficient at producing the product. This meant that prices could be kept lower. The improved **efficiency** meant that more finance was available for research and development. Existing products were updated more frequently and new innovative products were being brought to the market.

Having realised they were not as efficient as their Japanese competitors, some American and British companies started to look at what these competitors were doing. They began to incorporate some of the Japanese ways of doing things in order to try to catch up.

Benchmarking as a management tool started to be mentioned in 1980s. In 1985 none of the top 500 US companies were engaged in benchmarking. By 1990 over half of them were using the technique. In the UK the use of benchmarking continues to grow. The Confederation of British Industry (CBI) has a set of diagnostic and benchmarking tools that are available to both its members and non-members. PROBE stands for **PRO**moting **B**usiness **E**xcellence. It was designed by the CBI in conjunction with industry leaders and leading academics.

The Department of Trade and Industry (DTI) has published a guide to benchmarking aimed at small businesses.

## Business IN

### BIG BUSINESS, BETTER BUSINESS

Type the word 'benchmarking' into your internet search engine and the number of results gives a good indication of the growth in interest in benchmarking. Not only are there a huge number of firms who will assist but there are also plenty of opportunities for businesses to join in benchmarking activities.

In the UK the Department of Trade and Industry (DTI) runs a scheme that encourages businesses to share information about their processes and to find partners for benchmarking (www.dti.gov.org).

The US web-based Benchmarking Exchange claims to have 44,000 members in 79 countries. Through this website members can share information and views and find other similar firms to benchmark against. They conduct a regular survey of the most popular benchmarking activities.

In September 2002 the top ten were:

1  Customer service/satisfaction
2  Information systems/technology
3  Employee Development/training
4  Process improvement
5  Call centres/help desks
6  Performance measurement /improvement
7  Employee recruiting/staffing
8  Manufacturing assembly
9  Human resources
10  Project management.

Although the list is continually changing it shows the range of activities that are being benchmarked as businesses attempt to improve performance.

(Top ten list from www.benchnet.com)

## 37.2 Who do you benchmark against?

Early benchmarking exercises used Japanese companies for comparison. Now companies are looking at the best performing company, worldwide.

The British chemicals giant ICI has pledged to improve its profit margins. They lag behind those of its American competitors. It will do this by benchmarking itself against the best of its international rivals. Benchmarking initially tended to be industry specific. A car maker would benchmark against another car maker. Today this is less likely to be true. Companies benchmark against a best performer even if the other company is in a totally different industry. This has often produced new ways of thinking about **processes**. Xerox used LL Bean, a mail order clothing company, when it was looking to improve the way it dealt with customer orders in its warehouse. IBM looked at casinos in Las Vegas when it was trying to solve problems of theft by employees. Businesses may use one company as a benchmark for one activity and a completely different company for another activity.

### Example:
Vin by Van Ltd is a mail order wine company. After three years of successful operation it has decided to review its performance. It has employed an industry specialist who has produced the statistics shown in the table at the bottom of the page.

The company is happy with its pricing policy. It feels that this reflects its marketing theme of value for money coupled with quality. In order to improve performance it will benchmark against:

- company X to improve order processing and delivery times
- company Y to reduce order processing costs
- company Z on order fulfilment.

An analysis of complaints shows that most are about slow or non-delivery of the product. It must improve its order processing time and get a higher level of order completion. Then customer complaints will fall significantly.

## 37.3 What functions within the business are suitable for benchmarking?

The objective of benchmarking is to improve performance. It is often used as a tool for improving quality. It is also appropriate for any other activity in the organisation. Benchmarking can be an appropriate way to:

- improve waste management
- improve personnel practices
- simplify office systems
- control manufacturing costs.

As long as the process or activity is measurable it can be benchmarked.

Benchmarking does not aim to alter the product. It focuses on the processes involved in bringing the product to market. This can be any activity from design to after sales care. Inevitably, if the processes are improved this will impact on the product. This is particularly true when benchmarking is used for quality improvement.

Benchmarking is not about spying on competitors to discover their secrets. Benchmarking exercises are done with cooperation between the partners. If a company feels that information is sensitive for commercial reasons it can refuse to disclose the information. If companies do not form partnerships they can use information available on a database. This database will have been set up to collect benchmarking information for many companies within an industry. Often this is organised by the employer's association for the industry. Why should anyone be willing to share information? Because the only ones allowed to see the results are the companies which supplied information.

Benchmarking is not the same as competitive market research. Information about the products and performance of competitors is still a vital marketing activity.

| | | | COMPETITORS | | |
| | DESCRIPTION | VIN BY VAN | X | Y | Z |
| --- | --- | --- | --- | --- | --- |
| Price | Average price per case | £48 | £58 | £37 | £41 |
| Delivery | No. of days from receipt of order to customer receiving goods | 14 | 8 | 14 | 28 |
| Order processing | No. of days from receipt of order to dispatch | 12 | 7 | 10 | 24 |
| Cost of order processing | Average cost per order | £3.50 | £4.20 | £2.80 | £3.40 |
| Order fulfilment | Orders completed in 28 days as % of total orders | 74 | 72 | 37 | 80 |
| Customer complaints | Customer complaints as % of orders | 10 | 8 | 6 | 10 |

## 37.4 So how is it done?

A typical benchmarking system will involve:

1 **Identifying an area that is underperforming** – benchmarking begins when the company recognises it could do better. It may start with general worries about falling sales or lower profitability. It is then necessary to identify specific areas for benchmarking.

2 **Measuring the process** – businesses need to quantify the processes involved. If they cannot measure the activities they cannot compare performance. Most businesses have management information systems that provide the information. If it does not exist then it will be necessary to establish ways of collecting the information.

3 **Identifying the best company in the particular field** – the business may already be aware of the best performer in the industry. It may require more research to identify the best performer from another industry. Government-sponsored schemes and industry databases may provide information. Some companies use management consultants to find the best performer.

4 **Agreeing with the best-practice business on exchange of information** – some companies are willing to disclose information directly to another company. Others may put information on a general database. The level of cooperation may depend on how directly the firms are competing. Firms that are not in the same industry will have less reason for withholding information. The best-practice business may be unwilling to cooperate for reasons of cost rather than confidentiality. Providing information can be a costly and time-consuming activity. Partners are more likely to co-operate if a reciprocal arrangement can be made. Hewlett Packard found this when it approached Direct Line.

5 **Comparing processes and identifying areas for change** – by comparing how the best company operates, the business can identify activities which could be changed to improve performance.

6 **Changing processes** – specific changes can now be made. This may mean changing a whole process or just a small part. It may involve tackling a process in a completely different way or adjusting part of the existing activity.

7 **Remeasuring** – once the process has been completed the whole cycle will start again to determine if the changes have had the desired effect. It will show if there is still scope for further improvement.

This cycle will be ongoing. Even when the business has 'caught up' it will still need to ensure that it does not fall behind again.

## 37.5 Requirements for successful benchmarking

Successful benchmarking requires:

- Commitment from management – management needs to be totally committed or the exercise will fail. Managers may not recognise the need to benchmark. They may consider that the performance of the company is good enough. Managers may also feel threatened by the exercise. They may worry that it will expose their own weaknesses. They need to make sufficient resources available such as manpower and finance.

- Commitment from workers – workers will be required to cooperate with the benchmarking exercise. The objective of the exercise is to increase efficiency. This will often involve changing working practices and may reduce the work available. If workers feel threatened they may not cooperate in making changes. When Rover Cars introduced benchmarking it was tied to a commitment to jobs for life. This gave staff the confidence to cooperate.

- Adequate funding – the exercise will require funding. Time is needed for measuring and comparing processes. Changes initiated following the benchmarking exercise may require additional expenditure. The exercise may identify changes to factory layout or the purchase of additional machinery. As with any other financial expenditure, care needs to be taken to ensure that it is cost effective.

- Best-practice information available for comparison – companies may be aware that they are not performing as well as another firm but the comparative information may not be available. It may not be possible to find the best performer from either inside or outside the industry. Businesses may be unwilling to disclose information, especially if the information is competitively sensitive.

> *Requirements for successful benchmarking:*
>
> - *Commitment from management*
> - *Commitment from workers*
> - *Adequate funding*
> - *A system for measuring the process to be benchmarked*
> - *Best-practice information available for comparison*

Benchmarking is *most successful* when it concentrates on specific activities. It is easier to benchmark part of a process. If a business has a problem with labour turnover it is easier to benchmark the levels of pay or the working hours rather than trying to address the whole problem. In a quality context it will often help to identify the major problem areas and benchmark those first.

**Benchmarking will not work if:**

- *The process or activity being benchmarked cannot be measured*
- *It is not possible to find a best-practice company*
- *The best-practice company is unable or unwilling to disclose information*
- *There is insufficient funding available*
- *The changes that are identified are too costly to implement*
- *The systems used by the best company are not appropriate*

## 37.6 Advantages of benchmarking

- Benchmarking saves companies from having to solve problems from scratch. Companies can incorporate processes that are already working successfully rather than relying on 'trial and error'. With benchmarking they can 'import' working solutions.
- Benchmarking makes companies aware of their relative performance. Benchmarking data allows companies to see how they are performing. If their performance lags behind they can take action to catch up.
- Benchmarking can spark ideas about other ways of doing things. A process that might help to improve performance in one area might also be applied to another activity.
- Benchmarking can improve **international competitiveness**. As individual companies become aware of the need to compete with the best in the world this will improve their international performance.

## 37.7 Disadvantages of benchmarking

- If companies are just copying others then they will not develop new ideas. These new ideas contribute significantly to improvements in business performance.
- The company may focus on processes and may lose sight of its primary objectives.
- The costs may not be recovered in savings or increased efficiency.
- Successful companies may become complacent. This is particularly true if they are used as a benchmark within their industry. They may fail to recognise problems or realise that they are being overtaken by their competitors.

## 37.8 Benchmarking in the future

Benchmarking, although a fairly recent management tool, is now well established and is used by both large and small organisations. As the 'In Business' on page 232 shows, it is also used across the whole range of business activity. The help available to companies from organisations such as the CBI and the DTI, has helped not only to promote the use of benchmarking but also to make the process far simpler. The availability and sharing of data has made finding partners and information easier. Benchmarking has also become big business itself with many business consultancies getting involved. It has now become a favourite management tool for improving performance. It is likely that this will continue into the future. The attitude towards benchmarking can perhaps be best summed up by this quote from Tony Jarram, the quality manager of the Burton-on-the-Wolds site of Hawker Fusegear: 'It is the duty of every manager in industry to say, "is this the best I can do?" If he sees something better he should emulate it, then improve it.'

ISSUES FOR **analysis**

When answering questions on benchmarking, the following issues may need to be considered:

- The usefulness of benchmarking as a management tool.
- The difficulties involved in benchmarking.
- The limitations of benchmarking as a management tool.
- The difference between benchmarking and inter-firm comparisons.

## 37.9 Benchmarking
### an evaluation

Benchmarking has proved to be a useful exercise for many businesses. One of its major contributions has been to encourage businesses to recognise that they could do better. Having recognised that there may be a problem in the operation, it is easier to find solutions. Some businesses have found that they can usefully copy methods or processes used by other businesses. Others have discovered that it does not work to try to 'bolt on' someone else's processes to their existing way of working. The concept of benchmarking is fairly simple, but the practice is rather more complicated. It is often not a case of using the 'best', rather what is available. Comparing processes may also be a problem in that it is not always a case of comparing like with like. Nevertheless companies have found that even if benchmarking does not provide a quick fix solution, it does encourage people to think about the problem. This often leads to the discovery of alternative solutions.

**efficiency** – making the best use of the resources available to the business. It can be measured in several ways, such as output per worker or cost per unit produced.

**inter-firm comparison** – looking at statistical information that is available about other firms in an industry. It may take the form of accounting ratios or efficiency measures.

**international competitiveness** – the ability of firms to compete with overseas firms in overseas markets and on the home market.

**processes** – the activities that enable the company to produce and deliver its goods and services to the consumer.

# Exercises

## A. REVISION QUESTIONS

*(40 marks; 70 minutes)*

Read the unit, then answer:

1 What is the purpose of benchmarking? (3)
2 Identify two activities that might be suitable for benchmarking. (2)
3 State three requirements for successful benchmarking. (3)
4 State and explain three criteria you would use to benchmark the performance of:
  **a** a supermarket (6)
  **b** a manufacturer of toothbrushes. (6)
5 Identify three advantages to a firm of conducting a benchmarking exercise. (3)
6 List two possible problems that benchmarking might cause. (2)
7 Why might a leading business allow its confidential performance to be included in a benchmarking exercise?(4)
8 Give three reasons why benchmarking does not always work. (3)
9 Why do you think the government is encouraging benchmarking? (4)
10 What is the government doing to promote the use of benchmarking? (4)

## B. REVISION EXERCISES

### B1 Data Response
Sawbridge Manufacturing makes doors and timber frames used by the building trade. Over the last few months orders for internal doors have been falling. Sawbridge appears to be losing sales to overseas rivals. The firm has decided to conduct a benchmarking exercise and has gathered the data shown in the table below.

The company has also identified a local car component supplier whose order response time is only five days.

**Questions** *(25 marks; 30 minutes)*
1 Outline two reasons why Sawbridge is losing orders. (4)
2 Which company would be the most suitable partner for Sawbridge to benchmark:
  **a** production costs
  **b** quality? (4)
3 Discuss whether it would be better to use the car component firm or the French firm to benchmark delivery time. (8)
4 Identify and discuss three advantages to Sawbridge of conducting the benchmarking exercise. (9)

| | Sawbridge | Other Competitors | |
| --- | --- | --- | --- |
| | | Leading British Company | Leading French Company |
| Price | £15 | £16 | £16 |
| Delivery time | 14–21 days | 10 days | 8 days |
| Cost per door | £12 | £10 | £13 |
| Production time – no. of man hours per door | 2.4 | 1.6 | 1.9 |
| Quality index – no. of returns per 100 doors | 8 | 6 | 5 |

# QUALITY MANAGEMENT

## DEFINITION

Quality control is the maintenance of consistent levels of quality. Levels of quality are defined by product specifications and customer requirements.

Quality control prevents defects, controls costs and generates customer satisfaction.

## 38.1 What is quality?

Quality is very hard to define. W Edward Deming, the American quality guru, said that 'quality is defined by the customer'. The customer may define quality by insisting on certain specifications. Or by exercising choice in the market. Another definition of quality is 'fit for use'. Although hard to define, there is no doubt that customers are now very aware of quality. They use perceived quality as part of the buying decision. The importance of quality in that decision will depend on the choice available and the balance of power between the customer and the supplier.

Branded goods: are you paying for real, or perceived, quality?

In a competitive market where there is a range of goods available, quality is one of the ingredients in purchasing decisions. The customer will accept some trade-off between price and quality. There is, however, a minimum level of quality that is acceptable. The customer wants the product to work (be fit for use) regardless of the price. Below a minimum level customers will not buy the product. Above the minimum level of acceptable quality customers will expect to get more as they pay more.

When competition is fierce, businesses have to meet or exceed the quality offered by their competitors. The one hairdresser in a village can relate quality to customer satisfaction. If there are four competitors, though, quality may require customers to be delighted rather than satisfied.

### A CLOSER SHAVE

In 2001 Gillette achieved a staggering 71.1% global market share in the razor market. Not even Coca-Cola, Levi's or McDonald's come close to this level of market dominance. By 1997 sales of its leading razor, the Sensor, were at maturity. The company spent $200 million dollars on research and development. The company objective was clear. It wanted a product that would expand the market for non-electric shaving but at higher prices. This required a product with considerable added value. The Mach3 was the result and was launched in April 1998. Since then it has captured 23% of the global market with worldwide sales totalling over $3 billion.

Although it took sales from the Sensor this was not a problem for the company as the Mach3's price premium ensured increased profitability. Gillette's assumption that customers would be prepared to pay a premium for higher quality has been proved correct.

The company is hoping that this will again prove to be true. It has now launched a new product: the Mach3Turbo. In March 2002 when launching an advertising campaign to support the new product, Peter K. Hoffman, President, said, 'With more than 60 million men around the world already shaving with Mach3, we are confident that this campaign will inspire many of them to trade up to the even better performing Mach3Turbo, as well as introduce entirely new users to the razor's benefits.'

Dell is a hugely successful computer manufacturer which sells directly to customers through the Internet or newspaper advertising. Its mission statement says:

'*Customers must have a quality experience and be pleased not just satisfied.*'

Gillette's Mach3 Turbo: better quality at a higher price ©Gillette

## 38.2 Quality defined by specifications

Where the customer is in a powerful position, quality is directly defined by the customer. Many firms lay down minimum standards for their suppliers. This in turn helps them to maintain their own quality standards. Large businesses such as supermarkets and chain stores are able to insist on quality standards. They have the buying power to force their suppliers to conform. For many years, Marks and Spencer has worked with suppliers to ensure that standards are met. Other large purchasers such as government departments and local authorities are also able to insist on high standards for supplies. As new roads and motorways are built, the surface is checked to ensure its quality. If the surface does not conform to the required standards the contractor will have to re-lay the area.

## 38.3 Quality defined by law

The law lays down minimum quality standards. This applies particularly to products where health or safety are involved. Food must be fresh and has to be handled with care, by trained staff. It is illegal to sell electrical equipment without a plug fitted.

There are also trading standards. These are often industry based. They set minimum standards for particular goods and services. Some trade associations offer guarantees for work done by members of their association. The National House Building Council offers purchasers a 10-year guarantee for work done by their members. Some industries have watchdogs. They ensure that minimum standards are met. OFWAT, the water industry regulator, has the task of ensuring that water quality is maintained.

Other firms, and in particular local and central government agencies, will insist that their suppliers have obtained BS 5750 or the international equivalent ISO 9000 (see below). This ensures that suppliers are operating within a quality framework.

*ISO 9000 is an international standard for quality systems. It is a British standard that is recognised worldwide. It was previously known as BS 5750. Companies who are registered can display the BSI symbol. In order to register, companies have to document their business procedures, prepare a quality manual and assess their quality management systems. They are assessed by an independent assessor. After obtaining the award, businesses are visited at regular intervals to ensure compliance. It is necessary that everyone in the organisation follows the processes outlined in the quality manual.*

*Firms who have registered say that it has provided a range of benefits to the business. These include:*

- *increased competitiveness*
- *increased customer satisfaction*
- *less waste*
- *cost savings*
- *fewer mistakes*
- *increased efficiency*
- *better motivated employees*
- *improved communications*
- *increased profits.*

For all customers, quality is about satisfying their expectations. Customers expect products to work and to be of a consistent standard. For many customers the issues are not limited to reliability. The customer will take into account the total buying experience. Customer service and after-sales service may be as important as the product itself. The inability to obtain spare parts is also a quality issue. The way the product is sold, even where it is sold, all contribute to the customers' feelings about the quality of the product.

Quality is a moving target. Quality that is acceptable today may not be in the future. Customer expectations of quality are constantly changing. As quality improves, customer demands also increase.

*Quality:*
- *is satisfying customer expectations*
- *applies to services as well as products*
- *involves the whole business process, not just the manufacturing of the product*
- *is always changing.*

## 38.3 Why is quality control important?

Quality is an important competitive issue. Its importance will depend on how competitive the market is. Where the consumer has choice, quality is vital.

A reputation for good quality brings marketing advantages. A good quality product will:

- be easier to establish in the market
- generate repeat purchases
- have a longer life cycle
- allow brand building and cross marketing
- save advertising costs
- allow a price premium (This is often greater than any added costs of quality improvements. In other words, quality adds value. It therefore generates additional profit.)
- make products easier to place (Retailers are more likely to stock products with a good reputation.).

Implications of poor product or service quality

| MARKETING COSTS | BUSINESS COSTS |
|---|---|
| Loss of sales | Scrapping of unsuitable goods |
| Loss of reputation | Reworking of unsatisfactory goods – costs of labour and materials |
| May have to price discount | Lower prices for 'seconds' |
| May impact on other products in range | Handling complaints/warranty claims |
| Retailers may be unwilling to stock goods | Loss of consumer goodwill and repeat purchase |

## 38.4 How can firms detect quality problems?

The ideal is to detect quality problems before they reach the customer. This can be done by:

- Inspection of finished goods before sale – this has been the traditional method. It may be all goods or only a sample.
- Self-inspection of work by operatives – this is being used more as businesses recognise that quality needs to be 'everyone's business'. Thirty years ago, Professor Herzberg was emphasising the psychological importance of self-checking. Today it is a common feature of progressive factory managements.
- Statistical analysis within the production process – this can be used to ensure that specifications stay within certain limits. For example, Mars might set a target weight for 100 g bags of Maltesers of between 96 and 104 g (see Figure 38.1). Only if the weight slips outside this range will an alarm indicator be

triggered to warn that the specifications are not being met. Staff could then stop the production line and readjust the machine to ensure that the correct weight is being given.

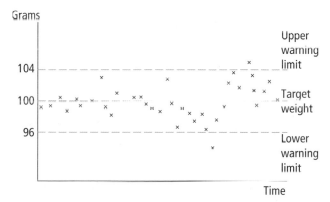

**Figure 38.1** Actual weight of 100 g bags of Maltesers coming off the production line

When problems are not detected before reaching the market they can be identified by:

- Market research – if the company is aware of quality it can build it into its market research. This allows the company to discover customer attitudes towards quality. It can be used to detect quality problems. Market research can include competitive analysis. This ensures that competitors are not gaining advantage by quality initiatives.

> 'Reducing the cost of quality is in fact an opportunity to increase profits without raising sales, buying new equipment, or hiring new people.'
> Philip Crosby, American quality guru

> 'Quality is remembered long after the price is forgotten.'
> Gucci slogan

> 'The only job security anybody has in this company comes from quality, productivity and satisfied customers.'
> Lee Iacocca, successful boss of Chrysler Motors

> 'Good management techniques are enduring. Quality control, for instance, was treated as a fad here, but it's been part of the Japanese business philosophy for decades. That's why they laugh at us.'
> Peter Senge, American business author

> 'Quality has to be caused, not controlled.'
> Philip Crosby

> 'Quality is our best assurance of customer allegiance, our strongest defence against foreign competition, and the only path to sustained growth and earnings.'
> Jack Welch, General Electric chief

Source: *The Ultimate Book of Business Quotations*, Stuart Crainer, Capstone Publishing, 1997

- Customer complaints and returned goods – this is one of the most immediate ways of identifying problems. It will only work if there is a system to collect and process the information. A store manager may be able to make an exchange or refund. If the problem is only dealt with at this level the customer may be satisfied but the problem could persist. The business needs to ensure that information is passed back to head office.

---

## Business IN

### QUALITY PROBLEMS ADD TO FORD'S WOES

Ford, the once great motor company, is ailing. It has now fallen behind its great rival General Motors after suffering a £3.6 billion loss in 2001. In the late 1990s it expanded horizontally with the purchase of Land Rover and Volvo and vertically by buying workshops and distributors such as the Kwik-Fit chain. The new chief executive Billy Ford, the great grandson of Henry Ford the company founder, has set about restructuring the business in an attempt to reverse its fortunes. In August 2002 the company sold the Kwik-Fit chain and has announced factory closures and job losses.

However, over-expansion has not been the sole cause of the company's problems. It was seriously affected by a quality control problem in 2001. After road deaths were linked to faulty Firestone tyres, it was forced to recall millions of vehicles and replace the tyres. This cost the company around £2 billion but probably the largest cost was to its reputation.

Adapted from *The Times*

---

## 38.6 How do businesses control quality?

Traditionally, quality control has been the responsibility of the production department. In the past, most quality control processes were concentrated in the factory. These were intended to prevent faults leaving the factory. The methods of quality control focused on statistical analysis and inspection. Today, firms are more likely to see quality as having product *and* service aspects.

There are four stages to quality control. They are prevention, detection, correction and improvement.

### 1 Prevention

This tries to avoid problems occurring. It can be applied to any part of the business. For example, at the design stage consideration may be given to quality by:

- ensuring the product is safe
- ensuring the product is easy to use
- ensuring the product is reliable and long lasting
- building in features that minimise production errors.

### 2 Detection

This ensures that quality problems are spotted before they reach the customer. This has been the traditional emphasis of quality control. The use of computer-aided statistical analysis has given firms better tools to detect faults. It has also enabled firms to keep production standards within certain tolerance levels. Increasingly, businesses are making detection the responsibility of every employee.

### 3 Correction

This is not just about correcting faults. It is also about discovering why there is a problem. Once the problem is identified steps can be taken to ensure it does not recur.

### 4 Improvement

Customer expectations of quality are always changing. It is important that businesses seek to improve quality.

---

## 38.7 Quality initiatives

As the importance of quality has been recognised, there has been a growth in initiatives to control and improve quality. Techniques for quality control such as inspection and statistical control continue. They have been supplemented by other initiatives aimed at controlling and improving quality. These include:

- **Total quality management**

  TQM was introduced by American business guru W Edward Deming in the early 1980s. He worked with Japanese firms and his techniques are said to be one of the reasons for the success of Japanese businesses. TQM is not a management tool. It is a philosophy. It is a way of looking at quality issues. It requires commitment from the whole organisation, not just the quality control department. The business considers quality in every part of the business process. This will include design right through to sales. Total quality management is about *building in rather than inspecting out*.

- **Continuous improvement**

  This is a system where the whole organisation is committed to making changes on a continual basis. The Japanese call it kaizen. It is an approach to doing business that looks for continual improvement in the quality of products, services, people and processes.

- **Zero defects**

  The aim is to produce goods and services with no faults or problems. It is a management philosophy and requires commitment throughout the organisation. It emphasises that each employee must contribute to quality.

- **Quality circles**

  A quality circle is a group of employees who meet together regularly for the purpose of identifying problems and recommending adjustments to the working processes. This is done to improve the product or process. It is used to address known quality issues such as defective products. It can also be useful for identifying better practices that may improve quality. It also has the advantage of improving employee morale through employee involvement. It takes advantage of the knowledge of operators.

- **Training**

  Training can make an enormous contribution to quality. It might be specifically job oriented, such as training a machinist or a sales assistant in customer care. It could be induction, or more general such as an introduction to the objectives of the company.

This is important where the company is trying to introduce a 'quality culture'.

- **Benchmarking**

  This is a process of comparing a business with other businesses. Having identified the best, businesses attempt to bring their performance up to the level of the best, by adopting its practices.

- **Obtaining quality accreditation**

  This includes schemes such as ISO 9000. Companies have to have in place a documented quality assurance system. This should be an effective quality system which operates throughout the company and involves suppliers and subcontractors.

- **Cross-functional improvement groups**

  These are groups set up within the organisation. They look at how interactions between departments can be improved. They may be quality oriented. They may also reduce costs or increase efficiency.

Most of these initiatives rely on employee involvement. In addition to quality improvements and cost reductions, most businesses find that the initiatives in themselves deliver benefits. These include better working practices, improved employee motivation, increased focus on tasks and the development of teamworking.

## 38.8 Problems with quality initiatives

Although most businesses benefit from introducing quality initiatives, there can be problems. These include:

1  Cost of the initiatives – costs include:

   - inspection costs
   - training costs
   - material costs
   - equipment costs
   - costs of changes to production methods
   - cost of specific quality initiatives such as quality circles.

   The traditional belief was that it is only possible to get 100% quality at a cost. It is necessary to balance the cost of quality control and improvement with the costs of poor quality. The company needs to be aware of how much the customer is prepared to pay. The alternative approach, put forward by the American guru Philip Crosby, is that 'quality is free'. The latter view suggests that getting things right first time can save a huge amount of time and money.

2  The time required to make it work – quality initiatives take time. Workers may be away from their jobs while attending training or quality groups.

**NOT SUCH PAINLESS INJECTIONS**

PowderJect Pharmaceuticals plc is a company that makes and sells vaccines. Many of the vaccines that PowderJect is developing incorporate its unique delivery technology, powder injection. This patented technology delivers vaccines into the outer layer of skin in a simple-to-use needle-free system. One of its products is the BCG (tuberculosis) vaccine that is given to most school children in the UK. Sales of this vaccine account for revenue of approximately £10 million each year.

In 2002 it ran into problems with quality. There were concerns about the shelf life of the product. The company withdrew the vaccine in spite of issuing statements that this problem did not affect the potency of the vaccine. The company estimated that the withdrawal would cost the business £5 million in lost profits but the effect is likely to be deeper than that. In one day following the announcement the share value of the business fell by over 20%. This reflects the fact that the City feels this problem will make it much harder to sell the company's products in the future and will affect long term profitability.

**3** Short-term versus long-term viewpoints – there may be a conflict between short-term costs and longer term results. Shareholders may want returns today, but often quality initiatives require a long-term view. The investment will be a current cost. The benefits, however, may take some time to show. They may also be difficult to measure.

ISSUES FOR **analysis**

When looking at quality issues in a case study or essay question, the following are issues that need to be considered:

- The importance of quality to the business. This will depend on the type of business, the type of product or the service. It will also depend on the market in which the business is operating.
- How businesses approach quality control. It is important to consider not only how the initiatives work but the problems they may cause.
- Quality issues are often closely interwoven with other parts of the business. The role of the employee in quality control is an important issue. Interlinked with this are the changes in management styles and philosophies that come with many of the quality initiatives.
- The balance within the business between the shareholders, customers and employees.
- The change of emphasis towards quality in businesses and the reasons underlying this change.

**242**

---

## 38.9 Quality management
### an evaluation

In recent years there has been a change in the emphasis on quality. The quality business has itself grown. The management section of any bookstore reveals several titles dedicated to quality management. The growth of initiatives such as TQM and continuous improvement goes on. The number of worldwide registrations for

ISO 9000 increases by more than 25% a year. Not all of these are from British businesses – there has been a rapid rise in overseas registrations. In 1996 some countries such as Barbados and Iran appeared in the list for the first time. With this increase in the international awareness of quality, British businesses will have to ensure that they continue to be competitive.

This growth in emphasis on quality has undoubtedly brought benefits to business. Increased quality brings its own rewards in the marketplace. Companies have also found that the initiatives, especially where they are people based, have also brought other advantages. Changes in working practices have improved motivation and efficiency and have reduced waste and costs.

This change in emphasis has not been without problems. The shift to a focus on the customer and the role of the employee could result in shareholders losing out. Some businesses have found that changing cultures is not easy. Resistance from workers and management have often caused problems. Today's great quality initiative often becomes tomorrow's damp squib. In a recent survey, City consultants Ernst and Young found that the TQM movement is floundering. The evaluative approach to quality, therefore, is to treat every initiative with equal amounts of interest and scepticism.

**KEY terms**

**benchmarking** – comparing a firm's performance with best practice in the industry.

**marketing mix** – the elements involved in putting a marketing strategy into practice. They are product, price, promotion and place.

**zero defects** – eliminating quality defects by getting things right first time.

---

**38.10 Workbook**

# Exercises

## A. REVISION QUESTIONS
*(35 marks; 60 minutes)*

Read the unit, then answer:

**1** State two reasons why quality management is important. *(2)*
**2** How important is quality to the consumer? *(3)*
**3** Suggest two criteria customers might use to judge quality at:
  **a** a budget-priced hotel chain *(2)*
  **b** a Tesco supermarket *(2)*
  **c** a McDonald's. *(2)*

**4** Why has there been an increase in awareness of the importance of improving the quality of products? *(3)*
**5** Give two marketing advantages that come from a quality reputation. *(2)*
**6** What costs are involved if the firm has quality problems? *(3)*
**7** What are the four stages of quality control? *(4)*
**8** What is total quality management? *(4)*
**9** What are quality circles? *(4)*
**10** Outline two additional costs that might be incurred in order to improve quality. *(4)*

# B. REVISION EXERCISES

## B1 Data Response

### Trac Parts

Trac Parts is a major manufacturer of parts for farm and construction machinery. It has been operating from a new centralised warehouse for four years. This year the company applied for BS ISO 9000. It gained accreditation. The main reason for applying was that several large customers had indicated that they would only deal with BS ISO 9000 companies when negotiating new contracts. The warehouse manager has been pleasantly surprised by the operational performance figures since accreditation:

- orders completed on time up from 75% to 84%
- errors in completing orders reduced by 40%
- average time from order receipt to dispatch reduced by two days.

### Questions                              (25 marks; 30 minutes)

1 What is BS ISO 9000?                              (3)
2 Why might a business want this accreditation?                              (4)
3 Examine the benefits to Trac Parts of the performance improvements identified in the text.                              (6)
4 In order to gain accreditation, the firm will have had to introduce procedures to ensure that levels of quality are maintained. Using the four stages of quality control (prevention, detection, correction and improvement) suggest actions it might have taken.                              (12)

## B2 Case Study

### Tricolour

Tricolour is a French computer manufacturer. It has worries about falling sales. It believes it is losing sales to Japanese and American companies that have set up manufacturing facilities in Europe. It has also lost sales to other European competitors. An industry survey has produced data on industry levels of production defects. It has added its own figures and produced the chart shown below.

The firm realises that survival depends upon addressing the quality problems. It has decided to employ a quality manager, Celeste Dubois, to address the issues. Her first suggestion is to get together a group of workers from each department to discuss the problems and issues. Following a survey of the factory she has also suggested that the layout of the production facilities should be changed. This will be an expensive exercise and the management is reluctant to make the changes. The changes will require production to stop for a week and investment in new equipment. The firm's weak cash flow position makes it hard for the board to accept new capital spending. The other area that Celeste has identified is a problem with one particular component. She has suggested that a new supplier should be found, or that she should work with the existing supplier to improve the quality of the component.

### Questions                              (40 marks; 50 minutes)

1 a What does the chart show?                              (2)
  b What further data would help to make the bar chart more useful?                              (4)
2 From the case study identify two reasons for the quality problems experienced by Tricolour.                              (2)
3 What are the marketing implications for Tricolour of the data in the bar chart?                              (8)
4 Outline the advantages Tricolour might get from the discussion group formed to discuss the quality problems.                              (8)
5 How might Celeste convince the firm's management to change the layout of the production facilities?                              (6)
6 Once these changes have been made the firm needs to ensure that quality is maintained and improved. Discuss the implications for the firm of implementing a total quality management initiative.                              (10)

**Manufacturing defects – producer comparisons**

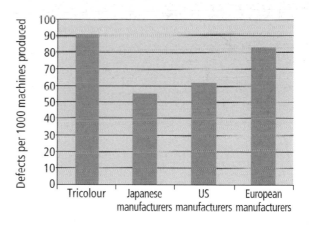

## C. ESSAY QUESTIONS

1 'Quality control is about building quality in, not inspecting it out.' Discuss.
2 Consider whether quality management is solely a matter for the production department.
3 To what extent is quality a major competitive issue in service businesses?

# STOCK CONTROL

**DEFINITION**

The management process that makes sure stock is ordered, delivered and handled in the best possible way. An efficient stock control system will balance the need to meet customer demand against the cost of holding stock.

## 39.1 Purchasing

Manufacturing businesses rely on stocks being bought in from other firms. These stocks can either be in the form of raw materials or components. These stocks are part of the inputs which manufacturing firms process into outputs.

The purchasing function acts as a service to the rest of the business. Its main objective is to meet the needs of those running the internal operations of the business. In a factory, inefficient purchasing may lead (in the extreme) to a shutdown if key materials or components have not turned up when needed. In a retail store, poor purchasing could mean empty shelves or an over-full stockroom. In order to avoid this, the purchasing function of a business will try to ensure that:

- a sufficient quantity of stocks is available at all times…
- …but not so much as to represent a waste of resources
- stocks are of the right quality
- stocks are available where they are needed in the factory
- the price paid for stocks is as competitive as possible
- good relations are built up with suppliers.

When purchasing stocks, a business must ask a range of questions about potential suppliers. The main two things that the buyer must be convinced of are that the supplier can meet its requirements on quality and on price.

- Quality can be checked through samples and/or a visit to the supplier's factory to inspect methods and conditions. If the supplier has achieved its BS 5750 certificate (or the European equivalent ISO 9000) it means it has an effective quality assurance system.
- The price may be negotiated, especially if the buyer is purchasing in bulk or is a regular customer. A lower price may be agreed, or longer credit periods established.

In addition, the buyer will have to consider other questions before deciding which supplier to use. This will include such things as:

- Will the supplier be consistent, supplying the quantity and quality needed on time, every time?
- Is the financial position of the firm sufficiently safe to guarantee, as far as possible, its future survival?
- If the needs of the buyer change, can the supplier change quickly to meet demand?
- Can the supplier expand if the buyer's demand grows?

In the past, firms tended to focus on short-term buying decisions based upon the lowest quoted price. Today's supplies might be from XZ Ltd; tomorrow's from PQ and Co. Companies such as Marks and Spencer and Toyota took a different approach. They aimed to form an effective and lasting partnership with suppliers. In that way both businesses benefit from the relationship. More and more British companies are following this lead.

The purchasing department will need to take a strategic decision on how best to operate. Key questions will be:

- Should the firm place large orders occasionally, or small orders frequently?
- Should the firm accept lower quality stocks at a lower cost?
- Should the firm rely on one supplier or use several?

## 39.2 Types of stock

Manufacturing firms hold three types of stock:

- Raw materials and components. These are the stocks the business has purchased from outside suppliers. They will be held by the firm until it is ready to process them into its finished output.
- Work in progress. At any given moment, a manufacturing firm will have some items which it has started to process, but which are incomplete. This may be because they are presently moving through the production process. It may be because the firm stores unfinished goods to give it some flexibility to meet consumer demand.
- Finished goods. Once a product is complete, the firm may keep possession of it for some time. This could be because they sell goods in large batches or no buyer has yet come in for the product. For producers of seasonal goods such as toys, most of the year's production may be building stock in preparation for the pre-Christmas sales rush. This process is known as producing for stock, or stockpiling.

As explained in Section 39.5, the firm's costs increase if it holds more stock. However, this needs to be set against the **opportunity cost** of keeping too little stock, such as not being able to meet customer demand. One theory is that a firm should try to keep as little stock as possible at all times. This system, known as just-in-time, is looked at in Section 39.7.

The firm must keep control of all the different types of stock to ensure it runs at peak efficiency.

## 39.3 Stock management

Stock management is the way a firm controls the stock within the business. If the purchasing function has been efficient, the business will receive the right quantity and quality of stock at the right time. However, once the stocks are inside the firm, they must be handled and used correctly. This is to make sure they are still in peak condition when the come to be used in the production process.

### STOCK ROTATION

Wherever possible, a firm will want to use its oldest stock first. This will mean stocks do not deteriorate, go past their sell-by date or become obsolete. Stock can go obsolete if new specifications are used or if the product of which they were a part is no longer manufactured. By using a system of **stock rotation**, the firm will ensure that the risks of stock going out of date are minimised. Supermarkets, for example, should always put new stock at the back of the shelf to encourage shoppers to take the older stock first. The principle behind stock rotation is first-in-first-out (FIFO). This is to avoid a situation in which new stock is used first, leaving older stock to become unusable at the back of a shelf or a warehouse.

### STOCK WASTAGE

This is the loss of stock in either a production or service process. Any wastage is a cost to the firm as it has paid for stock which it will not use.

In a manufacturing process, the main causes of stock wastage are:

- materials being wasted, such as scraps of cloth being thrown away as off-cuts from a dress maker; this can be minimised by careful planning – perhaps helped by computer-aided design (CAD) software
- the reworking of items that were not done correctly first time; good training and a highly motivated staff are the best ways to avoid this
- defective products that cannot be put right, which will often be sold off as seconds or damaged goods.

For a retailer, the main causes of stock wastage will be:

- products becoming damaged due to improper handling or storage

In massive warehouses like this, accurate stock management is crucial

- stealing from the shop, whether by customers or staff
- products such as food passing their sell-by dates.

In all of these cases, sound management and administrative techniques could reduce or even eliminate the problem of stock wastage. Any wastage is a cost to the firm, and procedures need to be set up to prevent such losses.

However, it is important that the cost of the processes set up is not more than the money being saved by them. Cost effective measures are needed to maximise the returns to the firm.

## 39.4 Stock control charts

One way in which a firm analyses its stock situation is by using stock control charts. These line graphs look at the level of stock in the firm over time. Managers will be able to see from these charts how stock levels have changed during the period, and will be able to note any unusual events with which they may need to be concerned.

A typical stock control graph is shown in Figure 39.1. On this chart there are four lines. These represent:

- Stock levels. This line shows how stock levels have changed over this time period. As the stock is used up, the level of stock gradually falls from left to right. When a delivery is made, however, the stock level leaps upwards in a vertical line. The greater the rise in the vertical line, the more stock has been delivered.
- Maximum stock level. This shows the most that the firm is either willing or able to hold in stock. It may reflect the physical size of the warehouse and be the maximum because no more can be taken in. It may

also, however, be set by management on the basis that:

– it is the most that be used by the production process
– it is the most that can be kept to ensure sell-by dates are not missed
– it is sufficient, given the time between deliveries and the rate of usage.

- Re-order level. This is a 'trigger' quantity. When stocks fall to this level a new order will be sent in to the supplier. The re-order level is reached some time before the delivery (shown by the vertical part of the stock level line). This is because the supplier will need some 'lead time' to process the order and make the delivery.
- Minimum stock level. This is also known as the **buffer stock**. The firm will want to keep a certain minimum level of stock for reasons of safety. It will have something to fall back on if an order does not arrive on time or if stock is used up particularly quickly, perhaps due to a sudden increase in demand.

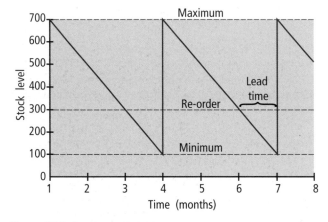

**Figure 39.1** Stock control chart

Diagrams such as this, showing a neat and regular pattern to stockholding, will not happen in reality. Orders may arrive late and may not always be in the correct quantity. The rate of usage is unlikely to be constant. The slope of the stock level line may be steeper showing more stock being used than normal, or shallower showing a slower use of stock.

However, as a basis for analysing stock levels over time, stock control charts such as these give managers a clear picture of how things have changed, and shows them what questions need to be asked. For example, it may show that stocks are constantly arriving late. Managers would then know to ask if suppliers were taking longer than the agreed lead time. Or if orders were not being placed when the re-order level of stock was reached.

Figure 39.2 shows a more realistic stock control graph. It is based on actual sales of Nestlé Lion bars at a newsagent in south-west London over a three-month period.

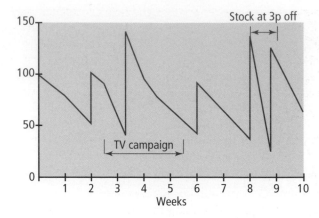

**Figure 39.2** Weekly sales of Lion bars at one newsagent

## 39.5 The costs of stock

The initial cost of purchasing stock is only one of the costs associated with a firm's stockholding. A firm can hold too much stock or too little stock. Both cases will add to the costs of the firm.

Too much stock can lead to:

- Opportunity cost. Holding the firm's wealth in the form of stock prevents it using its capital in other ways, such as investing in new machinery or research and development on a new product. By missing out on such opportunities the firm may put itself at a disadvantage compared with competitors.
- Liquidity problems. Holding the firm's wealth as stock may cause problems if it proves slow moving. There may be insufficient cash to pay suppliers.
- Increased storage costs. As well as the physical space needed to hold the stock, there may be increases in associated costs such as labour within the warehouse, heating and lighting or refrigeration. Stocks need to be insured against fire and theft, the cost of which will increase as more stocks are held.
- Increased finance costs; if the capital needs to be borrowed, the cost of that capital (the interest rate) will be a significant added annual overhead
- Increased stock wastage. The more stocks that are held, the greater the risk of it going out of date or deteriorating in condition.

This does not, however, mean that the business is free to carry very low stocks. Unless it can confidently run just-in-time systems the firm may well face increased costs from holding too little stock as well. These could be:

- Workers and machines standing idle as there are not enough materials or components to allow the process to operate. This costs the business in lost output and wages being paid for no work. It could also cost the business at a later date if extra overtime is needed to make up for the production lost.

- Lost orders as customers needing a specific delivery date which cannot be met go elsewhere.
- Orders not being fulfilled on time leading to worsening relations with customers. This could lead to future orders being lost as customers turn to more reliable suppliers. The firm may also have to pay customers financial compensation for missing delivery dates.
- The loss of the firm's reputation and any goodwill it has been able to build up with its customers.

The total cost to the firm of stocks will therefore be a combination of these factors. As the level of stocks grows, the costs of holding that stock will increase, but the costs of not holding stock will decrease. The cost of holding stock will therefore look like Figure 39.3.

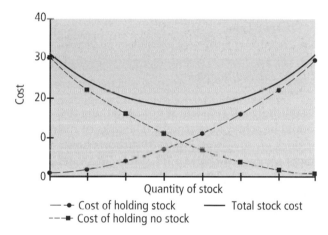

**Figure 39.3** Cost of stockholding

For a firm, the optimum level of stock to hold will be where the total costs of holding stock are the lowest.

A further consideration to the quantity of stocks being held is how much stock to order at any one time. Large orders need only be made a few times to keep sufficient stock levels, whilst smaller orders will mean that they have to be placed more regularly. The arguments for both of these are shown below:

*Advantages of many smaller orders:*

- *Less storage space needed*
- *More flexible to changing needs*
- *Less stock wastage*

*Advantages of few larger orders:*

- *Economies from buying in bulk*
- *Avoids chance of running out of stock*
- *Prevents machines and workers standing idle*

## 39.6 IT and stock control

As computers become cheaper and more powerful they are being used more and more in business. The management of stock is a good example. Stock control is all about the efficient handling of information about current and required stocks. Information technology can handle large quantities of data quickly and easily. Therefore the use of IT can make the task of stock control both easier and more accurate.

Most businesses will hold records of their stock on large databases. Stock control systems exist that allow these databases to be updated instantaneously as stock leaves the warehouse or goes through the checkout. The systems that achieve this are bar-code scanners which read the details of the stock coming in or going out. This data can be transferred immediately to the warehouse computer system which can then keep an accurate, up-to-the-second picture of how much stock is held at any given time. The need to re-order stock can be identified by the system, and the order sent automatically from the warehouse IT system to the supplier's IT system. Such a system largely does away with the need for human involvement in the stock control process once the system and the rules by which it operates are set up.

Stock control systems such as these add to the ability of managers to analyse stock movements. It should make it possible for more accurate decisions to be made on what stock to hold and in what quantities.

## STOCK CONTROL AT JAGUAR

When Jaguar began production of its new X-Type, it felt the need for a more tightly controlled stock management system to help increase efficiency, productivity and to meet consumer demand.

A particular area of concern was the availability of the welding tips used by robotic arms to seal the bodyshell. Thousands of such tips are used daily. Without them, car manufacture would slow down or even cease altogether. To prevent this happening, tips were usually overstocked – many more were held than were ever going to be needed.

Previously there had been no computerised tracking or controlled storage system in place. With the X-Type being produced, Jaguar felt the need to have a system to accurately manage and control stock levels, to allow production to be as cheap and efficient as possible.

It is believed that this new system has saved Jaguar up to £8,000 per year. In addition, staff have been given more responsibility for stock management, boosting their involvement and motivation.

Source: *The Engineer*

# Exercises

## A. REVISION QUESTIONS
*(35 marks; 70 minutes)*

Read the unit, then answer:

1 Why might it be important to maintain good relationships with suppliers? *(3)*
2 State the three main categories of stock. *(3)*
3 What is meant by 'internal customers'? *(3)*
4 How would stock rotation help a firm manage its resources better? *(4)*
5 Sketch a typical stock control chart. *(6)*
6 State three costs associated with holding too much stock. *(3)*
7 Give three costs associated with running out of stock. *(3)*
8 What is meant by 'just-in-time' stock control? *(4)*
9 Explain the meaning of the phrase in the text that: 'The purchaser's reputation is placed in the hands of the external supplier.' *(3)*
10 Why is stock control of particular importance to a greengrocer? *(3)*

## B. REVISION EXERCISES

### B1 Activities
*(35 marks; 40 minutes)*

1 A firm sells 40,000 units a month. It receives monthly deliveries. Its maximum stock level is 50,000 and minimum (buffer) stock is 10,000. After two months (8 weeks) it decides to switch to weekly deliveries.
  a Sketch a 12-week stock control graph to illustrate this situation. Assume the firm starts the first week with 50,000 units of stock. *(10)*
  b What short-term problems might the firm face in switching to weekly deliveries? *(6)*
  c Consider the long-term benefits that may result from the change. *(9)*
2 Sketch a graph to show the impact upon stock levels of a downturn in demand for a product for which a company has a non-cancellable fixed order from its suppliers. Fully label the graph to explain *what* happens *when*. *(10)*

### B2 Data Response
Ann Brennan established a bakery in Wigan in the early 1980s. Although the firm is profitable, Ann is considering the introduction of modern techniques to help the company develop. In particular she wishes to introduce information technology to improve communications between her five shops and the central bakery and to help her manage her stock of raw materials more effectively.

Stocks of raw materials at the business are currently purchased in response to usage. For example, the bakery uses on average 500 kilos of flour per week. The most Ann wishes to hold at any time is 2,000 kilos. She would be worried if the stock fell below 500 kilos. An order takes one week to arrive, so Ann always re-orders when her stock falls to 1,000 kilos.

**Questions** *(30 marks; 35 minutes)*
1 What is meant by the terms:
  a re-order level
  b buffer stock
  c lead time? *(6)*
2 a Draw a stock control graph for flour at Brennan's Bakery over a six-week period. *(6)*
  b Draw a second graph showing the situation if twice the normal amount of flour were used in the fourth week. *(6)*
3 How might information technology be used to improve communication between Ann's shops and between the bakery and its suppliers? *(6)*
4 Assess the effect of a 'stock-out' on Brennan's Bakery. *(6)*

### B3 Case Study
A recent survey by accountancy firm KPMG painted a gloomy picture for British car component suppliers. Car manufacturers were dissatisfied with the service they were receiving. Their main concerns were:

| Concern | % of Manufacturers Reporting Concern |
|---|---|
| Cost | 100 |
| Quality | 68 |
| On-time delivery | 60 |

The report found that many suppliers had only survived by having historical relationships with manufacturers and by advantageous exchange rates rather than by adapting to new global markets.

However, the exchange rate is now much less favourable, and improvements in transport mean having local suppliers is less important than it once was. If component suppliers are to survive, they must quickly reassess and respond to the needs of their customers.

Source: West Midlands Automotive Supply Chain Development Study, KPMG

39.10 Workbook

**Questions** *(30 marks; 35 minutes)*

1 What is meant by historical relationships in this context? (3)

2 What is meant by an 'advantageous exchange rate'? (4)

3 Why might some firms be especially worried about 'on-time delivery'? (5)

4 Assess the impact external factors might have on suppliers. (8)

5 'Suppliers should consider themselves part of the firms they supply.' Evaluate this statement. (10)

**B4 Case Study**

After many years working for Toy Town, the well known chain of toy shops, Moira Gradwell had recently been appointed manager of the company's distribution system. Most of the company's toys were imported, either from the United States or the Far East.

One particular problem facing all toy retailers is the 'must-have' toy. It seems that almost every year one toy grabs the imagination of children across the country, demand soars and toy shop shelves quickly empty. New stock can take months to arrive, leaving children, parents and retailers all very frustrated. Recent examples of this have been Harry Potter Lego, Thunderbird Tracy Islands and Yo-yos.

Moira's key task is to ensure that Toy Town isn't caught out by the next craze.

**Questions** *(25 marks; 30 minutes)*

1 Normally, stock patterns for Toy Town are fairly regular, as shown in Figure 39.5.
From this chart, what is:
  a the normal re-order quantity (2)
  b the normal re-order level (2)
  c the normal time for an order to arrive (2)
  d the firm's minimum stock level (2)
  e the firm's maximum stock level? (2)

2 Sketch a chart to show what would happen if a toy suddenly became a 'craze'. (5)

3 Assess the steps Moira could take to ensure Toy Town doesn't face a 'stock-out' of the latest craze. (10)

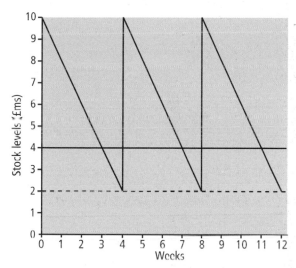

## C. ESSAY QUESTIONS

1 'The use of information technology makes stock control an automatic function, requiring little input from human beings.' Assess this statement.

2 Evaluate whether a medium-sized retailer such as Next would be wise to move to just-in-time stock control.

3 Assess the view that with today's information technology, no firm ought to experience stock control problems.

# INTEGRATED OPERATIONS MANAGEMENT

## 40.1 Operations management – an overview

### INTRODUCTION

All departments in an organisation tend to see themselves as the most important. Marketing people argue that without successful marketing even the greatest product in the world would fail. Those who work in personnel point out that without motivation, marketing and sales staff will achieve little.

Operations management can also claim a position of importance in the same way. Mercedes cars, Sony electronics and Boeing airplanes are not just well packaged. They are brilliantly conceived and developed, and superbly made. They are wonderful examples of the potential of top-class operations management.

These days there is a growing recognition of the need for productive efficiency. The globalisation of business has placed a great emphasis on the ability of firms to compete internationally. How is this done? Through the adoption of production techniques and ideas which set standards (benchmarking) and then make the best possible use of the available resources (lean production) to produce the best possible products (R&D, efficiency).

### WHAT IS OPERATIONS MANAGEMENT?

Operations management is a very wide-ranging term. While the basis of operations management can be seen in the management of the production process, the phrase covers a much wider range of ideas. In particular, the term is applied equally to firms who provide a service as to those involved in production. The same sorts of questions need to be answered, such as:

- Where should the firm be located?
- How can the firm develop more innovative products and services?
- How can the firm become more efficient?

- How can the firm maintain control of its quality?
- How best can the firm control its stock?
- How best can the workforce be organised?

The management of operations ties in very closely to the management of people. The two functions will often be carried out by the same managers at the same time. Motivation of the workforce is tied up very closely with management style. This will show itself most directly through the way in which the workplace is organised and tasks are allocated.

### 'A' GRADE OPERATIONS MANAGEMENT

More than perhaps any other area of business, operations management is intertwined with the other areas of the syllabus. This is most obvious in the links between operations management and personnel management. A fundamental reason for altering production methods is to improve the motivation and productivity of labour. In a similar way, the design and development function of operations management must tie in closely with the results of market research and the firm's competitive position. Top grade writing will consider the broader impact of operations management rather than taking a narrow, one-dimensional view.

The implications of some of the ideas must also be considered with care. The notion of kaizen, for example, is readily accepted by most students but its wider implications are rarely considered. Continual improvement implies a high degree of uncertainty and a constant state of change. What will the effect be on a firm, its workers and managers of such uncertainty? An 'A' grade answer would be able to reconcile the contradiction between the problems caused by change and uncertainty and the benefits of a policy of kaizen.

'A' grade operations management requires a grasp of big underlying issues such as those that follow. These are areas of discussion for conclusions to answers or case studies. They represent ways of evaluating the wider significance of the concepts covered.

## ISSUE 1  How important is operations management for international competitiveness?

A major reason for the growing importance of operations management is the need for firms to compete more effectively on an international stage. The start of the Euro on 1 January 2002 is the latest in a series of European developments that have forced firms such as Tesco and Kingfisher to look beyond Britain. Nor is it just a matter of looking to Europe. The 'shrinking' of the world through improvements in transport and communications have made many UK firms adopt a more international perspective.

While all areas of business need to be effective if a firm is to compete on the international stage, the foremost areas of concern revolve around the cost and quality of products. It is only by firms producing the best quality products at competitive costs that they stand a chance of winning a share of the international market. However, getting everything right internally is still not a guarantee of success. External factors such as high exchange rates can damage the competitiveness of the most efficient firms.

## ISSUE 2  When does a fad become a trend?

The 'Japanisation' of UK businesses has become a widely established phenomenon in recent years. The idea of kaizen, quality circle groups and aiming for zero defects are now common in both business literature and the workplace. There are, however, detractors who feel that these ideas are either:

- a restatement of established ideas, or
- broad generalisations with little application to the real world.

They argue that these ideas are more for the benefit of business 'gurus' who can earn a good living selling books and giving lectures based on these 'new' ideas than for the benefit and development of businesses.

For evidence, they can point to many examples of businesses that have applied these ideas but shown no sign of significant improvement or have even gone into further decline.

'A' grade students realise that the newer developments in operations management are no miracle cure for businesses. There is no one solution that will raise every business to levels of international competitiveness. The real task for managers is to adapt the principles and culture to their own individual circumstances, and continue adapting them over time as those circumstances change. Good students analyse answers by weighing up the suitability of a management method to the circumstances of the company.

## ISSUE 3  Operations management in the service sector

It is sometimes easy to think of operations management purely in terms of manufacturing firms. Clearly, though, the same issues apply to the service sector. If operations management is thought of as 'what, where, when and how' to produce, then service producers should have to answer these questions in the same way.

There will, of course, be some key differences. Service providers will have much more contact with the firm's final customers while goods manufacturers will have much more distant relations. In addition, services will often be very labour intensive while a lot of manufacturing firms today are highly automated. Perhaps the most important difference of all is in location. For services such as retailing, location is central to the marketing strategy of the business. For manufacturers, location is more likely to be a relatively minor factor.

A final difference will lie in the issue of stocks. Manufacturing firms will need to manage stocks of raw materials, work in progress and finished goods, even if they are using a just-in-time system that minimises the quantities of each held. Many service businesses, however, will have very little in the way of stocks. A firm of solicitors, for example, may keep a stock of stationery, but the output of the firm, its legal advice and work, will not appear as any sort of stock at all. Needless to say, the same does not apply to retailing, where stocks are a vital issue, nor catering, where stocks and work-in-progress are key elements in success.

# Operations management

## A. SHORT-ANSWER QUESTIONS

1  Identify two resources that lean production aims to minimise. *(4)*
2  Name two internal diseconomies of scale. *(2)*
3  What is meant by batch production? *(2)*
4  Outline two ways firms operating a lean production system might be affected by a national blockage in the supply of petrol and diesel. *(6)*
5  Give two ways a firm could increase its level of capacity utilisation. *(2)*
6  List four difficulties a business may face when automating production. *(4)*
7  Give two advantages to a company of introducing a quality assurance system such as BS 5750? *(2)*
8  State two factors that would affect the minimum amount of stock held by a company. *(2)*
9  Why is an efficient stock control system important to a manufacturing business? *(2)*
10  State two pieces of information a manufacturer might require before choosing a new supplier of components. *(2)*
11  Explain one factor a firm should take into account when implementing a just-in-time (JIT) manufacturing system. *(2)*
12  Explain two benefits a firm might derive from its employees participating in quality circles. *(4)*
13  What is meant by a kaizen group? *(2)*
14  What is meant by cell production? *(2)*
15  Define the term benchmarking. *(2)*

## B. DATA RESPONSE

### Stocking for Seasonal Demand at Cadbury

For Cadbury, Easter is one of the busiest times of the year. It supplies around 350 million Easter eggs to almost 30,000 delivery points across the country. The sales value is over £250 million.

As a production problem, gearing up to meet such targets in a brief span of time requires timing and coordination. Marketing may create the demand but delivery and, before that, the purchase of stocks needs to be carefully planned. As with bonfire night for fireworks manufacturers, there is an externally set deadline that will not move to accommodate any problems an individual firm may face.

To put the supply problem into perspective, Cadbury will purchase 60,000 tonnes of cocoa from West Africa, 180,000,000 litres of milk from farms in the UK, mainly around Herefordshire, and 80,000 tonnes of sugar. In total, Cadbury spends £300 million a year on raw materials and an additional £200 million on gas, electricity, water and transport.

The profit that Cadbury makes from its operation will depend largely on how it manages its extended supply chain. Cadbury's manager of logistics (supply and transport), Andy Phythian, is responsible for running an almost military-style operation to ensure the least possible wastage across the extended supply chain. He has conducted a five-year review of supplies to Cadbury with the stated aim of improving the level of service at a greater speed with less cost.

As an example of the improvements made following the five-year review, Cadbury reduced its packaging suppliers from 45 to 22. To encourage the remaining suppliers, it gave them three-year contracts to improve relationships and the quality of service. As a result, its packaging costs fell by 16%. In a similar way, the number of non-edible materials suppliers was halved from 3,000 to 1,500.

Cadbury's efforts to apply modern business practices to its purchasing and supply functions reflects a broad business trend. Businesses are forming partnerships with their suppliers to work together for the benefit of all.

**Source:** Adapted from *The Independent on Sunday*, 12/4/98

### Questions *(25 marks; 35 minutes)*

1  a  What is meant by the term 'supply chain'? *(2)*
   b  Assess the reasons for the changes introduced by Cadbury in the management of its supply chain. *(6)*
2  Assuming that the Easter period accounts for one-fifth of all Cadbury's business, calculate the average added value for each egg sold. *(4)*
3  Taking the whole article into account, what is the evidence that Cadbury's needs 'timing and coordination' to meet its production targets? *(7)*
4  Outline the problems Cadbury's might face if it moved to just-in-time production methods? *(6)*

# C. ACTIVITY

Working in groups of three or four, you are to investigate local engineering, manufacturing or assembly firms. The aim is for each group to report on a different firm so that a range of experiences are recorded. This should provide insight into the extent to which production theory is actually put into practice.

Each group is to identify a suitable local firm and arrange a visit, preferably to be shown around the plant or, if this is not possible, to be able to put questions to the firm.

Possible areas for questions could be:

- Who are the customers? Who has the greater say in design and specifications – the firm or its customers?
- How is production organised (job, batch, flow or cell production)? How are relations between the sections of the shop-floor organised?
- What quality control procedures are in place? Who is responsible for quality control?
- How far has the firm incorporated new technology in its operations?
- Are workers involved in a variety of tasks in their working lives?
- How much involvement has the firm with research and development?
- How did the firm come to be located where it is? What is its history?
- What stock control procedures are in place?

Each group can feed back to the whole group through a short presentation, allowing an overall picture to be compiled of the state of local manufacturing firms.

# D. ROLE PLAYS AND SIMULATIONS

You work in the operations management department of PB Bearings plc, an engineering company based in Durham. The department has recently acquired a new head, Doug Travis, who has been reviewing the firm's current position and planning for the future.

He summarises the position as follows: 'There has recently been a disappointing downward trend in the performance of the firm. Our competitive position has been further eroded by the entry of Deutsches Mechaniks.' This large multinational company is entering the UK market for the first time.

Doug has outlined three possible strategies to the board of directors:

- Option A – stay in the current factory with the existing level of technology
- Option B – stay in the current factory with investment into state-of-the-art technology
- Option C – move to a smaller, purpose-built factory unit with state-of-the-art technology.

Now he has asked for your views before he makes a recommendation to the directors about his preferred option. Using the following information, write a report, making a justified recommendation as to which option you think the firm should choose.

## Appendix A – Sales data (£m), past, present and forecast future

| Year | 1 | 2 | 3* | 4 | 5 |
|---|---|---|---|---|---|
| Total UK sales | 2.3 | 2.7 | 3.0 | 3.3 | 3.8 |
| PB Bearings sales | 0.5 | 0.6 | 0.6 | 0.65 | 0.7 |
| Deutsches Mechaniks sales | – | – | – | 0.5 | 0.75 |

## Appendix B – Capacity utilisation

| | |
|---|---|
| Current level of capacity utilisation at existing plant (option A) | 68% |
| Current output as a % of new machinery capacity at existing plant (option B) | 47% |
| Current output as a % of new plant capacity (option C) | 60% |

## Appendix C – Research and development spending (as a % of sales), past present and future

| Year | 1 | 2 | 3* | 4 | 5 |
|---|---|---|---|---|---|
| PB Bearings | 7% | 6% | 5% | 6% | 6% |
| Industry average | 8% | 8% | 8% | 10% | 10% |
| Typical cost of developing a successful new product = £200,000 | | | | | |

\* This year

## Appendix D – Personnel data

| Average travel to work: | | |
|---|---|---|
| | Old factory | New site |
| Distance | 1.75 miles | 2.5 miles |
| Time | 25 mins | 35 mins |
| **No. of staff required at full capacity:** | | |
| Current plant | 150 | |
| New machinery | 120 | |
| New location | 160 | |

## Appendix E – Net costs of change

| | |
|---|---|
| Net investment in new technology at existing plant | £5m |
| Net investment in new technology and new factory | £4m |

# EXTERNAL INFLUENCES AND MARKET FORCES

External influences are factors outside a firm's control, such as changes in the economy or the law. Market forces are the influences of customer demand and producer decisions on supply upon price and customer satisfaction.

## 41.1 Introduction

The external environment of the business creates opportunities as well as threats. Successful businesses have to be flexible enough both to cope with the threats and to exploit the opportunities. By careful analysis of market trends they can plan ahead. Then external change can be treated as an opportunity. For example, in recent years, car owners have become more worried about car thefts. The figures are actually falling, but the fear of it is not. So BMW put particular effort into making their cars harder to steal.

Some businesses watch their markets, adapting their products to consumer preferences, and looking out for potential new possibilities. These firms are unlikely to face falling sales when consumers change their habits. These are aspects of change management – the process by which businesses adapt to external influences by planning and implementing new strategies and methods of working.

External influences can be divided into four categories:

- Demand – a whole range of influences arise from customer demand
- Inputs – many external influences have their impact on the business through its requirements for inputs
- Government – all businesses are affected by government policies; some very significantly
- Social factors – businesses are increasingly sensitive to ethical issues, including environmental considerations.

These categories of external influence are not watertight – they link together and sometimes overlap. Units 42–45 deal with these areas in more detail. This introductory unit focuses upon demand and the market mechanism. Both factors are crucial to an understanding of business economics.

## 41.2 Demand for the product

Some products sell for a long time. Cadbury's Dairy Milk chocolate has been around since 1905, in much the same form as it is sold now. Other products have a very short life. Some recordings by Atomic Kitten may have sold quite briefly and there may be some uncertainty as to their long-term prospects. An important factor in what happens to a particular product is the level of demand and how it changes over time.

Often changes occur simply because people's preferences change. This may be a matter of taste or fashion. No matter how they are promoted, Atomic Kitten's recordings may be selling well, or poorly or not at all by the time you are reading this. Consumer choices are often fickle and unpredictable.

For some products, incomes can be important. In the UK, over the long run, output usually rises by an average of around 2% per year. This is known as the long-term trend rate of economic growth. This means that real incomes and standards of living rise over time. (Real incomes are incomes measured in terms of their purchasing power, i.e. not influenced by inflation). As a result it may become possible to sell large volumes of products which few people could have afforded in the past. 700,000 Rolex watches, for example, are sold each year. In the early 1980s the figure was below 100,000. Considerable business opportunities can be created in this way, and businesses which can predict accurately how rising real incomes will affect them are in a good position to exploit these opportunities.

**Competition** is often of crucial importance in determining the level of demand for the product. Often, we find that we are choosing from a range of competing products. Many of them are quite good substitutes. A change in the price or marketing strategy of a competing substitute can be a very important external influence on the business concerned. In the extreme there may be a price war in which competing sellers keep on undercutting each other. They may find they are under pressure to set prices below their costs of production, at least temporarily.

These many and various influences on demand are an important part of the subject matter of Units 42 and 43.

## THE BUSINESS CYCLE AND DEMAND

Economies as a whole are subject to a pattern of ups and downs in demand. Demand for all products taken together is known as *aggregate demand*. When aggregate demand is rising, the economy is enjoying a recovery. If this has gone on for a while, total output will be rising and the economy may be said to be booming. Economic growth will be higher than the long-run average, measured in percentage terms. The reverse, a downturn in aggregate demand is often called a recession and, if this is very prolonged, a depression or slump. During this time economic growth may be negative, meaning that output declines.

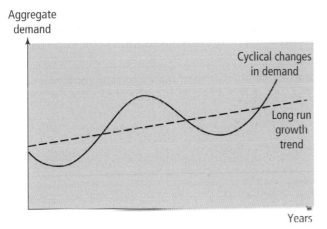

Figure 41.1

Some products are very vulnerable to **business cycle** fluctuations. When aggregate demand is falling, incomes will be falling and there will be some products which people feel they can do without. Between 1998 and 1999, for example, sales of Rolls Royce cars fell by 31% as the economy grew more slowly. The business which relies on sales of luxury items may experience serious problems unless it has other products for which demand is falling less or not at all. So recession can spell trouble for builders of yachts and swimming pools. Producers of biscuits may have little to worry about. When the recovery comes, however, it will be the yacht and swimming pool businesses which will experience increasing demand. The biscuit manufacturers may gain very little.

The nature and impact of the business cycle are looked at in more detail in Unit 43. Unemployment is invariably a feature of recession. Equally, accelerating inflation can be a consequence of prolonged, above average economic growth. These problems figure large in government thinking, and are often the reason for changes in a range of government policies.

In the long run, most economies experience fairly steady economic growth. It is this which provides the rising standards of living which have been a feature of the past hundred years or so.

## DEMAND FROM ABROAD

If times are hard on the home market, international trade may provide a solution. The business may look for foreign markets and export. The level of demand abroad is an important external influence for any business which is able to export. There are some industries where exporting has always been important, such as cars and chemicals. But large numbers of firms need to be more enterprising to develop export markets.

### FINDING NEW MARKETS

Americans don't like front-loading washing machines. What they want is a top-loader, a big one, with twice the average capacity of European machines. But Whirlpool wanted to break into the US market without having to design a special product for that market alone.

Front-loaders are generally more efficient than top-loaders in the use of energy and water. So Whirlpool used the 'platform' principle, which means using a single basic design for a wide range of different markets. This can be given small modifications to suit individual market expectations. In the planning stages, the engineers posed as market researchers, so they could get to talk with individual families in the US, finding out their preferences.

The company came up with a large front-loader. This meant that it could market the product as environmentally friendly *and* big enough for the US market. It went on sale in 2002. It's the Duet in the US and the Dreamspace in Europe. Asia next?

Business IN

Of course an exporting business has to contend with business cycle fluctuations in other countries. This adds a degree of complexity to its trading position. But it may be able to compensate for low demand in one country by selling in another country which is in a recovery phase. This is a way of spreading risk. Sometimes recessions coincide in many countries of the world, but this is rare.

Where international trade is important as a source of business, governments' trade and exchange rate policies will be major external influences. The role of trade and the importance of competitiveness are looked at in Unit 44. In looking at these issues, the likely impact of European Monetary Union will be considered in detail.

## 41.3 How decisions affect the economy

A business which is about to take the decision to produce a new brand has to be reasonably confident it can make a profit. It must be able to cover all the costs of production, including the **capital** costs. In fact it will be hopeful of making a little more than that. The better the prospect of profit, the more ambitious its plans are likely to be. In economics, this decision is described as leading to an increase in supply.

If the business fails to cover its costs, and cannot see that the situation will change in the near future, it will decide to cut or even end production. There is no point in producing something which makes continuous losses. The outcome will be a decrease in supply.

Obviously the nature of this decision depends greatly on the price at which the product can be sold. Consumers' decisions will depend on the price too. No-one is going to buy the product if they can get an equally satisfactory one for a lower price.

### THE PROFIT SIGNALLING MECHANISM

Many years ago economists tried to answer three questions:

- What will be produced?
- How will it be produced?
- For whom will it be produced?

They were trying to work out how society as a whole would use the resources available. Why would large quantities of some items be produced and only small quantities of others? What would be the best way to produce the things people want? Why do some people have the chance to enjoy many different consumer goods, while others have barely enough to keep themselves alive? These questions are all part of one big question: How are resources allocated?

When a business identifies a profitable opportunity, it decides to allocate more resources to that line of production. In order to produce more chrysanthemums, Ian Wade bought a piece of land adjoining his existing site, built another glasshouse, and took on two more people to help with the planting, picking and other tasks. The resources he needed to do this were land, labour and capital. Of course these resources were quite costly for him, but he reckoned the extra sales revenue he would get would be more than enough to make expansion worthwhile. The profit signalling mechanism was telling him that it would be worth increasing his output.

### — BLOOMING BUSINESS

*Business in*

Ian Wade grows and sells chrysanthemums, all year round. He has six big heated glasshouses with lights and blackout which can be used to fool the plants into thinking it is autumn even when it is actually winter or spring.

He sends some of the flowers to Covent Garden Market where they are sold on to florists. Others he sells direct to local florists and greengrocers. How does he decide what price to charge to local shops?

'You charge what you can get away with. You think what the florist will be able to charge the type of customers they will be getting, and offer a bit less. I'm confident that if I can continue to get £2 per bunch in local shops and £1.50 in the market, it will be worth putting up another glasshouse next year. It's a big investment but sales are rising and it should be profitable.'

### ENTRY AND EXIT

When a new business starts up, it is entering the market. A business which is making losses will probably **exit** from the market. When businesses are free to enter and exit the market, it is described as a free market. That means that market forces are free to operate, drawing resources into particular lines of production where there is some demand for them. Equally, resources will be moving out of lines of production which no-one wants. In this way resources are free to move so that the pattern of output reflects consumer demand.

When resources are reallocated in this way, we think of the market as 'working'. Resources won't be wasted on valueless production. Consumers will reject low quality items offering poor value for money, and it simply won't be worthwhile for anyone to produce them. Instead they will buy the things which offer the best value. It will be hard for businesses to survive unless they can offer good value. The market will force them to be efficient, and if they can't be, they will make losses and exit from the market. Efficient producers will find they have opportunities to expand.

So when markets are working well, they help people to get what they want.

### CONSUMER SOVEREIGNTY

Market forces work to produce a combination of products which match the pattern of consumer demand. Products people do not want will not be profitable and the businesses producing them will have to close down. This means that the ultimate decision takers in a free market economy are the consumers. Economists say, consumers have sovereignty. The customer is king.

In practice there is no economy in the world which is organised completely freely. Everywhere governments intervene to manage and control market forces. Sometimes one business can become so large that it can influence the market in such a way that consumers are not making completely free choices. The important factor in deciding whether consumers have the ultimate market power is whether there are many businesses competing in the market. Unit 42 looks in detail at how competition works in practice.

In this unit, markets are analysed on the assumption that most are reasonably competitive. This approach is very characteristic of how economics works. To get a good understanding of the relationships in the economy, it helps to assume that some of life's complicating factors do not exist. Later on, this assumption will be relaxed. Then the real world of business can be analysed in full.

## 41.4 How market forces work

### SUPPLY

Businesses which can foresee potential profits have an incentive to increase production. The more profit they can make, the bigger the incentive. So the quantity businesses want to supply is related to the price which can be charged. The higher the price, the greater the potential profit and the larger the quantity supplied. This relationship can be presented in the form of a graph or supply curve, as shown in Figure 41.2. If the price falls, businesses will reduce output and look around for other products which are more profitable.

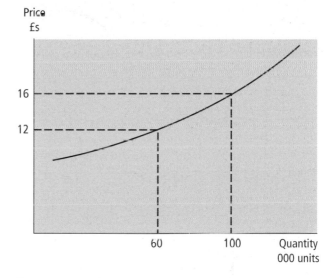

**Figure 41.2** Supply curve

### DEMAND

When businesses identify a profitable opportunity they are observing the existence of potential demand for the product. Whether they can create this opportunity for themselves depends very much on the price at which they are proposing to sell the product. There is a very easily understood relationship between the quantity which consumers wish to buy and the price they will be charged. You have only to think of what happens during the January and July sales to appreciate the nature of this relationship. It can be presented in the form of a demand curve, as shown in Figure 41.3.

The price cuts in the January sales move the consumer down the demand curve. If the price is cut they become active potential buyers. For some products, a price cut means that they will buy larger quantities. More winter weekend mini-breaks are possible for many people if the price looks a good deal. The demand curve plots the relationship between price and quantity bought.

### WHAT WILL THE PRICE BE?

Markets always have at least two players – a buyer and a seller. The price depends on the interaction between them. If you want to sell something such as a car, no matter how valuable you think it is, the price will depend on what the buyer is prepared to pay. However, the price on offer may be so low that you don't think it is worth selling. The deal will take place only if both buyer and seller can settle on an acceptable price.

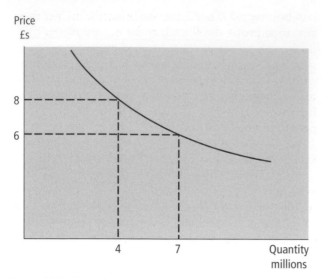

Price
£s

**Figure 41.3** Demand curve

This acceptable price is called the **equilibrium price**. This can be represented on a diagram as the intersection of the supply and the demand curve, as shown in Figure 41.4. The idea of an equilibrium price is important because at that price the amount which sellers wish to sell is equal to the amount which buyers wish to buy. There are no unsold stocks and no customers standing in a queue waiting for more deliveries. A market which has either unsold stocks or unsatisfied customers is in disequilibrium.

Many markets are in a state of constant change, moving from one equilibrium to another. Similarly, some markets are often in a state of disequilibrium. Analysing these changes is the subject of the next section.

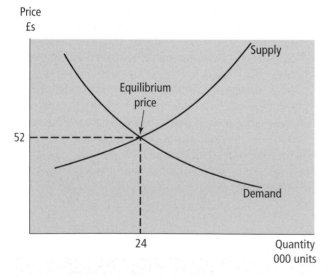

Price
£s

**Figure 41.4** Supply and demand in equilibrium

**Situations of disequilibrium:**

- Late in the day, supermarkets may mark some of their stock 'reduced to clear', as some items reach the end of their shelf life. They realise that they set the price a little above the equilibrium level for that

item and they will have unsold stocks of perishable items if they do not reduce the price.
- Tickets for some sporting events are fewer in number than the people who would like to buy them. The equilibrium price is above the face value of the ticket.

## 41.5 Dynamic markets

Markets in disequilibrium usually have symptoms. Reasons will vary, but the evidence takes the form of **excess demand** or **excess supply**.

### EXCESS DEMAND

You can sometimes *see* excess demand. Symptoms might include a long queue for tickets at the Wimbledon tennis championships. If there is a fixed supply of something which is popular, and for some reason the price does not go up, there will be rationing by queues or waiting lists, as with popular schools.

There have been times in recent years when the excess demand for flats and houses in central London has been visible in the estate agents' windows. They would put 'wanted' signs in the window, or if they had, say, three windows, put the same set of properties in each window.

Disequilibrium situations can persist for quite a while if people are slow to adjust their expectations or actions. Sellers may have reasons for not putting up prices. But over time, property prices have risen and that has meant less of a shortage of places for sale in London. Between mid-2001 and mid-2002 UK property prices rose 20.9%, on average. The estate agents' windows filled up again, indicating much less excess demand at the new prices. Equilibrium was gradually restored.

The existence of excess demand usually implies that there is a shortage of the productive capacity needed to satisfy demand. Unsatisfied demand will tend to drive up prices and increase the potential profits. In time, businesses have an incentive to come into the market and expand production so that the excess supply will usually disappear.

### EXCESS SUPPLY

Unsold stocks of any product suggest that the price is above its equilibrium level. Not enough customers are being attracted to buy the product. At current prices, the quantity supplied exceeds the quantity demanded. Only a price cut will clear the market, and in the long run it may be necessary to cut production. A situation of excess supply is shown in Figure 41.5.
Something like this happened with beef after the BSE crisis. When people discovered that eating beef might cause the fatal disease CJD, demand for beef fell. Farmers were left with beef cattle they could not sell at current prices; an excess supply.

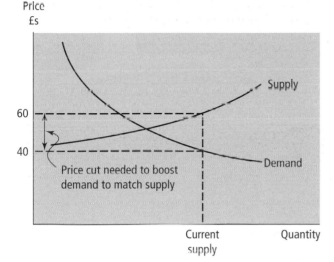

Price
£s

60

40

Price cut needed to boost
demand to match supply

Supply

Demand

Current
supply

Quantity

**Figure 41.5** Excess supply

## SUMMARY

Markets bring together buyers and sellers so that transactions can take place, allowing people to exchange what they have for what they want. Businesses have an incentive to produce in response to market demand. This means that consumers ultimately determine the pattern, or structure, of output.

Supply and demand (price theory) can be useful because:

- the impact of changes in demand and supply can be predicted
- different kinds of changes can be identified and classified according to their causes
- the theory can be used to analyse the relationships which determine prices and quantities.

Competition forces businesses to produce efficiently in order to survive. They need to be market oriented in their decision taking. Otherwise their costs will rise above the minimum necessary. This will reduce their profits.

## 41.6 Structural change

All the time, patterns of consumer demand are shifting and the structure of output changes in response. This means that resources are constantly being reallocated from one use to another. Sometimes this reallocation takes place within a business, as it diversifies its products. Reallocation also occurs as new businesses are set up and old ones close down. The land, labour and capital which is made redundant from a closing or shrinking business becomes available to one which is setting up or expanding. In the 1970s, high streets were full of shops. In the 1980s estate agents and building societies had taken over. In the 1990s these were taken over by restaurants and cafés and that process is continuing in the 2000s.

Technology also plays a big part in the process of structural change. The invention of a completely new *product* leads to structural changes as production facilities for that product are set up. Even more importantly, many lines of production benefit from new *process* technologies which lead both to cost reductions and quality improvements.

Looking at the structure of production nationally, we can identify a number of broad trends. Some changes take place swiftly as people respond to short-term changes. Other changes are part of very long-term trends.

As economies develop industrially, they move resources out of agriculture and into manufacturing. Later on in the process there is a shift towards services. All developed economies (broadly, North America, Japan, Australia and New Zealand and most of Europe) have shown a shift away from manufacturing and towards the production of services. So resources have tended to move into restaurants, hotels and holidays, hairdressers, leisure and financial services. Consumers often want to acquire a certain number of manufactured products, but once they have them, they spend more on services. A household's need to cook is satisfied by the possession of one cooker. As incomes rise further, people opt for more and more take-away food. So goods are more likely to reach market saturation than services.

The table below shows the changes in output by sector for the UK, with figures for Japan and India (a developing country with much lower income levels) for comparison.

When looking at the process of structural change, growing and declining industries can be identified. Declining industries are having to contract because demand for their products is either falling, or growing more slowly than the rest of the economy. The most obvious declining industry in recent years has been

The structure of production — % of gross domestic product

| COUNTRY | AGRICULTURE | | INDUSTRY | | SERVICES | |
|---|---|---|---|---|---|---|
| | 1980 | 2000 | 1980 | 2000 | 1980 | 2000 |
| UK | 2 | 1 | 43 | 25 | 55 | 74 |
| Japan | 4 | 2 | 42 | 36 | 54 | 62 |
| India | 38 | 27 | 26 | 27 | 36 | 46 |

Source: World Bank, World Development Report, 2002

coal mining. A combination of factors (some political) have led to a fall in demand for coal. Increasingly, power stations have switched to gas. Many mines have closed down and employment in the industry has dropped away to almost nothing. The number of butchers, fishmongers and bakers has declined in response to the relentless expansion of supermarkets.

An example of a growing industry is electronics. Chemicals have done well too. These are industries where technology has played a part in the story. Leisure, media and financial services have also grown robustly.

Coal mining has declined due to external factors
© Zen Icknow/CORBIS

## 41.7 Other kinds of markets

So far this unit has focused on markets for end products and services. Yet any resource which has a money value can be traded in a market. There are markets in the inputs to the production process – land, labour and capital, the three factors of production.

In the labour market, people seeking employment are selling their labour. Potential employers are buying it. The equilibrium price is the wage rate. It is possible to use the same principles of supply and demand and equilibrium price to analyse labour markets. If demand is high for computer analysts, their wage rate will rise.

Similarly, money markets are subject to market forces. Interest rates are the price which brings the funds available into line with the demand for loans. These markets are examined in more detail in later units. It will be important to be able to apply the understanding of markets gained in this unit.

ISSUES FOR **analysis**

When examining the impact on a firm of the external environment, there is an enormous range of different influences. The first issue for analysis is to select the most significant influences. These are some of the questions which address the issues:

- What kind of market will the business operate in?
- Will the necessary employees, with the skills required, be readily available?
- Is government policy likely to change demand for the product?
- Will inflation or exchange rate changes force the business into rethinking pricing policies?
- Are there important regulations which will constrain the business?
- Does the possibility of international trade lead to larger markets?
- Are technical changes going to alter cost structures or the nature of the competition?

**KEY terms**

**business cycle** – the fluctuations in demand and output which show a pattern of boom, recession, slump and recovery over a period of years, which affects the whole economy.

**capital** – the buildings, plant and machinery needed in the production process. These must be combined with land, labour and other inputs in order to create the final product.

**competition** – the process by which businesses act as rivals with one another in order to attract customers and increase sales.

**consumer sovereignty** – the process by which consumer choice signals to businesses what they should be producing.

**entry** – the process by which businesses may set up new lines of production where they think profitable opportunities exist.

**equilibrium price** – the price at which quantity demanded equals quantity supplied.

**excess demand** – a situation in which quantity demanded is greater than quantity supplied at current prices.

**excess supply** – a situation in which quantity supplied is greater than quantity demanded at current prices.

**exit** – the process by which businesses withdraw from markets where they are making disappointing profits.

**macro-economic** – a factor which affects the whole economy.

# Exercises

## A. REVISION QUESTIONS
*(40 marks; 70 minutes)*

Read the unit, then answer:

1 Outline three external influences upon a chocolate manufacturer such as Cadbury's. *(6)*
2 Give four examples of products for which sales are likely to rise as incomes rise. *(4)*
3 From your awareness of current events, outline the stage in the business cycle you believe the economy is in currently. *(4)*
4 What is the role of profit in business decisions? *(4)*
5 What is meant by the term 'allocation of resources'. *(3)*
6 Identify three major influences on the demand for Quality Street. *(4)*
7 What is meant by 'equilibrium price'? How is it determined? *(4)*
8 Give an example of a market in disequilibrium which you have observed personally, and explain why the disequilibrium situation occurred. *(4)*
9 Explain why the disequilibrium which you described in your answer to question 8 will or will not persist over time. *(4)*
10 What problems may arise in the process of structural change? *(3)*

## B. REVISION EXERCISES

### B1 Activities
1 Identify a local business which started up fairly recently. Gather as much information about it as you can. Write a report covering the following points:
   a Why did the business believe there was a potential market for its product?
   b What sort of competition did it face at the outset?
   c What impact did its entry to the market have on other businesses?
   d What future changes do you think may be important in determining the future of the business?

2 In the early 1990s trainers became hugely fashionable, then faded away. In 1998 yo-yos became the must-have item for 10–12-year-olds. Consider the market for a fashion item which you have recently observed in the process of rising and then falling demand.
   a Using supply and demand analysis describe what happened to price and quantity sold. *(15)*
   b Explain what you think will happen next. *(10)*

### B2 Data Response
Output in three industries
Index: 1990 = 100

| Year | Clothing & Footwear | Food, Drink & Tobacco | Electrical Investment Goods |
|------|------|------|------|
| 1986 | 111 | 93 | 73 |
| 1987 | 112 | 96 | 78 |
| 1988 | 107 | 98 | 91 |
| 1989 | 103 | 98 | 101 |
| 1990 | 100 | 100 | 100 |
| 1991 | 89 | 98 | 99 |
| 1992 | 89 | 100 | 105 |
| 1993 | 88 | 100 | 116 |
| 1994 | 91 | 101 | 136 |
| 1995 | 89 | 103 | 151 |
| 1996 | 90 | 104 | 159 |
| 1997 | 85 | 108 | 172 |
| 1998 | 76 | 105 | 198 |

**Source:** ONS Monthly Digest of Statistics, Crown copyright, Jan 1999

**Questions** *(30 marks; 35 minutes)*
1 Choose a suitable way to show the above data on graph paper. Label your diagram carefully. *(10)*
2 Explain how the changes in output have differed in the three industries in the table. *(8)*
3 Analyse the changes in each industry and explain the trends. *(12)*

### B3 Case Study

#### A market for business Jets?
If you want an executive jet right now, you will be looking at a price of around US$3.5 million. Eclipse Aviation is building one that will cost $838,000. It's a six-seater that can fly 1,300 miles at around 400 mph and it had its first test flight in summer 2002. The low price reflects developments in the use of cheaper electronic systems and new welding techniques. Also, the price assumes that volume manufacturing will be possible – in other words, it has to sell in quantity (at least 1,000 a year) to keep the price down.

Will it make it? There are big risks associated with developing a new aircraft. To succeed, this project depends on the development of a new concept, the air taxi. This will cash in on business executives' frustration with scheduled flights and people who need to fly to small airports. Eclipse has an initial order for 1,000 jets, destined for the air taxi service, with production scheduled to start in 2004. The current market for business jets is around 1,900 a year.

#### Questions
1 List three possible reasons why this project might fail.
2 To what extent do you think Eclipse is depending on new buyers emerging? What sort of market can it expect from businesses replacing an older executive jet?
3 Describe what will happen if this aircraft does not sell in the required quantities.

# MARKETS AND COMPETITION

## DEFINITION

Competition occurs when people can choose from a range of similar products, selecting the ones which most closely fit their needs. It occurs when a number of sellers are rivals with each other. Or when many buyers are competing to obtain something which is scarce. It can occur in the labour and capital markets as well as the markets for goods and services.

## 42.1 Markets

As a general rule a market consists of many buyers and many sellers. You can easily see this in a street market. For each type of product sold, there may be five or six competing sellers. You wander around looking for bargains and find that all the traders are selling at roughly the same price! In fact they have to. If one trader sold at much lower prices all his or her stock would be gone in a short time, but at very low profit margins. Lower than if he or she had more patience and stood there all day. Similarly, a trader who charges more than others will sell little because potential customers will go to another stall.

The term 'market' is used broadly and includes anyone who might buy or sell the product wherever they happen to be. The famous London stock market used to be a building where traders met to buy and sell shares. Today shares are bought and sold over the telephone by people who may never meet each other.

Businesses spend a lot of time working out how to defeat the competition. To get themselves into a position where **market forces** create fewer problems. What are you doing right now? You are studying for qualifications which will give you skills that you hope will be scarce. The more skills you have, the more attractive you will be to employers. And the easier it will be to defeat the competition when it comes to landing that difficult first job. You are striving for a competitive advantage.

People in business are constantly trying to defeat the competition and sometimes they succeed. If they actually manage to create something that no-one else can produce, they will have a **monopoly**. They will be able to charge a much higher price. Their profits will soar.

### MICROSOFT

Many people would say that Microsoft has a monopoly with its Windows operating system. Most computer users want it because it makes their system compatible with the rest of the world.

The US government's competition authorities certainly thought Microsoft was a monopoly, and that the company had abused its market power. The case against Microsoft spelt out how it had seriously damaged the much smaller competing software, Netscape, and the Java programming script. The courtroom arguments will run and run.

When Bill Gates took the witness stand in the US Court of Appeals, he said that without Windows in its current form, there would be a digital disaster. There would be widespread confusion amongst computer users, incompatible programs, failing software firms and a fall-off in the rate of innovation. He opposed the idea that customers should be able to choose rival companies' software to replace certain parts of the Windows system.

**Business IN**

Buying and selling in the 'market'
© The Image Bank/Getty Images

## 42.2 Choices for all

Every choice has an **opportunity cost**. Therefore all the alternatives should be considered before making a business decision. Similarly, consumers make the most of their spending power by thinking hard about the alternative uses of their money. This process ensures that a complacent producer will soon find customers are looking elsewhere. Competition is good for consumers.

The drive for profit which motivates many business decisions also has a very important implication. It means businesses will always be striving to defeat the competition. Direct competition is bad for business, because it forces prices down. So businesses strive for competitive advantage which makes them stand out from their rivals.

This tension between the needs of consumers and the needs of business points to many interesting issues. Governments try to promote competition because it forces businesses to be efficient. This keeps costs and prices down. Businesses can be less than thrilled by these efforts to promote competition.

In order to survive competition, many businesses make a major effort to cut costs and increase efficiency. This often leads to lower prices for consumers. In trying to increase long-term profits, businesses may spend large sums on research and development and find important new ways of implementing new technologies. These efforts may increase profits and may lead to lower prices for consumers.

These last two points are important reasons why in recent years market forces have come to be seen as a crucial element in an efficient, modern economy. Market forces have the power to make society better off. But they work in complicated ways and the outcome of the free play of market forces is not always what everyone wishes. How market forces work depends on the circumstances. Indeed, market forces do not always work. Governments can both encourage and discourage market forces. The reasons why they intervene in markets may be very varied.

## 42.3 Scale and competition

Some products need to be produced on a large scale to be cost effective. In other cases scale is unimportant. For example, small-scale production of cars works only if the car is to be marketed as a high status or specialist vehicle. The value added has to be high enough to justify the high price the producer will need to charge. Volume car producers need to produce 1–2 million cars per year to compete on world markets. Only then do **economies of scale** allow production costs to be low enough to compete.

Businesses which encounter severe diseconomies of scale will tend to flourish using relatively small-scale production methods. In some sectors, small- and large-scale operations coexist quite comfortably. In the hotel sector, small guest houses and huge hotel chains both flourish. This pattern is common in the service sector.

## 42.4 The degree of competition in the market

It can be useful to look at the range of competitive situations which occur. This is illustrated in Figure 42.1. At one extreme is the situation of the stalls on market day. There are many sellers, each aware that people can shop at the neighbouring stall. Very similar products are on offer. Prices are set just high enough to cover costs and make a reasonable profit.

This is known as **perfect competition**. It defines the perfect market, where market forces ensure that the only successful seller is the one who offers customers what they want. In this situation:

- production is efficient (i.e. lowest cost) because only the most efficient businesses can survive the competition
- consumers are free to choose the combination of products they most want, subject to the constraint of their income
- prices are kept low and quality kept high by the forces of competition.

Perfect competition has a set of essential features (see the table below). They give us a yardstick with which we can measure deviations from the state of perfect competition (i.e. market imperfections). All other competitive situations are categorised as imperfect competition.

| Perfect competition | Monopolistic competition | Oligopoly | Monopoly |
|---|---|---|---|
| ● homogenous product | ● differentiated product | ● differentiated product | ● no substitutes |
| ● free entry | ● free entry | ● barriers to entry | ● barriers to entry |
| ● many sellers | ● many sellers | ● few sellers | ● single seller |
| ● price takers | ● price takers | ● price makers | ● price makers |
| | | ● interdependence | |

**Figure 42.1** The spectrum of competition

The essential features of perfect competition

| Features | What They Mean in Practice |
|---|---|
| Homogeneous products | It is impossible to distinguish one seller's product from that of another |
| Free entry and exit | It is easy for new businesses to set up production and compete with existing sellers |
| Large numbers of buyers and sellers | The buyer has access to a large range of sellers |
| Full information is obtainable | Buyers can easily find out where the product is being sold most cheaply |

At the other extreme of the spectrum of competition there is monopoly, the single seller. This too is rare, though individual railway companies have a monopoly on particular routes. Virgin, for instance, has a monopoly on the busy London - Manchester route and most travellers condemn the poor service and high prices.

Two market categories come in between the extreme cases of monopoly and perfect competition: **monopolistic competition** and **oligopoly**. Monopolistic competition occurs when there are many sellers, but each has a differentiated product. So it is possible to distinguish the different brands. An example of this would be in football club shirts. The shirts compete with each other in a way, but not fully. Product differentiation is achieved through the club name and the product design.

Oligopoly is competition between the few. For example, 90% of chocolate sales in Britain come from Mars, Cadbury's and Nestlé. Branding is very important and businesses will copy and counter each other's marketing strategies all the time. Defeating the competition is everything. Prices may be well above average costs, and sometimes oligopolists will avoid competing on price so that all of them achieve high profit margins. Then non-price competition through advertising and promotions becomes very important.

For this situation to persist, there must be **barriers to entry**. These may arise because high minimum efficient scale means that entry cannot be achieved through small-scale production. The amount of capital needed to set up a large, competitive business may be prohibitive. In markets such as for chocolate, however, the underlying strength of the brand names is as important as any other feature.

These categories help clarify the nature of competition in different situations. Competition between oligopolists is quite different from all other competitive situations. Some of the time they may collude, quietly collaborating with each other. Where possible the government will try to control this type of behav-

iour through the Office of Fair Trading and the Competition Commission. If one firm is suffering loss of market share, it may shake the market up in its attempt to restore its position. In such circumstances, price wars may break out. This occurred in the newspaper business in 2002, with the *Mirror* losing out to ferocious price competition by the *Sun*.

## 42.5 Competition and profit

The profitability of a firm depends, in part, on the nature of the market. It is useful to use the idea of price takers and price makers. Price takers have to set the price close to that of competing products, otherwise they will have low sales. So they look at the market and consider what price will be competitive. Or in other words, what the market will bear. Price takers are found in situations which resemble perfect competition. They are also found among the smaller companies in an oligopolistic market.

Price makers, by contrast, are able to decide prices. They are products or services with the market power to set the price which others will follow. Heinz can do this in the salad cream market. British Airways can do the same on routes such as to Australia or South Africa. There are few satisfactory substitutes for their product so they can choose the price which will give them a commanding market position. This will not always be the highest price they might charge. It may be a price which is very profitable, but not so high as to encourage new entrants to the market. New entrants would create a more competitive market, which is the last thing the price maker wants. This kind of situation is very characteristic of an oligopoly.

To the extent that businesses succeed in increasing their market power, they will be more insulated from competition. That makes them able to make more

### BANKS AND SMALL BUSINESSES

'The report from the Competition Commission is crystal clear – competition in the market for banking services to small and medium sized enterprises (SMEs) is not working properly.

'As a result, SMEs in England and Wales are being overcharged. We cannot allow small businesses to continue paying a higher price for banking services than is right. SMEs are a vital part of our economy, employing over half the workforce. It is essential that they have a proper choice of banking services, supplied at competitive prices.'

Patricia Hewitt, Secretary of State for Trade and Industry.

profit by increasing prices. But complacency may set in. Weak competitive pressure may result in less efficiency and less focus on the customer. There is evidence that this happened with the banks' small business accounts in recent years.

## 42.6 Unfair competition

There is a very fine line between fair and unfair competition. Successive governments have attempted to draw that line in order to distinguish legal from illegal behaviour.

Where oligopolists avoid competing on price, there may be tacit agreement. This means that they all charge rather similar prices which are above the minimum needed to cover costs. This is not in itself illegal, although it may still be investigated by the Office of Fair Trading if a complaint has been lodged.

Market sharing agreements are definitely illegal. Businesses which agree to carve up the market by operating in different geographical areas are indulging in a restrictive practice. Cartels are usually found to be illegal – they allow producers to agree upon a way of limiting competition between them. They may decide to restrict supply so as to force up the price. There are many other ways in which businesses may try to avoid having to compete on a level playing field.

Unfair competition is never good for the consumer. It can limit the possibilities for businesses too. So governments in all developed countries have competition policies.

Air pollution by this factory could be indicative of market failure
© W. Cody/Corbis

## 42.7 Market failure

Market failure occurs where market forces lead to the production of more or less of a product than consumers require, given the costs of production in terms of real resources. It is best explained with a range of examples. Pollution is an indication of market failure. There is a cost to society which is not being paid fully by the producer. And therefore not being passed on to the consumers of the polluting product. Ideally all the costs of production, including those created by the pollution, should be covered by the price to the consumer. Then less of the polluting product would be bought because the price would be higher. Similarly, markets fail when there is a monopoly. Monopolists usually produce less, and charge higher prices, than would be the case in a competitive market.

Market failure often involves an element of unfair competition. Some people argue that it is unfair that rail users usually have to pay the full cost of their travel, which is clean and safe and creates no external costs for society. The railways compete with road transport. Road building is funded through the tax system, so motorists only have to cover the marginal cost of their own vehicle and fuel. Road travel creates considerable environmental costs. Effectively the polluting product is subsidised while the rail system is not.

The fact that markets *can* fail to allocate resources effectively means that government action may be needed. In the old communist economies of Eastern Europe, the government made all the economic decisions. Government officials decided on the number of chocolate bars to be produced, the number of staff who should work on the railways and so on. The Western reliance upon the free market to determine these issues has proved far more effective. Yet there is still an important role for government to step in when markets fail. Pollution can be controlled by laws and regulations, poverty wages can be avoided by setting a legal minimum wage, and traffic congestion could be reduced by massive investment in public transport.

ISSUES FOR **analysis**

Studying market systems provides numerous possibilities for analysis of business situations:

- Business cases can be considered in relation to the underlying market structure. Is the XYZ Company in an oligopolistic market? If so, that will need to be reflected in its actions and strategies.
- Business strategies can be analysed in terms of their impact on the competition. The outcome can then be examined from the point of view of both consumers and producers.
- In most markets, competition is fierce, but not as direct as in perfect competition. This is why product and marketing innovations are so vital for most firms. Standing still is rarely an option.

- Market failure points not only to the occasional need for government intervention, but also to the important potential role for pressure groups. Groups such as Greenpeace can draw public attention to the downside of business activity. This can force firms to change their ways or, if not, alerts politicians to the need for tighter regulation.

## 42.8 Markets and competition
### an evaluation

Business Studies focuses largely on what an individual firm can and should do in a given situation. Management decisions are considered in terms of their effectiveness at achieving the company's objectives. It is often implied that top quality management makes a big difference in the strategies and performance of firms.

This unit has used economic analysis to show that the wider market structure may be at least as important an influence. A superb young manager working in an oligopoly may end up making the same, cautious decision as would anyone else. A 'let's not rock the boat' decision to avoid a radical new strategy. After all, if you are one of three firms each with a 30% market share, why risk shaking things up?

This acts as a useful counterpoint to the view put forward by so many top company directors: that their personal qualities are so vital as to justify huge salary and bonus packages. If competition between the few is usually quite straightforward, perhaps it is not that hard to be the chairman of Bird's Eye Walls or Heinz. It may be much more demanding to run a smaller firm in a market where competition is fiercer.

**KEY terms**

**barriers to entry** – obstacles which prevent new businesses from entering a particular market.

**economies of scale** – a fall in average total costs due to an increase in the scale of a firm's operation.

**market forces** – the pressure exerted on the price of a product by customer demand and the willingness of producers to supply. Growing demand will push prices up. Growing supply will tend to flood the market and drive prices down.

**monopolistic competition** – occurs when there are many sellers in the market but each has a slightly differentiated product.

**monopoly** – a single seller in the market.

**oligopoly** – a small group of sellers competing with one another, most commonly by means of non-price competition.

**opportunity cost** – the cost of missing out on the alternatives when making a decision.

**perfect competition** – where many sellers compete with each other to sell a homogeneous product.

## Exercises

### A. REVISION QUESTIONS
*(40 marks; 70 minutes)*

Read the unit, then answer:

1  Describe two ways in which businesses compete with one another. (4)
2  In your view, what kinds of competition does McDonald's face at the moment? (4)
3  Briefly explain whether each of the following markets is perfectly competitive, monopolistically competitive, an oligopoly or a monopoly:
   a  the UK market for chocolate bars
   b  the UK market for cars
   c  the wholesale market for potatoes
   d  the market for Premiership tickets in Manchester. (8)
4  What are the key features of an oligopoly? (3)

5  What is meant by the term 'barriers to entry'? (3)
6  What impact do barriers to entry have on
   a  producers
   b  consumers? (4)
7  Identify three ways in which a business may achieve a competitive advantage. (3)
8  What is meant by 'unfair competition'? (3)
9  What is market failure? (2)
10 Decide whether each of the following is an example of market failure or unfair competition:
   a  three firms agreeing to control output to push up prices
   b  acid rain in Scotland caused by polluting power stations in the Midlands
   c  firms poaching experienced staff from rivals instead of training their own.
   Briefly explain your reasoning. (6)

## B. REVISION EXERCISES

### B1 Investigation

Write a report analysing the competitive position of a business in your area, or one which you have studied. Cover the following points:

- How competitive is the market?
- In what category would you place it, e.g. monopolistic competition?
- How does the business cope with the competition? What is its competitive advantage?
- What would happen to the business if competition increased?

### B2 Data Response

De Beers, which sells uncut diamonds, is one company which has managed to exert considerable control over the market since the late nineteenth century. It has ways of influencing the world supply and pricing of diamonds.

---

**De Beers Cuts Diamond Deal to Seal Cartel**

De Beers, the giant South African diamond cartel, has signed an agreement with Russia's biggest diamond producer giving the Russian company a role in regulating the world market and confirming the Russian diamond-cutting industry's rights.

The deal, which comes after months of wrangling, represents a significant concession by the South Africans. Under the agreement, De Beers will buy a minimum of £340 million worth of diamonds a year from the Russian company – 40% of its output. The bulk of the rest will be sold within the Commonwealth of Independent States (Russia and its neighbouring countries). The Russian company gains equal rights on the regulation of the volume, assortment and pricing of its exports. The agreement also gives the Russian diamond cutting and polishing industry preemptive rights in the selection of uncut gems. Some Russian cutting plants will be invited to London diamond sales organised by De Beers.

It was not clear yesterday what assurances De Beers had received from the Russian company on measures to stabilise the once chaotic supply of Russian diamonds. And to prevent frequently substantial 'leakages' onto the world market. In the past this had forced De Beers to buy increasing quantities of diamonds on second-hand markets in Antwerp and Tel Aviv to maintain price regulation.

---

De Beers emphasised that it was in the interests of both sides to keep to an agreement that it was sure would contribute to the stability of the market.

Source: Adapted from *The Times*, 22/10/97

**Questions** *(30 marks; 35 minutes)*

1 Why would it be in De Beers' and the Russian company's interests to regulate the export of diamonds? (8)
2 What impact may this deal have on consumer buyers of diamonds? (8)
3 De Beers tries to keep up the world price of diamonds not only by controlling supply but also by extensive advertising in magazines worldwide. Analyse the company's reasoning using supply and demand theory. (6)
4 Ought this kind of deal to be prevented? If so, by whom? (8)

### B3 Data Response

Antony Buck and Robert Calcraft were running a market research business but what they really wanted was to have their own products and sell them. They set up REN, which is Swedish for 'clean'. They manufacture and sell a range of pricey natural skin care products. This looks like a product area with barriers to entry due to the need for heavy advertising to create a market. Not so, says Mr. Buck, 'It's an unusual market, in that it's not so much driven by advertising as by public relations. Beauty journalists, celebrities, people who write about it'. The two had already had some experience of marketing cosmetics. Already they have two London shops, a growing Internet sales department and supply deals with department stores.

**Questions** *(30 minutes; 25 marks)*

1 Give reasons for the success of this business. (4)
2 What type of market is this? Explain the extent of competition within it. (7)
3 How might competitors react to the arrival of a new business in their midst? (7)
4 What opportunities and what threats might the business face in the future? (7)

## C. ESSAY QUESTIONS

1 Why are most washing products produced by one of two large firms, while the construction business is made up of a huge variety of large, small and medium-sized businesses?
2 'The companies which *sustain* monopolistic market shares do so, paradoxically, by acting as if they were beset by formidable competitors on every side.'

*Robert Heller.*

Why may a monopoly business lose its strong position unless it adopts the approach recommended by Robert Heller?

# DEMAND AND THE BUSINESS CYCLE

## DEFINITION

Over time, most businesses experience a sequence of changes in the level of demand for their products. This sequence is called the business cycle. Demand will grow for a period of years, peaking in a boom phase. This is followed by a downturn in which business conditions become difficult and demand slackens. For a time, demand may grow very slowly, be static, or actually decline. Eventually, demand picks up and most businesses begin to recover. Some businesses are affected by the business cycle very much more than others.

**43.1** Cyclical changes

The business cycle is easily observed. Do you know where the UK economy is in the business cycle right now? In the newspapers you will see words such as **recovery**, **recession**, **boom**, skill shortages and so on. These indicate that there are trends in the economy which affect not just one business but all of them. This unit is about how these movements can be recognised as they happen, how the pattern of events can be used to aid understanding, and how businesses are affected.

Figure 43.1 shows the annual growth rate of GDP at constant prices for the years 1988–2002. GDP stands for gross domestic product. It means the value of all output from the economy for the year. It is one of the standard measures of the size of the economy, used all over the world to provide information. It is very useful for making comparisons over time. It is given here in constant prices. This is important – it means that the figures have been 'deflated' to remove the effects of inflation. So it can be used as a measure of **real income** for the year. Real income tells us the actual value of what we produce, year by year. Money values can be misleading because some of the change they show reflects price changes.

Figure 43.1 shows that the UK has experienced some very rapid growth. The peak reached in 1988 was far above the average. That was the year in which the economy was in a massive boom. The next year growth slowed dramatically as the economy moved into recession. By 1991, output and sales were actually falling. Yet the recovery, when it came in 1992, again led to high rates of growth up until 1998. Then the economy began to slow a little. Output grew every year but by less, especially in 2001.

The business cycle consists of a sequence in which a recession is followed by recovery which leads into a boom. After a period of boom conditions there will be a downturn leading to recession. This is usually characterised as a period of slower growth or stagnation. It can be followed immediately by a period of recovery.

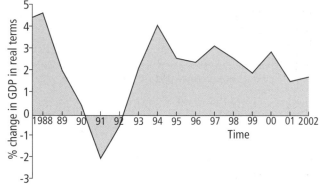

*Source:* Annual Abstract of Statistics, Crown copyright 2002

**Figure 43.1** Economic growth, 1988–2002

Or persist to the point where incomes and output are actually falling, in which case there is a depression or **slump**. These are the terms used to describe the phases of the business cycle.

In recent years the UK has felt slump threatening but the data shows that it did not actually happen. It is not easy to predict what will happen in the economy. This can mean businesses are caught out by events. They try to study the trends and evaluate the likely consequences

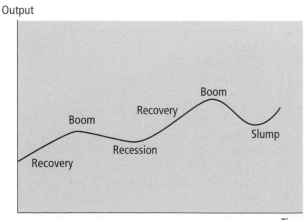

**Figure 43.2** The business cycle

for themselves. They always hope that the Government will be able to smooth out the fluctuations in demand. Changes in economic policy can have important effects. But governments also find economic forecasting difficult and quite often predict wrongly. Sometimes they add to uncertainty rather than reduce it.

## 43.2 The phases of the business cycle

It used to be thought that the business cycle consisted of a sequence of events which would recur at fairly regular intervals, usually taking about nine years. If this were ever true, it certainly does not provide an accurate picture now. For a while after World War Two it seemed possible that government policies would keep the economy growing smoothly. But in 1974 and 1981 severe recessions occurred. The slump which occurred in 1990–1992, clearly visible in Figure 43.1, was also quite severe. Although growth has been fairly steady in recent years, recession could become a problem still.

### RECESSION

In a recession, you will probably observe the following:

- businesses complaining of falling demand
- cuts in output
- rising unemployment
- few job opportunities
- gloomy expectations
- low levels of capacity utilisation
- falling levels of **investment**
- many businesses making losses
- some businesses closing down.

A recession starts with falling sales. At first, the business tries to keep things going, making extra marketing effort. It will be intensely conscious of increased competition; customers may seem very price sensitive. If the situation continues, cuts in output and employment follow. Though most businesses keep their 'key' workers – people with skills which are hard to replace when times improve. Few businesses implement the expansion plans they may have had. Investment in increased capacity is usually postponed. Indeed, with much under-used capital equipment the temptation is to cut rather than increase capacity.

### RECOVERY

When it comes, recovery is usually rather halting. Businesses are unsure that the improvement in demand will be sustained. Their expectations remain depressed and they continue to be unenthusiastic about taking the risk of investment. In particular, they will not want to take on more labour until they are sure that the recovery is real. Unemployment is likely to stay high. Lack of business confidence can become a self-fulfilling prophecy.

## BOEING TAKES A DIVE

Late in 1997, aircraft sales were booming. Boeing, the world's largest aircraft manufacturer, tried hard to expand to meet the demand. People were flocking to foreign destinations and airlines were making big profits. They wanted more jumbo jets, fast.

But by 2002, Boeing was in trouble. Of course, the terrorist attacks of September 11 2001 were a problem. For a while, many Americans did not want to travel. When they did start again the recovery in their confidence was slow.

There was much more to Boeing's problems than fear of flying. All across the US west coast, businesses were in difficulty. A spokesman for the AFL CIO (the American TUC) said 'You had the dotcom bust, but here there is a lot of industrial unemployment. Take aluminium, where 7,000 are unemployed. It's the same with logging and with Boeing. Recessions roll across from east to west. We get them last and often it lasts the longest.'

Boeing made 527 planes in 2001. It made 380 in 2002 and planned 275–300 for 2003. Faltering growth in US incomes meant less demand for air travel and aircraft. Many employees found themselves redundant.

Recovery phases can last a long time. So long as there is spare capacity in the economy, output can increase quite sharply. Initially, businesses use their under-utilised capital equipment to increase output. When they are running at full capacity, they put expansion plans in motion, investing in new buildings, plant and machinery.

### THE BOOM

As the recovery turns into a boom, various features emerge:

- as investment increases, equipment suppliers have difficulty supplying all customers
- most businesses are working flat out
- many businesses experience shortages of skilled labour
- in order to attract the people they need, businesses bid against each other so that wages begin to rise faster than inflation
- prices are increased
- high levels of demand mean that higher prices have little effect on the growth of sales
- inflation, i.e. a general rise in the level of prices, increases.

When a recovery turns into a boom it 'overheats'. The economy is growing at too fast a rate to be sustainable in the medium term. The reason is that growth requires resources. At any given time there is a limit to the quantity of resources available. So long as there are unemployed people who have the skills required by employers, businesses can go on hiring. Once all those people have jobs, the only way a business can hire more people is to poach them from each other. This requires an incentive, usually higher wages. Even that may not attract enough people with scarce skills. It may be necessary to pay *more* and wait for staff to undergo the necessary training. That takes time. Employers want people *now*.

Economists call this a supply constraint; businesses call it a bottleneck. There are others. If capital equipment producers are working flat out, orders for labour-saving equipment will go on the order books, but won't be produced for some time. This is called having a full order book. It is highly profitable for the supplier but indicates a shortage of capacity.

Full capacity output in the economy is the maximum production level possible when all resources are working flat out. The closer the economy gets to full capacity output, the greater the supply constraints. Therefore costs tend to rise. As costs rise, inflation accelerates. Then governments (and businesses) start to worry about the unpredictable consequences of high and rising inflation. They usually respond by raising interest rates.

### DOWNTURN

The rising costs associated with a boom will, in time, discourage continuing growth. They have a tendency to reduce profitability and the attractiveness of further investment. But usually government anticipates the need to damp down the economy. Rising interest rates put people off spending. Consumers who have to pay more for their mortgages spend less on consumer goods. Businesses which borrow to finance investment find their calculations less favourable when they have to pay higher interest charges.

The result is that demand for all sorts of products will fall. This has a cumulative effect on the economy. It has a big impact on construction. Higher mortgage rates mean lower demand for housing. Builders find that the houses they are working on are less profitable than they had hoped. So they cut back their plans and let some of their employees go. These people have difficulty finding a new employer and may have to rely on unemployment benefit. The cut in their incomes means less spending on luxuries. Businesses such as theme parks and restaurants face a drop in demand. Incomes fall there too.

In this way, the impact of higher interest rates is felt in lower levels of demand all through the economy. Once demand starts to fall, reduced real incomes cause demand to fall further. Some sectors will be affected less than others. Cadbury's feels a recession less than

most, because chocolate consumption is largely unaffected. Sales of **consumer durables** such as cars and carpets may fall sharply. As will luxuries such as malt whisky or Chanel No 5.

Producers of investment goods are affected the most. Plans to invest can be postponed. Figure 43.3 shows the volatility of consumption spending. Household incomes are protected somewhat by benefits. Also many people draw on past savings when they become unemployed. This helps to stabilise their spending over time.

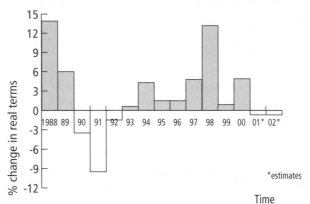

*Source:* Annual Abstract of Statistics, ONS, Crown copyright 2002

**Figure 43.3** Investment spending, 1988–2002

## 43.3 The role of investment

Experience shows that investment fluctuates far more than consumption. This can have a major effect on the business cycle. Supposing the economy has been weak, leading to a fall in interest rates. Some people in business become a little more optimistic and make some positive investment decisions. The increase in spending produces rising incomes for some. Their increased spending generates a further increase in incomes. Aggregate demand continues to rise and business expectations improve further.

The reverse process occurs at the end of a boom. Rising costs coupled with rising interest rates depress business expectations. Investment starts to drop away as it becomes less profitable. The result is a cumulative fall in incomes and a slowing down of aggregate demand. If the process continues, incomes and output will fall.

### STOCKS AND THE BUSINESS CYCLE

Investment in stocks of inputs or finished goods can also be an important factor in the cycle. When demand is rising, businesses will meet it partly by selling stocks. This is a signal to them that they should increase output. Similarly the early signs of recession may include rising stock levels as buyers spend less.

A decision to hold lower levels of stocks can mean that output will fall sharply for a while. This is known as **destocking**. The resulting fall in incomes is likely to affect aggregate demand. If it is widespread enough it will affect the whole economy. The converse is true too: if firms increase their stock levels there will be a rise in output, incomes and employment, which will stimulate the economy.

Although stocks are important in the analysis of real world events, their significance as determinants of the business cycle has been reduced by just-in-time production. If the policy is to minimise stocks at all times, changes in the level of stockholding will have little impact.

## CONSUMER DURABLES

Figure 43.4 shows that car sales are very sensitive to changes in income over the course of the business cycle. Changes in spending on consumer durables affect the economy in the same way that investment spending does. This is because purchases can be postponed or brought forward. Like changes in stocks, changes in demand for durables can explain the nature of business fluctuations.

## 43.4 How businesses are affected

It has already been pointed out that business fluctuations have a very variable impact on the individual firm. Producers of pickled onions may hardly notice the difference. People may even want to buy *more* of them when incomes fall, to spice up some cheaper food items. Toothpaste producers will probably notice no change at all. Producers of machinery for manufacturing – machine toolmakers – may be so badly affected that they cannot survive a recession.

Figure 43.5 shows how many business failed during the early 1990s. The data is for net registrations. So a positive figure indicates more new businesses setting up than business failures. During 1991, business start-ups just about balanced business failures, but in the next two years vast numbers of businesses closed down as the recession created increasingly difficult conditions.

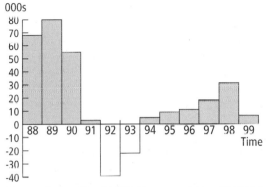

*Source:* Regional Trends, ONS, Crown copyright and ONS Website

**Figure 43.5** Business registrations and deregistrations

Often it is during recessions that businesses address their weaknesses. If they survive the recession they may emerge stronger and better able to compete. They may use improved human resource management strategies, new technologies, or more efficient approaches to organisation generally. They may try to predict the start of a recession to be ready for it when it comes.

One way to survive recession is to diversify the product range so that the business is not too dependent for its profits on items which are likely to experience wide variations in demand over the course of the cycle. This can be a good strategy for suppliers of consumer goods but may be of little help to a supplier of specialist steels. Falling investment will mean a sharp decrease in demand for steel. A steel company would need to make sufficient profits during economic upturns to survive the difficult times. Shareholders should come to expect wide variations in profits over time.

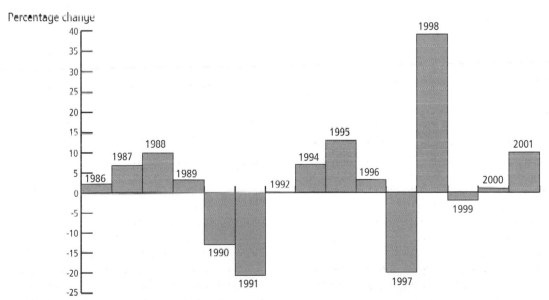

*Source:* Society of Motor Manufacturers and Traders Ltd

**Figure 43.4** New car registrations in the UK

IN **Business**

## TV, TOYS AND PENSIONS

Even when the economy is performing well, some businesses will get to the end of the road. But then, in unfavourable trading conditions, others will be expanding. On one weekend in 2002, Equitable Life, the pensions and insurance company, was in desperate trouble while HIT Entertainment, the animators behind *Bob the Builder*, reported increased profits.

Lengthening life expectancy was putting pressure on all pension funds. Promises about pensions made decades ago to contributors are now hard to keep; they have to be paid for so many years. Falling share prices added to the woe, increasing as profit forecasts worsened and confidence declined. It looked as though at least one pension fund could become insolvent (i.e. have insufficient funds to meet its obligations).

A disaster scenario of this sort does not mean that all businesses are in trouble. HIT (founded to help create the *Muppets*) had bought the rights to *Thomas the Tank Engine* and *Barney the Dinosaur*, and had sold *Rubbadubbers* to the BBC and some European TV stations.

ISSUES FOR **analysis**

Many business decisions are affected in some way by the business cycle. In considering business strategies, therefore, always consider the effect of trading conditions in the economy as a whole.

Particular points to consider:

- Is the product one which is significantly affected by the business cycle? Some products are much less vulnerable than others.
- Are sales forecasts or budgets likely to be disrupted by an impending recession?
- If the economy is entering a boom phase, might there be some difficulty in recruiting skilled labour?
- Could higher interest rates raise the cost of investment?
- Is the balance sheet strong enough to cope with a sharp recession? Is liquidity high enough and gearing low enough?
- If recession is imminent, ought the business to consider diversifying into products less prone to falling demand?

## 43.5 Demand and the business cycle
### an evaluation

The problem with the business cycle is similar to the difficulty in using the concept of the product life cycle.

In both cases, you can only draw the graph *after* the event. In other words, neither is easy to predict. The past does not necessarily tell you about the future. Therefore it is not easy to decide how significant its impact is likely to be in any given situation. Some businesses survive recessions with little difficulty, while others are pushed to the limits or collapse altogether.

However, difficult conditions can force businesses to address their weaknesses. In this way they may emerge from recession leaner and more competitive. Managements may tackle organisational problems they should have solved a long time ago. The early 1990s' recession saw a wave of 'de-layering', as companies removed entire layers of management from top-heavy, bureaucratic companies. Such cutbacks inevitably cause short-term difficulties but can have beneficial effects in the long term.

The existence of a rather unpredictable business cycle justifies the use of contingency planning by all firms. Today's successes should not lead to complacency but to careful thought about tomorrow's possible dangers. Similarly, during a recession a wise firm starts to think about consumer tastes in the next boom.

**KEY terms**

**boom** – a time of rapid economic growth, above the level which can be sustained in the long run, during which large numbers of businesses experience buoyant trading conditions.

**consumer durables** – the household equivalent of fixed assets, i.e. products used over many years such as cars, fridges and carpets.

**destocking** – running down stocks in response to a fall in demand

**investment** – spending today which will generate income in the future.

**real income** – the value of spending power for the population as a whole, or the value of output produced by the economy as a whole, with the effects of inflation removed.

**recession** – a period in which demand is growing more slowly than before, so that large numbers of businesses find they are selling less than they expected to.

**recovery** – a period of economic growth starting from a depressed situation in which the economy moves towards its full capacity, maximum possible output.

**slump** – a time of falling output and real incomes, accompanied by rising unemployment and gloomy business expectations.

# Exercises

## A. REVISION QUESTIONS
*(30 marks; 60 minutes)*

Read the unit, then answer:

1 Briefly describe each of the four phases of the business cycle. *(4)*
2 How are fluctuations in output measured? *(2)*
3 What problems are likely to arise during a boom? *(3)*
4 Why does investment fluctuate more than consumption? *(4)*
5 How can changes in stock levels affect the business cycle? *(3)*
6 Outline two ways a firm may benefit from a recession. *(4)*
7 Why is a recession difficult to predict? *(4)*
8 Explain three ways in which a firm might react to a recession. *(6)*

## B. REVISION EXERCISES

### B1 Data Response

#### Interest Rate Cuts 'Needed to Avoid Recession'

> The Bank of England should continue cutting interest rates to ward off the threat of recession, according to two of Britain's leading independent economic forecasting groups. Oxford Economic Forecasting and the London Business School believe the economy is likely to avoid recession narrowly next year, but with the risks clearly on the downside.
>
> The groups predict the economy will expand by 0.9% in 1999. They argue that there are several factors that could nonetheless push the economy into recession: for example weaker-than-expected world demand, aggressive destocking and higher saving.
>
> Meanwhile inflation is expected to undershoot the government's 2.5% target, reaching a trough just below 2% in the middle of next year.
>
> Source: *The Financial Times*, 24/11/98

**Questions** *(30 marks; 35 minutes)*

1 Explain how cutting interest rates might help 'ward off the threat of recession'. *(6)*
2 The UK economy grows, on average, by about 2.5% per year. What are the implications for firms of the economy growing at only 0.9%? *(8)*

3 a Explain the meaning of the term 'destocking'. *(2)*
 b Why might some firms undertake 'aggressive destocking'? *(7)*
4 Outline why inflation might be expected to 'undershoot' its target during an economic slowdown. *(7)*

### B2 Data Response

#### Labour shortage worst for 25 years

> The threat of a shortage of unskilled labour is at its most extreme for 25 years, according to a report yesterday that will raise fears that the jobs market is overheating.
>
> The number of manufacturers warning that recruitment difficulties could hit their businesses has hit levels not seen since 1974 – higher, even, than the boom of 1989, the last time the survey recorded major unskilled labour shortages.
>
> The Confederation of British Industry (CBI), the employers' organisation, said firms were worried that shortages of semi- and unskilled labour would hit output in the next four months.
>
> The most recent detailed unemployment figures show that the number of people claiming benefit in parts of the south-east has fallen as low as 1%. On this measure, Newbury in Berkshire and Crawley in West Sussex have unemployment rates of 1.1%. But towns in the industrial areas of northern England suffer high jobless rates. Hartlepool has 11.5% and Liverpool 8.7%.
>
> The CBI found businesses were almost as worried about shortage of manual workers as they were about difficulty in recruiting skilled employees.
>
> Source: The *Independent*, 28/7/99

**Questions** *(30 marks; 35 minutes)*

1 What is indicated by the data about the position of the UK economy with respect to the business cycle in late 1999? *(2)*
2 What are the options open to businesses that want to expand but have difficulty recruiting skilled labour? *(3)*
3 What options are available when unskilled labour is hard to recruit? *(3)*
4 Why are there big differences in the availablity of labour between different regions within the UK? *(8)*
5 What consequences for the economy as a whole would you expect as a result of labour shortages becoming a problem? *(14)*

# INTERNATIONAL TRADE, EXCHANGE RATES AND COMPETITIVENESS

Trade refers to the process of buying and selling goods and services. This makes it possible for people to specialise in the type of production they do best. They concentrate on producing items in which they have a competitive advantage. Then they exchange these for other products they need or want. When goods and services are exchanged by people in different countries, international trade takes place. In order to engage in international trade, a business must offer good value and attractive products; it must be competitive.

## 44.1 International trade

For some businesses, the market consists of a group of buyers who are close at hand. For other businesses the market could be anywhere in the world. In between there are large numbers of businesses which have some export markets. The Covent Garden Soup Company exports its cartons of soup to France. Because it has a perishable product it probably cannot extend its markets too far beyond this. Many businesses share this pattern of primary dependence on one market, with some sales overseas. This is a way of enlarging the market without becoming heavily dependent on overseas sales.

Many businesses face competition from imports. Growers of lettuces in the UK face strong competition from Dutch growers. The price at which they can sell their lettuces in UK markets will be limited by the price of the competition.

Figure 44.1 shows how the UK earns export revenue. Within these categories machinery, vehicles and chemicals are the important items. In practice, huge numbers of UK firms are involved in exports, sometimes of seemingly improbable items. Chemicals and cars are important UK exports, as are North Sea oil, Scotch whisky and marmalade.

Remember that the data in Figure 44.1 cover goods only; there are also significant exports of services. For instance, Americans wanting to travel on a Virgin Atlantic flight. 40% of Virgin Atlantic's customers originate outside the UK. The American pays dollars in the New York travel agent, but Virgin must be paid pounds. So the travel agent exchanges the dollars for pounds in order to pay the fare. This is known as an *invisible export*. Invisible because the product is a service, an export because it earns foreign currency.

International trade greatly increases the number of businesses competing with one another for most

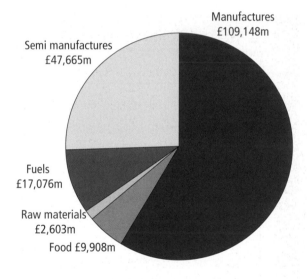

Source: Monthly Digest 2002, ONS

**Figure 44.1** UK exports of goods by category, 2000

products. It almost always leads to prices being lower than they would be without trade. This creates a very satisfactory situation for consumers because they have more choice and pay lower prices. This increases their spending power and, in turn, their standard of living.

Businesses which are involved in international trade have to cope with some uncertainties. Deliveries take longer and cost more. They may be subject to unforeseen delays. Even more importantly, at least one party to the deal will be making payments in foreign currency. Floating exchange rates can make the real value of payments unpredictable.

### THE SHIFTING PATTERN OF TRADE

The pattern of trade – the quantities and the products traded and the markets to which they go – does not stand still. It shifts continuously for all sorts of reasons:

- new businesses set up and develop their export markets
- new technologies open up previously impossible export and import markets
- businesses which are constantly striving to improve their competitive performance acquire advantages they did not previously have
- changes in exchange rates alter the prices at which goods and services can be sold abroad.

Export marketing is often a matter of extending market orientation to an unfamiliar market. The nature of that market and the particular requirements of customers there must be studied carefully. All aspects of marketing must be adapted to fit the circumstances. The impact of new technologies will be discussed in a later unit. Striving for competitive advantage involves good decision making in production and human resource management. Exchange rate changes present problems, and these must be studied in some detail.

## 44.2 Exchange rates

The exchange rate is the value of a currency measured in how much foreign currency it can buy. In 1980 a pound could buy 525 Japanese yen. By 1995 the pound had fallen to only 135 yen. In 2002 it was again touching 140 yen, after some fluctuations. Clearly, exchange rates vary. They may be stable for a while, but then enter a period of instability in which they rise or fall sharply. In the long term the exchange rate is determined by the pattern of international trade – supply and demand for imports and exports. In the short term, however, speculation can cause wide variations in a currency's value.

This speculation can be based upon:

- expectations about the future level of interest rates
- expectations about a country's future trade performance
- political uncertainties.

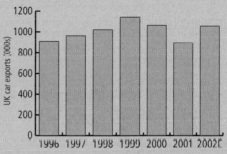
Figure 44.2 shows how the **sterling index** has fluctuated since 1988. The business uncertainties implied by

these variations have encouraged many companies to press for Britain to join the single European currency. This pressure increased after the successful launch of Euro notes and coins in January 2002.

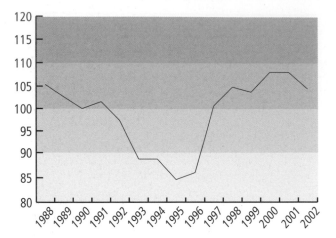

**Figure 44.2** Sterling exchange rate index (1990 = 100) (Source: Eurostat, © European Communities, 2002

## 44.3 The impact of exchange rate changes

Businesses which are exporting and importing on a regular basis find fluctuations in exchange rates a source of considerable uncertainty. This can be enough to stop them from developing export markets. It is not too much of a problem for exporters if the exchange rate falls because the effect is to increase competitiveness. But if the exchange rate rises, the loss of competitiveness erodes profit margins. This makes exporting unattractive. The resulting loss of markets can be very painful. Look back at Figure 44.2. Notice the rise in the value of the pound in 1996. Prices set in pounds rise sharply in foreign currency terms when the exchange rate rises.

The reverse effect can be expected for importers. If the exchange rate rises, the price they have to pay in pounds for the goods they import will fall. They can either cut prices in pounds or maintain prices and increase their margins. If they cut prices sales revenue may rise. What exactly are the effects on companies of changing exchange rates? The table below provides a step-by-step guide.

Overall, an **appreciation** of the exchange rate leads to a loss of competitiveness, while a **depreciation** leads to a gain in competitiveness. The unstable nature of floating exchange rates creates difficulties for businesses. So governments have made repeated attempts to fix their currency values in terms of other currencies. Some peg the value of their currency to the US$. The European Exchange Rate Mechanism limited the extent to which member currencies could diverge from one another. European Monetary Union goes one step further by creating a single currency, the Euro, for member countries. These policies will be discussed later.

*The effect on firms of changes in the value of the pound – a step-by-step guide:*

**1 The effect upon exports of a falling pound**

*The external value of the pound is measured by what it will buy. If it once bought $2 but now only buys $1.60, it has fallen by 20%.*

*Pound down means fewer $s per pound. So UK exporters don't need to charge as many dollars per pounds' worth of exports. For example, if a £200 coat is exported to the US:*

- *At $2 to the pound the coat must be priced at $400 to get a UK revenue of £200.*
- *At $1.60 to the pound you only have to charge $320. So a 20% fall in the pound improves UK export competitiveness by 20%.*

*Summary: A devaluation of the pound makes our exports more competitive; this boosts UK export sales, as foreign buyers switch to cheaper UK goods.*

**2 The effect upon imports of a falling pound**

*When £1 = $2 a US company selling Superman comics in Britain for £1 will receive $2 per unit. If the pound falls to $1.60, then each £1 comic generates only $1.60 in US revenue.*

*So a falling pound hits the revenue of those importing goods into the UK. As their revenues are hit, importers are likely to push up their UK prices (e.g. to £1.25 so that the dollar revenues are £1.25 × 1.60 = $2).*

*Summary: Devaluation pushes import prices up, which reduces their competitiveness. So import levels should fall. However, the increased import prices include food and fuel. So they can be expected to push the inflation rate up.*

**3 Effect of rising pound upon exports**

*If £1 rises to equal $2.40, exporters may have to increase their overseas prices.*

*The £200 coat must now be priced at $480 if the exporter wants to go on receiving £200 per export. This will cut demand. The % fall in sales will be determined by the price elasticity of the product. The price increase will cause a sharp fall in sales for a highly price elastic product.*

*If UK firms choose to hold their export prices constant, each dollar they charge will translate back into fewer pounds, so exporting firms' profit margins will suffer.*

*The $400 coat will now only provide $400/$2.4 = £166.6 of revenue.*

*Summary: Pound up means export prices up and therefore export volumes down.*

**4 The effect on imports of a high pound**

*If the pound rises, importers will find that each pound they receive will be worth more of their local currency. Therefore their profit margins increase. This encourages them to increase their marketing effort in the UK, as selling here is so profitable. If they choose to do so, they could afford to cut their pound prices. If import prices are cut, UK firms will enjoy lower costs on imported materials and components. But they will suffer fiercer competition from importers of rival products.*

**Summary: Pound up means imports up, with foreign firms increasing their share of our market (at the expense of our firms/jobs).**

## CHINA TAKING A POUNDING

It's a long time since life was easy in the Potteries. All the big china and pottery producers in Stoke-on-Trent have had problems. Royal Doulton had a major restructuring. Wedgwood brought in big name designers. Some long-established firms closed down. The basic problem was labour-intensive production facing intensive competition from countries with cheaper labour, and the strong pound.

Churchill China was in trouble in 1990, and had a visit from BBC's 'troubleshooter', John Harvey-Jones. He advised investing more and delegating more and it seemed to work. By 1996, the company was exporting 60% of sales, mostly to European markets. Then in 1997 the pound rose and stayed high. For a while, Churchill was able to rely on its hotel and restaurant customers, who valued its reliability. Then, the company began to lose money again and decided to go up-market.

New designs continued the very English style of the traditional Churchill product. Stephen Roper, the third generation chair of this family business, said that, along with the 'Made in England' stamp on the bottom, this would help them to compete in this market.

No one in the china business ever thinks you can just stand still. Continental Europe, where Churchill was successful in the past, has been dogged by slow economic growth. Survival generally requires action.

may be buying imported inputs, or selling their products abroad. In time they may need to set up subsidiaries overseas, either for manufacturing or distribution or both. At that point they become multinational enterprises (sometimes also termed transnationals). Some companies are operating in so many countries that they should be seen as global companies selling global products. A good example is Coca-Cola.

The process by which this has taken place has come to be known generally as globalisation. It has been greatly aided over the years by the development of cheaper and easier means of transport and communication. Transport costs are now insignificant for many products. Unless the ratio of bulk to value is very high, they are unlikely to give local producers a telling advantage in the market.

Business thinkers sometimes say 'think globally, act locally'. This is really just a reminder that a market oriented attitude demands that each individual market be understood and catered for. For most products this approach is important. The product must be suited to the needs of the market, and the marketing strategies must be in tune with the culture of that market.

Some companies hardly need to bother; Coca-Cola is one example, Starbucks another. Actually they are rather special cases. They are selling an image of the American way of life. Adaptation to local markets is unnecessary. It is the image that is in demand. These two are exceptions. For most companies it is essential to understand the market they are selling into. And adapt both product and marketing accordingly.

## SELLING CHINESE UNDERWEAR

Marketing consultants in Hong Kong are keen to help Chinese manufacturers to market their products. They tell stories of mistakes which have been made. One Chinese manufacturer of men's underwear wanted to sell to Western markets. It decided it would be good to name its range after a flower. They rummaged around the dictionary and decided to call it the Pansy range. They found it simply would not sell in Europe. If only they had sought advice from marketing people in Hong Kong.

## 44.4 The implications for business strategies

Businesses are under pressure to buy their inputs from the cheapest source. They will also try to expand their markets wherever possible. Many businesses have become increasingly involved in overseas markets. They

## 44.5 What determines international competitiveness?

Businesses compete on a number of fronts. Price competitiveness is extremely important for some products. For others, non-price competition may be more important. In general, businesses seek to improve their competitiveness in order to secure a larger market.

The decisions involved here are internal to the business and involve aspects of production, marketing and human resource management. They revolve around two issues:

- How can efficiency and productivity (output per person employed) be increased?
- How can the business create new areas of demand for the product?

However, competitiveness may be affected by the business environment. Exchange rate changes may make them more or less competitive. Rising input prices will push managers to consider raising prices. A general rise in prices – inflation – will affect competitiveness too. A change in the rules of the World Trade Organisation (WTO) may mean that import duties change. All of these factors are external to the business and involve deciding the most effective reaction.

## REACTING TO EXCHANGE RATE CHANGES

The business which competes with imports and finds the exchange rate rising is under added pressure to improve its efficiency. It may consider increasing investment in labour-saving machinery and reducing the workforce. It may introduce new technologies and new organisational strategies. It will increase its marketing efforts. The fight will be on just to *maintain* competitiveness. Sometimes governments have allowed the exchange rate to rise in the attempt to force businesses to increase their competitiveness.

The business which is exporting when the exchange rate falls has a bonus. The value in pounds of its product will rise if the foreign currency price stays the same. It has a choice. It could leave prices the same and accept a higher profit margin. Or it could cut the price in the hope of higher sales. The best strategy will depend on the price elasticity of demand for its product. A high elasticity – greater than 1 – will mean that a price cut will bring a disproportionately large increase in sales.

Similarly, the exporter which has to contend with a rising exchange rate must decide how higher prices in foreign currency will affect sales. If they will tend to fall because foreign buyers will switch to competing substitutes whose price has remained the same, it may be better to accept lower profit margins. Staying competitive when the exchange rate is rising is very difficult. Most big businesses want a stable, and low, exchange rate if export markets are important to them. Staying competitive is further complicated for the business which imports inputs as well as exporting the final product. Deciding a strategy means thinking through all the angles.

In 2003, after several years of the pound being high against the Euro, Volkswagen decided to reduce its car prices in Britain. To avoid any dent to its image, it advertised its 'surprising' prices very subtly.

There are many issues for analysis regarding the effects on business of changing exchange rates and changing patterns of international trade. They include:

- Existing trade patterns give clues as to profitable opportunities for the future in markets abroad, and their likely growth potential.
- The advent of the Euro is likely to accelerate the trend towards international trade. Small and medium-sized firms could avoid exporting in the past. In future, they are likely to be hit by more imports. This may force them to fight harder for export sales.
- A decision to enter certain export markets will be affected by the likely exchange rate risk. Within the Eurozone, other member countries will have a great advantage over outsiders.
- No firm should allow itself to be overly reliant upon one foreign currency. If 50% of a British firm's sales go to one foreign country, a rise in the value of the pound could be crippling.

## 44.6 International trade
### an evaluation

For many businesses, selling abroad is absolutely essential. It is the only way they can expand their markets. However, there are always more uncertainties in export markets. Market change, exchange rate changes and changes in the rules of world trade can all create problems.

Special efforts must be made to ensure that good market knowledge is obtained in foreign markets. Cultural differences can have a big impact and an understanding of these is often necessary. Careful evaluation of the risks associated with uncertainty may be needed.

International markets are usually more competitive than those where the business focuses on local markets. This is partly because there are more companies competing. The result is that exporting companies are usually among the most progressive. They refuse to accept low quality standards or poor management. This makes them livelier (though less secure) places to work.

**KEY terms**

**appreciation** – a rise in the exchange rate such that prices of imports fall and prices of exports in foreign currency rise.

**depreciation** – a fall in the exchange rate such that prices of imports rise and prices of exports in foreign currency fall.

**sterling** – a widely used term meaning the British pound.

**sterling index** – an index of the value of the pound compared with other currencies.

# Exercises

## A. REVISION QUESTIONS
*(30 marks; 60 minutes)*

Read the unit, then answer:

1 Give three examples of services that are important in international trade. *(3)*
2 Identify three sources of business uncertainty for exporting firms. *(3)*
3 Why may market orientation be especially important for an exporter? *(3)*
4 How are importers to the UK affected by depreciation in the value of the pound? *(3)*
5 What will happen to exporters' profits if the exchange rate falls? Explain your answer. *(4)*
6 Briefly outline how each of the following exporters to America might respond to a sharp rise in the value of the pound against the dollar:
   a Rolls Royce
   b EIDOS (producers of games software such as *Tomb Raider*)
   c British Steel, selling sheet steel for making car body panels. *(6)*
7 What is likely to happen to consumer demand if import prices rise? *(2)*
8 Outline one type of business that would suffer severely and one type that would benefit greatly from a high pound. *(6)*

## B. REVISION EXERCISES

### B1 Data Response

> Exports of manufacturers from the UK depend heavily on being fully competitive on world markets. Between early 1996 and early 1998 the pound rose steadily on the foreign exchange markets, threatening competitiveness. The table below gives the change in the value of the pound against the US dollar and the Deutschmark.
>
> | | US$ | DM |
> | --- | --- | --- |
> | 1996 Quarter 1 | 1.53 | 2.26 |
> | 1998 Quarter 1 | 1.66 | 2.98 |
>
> **Source:** NIER, 1998

**Questions** *(30 marks; 35 minutes)*
1 Using cars as an example, calculate:
   a the price of a £12,000 car in both currencies at the beginning of 1996 *(4)*
   b the price of the same £12,000 car in both currencies at the start of 1998 *(4)*

c the percentage change in each currency over the two-year period. *(4)*
2 What would you expect to happen to sales of UK cars in the US and in Germany as a result of this appreciation? *(5)*
3 How would your answer to question 2 be affected by the knowledge that a British producer of sports cars believes the price elasticity of its products is approximately 0.5?( *(5)*
4 What impact would the rise in the pound have generally on UK car producers' sales turnover and profits? Explain your answer. *(8)*

### B2 Data Response

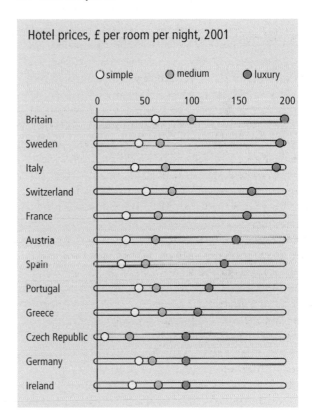

Hotel prices, £ per room per night, 2001

○ simple   ◐ medium   ● luxury

Source: The *Which?* Hotel Guide 2002

**Questions** *(30 marks; 35 minutes)*
1 How does the tourist trade affect exports and imports? *(4)*
2 Give three reasons that might explain why London hotel prices are exceptionally high. *(6)*
3 To what extent are London hotel prices likely to affect the level of tourism in the UK? *(4)*
4 What types of UK businesses are likely to be affected by the high price of London hotels? *(8)*
5 What might be done to make accommodation costs more competitive? *(8)*

# INFLATION AND UNEMPLOYMENT

## DEFINITION

Inflation is a general rise in prices across a wide range of goods and services. Inflation is a loss in the purchasing power of money.

Unemployment occurs when people who are available to work cannot find jobs.

## 45.1 Does inflation matter?

The simplest way to understand inflation is to see it as rising prices. This is true, but it leads to an unfortunate consequence. A price increase usually causes demand to fall. Therefore it seems logical to assume that rising inflation causes lower consumer spending – and therefore leads to recession. This is a misunderstanding. At a time of 5% inflation, not only prices are rising by 5% but also wages. So people can pay for their 5% higher shopping bill with their 5% extra income. **Aggregate demand** need not be changed.

Inflation is easiest to understand as rising prices, but *best* understood as a fall in the value of money. In other words, a pound is not worth as much as it used to be.

So does inflation matter? If people can pay the 5% higher prices with their 5% higher salaries, who loses? At these relatively low levels, no-one loses much at all. The fear of inflation is largely the fear of hyper-inflation. For example, inflation in Germany in 1923 was over 1,000,000%. In Russia it was over 2,500% between 1990 and 1996. At these high levels, families can find their life savings becoming worthless within months.

## 45.2 Measuring inflation

Over the years inflation has been very variable. You can see the dramatic changes in British inflation in Figure 45.1. This shows the annual rate of inflation, i.e. the percentage change in prices generally each year. During the 1970s and 1980s the rate of inflation fluctuated very considerably. It became apparent that inflation could also be very unpredictable. This makes it hard for businesses to forecast trends and make plans. An investment appraisal, for example, becomes much more uncertain if the inflation outlook is unclear.

In recent years inflation has not been a problem and there are fears that deflation, generally falling prices, may be more of a threat.

The figures on which Figure 45.1 is based are the outcome of a lengthy process of measurement from which the **retail price index** (RPI) is constructed. An **index** number is one which shows a time series using a base year which is given the figure 100. The table on the next page shows the RPI (inflation) figures as a series based on 1995 prices equalling 100.

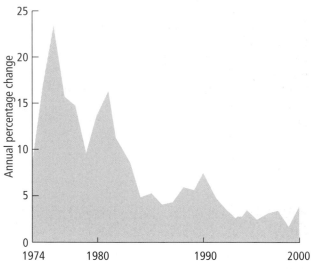

*Source:* Eurostat (© European Communities, 2002)

**Figure 45.1** UK inflation rate

The Office of National Statistics (ONS) is responsible for compiling the RPI. It is based on a vast amount of data. Prices are collected for a wide range of goods and services in different places and types of retail outlet. These prices are then weighted according to their relative importance in people's budgets. So an increase in the price of cars will have a bigger impact on the index than an increase in the price of potatoes. The data upon which these weightings are based comes from the Family Expenditure Survey, which records the expenditures of 7,000 households. These are representative of all types of household and all regions. In this way price changes are expressed as a weighted average which measures reasonably accurately the impact of inflation on consumers generally.

Retail price index, UK, 1992–2002 (1995 = 100)

| YEAR | RPI |
|------|------|
| 1992 | 92.9 |
| 1993 | 94.4 |
| 1994 | 96.7 |
| 1995 | 100.0 |
| 1996 | 102.4 |
| 1997 | 105.6 |
| 1998 | 109.3 |
| 1999 | 111.0 |
| 2000 | 114.2 |
| 2001 | 116.3 |
| 2002 | 118.1 |

Source: National Institute Economic Review, Crown copyright 2002

Expressing price changes in index numbers makes it easier to compare values over the years. At the time of writing the base year is 1995. Each figure after 1995 shows the percentage increase in prices compared with 1995. It does *not* show the percentage increase in prices year by year – that requires an additional calculation of each year's change as a percentage of the previous year's value.

Of course, prices are changing all the time and some go down. Think about air fares, or electronic products. Other products encounter price falls because demand is diminishing. These changes are included in the RPI because it is an average figure for the change in prices generally.

## 45.3 How inflation develops

Unit 43 discusses the business cycle. It shows how an upswing and then a boom might trigger an acceleration in the rate of inflation. During a boom, demand is growing faster than the capacity of businesses to satisfy it. This situation is sometimes called **excess demand**. It happens when the most crucial resources needed to expand output are becoming scarce because of recent rapid growth in output.

When the economy is growing strongly, employers look for people with the scarce skills needed to help them expand. In time, the shortage of skills becomes a supply constraint. Employers are then likely to try to attract employees with higher pay. As pay is increased, costs rise and businesses seek to recover these through higher prices.

At first this process is very gradual. It causes little alarm. If consumer spending is growing, it may be possible to raise prices without losing customers. But by degrees price increases become more numerous and begin to show up in a rising rate of inflation. As people observe the increase in the inflation rate, they build rising prices into their expectations.

### OVERHEATING

At some point in the upswing of the business cycle, a point is reached at which the economy is nearing its full capacity output. The result is that aggregate demand from all sources is growing faster than aggregate supply. This is known as excess demand; another term used to describe it is **overheating**. If it persists, inflation will accelerate as competition to obtain the available supplies intensifies.

This situation can be described as demand–pull inflation. Prices rise because people and businesses are trying to spend more. But the goods and services needed to satisfy demand cannot, in the short run, be produced. Another possible consequence of this is that imports will rise.

### EXPECTATIONS

At this point in the explanation of how inflation develops, it is important to think about how wages and prices are determined. Businesses can raise prices provided they are confident that customers will still buy the product. If they have sufficient spending power, they will. So whether they can or not depends on the extent to which earnings are rising to match inflation. In other words, prices can rise provided they are matched by rising earnings.

How can employees make sure that their earnings rise? One way, of course, is to ensure that they have the scarce skills that employers need. Another is to join a strong trade union and negotiate pay increases by means of collective bargaining. Recent research shows that union members in the UK still earn, on average, about 11% more than non-union members.

During the period 1970–1990, any increase in inflation quickly got built into the expectations of wage negotiators. It was extremely difficult for employers to avoid paying an increase in real wages every year. It was expected that in money terms pay would always increase by more than the rate of inflation. Anything else would be unacceptable. So earnings tended to rise at the existing rate of inflation plus a little more.

The result can be a **wage–price spiral**. Wages rise to cover expected inflation. Costs rise, so prices are increased and inflation continues. This kind of inflation is sometimes called **cost–push inflation**, because it can continue even when there is no excess demand in the economy. In order to reduce inflation in this situation, some way must be found to reduce expectations of inflation.

### THE EXCHANGE RATE AND TRADE

One way in which inflation may be given a twist upwards is through an exchange rate change. When the currency depreciates, imports get dearer and exports become cheaper. The increase in import prices will feed through into the RPI. This includes prices of imported consumer goods. The index also records price increases by British producers suffering higher costs of imported materials. A rising exchange rate will have the opposite effect. For that reason a strong exchange rate can be part of government policy to reduce inflation.

## 45.4 The impact of inflation on business

As already observed, when inflation is high it is also hard to predict. Forecasting expected sales revenue can be made very difficult. This is partly because of the price changes and partly because the presence of inflation makes it likely that the government will make changes to its economic policy.

When prices are changing quickly, businesses have more difficulty in keeping track of competitors' pricing strategies.

## 45.5 The impact of deflation on business

During the period 1998–2002, countries such as Japan suffered the opposite of inflation, which is **deflation**. This occurs when ferocious competition and a weak economy lead to falls in the average price level. This can be a far more serious economic problem than inflation. During 1999 and 2000 there were some signs of this in Britain, especially in the production and retailing of goods such as clothes and cars. However, the increasing price level of services such as restaurant meals, plus – especially importantly – rising wage levels, indicated that deflation was not a general problem.

Deflation hits businesses if the steady downward pressure on prices cannot be recouped by cost cutting. Even if there is scope for cutting costs, it may put severe pressure on relationships with suppliers. The hardest problem may be the effective management of a firm's most important supplier, its workforce.

### FITNESS FIRST

When incomes are growing, health clubs do very well. A little inflation is not a problem for them. Fitness First has 700,000 members at its network of clubs in the UK, Europe, Asia and Australia. While the economy looked strong, it opened many new clubs in the UK, only to find that they were not filling up very fast. The kind of people it was aiming for as members were finding that their incomes were at best growing rather slowly. Some were being made redundant as the economy slowed in 2001.

With overcapacity in the health club market generally, a price war seemed all too likely. Profits were falling and it was clear that some competition on price would be inevitable.

Deflation implies downward pressure on pay packets, or redundancies to allow the remaining staff to keep up their level of earnings. Either way staff suffer and so will morale.

## 45.6 The effects of government policy

When overheating occurs, governments feel threatened by rising inflation and a worsening balance of payments. Too many imports are sucked in by the spending boom. The usual government response is to tighten economic policy to dampen down demand. Taxes might be increased or interest rates pushed up. In 1997 and early 1998 the Bank of England increased interest rates to try to slow down a consumer spending boom. They did this again in 2000.

When economic policy changes such as this occur, the economy does not respond immediately.

| WAYS BUSINESSES BENEFIT FROM HIGH INFLATION | PROBLEMS FOR BUSINESS FROM HIGH INFLATION |
| --- | --- |
| Highly geared firms benefit from the cut in the real value of their loan repayments | Cash flow is squeezed by the rising cost of new materials and equipment |
| Balance sheets look stronger as rising property and stock values boost reserves | Forecasting is subject to greater uncertainty, which makes firms look for higher forecast rates of return |
| Smaller firms benefit from the reducing importance of brand names; they can compete on price/service | Owners of big brand names may struggle, as greater consumer price consciousness makes customers more price sensitive. This cuts the value added by brand names |
| It is easier to increase the price of your own product when prices are rising generally. So cost increases can be passed on to the consumer | Staff become much more wage conscious as inflation poses a threat to real living standards; therefore industrial disputes and labour turnover tend to rise |

Consumers used to high spending during a boom are reluctant to cut back. Firms have investment plans which may take months or years to complete. It is normal for a time lag to occur. The Bank of England usually anticipates a time lag of eighteen months or two years.

For firms, therefore, it is important to be aware of the possibility of changing government policy, but wrong to assume that demand will change straight away. So there should, therefore, be time to carry through strategies such as cutting stocks or carrying out a zero budgeting exercise.

## 45.7 Unemployment

Figure 45.2 shows what has happened to the percentage of the labour force which is unemployed in the UK. These figures show dramatic changes which had a marked effect on many people's lives. They are total figures and disguise the fact that unemployment is actually most serious within certain well-defined groups of people. The young, older people, men who previously worked in manufacturing, unskilled people and ethnic minorities are the groups most affected.

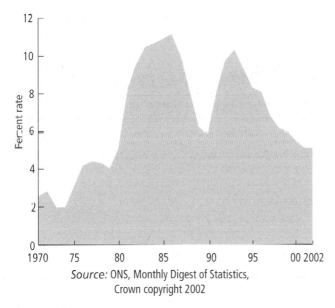

Source: ONS, Monthly Digest of Statistics, Crown copyright 2002

**Figure 45.2** UK unemployment

### TYPES OF UNEMPLOYMENT

There are many reasons why a person may become and then remain unemployed. Quite often it is difficult to separate the reasons when looking at an individual case. Sometimes an employee will lose a job for one reason but fail to find alternative employment for quite other reasons. Having said this, three broad categories of unemployment can be identified.

### 1 Cyclical unemployment:

- **Cyclical unemployment** occurs when firms cut back on staff during the recession phase of the business cycle. During recession and slump or

The real face of unemployment: outside a Job Centre in London (© Michael Ann Mullen/Format)

depression conditions, unemployment typically rises sharply. It will fall again as the economy recovers.
- When the economy is depressed, the main impact on incomes is born by those who lose their jobs. Those who remain employed typically manage to maintain real incomes most of the time.
- Counter-inflation policies which work by reducing the level of aggregate demand will necessarily tend to reduce the demand for labour and so create unemployment.

### 2 Frictional unemployment:

- **Frictional unemployment** occurs temporarily when people are between jobs. There are always some people who have left one job and are in the process of finding another. It has increased over the years because labour turnover has risen.
- Frictional unemployment can be reduced by developing improved flows of information about jobs available. It can also be affected by the level of income people have when their employment ceases. Redundancy payments give people time to look around for a job which suits them, rather than simply taking the first available job.

### 3 Structural unemployment: In 2000, the UK economy was booming. Unemployment was falling. Yet even then, 5.5% of the workforce was unemployed. How could this be, when employers were desperate to find people?

Unemployment which persists even when the economy is at its full capacity output is either frictional or structural in origin. It is definitely not cyclical. Yet when employers have many vacancies, frictional unemployment is not likely to be significant because people can find jobs easily. So the main problem has to be **structural unemployment**.

To understand structural unemployment, it is necessary to look at the rather complex problems which lie beneath it. There are four important factors to be considered:

- As shown in the following table, there has been a major shift away from manufacturing jobs to the service sector; skilled metal-workers do not take easily to switching to working at B&Q.
- Changing technologies have caused employers to look for a different range of skills.
- Efforts to stay competitive can lead to the installation of labour-saving equipment.
- New technologies sometimes require more capital and less labour.

Demand for individual products changes for many reasons. However, in modern economies certain broad trends can be observed. Changes in tastes and fashions affect demand. Rising incomes bring some products within reach which previously had been unaffordable. An imported substitute which is newly available can reduce demand for the domestic product.

Supply changes too. For example, new technologies affect both products and processes. Some items become cheaper, and then demand for competing substitutes will fall. These changes are summarised in Figure 45.3.

These changes entail the expansion of some businesses while others contract. Also, they entail changes in the mix of skills required by businesses. As the pace of changes gathers speed, the rate at which people are made redundant from businesses which no longer need them increases. More people are looking around for new employers. Changes in patterns of employment can be seen in the table on the right. It shows the long-term trend away from employment in agriculture and manufacturing and towards employment in the service sector.

## IMMOBILITIES

Two awkward factors get in the way of the process of movement from one job to another and so worsen structural unemployment. One is occupational immobility. This is when the skills people have are not the ones which employers are currently seeking. The solution to this is to retrain. But there are all sorts of problems. The person concerned must have the aptitude, must know that retraining is possible and must be aware of the existence of jobs in the relevant

Employment by sector, Great Britain (000s)

|  | 1979 | 2000 |
|---|---|---|
| Agriculture | 359 | 335 |
| Manufacturing | 7,113 | 4,162 |
| Services | 13,239 | 18,621 |
| Total employment | 22,639 | 24,314 |

Source: Crown copyright, ONS Annual Abstract, 1985 and 2001

field. Funds must be available from either the government or the individual to pay for retraining. For all these reasons, occupational immobilities have been very persistent in recent years.

The other awkward factor is known as geographical immobility. This is defined as a situation in which the unemployed person is unable (or unwilling) to move to a place where jobs are available. It is easy to see how this arises. House prices are higher in areas where jobs are available than in areas of high unemployment. Most owner-occupiers can't afford to move. If they are renting a council house, they will not qualify for one in an area of employment opportunity. When this situation is combined with the decline of a localised industry such as shipbuilding, high levels of structural unemployment can persist for decades.

## THE OUTLOOK

Structural unemployment does decline eventually, as people have time to adjust to economic change. However, the process can take a long time. Many people who are unemployed for long periods become 'discouraged workers'. They lose their skills and their work habit, and become steadily less attractive to employers. Attempts to arrest this process by retraining have been only partially successful, perhaps because too little finance was available to do the job properly. Structural unemployment remains one of the major economic problems of the times. It is very acute in other European countries and remains a problem in the UK.

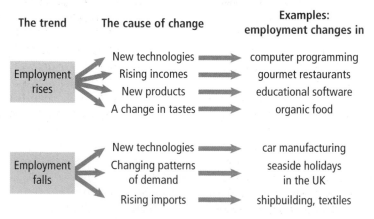

**Figure 45.3** Trends and changes

Inflation, or the threat of it, dominated economic policy making for many years. Governments tend to be very afraid of it. However, the long-term social effects of high unemployment are also very problematic. Inflation presents a range of issues for each individual decision taker.

- Higher rates of inflation are also usually more variable rates of inflation, so an accelerating rate of inflation may be creating an unpredictable situation. Both governments and businesses may find it more difficult to forecast accurately.
- Despite this, many businesses grow and prosper at times of inflation. For much of the past decade the problem for Japan has been deflation. In other words, economic depression leading to falls in average prices. This is very damaging to consumer and business confidence.
- Rising inflation may mean that governments want to reduce demand in the economy; policy measures such as higher taxes or higher interest rates will hit sales for many businesses.
- Different kinds of unemployment have different implications and it can be important to have a good understanding of the underlying causes of unemployment at any given time.
- Cynical though it sounds, many businesses benefit from moderately high unemployment. Workers are focused on job security, not on pay rises. Staff generally are more willing to accept change in methods and organisation.
- If unemployment is largely structural, the people who are seeking work may not be in the places where employers are creating jobs, or may not have the skills which happen to be required. In these circumstances it may be important to be able to retrain.

## 45.8 Inflation and unemployment
### an evaluation

In the past low inflation rates have been associated with high unemployment. This is what happens when the economy is in recession. The reverse is also true. This can mean that governments have to perform a balancing act. From 2000 to 2002, there was a happy balance of low inflation and fairly low unemployment too. For businesses, the difficulty is that the attempt by government to achieve a happy balance means that economic policy changes regularly. This was clear in 2000, when the interest rate was raised to 6%, but was falling again by the end of the year.

For individual firms, the problems caused by rising inflation or rising unemployment should be manageable. The most important thing is to have a well-diversified range of products selling into a wide range of markets. Then shortfalls in demand in one area can be cancelled out by successes elsewhere. A good example of this is Whitbread, whose low-priced Travel Inn hotels did well in 2002/03 at a time when luxury hotels were struggling.

**aggregate demand** – the total of all demand for goods and services throughout the economy.

**cost–push inflation** – when rising business costs force firms to increase prices in order to protect their profit margins.

**cyclical unemployment** – unemployment which results from a level of demand which is insufficient to buy all of current output

**deflation** – when the average price level is falling, i.e. negative inflation

**excess demand** – a level of demand which is greater, at current prices, than the capacity of the economy to supply goods and services

**frictional unemployment** – unemployment which occurs as people who have left one job seek out another. By definition, it covers only those unemployed for whom there is a job available once it can be found

**index** – a series of data which uses a base year with a value of 100 and expresses the data for all other years in relation to that base year

**overheating** – the phase in the business cycle in which demand is growing faster than the capacity of the economy to meet it by producing goods and services

**retail price index** – the data series used to measure the rate of inflation. It is a weighted average of the prices of all items commonly bought by consumers

**structural unemployment** – unemployment which occurs because the structure of the economy is changing, with some areas of production growing and others declining, while those people made redundant are unable to move to other areas of the economy because of immobilities

**wage–price spiral** – a sequence in which prices rise because of increased costs, which causes a rise in the rate of inflation, which in turn creates expectations of further inflation and increased wage demands leading to higher pay settlements.

# Exercises

## A. REVISION QUESTIONS
*(25 marks; 50 minutes)*

Read the unit, then answer:

**1** Why is inflation generally regarded as being undesirable?
*(3)*

**2** How is inflation measured? *(2)*

**3** In what way is inflation connected with the business cycle? *(4)*

**4** Why are expectations important in the inflation process? *(4)*

**5** Outline two advantages inflation can have for a business. *(4)*

**6** What is structural unemployment? *(3)*

**7** How is it possible for employers to have difficulty in recruiting, even when there are large numbers of unemployed? *(4)*

**8** What happens to unemployment in a recession? *(1)*

## B. REVISION EXERCISES

### B1 Data Response
Every three months, the Confederation of British Industry asks a sample of companies whether they expect that their output will be constrained over the coming four months by skill shortages. A rising percentage of positive answers indicates that skill shortages are on the increase. The data below shows half-yearly figures for expected skill shortages, average earnings increases and the rate of inflation for the year to that point. It covers the period 1994–97 when output was growing strongly (as shown in the last column). In looking at the connections between the figures, it is important to remember that there may be some time lags between cause and effect.

**Questions** *(35 marks; 40 minutes)*

**1** At what point did the level of expectation of skill shortages increase significantly? *(1)*

**2** Explain when the UK economy was operating close to full capacity. *(4)*

**3** What impact did this have on the rate of growth of average earnings? *(3)*

**4** Is there a connection between earnings growth and the rate of inflation? *(3)*

**5** From the figures, why do you think the Bank of England decided to increase interest rates in mid-1997? *(6)*

**6** From your library, find out what has happened to the rate of growth of output and the rate of inflation since mid-1997. Present both series of data as lines on a graph. *(10)*

**7** Try to predict what will happen in the economy over the next year. Forecast the rate of output growth (GDP) and the rate of inflation (RPI) in six months' time. Give a brief explanation of your reasoning. *(8)*

**Skill shortages, earnings and inflation**

| Half-year | | Expected Skill Shortages (%) | Yearly Growth in Average Earnings (%) | Inflation at Annual Rate (%) | Output Growth Since 12 Months Ago (%) |
|---|---|---|---|---|---|
| 1994: | I | 7 | 2.8 | 2.6 | 4.9 |
| | II | 10 | 3.3 | 2.6 | 3.4 |
| 1995: | I | 11 | 3.6 | 3.4 | 1.6 |
| | II | 10 | 4.1 | 3.2 | 2.1 |
| 1996: | I | 9 | 3.5 | 2.3 | 2.4 |
| | II | 11 | 3.0 | 2.6 | 3.4 |
| 1997: | I | 11 | 4.5 | 2.7 | 3.6 |
| | II | 17 | 5.0 | 3.6 | 3.7 |

Source: *National Institute Economic Review*, 1998/1

## B2 Case Study

### The Mobile Video-phone

Claire built her business from nothing. It started with a small, independent mobile phone shop in Taunton. By the time the national chains such as Carphone Warehouse and The Link started up, Claire had already made a great deal of money. On a business trip to Taiwan (she liked to cut out the middle-man) she saw her first mobile video-phone. And fell in love with it. Immediately she commissioned her own version, made with a royal blue plastic outer shell and branded *Claron*.

Within six months, the Claron video-phone had sales of over 500,000 in the UK. At an average price of £80, that came to an astounding £40 million. Claire built up her organisation hugely, with a sales force and a large administrative staff.

Then, just as Claire was starting to feel the effects of tougher competition, the economic environment became tougher. Two years of consumer spending boom had led to rising inflation. This was causing difficulties with staff, who were pushing for pay rises of around 10%. Several were urging others to join a trade union. Shocked into action by the widespread evidence of inflationary pressures, the government decided to raise interest rates sharply. This was to discourage consumers and firms from spending so much on consumable or investment goods.

Faced with this difficult marketplace, Claire could not decide what to do. Unfortunately others chose to cut prices to boost their market share. This had little effect at first, but after a month sales of the Claron started to slip. A radical new strategy was needed, or else it would be essential to cut Claron's price. Claire would have to make a decision – and very soon.

### Questions          (40 marks; 60 minutes)

1 Explain why Claire had such a success with the Claron. (6)
2 How might a consumer spending boom lead to rising inflation? (6)
3 If Claire does not make any changes, consider the possible effects upon her business of the market conditions outlined in the text. (12)
4 a Outline two new strategies Claire might consider, given her circumstances. (6)
   b Which of the two should she adopt? Make a fully justified recommendation. (10)

## B3 Case Study

### Employment puzzles

For nearly 1,000 workers at Black and Decker's Spennymoor plant in the north-east, the news that they had been dreading came last week. The American owned firm is moving production to the Czech Republic, where labour costs are lower.

John Bridge, Chairman of One NorthEast, the development agency, says that many more 'high volume, low value' manufacturing jobs will be moved offshore. The Engineering Employers' Federation (EEF) predicts 150,000 job losses this year.

There was also bad news for 850 workers at Prudential's Reading call centre, with the announcement that their work is being relocated to Mumbai to take advantage of India's lower labour costs and greater availability of skilled workers.

Digby Jones, director-general of the CBI, says Britain is in danger of 'sleepwalking into decline' as a result of increased labour market regulation and an erosion of low-tax advantages. An EEF survey of members shows that many are planning job cuts as a direct result of the national insurance rises next April.

Other job losses last week included more than 300 at Birds Eye in Grimsby and Hull, and more than 200 at Enterprise Jewellers in Bridgnorth. Unions are predicting another 10,000 job losses at Royal Mail.

There are puzzles about our employment market. While job losses continue, the unemployment count is at a 27-year low. The latest data suggests that growth is continuing even though manufacturing is struggling.

Source: *The Sunday Times*, 6/10/02

### Questions          (30 marks; 35 minutes)

1 What kinds of jobs were being cut at the time when the passage was written? (4)
2 List the four main reasons for job cuts, explaining the importance of each. (10)
3 To what extent could these changes be related to the business cycle? (6)
4 Evaluate the extent to which these job cuts matter at a time when employment is growing for the economy as a whole. (10)

# BUSINESS AND THE LAW

## DEFINITION

Laws are established by Acts of Parliament and by previous judgements made in courts. Businesses must work within the law to maintain their reputation and to avoid legal penalties.

## 46.1 Introduction

The government (and now the European Union) plays a major role in shaping the environment in which businesses operate. It does this by creating and implementing legislation which affects business. This unit considers the scope and impact of the key aspects of business legislation. It focuses upon the ways laws enhance or constrain business activity.

Almost all areas of business activity are affected by the law. These include marketing, production, financial activities, the employment of people and the establishment of the business itself. This unit looks at the relevant legislation in outline, then spends longer on the purpose of the legislation and its effects on firms.

## 46.2 Types of law

The sources of law which impact upon UK businesses are numerous, and are discussed below.

### ACTS OF PARLIAMENT

Throughout its period in office, each government passes a series of Acts through Parliament. These generally reflect the policies set out in its election manifesto. Legislation arising in this way is termed statute law. Recent examples of statute law include the Employment Act, 2002 (see In Business below).

### COMMON LAW (JUDICIAL PRECEDENT)

Despite the Acts passed by Parliament, much business legislation is the result of the decisions of judges. Legal decisions today may depend on the precedent set by a judge 40 years ago. Common law may involve the interpretation of a new statute or a decision when a new circumstance arises. Judicial precedent can only be set by the House of Lords, the Court of Appeal and the High Court.

### EUROPEAN UNION LAW

The UK joined the European Union on 1 January 1973. Since then the UK has been subject to EU legislation.

This is of particular importance to businesses since many of the EU's objectives are economic. The EU has passed laws affecting free competition between businesses, the free movement of labour and capital and conditions faced by employees. The **Social Chapter**, to which the UK became a signatory in 1997, extends EU legislation to health and safety, working conditions, collective bargaining and the right to strike.

### IN Business

## WORKERS' RIGHTS UPDATED

The Department of Trade & Industry has developed a new piece of workplace legislation designed to bring employment rights of British workers into line with their European counterparts. The DTI claims that the new law (the Employment Act, 2002) represents a compromise offering workers added protection without imposing many extra costs on employers.

The new measures increase paid maternity leave from 18 to 26 weeks and allow employees to have a further 26 weeks' unpaid leave. At the same time the Act grants fathers 2 weeks' paid paternity leave following the birth of a child. Many businesses, especially small ones, will be compensated by the government for additional costs arising from this legislation.

Much EU law is derived from the treaties which established the European Union. The legislation which originates from Brussels is applicable throughout the EU and overrides much of the law passed by national parliaments.

## 46.3 Health and safety legislation

Health and safety is the regulation of the working practices of organisations so as to discourage dangerous practices. It usually focuses upon the avoidance of accidents rather than the active promotion of good health.

The main legislation in Britain is the Health and Safety at Work Act of 1974. This was supplemented by extra regulations which came into effect on 1 January 1996. These set out new minimum standards to which employers must maintain the workplace and the working environment.

The Health and Safety at Work Act 1974 imposes on employers the duty 'to ensure, so far as is reasonably practicable, the health, safety and welfare at work' of all staff. 'Reasonably practicable' means that it is accepted that the risks of hazard can be weighed against the cost of prevention. The main provisions of the Health and Safety at Work Act are:

- firms must provide all necessary safety equipment and clothing free of charge
- employers must provide a safe working environment
- an obligation is placed upon employees to observe safety rules
- all firms with five or more employees must have a written safety policy on display
- union-appointed safety representatives have the right to investigate and inspect the workplace and the causes of any accidents.

Health and safety imposes significant constraints upon businesses. Businesses incur substantial additional costs of production. Firms have to appoint safety representatives who become non-productive personnel for at least part of their time at work. Further costs are involved in providing a safe working environment, for example guards for machinery and protective equipment and clothes for operatives.

Health and safety legislation does, however, provide advantages as well. A secure and safe working environment can provide a sound basis for building a motivated, participative workforce. Firms are also keen to improve their health and safety records (see the In Business article above). A good reputation for providing a safe working environment is likely to assist businesses in recruiting high calibre employees.

## HEALTH AND SAFETY AT WORK: THE EUROPEAN POSITION

The main European legislation dealing with health and safety relate to the following issues:

- pregnant workers
- working hours
- manual handling, especially heavy weights
- VDU equipment.

Health and safety matters in Europe are decided by the majority voting system, unlike employment matters which require unanimity. The UK can therefore not block health and safety directives.

## 46.4 Employment protection

There exists a wide body of legislation and judicial decisions relating to employment. Such labour law has two main forms. These are individual and **collective labour law**. The latter is not part of AS Business Studies.

### INDIVIDUAL LABOUR LAW

This body of law relates to the rights and obligations of individual employees. Over the last 30 years the amount of individual labour law has increased considerably. The increasing influence of the European Union has been a major factor behind this trend. Some of the major Acts in this area include:

- Equal Pay Act 1970 – this Act states that both sexes should be treated equally with regard to employment. Thus a woman employed in the same job as a man must have the same pay and conditions. This legislation has been strengthened by European Union law, most notably the 1975 Equal Pay Directive.
- Sex Discrimination Act 1975 – in the employment field this Act's main purpose is to outlaw discriminatory practices relating to recruitment, promotion, dismissal and access to benefits, facili-

### CONSTRUCTION WORKERS AT RISK

The Health & Safety Executive (HSE) has identified construction as one of the most dangerous industries in Britain. Construction workers are six times more likely to be killed than any other employees. In the last 10 years nearly 900 construction workers and over 50 members of the public were killed as a consequence of construction work. The HSE report announced that the construction industry accounts for over 32% of all employment-related deaths. The industry suffered 79 fatal accidents in the year March 2001–March 2002.

During an inspection of 223 construction sites in London in 2002 the HSE:

- ordered improvements to working practices at 110 sites
- stopped work on four sites because of the extent of danger to employees.

The construction industry has agreed a voluntary target to improve health and safety within the industry. This includes a planned reduction in fatal accidents and serious injuries of 66% by 2009.

In Business

ties or services. It is not directly concerned with discrimination in the matter of pay. The Equal Opportunities Commission was established to enforce the legislation.

- Race Relations Act 1976 – this Act makes it unlawful to discriminate in relation to employment, against men or women on the grounds of sex, marital status, colour, race, nationality or ethnic or national origins. These provisions apply to the recruitment of employees and to the way they are treated once employed. This legislation is enforced by the Commission for Racial Equality.
- Disability Discrimination Act 1995 – the main employment-related provisions of the 1995 Act are:
  - to make it unlawful for an employer to treat a disabled person less favourably than others
  - to require employers to make reasonable adjustments to working conditions and environment to help overcome the practical effects of disability.

## 46.5 Consumer protection legislation

Consumer protection describes various laws designed to protect consumers from unfair and unscrupulous business practices. Some of the legislation deals with consumer safety. Other laws attempt to protect the consumer from exploitation by strong or unethical firms.

Over the last decade or two consumers have become more sophisticated and informed purchasers. This trend was encouraged by the popularity of consumer organisations such as the Consumers' Association and its publication *Which?*. There has been a parallel growth in consumer television programmes such as *Watchdog* which has helped to highlight consumer issues. This has led to more calls for protection for consumers – often in the form of legislation. This trend, sometimes referred to as **consumerism**, has also served to make producers more aware of, and responsive to, the views of the consumer lobby.

In the UK, the Fair Trading Act of 1973 enables the **Office of Fair Trading** to:

- continuously review consumer affairs in general
- deal with trading practices which may unfairly affect consumers' interests
- take action against persistent offenders against existing legislation
- negotiate self-regulatory codes of practice to raise trading standards.

The major Acts comprising consumer legislation include the following:

- Sale of Goods Act 1893 and 1979 – the 1979 Act lays down the contractual arrangements implied by the purchase of an item. It specifies that goods must be of 'merchantable quality', i.e. fit for the purpose for which they were purchased.
- Weights and Measures Acts 1963 and 1985 – legislation making it illegal to sell goods below their stated weight or volume, together with an enforcement procedure through trading standards officers and the Office of Fair Trading. The 1985 Act allows metric measures to be used.
- Trade Descriptions Act 1968 – this prohibits false or misleading descriptions of a product's contents, effects or price. This affects packaging, advertising and promotional material. It is one of the key pieces of consumer protection legislation.
- Food Safety Act 1990 – this is a wide-ranging law which strengthens and updates consumer protection in the food sector. This brought food sources, and by implication farmers and growers, specifically under food safety legislation for the first time. It made it an offence to sell food which is not of the 'nature or substance or quality' demanded by the purchaser.

### THE IMPACT OF CONSUMER PROTECTION LEGISLATION

All firms supplying goods and services are affected by this legislation. The effects can take a number of forms:

**1 Ensuring customer satisfaction:** Consumerism has resulted in a new culture amongst those purchasing goods and services. Consumers are ready to complain if products are defective in any way. In order to maintain the business's image and standing and to avoid consumers resorting to the law, businesses regularly establish customer services departments. These are intended to rectify problems before they become serious. Similarly, firms might attempt to meet customer needs through the use of market research as part of a market oriented approach.

**2 Increased emphasis upon quality control:** Firms are nowadays more vulnerable to prosecution for supplying products which are unsuitable or damaged. Consumer safety and weights and measures legislation can be used against businesses who supply unsafe goods or do not supply the stated quantity, for example.

**3 Increases in production costs:** This is a consequence for firms of most business-related legislation. Food safety legislation, for example, means that those in the catering industry have to meet strict hygiene standards and offer staff appropriate training. Both factors result in increased costs for businesses.

## 46.6 Competition legislation

Competition legislation covers a number of aspects of business activity including mergers and takeovers, monopolies and **restrictive practices**. Competition legislation is a weapon deployed by government with the intention of promoting greater competition within markets. The aim of this aspect of government policy is enhanced consumer welfare with the cheapest possible supply. Governments aim to achieve a 'fair' price for the consumer and 'fair' profits for producers.

For many years UK governments have adopted a flexible approach to competition policy and the associated legislation. Unlike some governments, they have not determined that all anti-competitive practices (such as monopolies) are harmful and should be abolished. Rather they have argued that cases should be investigated and judged on their individual merit. The key criterion remains: is the practice against the public interest? This approach recognises that there may be benefits to be derived from mergers and from very large-scale production, particularly in international markets. It also acknowledges that there are disadvantages which may outweigh the benefits.

This approach has led to investigations into various business activities. The organisation created to carry out this work is the **Competition Commission**.

## THE COMPETITION COMMISSION

The Competition Commission is a government-financed organisation whose function is to oversee proposed mergers and to check that where monopolies do exist, they are not against the public interest. The Commission was established by the Competition Act 1998, although it had existed as the Monopolies Commission since 1948. As a general rule, any merger which is likely to lead to a 25% or greater market dominance will be investigated by the Commission. It will also look into existing cases of the apparent abuse of **monopoly** power. The Commission itself cannot take legal action. It can only advise the Office of Fair Trading that action is necessary.

## KEY ELEMENTS OF COMPETITION LEGISLATION

The Office of Fair Trading plays a key role in enforcing the government's competition policy. It has the power to investigate trading activities and to order investigations where it suspects that markets are not being operated in the 'public interest'.

**The Fair Trading Act 1973:** This set up the Office of Fair Trading, the government agency responsible for providing ministers with advice on legislation and action with regard to monopolies, mergers and restrictive practices. The Act granted the OFT the power to recommend which merger or monopoly situations should be investigated by the Competition Commission.

A preliminary investigation by the Competition Commission into the mobile phone industry has concluded that customers are overcharged.

One of the most controversial issues is high mobile termination charges. These are fees that mobile phone operators charge to rival companies for connecting calls to their networks. Inevitably the mobile phone companies pass these charges on to the consumer. The Competition Commission is contemplating limiting these charges, but a decision is not expected until 2003. Any restrictions on prices would be likely to affect all four British mobile network operators: Orange, Vodafone, T-Mobile and mmO2.

**Restrictive Practices Acts 1956, 1968 and 1976:** These comprise a body of legislation to control restrictive trade practices between rival suppliers. Restrictive trade practices are active interferences by producers into the free working of markets. This reduces competition and is therefore likely to lead to higher consumer prices and lower standards of customer service.

Examples of restrictive practices are market sharing and price fixing.

- A market-sharing agreement occurs when a number of firms in an industry agree to allow each a profitable part of the total market. Generally this is illegal as it means that price competition is being suspended (forcing consumers to pay excessive prices). A market-sharing agreement is only likely if supply is dominated by a small number of firms, and if it is hard for new competitors to enter the market. A commonly used term for market-sharing is a 'cartel'.
- Price fixing takes place when manufacturers instruct retailers as to the prices at which they may sell their products. Manufacturers may refuse to supply retailers who fail to follow their instructions. This prevents free competition between retailers resulting in higher prices for consumers. There have been allegations in recent years that manufacturers of household electrical equipment have engaged in covert price fixing.

The Restrictive Practices Acts make restrictive practices illegal unless specifically exempted by the Office of Fair Trading. This might occur after an investigation by the Restrictive Practices Court. The Restrictive Practices Court operates the reverse of the usual legal practice; practices are deemed to be illegal unless the business concerned can prove otherwise.

**Competition Act 1980:** The 1980 Act allowed anti-competitive practices such as the refusal to supply to be investigated by the Competition Commission.

**Competition Act 1998:** This Act strengthens competition policy in two areas. The first aspect reinforces legislation against anti-competitive practices and cartels. (A cartel is the name given to a group of producers who make an agreement to limit output in order to keep prices high). The second element strengthens penalties against the abuse of a dominant market position. Firms engaging in such anti-competitive practices will face huge fines – up to 10% of turnover.

## 46.7 European Union competition policy

The are distinct differences between UK and EU competition policy. There have, for many years, been calls for a reform of UK competition legislation to bring it in line with that operated by the European Union. As with most areas of business legislation EU law has primacy if a dispute exists over which code of law should be applied in any given circumstances.

EU policy towards restrictive practices concentrates on the *effects* of the restrictive agreement, whereas UK policy considers the *nature* of the agreement. A restrictive practice would be deemed illegal in the UK just because it contains certain terms and conditions. The EU would carefully assess the effect on the marketplace and would only declare it illegal if the agreement adversely affected consumers.

The abuse of monopoly power is dealt with severely by EU legislation. Large fines are levied on firms who compete unfairly, for example by pricing below cost. Critics have said that the EU's approach contains uncertainties. Only the dominant firm in the industry is considered to be acting illegally when setting its prices below production costs. In some cases it can be difficult to decide whether a firm is, in fact, dominant. The UK's approach is more pragmatic, judging the impact of each monopoly situation in terms of the criterion of public interest. In turn this is criticised for being weak and ineffective.

It is important when considering legislation relating to businesses not to get too bogged down in the detail of the Acts. A level Business Studies does not require an in-depth knowledge of the law but rather a clear understanding of its nature, scope and effects. You will not need to have detailed knowledge of the legislation such as that creating a minimum wage. However, you may be required to explain the possible consequences of the introduction of this legislation. You may also be asked to present arguments in favour of and against the policy. It is important to appreciate that there are two aspects to business legislation: it may constrain some aspects of business activity, but it can enhance it in other ways.

You could argue that the legislation discussed in this unit merely serves to constrain the activities of businesses. To some extent this is a valid argument. Small firms, particularly, may find the burden of legislation a struggle. It may damage their competitiveness within the world market. Legal controls increase the proportion of non-productive personnel (for example, health and safety officers) to ensure compliance with the relevant legislation. This increases costs which will be passed on to the consumer in the form of higher prices.

On the other hand, if a workforce feels well looked after and protected it is likely to be more productive. The workforce may also be more responsive to new techniques and ideas. Abraham Maslow (an American psychologist) would argue that this is because the workers' security needs have been met. This may result in improved industrial relations eliminating many of the costs associated with disputes.

A comparison of UK and EU competition policy

|  | **UK Policy** | **EU Policy** |
|---|---|---|
| Restrictive agreements | Dealt with by the Office of Fair Trading and possibly the Restrictive Practices Court. No fines for first offenders | Investigated by the EU under Article 85. Offenders may be fined up to 10% of worldwide turnover |
| Abuses of monopoly power | Dealt with by the Office of Fair Trading and the Competition Commission. No fines for offenders | Investigated by the EU under Article 86. Offenders may be fined up to 10% of worldwide turnover |
| Mergers | Investigated by the Office of Fair Trading and the Monopolies and Mergers Commission. Secretary of State for Trade and Industry plays a key role | Investigated by the EU's Merger Task Force. Political influence may determine which mergers are permitted |

One of the themes running through this unit has been that the impact of legislation has good and bad effects upon most businesses. Evaluation in the context of business legislation could centre upon assessing how the law may affect particular groups or types of businesses.

It could be argued that multinational businesses are less affected by business legislation. A prime argument is that strict legislation which forces up costs (such as the imposition of a generous minimum wage) will result in the business moving to other locations. Large businesses employ specialist lawyers who can advise on ways to minimise the impact of legislation. Furthermore, major businesses have considerable political influence and can lobby even the most independent of governments to change their policies. In 2002 small business in the UK lobbied the government to end the tax imposed on energy purchases. The government is considering changing the law in response to the activities of this lobby group.

Equally it is possible to put the case that large businesses are more affected by this kind of legislation. Much competition legislation is aimed at large firms. They are more likely to enjoy (and abuse?) monopoly power or to engage in mergers which are against the consumers' interest. They have reputations which they guard jealously. Large firms do not want to be prosecuted for infringing consumer protection legislation for fear of the consequent adverse impact upon sales. For example, between 1998 and 2003 there was fierce criticism (from the government and consumer bodies) of the financial services industry over advice given in relation to private pensions. Many firms in the financial services industry will have been embarrassed by this publicity and it is likely that their sales have suffered.

---

**KEY terms**

**collective labour law** – laws which relate to the activities of trade unions and the operation of industrial relations.

**Competition Commission** – a government-financed organisation whose function is to oversee proposed mergers and to check that where monopolies do exist, they are not against the public interest.

**consumerism** – an approach that places the interests of the consumer at the heart of discussions about business decisions or activities. This could be contrasted with trade unionism, which places the interests of workers first.

**EU directives** – the general term given to legislation enacted by the European Union.

**monopoly** – in theory, this is a single producer within a market, in practice it rarely exists because most products have close substitutes and because nowadays markets are international.

**Office of Fair Trading (OFT)** – the government body set up to ensure that firms are complying with the Fair Trading Act 1973.

**restrictive practice** – active interference by producers into the free working of markets. This reduces competition and is therefore likely to lead to higher consumer prices.

**Social Chapter** – a set of statutory and non-statutory measures designed to harmonise social legislation within the EU, alongside economic measures.

# Exercises

## A. REVISION QUESTIONS

*(35 marks; 75 minutes)*

Read the unit, then answer:

1 State three areas of business activity which may be affected by business legislation. *(3)*
2 Explain the term 'delegated legislation'. *(3)*
3 Why might a business follow a code of practice which has no legal authority but is, in fact, voluntary? *(3)*
4 State two provisions of the Health and Safety at Work Act, 1974. *(2)*
5 Outline one advantage to businesses of the Health and Safety at Work Act 1974. *(3)*
6 Give three examples of unfair dismissal under current employment protection legislation. *(3)*
7 Explain the term 'consumerism'. *(3)*
8 Outline the function of the Office of Fair Trading. *(3)*
9 Outline what the UK government and the EU hope to achieve through the operation of their competition policies. *(4)*
10 State two reasons why the authorities wish to outlaw restrictive practices. *(2)*
11 What is a cartel? Why might a cartel be against the public interest? *(4)*
12 State two differences between UK and EU competition policy. *(2)*

## B. REVISION EXERCISES

### B1 Data Response

#### A Week In Court

This is a week in the court life of West Yorkshire trading standards officers. Thousands of inspections are made each year, but prosecutions are only undertaken if traders are found to be seriously flouting the law.

**Monday – Wakefield**
This morning the bench hear four separate cases of goods vehicle overloading. All the defendants were caught out on the same day at a local weighbridge. Today everyone pleads guilty and the fines range from £150 to £1,200.

**Tuesday – Bradford**
A tour operator has advertised a holiday as 'exclusively for adults' and a couple booked on the strength of this statement. In fact the hotel was full of families with small children. The company pleaded guilty and was fined £1,450.

**Wednesday – Huddersfield**
Two off-licence owners are attending court, one for selling fireworks to a 15-year-old boy and the other for selling cigarettes to a 13-year-old girl. They are found guilty and fined £200 and £150 respectively.

**Thursday – Halifax**
A publican is pleading not guilty to selling short-measure beer to an undercover officer. After the evidence is heard the publican is found guilty and fined £300 plus (substantial) costs.

**Friday – Leeds**
A prosecution is taken out against a retailer selling goods described as 'Russian Vodka'. The bottles are found to contain diluted methylated spirits. The retailer is found guilty and fined £500 plus substantial costs.

Source: *Trading Standards Update*, Winter 1998, West Yorkshire Trading Standards Service

**Questions** *(30 marks; 35 minutes)*

1 Outline the benefits of the work of trading standards officers in implementing laws affecting:
   **a** consumers *(6)*
   **b** the general public. *(6)*
2 Firms worry about the cost of meeting rules and regulations, but how may responsible business owners benefit from legislation being enforced as in the cases above? *(10)*
3 The law also tries to protect consumers from anti-competitive practices such as price fixing between 'rival' firms. Why may this be beneficial to the firms concerned in the long run? *(8)*

### B2 Stimulus Question

#### Car Dealers Exposed in Price-fixing Investigation

Volvo, the Scandinavian motor manufacturer, was accused yesterday of 'price fixing' under European law by discouraging dealers from offering customers discounts. In a further example of the influence of consumerism, an undercover researcher from *Which?* magazine posed as an interested buyer at 12 Volvo dealerships. The researcher could only get a 'very small' discount on a car worth £16,675.

Some dealers allegedly went further, telling the researcher that Volvo told them not to offer discounts. According to this month's *Which?* report, one dealer in Farnham told the researcher that the car maker 'would rap the knuckles' of dealers caught discounting.

In a statement, the company said it did not engage in restrictive practices and that it did not '...restrict in any way the price at which dealers may sell cars'. The motor vehicle industry is an oligopoly with a few large manufacturers supplying the market. In spite of this, research revealed a significant variation in practices amongst dealers. Ford, for example, offered 'substantial discounts of up to £1,000'.

Despite reports such as this there is a strong lobby which contends that European firms face legislative controls which are too strict. Some employers have argued that they are placed at a disadvantage when trading in world markets because of the tight legislative control they face in their home market.

Source: Adapted from the *Independent*, 8/1/98

**Questions** *(30 marks; 35 minutes)*

1 Explain the meaning of the following terms:
   a price fixing
   b oligopoly. *(4)*
2 Outline two benefits a firm may enjoy as a result of engaging in restrictive practices. *(6)*
3 Consider the factors which have led to the rise of 'consumerism' in recent years. *(8)*
4 Discuss the view that European firms are hampered from competing effectively in world markets because of '...the tight legislative controls they face in their home market'. *(12)*

## C. ESSAY QUESTIONS

1 Some business leaders suggest that scrapping legal constraints upon firms would significantly improve Britain's international competitiveness. Discuss this view.
2 Economists such as Milton Friedman believe people should be free to choose what to sell and what to buy. Others believe regulation is needed to save the consumer from unscrupulous traders. Discuss these views and draw your own conclusions.

# STAKEHOLDING

### DEFINITION

A stakeholder is an individual or group which has an effect on and is affected by an organisation.

## 47.1 Introduction

All firms are affected by the environment in which they operate. For example, the managers of an organisation come into contact on a daily basis with suppliers, customers, the local community and employees. Each of these groups has an impact on the firm's success and at the same time is likely to be affected by any change in its activities. If, for example, the managers decide to expand the business, this may lead to:

- overtime for employees
- more orders for suppliers
- a wider range of products for consumers
- more traffic for the local community.

Groups such as suppliers, employees and the community are known as the firm's **stakeholder** groups because of their close links with the organisation. A stakeholder group both has an effect on and is affected by the decisions of the firm. Each stakeholder group will have its own objectives. The managers of a firm must decide on the extent to which they should change their behaviour to meet these objectives. Some

managers believe it is very important to focus on the needs of stakeholder groups. Others believe that a company's sole duty is to its **shareholders**.

The traditional view of an organisation is known as the 'shareholder concept'. Under this view managers are responsible solely to the owners of the organisation – the shareholders. The logic is clear: the shareholders employ managers to run the company on their behalf. So everything the managers do should be in the direct interests of shareholders. The managers should not take the needs or objectives of any other group into consideration. If the owners want short-run profit, for example, this is what the managers should provide. If the owners want expansion then this is what the managers should aim for. According to this view, the only consideration managers should have when making any decision is to meet their owners' objectives. Generally, this means maximising **shareholder value**, e.g. increasing the share price.

The alternative view places emphasis on the need to meet the objectives of a wider group. This has led to the growth of 'the stakeholder concept' as opposed to 'the shareholder concept'. The stakeholder approach suggests that managers should take into account their responsibilities to other groups, not just to the owners, when making decisions. The belief is that a firm can benefit significantly from cooperating with its stakeholder groups and incorporating their needs into the decision making process. Examples include:

- improving the working life of employees through more challenging work, better pay and greater responsibilities so that the firm benefits from a more motivated and committed workforce
- giving something back to the community to ensure greater cooperation from local inhabitants whenever the firm needs their help, for example when seeking planning permission for expansion
- treating suppliers with respect and involving them in its plans so that the firm builds up a long-term relationship. This should lead to better quality supplies and a better all-round service. If, for example, your supplier has limited availability of an item, it is more likely you would still get supplied because of the way you have treated the supplier in the past.

The stakeholder approach is, therefore, based on an inclusive view in which the various groups which the firm affects are included in its decision making rather than ignored. This, it is argued, can lead to significant advantages for the firm.

### Business IN

#### RAILTRACK

In 2002 the government ensured that Railtrack, the company that controlled the UK's railway lines, was taken over by a not-for-profit organisation called Network Rail. Various disasters on the railways such as Hatfield in 2000 had led to upgrading of the rail system which ultimately Railtrack could not afford to pay for. Also, many people felt that Railtrack had been so actively pursuing profit that safety standards had suffered, thereby endangering the lives of passengers. With a not-for-profit organisation running the railways, this conflict should not exist. The Board of Members for the new company includes stakeholders such as the train operating companies, passengers, train drivers and unions. Critics, however, question whether a not-for-profit organisation will have any incentive to be efficient.

## STAKEHOLDERS: ENRON

In 2001 Enron, a huge American company, was discovered to have been falsifying its accounts. Senior executives of both Enron and Andersen, its auditors, were taken to court because they had lied about the company's financial position. The fall out from the Enron scandal was enormous. People became wary of investing in companies because they felt the accounts departments could not be trusted (especially when another giant, WorldCom, was found to have been falsifying its accounts as well); as a result share prices fell significantly.

At the heart of this scandal was the enormous pressure on managers at both Enron and Andersen to deliver ever better results for their bosses and owners. At Enron managers who were able to produce improved growth figures each year received tremendous bonuses and rapid promotion; at Andersen the Enron account was extremely important and they were terrified of losing it. The desire for personal rewards meant that the needs of other stakeholder groups were ignored. Enron shareholders were misled only to discover, once the scandal broke, that their shares were worthless.

### 47.2 What are the gains of the stakeholding approach?

There are numerous gains which might result from the stakeholding approach. For example, existing employees might be more willing to stay with the firm. It may also attract people to work for the organisation. Employees are increasingly concerned about the ethical behaviour of the organisation they work for. Firms which put the shareholders above all else may deter some people from applying or accepting a job there. The stakeholder approach is also increasingly popular with investors. There are a growing number of financial institutions which specifically seek to invest in organisations which follow the stakeholder approach in the belief that it will lead to long-term rewards. A firm can also gain from better relations with the community, suppliers and distributors and more favourable media coverage. By working with other groups rather than against them a firm is also less likely to be targeted by a **pressure group**.

While this approach may seem attractive in theory there are a number of problems in practice. First, the owners may insist that the managers serve their interests and no-one else's. Many shareholders of public limited companies, for example, demand short-term rewards and may take some convincing that the firm should be paying attention to the needs of other groups. After all, it is their money which is invested in the business. Second, the managers may not be able to meet all their potential responsibilities to these various groups and may have to make some decisions regarding priorities. They may also have to decide between what they regard as their obligations to society and what is commercially viable.

Interestingly, society's view of the responsibilities of business seems to grow each year. This means we are expecting firms to take a much broader view of their activities than in the past. At one stage, for example, we would not have expected firms to be responsible for the political activities of the governments in the countries where they operate. However, the criticism of Shell in the late 1990s for failing to influence the Nigerian government over its human rights policy highlights that firms are now being held responsible for the actions of others, not just themselves. Similarly, Nike was heavily criticised for the behaviour of suppliers which employed child labour. Even though Nike was not directly responsible for this, pressure group activity forced the company to take action to prevent this occurring again.

## GREGGS THE BAKERS

In 1964 Ian Gregg reluctantly took over the family bakery shop in Newcastle when his father died. In 2003 he is retiring from the business, though he remains the biggest shareholder. In those years, he has built Greggs into Britain's biggest chain of bakery outlets, with more than 1,000 stores and sales of nearly £400 million a year.

To help fund the huge expansion, Greggs was floated onto the stock market in 1984. In the following 20 years the share price rose by more than 2,000%. Yet Ian Gregg makes it clear that he sees shareholders as the third most important stakeholder behind employees and customers. This, he says, reflects the values and sense of responsibility that underpin the business. Of the future, he is sure that, 'We will not seek to maximise shareholder value in the short term. We take a lot of flak about it.' He can point to the past profit and share price growth to show that there are long term benefits from such an approach. And he points to the company's plan for £1 billion annual sales by 2010 to show that there is no lack of ambition.

Source: Adapted from *The Financial Times*

In recent years people have come to expect more from business organisations. In the past they were just expected to provide good quality goods. Now many consumers want to know exactly how the goods are produced, what the company does for the environment and how it treats its employees. Stories about the use of child labour, the sale of goods to a military regime or

## STAKEHOLDERS: BAT

In July 2002 British American Tobacco (BAT) launched its first corporate social responsibility report. Unfortunately many stakeholders who had been asked to contribute to the report refused to take part. BAT's chairman said, 'You demonstrate a willingness to be responsible and to get a better understanding of what other parties want of you, but when it comes to the opportunity to talk they refuse because they'd rather shout from the sidelines than play a constructive role'. Groups that refused to take part included Action on Smoking and Health which said, 'It is quite possible and likely that well-meaning engagement with BAT will strengthen a public relations exercise, lend credibility to worthless and damaging initiatives, and work against public health and sustainable development'.

In BAT's report the chairman directly asked the question which has puzzled many an observer, 'Can a business be socially responsible if its core product can harm people?'

BAT's chairman firmly believes the answer is yes, saying, 'Our products pose risks to health, and if a business is managing such products, we believe it is all the more important that it does so responsibly. We acknowledge the significant responsibilities that go with our business, and we are working hard to demonstrate that we are carrying them out … We do not see Corporate Social Responsibility as about 'PR spin' or window dressing. It is about ensuring best practice in all aspects of our business conduct. We are committed to working to build trust, to listening and responding, and to balancing contrasting stakeholder expectations with each other and with our proper commercial goals.'

Martin Broughton, Chairman, British American Tobacco plc, *The Financial Times,* July 2002

the pollution of the environment can all be very damaging to firms. The fact that consumers and investors are becoming more demanding and have set higher ethical and social standards for organisations means that more firms have chosen to adopt the stakeholder approach. However, there are a number of companies such as the John Lewis Partnership which pioneered this approach long before the term 'stakeholder' was even thought of. Many of the origins of this approach go back to the paternalistic style of companies such as Rowntree and Cadbury in the nineteenth century. These family companies were the major employers in an area and built a reputation for treating customers, employees and suppliers with great respect.

**47.4** ## Can a firm satisfy all stakeholder groups?

According to the shareholder concept a firm's responsibilities to other groups directly conflicts with its responsibilities to shareholders. If the firm tried to help the local community, for example, this would take funds away from the shareholders. Similarly, more rewards for the owners would mean less resources for employees. In the shareholder view all these different groups are competing for a fixed set of rewards. If one group has a larger slice of the profits this leaves less for others.

Under the stakeholder approach, however, it is believed that all groups can benefit at the same time. By working with its various stakeholder groups the firm can generate more profit. Imagine, for example, that more rewards are given to employees out of profits. In the short run this may reduce rewards for the shareholder. But in the long run it may generate more rewards for everyone. Better quality work can lead to improved customer loyalty and therefore less marketing expenditure to achieve the same level of sales. Similarly, by building up better relations with suppliers the firm can produce better quality goods leading to more orders and more business for both parties.

ISSUES FOR **analysis**

When answering a case study or essay question it might be useful to consider the following points:

- An increasing number of firms claim to be adopting the stakeholder approach. They recognise their responsibilities to groups other than the shareholders and are taking their views into account when making decisions.
- It should be remembered, though, that the claims made by firms may largely be for public relations reasons. Companies should be judged on what they do, not what they say.
- Even firms which genuinely mean to change will find many managers stuck in the previous culture of profit/shareholder first. Changing to a stakeholder culture will take years.
- The stakeholder approach can lead to many benefits for organisations, such as attracting new customers, attracting and

keeping employees and building a strong long-term corporate image. However, the firm may not be able to fulfil the objectives of all groups. Meeting the needs of one group may conflict with the needs of others.

- The stakeholder approach may prove to be a fad. When the profits of firms fall, for example, they sometimes decide that short-term profit is much more important than obligations to other groups. So a sharp recession would be likely to make every business more profit/shareholder focused.

However, it may not be possible to meet the needs of all interest groups. Firms must decide on the extent to which they take stakeholders into account. Given their limited resources and other obligations, managers must decide on their priorities. In difficult times it may well be that the need for short-term profit overcomes the demands of various stakeholder groups. It would be naïve to ignore the fact that TV consumer programmes such as BBC's *Watchdog* keep exposing business malpractice. Even if progress is being made in general, there are still many firms which persist in seeing short-term profit as the sole business objective.

## 47.5 Stakeholding
### an evaluation

In recent years there has been much greater interest in the idea that firms should pay attention to their **social responsibilities**. Increasingly firms are being asked to consider and justify their actions towards a wide range of groups rather than just their shareholders. Managers are expected to take into account the interests and opinions of numerous internal and external groups before they make a decision. This social responsibility often makes good business sense. If you ignore your stakeholder groups you are vulnerable to pressure group action and may well lose employees and investors. If, however, you build your social responsibility into your marketing this can create new customers and save you money through activities such as recycling.

**KEY terms**

**pressure group** – a group of people with a common interest who try to further that interest, e.g. Greenpeace.

**shareholder** – an owner of a company.

**shareholder value** – the 1990s' term widely used by company chairmen and chairwomen which means little more than the attempt to maximise the company's share price.

**social responsibilities** – duties towards stakeholder groups which the firm may or may not accept.

**stakeholder** – an individual or group which affects and is affected by an organisation.

**47.6 Workbook**

## Exercises

### A. REVISION QUESTIONS
*(20 marks; 45 minutes)*

Read the unit, then answer.

1 What is meant by a 'stakeholder'? (2)
2 Distinguish between the 'shareholder concept' and the 'stakeholder' concept. (3)
3 Some people believe that an increasing number of firms are now trying to meet their social responsibilities. Explain why this might be the case. (3)
4 Outline two responsibilities a firm may have to :
  **a** its employees (4)
  **b** its customers (4)
  **c** the local community. (4)

### B. REVISION EXERCISES

**B1 Data Response**

**Shell's Business Principles**

Shell is one the first UK companies to produce a statement of its business principles. The company recognises five areas of responsibility. These are:

- To shareholders – to protect shareholders' investment, and provide an acceptable return.
- To customers – to win and maintain customers by developing and providing products and services which offer value in terms of price, quality, safety and environmental impact.

- To employees – to respect the human rights of their employees, to provide their employees with good and safe conditions of work, and good and competitive terms and conditions of service, to promote the development and best use of human talent and equal opportunity employment and to encourage the involvement of employees in the planning and direction for their work, and in the application of these principles within their company.
- To those with whom they do business – to seek mutually beneficial relationships with contractors, suppliers and in joint ventures.
- To society – to conduct business as responsible corporate members of society, to observe the laws of countries in which they operate, to express support for fundamental human rights in line with the legitimate role of business and to give proper regard to health, safety and the environment consistent with their commitment to contribute to sustainable development.

Source: Adapted from *Shell Statement of General Business Principles*

**Questions** *(30 marks; 35 minutes)*
1 How is Shell making use of the 'stakeholder' concept? *(4)*
2 Why might Shell have published a statement of its business principles? *(8)*
3 Consider the possible implications for Shell of producing a statement of business principles. *(8)*
4 Discuss whether the responsibilities identified by Shell may conflict with each other. *(10)*

**B2 Case Study**
Sandler plc produces a range of paints which are sold in the major DIY stores in the UK under the brand name Lifestyles. The company has had a very successful few years and expects demand to be much higher than capacity in the next few years. The company has considered two options:

- extending capacity at the existing site, or
- moving to a new purpose-built factory 60 miles away.

Although the second option is more expensive initially, building a completely new factory is estimated to be more profitable in the long run.

The problem is that the chosen site is close to an area of natural beauty and the firm is concerned that protesters might object to it building there. Also, the closure of the existing factory at Headington will lead to serious job losses in the area. The company has been based at Headington for over 50 years and has worked well with the community. Telling the workforce and local authorities will not be easy. On the other hand it will be creating jobs at the new location, which is an area of high unemployment, whereas Headington is booming at the moment.

**Questions** *(40 marks; 60 minutes)*
1 Identify four stakeholder groups which may be affected if Sandler closes the Headington factory. Explain briefly how each would be affected. *(8)*
2 Should Sandler plc close the Headington factory? Fully justify your answer. *(12)*
3 If the firm decides to close the Headington factory should it tell the employees immediately or wait until nearer the time? Explain your reasoning. *(10)*
4 Outline the difficulties Sandler might face with stakeholders other than the workforce if the decision is taken to move to the new site. *(10)*

# BUSINESS ETHICS

DEFINITION
Ethics are the moral principles that should underpin decision making. A decision made on ethical grounds might reject the most profitable solution in favour of one of greater benefit to society as well as the firm.

## 48.1 What are business ethics?

Ethics can be defined as a code of behaviour considered morally correct. Our individual ethics are shaped by a number of factors including the values and behaviour of our parents or guardians, those of our religion, our peers and the society in which we live and work.

Business ethics can provide moral guidelines for the conduct of business affairs. This is based on some assertion of what is right and what is wrong. An ethical decision means doing what is morally right. It is not a matter of scientifically calculating costs, benefit and profit. Most actions and activities in the business world have an ethical dimension. This has been highlighted recently in relation to whole industries (such as cigarettes) and to businesses which use cheap labour in less developed countries.

Two major influences shape the moral behaviour of businesses. First, an organisation is comprised of individuals. All of these have their own moral codes, their own values and principles. Naturally they bring these to bear on the decisions that they have to make as a part of their working lives. Second, businesses have cultures that shape corporate ethical standards. These two factors combine to determine the behaviour of businesses in a variety of circumstances having an ethical dimension.

The extract below illustrates a situation in which the corporate culture may well be dominant. Texas Instruments prepares its employees to take ethical decisions at all levels within the organisation. If unsure, employees are urged to seek advice from their line manager rather than make a decision that may be unethical.

## 48.2 Business ethics and business objectives

A useful starting point may be to consider business objectives in relation to ethical behaviour. We can pose the question: Why do businesses exist? For many businesses the answer would be 'to make the maximum profit possible in order to satisfy the owners of the business'.

Some notable academics support this view. Milton Friedman, a famous American economist, holds the view that all businesses should use the resources available to them as efficiently as possible. Friedman argues that making the highest possible profit creates the maximum possible wealth to the benefit of the whole society.

Friedman's view, however, ignores the fact that many individuals and groups have an interest in each and every business – the stakeholders. We could argue that to meet the demands of stakeholders means that a business has to take morally correct decisions. The following scenarios illustrate circumstances in which maximising profits conflicts with the interests of stakeholders.

**Scenario 1:**
Tobacco companies have responded to declining sales in the Western world by increasing production and sales in Asia and Latin America. Consumers in these countries are less knowledgeable about the dangers of smoking and more likely to purchase potentially harmful products.

### Ethics is the Cornerstone of TI

*Our reputation at TI depends upon all of the decisions we make and all the actions we take personally each day. Our values define how we will evaluate our decisions and actions ... and how we will conduct our business. We are working in a difficult and demanding, ever-changing business environment. Together we are building a work environment on the foundation of integrity, innovation and commitment. Together we are moving our company into a new century ... one good decision at a time. We are prepared to make the tough decisions or take the critical actions ... and do it right. Our high standards have rewarded us with an enviable reputation in today's marketplace ... a reputation of integrity, honesty and trustworthiness. That strong ethical reputation is a vital asset ... and each of us shares a personal responsibility to protect, to preserve and to enhance it. Our reputation is a strong but silent partner in all business relationships. By understanding and applying the values presented on the following pages, each of us can say to ourselves and to others, 'TI is a good company, and one reason is that I am a part of it'.*

*Know what is right. Value what is right. Do what is right.*

*Source: Texas Instruments website, October 2002*

## TOBACCO INDUSTRY SEEKS TO AVOID BAN

In March 2003, after a 30-year battle, cigarette advertising was finally banned in Britain. But the head of a cancer charity criticised the British tobacco industry right up to that point, for continually seeking ways to get round the legislation.

Allegedly the tobacco industry planned to use direct mail to communicate with households to encourage smokers to purchase tobacco products or to switch brands. Professor Gerard Hastings, of Cancer Research UK, said the tobacco industry lobbied government to exempt direct mail from any new legislation.

Unsurprisingly, the UK tobacco industry opposes the legislation. It believes that cigarette advertising raises no ethical questions because adults can make their own minds up about smoking.

**Scenario 2:**

Should a company seek to minimise its production costs to provide the greatest possible return to its shareholders or should it consider the wider community, particularly the less well-off members of that community? The In Business section below focuses on the activities of Monsanto, a biotechnology company. Following a merger in 1998 Monsanto is one of the largest corporations in the world and wields immense power.

## MONSANTO GUILTY OF POLLUTING RIVER

A decision by a court in Alabama in the United States in 2002 proved that the law has a long memory as well as a long arm. The court found bio-technology company Monsanto guilty of dumping many thousands of tons of chemicals into rivers near the town of Anniston during the period 1935–1971. The company only halted production of PCBs after complaints from many different groups.

The court's verdict means that Monsanto is likely to be sued by many local residents who claim that the company's actions in discharging polychlorinated biphenyls into the water system have resulted in severe illnesses including cancer.

## 48.3 Encouraging ethical behaviour

A number high profile accidents in the late 1980s led to calls for businesses to act in more socially responsible ways and to put moral considerations before profits. Incidents such as the disastrous fire on the North Sea oil rig Piper Alpha in 1988 prompted demands for greater ethical accountability. The pressures on UK businesses increased as a series of investigations exposed fraudulent activities at a number of high profile companies, including the Bank of Commerce and Credit International and Guinness.

This move towards changing corporate cultures was strengthened as a result of the report of the Cadbury Committee in 1992. One of the recommendations of the Committee was to reinforce the role of non-executive directors. It was hoped that these independent directors would encourage a more ethical culture in corporate decision making. Non-executive directors do not take an active role in the management of the company and are well placed to control unethical practices.

Changing corporate cultures is not easy to achieve even when external pressures are encouraging such change. Texas Instruments (profiled earlier) took the view that ethical behaviour began at the grassroots of the company. Its management contended that for a business to behave ethically all of its employees must behave ethically. The quote below highlights one of the ways in which the management team at Texas Instruments endeavours to create an ethical culture within the business.

> '*Is the action legal?*
> *Does it comply with our values?*
> *If you do it, will you feel bad?*
> *How will it look in the newspaper?*
> *If you know it's wrong, don't do it.*
> *If you are not sure, ask.*
> *Keep asking until you get an answer.*'
>
> **Source: Texas Instruments website, March 1998**

Texas Instruments issues this advice to all employees on a business card.

By attempting to ensure that all staff within the organisation behave in an agreed ethical manner, companies seek to avoid the potential conflict of ethics and delegation. In organisations where the culture of ethical behaviour does not extend beyond senior (and perhaps middle) managers, delegation brings risks. Delegation in such circumstances may result in junior staff taking decisions which may be regarded as immoral or unethical.

Other companies have operated on ethical principles since their inception. The Body Shop International is recognised as operating in a socially responsible and ethical manner and uses this as a major element of its marketing. That ethical behaviour is firmly rooted in

The Body Shop is indicated by this extract from its mission statement:

> *'To meaningfully contribute to local, national and international communities in which we trade, by adopting a code of conduct which ensures care, honesty, fairness and respect.'*

## 48.4 Ethical codes of practice

As a response to consumer expectations and competitive pressures, businesses have introduced **ethical codes** of practice. These are intended to improve the behaviour and image of a business. The extract below highlights the extent to which UK businesses have appreciated the importance of being seen to behave ethically. Furthermore, the very existence of the Institute of Business Ethics is evidence of the growing importance of this aspect of business behaviour.

---

*The Institute of Business Ethics*

*The aims of the Institute are to emphasise the essentially ethical nature of wealth creation, to encourage the highest standards of behaviour by companies, to publicise the best ethical practices and to demonstrate that business ethics involve positive initiatives as well as constraints.*

*A Report on a Survey on Corporate Codes of Conduct*
*By Simon Webley and Martin Le Jeune*
*Executive Summary*

*Every three years the IBE surveys larger companies known to have codes of ethics/conduct/business principles. The research asks about the use they make of these codes and their views about current business ethics issues. The main findings of the latest survey were as follows:*
*In 2001 (compared to 1998) more larger companies:*
- *provide a code of ethics for their employees*
- *provide procedures for asking questions in a confidential manner*
- *include conforming with the code in employment contracts*
- *show interest in ethical/social audits*
- *use their codes to 'give staff guidance' rather than for 'enhancing reputation'*
- *use the intranet to deliver ethics awareness and training.*
*But fewer:*
- *are training staff in business ethics*
- *are reporting on ethics in Annual Reports*
- *have a process for revision of their code.*

---

An ethical code of practice is a document setting out the way a business believes its employees should respond to situations that challenge their integrity or social responsibility.

The precise focus of the code will depend on the business concerned. Banks may concentrate on honesty, and chemical firms on pollution control. It has proved difficult to produce meaningful, comprehensive codes. The National Westminster Bank, for example, took two years to produce its 10-page document. The typical code might include sections on:

- personal integrity – in dealings with suppliers and in handling the firm's resources
- corporate integrity – such as forbidding collusion with competitors and forbidding predatory pricing
- **environmental responsibility** – highlighting a duty to minimise pollution emissions and maximise recycling
- social responsibility – to provide products of genuine value that are promoted with honesty and dignity.

A common feature of ethical codes of practice is that companies publicise them. This is because they believe that being seen to behave ethically is an important element of the marketing strategy of many businesses.

Critics of ethical codes believe them to be public relations exercises rather than genuine attempts to change business behaviour. What is not in doubt is that the proof of their effectiveness can only be measured by how firms actually behave, not by what they write or say.

Public outcry in the wake of the Piper Alpha disaster forced companies to reassess their ethical codes of practice (© Associated Press)

## 48.5 Pressure groups and ethics

The activities of **pressure groups** affect all types of businesses and most aspects of their behaviour. Most of the high profile pressure groups are multi-cause and operate internationally. Greenpeace is one of the best known pressure groups and lobbies businesses to restrict behaviour which might adversely affect the environment. Other single-cause pressure groups exist to control the activities of businesses in one particular sphere of operations.

- Action on Smoking and Health (ASH) is an international organisation established to oppose the production and smoking of tobacco. It publicises actions of tobacco companies that may be considered to be unethical. ASH frequently focuses on the long-term effects of tobacco on the consumers of the product.
- Compassion in World Farming is a UK-based pressure group campaigning specifically for an end to the factory farming of animals. The group engages in political lobbying and high profile publicity campaigns in an attempt to end the suffering endured by many farm animals.

### Business IN

### PRESSURE GROUP TARGETS McDONALD'S

McDonald's, the multinational fast food chain, is facing calls to introduce common animal welfare standards in all its operations worldwide. The company currently operates high welfare standards in the United States and Britain, but operates lower standards in the other 119 countries in which it trades.

An American pressure group People for the Ethical Treatment of Animals (PETA) has organised a resolution at McDonald's 2002 Annual General Meeting. The resolution, which is opposed by McDonald's Board, requires the burger chain to operate the highest animal welfare standards throughout the world.

If public opinion and pressure group activities force firms to take the publicity impact of their decisions into account, this may change the decisions made. This would not mean, however, that the firm was becoming more ethically minded. An ethical decision means doing what is morally right; it is not a matter of scientifically calculating costs and benefits.

## 48.6 The ethical balance sheet

### ADVANTAGES OF ETHICAL BEHAVIOUR

Companies receive many benefits from behaving, or being seen to behave, in an ethical manner. These are discussed below.

**Marketing advantages:** Many modern consumers expect to purchase goods and services from organisations that operate in ways that they consider morally correct. Some consumers are unwilling to buy products from businesses that behave in any other way. This trend has been accelerated by the rise of consumerism. This has meant that consumers have become increasingly well informed and are prepared to think carefully before spending their money.

Some companies have developed their ethical behaviour into a unique selling point (USP). They base their marketing campaigns on these perceived differences. An example of a high profile company adopting this strategy is The Body Shop International.

A key point is that not only does the company seek to support relatively poor communities in the less developed world, but it publicises these actions. By creating a caring image through its marketing The Body Shop hopes to gain increased sales.

Companies also gain considerable public relations advantages from ethical behaviour. Once again this can help enhance the image of the business with positive implications for sales and profits.

In 2002 the Co-operative Bank announced a 12% increase in pre-tax profits to £107.5 million whilst

### Business IN

### STARBUCKS TO SELL 'ETHICAL' COFFEE

In 2002 the Starbucks coffee chain took the decision to sell Fairtrade coffee in the UK. Farmers who grow Fairtrade coffee work in co-operatives and operate high environmental and ethical standards. This ensures that the communities who grow the coffee beans receive fair rewards.

The Fairtrade Foundation said the move would provide excellent publicity for its coffee, benefiting the environment and the coffee communities in the producer nations, even though the amount sold would be small. Due to global overproduction, the price of coffee beans dropped about 70% last year, causing severe economic and social hardship in coffee growing countries.

Starbucks, which buys about 1% of the global coffee crop, will promote its latest addition to its product range strongly.

confirming the maintenance of its ethical principles. The bank's chief executive, Martyn Pedelty, commented that the ethical position adopted by the company had attracted many customers from the wealthy A, B and C1 social groups. These customers held large, and profitable, balances with the bank.

**Positive effects on the workforce:** Firms who adopt ethical practices may experience benefits in relation to their workforce. They may expect to recruit staff who are better qualified and motivated. Employees can be expected to respond positively to working for a business with a positive ethical image and this can lead to greater competition for employment with such companies. A recent survey revealed that 75% of The Body Shop's UK employees were 'proud' to work for the company. Equally, employees may be less likely to leave employment because of dissatisfaction with their job. All of these factors can help to reduce the employment costs incurred by the business.

Creating an ethical culture within a business can also improve employee motivation. This may be part of a wider policy towards employee empowerment.

### DISADVANTAGES OF ETHICAL BEHAVIOUR

Inevitably, a number of disadvantages can result from businesses adopting ethical policies.

**Reduced profitability:** It is likely that any business adopting an ethical policy will face higher costs. It may also be that the company has to turn down the opportunity to invest in projects offering potentially high returns. Exploiting cheap labour in less developed countries may be immoral but it can be very profitable. Equally, The Body Shop International's commitment to purchasing its supplies from sustainable sources means that it incurs higher costs than if it purchased raw materials without regard to the environment.

Businesses adopting an ethical policy may also incur additional costs in training their staff to behave ethically in their decision making. Similarly, adapting production processes to protect the environment may result in increased costs of production.

It is possible to argue that, depending on the nature of the business and its market, profits may not be reduced as a consequence of adopting an ethical policy. A premium price may be possible, or new niche markets may be uncovered by a business marketing itself as ethical.

**Conflict with existing policies:** Introducing an ethical policy can create internal divisions within the business. A business with a tradition of delegation and empowerment might experience problems introducing an ethical policy. Staff may perceive the implementation as autocratic and a move towards centralisation. They could argue that such a concept conflicts with the philosophy of delegation. As a consequence they may resist the policy.

A company may also experience difficulty in spreading the message in a company which is decentralised. Even if employees view an ethical policy favourably, it may be difficult to implement it into everyday activities. Almost certainly considerable training will be required.

## 48.7 Ethical behaviour – future developments

It has been suggested that most of the interest in business ethics and its development has been in universities and colleges. However, there is evidence available to suggest that ethical awareness is becoming more firmly rooted in business practice. A number of arguments can be set out to support the view that ethics will be of increasing importance to businesses throughout the world.

**The adoption of ethical practices:** By 1998 over half the major businesses in the UK had implemented an ethical code of practice. The equivalent figure for 1988 was 18%. Over 30% of chairmen or chief executives see ethical practices and behaviour as their responsibility. Although everyone in a business needs to conform to an ethical code of practice, it is only senior managers who have the power to bring about the necessary changes in corporate culture.

**The commercial success of high profile 'ethical' companies:** Companies that are seen to have high ethical standards have enjoyed considerable commercial success over recent years. The Co-operative is well known for its ethical stance and has enjoyed rising profits since the mid 1990s. Similarly, Mitsubishi has benefited financially from its highly publicised decision to use sustainable resources in its factories.

A new ethical business was launched in October 2002 amid much publicity. The 'not-for-profit' Charity Bank will provide cheap loans to charities with no access to mainstream lending facilities. Investors in the new Bank will receive a flat rate of interest of 2% and will use any surpluses to support charities. The launch of The Charity Bank builds upon the commercial success of other ethical businesses.

**Public expectations:** The success of the 'ethical' companies mentioned above is evidence that the public respond favourably to a positive ethical stance. Consumers are likely to become better informed and better educated about products, processes and companies. They will demand products and services that do not pollute, exploit, harm or waste. Successful companies will need to respond positively to the demands of the 'new' consumer.

Cynics might well argue that many businesses may adopt so-called ethical practices simply to project a good public image. Such organisations would produce an ethical code of practice and derive positive publicity from a small number of 'token' ethical actions whilst their underlying business culture remained unchanged. Such businesses, it is argued, would not alter the way in which the majority of their employees behaved, and decisions would continue to be taken with profits (rather than morals) in mind.

This may be a realistic scenario for a number of businesses. But it is also a dangerous strategy in a society where increasing numbers of people have access to information. Certainly the media would be looking to publicise any breaches in a business's ethical code of practice. Being revealed as hypocritical is always a difficult position to defend.

Among the key issues for analysis are:

● What is the underlying intent? If a decision has been made on the basis of profit, it is not truly ethical. An ethical decision is made on the basis of what is morally correct.

● What are the circumstances? A profit-focused decision which might be considered questionable in good times, might be justifiable when times are hard. For example, a firm threatened with closure would be more justified in spending the minimum possible on pollution controls.

● What are the trade-offs? In many cases the key ethical question is profit versus morality. In others, though, the trade-offs are more complex. Making a coal mine close to 100% safe for the workers would be so expensive as to make the mine uneconomic – thereby costing the miners their jobs.

## 48.8 Business ethics
### an evaluation

Evaluation involves making some sort of informed judgement. Businesses are required to make a judgement about the benefits of ethical behaviour. Their key question may well be whether ethics are profitable or not.

In this unit, convincing arguments have been put together as to why this might be the case. For example, ethical behaviour can give a clear competitive advantage on which marketing activities can be based. However, disadvantages may lurk behind an ethical approach. The policy can be the cause of conflict and may be expected to reduce profits.

Operating an ethical policy gives a USP if none of your competitors has taken the plunge. Being first may result in gaining market share before others catch up. In these circumstances an ethical code may enhance profitability. It can also be an attractive option in a

market where businesses and products are virtually indistinguishable. In these circumstances a USP can be most valuable.

Ethical policies may add to profits if additional costs are relatively small. Thus for a financial institution to adopt an ethical policy may be less costly than that for a chemical manufacturer. Clearly companies need to weigh increased costs against the marketing (and revenue) benefits which might result.

Ethical policies are more likely to be profitable if consumers are informed and concerned about ethical issues. It may be that businesses can develop new niche markets as a result of an ethical stance.

**KEY terms**

**business culture** – the culture of an organisation is the (perhaps unwritten) code that affects the attitudes, decision making and management style of its staff.

**environmental responsibility** – this involves businesses choosing to adopt processes and procedures which minimise harmful effects on the environment. For example, placing filters on coal-fired power stations to reduce emissions.

**ethical code** – document setting out the way a company believes its employees should respond to situations that challenge their integrity or social responsibility.

**ethical investment** – a stock market investment based on a restricted list of firms that are seen as ethically sound.

**pressure groups** – groups of people with common interests who act together to further that interest.

**stakeholder interests** – stakeholders are groups such as shareholders and consumers who have a direct interest in a business. These interests frequently cause conflict, for example shareholders may want higher profits whilst consumers want environmentally friendly products, which are more costly.

**voluntary codes of practice** – these are methods of working recommended by appropriate committees and approved by the government. They have no legal authority. For example, much advertising is controlled by voluntary codes of practice.

# Exercises

## A. REVISION QUESTIONS

*(25 marks; 60 minutes)*

Read the unit, then answer:

1 Define the term 'business ethics'. *(3)*
2 State two factors that may shape the moral behaviour of businesses. *(2)*
3 Outline one circumstance in which a company might face an ethical dilemma. *(4)*
4 Explain the difference between a business behaving legally and a business behaving ethically. *(4)*
5 Why might decisions made upon the basis of a moral code (ethics) conflict with profit? *(4)*
6 Look at each of the following business actions and decide whether they were motivated by ethical considerations. Briefly explain your reasoning each time.
   a An advertising agency refusing to accept business from cigarette producers. *(2)*
   b A private hospital refusing to accept an ill elderly person whose only income is the state pension. *(2)*
   c A small baker refusing to accept supplies of genetically modified flour. *(2)*
   d A small baker refusing to deliver to a restaurant known locally as a racist employer. *(2)*

## B. REVISION EXERCISES

### B1 Stimulus Questions

#### BAe in Export Drive for Controversial Jet

> British Aerospace is looking for overseas orders worth over £2.5 billion for the Hawk trainer fighter. This aircraft is at the centre of the controversy over exports to Indonesia. John Weston, managing director of the company's military business division, said that the export business was worth £20 billion and created a large number of jobs in the UK.
>
> The company, Britain's biggest exporter, has been in close contact with the government over its decision to introduce a more ethical approach to military business overseas, but has no plans to change tactics.
>
> He said: 'We have always had an ethical guidelines policy from government to government. We take them very seriously.' Mr Weston said the group is waiting to assess the impact of the latest initiative taken by Robin Cook, the foreign secretary. He added: 'We are not rushing to make any amendments to our business plan for sales overseas.'
>
> The company has discussions with the Indonesian government about new business

> but is conscious of competition. Indonesia is in the market for surface-to-air missiles that could be supplied by Matra BAe, the joint French venture.
>
> So far BAe has supplied Indonesia with 60 Hawk aircraft and starts delivery of the final batch of 14 this year. The Hawk has won considerable business around the world, and BAe is involved in 14 marketing campaigns to attract new business.

#### Questions *(30 marks; 35 minutes)*

1 Explain the term '…a more ethical approach…'. *(3)*
2 Explain the ethical dilemma that British Aerospace might face in exporting fighter aircraft to a less developed nation. *(6)*
3 British Aerospace presents itself as a very moral company. Analyse the factors that might shape a moral business culture. *(9)*
4 Some business analysts have observed that the government's ethical policy will make firms such as British Aerospace less profitable. Discuss whether this is likely to be true. *(12)*

### B2 Stimulus Questions

#### Turning Iceland Green

> In 2001 the managing director of the Iceland Group, Malcolm Walker, resigned. Walker had established a reputation as one of the UK's greenest entrepreneurs and introduced an ethical code to the company. Walker built the Iceland Group from a roadside stall into a chain of 760 supermarkets. For many years the company was successful in the highly competitive supermarket field and enjoyed rising sales.
>
> The success of Iceland was based upon the increasing numbers of UK homes with a freezer. The company's stores sold predominantly frozen products, initially own brand, later other brands.
>
> Iceland first established its ethical credentials by refusing to sell tobacco products because of their potential to damage consumers' health. It was the first national food store to ban genetically modified products from own-label produce, much to the delight of environmental pressure groups. In 1999 the firm banned artificial colours and flavours from own-brand foods. And in 2000 the company bought 40% of the world's organic vegetable crop to become UK super-

**48.9 Workbook**

market leader in the pesticide-free field.

In 2001 Iceland suffered a slump in the sales of organic food and blamed its poor trading record on this. Malcolm Walker's downfall was sealed by his controversial sale of his shares in Iceland five weeks before the company announced a slump in profits.

Source: Adapted from www.news.bbc.co.uk. 31/1/01

**Questions** *(25 marks; 30 minutes)*

1 What is meant by the following terms:
  a 'ethical code'
  b 'pressure groups'? *(4)*
2 Explain one way in which the Iceland Group might encourage its staff to behave in an ethical manner *(4)*
3 Analyse two reasons why the Iceland Group may have chosen to adopt an ethical stance. *(8)*
4 Discuss whether Malcolm Walker's resignation suggests that ethical supermarkets are not viable in the long-term. *(9)*

# TECHNOLOGICAL CHANGE

Technological change involves developments both in terms of what is being produced by a firm, and how it is being made.

## 49.1 Introduction

Technology is changing at an extremely fast rate. New products and new processes are being developed all the time. In markets such as computers and mobile phones hundreds of new products are being launched every month. Almost the minute you buy the latest CD player, PC, mobile phone or fax machine you know it is about to be outdated! Firms face similar problems. If you visit a business and ask about its equipment you will inevitably find that the last piece of machinery it bought is already less efficient than the newest model on the market, which is probably available at a much lower price. Whatever you buy, whatever technology you use, the chances are someone somewhere is working on an improved version.

This rate of change seems to be getting ever faster. Product development times are getting quicker and, consequently, more products are getting to the market in less time. The result is that the typical product life cycle is getting shorter. Naturally this creates serious problems for firms. With more and more products being developed the chances of any one product succeeding is reduced. Even if it does succeed its life cycle is likely to be relatively short. Given the ever-higher quality demanded by customers firms are having to spend more on developing products but have less time to recoup their investment.

One of the main reasons for the rapid growth of technology is technology itself. The development of **computer-aided design** (CAD) and **computer-aided manufacture** (CAM) has enabled even faster development of other products and processes. Technology feeds off itself and generates even more ideas and innovations. This rapid rate of change creates both threats and opportunities for firms. The threats are clear. Firms which do not adopt competitive technology will:

- struggle to keep their unit costs down
- be unable to provide goods or services of sufficient quality relative to their competitors.

Imagine if you were still trying to sell typewriters in the UK against the latest Personal Computer, for example.

Technology can certainly make life a great deal easier for firms. Just think of how slow it would be to

### COMPUTER AIDED DESIGN

When Peter Fenn started Fenn Tool Ltd in 1982 it had 3 employees, was based in an old church hall and imported quality machine tools from Switzerland and Austria. It sold them to UK customers at competitive prices. Over time the business grew, moving into larger premises, taking on more staff and opening an office in Ireland. A few years ago the company realised there was a market for specialist cutting and grinding tools, especially in the aerospace and telecommunications industry. The typical waiting time to get these produced and imported into the UK was 6 to 10 weeks. This meant customers were kept waiting and so lost valuable production time.

After much discussion and worrying about the risks involved, Fenn Tool decided to spend £250,000 on a computer-aided design package linked to a computer-aided manufacturing system. This used up much of the firm's available capital, but cut customer lead times to just 48 hours from order to finished product. With its new equipment Fenn Tool has complete flexibility of design, and tools can be made in a variety of metals and finishes that will do the job more efficiently than a standard drill or cutter. The company has since bought a second machine and has been awarded the Parcel Force Worldwide Small Business of the Year and the prestigious Manufacturing Industry Achievement Award.

work out all of a large company's accounts by hand instead of using a computer spreadsheet. If one company avoids the latest technology while its rivals adopt it, it is likely to suffer real problems with competitiveness. The rivals may be able to offer lower prices or substantially better or faster service standards.

## 49.2 Problems of introducing new technology

Unfortunately, because of the costs, it is not always possible for a firm to acquire the technology it wants. New technology can represent a significant investment for a firm and cannot always be undertaken as and when the managers feel like it. This is particularly true when technology is changing at such a rate that any investment may be out of date very rapidly. The difficulty is knowing when to buy. Buy too late and you may well have lost the competitive advantage – your rivals will already be producing better quality, more cost-competitive work. Buy too early and you may find yourself committed to technology which is no longer relevant. Consumers who invested in Betamax videos, for example, found they were soon replaced by the present day VHS system.

Technology also creates problems within the firm. First, the managers must consider how it links up with what they have already. It is all too easy to buy one piece of equipment only to find it is not compatible with other parts of your production process. It is surprising how many firms have various elements of technology which do not match up. For example, a retailer may have scanning equipment which cannot feed information through to the manufacturer. Or some parts of the organisation may be on a computer network while others are not. Within factories you often find 'islands of **automation**'. Parts of the process are automated while others are not.

Second, technological change can create industrial relations problems. In some cases new technology may mean some employees lose their jobs. This often happens with relatively routine jobs such as repetitively cutting, pressing or moving items. In other cases people will still keep their jobs but will have to retrain or learn new skills to be able to use the technology successfully. This in itself may cause friction. Some employees will no doubt welcome the opportunity to use technology and regard retraining as a challenge. Others may be worried about their ability to cope. Imagine that you are very good at using one particular type of software, for example, and someone asks you to learn a new way of doing things. You may wonder what the point of changing is and you may be worried that you will not be able to cope quite so well with the new system. In this situation people will need reassuring. They will need to understand why the new technology is being introduced, and be trained and supported during the whole process of adjustment.

There will always be some people who object to change because they like things the way they are. There will also be some who object because they will actually be worse off. For example, they may have to transfer to a department headed by someone they dislike. In many cases, however, people object to change because they are scared by it or do not understand why it is needed. The management of technological change, therefore, needs careful handling. The process must be done at the right pace and employees must be involved wherever possible.

Resistance to change will come from:

- people who do not understand why it is necessary
- people who will be worse off (e.g. they no longer have the right skills)
- people who are worried about its effects, possibly unnecessarily
- people who disagree with it – they understand it, but are convinced it is a bad idea.

Firms must also consider the costs involved in training employees to be able to use new technology. These costs will include the direct costs of on-the-job or off-the-job training as well as the opportunity cost of the output lost while they are learning new skills. The firms also run the risk of training staff in the latest technology, only to have them leave for better paid jobs elsewhere.

### Business IN — ROBOTS

The purchase of robots in the UK continues to increase as more firms automate their production processes. The number of robots has risen, particularly in the automotive and engineering sectors. These areas were hit by the strength of the pound increasing the pressure on them to become more efficient. In 2001 around 2,000 robots were purchased in the UK; 75% of these were purchased in the automotive industry. By contrast, numbers bought in the plastics and rubber industries fell as production in these areas has been switched to lower cost locations overseas. In total the UK robot population is around 13,500. This is well behind Germany and Japan which have a much longer tradition of automation.

## 49.3 Benefits from introducing new technology

Technological change can provide enormous opportunities for firms. There is a tendency to think of technology as something which leads to mass unemployment. In fact it is an aid to us all. Imagine what life would be like without televisions, phones, videos, cashpoints, CDs or credit cards, for example. Similarly, technology makes working life considerably easier. Routine jobs can be replaced, work can generally be speeded up and problem solving made easier. Just think what it would be like solving some of your business problems without a calculator.

Technology also creates new markets. Telephone banking, computer games, e-mail, CD-ROMs, DVDs and Eurostar are all relatively recent developments which we now take for granted. These markets create huge opportunities for firms that are able to exploit them and for people with skills that are in demand.

## INTERNET USAGE

One of the most significant technological developments in recent years is the Internet. The use of the Internet is revolutionising the way firms communicate and the way they do business. The opportunities continue to grow as more people access the Internet. In the UK, for example, the number of regular home web users increased from just over 11 million to 16.5 million in 2002. The total number of people in the UK with Internet connections rose to around 30 million – around half the population. Globally, there are now 241 million active home web users.

As with any change, technological developments create potential gains and potential threats. Whether a particular firm wins or loses depends on its ability to predict this change and its ability to react. In the 1980s the American computer giant IBM provided a classic example of the dangers in failing to keep close to the market. It failed to anticipate the switch away from large mainframe computers to smaller desktop models and home computers. This meant it was very late to enter the home computer market and missed the chance to dominate it as an early entrant. By the time IBM appreciated the potential of the personal computer market it faced intense competition and had lost 'first mover' advantage. As technological change continues, firms must monitor their environments closely, look for the opportunities and protect themselves against the threats.

### ISSUES FOR analysis

When answering questions about new technology, bear in mind the following:

- Technology creates both opportunities and threats. It both destroys and creates new markets; it can provide a firm with a competitive advantage or make its product or service obsolete.
- The introduction of technology needs to be carefully managed. Managers have to consider issues such as the compatibility of the new technology with existing equipment, the financial implications and how best to introduce it.
- New technology can place additional stress on employees who might be worried about their ability to cope with the change.

Whether new technology provides an opportunity or a threat for an organisation depends on the technology itself, the resources of the firm and the management's attitude to change. Used effectively new technology can reduce costs, increase flexibility and speed up the firm's response time. In all areas of the firm, from marketing to operations, technology can provide increased productivity, reduced wastage and better quality goods and services.

However, it may not always be possible for a firm to adopt the most appropriate technology (perhaps because it does not have the necessary finance). Even if it does, the firm needs to ensure that the change is managed effectively. People are often suspicious or worried by new technology and managers must think carefully about the speed of the change and the method of introduction.

Organisations must also monitor the technology of their competitors. If they fail to keep up they may find they cannot match their competitors' quality standards. However, they may be limited by their ability to afford the technology. Typically, managers will be faced with an almost constant flow of demands for new technology from employees. Nearly everyone can think of some machine or gadget they would like in an ideal world. Managers must decide on priorities, given their limited resources, and also look for the gains that can be achieved with existing equipment. As the **kaizen** approach shows, success sometimes comes from gradual improvements rather than dramatic technological change.

**KEY terms**

**automation** – occurs when jobs which were previously done by people are now done by machines.

**computer-aided design** – software that provides 3D plans and designs for new products or processes.

**computer-aided manufacture** – a production process planned and controlled by a computer program. When linked with computer-aided design, CAD/CAM can be a highly efficient, fast and cheap way to produce small quantities of a wide range of products.

**kaizen** – an approach, originating from Japan, which aims to achieve continuous improvement in business.

**robot** – a programmable machine that handles tasks automatically.

# Exercises

## A. REVISION QUESTIONS

*(35 marks; 60 minutes)*

Read the unit, then answer:

1 What is meant by the term 'technology'? *(3)*
2 Explain how technology can improve a firm's performance. *(4)*
3 What benefits might a firm derive from linking CAD to CAM? *(3)*
4 Examine three possible problems of introducing new technology. *(6)*
5 Explain how technological change has helped in the following areas:
   a retailing *(3)*
   b stock control *(3)*
   c car production. *(3)*
6 Outline two factors that might explain why there are so few robots in the UK. *(4)*
7 Why may technology be an important factor in a firm's international competitiveness? *(3)*
8 How may staff benefit from the introduction of new technology? *(3)*

## B. REVISION EXERCISES

### B1 Data Response

**Tyre Technology**

A technical revolution is happening in the world tyre industry which should lead to better and cheaper products. For much of its history, tyre making has been multi-stage and highly labour intensive. Automation has been gradual involving activities such as automatic cutting and feeding of materials. Now new technology is being introduced which will cut the labour input, increase

productivity and provide a much greater degree of flexibility. Where commercially viable production meant continuous output of thousands of a single size and type of tyre it is now becoming possible to get a profit on a batch of just a few hundred.

The developments by the leading companies (the top six control more than 70% of the world market) is extremely worrying for the dozens of smaller players which lack the financial and technical resource to make their own developments. The new systems developed independently by the firms concerned are heavily computerised. Michelin's system is said to need half the workforce and one-tenth of the usual production space with a capital cost of $15 million per 500,000 of annual capacity. One perceived disadvantage is that it needs new and dedicated facilities. The introduction has tended to be gradual to minimise the social and employment disruptions associated with the process.

**Source:** Adapted from *The Financial Times*

**Questions**  *(30 marks; 35 minutes)*
1 Explain the meaning of the terms:
   a automation *(2)*
   b batch. *(2)*
2 Outline the factors involved when deciding whether to adopt new technology. *(7)*
3 Analyse the potential 'social and employment disruptions' associated with the new technology. *(9)*
4 'Without the latest technology firms cannot hope to compete effectively.' Critically assess this view. *(10)*

## B2 Case Study

### Brooks

Last Monday the management of Brooks plc announced the purchase of new equipment which would radically improve productivity levels. The investment would lead to some job losses, the management explained, but there was no doubt it was in the best interests of the company as a whole. Employees had not been consulted because management felt they had more than enough information to make the decision. Consultation would simply slow up the process. In the long run the new equipment should increase the firm's competitiveness and the purchase was an expensive necessity. Working practices would, of course, have to be altered and employees would certainly have to learn new skills. The managers promised to provide the necessary training although they could not guarantee everyone a job if they could not adapt successfully.

Following the announcement the employees were furious and considered taking industrial action. Hearing the rumours of possible strikes the management admitted that it might not have handled the issue in the best way possible but would not reconsider the decision.

**Questions** *(40 marks; 60 minutes)*

1 What factors may have made the management of Brooks plc decide to invest in new technology? *(8)*
2 Do you think the employees at Brooks plc would be justified in taking industrial action? Explain your answer. *(10)*
3 Analyse the factors which the managers at Brooks plc might have taken into account before acquiring the new equipment. *(10)*
4 The management of Brooks plc admitted it may not have handled the issue in the best possible way. In your opinion, how should the managers have handled it? Justify your answer. *(12)*

## C. ESSAY QUESTIONS

1 'Technology is something to be feared rather than welcomed.' Consider this view.
2 To what extent should a firm make introducing new technology a priority?
3 'The key to better performance is better management not more technology.' Critically assess this view.

# INTEGRATED EXTERNAL ISSUES

## 50.1 External influences – an overview

### INTRODUCTION

The external environment of the business affects all its decisions. When answering questions about production or finance or marketing decisions, the context will be all-important in determining whether a particular business decision is appropriate. Have interest rates just risen sharply? Is there ferocious competition from the Far East? Is a change in the law going to open up new opportunities?

A good example of the importance of the external context is the impact of the business cycle. It is clear that many business decisions will be different depending on whether the economy is booming or depressed. No less important is careful analysis of the strengths and strategies of a firm's main competitors. This will provide important information which should be fed into the decision making process.

### WHAT ARE EXTERNAL INFLUENCES?

External influences create both opportunities and constraints for the business. They stem from various sources, including economic, social, technological, legal and political factors. Different firms will be affected by different factors, but all will be subject to economic change.

Economics as a subject can help considerably to lead to an understanding of the external environment of the business. It is useful to be able to divide external economic influences into two groups. Macro-economic influences involve the whole economy and affect all businesses. Micro-economic influences affect specific sectors of the economy and may or may not be important for individual business decisions.

- Macro-economic influences include long-term growth rates, the business cycle, inflation and unemployment, macro-economic policies and international trade policy.
- Micro-economic influences include individual markets and government policies affecting the labour market or particular industries. Another important

part of the background for any business is the process of technological change. This will affect the inputs available to the business and the competition which it faces. The need to adapt to change is a factor of growing importance for many decision takers.

Social opportunities and constraints reflect the pressure on businesses to acknowledge responsibility for the well-being of different stakeholder groups. They include ethical and environmental considerations and lead businesses to change the way they do things for reasons other than those related to straightforward profit making.

### 'A' GRADE EXTERNAL ISSUES

The external environment of the business involves all those issues which are currently important in the world in which the business operates.

One strategy might be to keep in mind a checklist of the main external issues. Then when tackling any major question on business decisions, ask: are any of these factors relevant to this decision? The most important factors are:

- What kind of market is the business operating in?
- How stiff is the competition from other businesses?
- Is the business cycle going to have an important impact in this situation?
- Will the government's macro-economic policies influence the outcome of this decision?
- What opportunities might arise in overseas markets?
- Does economic growth provide opportunities which did not previously exist?
- Do the European Union or the World Trade Organisation have regulations which will affect the decision by creating threats or opportunities?
- Will changes in government micro-economic policy be important to this decision?
- Should ethical considerations dictate changes in the way decisions are made?
- Are stakeholders and pressure groups influencing decisions in ways which should be taken into account?
- Is technological change opening up opportunities which should not be ignored?

Often it will not be necessary to write about any of these questions in detail. What is required is to select the relevant questions for the case in hand, then develop an answer based upon the internal objectives and issues facing the business.

In addition to the above, three issues are especially worth looking at before facing an examination.

## ISSUE 1 When is the state of the economy most important to business?

Businesses want demand to grow in a steady and predictable fashion. Then all businesses can grow or at least continue producing and the pressures of competition are not too intense. When incomes start to fall because the economy is in recession, some businesses will be relatively unaffected. Suppliers of toothpaste may have quite an easy time but suppliers of luxury yachts, for example, may not survive if the recession persists. The construction industry typically faces great difficulties because fewer people have incomes sufficiently high to buy houses and fewer businesses are investing in new buildings. In general, most businesses will face reduced profits. The early 1990s' recession provided ample evidence of the problems.

## ISSUE 2 How big an influence should government have on business decisions?

Businesses want governments to keep the economy stable. So they tend to oppose big increases in government spending. Many people in business resent taxation of their personal gains and therefore oppose increased tax rates. So many business organisations support the view that reduced government intervention is desirable.

However, much government intervention is about ensuring fair treatment. In this, the welfare of consumers (who are also voters) can be very important. Most businesses dislike competition policies which constrain their activities. But competition can be very important in keeping prices down for consumers. In the long run, competition ensures that businesses produce efficiently and consider the needs of all their stakeholders.

## ISSUE 3 How important are ethical issues in business today?

Ethical issues have become increasingly widely publicised, but it is harder to say whether they have become more important. Many businesses have shown over the years that their own sense of social responsibility can ensure good decision taking, regardless of external pressures. Businesses which have pioneered customer service strategies or environmental friendliness have often believed in their approaches as being representative of good practice. However, while 'cowboy' businesses remain there will continue to be an assortment of legal and pressure group constraints upon business activity. Therefore ethical questions will remain central to the study of business.

# External issues

UNIT 50 | INTEGRATED EXTERNAL ISSUES

## A. SHORT-ANSWER QUESTIONS

1 How would an increase in incomes affect the following?
   a cauliflower producers
   b hairdressers
   c insurance advisers
   d building workers *(8)*
2 What effect might a fall in oil prices have on the British economy? *(3)*
3 What would happen to the price of burgers if McDonald's took over Burger King? *(3)*
4 How might an increase in interest rates affect a retail chain such as Woolworth's? *(3)*
5 How might tax cuts affect the following?
   a car owners
   b car manufacturers
   c road builders
   d petrol companies *(8)*
6 If the pound rose on the foreign exchange markets, what would happen to the price of scotch whisky in Japan? *(3)*
7 If economic growth slows down during recession, how would car producers react? *(2)*
8 During a period of high unemployment, large numbers of people may be forced to accept jobs at lower wage rates than they had previously. How would this affect employers? *(2)*
9 Identify two problems a firm might face during a period of deflation. *(2)*
10 How would UK businesses be affected by a reduction in import duties by a number of Far East countries? *(2)*
11 Distinguish between 'shareholder' and 'stakeholder'. *(3)*
12 Must ethical behaviour always be seen as an expensive luxury for firms? *(4)*
13 Explain the impact which improved telecommunications might have on the activities of a UK shoe manufacturer. *(4)*
14 Identify two ways in which firms can strengthen their ability to benefit from technological change. *(2)*
15 State three possible effects upon firms of the invention of cheap, efficient industrial robots. *(3)*

## B. DATA RESPONSE QUESTIONS

1 It is 1998. Your are working in the accounts department of a business producing commercial refrigerators with glass doors. They sell to pubs and restaurants and are used to both store and display drinks. Roughly half of production is exported and, of the exports, 40% is sold to EU buyers and 50% to Asian countries, principally Malaysia and Thailand.

Your employer is seriously considering a major expansion of capacity and has asked a team, including yourself, to assess the feasibility of the project. You are rather disturbed to find that all the discussion seems to be about production and marketing aspects of the decision. You decide to present the following information to the next planning meeting. The government's target for inflation is 2.5% and for earnings growth, 4.25%.

**Annual GDP growth, quarter 1 (%), 1998**

| UK | 3.0 |
|---|---|
| France | 3.4 |
| Germany | 3.8 |
| Italy | 2.5 |
| Malaysia | −1.8 |
| Thailand | 0.4 |

**UK data** (Source: *The Economist*, 25/6/98)

| Inflation (May) | 4.2% |
|---|---|
| Earnings increase (March) | 5.2% |
| Interest rate (Bank of England base rate, December) | 6.25% |
| Exchange rate (trade weighted index, June) | 106.9 |

**Questions** *(20 marks; 30 minutes)*
a How will you explain the relevance of the information you are providing? *(8)*
b What will your argument be as to how the information should be used in making the final decision? *(12)*

2 Study the figures below (adapted from the *Guardian*, 17/4/98):

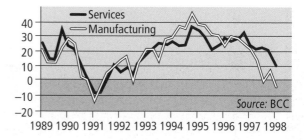

Export sales, percentage balance reporting sales increase

### Exchange rate index

| 1990 | 112.0 |
|------|-------|
| 1991 | 113.0 |
| 1992 | 108.7 |
| 1993 | 99.7 |
| 1994 | 100.0 |
| 1995 | 95.1 |
| 1996 | 96.7 |
| 1997 | 112.7 |
| 1998 | 106.9 |

Source: National Institute Economic Review, May 1998

### Questions                    (30 marks; 35 minutes)

**a** For what reasons might the exchange rate have been
changing during the 1990s?                    (6)
**b** How has the exchange rate affected exports of manufacturers and services?                    (6)
**c** Why might services have been less severely affected than
manufacturers?                    (6)
**d** What impact would you expect these trends to have on
the UK economy overall?                    (12)

## C.  ROLE PLAYS AND SIMULATIONS

### The Future of the Burger
On the basis of the evidence which follows, can McDonald's
and Burger King's expansion programmes succeed in
Britain?

### Appendix A

McDonald's had 830 restaurants in the UK at the
beginning of 1998. It planned to add a further 100
during 1998 and the same again in 1999. Burger King
had 445 restaurants in the UK at the beginning of 1998
and planned a further 55 outlets during 1998.

### Appendix B

Wages in McDonald's were raised in January 1998 from
£3.25 to £3.50 an hour. In May 1998 the minimum
wage in the UK was set at £3.60. McDonald's says its
average rates of pay are above the minimum wage.
However, prices may have to rise to recoup increased
costs.

### Appendix C

Burger King cut the price of its Whopper to gain market
share. It claims that its Big King, which has two burgers
and two slices of cheese, has increased its sales
substantially in the US. Also in the US, McDonald's is
facing a saturated market and has had to resort to new
product developments such as the Chilli McDonald's and
the McRibs, in an attempt to maintain its market share.
It has also abandoned batch cooking and now makes
burgers to order.

### Appendix D

Other kinds of fast-food outlets are gaining ground. Pret
a Manger and other chains are offering healthy and
interesting menus.
  The so-called McLibel case which ended in 1996
demonstrated that some members of the public have
considerable doubts about McDonald's environmental
stance. The 'McLibel Two' were able to defend
themselves against McDonald's by showing that there
were doubts about how environmentally friendly their
packaging and purchasing policies actually were.

### Appendix E

Burger King promises a continuous programme of
new products. It says it has doubled its R&D
budget. McDonald's has exploited its partnership
with Disney to create added attractions for
customers.

## D.  INTEGRATED CASE STUDIES

### Making a Living
George Wheeler was a potter. He spent long years at art
college and emerged with skills and artistic flair which
made him well equipped to make a living. He had one other
major advantage. His mother had inherited some money
and was prepared to invest in his business.
  George was able to rent an old mill in a small town on
the edge of the Lake District. He was well placed to attract
tourists and he set about creating a viable business. He
developed his own personal style. His mugs, plates and
vases were distinctive yet very suitable for everyday use. The
future looked bright. He was able to invest in the equipment
he needed easily enough and within three months his
showroom was stocked and ready to open.
  Plenty of people came to look round the showroom.
Unfortunately many left without making a purchase. Even
though George had accepted a small mark-up, hand-made
pottery seemed expensive in comparison with the mass produced product. People enjoyed looking but did not always buy.
  At the end of six months, George knew he had to
rethink. He had covered his input costs and the rent on the
building but he had a pitiful sum left to live on. He decided
that he would stock a large range of gifts alongside his
hand-made pots, and see if that would increase turnover.
  The strategy worked quite well. The mark-up on the
glasses and ornaments he bought in was larger. It was

depressing to think that so many people preferred mass produced products to his own, but he made a living and still spent most of his time doing what he wanted to do, creating individual pots.

The crunch came after about five years. The 1998/9 recession brought an end to the real income growth which had helped George at the start. Sales in early 1999 were 18% down on the previous year. George realised that he would have a hard time paying back his loans. They were not large but it became clear that his business was barely profitable.

An old friend came to visit. He had stayed on in the art college where George had trained as a teacher. There was a vacancy there for a potter. George's design skills had developed while he worked and he agreed to apply for the job. He realised it would pay more than the profit he had been making in the pottery. Within three months he sold off the stock and closed down for good.

## Questions

*(30 marks; 40 minutes)*

1 What reasons did George have for thinking his business would be viable when he made his plans? (5)
2 Why did the business deteriorate under recession conditions? (6)
3 George never went bankrupt. Why then did he close down the business? (5)
4 In general, what types of products are vulnerable to recession? (5)
5 Could a business such as this survive in the long run? Give reasons for your conclusion. (9)

# BUSINESS START-UPS

**DEFINITION**

An 'entrepreneur' is prepared to take risks in order to exploit a business opportunity. This term is often used to describe a person starting their own venture, perhaps for the first time. A new firm operating in the marketplace for the first time is known as a 'business start-up'.

## 51.1 Personal characteristics

What kind of person is willing to take the risk of starting a business? What are the qualities needed for success? It is difficult to generalise, as each case must be viewed on its own merits. A great deal of academic research has been carried out to try and find out who makes a good entrepreneur.

### HARD WORKING

Successful entrepreneurs usually demonstrate high levels of energy. Research conducted with 40 successful business leaders concluded that many 'don't know how to stop working, they always seem restless, work 15–18-hour days, take few holidays, … and report great reserves of psychic/physical energy'.

### STRONG MOTIVATION TO SUCCEED

Evidence from research suggests that entrepreneurs tend to demonstrate a driving ambition to succeed. Many measure their success by the extent to which they satisfy their inner sense of achievement. David McClelland identified three traits of individuals with a high need for achievement. He considered them to be strongly connected with entrepreneurial success:

- a willingness to take personal responsibility for finding solutions to problems
- a desire to set moderate achievement goals and take calculated risks
- the need for concrete feedback on performance.

McClelland also identified the need for power as a possible source of the successful business leader's ambition. However, evidence suggests that entrepreneurs with a great need for power perform less well when starting their own business than those with a moderate need. The latter group are able to adopt a more democratic style of management and delegate decision making as the business grows.

Many people who start their own business do so to gain some control over their own working lives. This is more likely to reflect a desire for independence than for power over others. Motivation of this kind is particularly strong for members of minority groups who feel they may not rise to the top in large organisations because of discrimination.

### THE ABILITY TO INNOVATE

Research also shows that successful entrepreneurs are likely to be **innovative** and creative. The ability to develop new ideas for products or services, or think of new ways of satisfying customer needs, gives these individuals a head start in the marketplace when they set up their business.

The kind of person most likely to be successful in starting a business is an innovative and creative thinker. It is more important to be hard working than to be highly intelligent. Ambition to achieve and the desire for power and control are also key factors. Successful entrepreneurs are prepared to take the risks, and put in the time and effort, to make their business a winner.

## 51.2 Identifying an opportunity

It is estimated that one in three business start-ups fail in the first three years of operation. In contrast, this figure falls to one in six amongst those small firms which seek advice and then carefully plan their development. A common feature of those start-ups that

### THE AMAZING AMAZON

Business start-ups rarely come bigger than the story of Jeff Bezos and Amazon. In 1994 Jeff, aged 30, quit his well paid job in finance, borrowed $300,000 and set up the world's first internet bookshop. By 1997 the shares were quoted on the New York stock market and Amazon.com had already become well known worldwide. Amazon's unique selling point was that it was the easiest way to buy a book – easier than going into town to a bookshop, and easier to use than other on-line book stores. When the internet stock market boom pushed Amazon shares to $115 in 2000, Jeff Bezos was one of the richest men in the world. By November 2002 the shares had slipped, but his holdings were still worth over $1,000 million.

Business in

| METHOD | STRENGTH | WEAKNESS |
|---|---|---|
| Identifying a business suited to your personal qualities and skills | Should be personally satisfying ,if successful | May overemphasise personal needs rather than market needs |
| Analysing market gaps in your local area | Based on the customer, which should increase chances of success | The gaps may be due to lack of demand, or – if successful – rivals may be attracted in soon after |
| Innovative thinking based upon strong knowledge of the market | Good combination of market knowledge and product differentiation | Unless the market potential is too small to attract bigger competitors, major rivals will soon arrive |
| Acquiring a franchise in a business with proven success elsewhere | Relatively low risk start-up, so easier to get bank loans | You must look beyond the franchisor's claims; careful research is still essential |

struggle to survive is lack of initial market research. Many people assume they know about the customers within a market and therefore that they do not need research.

Before conducting background research, it is necessary to decide upon a specific market in which the business will operate. Some people find this decision very simple. A person made redundant with long experience of a particular market sector will already have the knowledge and personal contacts needed to build a business. But is there necessarily a gap in the market?

## 51.3 Small budget research and marketing

The first stage for a business start-up when conducting small budget market research is to look at what potential competitors are doing. Business directories like *Yellow Pages* are useful for identifying these. What are they offering and where? By marking local competitors on a map, it may become clear that one area is underserved by kebab shops, off-licences, or whatever.

**Market mapping** can also be used in a non-geographical way (see Figure 51.1). It provides an analytical tool to judge the market segments each business is covering. This may provide insight into which areas of the market are not being covered by any product offering at present. This will lead naturally into the second phase of the research process which is to build up a clear understanding of the customer-base.

Secondary sources, such as local census data, can give an indication of likely customer profiles (age, income, etc.). Primary research is also important. Small firms cannot afford to launch statistically significant investigations into the nature of the customer-base, particularly when it is geographically spread. However, a lot can be learned from listening to what individuals and small groups of customers have

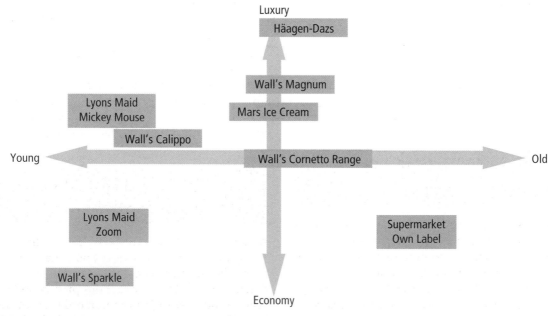

**Figure 51.1**

to say about the products and services available on the market. This approach is particularly useful for identifying potential market segments. As people express their ideas they will tend to polarise into different groups.

One key principle of successful business start-up is to decide who the firm will serve. A specific set of customers must be targeted. Only then will a small business be able to position itself in the market against its competitors. Market segmentation is a particularly useful technique for a start-up business with a limited marketing budget. General leaflet drops can be replaced with targeted campaigns concentrating on a specific housing estate or set of streets. Or a general advertisement in a local newspaper can give way to a carefully focused special offer aimed at attracting a particular group of customers. When resources are limited the key is to target directly those most likely to purchase.

Some potential advertising media which are ideal for business start-ups are given in the table below.

Advertising media suitable for business start-ups

| MEDIUM | ADVANTAGES FOR A SMALL FIRM |
|--------|------------------------------|
| Local newspapers | • Relatively low cost<br>• High penetration of local market |
| Trade/hobby magazines | • Well-defined, enthusiastic readership<br>• Low cost targeting of a market segment |
| Business directories, e.g. Yellow Pages | • Reference guide for local services<br>• Users often want to make an immediate purchase |
| Public relations (PR), i.e. obtaining free editorial coverage in suitable media | • Not only free but also editorial coverage has more credibility than advertising |

For most business start-ups the most important marketing aim will be to create satisfied customers. This will generate repeat purchases and develop a customer-base as the message of your success passes from person to person, via word of mouth.

## 51.4 Identifying a profitable product or service

Over the last 30 years, eight out of every ten new products launched have been a failure. Why do so many new products fail? Many customers do not like change. It is simply easier not to go to the trouble of learning how to use a new product, or to take the risk of trying out a new service. So a small firm with an innovative idea must help the consumer see how to use it – and

### IN THE SOUP

In 1990 two young entrepreneurs saw a gap in the market for premium-priced 'fresh soup'. Unusual recipes, top quality ingredients and packaging in fresh milk cartons rather than tins were all fundamental to the success of the New Covent Garden Soup Company. Sales went wonderfully well, and in 1997 a small publicly quoted company, S Daniels, bought the soup business for £22 million. By 2000, S Daniels was making profits of £5 million a year on a turnover of over £50 million, but according to chief executive Cyril Freedman this was still not enough to impress the stock market. Therefore, when the business needed to raise more capital, it was easier to allow a Singapore-based firm to buy into the business. In 2002 the Singapore investors bought the whole of the S Daniels business for just £23 million. The soup company had been swallowed up.

therefore see the benefit of the spending involved. A start-up business will find it difficult to overcome consumer resistance on a limited marketing budget.

Even if a product or service has immediate attractions, problems may remain. Few businesses are built on one-off purchases. Most require the steady income that comes from repeat business. It may be possible to create a situation in which this occurs. In the case of the New Covent Garden Soup Company (above), the strategy was to offer inventive new flavours and outstanding quality. Coupled with product variety (a 'soup of the month') it ensured regular purchasing and steady cash flow throughout the year. High quality also generated invaluable word of mouth advertising.

The majority of start-up businesses select an existing item and find a new innovative approach to providing it, which allows value to be added. To succeed, the entrepreneur needs a complete understanding of who the customers are and what they want. Careful market research is therefore the secret to identifying a profitable product or service.

## 51.5 Protecting a profitable product or service

A patent gives the holder the right to be the sole user of a production process, or the only manufacturer of a particular product. The Copyright, Designs and Patents Act of 1988 provides this protection for a 20-year period after registration. In order to register an invention, a set of drawings must be lodged with the

## OPPORTUNITY FOR ADDING VALUE: THE CASE OF THE FLYING SUITS

A small business start-up can be built around identifying a new way of adding value to an existing product or service.

Richard Branson found that business travellers on Virgin's flights to Hong Kong wanted to buy a new suit while there, but had no time to do so. An in-flight tailoring service was introduced which allowed individuals to be measured and their details sent by fax to a Hong Kong factory. The garment was manufactured and delivered to the airport for the customer's return flight.

A new business opportunity opened up for a Hong Kong tailor, and Virgin's business travellers appreciated the customer service.

Patent Office which shows that the product, or process, has original features. The inventor must state that these ideas are his or her own and have not been copied from another source. The work of authors, composers and artists is also legally protected against others copying it. However, in this case there is no requirement to register the copyright.

The holder of a patent has a potentially valuable asset which can be used to protect, or develop, a position in the marketplace. However, it is up to the individual to enforce the patent if he or she believes it is being infringed. This must be done through legal action, which is time-consuming and expensive.

Large organisations may be prepared to acquire smaller businesses if they hold an important patent. Given the expense of a product launch, many small businesses choose to sell patent rights rather than carry the financial burden themselves. A start-up business with a new product idea would be well advised to protect its main asset by patenting it.

## 51.6 The practical problems of business start-up

### FINANCE

Business start-ups face a problem in raising sufficient finance to establish themselves. New undertakings have no past track record by which their future potential can be judged. This means that any investor is taking a very high risk if they choose to supply finance. As a consequence lenders will charge high interest rates, if they are willing to lend at all. In fact many small firms are funded by loans from friends and relatives.

To avoid high interest charges, many individuals save, sell personal possessions, or mortgage their house to raise start-up finance. Another source is a lump sum resulting from redundancy or early retirement.

Estimating the cost of equipment or production facilities can be done with a degree of accuracy. In contrast, it is more difficult to judge the quantity of money required for working capital. Careful planning of cash flow is required to determine the finance required at start-up. It is important not to begin trading with too little capital, but it is equally sensible not to borrow more than is necessary. Cash lying unused in the business carries a high opportunity cost.

A potential lender, such as a bank, will wish to see the entrepreneur putting a substantial sum of his or her own money at risk in the business. This will ensure that the owner makes every effort to try and make the firm a success. In addition, some form of **security** will be required so that if the loan can not be repaid an asset of the borrower becomes the property of the lender. This will often be the premises of the business.

Banks provide approximately 60% of external finance for small business start-ups. The two most frequently employed forms of bank financing are:

- Loan capital – a commitment by the bank to provide a sum of money to the business for a defined period of time. A typical bank loan lasts for 2–3 years and is used to buy fixed assets.
- Overdrafts – these allow a firm to borrow up to an agreed maximum sum without a stated time limit. This is the most flexible form of borrowing and is therefore highly suitable for financing day-to-day working capital needs.

In recent years there has been a shift in the balance between these two forms of finance away from overdrafts towards loans. Banks claim that bank lending is increasingly based on the borrower's business plan, rather than on the security which can be offered. This approach has been developed in answer to the criticism that banks were not prepared to take the risks required to help foster new business formation in the UK. There remain, however, many commentators who believe banks are far too keen to avoid risks with small firms.

To help overcome the reluctance by banks to take risks with business start-ups, the **Loan Guarantee Scheme** was set up by the government. It promises a bank making a loan that if the business fails to repay, up to 80% will be provided by the government. This allows banks to support business start-ups which may otherwise be regarded as too risky. The government charges an interest rate premium of 1.5–2.5% of the annual value of the loan, which is paid by the borrower.

Other sources of finance exist for business start-ups in addition to banks:

- The **venture capital** industry exists to provide capital to small or medium-sized firms. In practice it has been criticised for its reluctance to provide 'seed corn' (start-up) investment, which represents only 4% of its total lending. Venture capitalists prefer to finance expansion by already established firms because this represents a lower risk. Few are willing to invest much less than £250,000.

- Business angels are people who have enough personal finance to fund start-ups which attract their interest. The capital they offer complements the formal venture capital industry because they provide money at an earlier stage in the firm's development. Evidence suggests that loans of £50,000 or less are involved, and that many individuals like to have some role in the business they are investing in.

## BUSINESS ANGELS FUND A FRESHER FUTURE

Fresh Approach is a business start-up based around an innovative new idea which allows fresh fruit and vegetables to be preserved for long periods of time. The technique employed is a type of packaging that uses high levels of gas to keep food fresh. This approach is the opposite of existing technology which removes oxygen to preserve the product.

The founders of the business are two food scientists, Alan English and Nigel Parker. The potential is great, given that the freshly prepared food market is worth £250 million each year and is currently growing at 15–25% per annum. Despite the profit potential this represents, raising financial backing for their venture proved far from easy.

Alan and Nigel approached a number of venture capitalists. None were prepared to take the risk of investing in the project, even though the pair were willing to use £100,000 of their own money. The Co-op Bank did feel able to match their contribution with a loan of the same amount, but this still left a large financial gap. As a result, the start-up was only possible because of the support of business angels. The further £80,000 capital required was raised by cash injections of between £2,000 and £30,000 by 32 different individual investors.

A shareholder's agreement has been drawn up which gives English and Parker 15% of the company each and sets target growth rates which the organisation must aim to achieve. The projected sales of the business are £1 million in the first year of operation with initial profits expected within nine months of start-up.

## LOCATION

A key consideration when selecting premises is the need to keep fixed costs to a minimum. When finance is limited, reducing the output required to break even makes the survival of the business more likely. As a result it may be appropriate in the first instance to operate from the owner's home, if this is practical. However, the difficulties this may create should not be underestimated. For example, it may be hard to escape the pressure of running the business.

If business premises are to be acquired, decisions are needed about size and location. This will involve an evaluation of the likely revenue generated compared with the purchase and running costs. In this context it is worth recalling an old retail saying that 'the three most important things in retail are location, location and location'. The same point holds good for most service businesses. So new firms are torn between the desire to keep costs down (poor location) and maximise revenue (costly location).

## BUILDING A CUSTOMER-BASE

The best and least expensive form of advertising available to a business start-up is word of mouth recommendation. The long-term strength of the business will depend on building a customer-base prepared to return to purchase products again and again. In order to achieve this, customers must be satisfied with the service they are offered by the business. There are a number of factors to consider when trying to build up customer loyalty:

- Provide a basic service that is efficient and meets the standards expected by the customer. For example, the business must ensure product availability.
- Develop an after-sales service. For example, deal effectively with consumer complaints, treating them as an opportunity to learn about how to improve customer service.
- Take every chance to understand more about the customer-base. For example, observe purchasing patterns at varying times of the day and week.
- Ensure positive contact between customers and staff to create a pleasant experience for the consumer each time they come into contact with the business.

The future success of any business start-up will be determined to a large extent by its ability to develop a group of satisfied customers.

## CASH FLOW

Research evidence suggests that approximately 70% of small business failure occurs because of poor cash flow management. Firms which are profitable find it impossible to continue trading because they are unable to meet their current debts. Often cash is tied up in stocks which can not be used immediately to pay bills.

It is therefore vital that even a profitable business, which has orders allowing it to work at full capacity, keeps enough cash available within the firm to ensure it does not run out of working capital. In order to do so, it is wise for business start-ups to prepare a **cash flow forecast** as part of the initial business plan. This will allow overdraft facilities to be arranged should a need for additional cash be identified at some future point in the firm's development. For a more detailed analysis of the role of cash flow forecasting in planning start-up business finance, see Unit 16.

Among the key lines of analysis are:

- Has the entrepreneur the drive, the personality and the vision to succeed at the start? If so, has the same person the leadership skills, the trusting nature and the human relations skills to manage growth effectively? At its simplest, most successful entrepreneurs are brilliant but arrogant workaholics. Those same qualities can become problems for a leader of a growing organisation.
- Apart from the abilities of the leader, the next most important issue is market knowledge. Can a real consumer desire be identified and met in an innovative way? Analysis should concentrate on identifying this group of customers and then considering the most cost effective means of communicating with them.
- Has the business plan been made prudently or is it window dressed to encourage financiers to put their money in? The founder should remember that his or her own money is as much at risk as that of any other shareholder (and more so than the banks, who will have insisted on security for any loans). Enthusiasm and optimism are vital qualities for entrepreneurs; but the optimism must not become blind.

## FLIKABALL

Leon and Vaughn Gingell were in the pub one Wednesday night when a business idea struck them. 'Why can't we put a football player in a marble?' They visualised a new craze. Instead of collecting stickers in an album, young children would collect Premiership marbles. Sold in packs of 3, there would be 240 to collect – 12 for each Premiership club. They could play with them, swop them, talk about them – all the hallmarks of a kids' craze.

The brothers spent some time trying to interest someone in their idea, but existing marble manufacturers simply said it was impossible. Eventually, though, a clever manufacturer managed to produce two marble halves that could have a tiny Alan Shearer photo put in the middle. The halves were then fixed together. Hey presto, a 'Flikaball'. Appearances on children's TV shows led Merlin Toys to sign a deal. Merlin bought the concept, paying the Gingells a small initial fee and a percentage of the sales turnover. If 'Flikaball' was able to sell the 14 million units forecast by Merlin Toys, the brothers would be rich.

It took 18 months to perfect the production method and the marketing, but finally the product was launched in Spring 1997. Despite Alan Shearer's help in launching the product and an expensive TV advertising campaign, Flikaball did not really take off. Children bought one or two packs (at 75p each), but saw no need to keep collecting. The actual sales of 4 million units left Merlin Toys with a hole in its annual sales turnover, and Leon and Vaughn with a very small pay-out.

## 51.7 Business start-ups
### an evaluation

Establishing a new business is risky. The potential for failure can be reduced by appropriate planning, but never completely removed. It is clear that initial market research, and the thorough monitoring of financial performance, are vital factors which make success more likely.

Within a short space of time, though, a growing business will rely increasingly on the effective management of its staff. This can be an acute problem for the founder whose personal objectives were not only to make money but also to be the boss. Staff who were there from day one will probably accept the founder's obsession with his or her own 'child'. New employees will be more inclined to treat the business as much the same as others, and may find it hard to fit in.

It is important to realise, therefore, that although initial success or failure may depend on financial and marketing issues, the management of people will soon become an issue. For any entrepreneur to be a master of all these aspects of business is a tall order indeed. Which is doubtless why most new businesses are financial disappointments.

At the end of the day the extent to which a start-up has been successful must be judged by the individual, or group of people, who took the risk of creating the business in the first place. Only they can know if their personal objectives have been achieved.

**cash flow forecast** – an estimate of the firm's cash inflows and outflows over the coming months.

**innovative** – describes a product or service that brings something new to the marketplace.

**Loan Guarantee Scheme** – government-funded insurance for banks against bad debts by small firms.

**market mapping** – analysing how existing products are rated in relation to customer preferences to identify whether any gaps exist in the market.

**security** – assets that can be used as collateral by a lender, i.e. can be sold for cash if the borrower fails to keep up the repayments.

**venture capital** – risk capital put into small to medium-sized businesses, usually as a mixture of loan and share capital.

## Exercises

### A. REVISION QUESTIONS
*(30 marks; 60 minutes)*

Read the unit, then answer:

1 Outline the personal qualities which academic research suggests successful entrepreneurs demonstrate. *(4)*
2 Why is innovativeness a valuable quality in an entrepreneur? *(3)*
3 Outline two ways market mapping might help when considering starting a new business. *(4)*
4 Explain the role of primary information sources in 'small budget' market research *(4)*
5 Why might a small builder decide to advertise only in a directory such as *Yellow Pages*? *(4)*
6 Why do 'patents' represent a strategic asset to a business? *(4)*
7 What are the most common sources of finance open to a small business? *(4)*
8 Explain the role of 'business angels'. *(3)*

### B. REVISION EXERCISES

#### B1 Data Response

A visit to an away game at Old Trafford proved the spur to Claire and Jon. They visited Roosters Rotisserie, a successful restaurant/café based around spit-roasted chicken. They enjoyed a good value meal and while Jon observed the cooking process in the open kitchen behind the service counter, Claire watched with interest the steady stream of take-away customers. Claire's mental arithmetic told her that the outlet had taken £200 in the half hour they had been there. Her guess was that weekly takings might be around £8,000 and the gross profit margins around 60%. So on their return journey to London, they talked about setting up Rotisserie de Paris in Fulham.

Within three days Jon had contacted suppliers about the costs of equipment: the five-spit, 30 bird spit-roasters costing £6,500 each; the extractor fans to keep the restaurant cool; the fixtures and fittings and much else. He estimated that £80,000 would be needed as an equipment budget. At the same time, Claire looked for a suitable location. On the third day she found a superb spot. A café had just closed down on the Fulham Road. It was a large site and planning permission would not be needed. The cost quoted by the estate agent was scary (£25,000 for a 10-year lease and then £60,000 per year) but Claire was convinced it was the right area.

Within a week they had arranged £200,000 finance from friends and family (all borrowed at an annual interest rate of 10%), had bought the lease and had hired an architect, a designer and builders to remodel the outlet as a Rotisserie de Paris on a budget of £50,000. While work proceeded, Claire interviewed and hired eight staff while Jon visited suppliers and drew up the menus and prices. Within six weeks the restaurant was ready and Claire and Jon had a great (but expensive) weekend inviting friends to visit for free, just to give the staff some practice.

The following Thursday's opening day proved a huge success. It seemed that Rotisserie de Paris was a winner.

**Questions** *(40 marks; 60 minutes)*

**1** What proportion of Jon and Claire's capital was invested in start-up costs, and therefore how much was left for working capital? *(6)*

**2** Jon and Claire were lucky enough to obtain finance from their own contacts.

  **a** How else might they have set about raising the £200,000 they needed? *(8)*

  **b** What constraints would have been placed upon Jon and Claire by each method you suggest? *(8)*

**3** If sales in the first year proved to be £400,000 and the fixed overheads of running the restaurant proved to be £80,000 on top of the annual lease payment, what profit would have been made? *(6)*

**4** Claire and Jon's business start-up went very smoothly. They naturally assume that they are brilliant entrepreneurs. Another possibility is that they were lucky. Which of the two views do you take and why? *(12)*

**B2 Case Study**
Read the In Business 'Flikaball' in the unit, then answer the questions.

**Questions** *(40 marks; 60 minutes)*

**1** How well do the Gingell brothers fit into McClelland's theory about the motivations of entrepreneurs? *(9)*

**2** Examine three types of market research you believe Merlin should have undertaken before launching Flikaball. *(9)*

**3 a** If the deal between Merlin and the Gingells had the following royalty structure, what sum would they have earned in the first year if the sales target had been met?

    0–5 million    0%
    5–10 million    5%
    10+ million    8%

    NB If 6 million sold, 5 million at 0%, 1 million at 5%. *(6)*

  **b** Why would Merlin Toys have negotiated a royalty structure such as this? *(6)*

**4** After the disappointment of the 1997/8 sales of Flikaball, Merlin Toys had to decide whether it was worth trying again. Analyse the appropriateness of the marketing of Flikaball to help decide whether Merlin should try again in the future. *(10)*

## C. ESSAY QUESTIONS

**1** An American business leader once defined an entrepreneur as a risk taker who would rather be a spectacular failure than a dismal success. Discuss.

**2** Consider the factors most likely to lead to success when starting a new hairdressers.

# BUSINESS ORGANISATIONS

DEFINITION

Business organisations are the different legal forms a business can adopt. The key distinction is that some provide the owners with limited liability for any debts the business incurs. Other forms of business organisation have unlimited liability.

## 52.1 Sole traders

A **sole trader** is an individual who owns and operates his or her own business. Although there may be one or two employees, this person makes the final decisions about the running of the business. A sole trader is the only one who benefits financially from success, but must face the burden of any failure. In the eyes of the law the individual and the business are the same. This means that the owner has **unlimited liability** for any debts that result from running the firm. If a sole trader cannot pay his or her bills, the courts can allow their personal assets to be seized by creditors in order to meet outstanding debts. For example, the family home or car may be sold. If insufficient funds can be raised in this way the person will be declared bankrupt.

Despite the financial dangers involved, the sole trader is the most common form of legal structure adopted by UK business. In some areas of the economy this kind of business dominates. Particularly where the finance required to run the business is small and customers demand a personal service. Examples include trades such as builders and plumbers, and many independent shopkeepers.

There are no formal rules to follow when establishing a sole trader, or administrative costs to pay. Complete confidentiality can be maintained because accounts are not published. As a result many business start-ups adopt this structure. Sole traders will usually be small organisations in which the owner is able to make rapid decisions giving the benefit of total control. They are also likely to create close contacts with customers and get to know employees on a personal basis. The result is the ability to respond quickly to changes in the competitive environment. This may allow survival even when faced with competition from much larger organisations able to charge lower prices.

The main disadvantages facing a sole trader are the limited sources of finance available, long hours of work involved (including the difficulty of taking a holiday) and concern with respect to running the business during periods of ill health.

## 52.2 Partnerships

The principal difference between a sole trader and a partnership is the number of owners. The key advantages and disadvantages which derive from multiple ownership are as follows:

### ADVANTAGES

- Additional skills – a new partner may have abilities which the sole trader does not possess. These can help to strengthen the business, perhaps allowing new products or services to be offered, or improving the quality of existing provision.
- More capital – a number of people together can inject more finance into the business than one person alone.
- Expansion – with the new skills, increased labour and greater capital a partner brings, the business will have an increased potential for future growth.

The primary reasons for taking on a partner are the need to put more money into the business, or to share the responsibility of running the firm.

### DISADVANTAGES

- Sharing profit – the financial benefits derived from running the business will have to be divided up between the partners according to the partnership agreement made on formation. This can easily lead to disagreements about 'fair' distribution of workload and profits.
- Loss of control – multiple ownership means that no individual can force an action on the business; decision making must be shared.
- Unlimited liability – it is one thing to be unlimitedly liable for your own mistakes (a sole trader); far more worrying, surely, to have unlimited liability for the mistakes of your partners. This problem hit many investors in the Lloyds insurance market in the 1990s. Certain partnerships (called syndicates) lost millions of pounds from huge insurance claims. Some investors lost their life savings.

## 52.3 Incorporation

The process of **incorporation** creates a separate legal identity for the organisation. In the eyes of the law the owners of the business and the company itself are now two different things. The business can take legal action against others and have legal action taken against it. This means that each owner will now have the benefit of **limited liability**. Their investment in the business will be represented by shares. The money which they have used to purchase these is the only finance they will lose if the business is unable to meet its debts. If a firm is declared insolvent, all the assets of the business will be sold off to raise money to repay the creditors. If that is insufficient, the creditors lose out. Unlimited liability sounds unfairly weighted towards the shareholders, but it encourages individuals to put forward capital because the financial risk is limited to the amount they invest.

In order to gain separate legal status a company must be registered with the **Registrar of Companies**. Two key documents must be completed:

- The Memorandum of Association which governs the relationship between the company and the outside world. This includes the company name, the object of the company (often recorded simply as 'as the owners see fit'), limitation of liability and the size of the authorised share capital.
- The Articles of Association which outline the internal management of the company. This includes the rights of shareholders, the role of directors and frequency of shareholder meetings.

The key advantages and disadvantages which result from forming a company limited by the issue of shares are as follows:

### ADVANTAGES

- Shareholders experience the benefits of limited liability.
- Companies have a separate legal identity.
- A limited company is able to gain access to a wider range of borrowing opportunities. This makes funding the growth of the business potentially easier.

### DISADVANTAGES

- Limited companies must make financial information available publicly at Companies' House. Small firms are not required to make full disclosure of their company accounts, so this requirement is not too onerous.
- By law, company accounts must be audited. This adds to the administrative costs of the business.
- Limited companies must conform with extensive formalities, such as holding the annual general meeting of shareholders and publishing annual returns.

## Business IN

### THE MICROSOFT STORY

In 1975, two teenage friends formed a company. It sold a form of computer language for a self-assembly kit computer based upon Intel processors. First year sales revenue amounted to $16,005. Profits were zero. The friends were Bill Gates and Paul Allen. They called the company Microsoft.

Revenues and profits rose dramatically in the following years. Microsoft developed a series of products before, in 1983, launching the amazingly successful Microsoft Windows. Before Windows the company's revenues were below $50 million. By 1988 they topped $500 million.

The great Microsoft success of the 1990s was the launch of Windows 95 in Autumn 1995. This product helped push sales towards $14.48 billion by 1998. By now Microsoft was one of the world's most profitable companies and Bill Gates was the world's richest man. Not a bad outcome for a couple of kids!

Microsoft Place, USA (© Corbis/Wolfgang Kaehler)

## 52.4 Private and public companies

Two types of company can be formed – private limited companies and public limited companies.

### PRIVATE LIMITED COMPANIES

The shares of a private limited company cannot be bought and sold without the agreement of the other directors. This means the company cannot be listed on the stock market. As a result it is possible to maintain close control over the way the business is run. This form of business is often run by a family or small group of friends and may pursue objectives other than pure profit maximisation. Share capital may not exceed £50,000 and 'Ltd' must be stated after the company name. This warns those dealing with the business that the firm is relatively small and has limited liability. By implication, therefore, its cheques are not as secure as ones from an unlimited liability business. This is why some petrol stations have notices saying 'no company cheques allowed'.

### PUBLIC LIMITED COMPANIES

The shares of public limited companies can be floated and then traded on the stock market. Any member of the general public can therefore become an owner of these organisations. The memorandum of association must state clearly that the business is a public company and it must be registered as such. The term 'plc' must appear after its name.

The principal differences between private and public limited companies are:

- A public company can raise capital from the general public, while a private limited company is prohibited from doing so.
- The minimum capital requirement of a public company is £50,000. There is no minimum for a private limited company.

- Public limited companies must publish far more detailed accounts than private limited companies.

The key advantages and disadvantages which result from forming a public limited company with a Stock Exchange listing rather than a private limited company are as follows:

Advantages:
- A listed company will find it easier to raise finance than a private limited company.
- Public limited companies will be regarded by lenders as representing a lower risk investment than private limited companies. They are therefore likely to benefit from smaller interest charges on any loans obtained.
- Suppliers are likely to offer listed companies more attractive credit facilities. This is because they will be thought less likely to default on payments than private limited companies.
- The standing of the organisation in its own markets, both with customers and suppliers, may be enhanced by a Stock Exchange listing.

**Disadvantages:**

- The cost of floating a business on the Stock Exchange is high. Some of the outlay is fixed and therefore falls heavily on small issues. This makes gaining a listing more cost effective as the size of the company increases.
- A public limited company must keep a wide range of people informed about its financial performance. As a result it will face greater administrative costs than a private limited company and more sensitive data will be available to the public and competitors.
- The extent to which any one individual, or group, can maintain control of an organisation is severely limited by the sale of its shares on the Stock Exchange. For example, a family may find their influence on a business diminished when a listing is obtained. In turn, this means that publicly quoted companies are always vulnerable to a takeover bid. This may affect the decisions taken by directors. For example, they may be more inclined to cut back on staffing during a recession, whereas a private firm would want to hold on to experienced staff for when the economy starts to recover.
- Stock market investors place a great emphasis on the short-term financial performance of the business in order to maintain dividends and share price, rather than other long-term objectives. This was the reason Richard Branson gave when he took the unusual step of withdrawing his Virgin empire from the stock market in the early 1990s. Private limited companies do not face the same immediate pressure for short-term profit maximisation.

## 52.5 Divorce of ownership and control

Shareholders are the owners of public limited companies, but they do not make decisions on a day-to-day basis. Many will have little detailed knowledge of the firm's operation. Through the mechanism of the annual general meeting, they appoint a board of directors who are entrusted to represent their interests and manage the organisation on their behalf. However, the AGM is often not well attended and even when it is, large institutional investors may dominate voting.

So shareholders are the owners, but they have no effective control over the day-to-day decisions made by directors. Once the ownership and control of the company are divorced it can no longer be certain that the decision takers (i.e. the managers) will always act in a way consistent with the interests of the owners (i.e. the shareholders). Managers may select a strategic approach based on improving their own careers or bank balances. For example, evidence suggests that over half of takeovers fail to achieve the objectives set for them. This may reflect the fact that a decision to acquire a business is taken in order to benefit management in some way, rather than shareholders.

## 52.6 Other forms of business organisation

### MUTUALITY

Building societies and mutual life assurance businesses are non-profit making organisations. They have no shareholders and no owners. They exist solely for the best interests of members, i.e. customers. In the 1990s this became regarded as an old-fashioned, inefficient structure. It was suggested that without a clear owner, such organisations were inevitably run by the staff for the staff. And therefore that they were inefficient and bureaucratic. In fact, there is no evidence that former building societies such as Abbey National have become more efficient since becoming public limited companies.

### COOPERATIVES

Whether worker owned or customer owned (such as the retail Co-op), cooperatives have the potential to offer a more united cause for the workforce than the profit of shareholders. Unfortunately, the retail Co-op has been in decline for many years, partly due to its unclear objectives. Is it a social service or a profit-making retailer? Worker cooperatives have become tainted with failures of the past. Often the problems lay in disagreements between management and the workforce – problems that the cooperative structure was supposed to avoid.

On a brighter note, retail Co-ops showed their first positive business move for years when they bid over £100 million to buy the Alldays group of convenience stores in 2002. Furthermore, the Co-op Bank's stance as 'the ethical bank' has brought it success.

### NOT-FOR-PROFIT ORGANISATIONS

Many important organisations within the business world have charitable status. These include pressure groups such as Greenpeace and Friends of the Earth. They also include conventional charities such as Oxfam and Save The Children Fund. Charitable status ensures that those who fund the charity are not liable for any debts. It also provides significant tax benefits.

ISSUES FOR **analysis**

When analysing which type of organisation is the most suitable for a business, consider:

- The financial risks involved. Manufacturing businesses require heavy investment in plant and equipment before anything is available for sale. Therefore a great deal of capital is put at risk. This suggests limited liability is essential. Some service businesses such as tax advisors or dry cleaners require relatively little capital outlay. If the owner intends to finance the start-up without any borrowings, there is no need to seek limited liability.

The image you wish to portray. Although cautious businesses may refuse company cheques, most people think 'M Staton Ltd' sounds more established and professional than 'Mervin Staton'. In the same vein, a small software production company called TIB Ltd thought of changing its name to TIB plc. It rightly thought it sounded bigger and more impressive. What's in a name? Ask Coca-Cola.

- An organisation considering a move to public company status and a stock market listing has far bigger issues to consider. It must weigh the benefits to be gained, particularly in terms of raising additional finance, against the costs incurred and the loss of control. Many business questions can be analysed fruitfully by considering short- versus long-term issues. Private (family) versus public (stock market investor) ownership is a classic case in point.

savings into a business, only to lose them. Sadly, there are thousands every year who end up personally bankrupt. In other words, in a business world in which risk is ever present, rewards for success should be accepted.

- Short-termism is a curse for effective business decision making. There is no proof that a Stock Exchange listing leads to short-termism, only the suspicion that in many cases it does. Of course, massive companies such as Unilever, Nestlé and Shell are likely to be above the pressures for short-term performance. In many other cases, though, there is a strong suspicion that directors focus too much on the short-term share price. Their worries about shareholder pressures or takeover bids may distract managers from the long-term business building of companies such as Sony, Mercedes and Toyota.

## 52.7 Business organisations
### an evaluation

Business organisation is a dry, technical subject. It does contain some important business themes, however. Three are particularly valuable sources of evaluative comment:

- The existence of limited liability has had huge effects on business. Some have been unarguably beneficial. How could firms become really big if the owners felt threatened by equally big debts? Limited liability helps firms take reasonable business risks. It also, however, gives scope for dubious business practices. Start a firm, live a great lifestyle, then go into liquidation leaving the customers/creditors out of pocket. Then start again. All too often this is the story told by programmes such as the BBC's *Watchdog*. Companies Acts try to make this harder to do, but it still happens. Such unethical behaviour is why government intervention to protect the consumer can always be justified.
- Bill Gates and Richard Branson are worth billions of dollars. How can such wealth be justified? The answer lies in the risks involved in business. For every Richard Branson there are hundreds of thousands of small entrepreneurs who sink their life

### KEY terms

**incorporation** – establishing a business as a separate legal entity from its owners, and therefore allowing at to have limited liability

**limited liability** – owners are not liable for the debts of the business; they can lose no more than the sum they invested.

**Registrar of Companies** – the government department which can allow firms to become incorporated. Located at Companies' House, where articles of association, memorandums of association and the annual accounts of limited companies are available for public scrutiny.

**sole trader** – a one-person business with unlimited liability.

**unlimited liability** – owners are liable for any debts incurred by the business, even if it requires them to sell all their assets and possessions and become personally bankrupt.

# Exercises

## A. REVISION QUESTIONS

*(30 marks; 60 minutes)*

Read the unit, then answer:

**1** Explain two types of business that should *not* start up as a sole trader. *(4)*

**2** Why might the proprietors of a business choose to apply for incorporation? *(4)*

**3** Explain the business implications of limited liability. *(5)*

**4** State two features that distinguish a private limited company from a plc. *(2)*

**5** Outline two reasons why a growing company might choose *not* to become a plc. *(4)*

**6** What is meant by the phrase 'divorce of ownership and control'? *(3)*

**7** Why might mutual organisations such as building societies serve customers better than companies such as the high street banks? *(4)*

**8** Why may retail Co-ops fail to serve their customers any better than companies such as Tesco? *(4)*

## B. REVISION EXERCISES

### B1 Data Response

> Planet Organic, the UK's only organic supermarket, has set an ambitious expansion plan for the next 10 years. Founder director Renee Elliott said financial restructuring within the next few months would pave the way for a nationwide chain. Established in 1995, the company's 13 investors are largely Elliott's family and friends. She is examining a number of options for refinancing the business including raising venture capital. Thirteen investors she describes as 'a bit unwieldy'.
>
> 'We will be consolidating over the next nine months then moving into an aggressive expansion programme,' Elliott said. 'I would like another 30 to 40 shops nationwide and I think that's achievable.'
>
> The principles behind a Planet store are about offering shoppers an environmentally friendly and healthier alternative to the usual supermarket. 'Our goal is to change food retailing in the UK. We'd like to see people eating food that sustains them and the environment.'
>
> The recent spate of food scares and ongoing concerns about genetically modified (GM) foods have boosted Planet's fortunes. The store received its first serious upturn in

> February 1996 when the BSE crisis broke. Elliott said there had been a noticeable boost over the last fortnight as the GM debate raged. She does not think it's a passing fad.
>
> Source: Adapted from *The Grocer*, 27/2/99

**Questions** *(30 marks; 35 minutes)*

**1 a** What type of business organisation is Planet Organic? *(2)*

  **b** Why do you think that? *(5)*

**2** Outline the ways in which Renee Elliott may be finding 13 investors 'a bit unwieldy'. *(7)*

**3** If Elliott had not been able to finance her start-up through family and friends, explain three other ways she might have obtained the capital. *(6)*

**4** Discuss how successful you believe Planet Organic is likely to be in the future. *(10)*

### B2 Case Study

#### Business Start-up Proposal: 'Flavours of the Sea'

Midshire Bank small business advisor Nicole James picked up the file marked 'Flavours of the Sea'. It was 15 minutes before her meeting with Andrew Ellis, just enough time to refresh her memory about his start-up proposal.

> *Midshire Bank Business Proposal Form*
> In order to be considered for our 'Acorn' small business loan scheme please complete each of the questions below:
>
> **What will your business be called?**
> 'Flavours of the Sea'
>
> **What product or service will it offer to customers?**
> The business will offer seafood buffets delivered to the customer's door. The intention is to sell our product to people holding dinner parties, wedding receptions or other special occasions. This is a catering service with a difference because our dishes will use fresh seafood products from the North Shields docks.
>
> **What quantities will be produced and what price do you propose to charge?**
> In the first few months it is anticipated that two to three orders will be filled each week, with most of the work being at weekends.

The fact that the meals are unusual should allow quite high prices to be charged, on average a buffet for 20 people should bring in about £300.

### How much competition do you expect your business to face?

In this region there are quite a few catering firms offering buffets of various types, the biggest is the Whitestone Hotel Group. We could not compete with this kind of 'mass' service on price, but we wouldn't want to. The *Yellow Pages* lists no catering business like ours.

### How will you make potential customers aware of your product or service?

The intention would be to advertise in the local paper at first, featuring primarily the dinner party element of the service. As we make a success of things, reputation should grow quite rapidly. Recommendation from past customers should be a very effective form of promotion.

### Who will work in the business?

There are two of us. I am Andrew Ellis, an ex-shop manager, with experience in running a small branch (four full-time staff) of a national electrical goods chain. I was made redundant five months ago when the company cut back and closed quite a number of its regional stores. I have always loved cooking and finished second in a regional heat of the BBC Master Chef programme two years ago. My partner John King has been employed in a number of local hotels and restaurants as an assistant chef, including recently at The Harbour where fish dishes are a major speciality.

### What premises and equipment will be needed?

We intend to work from my home at first. The kitchen is large and the basic facilities are adequate. It is possible that a number of smaller items will be needed, such as storage boxes to keep the food in good condition when we transport it. The only real large expenditure will be on a van. Our first contact with the customer will be as we pull up their driveway, so we must not give the wrong impression. A smart, well-decorated vehicle carrying the business logo (A swordfish and lobster interlinked) is vital. The local dealer says £10,000 should be enough to cover this.

### What is the likely cash flow position in the first four months of operation?

Again these are estimates. (We have assumed that the van is bought on hire purchase). We will have to pay for our fish on the day we buy it, but we do not anticipate customers settling their bills for approximately four weeks.

| | May | June | July | August |
|---|---|---|---|---|
| Opening balance | 7,000 | 5,100 | 5,810 | 6,520 |
| Total in | 0 | 2,160 | 2,160 | 2,160 |
| Money out: | | | | |
| Food | 720 | 720 | 720 | 720 |
| Advertising | 150 | 150 | 150 | 150 |
| Van | 880 | 430 | 430 | 430 |
| Admin. | 150 | 150 | 150 | 150 |
| **Total out** | 1,900 | 1,450 | 1,450 | 1,450 |
| Cash flow | (1,900) | 710 | 710 | 710 |
| Closing balance | 5,100 | 5,810 | 6,520 | 7,230 |

### How much money do you propose to put into the business yourself?

I intend to put the £2,000 which remains from my redundancy payment into the business. This sum may be enough to start Flavours of the Sea, but as you can see from the cash flow forecast above it would leave the firm with very little margin for error in the first few months of operations.

### How much do you wish to borrow from the Midshire Bank?

We are applying for a £5,000 loan over two years. If this is not possible then an overdraft facility of £2,000 would be appreciated.

## Questions (50 marks; 70 minutes)

1 a Does the start-up proposal provide sufficient indication that the market for seafood buffets has been adequately researched? (6)

b What further information about the potential market would you advise Andrew Ellis to gather to support his application for a loan? (6)

2 Having identified the potential competitors of Flavours of the Sea, how might Andrew analyse its relative strength in the marketplace? (6)

3 How realistic do you think Andrew's decision to work from home is? What advantages and disadvantages will result from making this choice? (10)

4 How useful do you regard the Flavours of the Sea cash flow forecast to the running of the business? (10)

5 Would you advise Nicole to grant Andrew Ellis the loan, the overdraft facility, or neither? (12)

# BUSINESS PLANNING

DEFINITION

A business plan is a document designed to provide sufficient information about a new or existing business to convince financial backers to invest in the business.

Every business, whether new or established, large or small, needs a plan for the future. In the case of large, established companies planning will be done by strategists or consultants. In small firms and new business start-ups, the owner of the business is likely to be both manager and planner. This unit is primarily concerned with the small business start-up and the vital role that the business plan has to play in attempting to ensure the success of these enterprises.

## 53.1 Purposes of a business plan

**To clarify the idea:** The process involved in creating a business plan means that the **entrepreneur** has to ask a number of key questions about their idea. This should ensure that before starting up, the business idea has been considered with care.

**To gain finance:** The plan will often be used as a means of showing potential investors or lenders why the business will succeed. Banks insist on seeing a business plan before any loan or overdraft is granted. Private shareholders might invest because they believe in the entrepreneur. Professional providers of **venture capital** will demand evidence of careful planning.

**To monitor progress over time:** The business plan can be used as a working document for the owner. Regular checks, particularly against the objectives and the financial forecasts included in the plan, can act as a useful indicator of how well the business is doing. This can be the start of an ongoing monitoring process to help the owner run an efficient organisation in the future.

## 53.2 What's in a business plan?

The contents of a business plan will vary tremendously, depending upon the type of business, the expertise of the entrepreneur, who the plan is aimed at and how much time is spent researching the plan. However, the sections outlined below will be found in most business plans.

### INTRODUCTION

The plan starts with a brief summary of what the business will do, where it will be done and why the entrepreneur has decided to set up this business. This section will provide little detail, but is designed to give the reader of the plan an overall impression of the business idea.

### PERSONAL INFORMATION

A curriculum vitae (CV) of each owner will be included, focused particularly on any previous experience, in this line of business, in previous business start-ups or in management generally. Also included may be personal details of other key staff within the business. The owner(s) may wish to make a statement of their own personal objectives in order to show the reader of the plan how committed they are and exactly what they hope to gain from the enterprise.

### OBJECTIVES

The business plan should provide a clear statement of the objectives the firm is aiming to achieve. These objectives should be quantifiable targets. In other words, it should be possible to measure whether or not the objective has been achieved within the timescale allowed for that target. In some cases, the objectives will be split into short, medium and long term. Short-term objectives will cover the first year of trading, perhaps stating that the business aims to break even in its first year of trading. Medium-term objectives will cover anything from two to five years in the future and may be less specific than the short-term objectives. They will often relate to the size of the business, specifically how the business may grow. Examples could include increase sales turnover by 20% per year for the first five years, or open up a second outlet within five years. Long-term objectives will be even less specific. Planning for the long-term future is far harder than planning in the short term. Examples may include diversification into other markets, products or regions.

### MARKETING PLAN

The reader of the plan will want to know why this business idea should succeed in the marketplace. What will make this product/service stand out? What will be its unique selling point (USP)? And how will this USP be communicated to potential customers? Practical details such as pricing and promotion will be judged by how well they fit in with this strategy. Is enough money being budgeted to communicate the USP successfully?

Apart from the 'product', the aspect of the marketing mix potential investors will look at with greatest care is 'place'. In other words, how, where and at what cost is distribution to be achieved? Someone may have found a way to make better breakfast cereals than Kelloggs. How will Tesco and Sainsbury's be persuaded to stock them, though?

The marketing plan may be structured around the four Ps, but it is important to remember that a small firm's marketing strategy is very different from that of a large firm. The topic of small business marketing is covered in Unit 51.

Pricing the product will often be based on breaking even. As a result, cost based methods, particularly mark-up pricing, will be used. However, small businesses must also consider the market within which they are operating – since they are likely to be price takers. An awareness of competitors' prices is vital and the small business must strike the right balance between covering costs and undercutting competitors in an attempt to gain market share. Often firms will begin by practising a form of penetration pricing in the first few months of trading. This is to build up a customer base, in other words gain a foothold in the market.

The single most important feature of the marketing plan, though, will be the sales forecast. This is, after all, not only the key marketing question. It is also the key financial issue. The revenue must be high enough to cover the costs. So the research and care put into the sales forecast will be checked with particular care by potential investors.

Overall, the marketing plan should aim to answer questions such as the following, taken from NatWest Bank's *Business Start-Up Guide*:

- What is the market size and potential? Is the market growing or getting smaller?
- Who are your customers? What are their needs?
- Who are the major competitors? What are their prices, strengths and weaknesses?
- What is your expected turnover in the first year?
- Why do you think you can achieve your expected turnover?
- Has your product or service been market tested?
- What marketing and sales methods will you use? What are the costs involved?

If the marketing plan is able to provide satisfactory answers to these questions, it is likely that any potential provider of finance will be satisfied that the business idea is sound. They will now be interested in seeing the production plan and financial information.

## THE BUSINESS PLAN

Chris and Becky Barnard risked everything on opening a restaurant in the country. Their sales projections had convinced the bank to provide a £40,000 overdraft (on top of a £110,000 mortgage on the property). They decided on the upmarket name Avins Bridge Restaurant and set their price at £17 a head for a three-course meal. The restaurant opened in the summer 1997.

Although the evening trade proved reasonable, the shock for them was that lunchtimes were dead. By February 1998 the situation was very worrying. With an average of just 16 meals a day, the business was operating well below break-even. Drastic action was needed. A special offer of a free dessert proved, if anything, that their middle-aged, affluent customers were not price sensitive. It did nothing for sales. So the Barnards decided to push prices up – and to cut costs by running the restaurant without any outside staff.

Although the restaurant is still struggling, the hope is to build up a summer daytime trade with more snacky food served in the garden. They have also started advertising in the local press. Chris and Becky have learned the hard way that good-looking figures on a business plan count for nothing when the business gets going.

Source: *Caterer & Hotelkeeper*

### PRODUCTION PLAN

The production plan is the section of the business plan which explains how the business will create the goods or services it intends to sell (see the table at the top of the next page). To be considered – staffing levels, knowledge and qualifications required and stocks of certain items (particularly relevant in a shop).

It is this section of the plan which is most flexible in format, depending upon the type of business being planned. Whatever type of business, the production plan must demonstrate that the entrepreneur has carefully thought through the exact details of how the business will run. In other words, the day-to-day, practical details of the activities involved.

### FINANCIAL INFORMATION

This, the heart of the business plan, will include a projected balance sheet for the end of the first year's trading, a projected profit and loss account for the

Details required in a production plan

| FOR A MANUFACTURING BUSINESS | FOR A SERVICE BUSINESS |
|---|---|
| The production process which will be used | How customers are to be serviced: personally? Or with automated systems such as voicemail and the Internet? |
| The materials needed to produce the product | The staff levels needed (and their training) |
| The labour and machinery required for production | The equipment required for information and communications technology; and the target stock levels |
| Details of production capacity and lead times from order to delivery | The planned customer service times |

first year and a cash flow forecast for the first six to twelve months. Also found in this section may be a break-even analysis. This will show either the number of units the business needs to sell, or the sales turnover needed, to cover the overheads. A statement of financial requirements will also be included, usually showing a prospective lender how much money is required and how that money will be spent.

## CALCULATING BREAK-EVEN REVENUE

For many businesses, traditional break-even analysis is impractical. This is because they may sell a range of different products at a range of prices. If this is the case, it is still possible to use break-even analysis to calculate the level of turnover required to break even. In order to calculate the break-even revenue, it is necessary to know the firm's overheads and to have an estimation of their average gross profit margin. With this information, the following formula can be used to calculate break-even sales revenue:

$$\frac{\text{fixed overheads}}{\text{average gross profit margin}} \times 100$$

If the firm is able to achieve this level of sales, and its gross profit margin does not fall below the average level, it will break even.

### Example:

Bell's Dried Fruits sells a range of dried fruit and nut products. Its average gross profit margin on each product is 50%. It has monthly overheads of £12,000. Therefore its break-even revenue is:

$$\frac{£12,000}{50} \times 100 = 240 \times 100$$

$$= £24,000$$

## COLLATERAL

However impressive the sales, cash flow and profit forecasts, banks are unwilling to lend money to finance business plans without **collateral**. This means security, in other words securing the loan against assets which can be sold to repay any debts. A bank lending £20,000 may require £25,000 of property

assets as security. If the business has these assets, there is no problem. Often, though, a new small firm has few assets. It rents property rather than buying it. If the business has no assets to use as collateral, the entrepreneur may have to offer personal assets as security, such as his or her house. In which case business failure may be a financial disaster for the family concerned.

All business plans directed at borrowing capital require a statement of assets of the business and the assets of the individuals concerned.

ISSUES FOR **analysis**

Analysing a business plan should involve the following issues:

- Is the idea a sensible one for starting a business? Perhaps the product itself is not attractive or the service being offered will not be wanted.
- Is the actual production of the product or service feasible? Perhaps the entrepreneur has overestimated how much his or her employees will be able to produce in a given time, or the employees may not be suitably skilled to do the job required.
- Is the financial side of the plan realistic? Any financial plan will be based on assumptions. This is particularly important for a new business start-up, with no track record upon which to base forecasts. It is important to consider whether or not the assumptions made in drawing up the forecasts are valid.
- What is the level of risk? Given the high rate of business failures amongst small business start-ups, any new business is at risk of failure. Some will close soon after opening and this will usually mean a substantial loss for the entrepreneur. Although a business plan is created as an attempt to reduce the risks involved, it does not eliminate risk.

## 53.3 Business planning
### an evaluation

Business planning questions lend themselves to offering opportunities for demonstrating evaluation. Two important themes to consider are:

1 One of the key themes to evaluation is the ability to be able to gauge appropriateness. When considering business plans, the appropriateness of each section must be considered. For example, should a business plan for a small plumber contain details of his planned television advertising campaign? Surely local newspapers or the *Yellow Pages* are more appropriate for advertising this type of business? Not only will this be more cost effective in reaching local consumers, it is also more appropriate in the context of the promotional budget for a small firm.

2 A second evaluative theme in business planning is an awareness of reality. Roughly 90% of small businesses cease trading within five years of starting up. Rates of business failure are high and those with detailed business plans can also fail. These failures may be the result of changes in tastes or fashions, unexpected competition, bad luck or a whole host of other, often external, constraints. Another important reminder of reality is that many small business start-ups are financed by redundancy payments or inheritances. So no additional finance is required. In these cases, it is highly likely that no formal business plan will exist. Entrepreneurs are, however, likely to have skill or expertise in their particular field. An electrician starting up as a sole trader may not know what a sole trader is, but does know how to re-wire a house. In reality, when you hire an electrician you would prefer them to have a detailed knowledge of electrical matters than business matters.

**KEY terms**

**collateral** – the assets needed as security on a bank loan.

**entrepreneur** – a person who is prepared to take business opportunities, often in the context of starting up a new business.

**venture capital** – risk capital put into a small to medium-sized business, usually as a mix of equity and loan capital.

**53.4 Workbook**

# Exercises

## A. REVISION QUESTIONS

*(35 marks; 50 minutes)*

Read the unit, then answer:

1 State the three main uses of a business plan. *(3)*
2 In what circumstances is a business likely to start up with no plan? *(2)*
3 Read the list of seven key questions from NatWest's *Business Start-Up Guide*. Which three do you consider the most important? Explain why. *(6)*
4 If a firm has a pricing policy of adding a 100% mark-up onto variable cost and has monthly fixed costs of £50,000, how much does it need to sell to break even? *(4)*
5 Explain why break-even analysis plays such an important role in assessing the validity of a new business idea. *(6)*
6 Why are banks so keen to have collateral on their loans to small firms? *(2)*
7 What benefits might there be to the economy of a relaxation by banks on their policy of insisting upon collateral before financing a businesses start-up? *(6)*
8 State and explain three reasons why a good business plan is no guarantee of success. *(6)*

## B. REVISION EXERCISES

### B1 Data Response

Fresh from college, Bhrijesh Patel used the money received in an inheritance to start up a sports shop in his local high street. He spent three months contacting suppliers in order to get a clear idea of the costs involved. He discovered that his £30,000 was sufficient to pay a year's rent on the shop, redecorate the shop just the way he wanted, buy the stock he needed and provide a small amount of working capital. His was the only sports shop on the local high street.

By the end of the first week, he was happy that so many people had come into the shop, but disappointed at the level of sales. Particularly weak were sales of branded trainers. As the weeks passed, the pattern continued. So Bhrijesh drew up a simple questionnaire for people entering the shop, but not buying. Within a week, he had identified his problem. Although he had no direct competition in the local high street, the large shopping centre just out of town had three sports shops. These shops sold little equipment or specialist clothing. They were mainly selling fashion items – particularly trainers – for up to 20% less than Bhrijesh.

Having discovered this, Bhrijesh dropped the prices on

the trainers he had in stock in order to prepare for a change in strategy. He spent the next few months developing a range of stock to differentiate his shop from those of his competitors. He repositioned his shop as a specialist, selling clothing and equipment that his fashion-conscious competitors did not stock.

The change of strategy worked. The shop gained a large number of regular customers and managed to survive its difficult first few years of trading.

### Questions                              (30 marks; 35 minutes)

**1** Examine the weaknesses in Bhrijesh's approach to starting up his business.                                   (6)

**2** Despite some weaknesses, a strength was that he did not stick rigidly to a plan that was not working.

   **a** Why may some small business proprietors do this? (4)

   **b** What would be the likely consequences?           (4)

**3** A common mistake made by those who are starting their first business is to underestimate their working capital needs. What are the implications of this?          (8)

**4** Nowadays Bhrijesh produces an updated business plan every year. What benefits is he likely to gain from it?  (8)

### B2  Case Study

Suzie Jones left college determined to make a success of the business idea that had occurred to her while travelling in the Middle East the previous summer. Along with many other young people of various nationalities, Suzie had spent her summer working on a Kibbutz in Israel, picking fruit by day and partying at night.

Suzie felt sure that this sort of summer job would be perfect for many students who wanted to spend summer in the sun, but needed to work to pay for their trip. She would form a private limited company called Summer Sun and run it from home to keep overheads low.

The service she proposed to offer was a choice of packages, covering one-, two-, three- and six-month trips. Customers would pay enough to cover the cost of their flight and a 25% mark-up to cover Suzie's overheads. Customers would then work on the Kibbutz where food and accommodation were provided, along with a small amount of 'pocket money' for entertainment.

Having travelled back to Israel and built up a collection of contacts at various Kibbutz sites, she felt that

she could cope with a maximum of 500 customers at any one time. Initial market research indicated that Suzie had no competition within a local market which included three large FE colleges and many school sixth forms. She felt confident that with the right marketing, her idea could be a great success.

The business plan she drew up included the following sections:

- an outline of her idea
- a marketing plan
- a production section detailing her plans to reserve blocks of seats on a number of flights to Israel for a 10% booking deposit. Seats would need to be booked in January of each year in order to achieve the greatest cost savings. Suzie would carry out market research in December to help her judge roughly how many seats to book each year and when customers would be most likely to travel.
- a financial plan detailing the expected costs and revenues of the business. This would detail the £3,000 overheads per year and provide information on the direct costs per customer, which would differ depending upon their length of stay and date of departure.

### Questions                              (30 marks; 40 minutes)

**1** In what ways does the case study reflect the importance of cash flow to new firms?                          (4)

**2** How would you advise Suzie to set about marketing her firm?                                              (8)

**3** Using examples, suggest how a business plan can aid the survival of new firms in the first few months of existence.                                           (8)

**4** Suzie decided to form a private limited company. Explain why this was ideal in her situation.           (6)

**5** What is Suzie's break-even revenue?                  (4)

## C.  ESSAY QUESTIONS

**1** 'I only did the plan to get the finance from the bank. Lots of it is guesswork so I can't see the point myself.' Try to persuade this business proprietor about the value of a business plan.

**2** Discuss whether the time and cost of devising a thoroughly researched business plan can ever be worthwhile.

# HANDLING RAPID GROWTH

'Rapid' growth is hard to define. For firms in the computer business such as Microsoft, a growth rate of 25% a year would seem slow. Whereas for Marks and Spencer it would be unmanageably fast. Rapid growth implies a sustained, substantial increase in sales turnover, sufficient to affect the managerial structure of the business.

## 54.1 Introduction

Growth is a common business objective. When a new market is opening up, it can be crucial to become the dominant supplier. Microsoft Windows dominated, then competitors fell by the wayside. VHS video recorders became the leading format, then Sony's Betamax system fell away. The dot com boom of 2000-2001 was driven by the desire by firms such as Lastminute.com to grow large enough to dominate online travel bookings. There can be no doubt, then,

Enron – mishandling rapid growth (© Greg Smith/CORBIS SABA)

that certain business circumstances make rapid growth essential.

For many other firms, growth may not be essential but certainly seems desirable. Which company chairperson would not like to stand up at the AGM and announce a 20% sales and market share increase? The reality is, though, that rapid growth is extremely difficult to manage. The same chairperson might stand up the following year and sheepishly announce a profit downturn.

The problems of growth are threefold:

- financial – especially the effects upon cash flow and gearing
- managerial – notably problems of coordination and control
- operational – especially the difficulty of boosting supply in line with demand.

The problems arise as a result of various internal and external causes of growth. The internal ones (such as a change in objectives) should at least be planned for. External causes of growth may be unexpected, though. This makes them far harder to manage. The following table sets out some possible internal and external causes of growth.

### ENRON

During the 1990s the American firm Enron grew from a small Texan company to become the world's biggest energy supplier. Between 1996 and 2000 sales revenues grew by more than 600%. This frantic growth was seen by the stockmarket as a huge tribute to Enron's innovative, dynamic leadership. Shares shot ahead by over 1,400% between 1990 and 2000. In January 2001 the share price of $85 meant the company had a stock market value of $60,000 million. Yet by December 2001 the shares were worthless.

Enron collapsed in 2001 because it became clear that the financial strains of extremely rapid growth had been covered up by highly questionable accounting. To achieve the growth, huge bonuses had been given to 'successes' and the sack given to 'failures'. This atmosphere of fear and greed had led staff to accept increasingly doubtful business practices. Meanwhile, cash flow was struggling to keep up with the firm's debts and declining profits.

The Enron case shows all three of the 'problems of growth' mentioned in the text.

| INTERNAL CAUSES | EXTERNAL CAUSES |
|---|---|
| • New growth objectives set by management<br>• Decision to open up new export markets<br>• Reorganisation makes increased output possible | • Rising consumer demand/ the product becomes fashionable<br>• Economic boom benefits a luxury product<br>• Closure/fire/strike hits competitor, boosting your sales<br>• New laws favour your product, e.g. new safety laws boost sales of first-aid kits |

## 54.2 Business effects of forecast rapid growth

In certain circumstances managers can anticipate a period of rapid growth. This may be temporary (such as the effect of a change in the law) or may seem likely to be permanent, such as the growth in demand for computer games software. The most successful firms will be those that devise a plan that is detailed enough to help in a practical way, but flexible enough to allow for the differences between forecasts and reality.

When rapid growth has been forecast, firms can:

• compare the sales estimate with the available production capacity
• budget for any necessary increases in capacity and staffing

### CASH EATEN BY SLUG

In October 2002 SFI, owner of the Slug and Lettuce and Bar Med pub chains, cancelled its dividend and admitted that it was struggling to pay its creditors. SFI shares collapsed to 25p. They had already fallen by 80% since September – the month before the cash flow problems emerged.

Andrew Latham, chief executive, 'admitted that rapid expansion had allowed too little room for error' (*The Financial Times*). SFI had opened 46 new outlets in its 2001/2002 financial year and another 8 in the first quarter of 2002/2003. This had put too great a strain on working capital, forcing it to become heavily overdrawn. Now SFI would need to sell off part of its operations to put more secure finance in place. It was a classic case of overtrading.

IN *Business*

• produce a cash flow forecast to anticipate any short-term financing shortfall
• discuss how to raise any extra capital needed.

Timescales remain important, though. The forecast may cover the next three months, but increasing capacity may involve building a factory extension which will take eight months. In which case there may be five months of excess demand to cope with (perhaps by subcontracting).

Smooth though all this sounds, there remains a lot of scope for error. The starting point is the increased workload on staff. Extra sales may put pressure on the accounting system, the warehouse manager and the delivery drivers. With everyone being kept busy, occasional things can start to go wrong. Invoices are sent out a little later, unpaid bills are not chased as quickly and stock deliveries are not checked as carefully. Suddenly the cash flow position worsens and costs start to rise. A strong, effective manager could retrieve this, but many are weak and woolly. Once they start to go wrong, plans are hard to sort out.

## 54.3 Management reorganisation during growth

**PROBLEM OF ADJUSTMENT FROM BOSS TO LEADER/MANAGER**

The typical creator of a successful new business is lively, energetic, creative, often impatient and always a risk taker. Such a person will have a strong personality, and quite possibly an autocratic though charismatic leadership style. When the business started, their own speed of decision making, attention to detail and hard work were fundamental to the firm's success.

With success comes a problem. How to cope with the additional workload. At first the boss works ever harder; then he or she takes on more junior staff. Then comes the crunch. Is he or she willing to appoint a senior manager with real decision making power? Or will a weak manager be appointed who always has to check decisions with the boss?

Staff will always find it hard to accept a new manager because everyone will know that it is really the boss's business. It is said that 10 years after Walt Disney died, managers were still rejecting ideas on the basis that 'Walt wouldn't have done it that way'. How much harder if the founder is still there: Richard Branson at Virgin, Bill Gates at Microsoft or Tim Waterstone at Waterstone's bookshops.

The boss must make the break, however. No longer should they attend every key meeting or demand regular reports on day-to-day matters. Delegation is necessary. In other words, authority should be passed down the hierarchy to middle managers without interference from above. And instead of looking for the next great opportunity the boss may have to focus on getting the right management structure to ensure a smooth running business.

Even if the founder of the company *is* able to adjust to managing a large organisation, there remains the problem of motivation. Will the new staff be as 'hungry' as the small team that built the business? Usually the answer is no. The drinks giant Diageo thinks it has a solution, though. Diageo is the giant result of the 1997 merger of Guinness and Grand Metropolitan. It is a business with annual sales of over £17,000 million, including Smirnoff, Baileys, Guinness and Burger King. To keep staff hungry, the chief executive gives managers a 'HAT' – a 'hairy audacious target'. In other words, a bold, challenging goal. Achieving these HATs will give each manager the chance to make huge bonuses. In 1998 Diageo set itself the goal of doubling the value of the business by the end of 2002 – and achieved it. The chief executive believes HATs can stretch 'our people's imaginations to achieve these aggressive targets'. It remains to be seen whether this approach works, but it shows the lengths to which large firms may have to go to achieve the growth they seek.

## CHANGE IN MANAGEMENT STRUCTURE/HIERARCHY

As a business grows, the management structure has not only to grow but also to change. New layers of management may be needed and completely new departments may be founded, such as personnel or public relations. And all the time, as the business grows, new staff are being recruited, inducted and trained. So there is constant change in personnel and their responsibilities. This can be disconcerting for customers and suppliers. Strong relationships are hard to build, making customer loyalty tough to achieve.

Even more important, though, is the internal effect of these personnel changes. With new staff appearing frequently and managerial changes occurring regularly, team spirit may be hard to achieve. Junior and middle managers may spend too much of their time looking upwards to the promotion prospects instead of concentrating on their own departments. The potential for inefficiency or even chaos is clear. Too many new staff may mean too many mistakes. If customer relations are relatively weak, the result could easily be loss of business.

These unpleasant possibilities can largely be set aside if a good example is set from the top. If the founder of the business continues to be involved – especially on customer service – all may still be well. The leader needs to make sure staff keep sight of the qualities that brought the business its success in the first place. If new management structures threaten to create communications barriers, the leader should set an example by visiting staff, chatting to them and acting on their advice. The leader must fight against being cut off from the grassroots – the staff and the customers.

## RISK OF LOSS OF DIRECTION AND CONTROL

Each year, Templeton College Oxford produces data on what it calls the *Fast Track 100*. These are the fastest growing 100 small companies in Britain. A recent survey showed that the average growth rate of these firms was:

- sales turnover: +93% per year
- employees: +75% per year

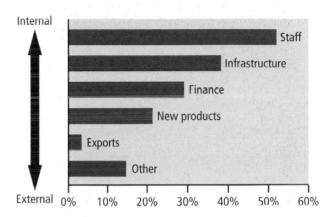

**Figure 54.1** Key challenges (Source: *Fast Track 100*, Templeton College)

The typical *Fast Track 100* firm had gone from 25 staff to 136 staff in the past three years. No wonder, then, that rapidly growing small firms can struggle to cope. The same survey showed that the key challenges faced by these companies were staff and infrastructure. As Figure 54.1 shows, the problems tend to be internal to the business, not external.

Faced with major challenges in managing the staff, the structure and the support infrastructure of the business (such as IT systems), there is a serious risk of losing focus. The successful small firms are those that keep sight of strengths that can maintain the level of innovation and competitive advantage. The survey showed the dominant growth strategy was to focus on customer service and meeting customer needs. Next most important was to focus on the company's own staff. Also important was to keep developing quality products and services. Figure 54.2 shows the findings in more detail.

The entrepreneurs who get swamped by the success of the business are those whose firms will fail to sustain their growth. They may become sidetracked by the attractions of expense account living. Or – the other extreme – become so excited by their own success that they start opening up several different businesses. They assume that their golden touch will ensure success in whatever they do. Instead, just as their core business becomes harder to handle, they are looking at a different venture altogether. Problems may then hit from several directions at once.

The key message is, therefore: focus on what you are good at.

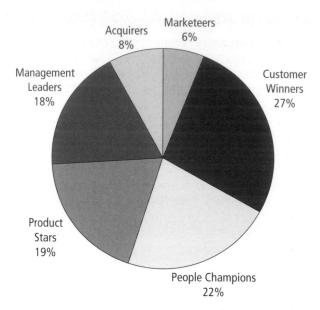

**Figure 54.2** Growth types (Source: *Fast Track 100*, Templeton College)

## 54.4 Problems of transition in size

### FROM PRIVATE TO PUBLIC

At certain points in a firm's life there are critical decisions regarding growth. Few are more fundamental than the decision to 'go public'. A private limited company is a family business, often dominated by the shareholdings of one person – probably the founder. Although its accounts must be published, it is still able to maintain a substantial veil over its activities. Its private status minimises the pressures upon the management. A year of poor trading may disappoint the family, but there is no publicly quoted share price to embarrass or to threaten the firm with a hostile takeover. This protection from outside pressures enables private companies to take a long-term view of what they want to achieve and how. The Virgin Group floated onto the stock market in the 1980s, but within four years Richard Branson took it back into private ownership. He blamed the short-term horizons of stock market investors which he thought would damage his business in the long term.

Switching from private to public company status is not, in itself, a difficult or expensive process. The big

change comes when a firm floats its shares onto the stock market. Only public companies are allowed to do this. From the protected world of the private company, the firm will enter the glare of public scrutiny. Before floating, the firm must issue a *prospectus* which sets out every detail of the firm's business, its financial record, its expectations and its key personnel. Newspapers and analysts will scrutinise this fully, and carry on writing about the firm when every set of financial results comes out.

The purpose of going public is usually to achieve a substantial increase in share capital. This can enable a highly geared private firm to achieve a more balanced capital structure, as shown in the table below.

### Business IN

### PROBLEMS OF RAPID GROWTH

In the mid-1990s, the American company Valujet became famous for opening up a new, super-low price sector of the US airline market. Its very low prices were achieved by stripping costs down to the bare minimum – including cutting out travel agents and their commission. Some wondered, though, whether there were cutbacks in safety too.

The company's growth was sensational. In the 18 months to May 1996 the number of Valujet aircraft jumped from 2 to 50 – growth of 2,400%! Then, on 11 May 1996, a Valujet plane crashed in the Florida everglades, killing all 100 passengers. Government safety investigations revealed widespread concern among safety inspectors about Valujet. The company's pace of growth had led to patchy maintenance procedures due to lack of staff. Over 58 safety incidents had occurred, 45 of which were attributed to maintenance problems. The bad publicity surrounding the crash may have done the business a favour by slowing down its pace of growth. Scant consolation, of course, for the families of the 100 passengers.

Source: Adapted from *Disaster*, BBC2

Cutting gearing by going public

| SHARPS LTD (BEFORE GOING PUBLIC) | | SHARPS PLC (AFTER RAISING £4M ON THE STOCK MARKET) | |
|---|---|---|---|
| Loan capital | £4m | Loan capital | £4m |
| Share capital | £1m | Share capital | £5m |
| Reserves | £3m | Reserves | £3m |
| **Capital employed** | **£8m** | **Capital employed** | **£12m** |
| Gearing level: | 50% | Gearing level: | 33% |

In the case of Sharps plc, the addition of 50% more capital (from £8 million to £12 million) will give a huge opportunity for major expansion. Indeed, if the management act slowly, the purchasers of the £4 million extra shares may get restless. So the managers will be inclined to make a big move. Perhaps they will make a takeover bid. Or perhaps a diversification, by launching a new product range. Either way, the risks

are substantial. Does this business have the expertise to succeed with either approach? What it needs is the confidence to keep focused upon what the management is good at. But the public pressure to make a big step forward may encourage the management to take a step too far.

## NATIONAL TO INTERNATIONAL

Most new businesses deal with local customers in their early months or years. Slowly they build up the customer contacts and the transport and distribution networks to operate nationally. Dealing with London customers may seem quite strange for a firm with its roots in Manchester, but adjustments can be made quite easily.

The next step is likely to be much harder. Many firms have struggled when building up a business overseas. In retailing, the list is endless: Tesco in France; Sainsbury's, Sock Shop, Tie Rack and Laura Ashley in America; and Marks & Spencer struggled so much overseas that in 2000 it closed all its branches outside Britain.

There are several underlying problems. These include:

- the assumption that a 'winning formula' in Britain will necessarily travel abroad
- insufficient understanding of the local market – from customer habits and attitudes through to the best locations for a retail store or for product distribution
- problems of control – if the decision is made to delegate full authority to a local managing director.

These difficulties are compounded by the view of many managers that sales success only occurs once a 'critical mass' has been achieved. Sometimes this is true. America's first serious attempt at building a national soccer league was based around the star-studded New York Cosmos, featuring football greats such as Pele and Beckenbauer. But who would they play, week by week? Football had not (and still has not) reached its critical mass as a spectator sport in America. So, when the first Sock Shop proved unsuccessful in America, the temptation was to say 'well, perhaps we need a bigger store with a wider range' or 'it's only when there's a Sock Shop at every station and airport that people will start taking them seriously'. Unfortunately, investing good money after bad is a very expensive approach. It nearly proved fatal for Sock Shop and Laura Ashley.

## RETRENCHMENT

Just as big steps forward can lead to problems, so can steps backward. Yet few firms will keep growing without the occasional sharp setback. Retrenchment means cutting back. This may be through a general reduction in staffing, or perhaps only a halt on recruitment. Most often, though, it will imply a rationalisation in which there are significant changes to the organisational structure and/or to the capacity level of the business.

In 2002 there were major worldwide rationalisations by giants such as Ford, Gap, Siemens and NEC. On a smaller scale, British Steel and Dr Marten's also cut back. In all cases, the key factor is to ensure that retrenchment does not cause lasting damage to morale, relationships and trust. Therefore it is vital to be honest, open, fair and as generous as possible to anyone who is losing a job.

When forced to cut back, firms have many options. These are described in the table at the bottom of the page.

When tackling questions about rapid growth, the following lines of analysis are helpful:

- Is the growth planned (internal) or unplanned (external)?
- Is the business leader's management style capable of changing as the business develops?
- Is there scope for containing the growth? For example, can some contracts be turned down without threatening the future health of the business? If so, this may be wise.
- Does the firm have the financial resources to cope with the growing needs for capital?
- How well does the firm cope with growth shocks, such as a stock market flotation? Can the management keep focused upon the strategy and the strengths of the business.
- Would managers who have handled growth well be equally good at handling retrenchment? Only if they have and deserve the trust of the staff.

## WARNING SIGNS OF COLLAPSE

Business consultant John Argenti says there are three phases in corporate collapse. The first involves gaps and imbalances appearing in a company's management, often because of rapid growth. In this phase, processes of monitoring fall apart, so managers start to lose touch with what is really happening within the business. In the second phase these defects lead managers to make wrong decisions. The final phase sees cracks appearing openly, such as rising staff turnover and signs of cash flow problems, e.g. late payment of bills.

Thirty years ago Argenti developed a way of measuring the risk of corporate collapse, which he called the A-score. As the table on page 347 shows, it is a mixture of leadership and managerial factors, plus financial measures. Argenti says it succeeds in predicting nine out of ten corporate crises.

### 54.5 Handling rapid growth
#### an evaluation

One of the hardest judgements to make about growth is when a rapid rate becomes excessive. Can firms cope with growth rates of over 50%, year after year? The *Fast Track 100* survey suggests that the answer is yes. A recent winner enjoyed turnover growth from £1 million to £26.4 million in three years. Such dramatic success is possible, but only if the management is well focused

| TYPE OF RETRENCHMENT | ADVANTAGES | DISADVANTAGES |
|---|---|---|
| Freezing recruitment and/or offering voluntary redundancy | • Not threatening; should not cause problems of job insecurity<br>• Viewed by staff as fair | • No chance to reshape the business<br>• Good people are always leaving, so they need to be replaced |
| De-layering, i.e. removing a whole management layer | • Should not affect direct operations (such as staff on the shop-floor)<br>• May empower/enrich remaining jobs | • May over-intensify the work of other managers, causing stress<br>• Risk of losing a generation of managers<br>• Loss of promotion prospects for those who remain |
| Closing a division, a factory or a number of loss-making outlets | • Sharp reduction in fixed overhead costs will reduce break-even point<br>• Capacity utilisation may rise in the firm's other factories | • Once closed, the capacity is unlikely to be available for the next economic upturn<br>• Lose many good staff |
| Making targeted cutbacks and redundancies in divisions throughout the business | • Can reshape the business to meet the future, e.g. no cutbacks among IT staff<br>• By keeping good staff, their average quality level may rise | • Huge problems of perceived fairness (unless there is a high degree of trust)<br>• Job security may be hit ('will it be me next?') |

and flexible. Many companies are dragged under by their failure to cope with success.

Why does rapid growth matter? Britain has for many years been one of Europe's leading economies for small business start-ups. Too often, though, they are part hobby and part self-employment. Rapid growth matters because job creation and economic growth depend upon small firms building up into medium or large businesses. Fifteen years ago, the American equivalent of the *Fast Track 100* identified unknown companies such as Microsoft, Oracle and Domino's Pizza. These are the growth stories that make a difference. All show that rapid growth can be managed. But all the managers would agree that it is never easy.

## A-SCORES – IS THE COMPANY A OK?

To calculate the A score, mark each criterion out of the total shown. Do not use half marks. If in doubt, score zero. Argenti's total scores are in the second column. In the third are the editor's estimates of Enron's position during 1999–2001. Enron collapsed in early 2002.

| DEFECTS | Total | Enron |
|---|---|---|
| Autocratic leadership | 8 | 8 |
| Combined chairman and chief executive | 4 | 0 |
| Passive board | 2 | 2 |
| Unbalanced skills | 2 | 0 |
| Weak finance director | 2 | 0 |
| Poor management depth | 1 | 0 |
| No budgetary control | 3 | 1 |
| No cash-flow plans | 3 | 0 |
| No costing system | 3 | 3 |
| Poor response to change (ageing product, plant, directors etc) | 15 | 0 |
| MISTAKES | | |
| High gearing | 15 | 12 |
| Overtrading (expansion under-financed) | 15 | 8 |
| Big project (overwhelming the rest of the business) | 15 | 2 |
| SYMPTOMS | | |
| Financial signs | 4 | 4 |
| Creative accounting | 4 | 4 |
| Non-financial signs (e.g. staff turnover) | 3 | 1 |
| Terminal signs | 1 | 0 |
| OVERALL TOTAL | 100 | 45 |
| Pass mark | 25 | 25 |

Stable companies score well under 25. Those at risk of insolvency score between 35 and 70.

# Exercises

## A. REVISION QUESTIONS

*(50 marks; 70 minutes)*

Read the unit, then answer:

1 Explain why rapid growth can cause problems for a company's:
   **a** cash flow *(2)*
   **b** management control. *(2)*

2 Distinguish between internal and external causes of growth, using examples. *(5)*

3 Why might there be a problem in adjusting from 'boss' to 'leader/manager'? *(4)*

4 How might large firms benefit from setting staff 'Hairy Audacious Targets'? *(3)*

5 Examine the bar chart headed 'Key Challenges'. Outline two important conclusions. *(6)*

6 Identify three problems for a fast-growing firm caused by changes in the management structure. *(3)*

7 Outline two strengths and two potential weaknesses of stock market flotation for a rapidly growing business. *(8)*

8 Explain the possible problems (and benefits) to a small computer software firm of changing status from private to public limited company. *(4)*

9 **a** Explain the meaning of the term 'retrenchment'. *(3)*
   **b** Outline two suitable methods of retrenchment for an airline that is losing market share. *(4)*

10 From your knowledge of current business events, identify two firms that have recently enjoyed very rapid growth. Analyse the likely causes of the growth in both cases. *(6)*

## B. REVISION EXERCISES

### B1 Data Response

#### Diseconomies at The Body Shop

The Body Shop was a huge 1980s' success story. It shot up from a single shop in Brighton to a multinational empire. Founder Anita Roddick was convinced that bulk buying and mass production would push costs down and profit margins up. By 1998, however, it was clear that things were not going according to plan. As the *Sunday Times* commented: 'As it has mushroomed from a company with 70 employees to an international retail group with more than 5,000, some of the arteries have clogged up.'

The directors had come to realise that it had become difficult to bring new ideas into their shops quickly. One pointed out that 'we are now in 47 countries with 19 languages … you have a pretty complicated business'. Problems had arisen of communication and coordination – but especially of motivation. When small, Anita Roddick had been able to inspire staff to care passionately about The Body Shop's mission to spread a message of social concern. Now the business was big and a little fat.

**Questions** *(30 marks; 35 minutes)*

1 Outline the ways in which a firm's arteries might be expected to clog up when its staff level has 'mushroomed' from 70 staff to 5,000. *(10)*

2 Examine the issues in the case study that indicate problems with diseconomies of scale. *(6)*

3 The Body Shop grew at a rate of nearly 100% per year during the 1980s, yet it never hit any serious cash flow or financing difficulties. What might be the reasons for this? *(6)*

4 One of The Body Shop's recent problems has been the weak performance of several of its overseas subsidiaries. How might the management tackle this problem? *(8)*

### B2 Data Response

#### Heinz Tries to Squeeze More out of the Ketchup Bottle

There are few better known brand names than HJ Heinz. Yet it is wrong to assume that well-known names always grow. The difficulty for Heinz has been transferring its success in bottled and canned foods to the faster growing chilled and frozen-food sectors. A 1997 retrenchment led to 20 plant closures, 2,500 job cuts and $200 million of savings per year. Even that was insufficient, however, and in 1999 a new plan was announced.

The 1999 plan (called Operation Excel) would cost $900 million and cost the jobs of 10% of the 40,000 staff worldwide. Three strategies lie at the heart of the programme:

- selling off the 30-year-old Weight Watchers business
- reorganising the group along product lines rather than geographically (making pan-European marketing easier to accomplish)
- increasing the marketing budget from 9% to 10% of the $9,000 million annual sales.

To its credit, Heinz is not content to cut back and cut back. It wants to transfer resources to marketing, in order to get sales moving again. As evidence of the potential of this approach, the company boasted that extra marketing spending in America on its mature Heinz ketchup products had boosted sales by 24% in January 1999. This will be little consolation to the 4,000 staff who will lose their jobs in 1999, but will reassure the remaining staff that management has a strategy for rebuilding the business.

Source: Adapted from *The Financial Times*, 19/2/99

## Questions                    *(30 marks, 35 minutes)*

**1** Use the text and the graphs below to explain why Heinz is carrying out a retrenchment programme.          *(8)*

**2** Outline two alternative approaches management might take to achieve the staff reduction by 4,000. Which of the two would you recommend and why?          *(12)*

**3 a** By how much is Heinz increasing its marketing spending (in $s)?          *(2)*

 **b** To what extent could this decision be expected to overcome the impact upon morale of the staff cutbacks?          *(8)*

## C. ESSAY QUESTIONS

**1** Dell Computers has grown at a rate of 50% per year for nearly a decade. Outline the problems this might cause. What might be the most effective way for management to tackle them?

**2** Charlie is a hugely successful hairdresser's in York. A wealthy client has offered to invest £500,000 to finance the establishment of Charlie outlets in Leeds and Harrogate. Discuss whether the proprietor should accept the offer or not.

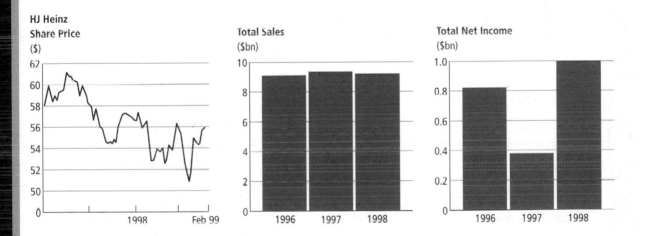

**HJ Heinz**
**Share Price** ($)

**Total Sales** ($bn)

**Total Net Income** ($bn)

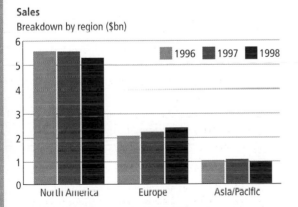

**Sales**
Breakdown by region ($bn)

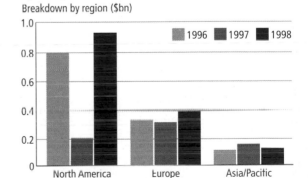

**Operating income**
Breakdown by region ($bn)

*Source:* Adapted from Datastream/ICV; company

# CORPORATE AIMS AND OBJECTIVES

## DEFINITION

Corporate aims express the long-term intention of the organisation to develop in a certain way. Their purpose is to create a common vision which everyone in the organisation should work towards achieving.

Objectives (or goals) are the targets which must be achieved in order to fulfil the corporate aims.

## 55.1 Corporate aims

Winning teams share a collective view of what it means to be successful in the long term. For a sports team the aim is simple, to finish first. Establishing aims for an organisation is more difficult. Yet it is equally important if sustained success is to be achieved. Corporate aims help build team spirit, encouraging commitment to the organisation and cooperation within it.

One of the stated aims of the McDonald's fast-food chain is to provide 'friendly service in a relaxed, safe, and consistent restaurant environment'. The success of the organisation depends upon turning this aim into practice. In order for this to be achieved employees must understand and share the aim. When a customer enters a McDonald's restaurant anywhere in the world they know what to expect. The organisation has the ability to reproduce the same 'relaxed, safe and consistent' atmosphere with different staff, in different locations. This has built the company's reputation. This corporate aim is effective because it recognises what lies at the heart of the organisation's success.

Many businesses do not write down their aims or even spend time trying to define them. This is particularly true of small organisations where employees know each other and understand their shared purpose. Staff in a small firm may work together to achieve a common vision with a commitment that may not exist in a large firm which sets out its aims in writing.

Whether stated or unstated, corporate aims act as a basis upon which to form goals or objectives for the organisation. These are the intermediate targets which must be achieved if the aims are to be realised. The success or failure of each individual decision within the firm can be judged by the extent to which it meets the business objectives. This allows the delegation of authority within the organisation, while at the same time maintaining coordination.

## LINKING AIMS AND OBJECTIVES AT ICI

When Miller Smith was appointed as chief executive officer of ICI (Imperial Chemical Industries) in 1994 he identified the need for the organisation to become more growth and profit oriented. He felt that in the past the company's strength had been 'in technical innovation rather than being market, or sales driven'.

In order to 'focus the hearts and minds' of its 65,000 workers, a new corporate aim was established to be 'the industry leader in creating value for our customers and shareholders'.

To communicate this corporate aim, a presentation to ICI's top 250 executives was followed by a television talk-in, hosted by Miller Smith. In this he answered questions from company sites worldwide – Asia in the morning, America and Europe after lunch.

The corporate aim was then turned into a specific, measurable goal for every part of ICI's business. This was to achieve an 'average return on net assets over the business cycle of 20%'.

*Business IN*

## 55.2 Corporate objectives

The larger the group, the more difficult it is to coordinate its actions towards a common goal. When a business is small its manager has personal contact with every employee. The long-term direction of the firm will be communicated clearly from day to day. Motivating the workforce to act together will be an easier task than in a large company. Objectives will be understood informally rather than written down.

As the firm grows the job of coordinating the actions of every employee becomes harder. A mission statement may be needed to provide a shared vision of the company's future. This may be needed to motivate the workforce. It is also the basis for developing **corporate objectives**. These represent the goals of the whole enterprise. These can take any form, but a number of targets are widely adopted:

**Maximising the amount of profit earned by the organisation:** This is usually regarded as the primary objective of any business in the private sector. In practice, profit maximisation is usually the principal target only when the firm's survival is threatened in the short run. It will govern decision making until the point at which the financial health of the organisation is restored. In the long run, if a business is functioning efficiently and healthily, alternative objectives will be of more importance such as growth or diversification.

In large public limited companies the owners of the firm (the shareholders) are not the decision makers (the management). A board of directors is elected to run the company on behalf of the shareholders. This group may develop aims for the business which recognise a wider group of **stakeholders** than just owners. As a result, the firm may not set profit maximisation as its key goal, even in the short run.

**Maximising shareholder wealth:** This is increasingly presented by the board of directors of large companies as the modern equivalent of profit maximisation. Share prices reflect the present value of the dividends the company is expected to pay out in the future. As a result this objective means taking actions which maximise the price of the organisation's shares on the stock market.

**Growth in the size of the firm:** The managers of a business may choose to take decisions with the objective of making the organisation larger. The motivation behind this goal could be the natural desire to see the business achieve its full potential. It may also help defend the firm from hostile takeover bids. If your firm is the biggest, who could be big enough to take you over?

**Diversification to spread risk:** In other words, to reduce dependence on one product or market. Such as Cadbury's developing soft drinks (Schweppes and 7-Up) to provide sales success in hot weather to counteract the fall in chocolate sales. In this way the long-term survival prospects of the business are improved. A firm may also diversify if it has a key product in the decline phase of the product life cycle; for example, cigarette manufacturers. Diversification will allow movement into 'growth' markets.

**Focus on core capabilities:** An increasing number of managers identify the key strengths which lie within their organisation, such as talent for innovation. Then focus the resources of the firm on developing the skills into profitable products.

**Increasing market standing:** If a business has a good reputation with its suppliers, distributors and customers then this will make it easier to launch new products.

In order to be effective, corporate objectives must be measurable. A target which is directional but with no given value, such as 'increasing market share', will not have the desired impact on employee motivation. A goal of 'boosting market share from 6% to 9%' provides a specific figure for individuals to work towards. However, the objective must be achievable. Otherwise it becomes demoralising. It is also important to provide a timescale within which the goal must be attained.

---

## SHORT-TERM PROFIT OBJECTIVES: A BRITISH DISEASE?

One of Britain's industrial successes of the 1990s was the TI Group. Dynamic and profitable, its methods were typified by the purchase in 1992 of Dowty – a 60-year-old, major supplier of landing gear (undercarriages) for aircraft. TI moved quickly to form a joint venture with the French producer Messier. Together Messier–Dowty held over one-third of the world market – a major European rival to the large US manufacturers. Here was a British firm with a major foothold in one of the world's largest, fastest growing and highest value-added industries – aircraft production.

Excellently run from Britain by Tony Edwards, the venture's chairman, the expectation was that TI would eventually buy out its French partner. Instead, in December 1997, TI announced the sale of its 50% stake in Messier–Dowty for £207.5 million. The Financial Times suggested a likely reason was that 'TI thought the 8.9% operating margin was too low'. Another possibility was that rapid growth called for more cash investment from TI Group than it was willing to provide. Whatever the reason, a profitable, high technology business was sold to delighted French owners. Perhaps the French were willing to consider longer term business objectives.

Source: Adapted from *The Financial Times*

## GROWTH BY DIVERSIFICATION CREATES DANGER FOR VIRGIN

During the mid-1990s, Richard Branson's Virgin Group made a series of bold strategic moves. Each was launched in a wave of favourable press and TV publicity. From its twin base in the music business and in air travel, Virgin moved into:

- the soft drinks market, with Virgin Cola
- the alcoholic drinks market, with Virgin Vodka
- the financial services market, with Virgin Direct
- rail travel, by taking a 17% stake in Eurostar and winning the privatised contract for West Coast Inter-City services
- the cosmetics market, through Virgin Vie.

By 1998, however, it was becoming clear that Virgin had expanded too far and in too many different directions. Bad publicity about the poor performance of Virgin trains was compounded by the weakening market position of Virgin Cola and Vodka. The Economist reported that these two brands had made losses of more than £4.5 million in the 1996/97 financial year. After several years boasting about new ventures, Virgin's corporate affairs director said 'We are going to consolidate around our core areas. We don't plan to extend the brand much further'. The objective of expansion through diversification had been reversed. Now Virgin was to focus on its core capabilities.

Source: Adapted from *Marketing Week*, 21/2/98 and © *The Economist*, 21/2/98

## 55.3 Business strategy

The managers of a business should develop a medium- to long-term plan about how to achieve the objectives they have established. This is the organisation's corporate strategy. It sets out the actions that will be taken in order to achieve the goals. And the implications for the firm's human, financial and production resources. The key to success when forming a strategy of this kind is relating the firm's strengths to the opportunities which exist in the marketplace.

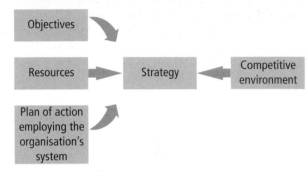

**Figure 55.2** Strategy formation

This analysis can take place at each level of the business, allowing a series of strategies to be formed in order to achieve the goals already established.

- Corporate strategy deals with the major issues such as what industry, or industries, the business should compete in, in order to achieve corporate objectives. Managers must identify industries where the long-term profit prospects are likely to be favourable. In 1998, for example, Boots decided to pull out of the DIY market by selling its Do It All subsidiary.
- Business unit (or divisional) strategy should address the issue of how the organisation will compete in the industry selected by corporate strategy. This will involve selecting a position in the marketplace to distinguish the firm from its competitors.

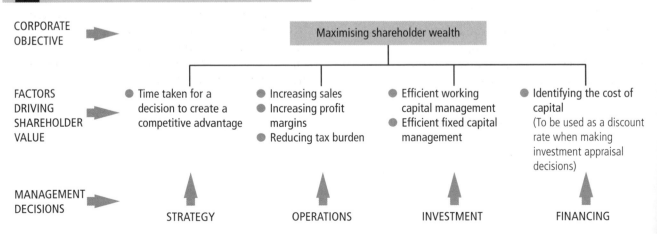

Adapted from *Shareholder Value* by Richard Barfield, published in *Accountancy*, October 1991

**Figure 55.1** Maximising shareholder wealth

- Functional (or department) strategy is developed in order to identify how best to succeed in the market position identified in the divisional strategy.

If targets are established for individual employees, it is quite possible that a personal strategy for achieving these goals may be established as part of the company's appraisal process.

Just as the objectives of the organisation cascade down to the lowest levels of the business ensuring consistent planning, so too do strategies. This is to establish coordinated action. If a strategy is to achieve the objectives set, it must match the firm's strengths to its **competitive environment**. Boots decided that its strength was in running the Number 1 chemist business in the UK. Its ability to hold on to the Number 1 position was not helpful at succeeding with Do It All – a DIY chain that was an also-ran. So Do It All had to go.

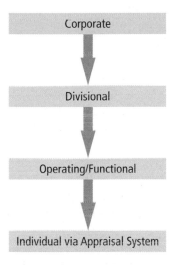

**Figure 55.3** Hierarchy of strategy

ISSUES FOR **analysis**

When analysing a firm's approach to establishing corporate objectives and developing strategic policy to achieve these goals, it is useful to consider the following points:

- Are the objectives of the business precisely defined? And are they understood and supported by staff?
- Is the outcome of each objective measurable so that it will be clear when it has been achieved?

- Does each objective have a target date for completion in order to ensure action?
- Are the organisation's objectives focused excessively on short-run profit maximisation at the expense of the long-term development of the business?
- Do the managers of the business clearly understand its strengths and weaknesses?
- Have opportunities in the competitive environment been identified?
- Does the strategic policy of the organisation 'match' the firm's strengths to opportunities in the competitive environment?
- Finally, and most importantly, do the strategies match the objectives?

## 55.4 Corporate aims and objectives
### an evaluation

In many organisations, particularly small businesses, the idea of stating objectives and developing strategy to achieve them may seem unnecessary. Some managers may claim their firm has no explicit strategy or planning process and yet is very successful.

The first issue here is the existence of strategy. Every organisation has a strategy. It may not be written down, or even clearly defined, but by observing the behaviour of the business over time a pattern will emerge in the actions which are taken. This pattern reflects the strategy adopted by the firm's management. Strategy in many businesses reflects a slow development towards a position in the market which is never formally identified, but is reached through a process of intuitive decisions. Managers shape the organisation's strengths to fit the competitive environment based on their knowledge and experience of that market.

A second issue is whether careful strategic planning can ever be as helpful in practice as in theory. It will always be difficult for managers or consultants to capture a complete picture of the current competitive environment. Especially in a global economy where change is occurring very quickly. Even harder, of course, is to anticipate how any market will look in one, five or ten years' time.

**business culture** – the culture of a business is a set of rules, usually unwritten, which govern the way employees behave. These are not formal procedures, but a set of practices which grow up over time and represent 'the way we do things around here'.

**business strategy** – a plan devised in order to allow an organisation to achieve a specific objective.

**competitive environment** – the strength, number and positioning of rival businesses within a firm's marketplace.

**core capabilities** – the strengths of the organisation, i.e. what it is good at doing.

**corporate objectives** – the goals established for the whole organisation. Examples include long-term growth and short-term profit maximisation.

**management by objectives** – divides the overall aim of the business into specific goals for each level of the organisation's hierarchy. In this way the actions of all employees are coordinated and individuals are motivated to behave in a way which helps the firm succeed.

**stakeholders** – groups with a direct interest in the way an organisation is performing and the action it takes. Examples include the firm's employees, shareholders, customers, suppliers and the local community.

# Exercises

## A. REVISION QUESTIONS
*(35 marks; 70 minutes)*

Read the unit, then answer:

1 Why might a formal statement of aims be unnecessary in a small business with a limited number of employees? *(3)*

2 **a** Explain the link between aims and goals. *(3)*

  **b** How do they combine to act in a way which allows authority to be delegated in a large organisation? *(4)*

3 **a** List four potential corporate objectives. *(4)*

  **b** Consider the extent to which each is focused on the short or long run. *(4)*

4 Explain why it might be more appropriate for a public limited company to set an objective of maximising shareholder wealth than annual profit. *(5)*

5 **a** What is a corporate strategy? *(3)*

  **b** Identify the factors an organisation might consider when forming strategy. *(4)*

6 Outline how strategies formed at different levels of the business might interlink to form a hierarchy. *(4)*

## B. REVISION EXERCISES

### B1 Data Response
### Wrapping It Up

In December 1993 Olivia Manduca struggled to find something glamorous to wear over her wedding dress. She made a satin and velvet stole which friends thought stunning. So she went into business. She produced half a dozen and persuaded Harrods to stock them. 1994's sales turnover of £50,000 persuaded her to form a limited company called Wonderful Wraps. She also found a factory in London's East End which has been making the wraps ever since.

By 1998 turnover reached £150,000 and net profit margins were over 50%. Making the business a lot more than a hobby. Olivia had started her business with an investment of just £500 and had never needed to borrow a penny. She was starting to face her first big decision. Whether to expand further or to keep Wonderful Wraps small.

**Questions** *(30 marks; 35 minutes)*

1 a Outline three possible business objectives that Olivia may have had from the start. *(6)*
  b From the text, which do you think was her main objective? Explain your reasoning. *(5)*
2 a In 1998 alone, what percentage return was Olivia receiving on her £500 investment? *(4)*
  b Can such returns ever be justified? *(6)*
3 Discuss the factors Olivia should take into account in deciding 'whether to expand further or to keep Wonderful Wraps small'? *(9)*

### B2 Data Response

In 1994, a 30-year-old New Yorker called Jeff Bezos read about the Internet. He moved to California and in a year had set up an Internet bookshop. When orders came in, he packed and posted the books from his garage. By February 1999 he employed 1,600 people and his shares were worth $2,500 million. Jeff Bezos is the founder and 40% shareholder in Amazon.com, the world's biggest Internet bookshop.

What are the aims that helped guide him to become one of the first Internet billionaires? His workforce mission is to 'Change the world in an important and fundamental way. Our motto is: Work hard, have fun, make history.'

The aim in relation to customers is to '...provide the best customer experience.... That means we have to have the biggest selection! The easiest to use website! The lowest prices! And the best purchase decision information!'

Asked about his huge wealth, Bezos replied: 'I don't think it matters much. The biggest change is that I don't have to look at menu prices any more.'

**Questions** *(30 marks; 35 minutes)*

1 Distinguish between aims and objectives with reference to this case. *(6)*
2 Do you consider that Mr Bezos was successful because of his aims, or that his success allowed him to adopt such aims? Explain your answer. *(10)*
3 What evidence is there in the text that business people are not only motivated by money. *(6)*
4 Outline four factors that might lead to a change in Amazon.com's aims in future. *(8)*

# BUSINESS STRATEGY

## DEFINITION

Strategic analysis is the process of examining the factors within the organisation which will have an impact on its long-term success, and comparing these with the conditions identified in the firm's competitive environment.

## 56.1 What is strategy?

In order to achieve a goal, it is necessary to develop a plan of action. For example, a timetable to guide examination revision and success. Organisations also have objectives to achieve. This process requires an outline of the steps that will be taken to reach a given target. A plan of this kind is called a strategy.

## 56.2 A model for conducting a strategic analysis

In order to form a strategic plan it is necessary to gather information about the business and its market-place. This will come from two sources:

- internal sources of information, such as the company's prices, costs and efficiency levels
- external data from organisations like the government and trade associations.

The planning should be undertaken regularly and involve the department managers closest to the key issues. It should not be a crisis measure, or else hasty decisions may be made.

The process of strategic analysis involves an *internal audit* to appraise the strengths and weaknesses of the firm. And an **external audit** to evaluate the threats and opportunities in the company's competitive environment (see Figure 56.1).

## 56.3 External audit

An external audit should investigate three key areas of the competitive environment facing an organisation:

1 The general business and economic conditions which exist within each of the countries which the firm serves.
2 The conditions within each specific market to which the business sells.
3 The nature of the competition in each market segment targeted by the organisation.

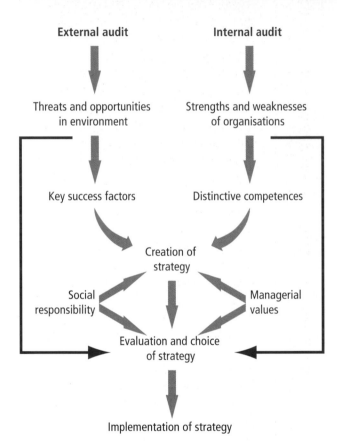

**Figure 56.1** Model guiding strategic analysis (After Mintzberg, 1990)

### BMW AND MERCEDES: SHARED OBJECTIVES BUT DIFFERENT STRATEGIES

*In Business*

BMW and Mercedes-Benz both built their reputations on large, luxury cars. However, strategic market analysis pointed both companies towards a change in strategy. The average age of a Mercedes owner was about 60, while BMW drivers were in their 40s. An ageing customer-base limits the prospects for sales growth.

In order to achieve the objective of long-term growth both companies made the decision to move into the market for smaller cars. Mercedes developed the A Class and BMW, using the Rover brand name, launched the Spiritual in Germany. Although both firms shared the common goal of producing a smaller car, the strategies they adopted to accomplish it were very different.

BMW made the decision to acquire Rover in 1994 for £800 million. This almost doubled its potential output immediately. However, the key benefit of the takeover was to add a number of smaller and cheaper cars to the BMW range. In this way the company gained a foothold in the mass market using the Rover name and the established reputation of models such as the Mini. At the same time the image of the parent company as a luxury car manufacturer was not jeopardised.

Mercedes also considered the purchase of Rover, but preferred the strategy of building its own small car. The A Class is an unconventional design, aimed at the market segment which purchase vehicles such as the VW Golf. This was always a high-risk strategy, because failure could tarnish the Mercedes image in its established market.

Each strategy was to prove costly. For BMW, the short term cost of purchasing the Rover brand was high because of the British company's poor trading performance plus the rise in the value of the pound in 1996. By late 1998, BMW was forecasting losses at Rover until at least 2001. The Mercedes approach proved even more accident prone. The late 1997 launch of the A Class was marred by worldwide headlines about the car rolling over when a journalist cornered sharply at just 30 miles an hour.

Both companies shared the view that their competitive position demanded a move into the small car market. Each developed a strategy which looked a mistake in the short term. For firms like Mercedes and BMW, though, the final verdict can only be made in five or ten years' time.

## BUSINESS AND ECONOMIC CONDITIONS

To analyse the business and economic conditions a firm faces, 'PEST-G' analysis is helpful.

## PEST-G analysis:

**l  P for Political**

Government policy can have a major impact on the operation of a business. For example, laws on competitive practices will influence the number of firms operating in an industry and therefore the strength of competition. Health and safety legislation will affect work practices and production costs. Marketing tactics will be limited by consumer legislation. It is important to study the political environment within which business operates, particularly in countries where governments are unstable and therefore investment risks are high.

- **E for Economic**

Economic factors will influence the future potential profit of a business. The level of consumer demand is a key variable affecting the quantity of sales and the price at which output can be sold. Interest rates will determine the cost of finance to the company. Final profits will be taxed by the government. The economic cycle of recession and recovery is an important influence on the opportunities and threats to the organisation.

- **S for Social**

Consumers reflect changes in lifestyles over time. This means businesses must observe shifts in the characteristics and habits of the population. Especially where these influence segments of the existing market. For example, as the UK population ages, new opportunities open up such as holidays aimed specifically at older people. Demographic variations may also represent a threat to companies. For example, a fall in the birth rate would jeopardise the competitive position of Mothercare.

- **T for Technology**

An external audit must monitor developments in technology. These can affect the production methods employed by the organisation, or the products/services offered for sale. A new manufacturing technique might make existing production too expensive for the business to remain profitable. A product may become obsolete because new technology has developed a more effective substitute. However, changes in technology also offer opportunities, such as the potential to break into new markets by producing a new, radically different, product offering.

- **G for Green issues**

Consumers and governments are becoming increasingly aware of the impact of business upon the environment. Organisations must now monitor their actions and consider their environmental implications. For example, Shell met with substantial opposition to its plan to sink a disused oil rig in the Atlantic Ocean. An issue of this kind can influence

Business IN

## PRODUCT REPOSITIONING: LUCOZADE

In the 1970s Lucozade was regarded by consumers as a glucose drink to be given to people who were not feeling well. Its slogan was 'Lucozade aids recovery'. The packaging and pricing reflected this. A premium price was charged for a large glass bottle wrapped in cellophane. Distribution was largely through chemists. This established an image radically different from that adopted by other soft drinks.

In the 1980s changes in consumer lifestyles led to a growth in health consciousness and particularly personal fitness. Lucozade was radically repositioned in the market. Advertising was used to promote the product as an energy-giving sports drink. A series of nationally known personalities, such as John Barnes, the England football player, appeared in Lucozade commercials. The packaging of the product was changed to conventional soft drink cans and much smaller bottles. These were designed to be consumed as a single drink during or after sport rather than stored away for repeated use. General retailers were encouraged to stock the relaunched product alongside other canned soft drinks.

Lucozade is now firmly established as an energy-giving soft drink for health conscious consumers. This offers the potential for a greater sales volume than the original target segment of those recovering from illness. It is this kind of dramatic revival of a product's sales potential which reflects the benefits which can result from a careful analysis of the market environment.

the corporate image of an organisation. The resulting publicity may damage the effectiveness of the firm's promotional activities.

### THE MARKET ENVIRONMENT

An external audit should consider each of the major markets in which the firm competes. Key factors of importance are:

- Market size – measured by value and volume of sales.
- Market growth – measured by the percentage change in the value and volume of sales.
- Market trends – such as the position of the product in its life cycle.

- Market share of each manufacturer – based on product type and brand name.
- New products introduced to the market – not just those items which compete directly with the company's output, but also complementary and substitute goods.
- Product positioning – a process widely adopted by marketers is to 'map' consumer impressions of the goods available for purchase, based on the most important benefits the product offers consumers. This method allows managers the opportunity to analyse the potential for changes in strategic approach towards a particular brand.

### THE COMPETITIVE ENVIRONMENT

The final phase of the external audit concentrates on the organisation's direct competitors (see Figure 56.2).

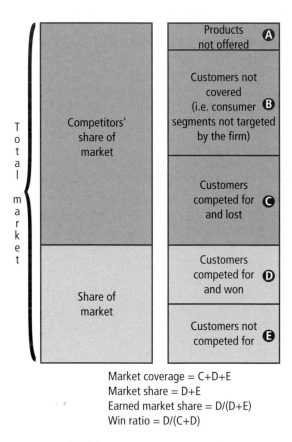

Market coverage = C+D+E
Market share = D+E
Earned market share = D/(D+E)
Win ratio = D/(C+D)

**Figure 56.2** Audit of the competitive environment (K. Ohmae, 1983)

- Identify who they are and how they conduct their business.
- Determine their approximate size in terms of sales value and volume.
- Assess their production capabilities, including the maximum volume of output of which they are capable and the extent to which machinery is currently being utilised.
- Use their published annual accounts to assess their financial strength.
- Consider the extent to which the organisation has diversified into a range of different product types

and is involved in trading across international markets.

- Investigate the channels of distribution which they use.
- Judge their market standing with consumers and the extent to which each item in the product range contributes to their reputation.

The information gathered in the audit of competitors should be used to assess the likely objectives and strategies that the firm may adopt in the future.

## SHARING INFORMATION WITH COMPETITORS: BEST PRACTICE BENCHMARKING

An audit which aims to gather information about competitors in the same industry is difficult to conduct. Many firms make very few facts about themselves public, except when required to by law. Best practice benchmarking breaks with the idea of keeping material secret. Companies form alliances in order to share knowledge about how to conduct their business as efficiently as possible. The purpose of the approach is to gain an understanding of how to undertake specific processes in the most efficient way possible. By copying best practice in each area of the business a company which is second best at each activity can become the best company overall.

## 56.4 Internal audit

An **internal audit** is a way of compiling a list of a firm's main strengths and weaknesses. Robert Townsend, former chairman of Avis Car Rental, said the first thing he did when taking charge was to 'go and talk to all 1,000 employees and find out what they do. And what stops them being the best in the world at what they do.' Today, internal audits are more likely to be carried out by a **management consultant**.

An organisation undertaking an internal audit must seek to identify the strengths and weaknesses of the firm *relative to its competitors*. A business may have modern, highly efficient machinery, but if every other company in the industry has access to similar technology then this is not a strength.

Managers should be objective in assessing their own departments. An internal audit will be of little use if it is the result of over-optimistic analysis. Fortunately, it should be possible to base much of the evidence on facts (such as product costs) rather than estimates.

An internal audit should analyse financial data such as cost trends, actual performance against budget estimates and the profit in relation to capital employed. Much of the relevant data will already have been produced by management accountants to guide decision making within the firm.

In addition to financial information, marketing, human resource and operations strategies must be considered in detail. In each case direct comparisons

with competitors can be made as a result of the knowledge gathered in the external audit, or via benchmarking.

The following table gives examples of internal auditing in practice:

| DEPARTMENT BEING AUDITED | CRITERIA FOR AUDITING |
| --- | --- |
| Human resources | Labour turnover, employee satisfaction surveys, absenteeism, skills audit |
| Marketing | Sales trends for each of the firm's products, advertising spending per product, size and skills of sales force |
| Operations management | Trends in defect rate (production quality), productivity, lead time, stock turnover |
| Financial management | Production costs, analyses of sales and cost variances, audits of profitability of past capital investments (did the appraisal of cash flow data prove accurate?) |

## 56.5 Presenting the strategic analysis: SWOT diagrams

A large quantity of information will result from the external and internal audit. These facts must be organised into a format which allows them to be understood by managers in order to aid their decision making. A SWOT (Strengths, Weaknesses, Opportunities and Threats) diagram is the most widely adopted method used for presentation purposes (see Figure 56.3).

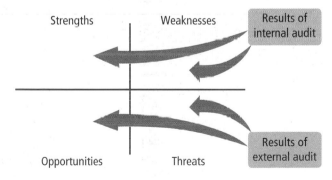

**Figure 56.3** SWOT diagram

The results of the internal audit are divided into two groups:

- factors which are positive relative to competitors are recorded as strengths

- factors which are negative relative to competitors are recorded as weaknesses.

The results of the external audit are also divided into two groups:

- factors in the external environment which have the potential to bring benefits to the organisation are recorded as opportunities
- factors in the external environment which have the potential to cause a negative effect on the organisation are recorded as threats.

The SWOT diagram should focus on the relevant key factors in each case. A brief outline highlighting the reasons for good or bad performance should accompany the diagram. In order to be effective it must be relevant to those managers using it and creative in its interpretation of the internal and external audit data.

ISSUES FOR **analysis**

In order to consider the approach adopted towards strategic analysis by an organisation there are a number of key issues which should be reviewed. These include:

- Do the managers of the business undertake a regular planning exercise, including an internal and external audit?
- If an external audit has been completed, has sufficient attention been paid to the business and economic environment, market conditions and the nature of competition?
- Has the firm used best practice benchmarking in order to establish an external measure of success and the most efficient way to conduct specific operations?
- If an internal audit has been completed, is the resulting assessment of the organisation's strengths and weaknesses realistic and placed in the context of the competition faced?
- Have managers of the business developed a SWOT analysis of the firm's position? If so, to what extent are its findings used to shape a strategy for achieving the long-term aims and objectives of the organisation?

## 56.6 Business strategy
### an evaluation

All successful organisations conduct strategic analysis. This does *not* have to mean a formal process.

The owner of a small business may monitor competitors' prices, or recognise a particular employee's

skills, without any conscious decision to study strengths, weaknesses, opportunities or threats in detail. The formal process set out in this unit is a large firm's way of trying to match the market knowledge and instincts of a successful small trader. Strategic policy which emerges as a pattern in action over time can be highly effective.

The key issue here is the size of the firm. The larger the organisation, the more likely it is that formal strategic analysis will be required in order to establish and maintain competitive advantage. This is because coordination of employee action becomes increasingly complex as a business grows. The process of preparing a SWOT diagram provides a focus to strategic analysis. There is always a risk, however, that a formal planning process can come to seem an annual ritual – more boring paperwork. In the long term, strategic analysis will only keep being successful if all staff are made fully aware of its effects upon decision making. The process of **SWOT analysis** is not enough. Its findings and consequences must be communicated effectively to staff.

**KEY terms**

**internal audit** – the process of analysing the organisation and effectiveness of each business department and activity. The results can inform a SWOT analysis by highlighting the firm's strengths and weaknesses.

**external audit** – the process of analysing the business and economic environment, market conditions and the nature of competition facing an organisation. The results can inform a SWOT analysis by highlighting the firm's opportunities and threats.

**management consultant** – independent advisors brought in to analyse a problem and recommend solutions in an objective way.

**SWOT analysis** – a four-box summary of the results of internal and external auditing. Strengths and weaknesses represent the internal position of the business today. Opportunities and threats represent the external position of the business which will influence its future development.

# Exercises

## A. REVISION QUESTIONS
*(45 marks; 70 minutes)*

Read the unit, then answer:

1 Identify the two sources of information gathered for the purposes of strategic analysis and give examples of each. *(6)*

2 a Consider Figure 56.1; is a large or a small business more likely to adopt this formal approach to strategic analysis? Why? *(4)*
  b Explain who should conduct a strategic analysis and why it should be undertaken regularly. *(3)*

3 What is the purpose of:
  a an internal audit *(3)*
  b an external audit? *(3)*

4 Outline the purpose of the three main elements of an external audit and provide an example of the kind of analysis which takes place in each. *(6)*

5 What is 'best-practice benchmarking'? Why might competitors choose to share information in this way? *(6)*

6 a How are the results of the internal and external audit used to prepare a SWOT diagram? *(5)*
  b What is the purpose of this analytical technique? *(4)*

7 How can strategic analysis be employed by managers in order to help achieve the organisation's aims and objectives? *(5)*

## B. REVISION EXERCISES

### B1 Case Study
#### Analysing the Strategic Position of ULV

ULV is a British manufacturer of motor components. It supplies major car makers in the UK and abroad. Every six months senior managers hold a key meeting. They review the firm's present position in the light of immediate planning targets and its longer term strategic position. The following are extracts from the most recent of these discussions:

#### Stephen Cross (Finance Director):
'Let's start with the good news. We are going to meet our objective of increasing return on capital employed by 2% this year. We should be able to pay a higher interim dividend to shareholders. If we are still thinking about expansion I believe we have the potential to raise additional capital. We are very lucky to have access to the kind of financial expertise available in the City of London. On the other hand, we have to be alert to the threat of takeover. Actions are sometimes necessary to protect our independence in the short term, even if it means sacrificing future growth.'

#### Lisa Taylor (Marketing Director):
'The expansion of the European Union is very promising for us. The potential of trading, without barriers, in some of the Eastern European economies is very excit-

ing. There is no reason we can't develop our two main product lines to become familiar to customer firms right across Europe. That would allow us to enjoy economies of scale and establish a position in the market as cost leaders. However, the low labour costs of the Eastern European manufacturers make them very serious competitors. In addition the slow down in the Asian economies is concerning. Not just because it might lead to world recession, but because we have built up a good reputation with our customers in that part of the world and as a result it is a growing source of demand.'

#### Peter Collins (Operations Director):
'It's a shame we closed down the Birmingham plant. I know the 1991 recession hit us hard, but we sometimes find ourselves turning away orders now because our capacity is so limited. The Long Eaton facility is still in need of new machinery and I am concerned about some of our equipment getting out of date. We need to look more closely at modernising our operations before any thoughts of expansion.'

#### Brian Shaw (Human Resource Director):
'I am concerned that the reintroduction of a minimum wage and other new European laws might cause us problems and eat into our competitive advantage. At least our training programme is taking effect and we are starting to reach a position where we can work in a more flexible way. As you know for a long time we have had a real shortage of skilled staff, particularly with appropriate computing knowledge, but the recruitment drive has been successful and the new employee share scheme has helped cut down labour turnover and improve motivation significantly.'

#### Questions *(40 marks; 60 minutes)*

1 Analyse the extracts from ULV's planning meeting to indicate those factors which would have been identified in an external business audit. *(6)*
2 Analyse the extracts from ULV's planning meeting to indicate those factors which would have been identified in an internal business audit. *(6)*
3 Prepare a SWOT diagram based on the analysis presented in your answers to questions 1 and 2. *(16)*
4 Identify and evaluate potential strategic policy options available to ULV by using the SWOT diagram prepared in your answer to question 3. *(12)*

## C. ESSAY QUESTION

Many successful organisations do not undertake formal strategic analysis. Consider the issues which might make the preparation of a SWOT diagram worthwhile and discuss how it could be used to shape a firm's strategic policy.

# INTEGRATED OBJECTIVES AND STRATEGY

## Objectives and strategy

### A. AS LEVEL REVISION QUESTIONS
*(30 marks; 30 minutes)*

1 Identify three possible aims for a small, family-run bakery. *(3)*
2 Distinguish between aims and objectives. *(3)*
3 Suggest two reasons why many firms have mission statements. *(2)*
4 What is meant by the term 'venture capital'? *(3)*
5 Outline two problems that might be encountered when starting a business. *(4)*
6 List two documents which must be submitted when applying to incorporate a company. *(2)*
7 Explain why a firm might obtain a patent. *(4)*
8 State three groups to which a business has some responsibility. *(3)*
9 What is meant by the term SWOT analysis? *(2)*
10 How might a firm set about determining its opportunities and threats? *(4)*

### B. AS LEVEL REVISION EXERCISES

**B1 Data Response**

**The Management Buyout**

**Streamer plc annual accounts**
**Profit and loss account, year-end 31 March**

|  | This Year (000s) | Last Year (000s) |
|---|---|---|
| Turnover | £91,178 | £92,846 |
| Cost of sales | £61,969 | £63,542 |
| Gross profit | a | a |
| Selling & distribution costs | £14,814 | £15,365 |
| Administrative expenses | £9,006 | £9,568 |
| Interest | b | b |
| Operating profit | £3,136 | £2,027 |
| Taxation | £791 | £581 |
| Dividends | £684 | – |
| Retained profit | c | c |

**Balance sheet as at 31 March**

|  | This Year (000s) | Last Year (000s) |
|---|---|---|
| Intangible assets | 1,560 | 1,672 |
| Tangible assets | 593 | 546 |
| Stocks | 24,553 | 29,392 |
| Debtors | 22,982 | 21,645 |
| Cash | 8,338 | 1,070 |
| Creditors (falling due within one year) | 37,000 | 33,793 |
| Net current assets | w | w |
| **Assets employed** | x | x |
| Loans | 158 | 581 |
| Share capital | 28,655 | 28,655 |
| Reserves | y | y |
| **Capital employed** | z | z |

**Questions** *(30 marks; 35 minutes)*

1 Look at the above accounts and fill in the gaps (a–c and w–z). *(7)*
2 If you were managers of Streamer plc, considering a management buyout, what is the maximum price you would consider offering the shareholders of the business, to buy them out? Explain your logic. *(9)*
3 Outline two ways you might finance the buyout. *(4)*
4 The managers have met to discuss their approach if they succeed with an offer. Their new objective will be to 'grow the business by 50% over the next three years and then re-float onto the stock market'. Consider the possible effects of this objective upon the performance of Streamer. *(10)*

## C. NUMERICAL REPORT
**AEB Summer 1998 Paper 3**

### Section A
Answer this question. You should spend up to 50 minutes on this section.

**1** Total for this question: 25 marks

### Making Dough
The Grayton Bakery owns three shops, each selling bread, sandwiches and cakes. Each shop is supplied daily from the bakery itself, which is in the heart of Grayton. The family owners have recently appointed a new managing director. He is critical of the 'poor profit record' of the business. He often points to the shops' 6% profit margin as an example of past managerial weakness.

The Chairman Grayton's Board has asked you, as a local management consultant, to write a report analysing the strengths and weaknesses of the business and 'to recommend a strategy for the 21st Century'. (2 marks are included for appropriate report format.)

### Appendices

Appendix A     Contribution Statement per Shop (£000s)
Appendix B     Shop Efficiency Data
Appendix C     Workforce Performance Data per Shop
Appendix D     Sales Growth per Shop (Indexed)
Appendix E     Sales Profile (1997 by value)

## D. ESSAY QUESTIONS
Answer one question from this section.

**1** The Plastics Division of Horlock Engineering plc has made losses in two of the last four years. Now Horlock has suggested a management buyout of the Division at a price of £26 million.

Consider the issue which might determine whether or not the management decides to buy the Division.

*(25 marks)*

**2** Shortly after being appointed, the new Chief Executive announced her determination to 'change the culture of the organisation'. Discuss the effect this might have.

*(25 marks)*

**3** A sharp recession sends some firms into receivership, while others emerge stronger than ever. Discuss the factors which may determine the effect of a sharp recession upon a firm. *(25 marks)*

**4** 'At their best, UK companies are as good as any in the world. But there is a long grey tail of poorly performing small and medium-sized companies.'

**Source:** John Neill, Group Chief Executive, the Unipart Group (The Guardian) 21 December 1996

Consider the factors which might enable this 'long grey tail' to improve its performance over the coming years.

*(25 marks)*

### Appendix A – Contribution statement per shop (£000s)

|  | Darton Road | Beamish Avenue | The Grange |
|---|---|---|---|
| Sales turnover | 165 | 145 | 220 |
| Contribution | 42 | 18 | 62 |
| Allocated overheads | 30 | 30 | 30 |
| Profit per shop | 12 | (12) | 32 |

### Appendix B – Shop efficiency data

|  | Darton Road | Beamish Avenue | The Grange |
|---|---|---|---|
| Sales per employee (£000s) | 27.5 | 29 | 34 |
| Sales per square foot (£) | 360 | 330 | 410 |
| Stock wastage (£000s) | 8 | 14 | 11 |

### Appendix C – Workforce performance data per shop

|  | Darton Road | Beamish Avenue | The Grange |
|---|---|---|---|
| Staff (full-time equivalent) | 6 | 5 | 6.5 |
| Staff employed in last year | 8 | 14 | 7 |
| Labour turnover | 33% | 180% | 8% |
| Absence rate | 4% | 11% | 2% |

### Appendix D – Sales growth per shop (indexed: 1990 = 100)

| Year | Darton Road | Beamish Avenue | The Grange |
|---|---|---|---|
| 1993 | 118 | 114 | 122 |
| 1994 | 123 | 117 | 134 |
| 1995 | 127 | 120 | 143 |
| 1996 | 133 | 123 | 146 |
| 1997 | 138 | 127 | 150 |

### Appendix E – Sales profile (1997 by value)

|  | Darton Road | Beamish Avenue | The Grange |
|---|---|---|---|
| Bread | 44% | 52% | 36% |
| Sandwiches | 18% | 22% | 24% |
| Cakes | 38% | 26% | 40% |

# TACKLING EXAMINATION PAPERS

**DEFINITION**

Levels of response mark scheme – a way of marking answers based upon different academic skills rather than the quantity of knowledge shown.

Time allocation – the amount of time available to each element of an examination paper. This is calculated by dividing the minutes available by the total marks on offer.

Analyse – to break a topic down into its component parts. This should help to identify the causes and effects of the issue. It is important, when analysing, to follow a line of argument.

Evaluate – this vital term means to weigh up evidence in order to reach a judgement.

Many examiners have been heard to comment: 'The candidate had a pretty good knowledge of the subject, but was not well prepared for the examination'. Knowing your subject matter is not enough. You have to prepare carefully for examinations by practising the skills you need on a regular basis.

## 58.1 Methods of assessment

Students taking AS level Business Studies are likely to encounter a variety of methods of assessment. The precise composition will depend upon the syllabus followed. The main methods include:

### 1. DATA RESPONSE QUESTIONS

These are series of questions relating to stimulus material in the form of graphs, charts, pictures or prose. Some, or all, of the questions will be based upon this information. However, you will be required to apply your subject knowledge and demonstrate your examination skills.

### 2. CASE STUDIES

A case study places you within a business scenario and invites an analysis of the situation. You will be required to offer solutions to problems and to propose business actions in a variety of circumstances. Commonly, case studies are employed to integrate the assessment of the various elements of Business Studies. To find out more about case studies you should read Unit 59.

## 58.2 Examination hints

### BEFORE THE EXAMINATION

In spite of the increasing need for examination skills, it is important to revise thoroughly for examinations. The strategy adopted for revision is a matter of personal preference. However, there are a number of steps you should take:

- plan your time carefully – you should work to a revision timetable
- ensure that you have covered the entire syllabus – check your class notes against the exam board's syllabus and repair any gaps
- organise your notes into the sections covered by the various examinations to assist your preparation
- devise a system for working through your notes – perhaps by writing revision notes
- make extensive use of past papers in your revision and ask your teacher or lecturer for copies of the mark schemes
- practise writing answers to past papers working within the actual time limits of the examination
- focus your revision on topics which have not been tested for some time as these are more likely to come up in the forthcoming examination.

### DURING THE EXAMINATION

There is a trend in Business Studies (and other subjects) towards shorter examinations. This places more pressure upon students to make effective use of the limited time available. Any errors in examination technique are highlighted as there is little time for recovery. Some key principles include:

- It is vital to read the question paper carefully and to ensure that you do exactly what is required of you. It is also important to read case studies, stimulus materials, charts and figures carefully as well as the associated questions. You must resist the desire to start writing as soon as possible – remember, it is quality that matters, not quantity.
- Plan your answers. Even for answers worth just a few marks, a little planning can avoid irrelevance and maximise your mark scoring potential. Too many examination candidates begin writing whilst still thinking about their answers. This results in fairly meaningless opening sentences and a tendency to repeat the wording of the question. For longer responses it is worth writing out a very brief plan at the top of your answer and adding to it as ideas occur to you.
- Timing is an important aspect of any examination. You should calculate how much time is available for each mark on the paper. Thus, if an examination lasts for 90 minutes and is worth 80 marks, the calculation might be as follows :

| ALLOCATING TIME WITHIN EXAMINATIONS | |
| --- | --- |
| Time available: | 90 minutes |
| Reading time: | 10 minutes |
| Time for writing answers: | 80 minutes |
| Marks available: | 80 |
| Minutes available per mark: | 1 |

- Ensure that you answer the correct number of questions. It will limit your performance severely if you answer fewer questions than required. It is important to read the wording on the paper, but you should be familiar with the format of the examination before you sit it.
- Layout is important. Numerical responses are often poorly presented and this can make marking very difficult. You should lay out work clearly, spacing it out and showing workings. Key figures within answers (for example, total sales income, gross profit, etc.) should be labelled to assist the examiner. If the question calls for a graph, then as a matter of routine this should be titled, and all lines, as well as both the axes, should be labelled.

# TACKLING AQA CASE STUDY PAPERS

## 59.1 Exam technique for all AQA case studies

Good case study answers combine a firm grasp of the case material with the ability to apply business concepts and theory to the questions set.

### 1. THE CASE MATERIAL

Writing an exam case study takes a great deal of time. Care is taken over the plot, the characters, the external context and over the underlying business themes. Weak answers reveal little grasp of even the most obvious parts of the text. Good candidates show a thoughtful approach to the key issues and characters. They appear not only to have read the material a couple of times, but also to have sat back for a moment or two to reflect upon it.

### 2. BUSINESS CONCEPTS

The job of every exam is to test the candidate's grasp of the concepts and content of the syllabus. Therefore, when reading a case study, it can be very helpful to note in the margin the business concepts hinted at in the text. When the case says 'they came up with a radical new design', your note in the margin might read 'value added' or 'price inelastic'. Then, when answering questions, there is a greater likelihood that your answer will be rooted in the theory of the subject.

### 3. THE QUESTIONS

The third crucial variable in exam success is the questions themselves. Mastering the precise wording of the questions is important for all exams, but with case studies there are other issues relating to the questions. The biggest is that a student may answer question 2a using material they later realise would have been more appropriate for answering question 3. Case study questions are much easier to answer if *all* the questions have been read at the start.

Taking all of the above points together, it is possible to come up with ground rules for how to tackle a case study exam. When you open the exam paper, follow this method:

1 Skim-read the text.
2 Briefly analyse any numerical material contained, perhaps, in an appendix. The reason for doing this now is that you have to understand the business fully before you can tackle the first question. If market share figures show a declining picture, you would need to know this to answer a question on marketing, finance, people or operations management.
3 Reflect for a moment on case material, then jot down the objectives of the featured business. Most business decisions are made with company objectives in mind. A candidate who has not thought about the firm's objectives is in a weak position to give a mature answer.
4 Read *all* the questions.
5 Re-read the case, jotting down relevant concepts in the margin of the exam paper.

Taking 10-15 minutes to digest and think about the material at the start of a 90-minute case study exam is time well spent. Top marks go to those who understand the business and its problems, have thought about how they relate to the theory of the subject, and make sure they answer the precise wording of each question.

## 59.2 Exam technique for the AS level AQA case study

This case study paper covers two sections of the AS syllabus: Units 2 and 3. The business case will focus upon the personnel and operations issues faced by a firm that also needs to think hard about strategy in the face of important external, e.g. economic, opportunities or threats. Top candidates will be those who can write lengthy, analytic answers to the questions posed. Such answers will require a good grasp of the syllabus material plus a great deal of practice at case studies for homework or in the lead-up to the examinations.

Among the most common question styles will be:

- Short-answer questions of fact, such as definitions.
- Questions asking for an outline or an explanation of subject matter. This will test the ability to show detailed knowledge and understanding of syllabus material.
- Analytic questions, asking for the application, examination or analysis of an issue in the context of the case material.

- Evaluative questions, which look for judgements to be made, often by weighing one series of factors against another. These would be provoked by phrases such as 'make a fully justified recommendation …' or 'discuss' or even 'evaluate'. These questions carry 15 marks, and all have a mark allocation of:

> Knowledge 3 marks
> Application 3 marks
> Analysis 4 marks
> Evaluation 5 marks.

# SUCCESS AT OCR BUSINESS STUDIES

## 60.1 The new OCR modular examinations

September 2000 sees a new OCR (Cambridge) syllabus for those following an AS course. The AS consists of 3 units of examination comprising:

1 An unseen case study on Businesses, Their Objectives and Environment
2 A data response paper on Business Decisions
3 A pre-issued case study on Business Behaviour.

Unseen case studies are covered in Unit 40. This unit concentrates largely on pre-issued case studies. It is essential to obtain a syllabus from OCR, together with specimen papers.

## 60.2 Pre-issued case studies

Pre-issued case studies allow tutors and students to focus on specifically relevant material before the examination, when candidates see the questions for the first time.

The case-material will touch on all, or virtually all, syllabus areas and so it is not possible to ignore the 'harder' or less interesting parts of the subject. The best advice to teachers and students is to cover the whole syllabus, explore the case study thoroughly, and to avoid question-spotting.

When the case material arrives, tackle it systematically. The cases are written to test the syllabus, so have a copy to hand. Go through the text looking for the main syllabus areas. For example, in a Marketing case, there might be a reference to cutting price to beat competition. This immediately suggests revision of price elasticity of demand and a study of the role of price in the marketing mix, among other areas. If the competitive environment has become more hostile, then this raises questions of strategy or planning to face new circumstances. By its nature, marketing is an all-embracing activity and issues of overall strategy, planning and evaluation should arise. Pre-issue does not limit the scope for study but helps to focus it.

It is important to check if the syllabus contains a quantitative element, for example, investment appraisal or sales forecasting. There is no need to fear quantitative questions as the emphasis will be on understanding and analysis rather than calculation. The use, suitability and limitations of a technique in a context are important.

New information can be introduced in the questions but only in a limited way. For example, if depreciation of a fixed asset is being considered, the method or rate of depreciation might be given in the question paper only. Further assumptions about the context might be given in the question papers.

The cases are generally written as contemporaneous so any useful up-to-date background knowledge of the economy, the EU or the market is sensible: credit could be given for this.

## 60.3 Levels of response

Examiners award marks using a 'levels of response' marking strategy. This has replaced the traditional approach of rewarding basic points made and the development of those points. The net effect of the change is to reward the depth of an answer rather than the breadth.

The four levels of response correspond to the level of skill used in the answer. At the end of each statement is an example of the marks that might be awarded out of 12.

### LEVEL 1

Level 1 is a response based on knowledge only, unrelated to the context, simply rehearsing pre-learnt material. Suppose a candidate answers a question about the marketing of a specific business by writing a long answer explaining the marketing mix, its content, its advantages and disadvantages etc. However 'good' or 'comprehensive' this answer may be, this is a Level 1 answer because it is unconnected with the context of the question set. It would typically receive 1–3 marks out of 12.

### LEVEL 2

Level 2 responses are characterised by explanation and understanding rather than pure regurgitation of knowledge. Also, there is reference to the case material so that application to the context is effected. At Level 2 answers tend to be explanatory or descriptive, rather than exploring causes or setting out the links in a chain of argument or logic. They might receive 4–6 marks out of 12.

## LEVEL 3

At Level 3 candidates show strong grasp of the concepts and theoretical underpinnings of the subject and demonstrate a chain of logic and analysis. An example would be an analysis of the effects of a rise in interest rates on a firm. For example: 'Investment plans are affected by an increase in the cost of capital. Marketing decisions are altered as a rise in interest rates affects aggregate demand and hence the market for its products via the income elasticity of demand. Employment plans change given the possible downturn in demand and the derived effects on the demand for labour.' Analytic answers receive 7–9 marks out of 12.

## LEVEL 4

A Level 4 response is evaluative showing not only a command of analysis but also an ability to reach a judgement using the analysis and weighting it. For example, a question may be about the best time to launch a new product. There might be several arguments for and several against, based on different analyses or approaches. The evaluative answer discriminates or weights these different examples of analysis and comes to reasoned judgement. It is not necessary for the examiner to agree with the judgement reached to award Level 4 marks, merely to recognise that evaluation has taken place. Level 4 answers are likely to receive 10–12 out of 12.

Finally, by way of reassurance, Level 4 responses are relatively rare and Level 3 not as common as examiners would wish. A strong performance at A Level can be achieved by consistently achieving a high Level 2 with some Level 3 or 4.

# HOW TO REVISE FOR BUSINESS EXAMS

Studies have shown that good revision can add as much as two grades to a student's result at A level. The aim of this unit is to help you to appreciate what makes up a quality revision programme.

## 61.1 Aims and objectives

A good revision programme will be aimed at achieving specific targets that will maximise your chances of success in the exam. How should these targets be set?

The basis for setting revision targets can be found in two places:

- the syllabus
- past papers.

### THE SYLLABUS

The content of the course will be outlined in some detail. Since the questions in the exam will be based closely on this document, you must ensure that you have sufficient knowledge of each area.

The specification will tell you what skills the examiner will be looking for. As well as basic factual recall as appropriate to the case being discussed, there will be a range of other skills you must demonstrate if you are to score highly. An example is given below.

---

*Definitions of higher academic qualities:*

*Application (relating answers to the case)*
- *Drawing business themes from the case material.*
- *Identifying and using the distinctive features of the business context.*

*Analysis (breaking down)*
- *Identification of cause, effect and interrelationships.*
- *The appropriate use of theory or business cases/practice to investigate the question set.*
- *Breaking the material down to show underlying causes or problems.*
- *Use of appropriate techniques to analyse data.*

---

*Evaluation (judgement)*
- *Judgement shown in weighing up the relative importance of different points or sides of an argument, in order to reach a conclusion.*
- *Informed comment on the reliability of evidence.*
- *Distinguishing between fact and opinion.*
- *Judgement of the wider issues and implications.*
- *Conclusions drawn from the evidence presented.*
- *Selectivity – ensuring material is all relevant to the question.*

Source: Ian Marcousé 2003

---

Knowing what skills the examiner is looking for will help you produce better quality answers in an exam. However, these are skills and like all skills they can only be developed through practice.

### PAST PAPERS

Previous exam papers are also very important in helping you to prepare for your exam. They will show you exactly what sort of questions you will face and the number of marks available. They will also give you a feel for the type of words used in the question. It goes without saying that exam questions must be read carefully. However, there will be key words used in the questions that tell you how to answer them. There is, for example, a great difference in the expected answers for the following two questions:

1 Outline Maslow's motivation theory.
2 Evaluate Maslow's motivation theory.

Unless you know what is expected from these two questions, you are unlikely to know how much detail is required or how your answer ought to be structured.

## 61.2 Resources

The following list contains items which will be of enormous value in preparing for an exam. They should all be familiar to you before you begin revising, and should have played a constant part of your studies throughout the course.

1  class notes
2  a copy of the specfication
3  past exam papers and mark schemes
4  a revision plan
5  newspapers/cuttings files
6  a good textbook
7  access to your teacher
8  other students.

**Class notes:** Since these are the product of your work and a record of your activities, they will form a vital part of your understanding of the subject. Hopefully they will contain past work you have done on exam-style questions and model answers that will help prepare you for the exam.

**A copy of the specification:** The specification tells you several important things:

- what knowledge you could be tested on
- what skills the examiner will be looking for
- how the marks will be allocated
- what you will be expected to do in each exam paper you will sit.

**Past exam papers and mark schemes:** By working from past papers you will develop a feel for the type of question you will be asked and the sorts of responses you will be expected to give.

**A revision plan:** As described in the previous section. It will help keep you on target to achieve everything that you need to cover before the exam.

**Newspapers/cuttings files:** Since Business Studies is a real-life subject, the ability to bring in relevant examples will boost your answers and their grades.

**A good textbook:** One that will help clarify any points that you are still unsure about.

**Access to your teacher:** To be able to receive help and advice, to quell sudden panics and to help review your progress by marking work done and suggesting ways to improve your performance.

**Other students:** To help discuss points and clarify ideas.

## 61.3 Learning the language of the subject

Clear definitions of business terms are essential for exam success. They count for much more than the odd two-mark question here or there. In June 2002, many students who tackled an AQA paper 6 question on 'Ethics' knew the term too vaguely to be able to construct a valid answer.

There are many possible sources of good definitions of business terms. In this book, key terms have been given clear and concise definitions. The defini-

tions should be written without using the word in question.

> **Revising business definitions:**
> - **Definition cards**
> - **Past papers**
> - **Crosswords/word games**
> - **Brainteasers**

It is important, then, that you can produce high quality definitions in an exam. This can only be done through learning and practice. Possible ways to achieve this are as follows.

### DEFINITION CARDS

Take a pack of index cards or postcards, or similar-sized pieces of thick paper. On each, write each term or phrase that you can find in the specification document. Remember to include things like motivation theories where a clear definition/description can give an excellent overview. It is extremely unlikely that you will be asked to know a precise definition for any term that is not specifically in the syllabus.

On the back of each card write an appropriate definition. This could come from your class notes, a textbook or a dictionary such as *The Complete A–Z Business Studies Handbook* 4th edition, Lines, Marcousé and Martin, Hodder and Stoughton 2003. Make sure that the definition you write is:

- concise
- clear
- does not use the word being defined in the definition.

Learn them by continual repetition. Put a tick or cross on each card to show whether or not you came up with an acceptable effort. Over time, you should see the number of ticks growing.

Shuffle the cards occasionally so that you are not being given clues to some definitions because of the words or phrases preceding them.

Try the exercise backwards by looking at the definitions and applying the correct word or phrase.

### PAST PAPERS

By using as many past papers as possible you can find out exactly what type of definition questions are asked. More importantly, you can see how many marks are available for them, which will tell you exactly how much detail you need to go into in your answer.

If possible, get hold of examiners' mark schemes. These will again give you a clear idea of what is being looked for from your answer.

You will be able to find many examples of 'word games' in magazines such as *Business Review* (Philip Allan, Market Place, Deddington, OX15 OSE). By completing these you are developing your business vocabulary and linking words with their meanings.

For a fuller, alphabetical source of exercises such as these, Ian Marcousé's *A-Z Business Studies Workbook* is very helpful. It contains literally thousands of questions - all with answers in the back of the book.

## 61.4 Numbers

All business courses contain aspects of number work which can be specifically tested in exams. It must be remembered, however, that there are two clear aspects to numbers:

1 calculation
2 interpretation.

The calculation aspects of business courses are one area where practice is by far the best advice. Each numerical element has its own techniques that you will be expected to be able to demonstrate. The techniques can be learnt, and by working through many examples they can become second nature. Even if mathematics is not your strong point, the calculations ought not to cause problems to an A level student. Something that at first sight appears complex, such as decision trees, requires only simple techniques such as multiplying fractions, adding and subtraction. Going through the workbook sections of this book will be invaluable. Ask your teacher for a photocopy of the answers available in the Teachers Guide.

Once calculated, all business numbers need to be used. It is all very well to calculate the accounting ratios, but if the numbers are then unused the exercise has been wasted. You must attempt to follow each calculation by stating what the numbers are saying and their implications for the business.

## 61.5 General tips for revision

1 start early
2 know the purpose of your revision
3 work more on weaker areas
4 use past papers as far as is possible
5 keep a clear perspective.

And finally, do no more revision on the night before the exam – it won't help and can only cause you anxiety. Eat well and get a good night's sleep. This way you will be in good physical shape to perform your best in the exam.

# MARKING BUSINESS STUDIES PAPERS

If you understand how AS level papers in Business Studies are marked then it will be easier for you to obtain high marks.

## 62.1 Levels of response marking

Almost all Business Studies papers are now marked using levels of response marking schemes. This type of marking scheme operates through the application of a number of descriptors against which your work is assessed. The levels of response are based on assessment objectives such as analysis and evaluation.

The most important thing to understand about levels of response marking is that it rewards quality and depth. It penalises those who write a large quantity of brief, simple points. Full paragraphs that develop a theme will always do better, therefore, than lists of bullet points. The reason is simple. Examiners want to award good grades to those who can write thoughtfully about the subject.

Questions that are only worth up to four marks are unlikely to require more than subject knowledge. They might merely require the appropriate knowledge to be stated or perhaps expressed in the form of explanation. However, questions with higher mark allocations inevitably require application as well as analytic and evaluative writing.

A question worth 10 marks might be assessed using the levels of response set out in the table opposite.

As you can see simply basing your argument on your subject knowledge will severely restrict the number of marks available to you. In this case you may only receive two marks out of the ten available. To gain full marks it is essential to:

- relate your answers to the scenario
- develop your arguments
- offer some judgement in the form of evaluation.

Not all questions require all these skills. It is important that you learn to recognize the skills that each question requires of you.

The example shown on the following page is based on a part of a recent examination set by AQA. You will note that the verb in the question (**discuss**) highlights clearly what was required of candidates sitting this

| LEVEL | CONTENT 2 MARKS | APPLICATION 2 MARKS | ANALYSIS 3 MARKS | EVALUATION 3 MARKS |
|---|---|---|---|---|
| 2 | **2 marks** Candidate offers two or more relevant arguments. | **2 marks** Candidate applies knowledge effectively to scenario. | **3–2 marks** Good analysis of argument. | **3–2 marks** Sound judgement shown in answers and conclusions. |
| 1 | **1 mark** Candidate offers single relevant argument. | **1 mark** Candidate attempts to apply knowledge to scenario. | **1 mark** Limited analysis of argument. | **1 mark** Some judgement shown in response. |
| 0 | **0 marks** No relevant content present. | **0 marks** No discernible attempt to apply knowledge | **0 marks** No analysis present. | **0 marks** No evaluation present. |

examination. If you answered this question without writing evaluatively, then the maximum mark you could achieve would be 10 out of 15. Similarly, failure to apply your knowledge to the scenario of the question (in this case a firm of tailors) or to use relevant theory to develop analytical arguments, would limit the mark you might achieve.

If you simply wrote a list of points stating whether or not health and safety laws constrain any businesses, you would only receive marks under the 'content' heading; thus three is the maximum mark you would achieve. If however, you related your answer to the circumstances of 'Fitz' then the marks under the heading application could be awarded to you. In the same way the use of analysis and evaluation makes marks in these categories available. You should appreciate that to have good subject knowledge is not enough. You should be able to use that information effectively to demonstrate that you have the necessary examination skills.

The same principles apply to case study and essay writing. Analysis and evaluation are the key skills for exam success. This is why this book has sections within every unit headed 'Issues for Analysis' and 'An evaluation'. When preparing a revision programme, these sections are invaluable. They act as both a summary of the key themes within each unit and as a pointer to the issues most likely to generate the lines of argument for answering the longer, tougher questions.

The key points to remember about exam marking, then, are:

- Markers admire well-developed argument, as long as it is relevant to the question set.
- Bullet point lists generate only knowledge marks – the lowest level of response.
- Arguments should ideally be developed using the theory of the subject …
- … and then be weighed up, in order to show the ability to evaluate (judge) the appropriate answer to the question set.

### QUESTION FROM JUNE 2003 EXAMINATION

'Many commentators suggest that employment and health and safety laws are a constraint that damages business competitiveness. Discuss whether this could be said to apply to the case of Fitz.'

Possible answers include:

**Case for such laws**

- As in this case, managers can act unfeelingly towards staff, and ignore the potential long-term damage to morale and trust caused by short-term fixes; legislation may save them from themselves.
- The same case was made against legislation to ban child chimney sweeps in nineteenth-century Britain, but social improvements are an essential part of economic progress. Society cannot be held back to the level of the world's worst standards.
- Highly interventionist countries such as Sweden and Germany are at least as successful as Britain.

**Case against such laws**

- Given the acute competitiveness problem of the textile industry, UK legislation may make life too easy for Far East, low-cost producers.
- Followers of a laissez-faire approach emphasise that laws are often ineffective and that 'red tape' can dissuade potential entrepreneurs from taking the plunge … but there is no evidence of this in the case of Fitz.
- The Fitz case shows that people do not lie down and let themselves be exploited. If people are unhappy with the working conditions they can leave; the resignation of five staff was the catalyst for change, not the laws.

Source: AQA Marking Scheme, Unit Three, Summer 2002

| LEVEL | CONTENT 3 MARKS | APPLICATION 3 MARKS | ANALYSIS 4 MARKS | EVALUATION 5 MARKS |
|---|---|---|---|---|
| 3 | | | | **5 marks** Judgement shown in weighing up the impact of legislation on the competitiveness of "Fitz", giving clear conclusions. |
| 2 | **3 marks** At least one point explaining about legislation, showing understanding. | **3 marks** Point or points made are applied in detail to the case. | **4–3 marks** Analysis of the question set using relevant theory. | **4–3 marks** Judgement shown in weighing up the impact of legislation. |
| 1 | **2–1 marks** One or more relevant points made about legislation. | **2–1 marks** Point or points made are applied to the case. | **2–1 marks** One or two points applied in a limited way to analyse the question set. | **2–1 marks** Some judgement shown in text or conclusions. |
| 0 | **0 marks** No relevant content present. | **0 marks** No relevant points applied to the case. | **0 marks** No analysis of the question set. | **0 marks** No judgement shown in text or conclusion. |

# AS EXAM REVISION FOR BUSINESS STUDIES

AS examinations are aimed to be 'at a level to be expected half way through an A level course'. In other words, about half way between GCSE standard and A level standard. They focus on the skills of Knowledge and Application, though also require some Analysis and Evaluation. It is therefore helpful to make good use of the final sections of each Unit of this book, entitled Issues for Analysis and An Evaluation.

A very valuable supplement to this book is the *Complete A-Z Business Studies Handbook* 4th Edition, by Lines, Marcousé and Martin, published by Hodder & Stoughton, ISBN 0 340 87263 2.

If you are studying this subject at evening classes or as a self-study student, you will find it helpful to obtain the accompanying Teacher's Book. It contains detailed mark schemes to show how best to tackle the Workbook questions, and is obtainable from good bookshops or from Amazon.co.uk; published by Hodder & Stoughton, ISBN 0 340 81113 7.

## 63.1 AQA

### DATA RESPONSE UNIT 1

For revision, read through a Unit, then immediately go through the Revision Questions in the Workbook section, referring back to the text when necessary. Make sure to revise the Key Terms listed, then consider the Revision Exercises.

Examination Unit 1 of the AQA scheme is a data response paper. It has a running time of 60 minutes and contains two questions, both out of 25 marks. At the end of every Unit of this textbook is a Workbook section that includes data response questions. The style, level and timing of these data response questions is a good indication of the actual AS level exams. Do take care to note, though, that some Workbooks contain both AS and A2 questions. Needless to say, make sure you choose the AS ones.

For daily revision of approximately 90 minutes:
1  Read a Unit and answer the Revision Questions
2  Learn the Key Terms
3  Do one data response question

In the case of the Examination Unit 1, this revision programme will require 20 days. In addition allow two days for going back over the chapters of the book, re-reading the short sections called Issues for Analysis and An Evaluation. At the same time, check your recall of the Key Terms.

The key subject content for AS level is in the following Units:

### Examination Unit 1 AS Marketing and Finance
- Marketing: 1, 2, 3, 4, 5, 6, 7, 8, 9, 10 and 11
- Finance: 12, 13, 14, 15, 16, 17, 18, 19, 20 and 21

### EXAMINATION UNITS 2 AND 3

Whereas a data response paper focuses on knowledge, understanding and application, case studies have a tighter focus on analysis and evaluation. This makes it important to write longer, deeper answers focusing upon one or two key themes, rather than broad answers that make many points. Naturally, the sections called Issues for Analysis and An Evaluation become even more important than for the first paper.

Recommended revision approach:

1  Read each Unit at a time, briefly answering the Revision Questions
2  Learn the Key Terms
3  Tackle one AS level data response question
4  Try the following case studies:
   - The Mobile Video Phone, page 289
   - Brooks, page 315
   - Integrated Case Study, page 319
   - Case Study, page 340

The key subject content for AS level is in the following Units:

### Examination Unit 2 AS People and Operations
- People: Units 22–31
- Operations management: Units 32 –40

### Examination Unit 3 AS External Influences, Objectives and Strategy
- External Influences: 41, 42, 43, 44, 45, 46, 48, 49, 50
- Objectives and Strategy: 47, 51, 52, 53, 55

## 63.2 OCR

### EXAMINATION UNIT 1 BUSINESSES, THEIR OBJECTIVES AND ENVIRONMENT

This 60-minute exam consists of pre-issued questions based upon a case study. In fact the material will often be drawn from newspaper articles, therefore the exam is very similar to a data response paper. It is therefore wise to use the data response questions as well as the case studies that come at the end of each Unit of this book.

For AS revision, the following Units are recommended:

- Nature, Classification and Objectives of Business: 51, 52, 53, 47, 54, 55
- External Influences: 41, 42, 43, 44, 45, 46, 48, 49, 50

For revision, read through a Unit, then immediately go through the Revision Questions in the Workbook section, referring back to the text when necessary. Make sure to revise the Key Terms listed, then consider the Revision Exercises. For the OCR Examination Unit 1 it will be helpful to tackle a mixture of data response and case study questions. The following are recommended especially:

- Data Response B2 on page 269
- Data Response B1 on page 275
- Data Response B1 on page 281
- The Mobile Video-phone, page 289
- Brooks, page 315
- Integrated Case Study, page 319
- Data Response B1 on page 328
- Data Response B1 on page 327
- Case Study, page 340

For daily revision of approximately 90 minutes:

1 Read a Unit and answer the Revision Questions
2 Learn the Key Terms
3 Do one AS level data response or case study exercise

### EXAMINATION UNIT 2 BUSINESS IN ACTION

This 45-minute exam consists of one compulsory data response question based upon unseen material. The stimulus material is likely to be drawn from newspaper articles or devised by the examiners to test numerical aspects of the subject. Comparable questions are included at the end of each Unit of this book.

For AS revision, the following Units are recommended:

- Marketing: 1, 2, 3, 4, 5, 8.1–8.6, 9, 11
- Finance and Accounting: 12, 13, 14, 16, 19
- People: 22, 23, 24, 25, 26, 27, 28, 31
- Operations Management: 32, 33, 34, 35, 37, 38, 39, 40

When revising, particular care should be taken over numerate topics such as price elasticity, cash flow, investment appraisal (pay-back and ARR) and break-even analysis. These are likely to be tested quite regularly within this exam. Make a particular effort to practise:

- Price elasticity: Revision questions A1–10 and B1 on page 54
- Cash flow: Revision Exercise B1 on page 106
- Investment appraisal: Revision Questions A1–10 and Revision Exercise B1 Question 1
- Break-even: Revision Exercises B1 and B2 on page 95

Leading up to the exam, for daily revision of approximately 90 minutes:

1 Read a Unit and answer the Revision Questions
2 Learn the Key Terms
3 Do one AS level data response exercise

### EXAMINATION UNIT 3 BUSINESS BEHAVIOUR

This 75-minute exam consists of four compulsory questions based upon a pre-issued case study. The subject content combines the above Examination Units 1 and 2. Therefore the only extra work involved is to look carefully at the pre-released case material and to prepare for the particular demands of case study technique. Read Unit 60 of this book for guidance from a senior OCR examiner.

In addition to the revision suggestions for Exams 1 and 2 (above) it would be helpful to tackle the following case studies from this book:

- Page 75: Integrated (Marketing) Case Study
- Page 147: B2 Case Study
- Page 204: B2 Case Study 'Expanding European Airways'
- Page 211: B2 Case Study
- Page 243: B2 Case Study 'Tricolour'

## 63.3 Edexcel

### EXAMINATION UNIT 1 BUSINESS STRUCTURES, OBJECTIVES AND EXTERNAL INFLUENCES

All three examination units will be based upon a comon pre-issued case study. This 60-minute examination consists of three compulsory questions. For revision, read through one of the Units of this book, then immediately go through the Revision Questions in the Workbook section, referring back to the text when necessary. Make sure to revise the Key Terms listed, then consider the Revision Exercises. The style, level and timing of the data response questions is a good indication of the actual AS level exams. Do take care to note, though, that some Workbooks contain both AS and A2 questions. Needless to say, make sure you choose the AS ones.

For daily revision of approximately 90 minutes:

1 Read a Unit and answer the Revision Questions
2 Learn the Key Terms
3 Do one AS level data response question

In addition, allow two days for going back over the chapters of the book, re-reading the short sections called Issues for Analysis and An Evaluation. At the same time, check your recall of the Key Terms.

The key subject content for AS level Exam Unit 1 is in the following Units:

- External Factors: 8, 42, 43, 44, 45, 46, 47, 51, 52, 55
- Internal Factors: 23, 24, 25, 26, 31

### EXAMINATION UNIT 2 MARKETING AND PRODUCTION

This Unit is examined by 60 minutes of questions based on pre-seen material. Case studies have a focus on analysis and evaluation. This makes it important to write relatively long answers focusing upon one or two key themes, rather than broad answers that make many points. The textbook sections called Issues for Analysis and An Evaluation become especially important.

Recommended revision approach:

1 Read each Unit at a time, briefly answering the Revision Questions
2 Learn the Key Terms

3 Tackle one AS level data response question
4 Try the following case studies:
   - Case Study B2, page 20
   - Integrated Case Study, page 75
   - Case Study B2 page 204
   - Case Study B2, page 243

The key subject content for AS level Exam Unit 2 is in the following Units:

- Marketing: 1, 2, 3, 4, 5, 6, 7, 8, 9, 10, 11
- Operations management: 32, 33, 34, 38, 39

### EXAMINATION UNIT 3 FINANCIAL MANAGEMENT

This Unit is examined by 60 minutes of questions based upon pre-seen case material. This exam will place especial importance upon business calculations, particularly break-even analysis and ratio analysis.

Recommended revision approach:

1 Read each Unit at a time, briefly answering the Revision Questions
2 Learn the Key Terms
3 Tackle one AS level data response question

The key subject content for AS level Exam Unit 3 is in the following Units:

- Finance and Accounting : 12, 13, 14, 15, 16, 17, 18, 19, 21

# INDEX

Page numbers in *italics* refer to diagrams and figures, those in **bold** type refer to definitions.

INDEX